HAP PALMER

BABY SONGS™

A Collection of Songs for the Very Young
from the Videos <u>Baby Songs</u>™ and
Illustrations by Susannah

Crown Publishers, Inc.
New York

For Kelly, Wesley, and Danny

Text copyright © 1990 by Hap Palmer
Illustrations copyright © 1990 by Susannah Ryan
Published by Crown Publishers, Inc., a Random House
Company, 225 Park Avenue South, New York,
New York 10003.
CROWN is a trademark of Crown Publishers, Inc.

Manufactured in Italy.

Library of Congress Cataloging-in-Publication Data
Palmer, Hap, 1942–   Baby Songs / by Hap Palmer.
Summary: A collection of songs from Hap Palmer's first
two videos for very young children: "Baby Songs" and
"More Baby Songs." Both music and texts are included.
ISBN 0-517-57593-0 1. Children's songs. 2. Songs. [JUV]
I. Baby Songs (Motion picture) II. More baby songs.
III. Title   M1990.P233B3   1990   89-753454

10 9 8 7 6 5 4 3 2 1

First Edition

Piano arrangements by William Komaiko
Music copying by Christina Davidson
Music editing by Carol Nethen

The songs in this collection are
recorded by Hap Palmer on the
albums *Baby Song* and *Tickly Toddle,*
Educational Activities, Inc., and
on the videos *Baby Songs*™ and *More
Baby Songs,*™ Hi-Tops™ video.

Contents

Guitar Chords

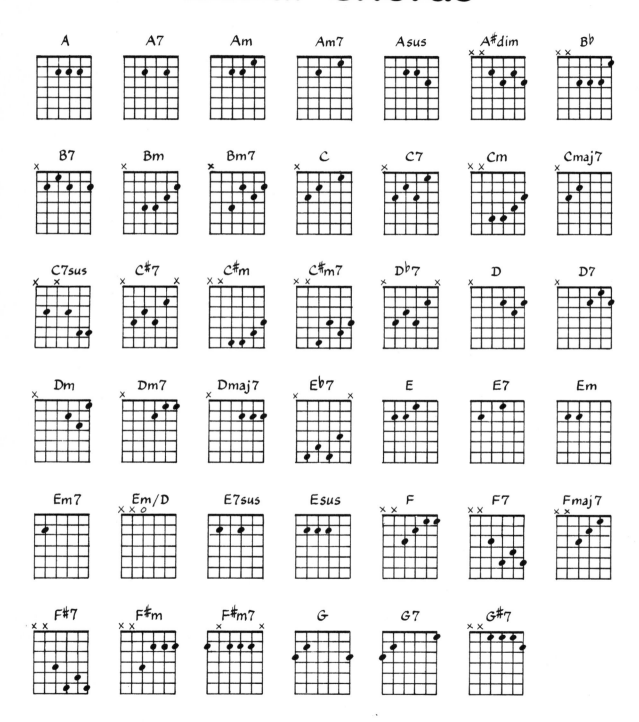

Note to guitarists: The guitar chords shown here have been simplified. Refer to a standard chord chart for barre chords.

Introduction

This collection of songs about the world of very young children will help you make music an integral part of your child's day. Music can accompany and enhance a child's activities anytime. There are songs to sing with daily activities such as taking a bath, changing diapers, eating in a high chair, or taking a walk. Other songs are supportive and reflect a child's emotional concerns—separation from mother, sharing of toys, or attachment to a favorite blanket. A variety of playful and imaginative situations, such as bathing a dolly or riding a bucking bronco, naturally suggest ways children can move as they sing along.

Parents and children make music together. You can play the piano, strum an autoharp or guitar, shake a tambourine, clap your hands, or just plain sing out—you don't have to have a great voice. Letting your child hear the reassuring sound of your voice is what's important. The songs are simple and repetitive, making it easy for the young child to join in and sing. While you are enjoying the music, you and your baby will recognize these songs as true experiences for a little person learning about the big world.

Hap Palmer

Piggy Toes

Medium tempo Caribbean-style

Words: Martha Cheney
Music: Hap Palmer

1. Ten lit-tle pig - gies run
2. Ten lit-tle pig - gies dig
3. (Instrumental)

thum-pi-ty thud, _____ Ten lit-tle pig-gies squish in-to the mud, _____
in - to the rug, _____ Ten lit-tle pig-gies curl up like a bug, _____

Ten lit-tle pig - gies so soft and so sweet, _____ Don't you think toes are the
Ten lit-tle pig - gies go tip - py tip toe, _____ Toes are the best part of

7

Shout and Whisper

Gentle medium tempo

Words: Martha Cheney
Music: Hap Palmer and Martha Cheney

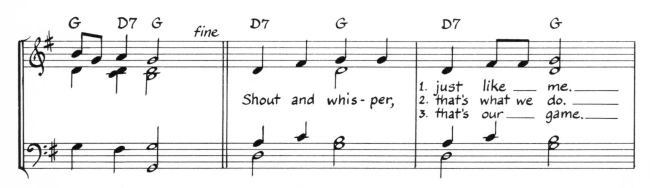

Shout and whis-per,
1. just like ___ me. ___
2. that's what we do. ___
3. that's our ___ game. ___

8

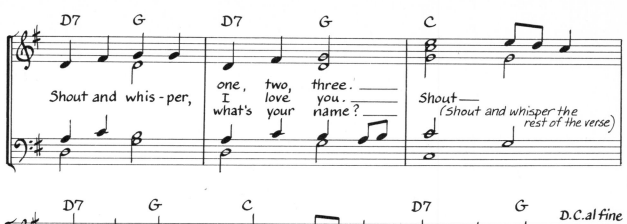

Shout and whis-per, | one, two, three. ___ | Shout ___
  | I love you. ___ | (Shout and whisper the rest of the verse)
  | what's your name? ___ |

D.C. al fine

one, two, three. | Whisper ___ | one, two, three. ___
I love you. | | I love you. ___
what's your name? | | (say your own name) ___

9

Share

Medium bounce

Words: Martha Cheney and Hap Palmer
Music: Hap Palmer

Verses A

1. Son - ja share your sand - box with Em - i - ly Ann, _____
2. Chris - ty share your cray - ons with Ca - mille and Kay, _____
3. Shei - la share your sho - vel with San - dy and Sam, _____

sim.

A / E7

De - rek share your dump truck with lit - tle _____ Dan, _____
Dus - tin share your dol - ly with Ka - ri - ne, _____
Pa - trick share your puz - zle with Paul and _____ Pam, _____

A

A - dam share your an - i - mals with An - drew, _____ And
Mi - key share your mon - key with Ma - ry Lou, _____ And
Ti - na share your tri - cy - cle with Tom - my too, _____ And

then they'll share their toys with you. ___ Your ___
you can play with their toys with you too! ___ Your ___
then they'll share with their toys with you.

Chorus

friends (your friends) just want a turn to play, ___ They won't take your

toys a-way. ___ Good friends (good friends) can have a

lot more fun ___ When they share with ev-ery-one. ___

ev-ery - one. ___

11

My Mommy Comes Back

Happy tempo

Words: Martha Cheney and Hap Palmer
Music: Hap Palmer

Verses

1. Some-times my mom-my takes me o - ver ____ To an-oth - er friend's house to
2. Some-times I wor - ry when she leaves me. ____ I hope she won't be gone
3. Some-times I vi - sit with my grand-ma ____ While my mom-my goes some-

get me. _____ My mom-my comes back, She al-ways comes back, She

nev - er would for - get me. _____

Baby's Good Doggy

Light swing (♫ = ♪³♪)

Words: Martha Cheney and Hap Palmer
Music: Hap Palmer

I'm a good dog - gy, ba - by's good dog - gy,

$\oplus$ CODA

| Bb | | G7 | | C7 sus | |

me. _____ There'll be no ____ oth - er

| F7 | Bb |

ba - by for me. _____

Rolling

Bright medium swing

Words: Martha Cheney
Music: Hap Palmer

1. Ba - by has a stroll-er with ___ four round wheels. ___ It
2. Broth-er has a trike to pe-dal with his feet. ___ He
3. fa - mi-ly car ___ has room in - side ___ For

A C#m7   Bm7 A

rolls down the side - walk and up the hills. _____ The
rides on the side - walk but not the street. _____ When
ev - ery - one to _____ come and ride. _____

A C#m7   C#7 F#m

stroll - er takes __ ba - by _____ ev - ery - where, _____ It's a
dad - dy takes __ ba - by for a stroll - er ride, _____ Broth - er
Mom-my buck-les up __ the __ seat - belts tight, _____ Then the

Security
(Don't Wash My Blanket)

Quick lyric waltz

Words: Martha Cheney and Hap Palmer
Music: Hap Palmer

Don't wash my blan-ket, don't take it a - way, ___

I want to drag it a- round while I play.__ To me it's o- kay,___

dir-ty and gray, Please don't wash my blan-ket to- day.___

Verses

1. I ___ might get lone – ly,___ I ___ might get
2. I ___ might get an – gry,___ I ___ might ___

scared,___ I ___ need to know___
cry,___ I ___ need to know___

that ___ my blan – ket ___ is there. ___ So
that ___ my blan – ket's ___ near- by. ___

(To Chorus)

22

CODA

To me it's o-kay, ___ dir-ty and gray, ___ Please don't wash my blan-ket to - day. ___

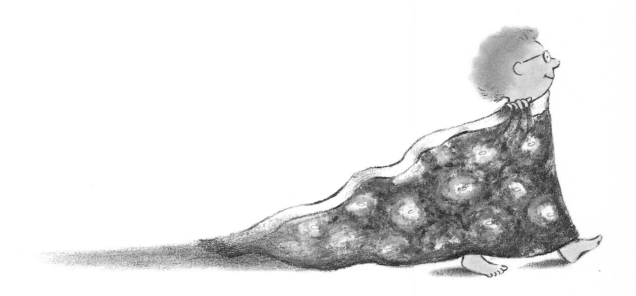

Rub-a-Dub

Happy tempo

Words: Martha Cheney
Music: Hap Palmer

A

Don't you

Chorus

A   B7   E7

love to have   fun __ in the   tub, Rub-a-   dub.   Just   hop __ in the

24

tight.
hope. ___Then ears in and out___ ___and

Wash your bot - tom and legs,___ scrub 'on

neck round and round,
down to those feet,

Then move on ___ to your
___ Then up,___ down and

(To Chorus)

shoul - ders and arms___ up and down.
side - ways, you're all ___ clean and sweet.

Don't you

Today I Took My Diapers Off

Medium Country-Western

Words and Music: Hap Palmer

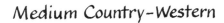

Verses

1. day I took my dia-pers off, I do not need them now.___
2. day I took my dia-pers off, I've nev-er felt so free.___ My

I Sleep 'til the Morning

Gentle Irish Jig

Words: Martha Cheney and Hap Palmer
Music: Hap Palmer

Chorus

I sleep 'til the morn-ing, I do not wake too soon.___ I rest un-til the

30

Walking

Quick, perky walk

Words: Martha Cheney
Music: Hap Palmer

Chorus

Walk-ing walk-ing walk-ing walk-ing Seems so ea-sy now,____ But

I re-mem-ber when I was small And I did not know

The Hammer Song

Slow rock 'n' roll tempo
Hammer away!

Words and Music: Hap Palmer

Bang Bang Bang Bang   Watch me ham-mer-in',   Bang Bang Bang Bang

pound-in' nails in.   Bang Bang Bang Bang   I try to pound them straight,

35

Sittin' in a High Chair

Quick, with good mountain spirit

Words: Martha Cheney and Hap Palmer
Music: Traditional

Chorus

Sit - tin' in a high chair, big chair, my chair,

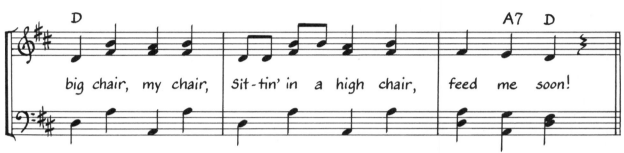

Sit-tin' in a high chair, bang my spoon! Sit-tin' in a high chair,

big chair, my chair, Sit-tin' in a high chair, feed me soon!

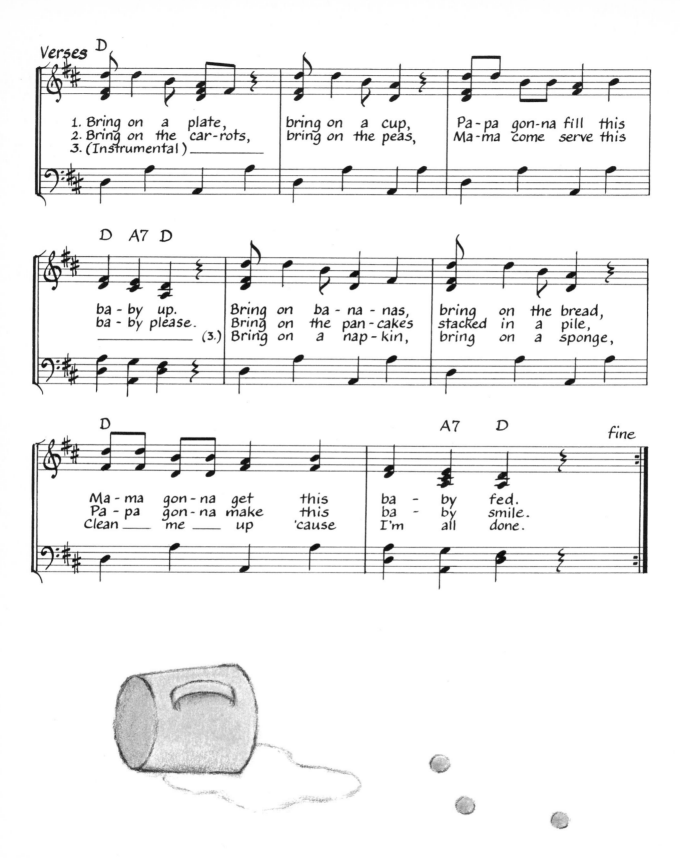

Daddy Be a Horsie

Playful riding tempo

Words and Music: Hap Palmer

Verses

1. Dad-dy loves to squeeze ___ me and bounce me on his knee, ___
2. tick-les me and makes me laugh when giv - ing me a bath. ___ He
3. (Instrumental)

39

40

please. _____

2. He
3. _____

3.
Take __ me __ rid – ing __ please. _____

My Baby

Moderate rocking waltz

Words: Martha Cheney and Hap Palmer
Music: Hap Palmer

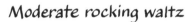

1. My

Verses

1. ba - by wants ___ her bot - tle now, She's hun - gry as ___ can
2. ba - by's dia - per is all wet, He needs one nice ___ and
3. ba - by is ___ all dir - ty 'cause We went out - side ___ to
4. ba - by has ___ a sleep - y face, He needs a lit - tle

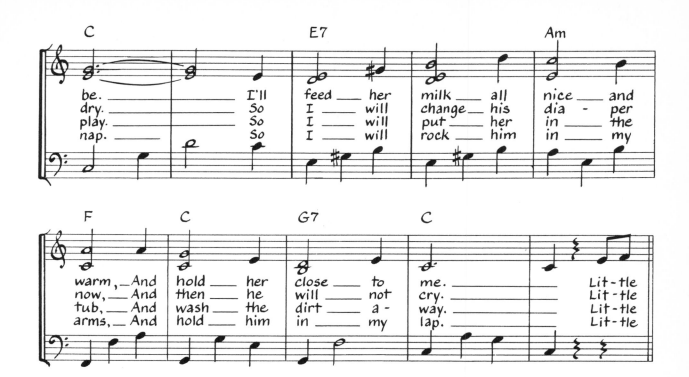

C		E7		Am

be. _____ I'll | feed ___ her | milk ___ all | nice ___ and
dry. _____ So | I ___ will | change ___ his | dia - per
play. _____ So | I ___ will | put ___ her | in ___ the
nap. _____ So | I ___ will | rock ___ him | in ___ my

F	C	G7	C

warm,_And | hold ___ her | close ___ to | me. _____ Lit-tle
now,__And | then ___ he | will ___ not | cry. _____ Lit-tle
tub,_And | wash ___ the | dirt ___ a- | way. _____ Lit-tle
arms,_And | hold ___ him | in ___ my | lap. _____ Lit-tle

Tickly Toddle

Smooth medium tempo

Words: Martha Cheney
Music: Hap Palmer

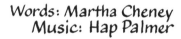

Verses

1. Ti - ck - ly tod - dle, a goose ___ likes to
2. Ti - ck - ly jig - gle, a worm ___ likes to
3. Ti - ck - ly tum - ble, a bee ___ likes to

Crazy Monster

Crashing monster tempo

Words: Martha Cheney
Music: Hap Palmer

I'm a cra-zy mon-ster, I live in a cave.___ I'm a cra-zy mon-ster

(Spoken) I will not be-have! (Sung) I'm a cra-zy mon-ster, I jump up with the sun, 'Cause

I can't wait to run out-side ___ and scare ev-ery-one! ___

Ha ha ha ha ha!

I'm a cra - zy mon - ster, I

stomp and scream and moan.____ I'm a cra - zy mon - ster, I

smash and crash and groan.____ I'm a cra - zy mon - ster and

when the day is through,___ I crawl back in my cave and sleep

just like you, Just like you.____

53

Wild and Woolly

Medium fast Elvis rock 'n' roll

Words: Martha Cheney and Hap Palmer
Music: Hap Palmer

(Opt. Play left hand octave lower throughout song)

Verses

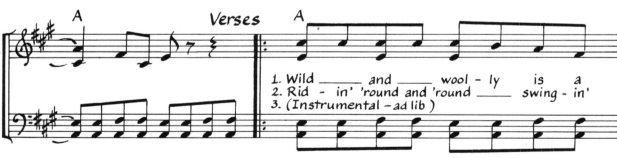

1. Wild _____ and _____ wool - ly is a
2. Rid - in' 'round and 'round _____ swing - in'
3. (Instrumental – ad lib)

cow-boy   show, _____   Rid - in' buck - in' bron-cos in a
your las - soo, _____   Wave your hat to ma - ma shout-in'

ro - de - o. _____ Boun - cin' up and down ____ and a
woo ya - hoo! _____ When the wes - tern Ar - i - zo - na

turn - in' a - round, ____ Jump - in' and a jolt - in' till you
sun ____ goes down, You're dan - cin' and a sing - in' at the

fall on the ground. _____ Wild ____ and wool - ly _____
big ____ hoe - down. _____

Chorus   C#7

Family Harmony

Happy country waltz

Words: Martha Cheney and Hap Palmer
Music: Hap Palmer

Chorus

We play our song to-ge-ther,___ A hap-py___

___ me-lo-dy,___ It al-ways sounds___ much bet-ter,___

In fam - i - ly har - mo - ny. ____

Verses

Ba - by plays ___ the bon - go drums, ____
Aun - tie plays ___ the xy - lo - phone, ____
Grand - pa plays ___ the slide trom - bone, ____

58

Dad – dy   plays   a   big   gui –
Sis – ter   plays   the   sax – o –
Ma – ma   plays   pi –   a – no, ___

tar, ___   Grand – ma
phone, ___   Un – cle
                  Bro – ther

59

plays ___ the | vi - o - | lin, ___ ___ |
plays ___ the | sil - ver | flute, ___ |
plays ___ the | tam - bou- | rine, ___ |

___ | Oh, what | pret - ty | sounds they
Oh, what | love - ly | lilt - ing
With | love they | make the | mu - sic

G   Am   D7   G   (to Chorus)

are. ___ |
tones. ___ |
flow. ___ | We

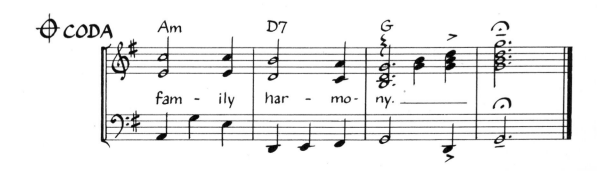

✠ CODA   Am   D7   G

fam - ily | har - mo- | ny. ___ |

60

Babysong

Easy swing tempo (♫ = ♩³♪)

Words: Martha Cheney
Music: Hap Palmer

It's a
won-der-ful day ____ to go out and play, ___ Hey, may-be you could come a-long.
____ All you need to bring is a song to sing, ___ A hap-py lit-tle ba-by song.

62

Index

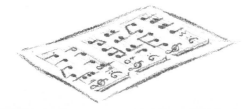

Everyday Mathematics®

The University of Chicago School Mathematics Project

GRADE
3

TEACHER'S LESSON GUIDE
VOLUME 1

Mc
Graw
Hill
Education

The University of Chicago School Mathematics Project

Max Bell, Director, *Everyday Mathematics* First Edition; James McBride, Director, *Everyday Mathematics* Second Edition; Andy Isaacs, Director, *Everyday Mathematics* Third, CCSS, and Fourth Editions; Amy Dillard, Associate Director, *Everyday Mathematics* Third Edition; Rachel Malpass McCall, Associate Director, *Everyday Mathematics* CCSS and Fourth Editions; Mary Ellen Dairyko, Associate Director, *Everyday Mathematics* Fourth Edition

Authors
Jean Bell, Max Bell, John Bretzlauf, Mary Ellen Dairyko, Amy Dillard, Robert Hartfield, Andy Isaacs, Kathleen Pitvorec, James McBride, Peter Saecker

Fourth Edition Grade 3 Team Leader
Mary Ellen Dairyko

Writers
Lisa J. Bernstein, Camille Bourisaw, Julie Jacobi, Gina Garza-Kling, Cheryl G. Moran, Amanda Louise Ruch, Dolores Strom

Open Response Team
Catherine R. Kelso, Leader Amanda Louise Ruch, Andy Carter

Differentiation Team
Ava Belisle-Chatterjee, Leader Martin Gartzman, Barbara Molina, Anne Sommers

Digital Development Team
Carla Agard-Strickland, Leader John Benson, Gregory Berns-Leone, Juan Camilo Acevedo

Virtual Learning Community
Meg Schleppenbach Bates, Cheryl G. Moran, Margaret Sharkey

Technical Art
Diana Barrie, Senior Artist; Cherry Inthalangsy

UCSMP Editorial
Lila K. S. Goldstein, Senior Editor Kristen Pasmore, Molly Potnick, Rachel Jacobs

Field Test Coordination
Denise A. Porter

Field Test Teachers
Eric Bachmann, Lisa Bernstein, Rosemary Brockman, Nina Fontana, Erin Gilmore, Monica Geurin, Meaghan Gorzenski, Deena Heller, Lori Howell, Amy Jacobs, Beth Langlois, Sarah Nowak, Lisa Ringgold, Andrea Simari, Renee Simon, Lisa Winters, Kristi Zondervan

Digital Field Test Teachers
Colleen Girard, Michelle Kutanovski, Gina Cipriani, Retonyar Ringold, Catherine Rollings, Julia Schacht, Christine Molina-Rebecca, Monica Diaz de Leon, Tiffany Barnes, Andrea Bonanno-Lersch, Debra Fields, Kellie Johnson, Elyse D'Andrea, Katie Fielden, Jamie Henry, Jill Parisi, Lauren Wolkhamer, Kenecia Moore, Julie Spaite, Sue White, Damaris Miles, Kelly Fitzgerald

Contributors
John Benson, Jeanne Mills DiDomenico, James Flanders, Lila K. S. Goldstein, Funda Gonulates, Allison M. Greer, Catherine R. Kelso, Lorraine Males, Carole Skalinder, John P. Smith III, Stephanie Whitney, Penny Williams, Judith S. Zawojewski

Center for Elementary Mathematics and Science Education Administration
Martin Gartzman, Executive Director, Meri B. Fohran, Jose J. Fragoso, Jr., Regina Littleton, Laurie K. Thrasher

External Reviewers
The *Everyday Mathematics* authors gratefully acknowledge the work of the many scholars and teachers who reviewed plans for this edition. All decisions regarding the content and pedagogy of *Everyday Mathematics* were made by the authors and do not necessarily reflect the views of those listed below.

Elizabeth Babcock, California Academy of Sciences; Arthur J. Baroody, University of Illinois at Urbana-Champaign and University of Denver; Dawn Berk, University of Delaware; Diane J. Briars, Pittsburgh, Pennsylvania; Kathryn B. Chval, University of Missouri–Columbia; Kathleen Cramer, University of Minnesota; Ethan Danahy, Tufts University; Tom de Boor, Grunwald Associates; Louis V. DiBello, University of Illinois at Chicago; Corey Drake, Michigan State University; David Foster, Silicon Valley Mathematics Initiative; Funda Gönülateş, Michigan State University; M. Kathleen Heid, Pennsylvania State University; Natalie Jakucyn, Glenbrook South High School, Glenview, IL; Richard G. Kron, University of Chicago; Richard Lehrer, Vanderbilt University; Susan C. Levine, University of Chicago; Lorraine M. Males, University of Nebraska-Lincoln; Dr. George Mehler, Temple University and Central Bucks School District, Pennsylvania; Kenny Huy Nguyen, North Carolina State University; Mark Oreglia, University of Chicago; Sandra Overcash, Virginia Beach City Public Schools, Virginia; Raedy M. Ping, University of Chicago; Kevin L. Polk, Aveniros LLC; Sarah R. Powell, University of Texas at Austin; Janine T. Remillard, University of Pennsylvania; John P. Smith III, Michigan State University; Mary Kay Stein, University of Pittsburgh; Dale Truding, Arlington Heights District 25, Arlington Heights, Illinois; Judith S. Zawojewski, Illinois Institute of Technology

Note
Many people have contributed to the creation of *Everyday Mathematics*. Visit http://everydaymath.uchicago.edu/authors/ for biographical sketches of *Everyday Mathematics* 4 staff and copyright pages from earlier editions.

www.everydaymath.com

Send all inquiries to:
McGraw-Hill Education
8787 Orion Place
Columbus, OH 43240

ISBN: 978-0-02-140996-9
MHID: 0-02-140996-X

Printed in the United States of America.

1 2 3 4 5 6 7 8 9 RMN 20 19 18 17 16 15

Welcome to *Everyday Mathematics*

The elementary program from the
University of Chicago School Mathematics Project.

Dear Teacher,

Everyday Mathematics 4 is designed to help you teach the content required by the Common Core State Standards. In third grade, that content focuses on procedures, concepts, and applications in four critical areas:

- understanding of multiplication and division and strategies for multiplication and division within 100;
- understanding of fractions, especially unit fractions;
- understanding of the structure of rectangular arrays and of area; and
- describing and analyzing two-dimensional shapes.

As you teach this content, *Third Grade Everyday Mathematics* lessons consistently provide you with opportunities to engage children in the Common Core's mathematical practices and to foster the attitudes and habits of mind of those who know and enjoy mathematics and use it effectively. The practice standards emphasize problem solving, the use of multiple representations, reasoning, mathematical modeling, tool use, communication, and other ways of making sense of mathematics. These practices will gradually shape children's ways of thinking about mathematics and will promote the development of their mathematical intuitions and understandings. Every lesson in *Everyday Mathematics* systematically integrates instruction in mathematical content with instruction in the mathematical practices.

Throughout *Everyday Mathematics,* emphasis is placed on

- problem solving in everyday situations and mathematical contexts;
- an instructional design that revisits topics regularly to ensure depth of knowledge and long-term learning;
- distributed practice through games and other daily activities;
- teaching that supports "productive struggle" and maintains high cognitive demand; and
- lessons and activities that engage *all* children and make mathematics fun!

This *Teacher's Lesson Guide* and other program features provide support as you implement the program. See Getting Ready to Teach on pages xxxvi–xxxix for some advice about how to begin. As you gain experience with *Third Grade Everyday Mathematics,* you will become more comfortable with its content, components, and approaches. By the end of the year, we think you will agree that the rewards are worth the effort.

Have an exciting and productive school year!

Ellen Dairyko
and the *Third Grade Everyday Mathematics* Development Team

Everyday Mathematics: How Children Learn

Your students deserve a mathematics program based on decades of research and engineered to make sure that all have the opportunity to succeed. For over 30 years *Everyday Mathematics* has been helping students all over the world develop enduring mastery of mathematics.

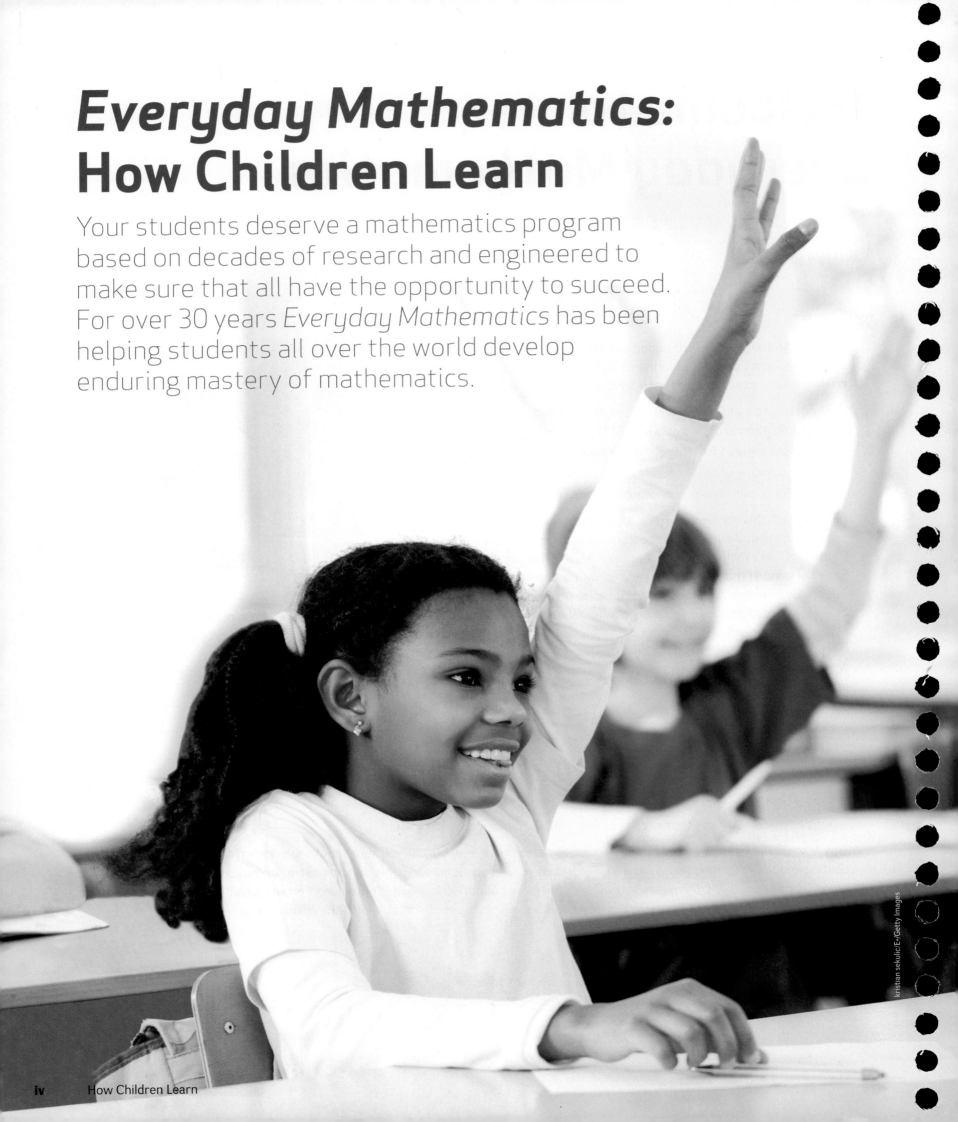

kristian sekulic/E+/Getty Images

Connects Math to Everyday Situations

Everyday Mathematics makes math fun and meaningful inside the classroom by helping children connect math to the world outside the classroom.

Encourages Creativity

Everyday Mathematics encourages children to be creative problem solvers and flexible thinkers. Children are challenged to work through problems on their own, fostering independence and persistence.

Gives Every Child the Opportunity to Succeed

Everyday Mathematics helps children find the methods that work for them, building confidence and ensuring positive feelings about math.

Adapts to Fit Your School

Everyday Mathematics offers a wealth of guided support through structured lesson plans, tailored training, and in-depth professional development—all helping teachers become more confident math teachers. The program can be implemented in a fully digital environment, adapting to meet all your children's needs and capabilities.

A Research-Based Curriculum

Acknowledgements from the Authors

Everyday Mathematics grew out of groundbreaking work carried out by Max Bell at the University of Chicago in the 1960s and 1970s. Research projects led by Max and supported by the National Science Foundation, the National Institute of Education, and the Benton Foundation developed new insights into young children's surprising mathematical abilities and new approaches to teaching mathematics in elementary school. Max's insights and approaches are the foundation for *Everyday Mathematics*.

The development of *Everyday Mathematics* itself has been supported over the years by the GTE Corporation, the National Science Foundation, the Amoco Foundation, the University of Chicago, McGraw-Hill Education and our other publishers, and the Authors. We are deeply grateful for our funders' faith in our work.

Everyday Mathematics has also benefitted enormously from teachers willing to try out draft materials and from our many close advisors, especially John P. Smith III and his colleagues at Michigan State University, who helped us with measurement; Susan C. Levine, Susan Goldin-Meadow, and their colleagues at the University of Chicago, who helped us with early number and geometry; Gina Kling at Western Michigan University, who helped us with basic facts; and Judith S. Zawojewski at the Illinois Institute of Technology, who helped us with assessment and open response tasks. Many others, too many to list, have also contributed, which we gratefully acknowledge.

Finally, we would like to thank our colleagues here at the University of Chicago School Mathematics Project and at our publisher, McGraw-Hill Education. Debbie Leslie, Cheryl Moran, Rebecca Maxcy, Sarah Burns, Kathleen Pitvorec, Cathy Kelso, Ava Belisle-Chatterjee, Denise Porter, and Marty Gartzman joined us on a committee that provided guidance on many key issues. Working with such energetic, dedicated, and good-humored people made our work a pleasure.

Andy Isaacs
Director

Ellen Dairyko
Associate Director

Rachel Malpass McCall
Associate Director

A program designed to fit how children learn.

High Expectations

Everyday Mathematics began with a mission to improve school mathematics by establishing high expectations. We continue that mission today, maintaining high expectations for all children and providing the resources they need to meet them.

Strong Foundations

Everyday Mathematics continues to be developed by educators at the University of Chicago School Mathematics Project (UCSMP) who are dedicated to helping teachers gain confidence in their mathematics teaching so that children achieve their full potential.

Extensive Field Testing

Everyday Mathematics 4 has been rigorously field tested and iteratively improved using feedback from administrators, teachers, and children, making it the most research-grounded and field-tested elementary mathematics program available today.

Engineered for Learning

A powerful instructional design to maximize student learning.

Master the Common Core

Seamless integration of the Common Core State Standards helps ensure that your children will succeed.

Build Conceptual Understanding

Concrete modeling, strategy development, and mathematical discourse in the curriculum build conceptual understanding.

Develop Depth of Knowledge

Everyday Mathematics develops depth of knowledge by building connections among concepts, procedures, and applications.

Carefully Engineered Spiral

Everyday Mathematics strategically distributes instruction and practice in a research-proven design that is the best way to help your children develop enduring mastery and depth of knowledge.

Focused Instruction

Careful learning progressions develop concepts, skills, and applications over time, in new ways, increasing in sophistication, and in a variety of contexts.

Clear Expectations of Mastery

Tools are embedded throughout the program to help you easily see what your children should master at each point in the learning progression.

 Go Online ⟩ to **everydaymath.com** for more on how *Everyday Mathematics* is engineered for learning.

A Shared Vision with the Common Core

Both *Everyday Mathematics* and the Common Core State Standards are designed to ensure that all students are prepared for success in college and careers.

Depth of Knowledge through Focus, Coherence, and Rigor

Depth of knowledge cannot be developed in a single lesson or unit but requires repeated exposures to key ideas in different contexts over time. Research over many decades has shown that children learn best through a spiral curriculum such as *Everyday Mathematics*.

Focus on Common Core State Standards

Each activity and each problem directly addresses specific content standards to ensure mastery.

Coherence Across and Within Grades

Carefully crafted, research-based learning progressions are interwoven to help children connect skills, concepts, and applications. Children develop deep understandings and long-term learning by repeatedly returning to big ideas.

Rigorous Content

Everyday Mathematics provides teachers the tools they need to teach conceptual understanding, procedural fluency, and application with equal intensity.

Engineered for the Common Core

The careful design of *Everyday Mathematics* ensures that students will master Common Core expectations.

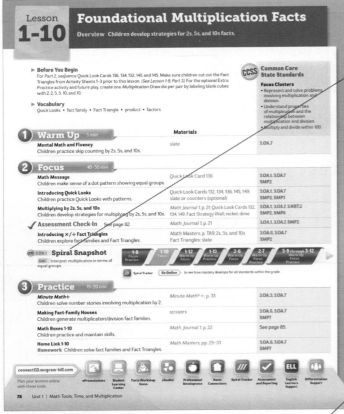

Goals for Mathematical Content

Each Common Core content standard has been decomposed into *Everyday Mathematics* Goals for Mathematical Content to enable finer-grained tracking of student progress. These Goals for Mathematical Content help teachers monitor children's progress, differentiate appropriately, and ensure that students fully meet the standards.

See page EM3 for a complete list of the Common Core content standards and the Goals for Mathematical Content (GMCs).

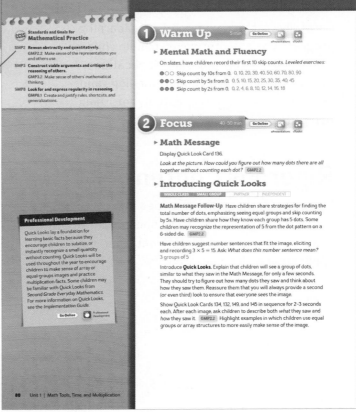

Goals for Mathematical Practice

To help teachers build the Standards for Mathematical Practice into classroom instruction, *Everyday Mathematics* specifies Goals for Mathematical Practice that unpack each Common Core practice standard appropriately for elementary school children.

See page EM6 for a complete list of practice standards and the Goals for Mathematical Practice (GMPs).

Open Response Problems

Lessons Built for Common Core Classroom

- Lessons are designed to focus on grade-level content, with every activity tagged to a standard.
- Goals for Mathematical Practice are embedded in daily lessons.
- Entire lessons dedicated to solving non-routine problems

CCSS-Enabled Reporting and Tracking

Everyday Mathematics provides assessment and reporting tools designed to help you track progress toward mastery of the Common Core standards and adjust instruction to meet the needs of all students.

Correlation to the Common Core State Standards

The *Everyday Mathematics* curriculum is completely aligned to the *K-12 Common Core State Standards* for Kindergarten through Grade 6. See each Lesson Opener for specific Content Standards and Standards for Mathematical Practice focused on in every lesson. The chart below shows complete coverage of each Content Standard throughout the grade level.

*Bold lesson numbers indicate that content from the standard is taught in the Focus part of the lesson. Lesson numbers not in bold indicate that content from the standard is addressed in Warm-Up or Practice parts of the lesson. The second set of lesson numbers, which are in parentheses, indicate that content from the standard is being addressed in Home Links or Math Boxes.

Common Core State Standards for Mathematical Content for Grade 3	*Everyday Mathematics* Grade 3 Lessons*
Operations and Algebraic Thinking 3.OA	
Represent and solve problems involving multiplication and division.	
3.OA.1 Interpret products of whole numbers, e.g., interpret 5×7 as the total number of objects in 5 groups of 7 objects each. *For example, describe a context in which a total number of objects can be expressed as 5×7.*	**1-8, 1-10, 1-12,** 1-13, **2-6, 2-7, 3-9, 3-10, 3-11, 3-12,** 3-13, 4-2, 4-5, **5-4, 5-6,** 5-9, **5-11,** 6-3, **6-4, 7-2, 9-1** (1-11, 2-1, 2-2, 2-3, 2-4, 2-10, 2-12, 3-2, 3-4, 3-5, 3-7, 4-1, 4-3, 4-4, 4-7, 4-9, 5-5, 5-7, 8-3)
3.OA.2 Interpret whole-number quotients of whole numbers, e.g., interpret $56 \div 8$ as the number of objects in each share when 56 objects are partitioned equally into 8 shares, or as a number of shares when 56 objects are partitioned into equal shares of 8 objects each. *For example, describe a context in which a number of shares or a number of groups can be expressed as $56 \div 8$.*	**1-9, 2-7, 2-8, 2-9, 2-10,** 2-12, 3-10, 4-1, 4-10, **5-10,** 6-2, **6-6, 7-3, 7-12, 8-3, 8-4, 8-6, 9-6** (1-11, 2-5, 3-1, 3-2, 3-3, 3-6, 3-8, 3-13, 4-6, 4-8, 4-11, 5-1, 5-3, 5-8, 6-9, 6-11, 7-1, 7-9, 8-2, 9-1, 9-3)
3.OA.3 Use multiplication and division within 100 to solve word problems in situations involving equal groups, arrays, and measurement quantities, e.g., by using drawings and equations with a symbol for the unknown number to represent the problem.[1]	1-2, **1-8, 1-9,** 1-10, **2-5, 2-6, 2-7, 2-8, 2-9, 2-10,** 2-11, 3-8, 3-9, **3-10, 3-11, 3-12,** 4-1, 4-5, 4-8, 4-10, 5-4, **5-5, 5-10, 5-11,** 6-2, 6-4, **6-6, 7-2, 7-3, 8-2, 8-3, 8-4, 8-6, 9-2, 9-3, 9-5** (1-11, 1-13, 2-1, 2-2, 2-3, 2-4, 2-12, 3-1, 3-3, 3-4, 3-5, 3-6, 3-7, 3-13, 4-2, 4-4, 4-11, 6-5, 6-7, 6-9, 6-11, 7-1, 7-4, 7-5, 7-7, 7-9, 9-1)
3.OA.4 Determine the unknown whole number in a multiplication or division equation relating three whole numbers. *For example, determine the unknown number that makes the equation true in each of the equations $8 \times ? = 48, 5 = \boxed{?} \div 3, 6 \times 6 = ?$.*	**2-7, 2-8, 3-1,** 3-12, **5-4,** 5-6, **5-8,** 6-1, **6-4, 6-6, 6-7,** 6-9, 7-3, 8-2, **8-3,** 8-4, **8-5,** 8-7, **9-1, 9-2,** 9-3, 9-4 (2-9, 3-5, 3-7, 3-9, 4-1, 4-3, 4-7, 6-2, 6-3, 6-9, 6-10, 6-11, 7-1, 7-2, 7-4, 7-9, 7-10, 7-12, 8-1, 8-6, 9-5, 9-6, 9-7)
Understand properties of multiplication and the relationship between multiplication and division.	
3.OA.5 Apply properties of operations as strategies to multiply and divide.[2] *Examples: If $6 \times 4 = 24$ is known, then $4 \times 6 = 24$ is also known. (Commutative property of multiplication.) $3 \times 5 \times 2$ can be found by $3 \times 5 = 15$, then $15 \times 2 = 30$, or by $5 \times 2 = 10$, then $3 \times 10 = 30$. (Associative property of multiplication.) Knowing that $8 \times 5 = 40$ and $8 \times 2 = 16$, one can find 8×7 as $8 \times (5 + 2) = (8 \times 5) + (8 \times 2) = 40 + 16 = 56$. (Distributive property.)*	**2-6, 3-10, 3-11, 3-12, 5-4, 5-5, 5-6, 5-9, 5-11, 6-3, 6-7,** 8-3, **9-3, 9-5** (3-5, 3-7, 4-1, 4-2, 4-3, 4-4, 4-5, 4-7, 4-9, 5-7, 6-2, 6-4, 6-9, 6-11, 7-1, 7-2, 7-3, 7-4, 7-12, 8-1, 8-4, 8-7)
3.OA.6 Understand division as an unknown-factor problem. *For example, find $32 \div 8$ by finding the number that makes 32 when multiplied by 8.*	**1-9, 1-10,** 4-5, 5-6, **5-8,** 6-1, 6-2, **6-6,** 6-9, 7-3, **8-2, 8-3, 8-5, 8-7,** 9-1, **9-2,** 9-4 (2-1, 2-3, 3-6, 3-8, 4-1, 4-3, 6-4, 6-10, 6-11, 7-5, 7-7, 8-8, 9-5, 9-7)

[1] See Glossary, Table 2.
[2] Students need not use formal terms for these properties.

Common Core State Standards for Mathematical Content for Grade 3	Everyday Mathematics Grade 3 Lessons*
Multiply and divide within 100.	
3.OA.7 Fluently multiply and divide within 100, using strategies such as the relationship between multiplication and division (e.g., knowing that $8 \times 5 = 40$, one knows $40 \div 5 = 8$) or properties of operations. By the end of Grade 3, know from memory all products of two one-digit numbers.	1-1, 1-5, **1-8**, 1-9, **1-10**, 1-11, 1-12, 1-13, 2-2, 2-3, **2-4, 2-5, 2-6, 2-7**, 2-8, **2-9, 2-10, 2-11**, 2-12, **3-1**, 3-5, 3-8, **3-9, 3-10, 3-11, 3-12, 3-13**, 4-1, 4-2, 4-3, 4-4, 4-5, 4-7, 4-9, 4-10, 4-11, **4-12**, 5-1, 5-2, 5-3, **5-4, 5-5, 5-6, 5-7, 5-8, 5-9**, 5-10, **5-11**, 6-1, **6-2, 6-3, 6-4**, 6-5, **6-6, 6-7, 6-8**, 6-9, **6-10, 6-11**, 7-1, **7-2, 7-3**, 7-4, 7-6, 7-12, **8-2, 8-3**, 8-4, **8-5, 8-6**, 8-7, **9-1, 9-2, 9-3**, 9-4, **9-5, 9-6**, 9-7 (2-1, 3-3, 3-6, 3-7, 4-6, 4-8, 7-5, 7-7, 7-8, 7-9, 7-10, 7-11, 8-1, 8-8)
Solve problems involving the four operations, and identify and explain patterns in arithmetic.	
3.OA.8 Solve two-step word problems using the four operations. Represent these problems using equations with a letter standing for the unknown quantity. Assess the reasonableness of answers using mental computation and estimation strategies including rounding.[3]	**2-2, 2-3, 2-4, 2-5**, 2-10, **3-2, 3-3, 3-4, 3-5, 3-6**, 3-8, 3-9, 4-1, **4-12**, 5-4, **5-10**, 6-1, **6-7, 6-8, 6-9, 6-10, 6-11**, 7-1, **7-2**, 9-1, 9-7 (2-12, 3-1, 3-7, 3-10, 3-12, 3-13, 4-2, 4-4, 4-5, 4-6, 4-8, 4-11, 5-7, 5-8, 6-5, 7-4, 7-5, 7-6, 7-7, 7-8, 7-11, 8-1, 8-2, 8-4, 8-6, 9-3, 9-6)
3.OA.9 Identify arithmetic patterns (including patterns in the addition table or multiplication table), and explain them using properties of operations. *For example, observe that 4 times a number is always even, and explain why 4 times a number can be decomposed into two equal addends.*	**2-6, 3-10, 5-4, 5-5, 5-6, 5-7, 5-9, 6-7, 9-3, 9-5** (3-5, 4-5, 6-3)
Number and Operations in Base Ten 3.NBT	
Use place value understanding and properties of operations to perform multi-digit arithmetic.[4]	
3.NBT.1 Use place value understanding to round whole numbers to the nearest 10 or 100.	**1-4**, 1-7, 1-13, 2-4, **3-2, 3-3**, 3-4, 3-5, **3-6** (1-6, 1-8, 1-10, 1-14, 2-2, 2-9, 3-7, 3-9, 3-12, 3-13, 4-2, 4-5, 4-6, 4-8, 4-11, 7-4)
3.NBT.2 Fluently add and subtract within 1000 using strategies and algorithms based on place value, properties of operations, and/or the relationship between addition and subtraction.	**1-1, 1-2, 1-3, 1-4**, 1-7, 1-8, **1-10**, 1-13, **2-1, 2-2, 2-3, 2-4, 2-5**, 2-10, **2-11**, 2-12, **3-1, 3-2, 3-3, 3-4, 3-5, 3-6**, 3-7, **3-8**, 3-9, **3-13**, 4-1, 4-3, 4-6, 4-7, 4-9, 5-1, 5-4, 5-5, 5-6, **5-7**, 5-9, **6-1, 6-8, 6-10, 6-11**, 7-1, 7-2, **7-3**, 7-4, 7-6, 7-12, **8-2**, 9-5, **9-6**, 9-7 (1-5, 1-6, 1-9, 1-11, 1-12, 2-6, 2-7, 2-8, 2-9, 3-10, 3-12, 4-2, 4-4, 4-5, 4-8, 4-10, 4-11, 4-12, 5-8, 6-5, 6-6, 6-7, 6-9, 7-5, 7-7, 7-8, 7-10, 7-11, 8-6, 8-7, 9-3)
3.NBT.3 Multiply one-digit whole numbers by multiples of 10 in the range 10–90 (e.g., 9×80, 5×60) using strategies based on place value and properties of operations.	1-9, 4-7, **7-2, 7-3, 8-2, 8-3**, 8-5, **9-2, 9-3**, 9-4, **9-5** (7-9, 8-6, 8-7, 8-8, 9-6, 9-7)
Number and Operations—Fractions[5] 3.NF	
Develop understanding of fractions as numbers.	
3.NF.1 Understand a fraction $1/b$ as the quantity formed by 1 part when a whole is partitioned into b equal parts; understand a fraction a/b as the quantity formed by a parts of size $1/b$.	1-12, 2-9, 2-12, 5-1, 5-2, **5-3**, 5-7, 6-4, 6-6, 7-2, **7-4**, 7-5, **7-6**, 7-7, 7-8, 7-9, 7-10, **7-11, 7-12, 8-1, 8-6, 8-7**, 8-8, 9-5 (2-5, 2-7, 2-10, 3-2, 3-4, 4-9, 5-5, 6-5, 6-7, 6-8, 7-1, 7-3, 8-2, 8-3, 8-4, 8-5, 9-2, 9-4, 9-6)

[3]This standard is limited to problems posed with whole numbers and having whole number answers; students should know how to perform operations in the conventional order when there are no parentheses to specify a particular order (Order of Operations).
[4]A range of algorithms may be used.
[5]Grade 3 expectations in this domain are limited to fractions with denominators 2, 3, 4, 6, and 8.

Common Core State Standards for Mathematical Content for Grade 3	*Everyday Mathematics* Grade 3 Lessons*
3.NF.2 Understand a fraction as a number on the number line; represent fractions on a number line diagram.	**4-3**, 5-2, **7-5**, **7-6**, **7-9**, **7-10**, **7-11**, 8-1, **8-7**, 9-5 (6-8, 7-8, 7-12, 8-3, 8-4, 8-5, 8-8, 9-1, 9-2, 9-4, 9-7)
3.NF.2a Represent a fraction *1/b* on a number line diagram by defining the interval from 0 to 1 as the whole and partitioning it into *b* equal parts. Recognize that each part has size *1/b* and that the endpoint of the part based at 0 locates the number *1/b* on the number line.	**4-3**, 5-2, **7-5**, **7-6**, **7-9**, **7-10**, 7-11, 8-1, 8-5, **8-7**, 9-5 (6-8, 7-8, 8-8, 9-2, 9-4)
3.NF.2b Represent a fraction *a/b* on a number line diagram by marking off a lengths *1/b* from 0. Recognize that the resulting interval has size *a/b* and that its endpoint locates the number *a/b* on the number line.	5-2, **7-5**, **7-6**, **7-9**, **7-10**, **7-11**, 8-1 8-5, **8-7**, 9-5 (7-8, 7-12, 8-3, 8-4, 8-8, 9-1, 9-2, 9-7)
3.NF.3 Explain equivalence of fractions in special cases, and compare fractions by reasoning about their size.	**5-2**, **5-3**, 5-7, 6-4, **7-2**, **7-4**, **7-5**, **7-6**, **7-7**, **7-8**, **7-9**, **7-10**, **7-11**, **8-1**, 8-5, **8-7**, 9-5 (3-4, 5-5, 5-6, 5-10, 6-2, 6-8, 8-2, 8-3, 8-4, 8-6, 8-8, 9-1, 9-2, 9-3, 9-4, 9-7)
3.NF.3a Understand two fractions as equivalent (equal) if they are the same size, or the same point on a number line.	**5-3**, 6-4, **7-2**, **7-4**, **7-5**, **7-7**, **7-9**, **7-10**, 8-1, 8-5, **8-7**, 9-5 (3-4, 6-2, 7-6, 8-2, 8-3, 8-8, 9-2, 9-4)
3.NF.3b Recognize and generate simple equivalent fractions, e.g., 1/2 = 2/4, 4/6 = 2/3. Explain why the fractions are equivalent, e.g., by using a visual fraction model.	**5-3**, 5-7, 6-4, 7-2, **7-4**, **7-5**, **7-7**, 7-8, **7-10**, 8-5, **8-7**, 9-5 (5-5, 6-2, 7-6, 8-2, 8-3, 9-2, 9-4)
3.NF.3c Express whole numbers as fractions, and recognize fractions that are equivalent to whole numbers. *Examples: Express 3 in the form 3 = 3/1; recognize that 6/1 = 6; locate 4/4 and 1 at the same point of a number line diagram.*	**5-2**, **5-3**, 5-7, 7-2, **7-4**, **7-5**, **7-6**, 7-8, **7-9**, **7-11**, **8-1** (7-7, 8-2, 8-5, 8-6, 8-8, 9-2)
3.NF.3d Compare two fractions with the same numerator or the same denominator by reasoning about their size. Recognize that comparisons are valid only when the two fractions refer to the same whole. Record the results of comparisons with the symbols >, =, or <, and justify the conclusions, e.g., by using a visual fraction model.	**5-3**, 6-4, 7-2, **7-4**, **7-6**, **7-7**, **7-8**, 7-9, **7-10**, **7-11**, 8-1, 8-5, **8-7**, 9-5 (5-6, 5-10, 6-2, 6-8, 8-2, 8-4, 8-6, 8-8, 9-1, 9-2, 9-3, 9-4, 9-7)

Measurement and Data   3.MD

Solve problems involving measurement and estimation of intervals of time, liquid volumes, and masses of objects.

3.MD.1 Tell and write time to the nearest minute and measure time intervals in minutes. Solve word problems involving addition and subtraction of time intervals in minutes, e.g., by representing the problem on a number line diagram.	**1-3**, **1-5**, **1-6**, **1-11**, 2-1, 2-6, **7-3**, **9-4**, 9-7 (1-7, 1-8, 1-9, 1-10, 1-12, 1-13, 2-3, 2-5, 2-7, 3-6, 3-8, 3-9, 3-12, 4-1, 4-3, 5-6, 5-10, 6-1, 6-3, 6-8, 6-9, 6-11, 7-2, 7-4, 7-6, 7-8, 7-11, 8-1, 8-4, 8-7, 9-1, 9-2, 9-3)
3.MD.2 Measure and estimate liquid volumes and masses of objects using standard units of grams (g), kilograms (kg), and liters (l).[6] Add, subtract, multiply, or divide to solve one-step word problems involving masses or volumes that are given in the same units, e.g., by using drawings (such as a beaker with a measurement scale) to represent the problem.[7]	1-3, **1-12**, **1-13**, 2-9, **2-12**, **4-3**, 5-4, 6-7, **7-1**, **7-2**, **7-3**, 7-7, 8-7, 8-8, **9-2**, **9-3**, **9-4** (2-2, 2-4, 2-6, 2-8, 2-11, 3-6, 3-8, 5-6, 5-10, 6-8, 7-5, 7-10, 7-12, 9-5, 9-6, 9-7)

Represent and interpret data.

3.MD.3 Draw a scaled picture graph and a scaled bar graph to represent a data set with several categories. Solve one- and two-step "how many more" and "how many less" problems using information presented in scaled bar graphs. *For example, draw a bar graph in which each square in the bar graph might represent 5 pets.*	**1-7**, 3-6, **3-7**, **3-8**, 4-2, 5-5, 5-6, **9-7** (1-9, 1-12, 2-2, 2-4, 2-9, 3-2, 3-4, 3-10, 3-13, 4-4, 8-7)
3.MD.4 Generate measurement data by measuring lengths using rulers marked with halves and fourths of an inch. Show the data by making a line plot, where the horizontal scale is marked off in appropriate units—whole numbers, halves, or quarters.	1-3, **4-1**, **4-2**, **4-3**, **4-6**, **4-7**, 4-8, **6-5**, **8-1**, 8-2 (1-9, 3-11, 4-5, 4-11, 5-2, 5-4, 5-6, 5-10, 6-1, 6-3, 7-9, 8-3, 8-5, 8-8, 9-6)

[6]Excludes compound units such as cm3 and finding the geometric volume of a container.
[7]Excludes multiplicative comparison problems (problems involving notions of "times as much"; see Glossary, Table 2).

Common Core State Standards for Mathematical Content for Grade 3	*Everyday Mathematics* Grade 3 Lessons*
Geometric measurement: Understand concepts of area and relate area to multiplication and to addition.	
3.MD.5 Recognize area as an attribute of plane figures and understand concepts of area measurement.	**2-12, 3-7, 4-7, 4-8, 4-9, 4-10, 4-12,** 5-3, 5-11, 7-10 (3-11, 5-1, 5-2, 5-6, 5-10)
3.MD.5a A square with side length 1 unit, called "a unit square," is said to have "one square unit" of area, and can be used to measure area.	**2-12, 3-7, 4-7, 4-8, 4-10, 4-12,** 5-3 (3-11, 4-9, 5-1, 5-2, 5-6, 5-10)
3.MD.5b A plane figure which can be covered without gaps or overlaps by n unit squares is said to have an area of n square units.	**2-12, 3-7, 4-7, 4-8, 4-9, 4-10,** 5-3, 7-10 (3-11, 4-12, 5-1, 5-2, 5-6, 5-10)
3.MD.6 Measure areas by counting unit squares (square cm, square m, square in, square ft, and improvised units).	**2-12, 3-7, 4-7, 4-8, 4-9, 4-10,** 5-1 (3-11, 5-3)
3.MD.7 Relate area to the operations of multiplication and addition.	**3-7, 4-7, 4-8, 4-9, 4-10, 4-11, 4-12,** 5-1, 5-3, 5-4, **5-5, 5-6, 5-11,** 6-5, 7-10, 8-3, **8-7,** 9-1, **9-5** (5-2, 5-9, 5-10, 6-1, 6-2, 6-3, 6-4, 6-6, 6-10, 7-1, 7-2, 7-3, 7-4)
3.MD.7a Find the area of a rectangle with whole-number side lengths by tiling it, and show that the area is the same as would be found by multiplying the side lengths.	**3-7, 4-7, 4-8, 4-9,** 5-3 (4-12, 5-1, 5-2, 5-9, 5-11)
3.MD.7b Multiply side lengths to find areas of rectangles with whole number side lengths in the context of solving real world and mathematical problems, and represent whole-number products as rectangular areas in mathematical reasoning.	**4-9, 4-10, 4-11, 4-12,** 5-1, 5-4, **5-5, 5-6, 5-11,** 7-10, **8-7,** 9-1, **9-5** (5-3, 5-9, 5-10, 6-1, 6-2, 6-3, 6-4, 6-6, 6-10, 7-1, 7-2, 7-3, 7-4)
3.MD.7c Use tiling to show in a concrete case that the area of a rectangle with whole-number side lengths a and $b + c$ is the sum of $a \times b$ and $a \times c$. Use area models to represent the distributive property in mathematical reasoning.	**5-5, 5-6, 5-11,** 8-3, **9-5** (7-1, 7-3)
3.MD.7d Recognize area as additive. Find areas of rectilinear figures by decomposing them into non-overlapping rectangles and adding the areas of the non-overlapping parts, applying this technique to solve real world problems.	**4-12, 5-5, 5-6, 5-11,** 9-1, **9-5** (4-9, 5-2, 5-4, 5-9, 6-6, 6-10, 7-2, 7-4)
Geometric measurement: Recognize perimeter as an attribute of plane figures and distinguish between linear and area measures.	
3.MD.8 Solve real world and mathematical problems involving perimeters of polygons, including finding the perimeter given the side lengths, finding an unknown side length, and exhibiting rectangles with the same perimeter and different areas or with the same area and different perimeters.	**4-3, 4-6, 4-7, 4-8, 4-10, 4-11, 5-1,** 5-11, **6-5,** 7-10, 9-1 (4-12, 5-3, 5-5, 5-6, 5-7, 5-10, 6-1, 6-3, 6-6, 6-10, 8-2, 8-6)
Geometry 3.G	
Reason with shapes and their attributes.	
3.G.1 Understand that shapes in different categories (e.g., rhombuses, rectangles, and others) may share attributes (e.g., having four sides), and that the shared attributes can define a larger category (e.g., quadrilaterals). Recognize rhombuses, rectangles, and squares as examples of quadrilaterals, and draw examples of quadrilaterals that do not belong to any of these subcategories.	**1-3, 4-4, 4-5, 4-6, 6-5,** 6-8, **8-8, 9-4** (1-6, 1-8, 2-10, 2-12, 3-11, 4-8, 4-10, 4-11, 4-12, 5-1, 5-2, 5-3, 5-4, 5-5, 5-7, 5-9, 5-11, 6-1, 6-6, 6-7, 6-10, 7-9, 8-5, 9-2, 9-6)
3.G.2 Partition shapes into parts with equal areas. Express the area of each part as a unit fraction of the whole. *For example, partition a shape into 4 parts with equal area, and describe the area of each part as 1/4 of the area of the shape.*	**1-12, 2-9, 3-7, 5-1, 7-4, 7-10, 7-11,** 8-5, **8-7, 9-4** (2-5, 2-7, 2-10, 2-12, 3-2, 3-4, 3-11, 4-9, 5-3, 5-5, 5-7, 6-5, 6-7, 6-8, 7-6, 8-3)

Adapts to Fit Your Classroom

From classroom organization to tailored training, everything you need is included in *Everyday Mathematics*.

Get Ready for Each Day

Everything you need to prepare for each lesson is available online and in print.

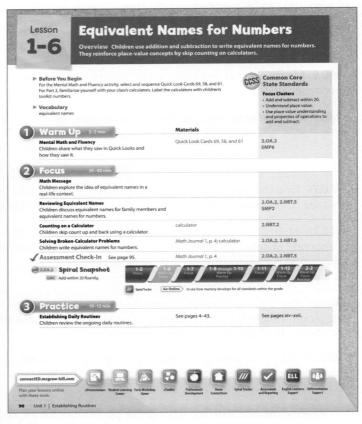

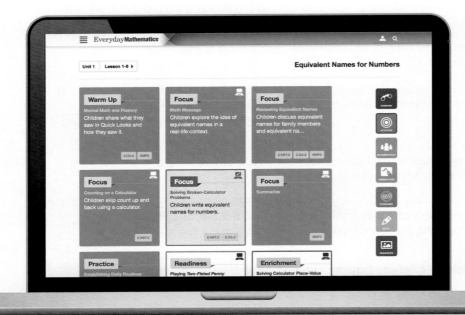

Organize for Success

Be confident with an easy-to-follow lesson plan.

Warm Up: Builds mental math and fluency skills and embeds daily routines

Focus: Introduces and develops new content with a focus on key CCSS standards

Practice: Develops and maintains skills over time

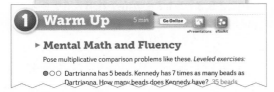

Plan, Teach, and Assess Digitally

Comprehensive digital resources put everything you need at your fingertips.

ePresentations

eToolkit

Assessment and Reporting

Interactive IWB-ready presentations to support your instruction for every lesson

Integrated virtual manipulatives for whole-class demonstrations and individual student explorations

Embedded digital tool allowing you to assign online assessments, monitor student progress in real time, and view student, class, school, and district reports

connectED.mcgraw-hill.com

Flexible access to complete lesson information by day, month, or unit.

Access Embedded Support for Each Lesson

Find support for professional learning, including Mathematical Background information in every Unit Organizer and point-of-use professional development notes in many lessons.

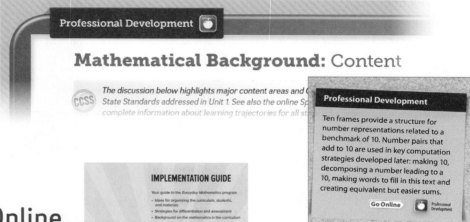

Access In-Depth Support Online

The *Implementation Guide* in your ConnectED Teacher Center provides information about assessment and differentiation, help teaching lessons, and much more.

Collaborate Online

Network in the Virtual Learning Community to share ideas, gather resources, view videos, and interact with other users, *Everyday Mathematics* authors, and other experts in mathematics education.

Virtual Learning Community

Connects Math to Everyday Situations

Help your students make connections between mathematical concepts and experiences in their daily lives.

Get Digital

A comprehensive digital learning environment allows children to

- complete and submit digital versions of lesson activities
- save work to an online portfolio
- access lesson resources with embedded tutorials and hints
- receive immediate feedback on selected problems
- collaborate with peers

Motivate Your Students

Fun and encouraging math games help keep your students motivated. Digital games challenge your students and let you track their progress.

Facts Workshop Game

EM Games

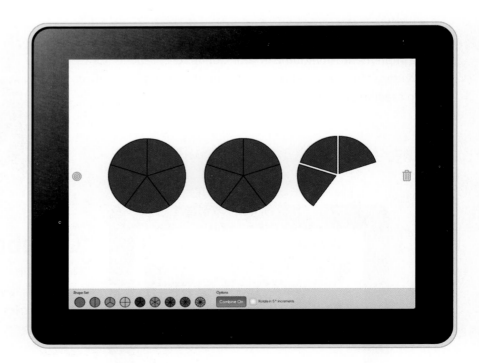

Connects Families to the Classroom

Access EM at Home

Help families support their children at home with complete digital access to classroom resources, including the *Student Reference Book*, Home Links, tutorials, and more.

Get Homework Help

Support families with online tips and tutorials as they help their children with Home Link assignments.

Reach Out with the *Home Connection Handbook*

Home Connections

Communicate easily and effectively using a collection of practical ideas and reproducible masters.

Keep in Touch with Family Letters

Keep families informed with unit-specific letters that communicate key information in English and Spanish, including a unit overview, suggestions for supporting activities, and answers to Home Links.

Give Every Child the Opportunity to Succeed

Everyday Mathematics helps all your students develop enduring mastery that prepares them for the rigor of Common Core assessments.

Assessing the Content Standards

Assess Daily

Assess the focus of each lesson with an Assessment Check-In to ensure children are making adequate progress toward mastery. Specific, actionable recommendations help teachers make instructional decisions and differentiate as appropriate.

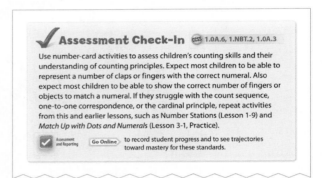

✓ **Assessment Check-In** ⓒⓒⓢⓢ 1.OA.6, 1.NBT.2, 1.OA.3

Use number-card activities to assess children's counting skills and their understanding of counting principles. Expect most children to be able to represent a number of claps or fingers with the correct numeral. Also expect most children to be able to show the correct number of fingers or objects to match a numeral. If they struggle with the count sequence, one-to-one correspondence, or the cardinal principle, repeat activities from this and earlier lessons, such as Number Stations (Lesson 1-9) and *Match Up with Dots and Numerals* (Lesson 3-1, Practice).

☑ Assessment and Reporting ⟨ Go Online ⟩ to record student progress and to see trajectories toward mastery for these standards.

Assess Digitally

Simplify gathering data and prepare children for digital assessments by assigning assessments online through the Student Learning Center.

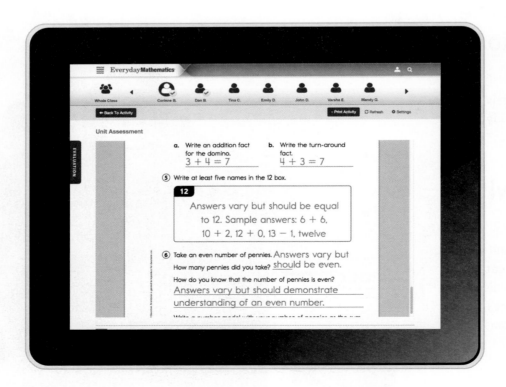

⟨ **Go Online** ⟩ to **connectED.mcgraw-hill.com** to the *Implementation Guide* for more on assessment and mastery.

Assess Unit Content

- *Unit Assessments* at the end of each unit provide formal opportunities to assess children's progress toward mastery of content and practices that are the focus of the unit.
- *Self Assessments* allow children to reflect on their understanding of content and practices that are the focus of the unit.
- *Challenge* problems extend important ideas from the unit, allowing children to demonstrate progress beyond expectations.
- *Cumulative Assessments* assess children's progress toward mastery of content and practices from prior units.
- *Open Response Assessments* provide information about children's performance on longer, more complex problems and emphasize the mathematical practices.

Provide Periodic Assessments

Monitor children's performance over time with interim assessments, including Beginning-of-Year, Mid-Year, and End-of-Year Assessments.

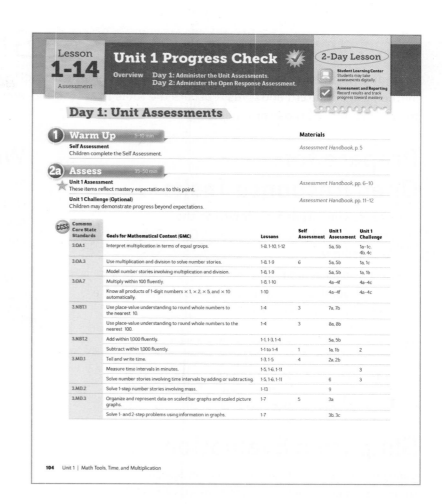

Assessing the Practice Standards

Everyday Mathematics engages children in the mathematical practices as they learn mathematical content and gives teachers the tools to assess and monitor each child's progress toward mastery of those practices.

Prepare for Open Response Tasks

- Assess your students' growth on the mathematical practices through Open Response Assessments.
- Access assessment and reporting tools designed to help you track progress towards mastery of the Common Core standards.

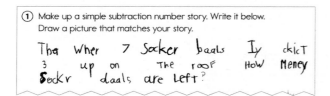

① Make up a simple subtraction number story. Write it below. Draw a picture that matches your story.

Tha Wher 7 Socker baals Iy ckicT
3 up on The rooF How Meney
Sockr daals are Left?

Simplified Evaluation

Easily evaluate performance with task-specific rubrics, student exemplars, ready-made checklists, and online assessment and reporting.

Writing/Reasoning Prompts

Students are given frequent opportunities to complete writing and reasoning tasks in Math Boxes, allowing teachers to observe and document communication skills and strategies for solving problems.

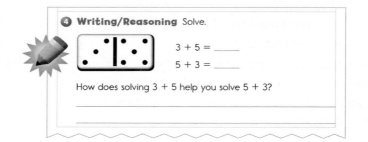

④ **Writing/Reasoning** Solve.

$3 + 5 =$ _____
$5 + 3 =$ _____

How does solving 3 + 5 help you solve 5 + 3?

Clear Mastery Expectations

Everyday Mathematics gives clear guidance regarding what children should know at every point in the year.

Plan for Mastery

Plan instruction more confidently by seeing how content develops across recent and upcoming lessons.

See the Big Picture

Easily grasp what children should know by the end of each unit.

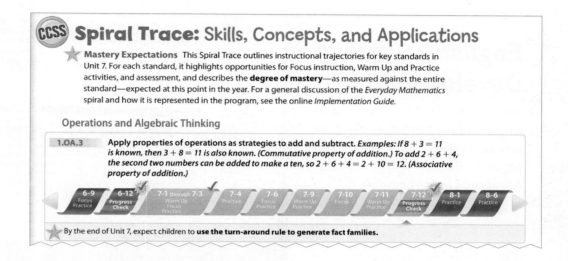

Build In-Depth Mastery

Go online to see a complete picture of how mastery develops for all standards within the grade. Preview upcoming activities and assessments to support instruction for each standard.

Monitor Student Progress

Use online assessment and reporting tools, Individual Profiles of Progress, and Class Checklists to monitor student progress toward mastery of each standard.

Differentiated Learning

Everyday Mathematics helps ensure that every child has the opportunity to achieve.

Response to Intervention

Differentiation Options for Readiness, Extra Practice, and Enrichment activities are included in every lesson and address the focus standards for that lesson.

English Language Development

Support is included in every lesson, with additional resources available through online Differentiation Support pages for Beginning, Intermediate, and Advanced English Learners.

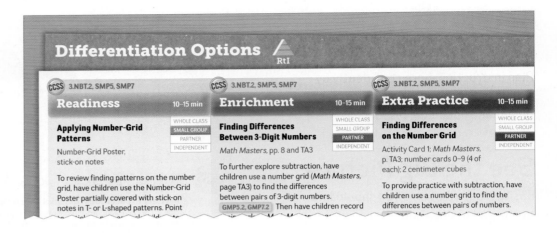

Differentiation Options △ RtI

CCSS 3.NBT.2, SMP5, SMP7

Readiness 10–15 min

WHOLE CLASS · SMALL GROUP · PARTNER · INDEPENDENT

Applying Number-Grid Patterns

Number-Grid Poster, stick-on notes

To review finding patterns on the number grid, have children use the Number-Grid Poster partially covered with stick-on notes in T- or L-shaped patterns. Point

CCSS 3.NBT.2, SMP5, SMP7

Enrichment 10–15 min

WHOLE CLASS · SMALL GROUP · PARTNER · INDEPENDENT

Finding Differences Between 3-Digit Numbers

Math Masters, pp. 8 and TA3

To further explore subtraction, have children use a number grid (*Math Masters*, page TA3) to find the differences between pairs of 3-digit numbers. GMP5.2, GMP7.2 Then have children record

CCSS 3.NBT.2, SMP5, SMP7

Extra Practice 10–15 min

WHOLE CLASS · SMALL GROUP · PARTNER · INDEPENDENT

Finding Differences on the Number Grid

Activity Card 1; *Math Masters*, p. TA3; number cards 0–9 (4 of each); 2 centimeter cubes

To provide practice with subtraction, have children use a number grid to find the differences between pairs of numbers.

English Language Learners Support

Beginning ELL Teach the slate routine with one-word signals and gestures. For example: LISTEN—Pulling on one ear; THINK—Closing your eyes and pointing with one finger to your temple; WRITE—Holding a writing tool and air writing; SHOW—Holding up a slate. Model each action with *I* _____, *We* _____, and *You* _____ sequences and have children show the actions along with you. Then have them show the appropriate action when you call out the one-word signal. **Go Online** **ELL** English Learners

Online Differentiation Support

Differentiation Support pages available in the online Teacher's Lesson Guide provide expanded, lesson-specific suggestions for working with English language learners and students who need more scaffolding.

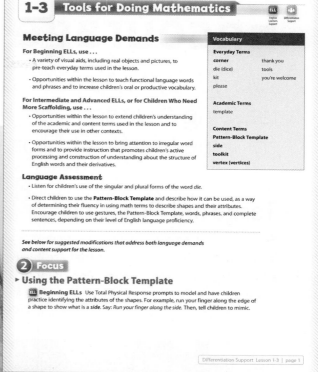

Academic Language Development

Explicitly plan instruction to develop all children's academic language. Academic Language Development suggestions are included in the *Teacher's Lesson Guide* and Differentiation Support pages for all lessons.

Point-of-Use Instructional Guidance

Easily identify common misconceptions and adjust activities immediately with differentiation support embedded within each lesson.

Academic Language Development

Some children may need to see what it means to put items in order. Have them order numbers from smallest to largest, or children from tallest to shortest. Encourage children to orally describe each member of a group: for example, small, bigger, and biggest. This will prepare them to look for patterns in the next activity.

Common Misconception

Differentiate **IF** children suggest number pairs that do not add to 10, **THEN** help them understand that if they start with a total of 10 pennies, then as long as they have picked up all the pennies on the table, the number of pennies in both hands should always add to 10.

Go Online | Differentiation Support

Differentiate Adjusting the Activity

- *Use sentence frames to help children name the pennies in each hand: I have _____ pennies in one hand. I have _____ pennies in the other hand. I have _____ pennies in all.*

- Draw two large hands on the board and record the numbers of pennies inside each hand using numbers and then circles. Give each child a copy of *Math Masters*, page 24. Children can put the pennies on the two hands and count them.

Go Online | Differentiation Support

Encourage Creative Thinking

Everyday Mathematics helps you create a dynamic learning environment that fosters creative mathematical thinking and flexible problem-solving skills.

Targeted Practice

Support children with leveled practice, including activities and games that are easily adapted to remediate or challenge children.

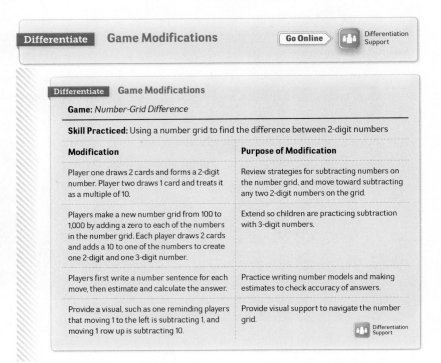

Differentiate	Game Modifications		Go Online	Differentiation Support

Differentiate   Game Modifications

Game: *Number-Grid Difference*

Skill Practiced: Using a number grid to find the difference between 2-digit numbers

Modification	Purpose of Modification
Player one draws 2 cards and forms a 2-digit number. Player two draws 1 card and treats it as a multiple of 10.	Review strategies for subtracting numbers on the number grid, and move toward subtracting any two 2-digit numbers on the grid.
Players make a new number grid from 100 to 1,000 by adding a zero to each of the numbers in the number grid. Each player draws 2 cards and adds a 10 to one of the numbers to create one 2-digit and one 3-digit number.	Extend so children are practicing subtraction with 3-digit numbers.
Players first write a number sentence for each move, then estimate and calculate the answer.	Practice writing number models and making estimates to check accuracy of answers.
Provide a visual, such as one reminding players that moving 1 to the left is subtracting 1, and moving 1 row up is subtracting 10.	Provide visual support to navigate the number grid.

Differentiation Support

Data-Driven Instruction

Online Assessment and Reporting provides easy-to-use, actionable information about children's performance, allowing teachers to make informed instructional decisions.

Assessment and Reporting

Set Up Small-Group Activities

Use Activity Cards in centers for small-group differentiation to support or extend the Focus part of the lesson.

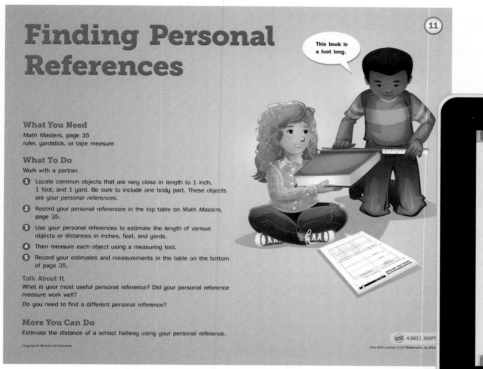

Finding Personal References

What You Need
Math Masters, page 35
ruler, yardstick, or tape measure

What To Do
Work with a partner.
1. Locate common objects that are very close in length to 1 inch, 1 foot, and 1 yard. Be sure to include one body part. These objects are your *personal references*.
2. Record your personal references in the top table on *Math Masters*, page 35.
3. Use your personal references to estimate the length of various objects or distances in inches, feet, and yards.
4. Then measure each object using a measuring tool.
5. Record your estimates and measurements in the table on the bottom of page 35.

Talk About It
What is your most useful personal reference? Did your personal reference measure work well?

Do you need to find a different personal reference?

More You Can Do
Estimate the distance of a school hallway using your personal reference.

This book is a foot long.

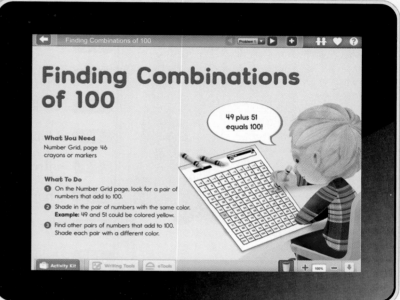

Finding Combinations of 100

What You Need
Number Grid, page 46
crayons or markers

What To Do
1. On the Number Grid page, look for a pair of numbers that add to 100.
2. Shade in the pair of numbers with the same color.
   Example: 49 and 51 could be colored yellow.
3. Find other pairs of numbers that add to 100. Shade each pair with a different color.

49 plus 51 equals 100!

Give Your Students Problem-Solving Power

Empower children to think critically, so they can identify the approach that works best for them and develop the confidence needed for success.

Choose Dynamic Grouping

Plan lessons for diverse classrooms using instructional grouping suggestions.

WHOLE CLASS	SMALL GROUP	PARTNER	INDEPENDENT

Contents

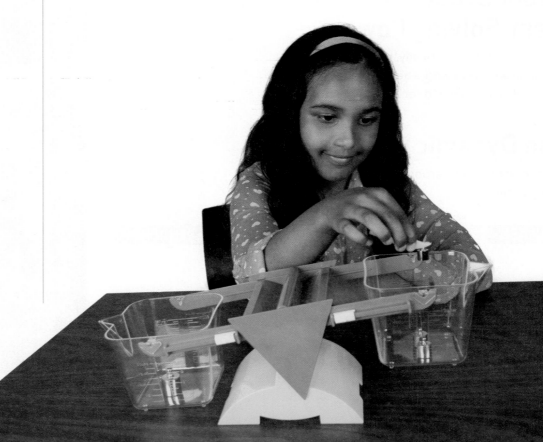

(t)McGraw-Hill Education/Mark Steinmetz, (b)McGraw-Hill Education

(t)McGraw-Hill Education/Ken Karp, (b)McGraw-Hill Education/Mark Steinmetz

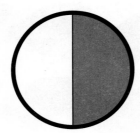

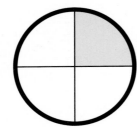

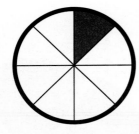

(t)©GoodSportHD.com/Alamy

McGraw-Hill Education

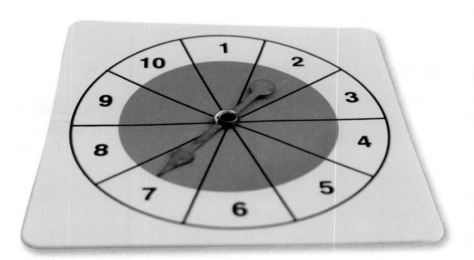

Getting Ready to Teach *Third Grade Everyday Mathematics*

Welcome to Third Grade Everyday Mathematics. This guide introduces the organization and pedagogy of Everyday Mathematics and provides tips to help you start planning and teaching right away.

Grade 3 has 108 lessons in 9 units. Plan to spend 60–75 minutes every day on math so that you complete 3–4 lessons each week and one unit every 3–5 weeks.

This pacing is designed for flexibility and depth. You will have flexibility so you can extend a lesson if discussion has been rich or if students' understandings are incomplete. You can add a day for "journal fix-up" or for differentiation—to provide an Enrichment activity to every student, for example—or for games. There will also be time to accommodate outside mandates, district initiatives, and special projects.

This pacing also gives you time to go deep, to create a classroom culture that values and supports productive struggle. You can expect your students to do their own thinking, to solve problems they have not been shown how to solve, to make connections between concepts and procedures, to explain their thinking, and to understand others' thinking. Creating such a classroom culture takes time, but it's what the Common Core asks you to do in its Standards for Mathematical Practice—and the pacing of Everyday Mathematics 4 is designed to give you the time you'll need.

The *Teacher's Lesson Guide* is your primary source for information on planning units and teaching lessons. In most lessons, children will complete pages in their *Math Journals* or digitally in the Student Learning Center. Additional pages that require copies are available as *Math Masters*. See the Materials section on pages xl–xlii for information on the teacher and student components.

▶ Preparing for the Beginning of School

- ☐ Use the list on pages xl–xlii to check that your **Classroom Resource Package** is complete.
- ☐ See page xliii for manipulatives and supplies you will need.
- ☐ Read the **Unit 1 Organizer** (pages 2–13) and the **first several lessons in Unit 1** to help you plan for the first week of school.
- ☐ Read the *Everyday Mathematics* in Grades 1–6 section of the ***Implementation Guide*** for more information on getting started.
- ☐ Prepare the **Unit 1 Family Letter** on *Math Masters,* pages 2–6 to distribute early in the school year.
- ☐ Review the **Beginning-of-Year Assessment** on pages 105–110 in the *Assessment Handbook* and consider when you will administer it.

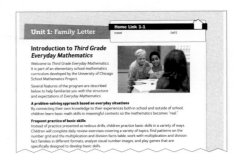

Go Online to join the Virtual Learning Community (VLC) to learn about *Everyday Mathematics* classrooms from other teachers and to find tips for setting up your classroom.

▶ Lesson Types

Third Grade Everyday Mathematics includes four types of lessons, which share many of the same features.

Regular Lessons are the most common lesson type. See the tables on the following pages for details about regular lessons.

Explorations Lessons occur once per unit and give children three unique opportunities to explore new concepts and tools in an informal small-group setting. Exploration A is often a teacher-led activity and focuses on the main content of the lesson. Activity Cards provide directions for children to complete most Explorations.

Open Response and Reengagement Lessons extend over two days and occur in every unit. On Day 1 children solve a challenging problem that involves more than one possible strategy or solution. On Day 2 children reengage in the problem and are asked to defend their reasoning and make sense of the reasoning of others.

Progress Check Lessons are two-day lessons at the end of every unit. All items on the Progress Check match expectations for progress at that point in the grade and, with the exception of the optional challenge assessment, are fair to grade. On Day 1 children complete a self-assessment, a unit assessment, and an optional challenge assessment covering the content and practices that were the focus of the unit. Day 2 includes one of the following types of assessments:

Open Response Assessments are included in odd-numbered units and allow children to think creatively about a problem. They address both content and practice standards and are accompanied by task-specific rubrics.

Cumulative Assessments are included in even-numbered units and cover standards from prior units.

▶ Lesson Parts and Features

Every regular lesson begins with two planning pages. The remaining pages of the lesson provide a detailed guide for teaching the three parts of a lesson: Warm Up, Focus, and Practice.

	Lesson Parts and Features	Description	Tips
PLANNING	**Lesson Opener**	An outline of the lesson to assist in your planning that includes information on content and standards, timing suggestions, assessment, and materials. **Go Online** to the *Implementation Guide* for information on *Everyday Mathematics* and the Common Core State Standards (CCSS).	• See **Before You Begin** for preparation tips. • Follow the time allotments for each part of the lesson.
	Differentiation Options	Optional **Readiness, Enrichment, Extra Practice,** and **English Language Learners (ELL) Support** activities that allow you to differentiate instruction. Additional Differentiation Support pages are available online for each regular lesson.	• Choose to complete Differentiation Options as a whole class, as a small group, with partners, or individually depending on the needs of your children. • Note that some children may benefit from completing the **Readiness** activity prior to the lesson. **Go Online** to the *Implementation Guide* for information on differentiation.

	Part 1: Warm Up	Description	Tips
INSTRUCTION	**Mental Math and Fluency**	Quick, leveled warm-up exercises children answer orally, with gestures, or on slates or tablets that provide practice towards fluency.	• Select the levels that make sense for your children and customize for your class. • For most lessons, spend 5 or fewer minutes on this feature. For Quick Looks, allow up to 10 minutes. **Go Online** to the *Implementation Guide* for information on Quick Looks.

	Part 2: Focus	Description	Tips
INSTRUCTION	**Math Message and Math Message Follow-Up**	An introductory activity to the day's lesson that usually requires children to solve a problem they have not been shown how to solve. The follow-up discussion connects to the focus activities of the lesson and gives children opportunities to discuss their strategies.	• Consider where and how you will display the Math Message and how children will record their answers. • Maintain high cognitive demand by expecting children to work through the problem without your help before the follow-up discussion begins.

Part 2: Focus, *cont.*		Description	Tips
INSTRUCTION	**Focus Activities**	Two to four main instructional activities, including games, in which children explore and engage in new content (skills, concepts, games).	• Encourage children to discuss and work together to solve problems during focus activities. • Remember that many focus skills, concepts, applications, and games will be revisited in later practice. Go Online to the Spiral Tracker to see the complete spiral. • Look for Goals for Mathematical Practice icons. GMP1.1 Use these to facilitate discussions about the practices. Go Online to the *Implementation Guide* for information on Mathematical Practices.
	Assessment Check-In ✓	A daily assessment opportunity to assess the focus content standards in the lesson. Assessment Check-Ins provide information on expectations for particular standards at that point in the curriculum.	• Use results to inform instruction. Expectation statements in the Assessment Check-Ins help you decide which children would benefit from differentiation activities. • Consider Assessment Check-Ins as "fair to grade" in most cases. Go Online to record children's progress and to see trajectories toward mastery for these and other standards. Go Online to the *Implementation Guide* for assessment information.

Part 3: Practice		Description	Tips
INSTRUCTION	**Practice Activity**	An opportunity to practice previously taught skills and content through a practice page or a game in many lessons.	• Allow time for practice pages and games because they are critical for children to meet expectations for standards. This is an essential part of the distributed practice in *Everyday Mathematics*. • Plan for all children to play *Everyday Mathematics* games at least 60 minutes per week. Go Online to the *Implementation Guide* for tips to ensure that all children have ample game time. See also the Virtual Learning Community (VLC) to observe many *Everyday Mathematics* games in action.
	Math Boxes	A daily *Math Journal* page, beginning in Lesson 1-5, that reviews skills and concepts which children have seen prior to that point in the program. Preview Math Boxes anticipate content in the upcoming unit.	• Aim to have children complete Math Boxes with as little teacher support as possible. • Complete Math Boxes at any point during the day.
	Home Link	A daily homework page that provides practice and informs families about the math from that day's lesson.	Encourage children to do these activities with someone at home, such as a parent, caregiver, or sibling.

	Differentiation and Language Features	Description and Purpose
DIFFERENTIATION	**Adjusting the Activity**	Allows for differentiated instruction by offering modifications to lesson activities.
	Common Misconception	Offers point-of-use intervention tips that address common misconceptions.
	Game Modifications	Provides suggestions online for modifying games to support children who struggle and challenge children who are ready.
	Differentiation Support	Offers two online pages of specific differentiation ideas for each lesson, as well as ELL suggestions and scaffolding for children who need it.
LANGUAGE NOTES	**Academic Language Development**	Suggests how to introduce new academic vocabulary that is relevant to the lesson. These notes benefit all children, not solely English language learners.
	English Language Learners (ELL) Support	Provides activities and point-of-use ideas for supporting children at different levels of English language proficiency.

Getting to Know Your Classroom Resource Package

Complete access to all digital resources is included in your Classroom Resource Package. To access these resources, log into **ConnectED.mcgraw-hill.com**.

Planning, Instruction, and Assessment

Resource	Description
Teacher's Lesson Guide (Volumes 1 and 2) ☑ digital ☑ print	• Comprehensive guide to the *Everyday Mathematics* lessons and assessments • CCSS alignment information: digital version includes online tracking of each content standard • Point-of-use differentiation strategies: Readiness, Enrichment, Extra Practice, English Language Learners Support, Academic Language Development, Adjusting the Activity, Game Modifications, Common Misconception • Additional Differentiation Support pages available digitally for virtually every lesson • Unit overviews • Planning and calendar tools
eToolkit ☑ digital ☐ print	• Online tools and virtual manipulatives for dynamic instruction • A complete list of Grade 3 eTools on page xliii
ePresentations ☑ digital ☐ print	• Ready-made interactive white board lesson content to support daily instruction
Math Masters ☑ digital ☑ print	• Reproducible masters for lessons, Home Links, Family Letters, and games
Minute Math+ ☑ digital ☑ print	• Brief activities that require little or no materials; useful for transition times and for spare moments throughout the day
Classroom Posters ☑ digital ☑ print	• Posters that display grade-specific mathematical content • Posters that display the Standards for Mathematical Practice

Planning, Instruction, and Assessment (con't)

Resource	Description
Assessment Handbook ☑ digital ☑ print	• Assessment masters for unit-based assessments and interim assessments • Record sheets for tracking individual and class progress
Assessment and Reporting Tools ☑ digital ☐ print	• Student, class, school, and district reports • Data available at point-of-use in the planning and teaching materials • Real-time data to inform instruction and differentiation
Spiral Tracker ☑ digital ☐ print	• Online tool that helps you understand how standards develop across the spiral curriculum

Professional Development

Resource	Description
Implementation Guide ☑ digital ☐ print	• Online resource with information on implementing the curriculum
Virtual Learning Community ☑ digital ☐ print	• An online community, sponsored and facilitated by the Center for Elementary Mathematics and Science Education (CEMSE) at the University of Chicago, to network with other educators and share best practices • A collection of resources including videos of teachers implementing lessons in real classrooms, photos, work samples, and planning tools

Family Communications

Resource	Description
Home Connection Handbook ☑ digital ☐ print	• A collections of tips and tools to help you communicate to families about *Everyday Mathematics* • Reproducible masters for home communication for use by both teachers and administrators

Student Materials

Resource	Description
Student Math Journal (Volumes 1 and 2) ☑ digital ☑ print	• Student work pages that provide daily support for classroom instruction • Provide a long-term record of each student's mathematical development
Pattern-Block Template ☑ digital ☑ print	• eTools to support mathematical concepts, including geometry and measurement • Also available as plastic templates
Student Reference Book ☑ digital ☑ print	• Resource to support student learning in the classroom and at home • Includes explanations of mathematical content and directions for many *Everyday Mathematics* games
Activity Cards ☑ digital ☑ print	• Directions for students for Explorations, Differentiation Options, and other small-group activities
Student Learning Center ☑ digital ☐ print	• Combines *Student Math Journal, Student Reference Book,* eToolkit, and Activity Cards, and other resources for students in one location • Interactive functionality provides access in English and Spanish • Interactive functionality provides immediate feedback on select problems • Animations that can help with skills and concepts and reinforce classroom teaching • Provides access to EM Games Online and Facts Workshop Game
EM Games Online ☑ digital ☐ print	• Digital versions of many of the *Everyday Mathematics* games that provide important practice in a fun and engaging setting
Facts Workshop Game ☑ digital ☐ print	• Games that build computation skill and fact fluency with *Everday Mathematics* routines such as fact families and fact triangles

► Manipulative Kits and eToolkit

The table below lists the materials that are used throughout *Third Grade Everyday Mathematics.* All of the items may be purchased from McGraw-Hill Education as a comprehensive classroom manipulative kit or as individual items. Note that some lessons call for additional materials, which you or your children can bring in at the appropriate times. The additional materials are listed in the Unit Organizers and in the lessons in which they are used.

Manipulative Kit Contents		eTools
Item	**Quantity**	**Item**
Attribute Blocks	Not in kit	✔
Base-10 Big Cube	Not in kit	✔
Base-10 Flats	6 packs of 10 flats	✔
Base-10 Longs	5 packs of 50 longs	✔
Base-10 Cubes	10 packs of 100 cubes	✔
Beakers, Nested Graduated Set	4 sets; 5 beakers in each set	
Clock Faces	1 pack of 25 faces	✔
Clock Face Stamp	2 stamps	
Connectors	1 pack of 2,000	
Counters, Double-Sided	Not in kit	✔
Counters, Translucent (red, yellow, blue, green)	1 pack of 200	
Counting Sticks	Not in kit	✔
Dice, Blank	1 pack of 16	✔
Dice, Dot	2 packs of 12	✔
Dice, Polyhedral	Not in kit	✔
Dice, 10-Sided, numbered 1-10	25 dice	✔
Dominos, Double-9	Not in kit	✔
Everything Math Deck	15 decks	✔
Fraction Circle Pieces	25 sets	✔
Geoboard, Two-Sided, 7" by 7"	8 geoboards	✔
Marker Boards	25 boards	
Medicine Dropper, 1 mL	12 droppers	
Metersticks, Dual Scale	2 packs of 10	
Number Line, -35 to 180	1 number line (in 3 parts)	✔
Pattern Blocks	2 sets of 250	✔
Play Money Bill Set	$1 Bills: 1 pack of 350 bills; $10 Bills: 1 pack of 150 bills	✔
Quick Look Cards	1 set Equal Groups; 1 set Fractions	✔
Rocker (Pan) Balance	1 balance	✔
Rubber Bands	1 pack of 400	
Ruler, 12 in.	5 packs of 5 rulers	
Standard Metric Masses	1 set	
Straws	1 pack of 500	
Tape Measure, Retractable	15 tape measures	
Thermometer, Classroom	Not in kit	✔

Unit 1 Organizer
Math Tools, Time, and Multiplication

In this unit, an active and collaborative learning environment is established. Children recall how to use a variety of math tools to solve problems, tell time to the nearest minute, and use mathematical models to calculate elapsed time. This unit also lays the foundation for developing multiplication and division strategies.

 ### Standards for Mathematical Content

Domain	Cluster
Operations and Algebraic Thinking	Represent and solve problems involving multiplication and division.
Number and Operations in Base Ten	Use place value understanding and properties of operations to perform multi-digit arithmetic.
Measurement and Data	Solve problems involving measurement and estimation.

Because the standards within each domain can be broad, *Everyday Mathematics* has unpacked each standard into Goals for Mathematical Content **GMC**. For a complete list of Standards and Goals, see page EM1.

For an overview of the CCSS domains, standards, and mastery expectations in this unit, see the **Spiral Trace** on pages 8–9. See the **Mathematical Background** (pages 10–12) for a discussion of the following key topics:

- Number Grids
- Computational Estimation and Rounding
- Multiplication and Division Representations
- Organizing and Representing Data
- Time
- Measuring Mass
- Quick Looks
- Explorations

Standards for Mathematical Practice

SMP4	Model with mathematics.
SMP5	Use appropriate tools strategically.

For a discussion about how *Everyday Mathematics* develops these practices and a list of Goals for Mathematical Practice **GMP**, see page 13.

 VLC **Virtual Learning Community** Go Online to **vlc.cemseprojects.org** to search for video clips on each practice.

McGraw-Hill Education

Go Digital with these tools at **connectED.mcgraw-hill.com**

| ePresentations | Student Learning Center | Facts Workshop Game | eToolkit | Professional Development | Home Connections | Spiral Tracker | Assessment and Reporting | English Learners Support | Differentiation Support |

Contents

*The standards listed here are addressed in the **Focus** of each lesson. For all the standards in a lesson, see the Lesson Opener.

Unit 1 Materials

VLC Virtual Learning Community

See how *Everyday Mathematics* teachers organize materials.
Search "Classroom Tours" at **vlc.cemseprojects.org**.

Lesson	Math Masters	Activity Cards	Manipulative Kit	Other Materials
1-1	pp. 2–8; TA2–TA3	1	counters (optional); number cards 0–9 (4 of each from the Everything Math Deck, if available); 2 centimeter cubes	slate; Number-Grid Poster; stick-on notes; *Minute Math+*
1-2	pp. 9–10; TA3; G2	2–3	number cards 0–9 (4 of each); 2 counters; base-10 blocks (optional); 2 centimeter cubes	slate (optional); Number-Grid Poster; calculator (optional); *Minute Math+*
1-3	pp. 11; TA3–TA4; G2–G3	4	toolkit items; toolkit clock; number cards 0–9 (4 of each); 2 counters	demonstration clock; brads (optional); scissors (optional); paper (optional); calculator; *Minute Math+*
1-4	pp. 12–13; TA3	5–6	number cards 1–9 (4 of each)	slate; half-sheet of paper; calculator; number grid (optional); *Minute Math+*
1-5	pp. 14–16; TA4 (optional); TA5	7–8	toolkit clocks; number cards 1–20	demonstration clock; scissors; brads; crayons; stapler; *Minute Math+*
1-6	pp. 17–18; TA6		toolkit clocks	demonstration clock; Class Data Pad or chart paper; Standards for Mathematical Practice Poster; colored pencils (optional); selected samples of children's work; children's work from Day 1
1-7	pp. 19–21; TA7; G4–G5	9	number cards 1–9 (4 of each)	Class Data Pad; pencil; large paper clip; paper; *Minute Math+*
1-8	pp. 22; TA8	10–12	72 counters; number cards 2–4 (4 of each); 6-sided die	slate; 4 quarter-sheets of paper; full sheets of paper; *Minute Math+*
1-9	pp. 23–26		counters or pennies (optional)	scissors; envelopes or resealable plastic bags (optional); paper clip; *Minute Math+*
1-10	pp. 27–33; TA9; G6		Quick Look Cards 132, 134, 136, 145, 149; counters (optional); number cards 1–10 (4 of each); per partnership: die labeled 2, 2, 5, 5, 10, 10	slate; paper; scissors; nickel; dime; Fact Strategy Wall; 2s, 5s, and 10s Fact Triangles; *Minute Math+*
1-11	pp. 34; TA10–TA12	13–14	toolkit clocks	demonstration clock; slate; marker; paper; scissors; paper clip; envelope; Length-of-Day Graph; Fact Triangles; *Minute Math+*
1-12	pp. 35–37; TA13; G6	15–17	Quick Look Cards 124, 125, 130; counters; Everything Math Decks including number cards 1–10 (4 of each); two 6-sided dice; die labeled 2, 2, 5, 5, 10, 10; pan balance; standard masses	calculator; scissors; paper; classroom objects; paper clips and tape (optional); slate; *Minute Math+*
1-13	pp. 38–40; G4–G5	18	Quick Look Cards 126, 127, 128; number cards 1–9 (4 of each); pan balance; standard masses	1-liter bottles of water; large paper clips; classroom objects of varying weights and sizes; Class Data Pad; resealable plastic bag; 20 nickels; stick-on notes; pencil; poster paper (optional); *Minute Math+*
1-14	pp. 41–44; *Assessment Handbook*, pp. 5–14			Standards for Mathematical Practice Poster

📖 **Literature Link** **1-9** *The Doorbell Rang* (optional); *A Remainder of One* (optional)

Go Online for a complete literature list in Grade 3 and to download all Quick Look Cards.

Problem Solving  Professional Development

Everyday Mathematics emphasizes equally all three of the Common Core's dimensions of **rigor:**

- conceptual understanding
- procedural skill and fluency
- applications

Math Messages, other daily work, Explorations, and Open Response tasks provide many opportunities for children to apply what they know to solve problems.

▶ Math Message

Math Messages require children to solve a problem they have not been shown how to solve. Math Messages provide almost daily opportunities for problem solving.

▶ Daily Work

Journal pages, Home Links, Writing/Reasoning prompts, and Differentiation Options often require children to solve problems in mathematical contexts and real-life situations. ***Minute Math+*** offers number stories and a variety of other practice activities for transition times and spare moments throughout the day.

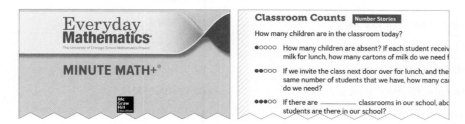

▶ Explorations

In Exploration A, children estimate and compare masses of objects. In Exploration B, children divide whole pancakes into equal shares. In Exploration C, children create equal groups.

▶ Open Response and Reengagement

In Lesson 1-6, children use mathematical models to measure elapsed time. Children will calculate the length of their school morning. During the reengagement discussion on Day 2, children share models and discuss strategies for calculating elapsed time and then revise their work. Using mathematical models to solve problems and answer questions is the focus practice for the lesson. GMP4.2

VLC Virtual Learning Community **Go Online** to watch an Open Response and Reengagement lesson in action. Search "Open Response" at **vlc.cemseprojects.org.**

▶ Open Response Assessment

In Progress Check Lesson 1-14, children interpret a graph and use the graph to solve a problem. They share their observations from the graph and their solutions to the problem. GMP4.2

Look for GMP1.1–1.6 markers, which indicate opportunities for children to engage in **SMP1:** "Make sense of problems and persevere in solving them." Children also become better problem solvers as they engage in all of the CCSS Mathematical Practices. The yellow GMP markers throughout the lessons indicate places where you can emphasize the Mathematical Practices and develop children's problem-solving skills.

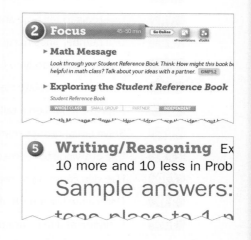

Assessment and Differentiation

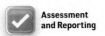
Assessment
and Reporting

See pages xxii–xxv to learn about a comprehensive online system for recording, monitoring, and reporting children's progress using core program assessments.

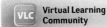
VLC | Virtual Learning Community | Go Online > to **vlc.cemseprojects.org** for tools and ideas related to assessment and differentiation from *Everyday Mathematics* teachers.

✔ Ongoing Assessment

In addition to frequent informal opportunities for "kid watching," every lesson (except Explorations) offers an **Assessment Check-In** to gauge children's performance on one or more of the standards addressed in that lesson.

Lesson	Task Description	CCSS Common Core State Standards
1-1	Find differences using a number grid.	3.NBT.2, SMP7
1-2	Find differences using a number grid.	3.NBT.2, SMP5
1-3	Use tools to tell time and measure length.	SMP5
1-4	Use number lines to round to the nearest 10 and 100.	3.NBT.1
1-5	Tell time accurately to the nearest 5 minutes.	3.MD.1, SMP5, SMP6
1-6	Accurately calculate elapsed time.	3.MD.1, SMP4
1-7	Represent data on a tally chart and set up a scaled bar graph.	3.MD.3, SMP6
1-8	Solve equal-groups number stories, and record number models.	3.OA.3, SMP4
1-9	Use drawings to represent and solve division number stories.	3.OA.2, 3.OA.3, SMP1
1-10	Use skip counting or repeated addition to solve multiplication problems.	3.OA.1, 3.OA.7, SMP2
1-11	Determine the length of day using strategies to find elapsed time.	3.MD.1, SMP1
1-13	Estimate and measure mass.	3.MD.2

► Periodic Assessment

Beginning-of-Year Assessment This benchmark test checks children's mastery of concepts and skills that are important for success in third grade. See the *Assessment Handbook*.

Unit 1 Progress Check This assessment focuses on the CCSS domains of *Operations and Algebraic Thinking, Number and Operations in Base Ten,* and *Measurement and Data.* It also contains an Open Response Assessment to assess children's ability to interpret a graph and use the information to solve a problem. GMP4.2

> **NOTE** Odd-numbered units include an **Open Response Assessment.** Even-numbered units include a **Cumulative Assessment.**

▶ Unit 1 Differentiation Activities

 **Differentiation Support**   **English Learners Support**

Differentiation Options Every regular lesson provides **Readiness, Enrichment, Extra Practice,** and **Beginning English Language Learners Support** activities that address the Focus standards of that lesson.

Activity Card 8

Activity Cards These activities, written to the children, enable you to differentiate Part 2 of the lesson through small-group work.

English Language Learners Activities and point-of-use support help children at different levels of English language proficiency succeed.

Differentiation Support online pages

Differentiation Support Two online pages for most lessons provide suggestions for game modifications, ways to scaffold lessons for children who need additional support, and language development suggestions for Beginning, Intermediate, and Advanced English language learners.

For **ongoing distributed practice,** see these activities:
- Mental Math and Fluency
- Differentiation Options: Extra Practice
- Part 3: Journal pages, Math Boxes, *Math Masters*, Home Links
- Print and Online games

Ongoing Practice  **Differentiation Support**

▶ Embedded Facts Practice

Basic Facts Practice can be found in every part of the lesson. Look for activities or games labeled with CCSS 3.OA.7; or go online to the Spiral Tracker and search using CCSS 3.OA.7.

▶ Games

Games in *Everyday Mathematics* are an essential tool for practicing skills and developing strategic thinking.

Lesson	Game	Skills and Concepts	CCSS Common Core State Standards
1-2 1-3	*Number-Grid Difference*	Practicing mental subtraction strategies	3.NBT.2, SMP5, SMP6
1-3	*Hit the Target*	Finding differences between 2-digit numbers and multiples of 10	3.NBT.2, SMP3
1-7 1-13	*Spin and Round*	Rounding 3-digit numbers to the nearest 10 or 100	3.NBT.1
1-10 1-12	*Multiplication Draw*	Practicing multiplication facts	3.OA.7, SMP6, SMP7

VLC Virtual Learning Community | Go Online ▷ | to look for examples of *Everyday Mathematics* games at **vlc.cemseprojects.org.**

(CCSS) Spiral Trace: Skills, Concepts, and Applications

⭐ **Mastery Expectations** This Spiral Trace outlines instructional trajectories for key standards in Unit 1. For each standard, it highlights opportunities for Focus instruction, Warm Up and Practice activities, as well as formative and summative assessment. It describes the **degree of mastery**—as measured against the entire standard—expected at this point in the year.

Operations and Algebraic Thinking

3.OA.1 Interpret products of whole numbers, e.g., interpret 5×7 as the total number of objects in 5 groups of 7 objects each. *For example, describe a context in which a total number of objects can be expressed as 5×7.*

| 1-8 Focus Practice | 1-10 Focus Practice | 1-12 Warm Up Focus | 1-13 Warm Up Practice | 1-14 Progress Check | 2-6 Focus | 2-7 Focus Practice | 2-13 Progress Check | 3-9 through 3-12 Warm Up Focus Practice | 3-13 Warm Up | 3-14 Progress Check |

⭐ By the end of Unit 1, expect children to **interpret multiplication in terms of equal groups for multiples of 5 and 10.**

3.OA.3 Use multiplication and division within 100 to solve word problems in situations involving equal groups, arrays, and measurement quantities, e.g., by using drawings and equations with a symbol for the unknown number to represent the problem.

| 1-2 Warm Up | 1-8 Focus Practice | 1-9 Focus Practice | 1-10 Practice | 1-14 Progress Check | 2-1 through 2-4 Practice | 2-5 through 2-10 Warm Up Focus Practice | 2-11 Practice | 2-13 Progress Check | 3-8 Practice |

⭐ By the end of Unit 1, expect children to **solve word problems in situations involving equal groups and arrays by using drawings to represent the problem.**

3.OA.7 Fluently multiply and divide within 100, using strategies such as the relationship between multiplication and division (e.g., knowing that $8 \times 5 = 40$, one knows $40 \div 5 = 8$) or properties of operations. By the end of Grade 3, know from memory all products of two one-digit numbers.

| 1-1 Warm Up | 1-5 Warm Up | 1-9 Warm Up Practice | 1-10 Warm Up Focus Practice | 1-11 through 1-13 Warm Up Practice | 1-14 Progress Check | 2-2 Practice | 2-3 Practice | 2-4 through 2-7 Warm Up Focus Practice | 2-8 Warm Up Practice |

⭐ By the end of Unit 1, expect children to **multiply using strategies for all products of one-digit numbers and 2 and 10.**

Spiral Tracker

Go to **connectED.mcgraw-hill.com** for comprehensive trajectories that show how in-depth mastery develops across the grade.

Number and Operations in Base Ten

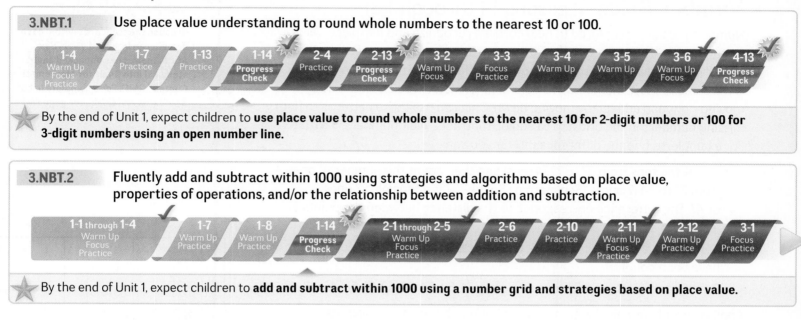

3.NBT.1 — Use place value understanding to round whole numbers to the nearest 10 or 100.

1-4 Warm Up Focus Practice • 1-7 Practice • 1-13 Practice • 1-14 Progress Check • 2-4 Practice • 2-13 Progress Check • 3-2 Warm Up Focus • 3-3 Focus Practice • 3-4 Warm Up • 3-5 Warm Up • 3-6 Warm Up Focus • 4-13 Progress Check

By the end of Unit 1, expect children to **use place value to round whole numbers to the nearest 10 for 2-digit numbers or 100 for 3-digit numbers using an open number line.**

3.NBT.2 — Fluently add and subtract within 1000 using strategies and algorithms based on place value, properties of operations, and/or the relationship between addition and subtraction.

1-1 through 1-4 Warm Up Focus Practice • 1-7 Warm Up Practice • 1-8 Warm Up Practice • 1-14 Progress Check • 2-1 through 2-5 Warm Up Focus Practice • 2-6 Practice • 2-10 Practice • 2-11 Warm Up Focus Practice • 2-12 Warm Up Practice • 3-1 Focus Practice

By the end of Unit 1, expect children to **add and subtract within 1000 using a number grid and strategies based on place value.**

Measurement and Data

3.MD.1 — Tell and write time to the nearest minute and measure time intervals in minutes. Solve word problems involving addition and subtraction of time intervals in minutes, e.g., by representing the problem on a number line diagram.

1-3 Focus Practice • 1-5 Focus Practice • 1-6 Warm Up Focus Practice • 1-11 Warm Up Focus Practice • 1-14 Progress Check • 2-1 Practice • 2-6 Practice • 2-13 Progress Check • 4-13 Progress Check

By the end of Unit 1, expect children to **tell and write time to the nearest 5 minutes and use a number line to add time intervals in minutes.**

Throughout Grade 3, children will regularly practice 3.MD.1 content by recording time on *Math Journal* pages and attending to the Length-of-Day Project.

Key ✓ = Assessment Check-In   ✦ = Progress Check Lesson   ▱ = Current Unit   ▰ = Previous or Upcoming Lessons

Mathematical Background: Content

 The discussion below highlights major content areas and the Common Core State Standards addressed in Unit 1. See the online Spiral Tracker for complete information about the learning trajectories for all standards.

▶ Number Grids (Lessons 1-1 through 1-3)

Number grids are structured to help children recognize and use place-value patterns. Numbers increase as you move to the right and down. Each row starts with a 1 in the ones place and ends in a decade number. The ones digit is the same in all the numbers in a column. This means you can add one by moving right and add ten by moving down. Children use these patterns to find missing numbers in the grid and to add or subtract 2-digit numbers. **3.NBT.2** For example, to find the difference 84 − 37 you can:

- Count the tens from 37 to 77 (4 tens) and then count the number of ones from 77 to 84 (7 ones). (*See margin.*) So 84 − 37 is 4 tens plus 7 ones, or 47. This difference corresponds to the distance between the points 37 and 84 on a number line.
- Start at 84 and count back to 37, noting as before how many numbers have been counted.
- Count back 37 from 84 by tens and ones: 74, 64, 54, 53, 52, 51, 50, 49, 48, 47.

Addition problems can also be solved on the number grid in similar ways.

▶ Time (Lessons 1-3, 1-5, 1-6, and 1-11)

Unlike measurements or counts, numbers in reference frames locate things only within definite systems or contexts. Examples include dates, times, and temperatures. Clock time is a reference frame with second, minute, and hour intervals. In third grade, children become more efficient and accurate at telling time to the nearest minute by using helpful "familiar times." **3.MD.1** Beginning in Lesson 1-5, children engage in daily time-telling practice by recording the time on every *Math Journal* page. The use of time units to measure the duration of an event or the time between events is called *elapsed time.* Children are encouraged to model and make sense of elapsed time situations using analog clocks or open number lines. **3.MD.1**

▶ Computational Estimation and Rounding
(Lesson 1-4)

Estimation in computation is a major thread in *Everyday Mathematics* because of its importance in both mathematics and everyday life. Estimation requires intuition about numbers, understanding of context, and a flexible range of techniques. Good estimation skills take years to develop but can help children develop mental flexibility, good number sense, and confidence that mathematics makes sense.

It is important for children to discuss the differences between exact and estimated answers. Help children identify situations in which an estimate is good enough or even makes more sense than an exact answer. In other situations, an estimate might

 Standards and Goals for Mathematical Practice

Because the standards within each domain can be broad, *Everyday Mathematics* has unpacked each standard into Goals for Mathematical Content **GMC**. For a complete list of Standards and Goals, see page EM1.

−9	−8	−7	−6	−5	−4	−3	−2	−1	0
1	2	3	4	5	6	7	8	9	10
11	12	13	14	15	16	17	18	19	20
21	22	23	24	25	26	27	28	29	30
31	32	33	34	35	36	37	38	39	40
41	42	43	44	45	46	47	48	49	50
51	52	53	54	55	56	57	58	59	60
61	62	63	64	65	66	67	68	69	70
71	72	73	74	75	76	77	78	79	80
81	82	83	84	85	86	87	88	89	90
91	92	93	94	95	96	97	98	99	100
101	102	103	104	105	106	107	108	109	110
111	112	113	114	115	116	117	118	119	120

One way to find 84 − 37

Unit 1 Vocabulary

array	equal grouping	kilogram	precise
bar graph	equal groups	length of day	product
close-but-easier numbers	equal shares	mass	Quick Looks
	equal sharing	masses	round
column	essay	mathematical model	row
data	estimate	multiplication	strategy
difference	fact family	multiplication symbol	weight
division	factors	number grid	zero
division symbol	Fact Triangle	open number line	
elapsed time	gram	pan balance	

provide insight into a difficult problem or verify the reasonableness of an answer after calculation. **3.OA.8** Children should become aware that there is no single "correct" estimate; the purpose of estimation is to find a reasonable answer, not the correct answer.

When solving problems, children sometimes use close-but-easier numbers to estimate answers. Rounding, a technique for finding close-but-easier numbers, is introduced in *Third Grade Everyday Mathematics.* **3.NBT.1** An open number line is a useful tool for rounding numbers to the nearest 10 or 100, as explained in detail in Lesson 1-4. Some children may not need a number line, having learned to look at the digit to the right of the target place. If that digit is 5 or greater, they round up. If it is less than 5, they round down. Encourage children to explain and compare the tools and strategies they use.

▶ Organizing and Representing Data
(Lessons 1-7 and 1-11)

In *Everyday Mathematics,* children participate in data collection and analysis. In Lesson 1-7 children collect, organize, and analyze data about how many letters are in their first and last names. They review elements of a scaled bar graph in preparation for more in-depth work with graphs in Unit 3. In Lesson 1-11 children begin an ongoing data collection activity called the Length-of-Day Project. **3.MD.1, 3.MD.3**

▶ Multiplication and Division Representations
(Lessons 1-8 through 1-10, 1-12)

In *Everyday Mathematics,* beginning work with an operation involves concrete representations of real-life situations. In Lesson 1-8 children make sense of multiplication situations, using intuition to put objects into equal-sized groups and invent strategies such as drawing pictures and counting, skip counting, and repeated addition. **3.OA.1** Children also use rectangular arrays to represent multiples of equal groups with *r* rows with *c* objects in each row. (*See margin.*) These strategies are

then formalized as children represent stories with multiplication number models. **3.OA.3** In Lesson 1-9 children are introduced to representations of equal-sharing and equal-grouping situations. **3.OA.2** In Lesson 1-10 children are introduced to multiplication/division Fact Triangles, which are the *Everyday Mathematics* version of flash cards. Fact Triangles emphasize fact families, which are collections of four related facts linking multiplication and division. (*See margin.*) **3.OA.6, 3.OA.7**

A progression of lessons helps children develop *fluency* with multiplication facts. **3.OA.7** This progression begins in Unit 1 when children develop strategies for the 2s, 5s, and 10s facts. These facts are foundational because they are "helper facts" for more sophisticated strategies in future units. Through strategy development and practice such as solving number stories, discussions, Quick Looks, and games, children will eventually develop automaticity with all multiplication facts. **3.OA.7**

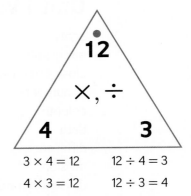

| $3 \times 4 = 12$ | $12 \div 4 = 3$ |
| $4 \times 3 = 12$ | $12 \div 3 = 4$ |

Fact family for the numbers 4, 3, and 12

▶ Quick Looks (Lesson 1-10 and following)

In the Quick Looks routine, the teacher displays a dot pattern that children look at briefly, but not long enough to count each dot. As children make sense of the patterns, they develop the ability to subitize, or instantly recognize a quantity without counting. In third grade, most Quick Looks involve arrays or equal groups, which encourage children to utilize skip counting, repeated addition, or instant recognition to build their understanding of multiplication. **3.OA.1, 3.OA.7**

Quick Look Card 136

▶ Explorations (Lesson 1-12)

Explorations provide an opportunity for children to work in small groups on several informal, open-ended activities. In Lesson 1-12 children estimate, compare, and measure masses of objects, create equal groups of eggs in nests, and divide whole pancakes into equal shares. **3.OA.1, 3.NF.1, 3.MD.2** Children are encouraged to explain their thinking and to follow the rules for cooperative learning.

▶ Measuring Mass (Lessons 1-12 and 1-13)

In the last two lessons of this unit, children are introduced to the tools and units used to estimate and measure mass of objects. **3.MD.2** Mass is a measure of the amount of matter in an object. Weight is a measure of the force of gravity given an object's mass. On a trip to another planet, an object's mass remains constant because the amount of matter in the object does not change. The object's weight, however, will vary depending on each planet's gravitational pull. Because gravity is fairly constant on Earth and because weight and mass are proportional when gravity is constant, mass and weight are difficult to distinguish in everyday life. Children will likely use the terms *weight* and *mass* more or less interchangeably; this should not be a concern at this time. According to the National Research Council's *Next Generation Science Standards,* "At this grade level [Grades 3–5], mass and weight are not distinguished . . . " (NRC, 2012, p. 233).

Children use a balance and standard masses to measure the masses of objects. They determine benchmark items that will assist them with estimating the masses of objects. Children then use these units in solving measurement number stories.

Mathematical Background: Practices

 In Everyday Mathematics, *children learn the **content** of mathematics as they engage in the **practices** of mathematics. As such, the Standards for Mathematical Practice are embedded in children's everyday work, including hands-on activities, problem-solving tasks, discussions, and written work. Read here to see how Mathematical Practices 4 and 5 are emphasized in this unit.*

▶ Standard for Mathematical Practice 4

"Mathematically proficient students can apply the mathematics they know to solve problems arising in everyday life, society, and the workplace." **SMP4** In Lessons 1-8 and 1-9, children model array, equal-sharing, and equal-grouping situations with drawings and number sentences. **GMP4.1** They are encouraged to use these mathematical models to solve problems and answer questions. **GMP4.2** In Lesson 1-12, children model division using concrete representations, and explore fractional parts of a whole by folding paper. They create mathematical models based on real-world situations and use them to solve problems. **GMP4.1, GMP4.2**

Using mathematical models to solve problems and answer questions is the focus of the Open Response and Reengagement lesson. Children are presented with the real-world problem of measuring the length of a morning at school, and model the problem using an open number line or a toolkit clock. An important element of mathematical modeling includes an ability to "identify important quantities in a practical situation and map their relationships." **SMP4** Children identify the start and end times, and break the elapsed time into easy-to-calculate increments to determine the total number of hours and minutes that have passed. Instruction focuses on having children show how they used a mathematical model to solve the problem, and on revisiting and revising their solutions after comparing and analyzing others' strategies. **GMP4.2** This reengagement with the problem allows children to deepen their understanding of the models used to calculate elapsed time and prepares them for the Length-of-Day Project beginning in Lesson 1-11.

▶ Standard for Mathematical Practice 5

Proficient problem solvers "consider the available tools" and "make sound decisions about when each of these tools might be helpful." **SMP5** *Everyday Mathematics* defines tools broadly to include anything that can be used to facilitate mathematical thinking and problem solving. By emphasizing the power of tools and helping children learn how to properly choose them, problem solving at school more closely resembles how mathematics is done in everyday life.

Many of the tools children use in this unit will be familiar from second grade. Children use number grids and number lines to count, to add and subtract, and to round numbers. Children also choose clocks, rulers, and Pattern-Block Templates from their math toolkits to answer a variety of questions. When solving problems with elapsed time, children decide whether to use toolkit clocks or open number lines to model the situations. They are introduced to pan balances and standard masses to measure the mass of a variety of objects. As children become more proficient problem solvers, they will become more flexible and strategic in choosing and using math tools.

 Standards and Goals for Mathematical Practice

SMP4 Model with mathematics.
> **GMP4.1** Model real-world situations using graphs, drawings, tables, symbols, numbers, diagrams, and other representations.
>
> **GMP4.2** Use mathematical models to solve problems and answer questions.

SMP5 Use appropriate tools strategically.
> **GMP5.1** Choose appropriate tools.
>
> **GMP5.2** Use tools effectively and make sense of your results.

Go Online to the *Implementation Guide* for more information about the Mathematical Practices.

For children's information on the Mathematical Practices, see *Student Reference Book*, pages 1–36.

NOTE Math toolkit tools can be stored in the zippered bags especially designed for the *Everyday Mathematics* program or in some other container, such as a resealable plastic bag or a school-supply box. See the *Implementation Guide* for suggestions about how to manage math toolkits.

Number Grids

Overview Children use number-grid patterns for computation.

▶ **Before You Begin**
Plan how you will keep track of math tools. See the online *Implementation Guide* for more details. For Part 2, you may want to copy, cut apart, and tape number grids from *Math Masters*, page TA2 onto children's desks.

▶ **Vocabulary**
number grid • difference

CCSS **Common Core State Standards**

Focus Cluster
Use place value understanding and properties of operations to perform multi-digit arithmetic.

1 Warm Up 5 min

	Materials	
Mental Math and Fluency Children skip count by 10s, 5s, and 2s.		3.OA.7

2 Focus 45–55 min

Math Message Children add 2-digit numbers.	slate	3.NBT.2
Sharing Strategies Children share strategies for adding 2-digit numbers.	Number-Grid Poster	3.NBT.2 SMP6
Reviewing Number-Grid Patterns Children identify patterns on the number grid.	*Math Journal 1*, p. 3; Number-Grid Poster (optional)	3.NBT.2 SMP7
Finding Differences Children use a number grid to help find differences.	*Math Journal 1*, p. 3; *Math Masters*, p. TA2 (optional); counters (optional)	3.NBT.2 SMP6, SMP7
✓ **Assessment Check-In** See page 18.	*Math Journal 1*, p. 3	3.NBT.2 SMP7

CCSS **3.NBT.2** **Spiral Snapshot**

GMC Subtract within 1,000 fluently.

1-1 Focus Practice	1-2 Focus Practice	1-3 Practice	1-4 Focus Practice	1-7 Warm Up Practice	1-8 Warm Up Practice	2-1 through 2-5 Warm Up Focus Practice

▰ Spiral Tracker   (Go Online) to see how mastery develops for all standards within the grade.

3 Practice 10–15 min

Minute Math+ Children find 10 more and 10 less.	*Minute Math®+*, p. 21	3.NBT.2
Home Link 1-1 **Homework** Children find differences between numbers.	*Math Masters*, pp. 2–7	3.NBT.2 SMP6

connectED.mcgraw-hill.com

Plan your lessons online with these tools.

 ePresentations
 Student Learning Center
 Facts Workshop Game
 eToolkit
 Professional Development
 Home Connections
 Spiral Tracker
 Assessment and Reporting
 English Learners Support
 Differentiation Support

Differentiation Options

RtI

CCSS 3.NBT.2, SMP5, SMP7

Readiness
10–15 min

	WHOLE CLASS
	SMALL GROUP
	PARTNER
	INDEPENDENT

Applying Number-Grid Patterns

Number-Grid Poster, stick-on notes

To review finding patterns on the number grid, have children use the Number-Grid Poster partially covered with stick-on notes in T- or L-shaped patterns. Point to a stick-on note and ask children to figure out which number is covered. **GMP5.2, GMP7.2** For example, point to the stick-on note that covers 63. Ask: *What number do you think this stick-on note covers?* 63 *How do you know?* Sample answer: It is between 62 and 64. *How could you figure out the other numbers?* Sample answer: To find the number under the bottom sticky note, start at 42 and count 10 to 52. One more than 52 is 53. Then count by 10s from 53 to 63, 73, 83. **Cover other patterns on the Number-Grid Poster and pose similar questions.**

41	42	43	44	45
51				55
61	62		64	65
71	72		74	75
81	82		84	85

CCSS 3.NBT.2, SMP5, SMP7

Enrichment
10–15 min

	WHOLE CLASS
	SMALL GROUP
	PARTNER
	INDEPENDENT

Finding Differences Between 3-Digit Numbers

Math Masters, pp. 8 and TA3

To further explore subtraction, have children use a number grid (*Math Masters*, page TA3) to find the differences between pairs of 3-digit numbers. **GMP5.2, GMP7.2** Then have children record their work on *Math Masters*, page 8.

> **Finding Differences**
>
> Lesson 1-1
> NAME DATE
>
> Use the number grid to find the difference between the pairs of numbers. Explain what you did.
>
> ① The difference between 324 and 351 is __27__.
>
> How did you use the number grid to find the difference?
> Sample answer: I used the number grid to count by 10s from 24 to 44 and got 20. Then I counted by 1s from 44 to 51 and got 7. The difference between 24 and 51 is 27, so I know that the difference between 324 and 351 is also 27.
>
> ② What number is 34 less than 173? __139__
>
> How did you use the number grid to find the number?
> Sample answer: I counted back by three 10s from 73 to 43. Then I counted back by four 1s: 42, 41, 40, 39. I know 34 less than 73 is 39, so 34 less than 173 is 139.
>
> ③ Do your own.
> The difference between _____ and _____ is _____.
>
> How did you use the number grid?
> Answers vary.
>
> 8   3.NBT.2, SMP5, SMP7

CCSS 3.NBT.2, SMP5, SMP7

Extra Practice
10–15 min

	WHOLE CLASS
	SMALL GROUP
	PARTNER
	INDEPENDENT

Finding Differences on the Number Grid

Activity Card 1; *Math Masters*, p. TA3; number cards 0–9 (4 of each); 2 centimeter cubes

To provide practice with subtraction, have children use a number grid to find the differences between pairs of numbers. **GMP7.2** Have children discuss how they used the number grid to help them solve the problems. **GMP5.2**

> **Finding Differences on the Number Grid**
>
> **What You Need**
> Number Grid, page TA3
> number cards 0–4 (4 of each)
> 2 centimeter cubes
> paper
>
> **What To Do**
> Work with a partner.
> ① Turn over four cards and make two 2-digit numbers.
> ② Place a centimeter cube on each of your numbers on the number grid.
> ③ Find the difference between the two numbers.
> ④ Fold a paper into two columns to make a chart.
> ⑤ Write "Numbers" over the first column and "Difference" over the second.
> ⑥ Write your numbers in the "Numbers" column. Circle the number that is more. Underline the number that is less.
> ⑦ Write the difference between the numbers in the "Difference" column.
> ⑧ Repeat Steps 1–7 until you run out of cards.
>
> **Talk About It**
> How did you use the number grid to find the differences?
>
> The difference between 65 and 80 is 15.

English Language Learners Support

Beginning ELL Teach the slate routine with one-word signals and gestures. For example: LISTEN—Pulling on one ear; THINK—Closing your eyes and pointing with one finger to your temple; WRITE—Holding a writing tool and air writing; SHOW—Holding up a slate. Model each action with *I* _____, *We* _____, and *You* _____ sequences and have children show the actions along with you. Then have them show the appropriate action when you call out the one-word signal.

Go Online **ELL** English Learners Support

SMP6 Attend to precision.
GMP6.1 Explain your mathematical thinking clearly and precisely.

SMP7 Look for and make use of structure.
GMP7.1 Look for mathematical structures such as categories, patterns, and properties.
GMP7.2 Use structures to solve problems and answer questions.

Professional Development

Finding differences on a number grid is a review from Grade 2. The focus of today's lesson is clearly explaining strategies using appropriate mathematical language. This is an important skill that will be emphasized and practiced throughout the year.

Number-Grid Poster

−9	−8	−7	−6	−5	−4	−3	−2	−1	0
1	2	3	4	5	6	7	8	9	10
11	12	13	14	15	16	17	18	19	20
21	22	23	24	25	26	27	28	29	30
31	32	33	34	35	36	37	38	39	40
41	42	43	44	45	46	47	48	49	50
51	52	53	54	55	56	57	58	59	60
61	62	63	64	65	66	67	68	69	70
71	72	73	74	75	76	77	78	79	80
81	82	83	84	85	86	87	88	89	90
91	92	93	94	95	96	97	98	99	100
101	102	103	104	105	106	107	108	109	110
111	112	113	114	115	116	117	118	119	120

Number Grid

TA3

1 Warm Up   5 min   Go Online
ePresentations   eToolkit

Mental Math and Fluency

Have children practice skip counting. *Leveled exercises:*

● ○ ○ Skip count by 10s from 0 to 100.
● ● ○ Skip count by 5s from 0 to 50.
● ● ● Skip count by 2s from 0 to 30.

2 Focus   45–55 min   Go Online
ePresentations   eToolkit

▶ Math Message

Distribute one slate and marker to each child. Establish a slate routine, such as LISTEN, THINK, WRITE, and SHOW. You may want to have children place their slates facedown to signal that they are finished writing. When you say *Show,* they can hold their slates so you can see them.

Pose the following problems orally and have children try to answer them in their heads. Then have children record the answers on their slates to practice the slate routine.

What number is . . .

20 more than 45? 65   *37 more than 50?* 87

40 more than 38? 78   *54 more than 31?* 85

Explain that in future lessons, the Math Message will be displayed in the classroom.

▶ Sharing Strategies

WHOLE CLASS	SMALL GROUP	PARTNER	INDEPENDENT

Math Message Follow-Up Invite children to share their solution strategies for the Math Message problems. Have them model their thinking on the Number-Grid Poster. Encourage them to clearly explain their thinking using place-value terms so others may follow the steps they took. **GMP6.1** Expect strategies such as the following:

- To find 20 more than 45: Point to 45. Then count 20 more by 10s, saying 55, 65. So 20 more than 45 is 65.
- To find 40 more than 38: Point to 38. Then count 40 more by 10s, saying 48, 58, 68, 78. So 40 more than 38 is 78.
- To find 37 more than 50: Point to 50. Count 30 more by 10s, saying 60, 70, 80. Then count 7 more saying 81, 82, 83, 84, 85, 86, 87. So 37 more than 50 is 87.

• To find 54 more than 31: Point to 31. Count 50 more by 10s saying 41, 51, 61, 71, 81. Then count 4 more saying 82, 83, 84, 85. So 54 more than 31 is 85.

Tell children that they will examine the number grid for patterns and then use those patterns to help find differences between pairs of numbers.

▶ Reviewing Number-Grid Patterns

Math Journal 1, p. 3

WHOLE CLASS	SMALL GROUP	PARTNER	INDEPENDENT

Distribute *Math Journal 1* to the class. Have children turn to journal page 3 and write today's date on the line provided. Note that there is no line for a name as the pages are not intended to be removed from the book. The journals are records of children's work that they can review throughout the year.

Ask partners to examine the **number grid** on page 3 and discuss any patterns they see. GMP7.1 After several minutes, invite them to share patterns their partner found. Encourage children to use prompts, such as: *I heard you say _____, did I get that right?* and *I see the pattern _____ described.* Elicit place-value patterns by asking:

• *What happens to the numbers in a row as you move from left to right?* They increase by 1. *From right to left?* They decrease by 1.

• *What do you notice about the ones and tens digits in the numbers as you go from left to right?* The tens digits stay the same until the ones digit becomes 9, and then it goes up by 1. The ones digit goes up by 1 until 9, and then it goes to 0.

• *If you add 1 to a number, where on the grid is the sum?* Usually it is to the right, but if the number has a 0 in the ones place, it is at the beginning of the next row. *If you subtract 1 from a number, where on the grid is the difference?* Usually it is to the left, but if the number has a 1 in the ones place, it is at the end of the row above.

• *What do you notice about the digits as you go from top to bottom?* The ones digit stays the same and the tens digit goes up 1 until you get to 100. Then you exchange all your tens for a hundred and start over with 0 in the tens place.

• *If you add 10 to a number, where on the grid is the sum?* It is the number below the original number. *If you subtract 10 from a number?* It is the number above the original number.

• *If you continue the number grid, what is the next number?* 121 *How do you know?* Sample answers: One more than 120 is 121. Ten more than 111 is 121.

• *Use the patterns on the number grid to predict what would happen if you add 100 to a number.* You increase the digit in the hundreds place by 1. *What happens if you subtract 100 from a number?* You decrease the digit in the hundreds place by 1.

Math Journal 1, p. 3

Finding Differences on a Number Grid   Lesson 1-1
DATE

									0
1	2	3	4	5	6	7	8	9	10
11	12	13	14	15	16	17	18	19	20
21	22	23	24	25	26	27	28	29	30
31	32	33	34	35	36	37	38	39	40
41	42	43	44	45	46	47	48	49	50
51	52	53	54	55	56	57	58	59	60
61	62	63	64	65	66	67	68	69	70
71	72	73	74	75	76	77	78	79	80
81	82	83	84	85	86	87	88	89	90
91	92	93	94	95	96	97	98	99	100
101	102	103	104	105	106	107	108	109	110
111	112	113	114	115	116	117	118	119	120

Use the number grid to help you solve these problems.

① Which is less, 83 or 73? 73   How much less? 10
② Which is less, 13 or 34? 13   How much less? 21
③ Which is more, 90 or 55? 90   How much more? 35
④ Which is more, 44 or 52? 52   How much more? 8

Find the **difference** between each pair of numbers.

⑤ 71 and 92 21   ⑥ 26 and 46 20
⑦ 30 and 62 32   ⑧ 48 and 84 36
⑨ 43 and 60 17   ⑩ 88 and 110 22

3.NBT.2, SMP7   three 3

21	22	23	24	25	26	27	28	29	30
31	32	33	34	35	36	37	38	39	40
41	42	43	44	45	46	47	48	49	50
51	52	53	54	55	56	57	58	59	60
61	62	63	64	65	66	67	68	69	70
71	72	73	74	75	76	77	78	79	80
81	82	83	84	85	86	87	88	89	90
91	92	93	94	95	96	97	98	99	100

→ +1   ↓ +10

One way to find the difference
between 35 and 83

Common Misconception

Differentiate To avoid having children count the start number as 1 (when counting by 1s) or as 10 (when counting by 10s), have them place counters on the start numbers. Then have children move their fingers to the next number to begin their counts. They may also draw hops to each new space to signal counting by 1s or 10s. (*See number grid above.*)

Go Online Differentiation Support

Adjusting the Activity

Differentiate Some children may count up or down by 1s, which is less efficient than counting by 10s and then by 1s. Provide number grids for children to tape onto their desks. See *Math Masters*, page TA2. Consider having children draw directional arrows showing + 1 and + 10 at the top of the number grid, as shown above.

Go Online Differentiation Support

▶ Finding Differences

Math Journal 1, p. 3

WHOLE CLASS **SMALL GROUP** **PARTNER** **INDEPENDENT**

Point out that the organization of the number grid can help children to think about counting up and back by tens and ones, and to identify the **difference,** or distance, between two numbers. Pose the following problem and encourage children to use patterns they observed on the number grid as they find differences. **GMP7.2**

Use the number grid on journal page 3. Start at 35. How many spaces is it to 83? **GMP7.2** 48

Ask volunteers to describe how they found the difference. **GMP6.1** Sample answer: I started at 35. I moved down one row to 45—that's 10 spaces. Then I moved down four more rows to 85—that's 50 spaces in all. Then I moved back two spaces to 83—that's 48 spaces. Remind children that 48 is called the difference between 35 and 83 because it is the number of spaces between those two numbers. It does not matter whether children count on from the smaller number to the larger number, count back from the larger number to the smaller number, or count back the smaller number from the larger number to find the differences. Complete a few more problems with the class and invite volunteers to share their strategies using the Number-Grid Poster. **GMP6.1, GMP7.2**

Suggestions:

- 83 and 33 *Which is more?* 83 *How much more?* 50
- 28 and 50 *Which is less?* 28 *How much less?* 22
- 37 and 25 *Which is less?* 25 *How much less?* 12
- 19 and 34 *Which is more?* 34 *How much more?* 15

When children seem comfortable with finding differences, have them complete journal page 3 on their own.

✓ **Assessment Check-In** **CCSS** 3.NBT.2

Math Journal 1, p. 3

Observe as children work on journal page 3. Though some children may find the differences mentally, expect most to use the number grid. **GMP7.2** For those who struggle, consider implementing the suggestions in the Common Misconception and Adjusting the Activity notes.

 Assessment and Reporting   **Go Online** to record student progress and to see trajectories toward mastery for this standard.

When most children have completed the page, review the answers and have them model strategies on the Number-Grid Poster.

Summarize Have partnerships discuss which patterns on the number grid can help them find differences between pairs of numbers.

3 Practice

10–15 min | Go Online | ePresentations eToolkit Home Connections

▶ Minute Math+

Minute Math+, p. 21

Minute Math+ is a collection of short activities that require little or no preparation. Most do not require any materials and are brief enough to do in a minute. *Minute Math+* activities can be used with large or small groups at any time, for example, regular class time, transitions between activities, waiting in lines, dismissal time, and so on. Teachers are often surprised at how beneficial these activities are for learning mathematics.

Minute Math+ activities that reinforce and review focus content are suggested throughout Unit 1, with the exception of Open Response and Reengagement and Progress Check lessons. Beginning in Unit 2, reminders to use *Minute Math+* activities appear in Part 3 of lessons.

To provide practice adding and subtracting 10, see *Minute Math+*, page 21.

▶ Home Link 1-1

Math Masters, pp. 2–7

Homework Children find differences between pairs of 2-digit numbers using a number grid and explain their strategies. **GMP6.1**

Distribute the Home Link. Briefly review the purpose of Home Links and talk about the children's responsibility to complete them. Have a volunteer read the Home Link aloud, and discuss any questions children may have.

Point out the "no calculator" icon on the page. (*See margin.*) Explain that whenever children see this icon, they should use a problem-solving strategy that does not include a calculator. Tell children that practice problems will appear on many Home Links.

In addition to Home Link 1-1, children should take home the Family Letter introducing *Third Grade Everyday Mathematics* and Unit 1.

Minute Math+

Everyday Mathematics®
The University of Chicago School Mathematics Project

MINUTE MATH+®

McGraw Hill Education

NOTE Some journal pages, *Math Masters*, and Home Links have been marked with a "no calculator" icon.

Math Masters, p. 7

Finding Differences on a Number Grid

Home Link 1-1
NAME   DATE

Family Note Today your child reviewed patterns on the number grid and used them to find differences between numbers. For example, one way to find the difference between 87 and 115 on the number grid is: Start at 87. Count the number of tens to 107. There are 2 tens, or 20. Count the number of ones from 107 to 115. There are 8 ones, or 8. The difference between 87 and 107 is 2 tens and 8 ones, or 28. Formal subtraction methods will be covered in the next unit.

Please return this Home Link to school tomorrow.

81	82	83	84	85	86	87	88	89	90
91	92	93	94	95	96	97	98	99	100
101	102	103	104	105	106	107	108	109	110
111	112	113	114	115	116	117	118	119	120
121	122	123	124	125	126	127	128	129	130

Use the number grid to help you solve the following problems.

① The difference between 83 and 109 is ___26___.
② The difference between 97 and 125 is ___28___.
③ Explain how you solved Problem 2. Sample answer: I counted by 10s from 97 to 117 and got 20. Then I counted by ones to 125 and got 8. So the answer is 28.

Practice
Solve.

④ $13 = 7 + \underline{6}$ ⑤ $13 = 6 + \underline{7}$
⑥ $6 = \underline{13} - 7$ ⑦ $7 = \underline{13} - 6$

Unit
pencils

3.NBT.2, SMP6   7

Introducing the Student Reference Book

Overview Children explore the *Student Reference Book* and play *Number-Grid Difference*.

▶ **Before You Begin**
For Part 2, plan how you will keep track of children's *Student Reference Books*. Prepare game materials for *Number-Grid Difference* (see *Student Reference Book,* page 251). Make a Class Data Pad using large chart paper to record information the class collects throughout the year. Plan to create a poster with children about rules for working with others. (*See page 23.*)

▶ **Vocabulary**
essay

 Common Core State Standards

Focus Cluster
Use place value understanding and properties of operations to perform multi-digit arithmetic.

1 Warm Up 5–10 min

	Materials	
Mental Math and Fluency Children solve number stories.	slate (optional)	3.OA.3, 3.NBT.2

2 Focus 45–50 min

Math Message Children think how the *Student Reference Book* will be helpful.	*Student Reference Book*	SMP5
Exploring the *Student Reference Book* Children explore the *Student Reference Book.*	*Student Reference Book*	SMP3, SMP5
Looking Up Information in the *Student Reference Book* Children locate information and game directions in their *Student Reference Book.*	*Student Reference Book; Math Journal 1,* p. 4; *Math Masters,* pp. 9–10, TA3, and G2; number cards 0–9 (4 of each); 2 counters; calculator and base-10 blocks (optional)	3.NBT.2 SMP5, SMP6
✓ **Assessment Check-In** See page 25.		3.NBT.2, SMP5

CCSS 3.NBT.2 Spiral Snapshot

GMC Subtract within 1,000 fluently.

| 1-1
Focus
Practice | 1-2
Focus
Practice | 1-3
Practice | 1-4
Focus
Practice | 1-7
Warm Up
Practice | 1-8
Warm Up
Practice | 2-1 through 2-5
Warm Up
Focus
Practice |

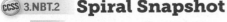 Spiral Tracker **Go Online** to see how mastery develops for all standards within the grade.

3 Practice 10–15 min

Minute Math+ Children use various operations to find a secret number.	*Minute Math®+,* p. 52	3.NBT.2
Playing *Number-Grid Difference* Children practice mental subtraction strategies.	*Student Reference Book,* p. 251; *Math Masters,* pp. TA3 and G2; number cards 0–9 (4 of each); 2 counters; calculator (optional)	3.NBT.2
Home Link 1-2 **Homework** Children play *Number-Grid Difference.*	*Math Masters,* pp. 9–10	3.NBT.2

 connectED.mcgraw-hill.com

Plan your lessons online with these tools.

 ePresentations
 Student Learning Center
 Facts Workshop Game
 eToolkit
 Professional Development
 Home Connections
 Spiral Tracker
 Assessment and Reporting
ELL English Learners Support
Differentiation Support

20 Unit 1 | Math Tools, Time, and Multiplication

Differentiation Options
RtI

Readiness
5–10 min

Finding Differences Between Numbers

| WHOLE CLASS |
| SMALL GROUP |
| PARTNER |
| INDEPENDENT |

Number-Grid Poster

To provide experience with subtraction, have children find the difference between two numbers on the Number-Grid Poster. Pose a difference problem involving a multiple of 10 such as: *What number is 30 less than 55?* 25 Have children use the structure of the Number-Grid Poster to help them locate the number. GMP5.2, GMP7.2 Once children are familiar with the activity, they can take turns posing problems to one another. Remind children to use a multiple of 10 as one of their numbers.

Enrichment
15–20 min

Finding Differences in Multiple Ways

| WHOLE CLASS |
| SMALL GROUP |
| PARTNER |
| INDEPENDENT |

Activity Card 2; *Student Reference Book*, p. 251; *Math Masters*, pp. TA3 and G2; number cards 0–9 (4 of each); 2 centimeter cubes

To extend finding differences, have children play *Number-Grid Difference* and find each difference using two different strategies. GMP1.5 Game directions are on *Student Reference Book*, page 251.

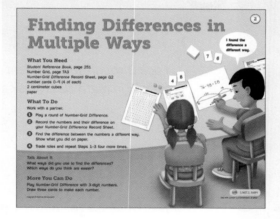

Finding Differences in Multiple Ways

Extra Practice
10–15 min

Finding the Mystery Number

| WHOLE CLASS |
| SMALL GROUP |
| PARTNER |
| INDEPENDENT |

Activity Card 3; *Math Masters*, p. TA3

To provide more experience finding differences, have children find mystery numbers using the structure of a number grid (*Math Masters*, page TA3). GMP7.2 You may want to model one or two mystery-number problems before children work in partnerships. For example: *I am thinking of a number that is 15 less than 50. What is my number?* 35 Encourage children to explain how they used the number grid to find the mystery numbers. GMP5.2

Finding the Mystery Number

English Language Learners Support

Beginning ELL Help children participate in reviewing the *Student Reference Book* by introducing terms prior to the lesson. Prepare displays for each of the sections to be discussed: *Contents, Answer Key, Glossary,* and *Index.* Encourage children to match the terms on the displays with the terms in their books. Display page numbers for children to see the pages to which they should turn. As needed, pair children with English-proficient partners who can demonstrate how to find the sections being discussed.

 Go Online ELL **English Learners Support**

Standards and Goals for
Mathematical Practice

SMP3 **Construct viable arguments and critique the reasoning of others.**
   GMP3.2 Make sense of others' mathematical thinking.

SMP5 **Use appropriate tools strategically.**
   GMP5.2 Use tools effectively and make sense of your results.

SMP6 **Attend to precision.**
   GMP6.1 Explain your mathematical thinking clearly and precisely.

NOTE Many teachers integrate the *Student Reference Book* into their nonfiction literacy instruction. Consider using it to build children's understanding of informational text features and reading comprehension, as well as to reinforce learning of Grade 3 mathematics concepts.

1 Warm Up   5–10 min   Go Online   ePresentations   eToolkit

▶ Mental Math and Fluency

Pose number stories and have children share their solutions.
Leveled exercises:

- ●○○ There are 9 softball players on the home team and 9 softball players on the visiting team. How many softball players are there in all? 18 softball players
- ●●○ There are 2 bags with 5 apple slices in each bag. How many apple slices in all? 10 apple slices
- ●●● There are 3 bicycles with 2 wheels each. How many wheels in all? 6 wheels

2 Focus   45–50 min   Go Online   ePresentations   eToolkit

▶ Math Message

Look through your Student Reference Book. Think: How might this book be helpful in math class? Talk about your ideas with a partner. GMP5.2

▶ Exploring the *Student Reference Book*

Student Reference Book

| WHOLE CLASS | SMALL GROUP | PARTNER | INDEPENDENT |

Math Message Follow-Up Have children share their ideas about how the *Student Reference Book* might be helpful. Explain that the *Student Reference Book* has several important sections that will help them learn mathematics. As you work through the various sections, you may want to record key features on the Class Data Pad. (*See Before You Begin.*)

- First have children turn to the *Contents*. Explain that these pages may be used to find information about a particular math topic. Point out the organization of the Contents pages: section headings and then essays within each section heading. Have children use the Contents to find Name-Collection Boxes in the Operations and Algebraic Thinking section. GMP5.2

- Explain that this is the title of an **essay,** or a short, informational text, about name-collection boxes. Note that the Contents provide the page number for the first page of each essay.

- Have children turn to the Name-Collection Boxes essay on pages 96 and 97. Point out the Check Your Understanding problem at the bottom of page 97.

- Next have children turn to the *Answer Key* to find the answers to this problem. Explain the purpose of the Check Your Understanding problems: to help children find out whether they understand the essay. When children read an essay, they should do the Check Your Understanding problems and then look up the answers in the Answer Key.
- Have children turn to the *Glossary.* Point out that this section lists important math vocabulary in alphabetical order and gives a brief definition of each word. Explain that children can use this section to look up the meanings of terms. GMP5.2 Have children look up the term *number grid.*
- Have children turn to the *Index.* Explain that the Index lists key words in alphabetical order and gives the page numbers on which these words appear. Ask children to use the Index to find the rules for the game *Spin and Round.* Support them as they find the name of the game and its page number in the Index. GMP5.2 Point out that this is one of many games described in the *Games* section. Ask: *Where else could we look to find the page number for directions to* Spin and Round? The Contents
- Finally have children turn to the *Data Bank.* Take a few minutes to browse this section together. Explain that it contains information that they will use throughout the year.

Tell children they will work with a partner or in a small group and use the *Student Reference Book* to look up information. Ask children to suggest what could make the classroom more pleasant when working in partnerships or in small groups. Develop a set of rules together. The list you generate may include:

- Be polite.
- Help each other.
- Share.
- Listen to each other.
- Take turns.
- Talk about problems.
- Speak quietly.
- Work to understand each other's thinking.

Emphasize that when working in groups it is important for children to make sense of their partners' or group members' thinking because it will help them become better problem solvers. GMP3.2 Children should ask for help from an adult only if the group cannot solve the problem together.

Academic Language Development

Build children's vocabulary by making connections between the words *refer* and *reference.* Use sentences, such as: *Let's refer to, or look at, the* Student Reference Book *to find that information.* Have children find the base word *refer* in *reference.* Point out that the two words are part of the same word family. Encourage children to use sentence frames, such as: *I refer to my* Student Reference Book *to find _____.*

Math Journal 1, p. 4

Looking Up Information — Lesson 1-2

Work with a partner. Use your *Student Reference Book* for Problems 2 and 3.

1 Write your partner's first name. _Answers vary._
Write your partner's last name. _Answers vary._

2 a. Locate and read the essay "Number Grids."
Describe what you did to find the essay.
Sample answer: I looked for Number Grids in the index and went to the essay that begins on page 89.

b. Do Check Your Understanding Problems 1 and 2 on page 92.
Check your answers in the Answer Key.
Problem 1a: _30_ Problem 1b: _25_ Problem 1c: _35_
Problem 2:

a. 58 59 / 66 67 68
b. 213 215 216 / 224 225
c. 31 33 / 40 42 44

3 Look up and read the rules for *Number-Grid Difference.*
On what page did you find the rules? Page 251

4 four 3.NBT.2, SMP5, SMP6

Number-Grid Difference

Materials	☐ number cards 0–9 (4 of each)
	☐ 1 Number Grid (*Math Masters,* p. TA3)
	☐ 1 *Number-Grid Difference* Record Sheet for each player (*Math Masters,* p. G2)
	☐ 1 counter for each player
	☐ calculator (optional)
Players	2
Skill	Using a number grid to find the difference between 2-digit numbers
Object of the Game	To have the lower sum.

Directions

1. Shuffle the cards. Place the deck number-side down on the table.
2. Players take turns. When it is your turn:
   • Each player takes 2 cards from the deck and uses the cards to make a 2-digit number. Players then place their counters on the grid to mark their numbers.
   • Find the difference between your number and your partner's number.
   • The difference is your score for the round. Record both numbers and your score on your record sheet.
3. Continue playing until each player has taken 5 turns and recorded 5 scores.
4. Each player finds the sum of his or her 5 scores. Players may use a calculator to add.
5. The player with the lower sum wins the game.

Number-Grid Difference Record Sheet

two hundred fifty-one SRB 251

Number-Grid Difference Record Sheet

My Record Sheet

Round	My Number	My Partner's Number	Difference (Score)
1			
2			
3			
4			
5			

Total: _____

G2

▶ # Looking Up Information in the *Student Reference Book*

Student Reference Book; Math Journal 1, p. 4; *Math Masters,* pp. TA3 and G2

WHOLE CLASS	SMALL GROUP	PARTNER	INDEPENDENT

Have partners work together to complete journal page 4. Circulate and have children explain their strategies for finding the differences in the Check Your Understanding problems. **GMP6.1**

Differentiate **Adjusting the Activity**

For children who struggle to find the difference between two numbers using a number grid, have them place a base-10 (centimeter) cube on each number they count. Next have them exchange every 10 cubes for a base-10 long and count the total number of base-10 blocks beginning with the longs, representing tens, and then the cubes, representing ones.

 Go Online ▶ Differentiation Support

---

Problem 4 directs children to locate and review the rules for *Number-Grid Difference.* When most children have completed Problem 4, ask: *How did you find the directions for* Number-Grid Difference? **GMP5.2** Sample answer: I looked under Games in the Contents and found *Number-Grid Difference* on page 251.

Children played *Number-Grid Difference* in *Second Grade Everyday Mathematics.* This game helps children develop mental subtraction strategies.

Distribute game materials. (*See Before You Begin.*) Review the directions as a class and play one or two rounds together. Emphasize the rules for working together. Invite children to model how to make a 2-digit number with two number cards and share strategies for finding the differences. When children are comfortable with the game, have them play in pairs and record their scores on *Math Masters,* page G2 while you circulate and observe.

Observe

You may use the following questions to help guide your observations.

• How do children use the number grid to calculate differences?
• Which children use a calculator to add their five scores? Which children use other strategies? What strategies do they use?

Discuss

You may use the following questions to guide discussion about the game.

• *What math did you use while playing this game?*
• *How did you use the number grid to find the difference between the two numbers?* **GMP5.2, GMP6.1**

Assessment Check-In CCSS 3.NBT.2

Observe as children play *Number-Grid Difference*. Expect most children to use the number grid to successfully find the differences between pairs of numbers. GMP5.2 For those who struggle, consider using the Readiness activity for this lesson. Some children may be able to determine differences between pairs of numbers without the use of a number grid.

☑ Assessment and Reporting | Go Online | to record student progress and to see trajectories toward mastery for this standard.

Summarize Distribute Home Link 1-2. Point out the *Student Reference Book* icon on the page. Explain that this icon will appear on many assignments throughout the year. Ask partnerships to discuss how they can use it to help them with their assignments. GMP5.2 Sample answer: We can look up pages it says to help us remember how to find differences on number grids.

3 Practice 10–15 min

Go Online | ePresentations | eToolkit | Home Connections

▶ Minute Math+

Minute Math+, p. 52

To provide addition and subtraction practice, see *Minute Math+,* page 52 levels 1 and 3.

▶ Playing *Number-Grid Difference*

Student Reference Book, p. 251; *Math Masters,* pp. TA3 and G2

WHOLE CLASS	**SMALL GROUP**	**PARTNER**	INDEPENDENT

Have children continue to practice finding differences between pairs of numbers by playing *Number-Grid Difference.*

Games are an integral part of the *Everyday Mathematics* program and are as important as Math Boxes and Home Links. They are an effective, interactive way to reinforce skills that are identified in the Common Core State Standards for Mathematics (CCSSM). Games in *Third Grade Everyday Mathematics* build computation and fact fluency throughout the year. Children also develop cooperative-learning skills in an engaging context. Establish a games routine with children and maintain it throughout the year, and make sure that all children are given time to play games. For more information on managing games, see the *Implementation Guide.*

▶ Home Link 1-2

Student Reference Book; Math Masters, pp. 9–10

Homework Children share their *Student Reference Book* and play *Number-Grid Difference* with someone at home.

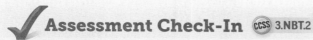

Minute Math+, p. 52

Secret Numbers

Operations and Algebraic Thinking

Say: *Each of you think of a secret number 1–10. When I call on you, **add 22** to your secret number, tell us only the answer, and call on someone else to guess your secret number. For instance, if **Debbie's** secret number is 4, she will say 26, and then call on someone to guess her secret number.*

●○○○○ Choose a 1- or 2-digit number to add to or subtract from the secret number. Example: Add 23 to the secret number.

●●○○○ Choose a 1-digit number to multiply by the secret number. Example: Multiply 8 by the secret number.

●●●○○ Choose two numbers; have the child add the first one to the secret number and then subtract the second one. Example: Add 31 to the secret number, and then subtract 10.

Variation Provide the whole class with an operation, and then have children take turns with a partner thinking of and calculating the secret number.

52 CCSS 1.OA.8, 1.NBT.4, 2.OA.2, 2.NBT.5, 3.OA.4, 3.OA.7, 3.NBT.2

Math Masters, p. 10

Number-Grid Difference (continued)

Home Link 1-2
NAME   DATE

Show someone at home how to play *Number-Grid Difference.*

−9	−8	−7	−6	−5	−4	−3	−2	−1	0
1	2	3	4	5	6	7	8	9	10
11	12	13	14	15	16	17	18	19	20
21	22	23	24	25	26	27	28	29	30
31	32	33	34	35	36	37	38	39	40
41	42	43	44	45	46	47	48	49	50
51	52	53	54	55	56	57	58	59	60
61	62	63	64	65	66	67	68	69	70
71	72	73	74	75	76	77	78	79	80
81	82	83	84	85	86	87	88	89	90
91	92	93	94	95	96	97	98	99	100
101	102	103	104	105	106	107	108	109	110
111	112	113	114	115	116	117	118	119	120

	My Record Sheet				My Partner's Record Sheet		
Round	My Number	My Partner's Number	Difference	Round	My Number	My Partner's Number	Difference
1				1			
2				2			
3				3			
4				4			
5				5			
		TOTAL _____				TOTAL _____	

10 3.NBT.2

Tools for Mathematics

Overview Children review and use a variety of math tools.

▶ **Before You Begin**
For Part 2, plan how you will manage toolkits and tools (clocks, calculators, rulers, and Pattern-Block Templates) before distributing them to the class. See the *Implementation Guide* for more details. If you need additional clocks, or would like to send clocks home, have children use scissors and brads to construct paper clocks from *Math Masters*, page TA4.

Common Core State Standards

Focus Clusters
- Use place value understanding and properties of operations to perform multi-digit arithmetic.
- Solve problems involving measurement and estimation.
- Reason with shapes and their attributes.

---

1 Warm Up 5–10 min

Materials

Mental Math and Fluency
Children solve basic facts and share their strategies.

3.NBT.2

---

2 Focus 40–50 min

Math Message
Children explore tools in their math toolkits.

toolkit (*See Before You Begin.*)

SMP5

Discussing Math Tools
Children share when and how their toolkit tools are used.

toolkit (*See Before You Begin.*)

SMP5

Reviewing Telling Time
Children review telling time.

demonstration clock; toolkit clock (*See Before You Begin.*)

3.MD.1
SMP5, SMP6

Reviewing Length Measurement
Children use tools to measure, calculate, and trace shapes.

Math Journal 1, p. 5; *Student Reference Book* (optional); toolkit tools

3.NBT.2, 3.MD.1, 3.MD.4, 3.G.1
SMP5

✓ **Assessment Check-In** See page 30.

Math Journal 1, p. 5

SMP5

CCSS 3.MD.1 Spiral Snapshot

GMC Tell and write time.

| 1-3 Focus Practice | 1-5 Focus Practice | 1-6 Practice | 1-8 Practice | 1-10 Practice | 1-11 Warm Up | 1-13 Practice | 2-1 Practice |

Spiral Tracker   **Go Online**   to see how mastery develops for all standards within the grade.

---

3 Practice 15–20 min

Minute Math+
Children identify tools for measuring time and length.

Minute Math®+, p. 106

3.MD.1, 3.MD.2, 3.MD.4
SMP5

Game Playing *Number-Grid Difference*
Children find differences between 2-digit numbers.

Student Reference Book, p. 251; *Math Masters*, pp. TA3 and G2; number cards 0–9 (4 of each); 2 counters; calculator (optional)

3.NBT.2
SMP5, SMP6

Home Link 1-3
Homework Children tell time using an analog clock.

Math Masters, p. 11, TA4 (optional)

3.MD.1

---

connectED.mcgraw-hill.com

Plan your lessons online with these tools.

ePresentations | Student Learning Center | Facts Workshop Game | eToolkit | Professional Development | Home Connections | Spiral Tracker | Assessment and Reporting | English Learners Support | Differentiation Support

Differentiation Options

RtI

CCSS 3.NBT.2, SMP5

Readiness
5–10 min

Making 10 on a Calculator

| WHOLE CLASS |
| SMALL GROUP |
| PARTNER |
| INDEPENDENT |

calculator

To review using a calculator and to practice addition and subtraction, have children make 10 on a calculator. First remind them to clear calculators by pressing the ON/C key. A zero should show in the display window. If an M is also visible, have children press the MRC key to clear it. Say: *Enter 2 into your calculator. Change the display to 10 by adding or subtracting a number using the + key or the − key. Then press the number and the = key.* As needed, model the steps on a display calculator. *What keys did you press?* GMP5.2 +, 8, = Have children push the ON/C button to clear the display and pose similar problems. For example enter 12 and change to 20. +, 8, =

CCSS 3.NBT.2, SMP7

Enrichment
10–15 min

Completing Calculator Puzzles with Negative Numbers

| WHOLE CLASS |
| SMALL GROUP |
| PARTNER |
| INDEPENDENT |

calculator

Have children extend their calculator-puzzle skills to working with negative numbers. Invite them to enter 5 and count aloud as they count back by 1s to −1. (On a Casio, enter 1, −, −, 5, =, =, . . . ; on a TI-108, enter 5, −, 1, =, =, . . .) Ask: *What does the calculator display show after zero?* −1 Explain that −1 is read *negative 1*. Have children continue to count back on their calculators while counting aloud until they reach negative 10. Next ask them to change their display from −10 to 10. Have children share their strategies and patterns they notice with negative numbers. GMP7.1 Some children may press +, 1, +, =, =, . . . until they reach 10. Others may press +, 2, 0, and reach 10 in one step. Remind children that there are many ways to solve the puzzles. Pose additional puzzles with negative numbers for partners to solve. For example, start at −5 and change to 5. Start at −15 and change to 20. Encourage children to record and solve their own calculator puzzles with negative numbers.

CCSS 3.NBT.2, SMP3

Extra Practice
10–15 min

Playing *Hit the Target*

| WHOLE CLASS |
| SMALL GROUP |
| PARTNER |
| INDEPENDENT |

Activity Card 4;
Math Masters, p. G3;
calculator

Have children practice finding differences between 2-digit numbers and multiples of 10 by playing *Hit the Target.* Then have them explain why they chose a particular number to add or subtract on their calculators. GMP3.1

English Language Learners Support

Beginning ELL To introduce children to reading the time aloud, use numerical expressions that closely relate to reading numbers, as this will limit language demands. For example: *four o'clock, four-oh-one* (4:01) through *four-oh-nine* (4:09), and *four ten* (4:10) through *four fifty-nine* (4:59). Provide children with oral language practice telling time using numerical expressions before introducing other time-related expressions such as *half-past four* and *thirty minutes after four.*

Go Online ELL English Learners Support

1 Warm Up 5–10 min Go Online ePresentations eToolkit

▶ Mental Math and Fluency

Children are expected to memorize basic addition facts by the end of second grade. You may use the exercises in Unit 1 to assess children's fact fluency in preparation for the addition and subtraction work in Unit 2.

Have children use the first fact in each pair (doubles) to help them solve the second fact (near doubles). Encourage them to share their strategies. *Leveled exercises:*

●○○ $4 + 4 = ?$ 8 $4 + 5 = ?$ 9
     $6 + 6 = ?$ 12 $6 + 7 = ?$ 13

●●○ $7 + 7 = ?$ 14 $7 + 6 = ?$ 13
     $8 + 8 = ?$ 16 $8 + 7 = ?$ 15

●●● $5 + 5 = ?$ 10 $5 + 7 = ?$ 12
     $6 + 6 = ?$ 12 $6 + 8 = ?$ 14

2 Focus 40–50 min Go Online ePresentations eToolkit

▶ Math Message

Explore the tools in your toolkit. Talk with a partner about how and when you could use each of the tools. GMP5.1

▶ Discussing Math Tools

| WHOLE CLASS | SMALL GROUP | PARTNER | INDEPENDENT |

Math Message Follow-Up Briefly display each of the tools from the toolkit—clock face, calculator, Pattern-Block Template, and ruler—and have children share what they remember about them from second grade, including when and how each is used. GMP5.1 Point out that the number grid and *Student Reference Book* are also examples of mathematical tools.

Ask for suggestions for how to take care of the toolkits. Remind the class that other children will use the same toolkits next year. You might consider establishing a Lost-and-Found Box as a repository for misplaced items.

Mention that additional mathematical tools will be added to the kits throughout the year. Explain that this lesson will review how to use the toolkit clock, calculator, Pattern-Block Template, and ruler.

▶ Reviewing Telling Time

| WHOLE CLASS | SMALL GROUP | PARTNER | INDEPENDENT |

Display two clock faces—one showing 2:00 and the other showing 3:00. Have children read the times. Remind them that in *Second Grade Everyday Mathematics,* they thought of the space between two numbers on a clock face (in this case, between 2 and 3) as a special container for all the minutes in the hour. When the hour hand moves from one number to the next, a whole hour (or 60 minutes) has passed. However, when the minute hand moves from 2 to 3, only five minutes have gone by.

Use the demonstration clock to model the movement of the hour and minute hands. Display 4:00 and ask children what time it shows. GMP5.2 4 o'clock Move the minute hand slowly forward to 4:30, pausing on each number 1 though 5. As needed, adjust the hour hand. At each pause, have children say the time. 4:05 or 5 minutes after 4; 4:10 or 10 minutes after 4; 4:15 or 15 minutes after 4; 4:20 or 20 minutes after 4; 4:25 or 25 minutes after 4; 4:30 or 30 minutes after 4 Encourage children to focus first on the location of the hour hand (in this case, between 4 and 5), so they know the time is within the 4 o'clock hour. Point out that the position of the hour hand between the 4 and 5 tells us about how much of an hour has passed. For example, if the hour hand is halfway between the 4 and the 5, it is about 4:30. Then have children note the location of the minute hand so they know the number of minutes that have passed since 4 o'clock. GMP5.2

Dictate a variety of times for children to display on their clocks. Have them either use their toolkit clocks or make paper clocks from *Math Masters,* page TA4. Begin with times on the hour, then on the half-hour, and finally with times in 5-minute intervals. Include times to the nearest 5 minutes in all quadrants of the clock, such as 3:05, 3:20, 3:40, and 3:55. Move sequentially through the times and remind children to reposition the hour hand as the minute hand moves to later quadrants. Ask volunteers to show each time on the class demonstration clock so children can check their answers. GMP5.2, GMP6.4

▶ Reviewing Length Measurement

Math Journal 1, p. 5

| WHOLE CLASS | SMALL GROUP | PARTNER | INDEPENDENT |

Display a few line segments of different lengths less than 12 inches long. Ask: *Which tool in your toolkit could you use to measure these line segments?* GMP5.1 Ruler Have partners discuss how to use rulers to measure the lengths of line segments to the nearest inch or centimeter. After a few minutes, invite volunteers to demonstrate. GMP5.2 Possible strategies include:

• Align the 0-mark on the ruler with one of the endpoints of a line segment. Read the number on the ruler aligned with the other endpoint of the line segment as the total length.

Children can make paper clocks from *Math Masters,* page TA4.

NOTE Measurement tools on screens may display units as larger or smaller than in real life. Ask children to compare the length of an inch and a centimeter on their rulers to the length of the displayed inch and centimeter. Remind children that the actual lengths of standard units, such as inch and centimeter, never change.

Math Journal 1, p. 5

Using Mathematical Tools

Lesson 1-3
DATE

For Problems 1 and 2, record the times shown on the clocks. For Problem 3, draw the minute and hour hands to show the time.

① **8:30** ② **2:45** ③ 6:10

④ Use your ruler to measure the line segment.

This line segment is about ___3___ inches long.

⑤ Draw a line segment 10 centimeters long.

Use your calculator. What keys did you press to make each change?

⑥ Enter 50. Change to 107.   ⑦ Enter 94. Change to 30.
Sample answer: +, 50, +, 7   Sample answer: −, 4, −, 60

⑧ Use your Pattern-Block Template. Trace two polygons that have exactly 4 sides.

Sample answers:

What are polygons that have 4 sides called? (Use your *Student Reference Book* if you need help.) _quadrilaterals_

3.NBT.2, 3.MD.1, 3.MD.4, 3.G.1, SMP5   five 5

- Align any number mark on the ruler with one of the endpoints of a line segment. Count the total number of inches or centimeters along the length of the segment.
- Find the difference between the two numbers on the ruler that are aligned with the endpoints of the line segment.

Differentiate **Adjusting the Activity**

Help children who struggle with measuring length to use their finger to swipe across the space between the numbers as they count units rather than just reading the number at the end of each unit. Understanding that the length is the number of units, not just the number at the end of the item being measured, is especially important when one end of the object to be measured is not aligned with the 0-mark on the ruler.

 Go Online   Differentiation Support

Have children independently complete journal page 5 using appropriate math tools. **GMP5.2**

The problems on the journal page provide an opportunity to assess a selection of time-telling, measurement, computation, and geometry skills that were taught in previous grades. These skills will be revisited and extended in future lessons.

 **Assessment Check-In**

Math Journal 1, p. 5

Expect most children to use the appropriate tools for completing each problem correctly on journal page 5. **GMP5.2** If children struggle with the tool usage, have them describe what the suggested tool does and reread the problem before attempting to solve it. They may also benefit from completing the Readiness activities (found in the Differentiation Options) before these topics are revisited: time in Lesson 1-5, addition and subtraction in Units 2 and 3, and measurement and geometry in Unit 4.

 Assessment and Reporting **Go Online** to record student progress for this standard.

Summarize Have children return their tools to their toolkits. Ask: *Which tools do you feel most comfortable using? Which tools do you still have questions about?*

Minute Math+, p. 106

Measuring Tools

Measurement and Data

Say: *I'm thinking of a measuring tool that can measure **amounts of time**. What is the tool?* (Clock or calendar) Also point out informal tools like the position of the sun and moon.

●○○○○ Think of a measuring tool that can measure length. (Ruler, tape measure, and meterstick or yardstick) Also point out informal measures like a person's foot or a piece of paper.

●●○○○ Think of a measuring tool that can measure mass. (Pan balance) Think of a tool that can measure capacity. (Liter beaker and measuring cups marked in milliliters and liters)

106 2.MD.1, 3.MD.1, 3.MD.2, 3.MD.4

---

3 Practice 15–20 min

Go Online

ePresentations   eToolkit   Home Connections

▶ *Minute Math+*

Minute Math+, p. 106

To provide practice identifying formal and informal measuring tools for length and time, see *Minute Math+,* page 106 levels 1 and 2.   GMP5.1

▶ **Playing *Number-Grid Difference***

Student Reference Book, p. 251; *Math Masters,* pp. TA3 and G2

| WHOLE CLASS | **SMALL GROUP** | **PARTNER** | INDEPENDENT |

Have children play *Number-Grid Difference* to practice finding differences between two 2-digit numbers. For detailed instructions, see Lesson 1-2.

Observe

- How do children use the number grid to calculate the differences?
- What other strategies do children use to find differences?
- Which children use a calculator to add their five scores? Which children use other strategies to add their scores?

Discuss

- *How did you add your five scores?*
- *How did you use the number grid to help find the difference between the two numbers?*   GMP5.2, GMP6.1

| Differentiate | **Game Modifications** | Go Online | Differentiation Support |

▶ **Home Link 1-3**

Math Masters, p. 11

Homework Children practice telling time on an analog clock. You may send home paper clocks (*Math Masters,* page TA4) for children to use.

Student Reference Book, p. 251

Games

Number-Grid Difference

Materials	☐ number cards 0–9 (4 of each)
	☐ 1 Number Grid (*Math Masters,* p. TA3)
	☐ 1 *Number-Grid Difference* Record Sheet for each player (*Math Masters,* p. G2)
	☐ 1 counter for each player
	☐ calculator (optional)
Players	2
Skill	Using a number grid to find the difference between 2-digit numbers

Object of the Game To have the lower sum.

Directions

① Shuffle the cards. Place the deck number-side down on the table.

② Players take turns. When it is your turn:
- Each player takes 2 cards from the deck and uses the cards to make a 2-digit number. Players then place their counters on the grid to mark their numbers.
- Find the difference between your number and your partner's number.
- The difference is your score for the round. Record both numbers and your score on your record sheet.

③ Continue playing until each player has taken 5 turns and recorded 5 scores.

④ Each player finds the sum of his or her 5 scores. Players may use a calculator to add.

⑤ The player with the lower sum wins the game.

Number-Grid Difference Record Sheet

two hundred fifty-one   SRB 251

Math Masters, p. 11

Telling Time   Home Link 1-3

NAME   DATE

Family Note Today your child explored some of the math tools commonly used in third grade. We reviewed how to read a ruler to the nearest inch and centimeter, and how to tell time to the nearest hour, half hour, and 5 minutes. Help your child read each time by paying attention to the position of both the hour and the minute hands.

Please return this Home Link to school tomorrow.

① Draw the hour hand and the minute hand to show the time right now. Write the time.
Answers vary.

____ : ____

Write the time shown.

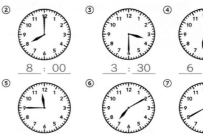

② __8__ : __00__   ③ __3__ : __30__   ④ __6__ : __15__

⑤ __11__ : __45__   ⑥ __7__ : __10__   ⑦ __5__ : __40__

⑧ Show someone how you solved the hardest problem on this page.

3.MD.1   11

Number Lines and Rounding

Lesson 1-4

Overview Children use open number lines to round numbers.

▶ **Before You Begin**
For the Math Message, display a unit box labeled "pencils."

▶ **Vocabulary**
estimate • close-but-easier numbers • round • open number line

 Common Core State Standards

Focus Cluster
Use place value understanding and properties of operations to perform multi-digit arithmetic.

1 Warm Up 5 min

	Materials	
Mental Math and Fluency Children identify the places in numbers and the values of digits in those places.	slate	3.NBT.1

2 Focus 40–50 min

Math Message Children solve addition problems.	half-sheet of paper	3.NBT.2
Reviewing Estimates Children make estimates.		3.NBT.2 SMP1, SMP6
Using Number Lines to Round Children round numbers to the nearest 10 or 100.	*Math Journal 1*, p. 6	3.NBT.1
✓ **Assessment Check-In** See page 38.	*Math Journal 1*, p. 6	3.NBT.1
Estimating Answers Children estimate sums and differences, and then add or subtract.		3.NBT.1, 3.NBT.2 SMP1

CCSS 3.NBT.1 Spiral Snapshot

GMC Use place-value understanding to round whole numbers to the nearest 10.

1-4 Warm Up Focus Practice	1-7 Practice	1-13 Practice	2-4 Practice	3-2 Warm Up Focus	3-3 Focus Practice	3-4 Warm Up	3-5 Warm Up

/// Spiral Tracker   **Go Online** to see how mastery develops for all standards within the grade.

3 Practice 10–15 min

Minute Math+ Children round numbers to the nearest 10 or 100.	*Minute Math®+*, p. 80	3.NBT.1
Solving Calculator Puzzles Children solve place-value puzzles.	*Math Masters*, p. 12; calculator; number grid (optional)	3.NBT.2
Home Link 1-4 **Homework** Children round numbers to the nearest 10 and nearest 100.	*Math Masters*, p. 13	3.NBT.1

connectED.mcgraw-hill.com

Plan your lessons online with these tools.

 ePresentations   Student Learning Center   Facts Workshop Game   eToolkit   Professional Development   Home Connections   Spiral Tracker   Assessment and Reporting   English Learners Support   Differentiation Support

Differentiation Options

RtI

CCSS 3.NBT.1, SMP5

Readiness
5–10 min

Identifying Close-but-Easier Numbers

Math Masters, p. TA3

WHOLE CLASS
SMALL GROUP
PARTNER
INDEPENDENT

To support children with identifying close-but-easier numbers, have them shade multiples of 10 on *Math Masters*, page TA3. Pose problems such as: *Put your finger on 57. Is it closer to 50 or 60?* 60 *How do you know?* **GMP5.2** Sample answer: It only takes 3 hops to get to 60 from 57, but 7 hops to get to 50. Repeat with other numbers.

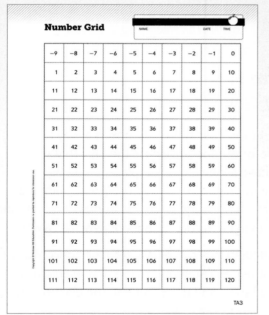

CCSS 3.OA.8, 3.NBT.1, 3.NBT.2, SMP1

Enrichment
10–15 min

Estimating Sums and Differences

Activity Card 5;
number cards 1–9 (4 of each)

WHOLE CLASS
SMALL GROUP
PARTNER
INDEPENDENT

To apply children's estimation skills, have them mentally estimate sums and differences and use their estimates to check whether their exact answers make sense. **GMP1.4**

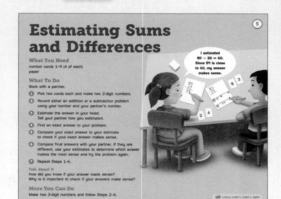

CCSS 3.NBT.1, SMP5

Extra Practice
5–10 min

Rounding to the Nearest 10

Activity Card 6;
number cards 1–9 (4 of each)

WHOLE CLASS
SMALL GROUP
PARTNER
INDEPENDENT

To provide practice rounding numbers, have children make a 2-digit number with number cards and round it to the nearest 10. Children may sketch open number lines and discuss how they used them to help round numbers. **GMP5.2**

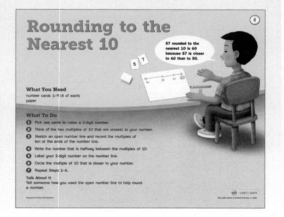

English Language Learners Support

Beginning ELL To help children understand and remember that numbers rounded to the nearest 10 end in zero, point out the similarity of the shape of the 0 and round shapes. Display several multiples of 10 in 2- and 3-digit numbers. Trace around the zero digit in a multiple of 10 as you say: *I can round ___ to this multiple of 10, ___.* Ask children to point to other round numbers and write them. Add non-examples to the multiples of 10 display, and use *yes* or *no* questions, such as: *Is this a round number?* as you point to different numbers.

Go Online **ELL** English Learners Support

Standards and Goals for
Mathematical Practice

SMP1 **Make sense of problems and persevere in solving them.**
  GMP1.4 Check whether your answer makes sense.

SMP6 **Attend to precision.**
  GMP6.2 Use an appropriate level of precision for your problem.

  GMP6.3 Use clear labels, units, and mathematical language.

NOTE Consider posting a unit box for the day so children will have a context in which to think about the abstract numbers used in the day's activities. Alternatively, children can supply the context themselves and choose topics of current interest or, if they prefer, fanciful or silly labels.

---

1 Warm Up 5 min

▶ Mental Math and Fluency

Dictate and have children write 2- and 3-digit numbers on their slates. Ask questions such as: *Which digit is in the tens place? Hundreds place? What is the value of the digit x? How many hundreds are there?*
Leveled exercises:

● ○ ○ 35; 47; 96
● ● ○ 356; 472; 405
● ● ● 1,452; 2,698; 2,097

2 Focus 40–50 min

▶ Math Message

Add. Record your answers on a half-sheet.

$28 + 37 =$ __65__
$49 + 18 =$ __67__

Unit
pencils

▶ Reviewing Estimates

| WHOLE CLASS | SMALL GROUP | PARTNER | INDEPENDENT |

Math Message Follow-Up Review using the unit box as a way to establish a real-world context for numbers. Discuss the idea that in everyday life, numbers often have a label (for example, apples, children, books) or a measurement unit (for example, inches, kilograms, minutes). Because the unit box for the Math Message is labeled *pencils,* explain that the problems can be thought of in terms of numbers of pencils. GMP6.3

Have children explain their calculation strategies. Listen for how children refer to the values of digits in their explanations. In the first problem, for example, if a child says, "I added the 2 and the 3," remind the class to say they added 20 and 30, or 2 tens and 3 tens. GMP6.3

Possible strategies for 28 + 37:

- 20 + 30 = 50; 8 + 7 = 15; and 50 + 15 = 65. This strategy uses partial sums, which will be reviewed in Unit 2.
- Take 2 from 37 to get 35, and add it to 28, so 28 + 2 = 30 and 35 + 30 = 65.
- Think of 37 as 30 + 7 and add 7 to 28, so 28 + 7 = 35. Then add 30, so 30 + 35 = 65.

Tell children that they should always check whether their answers make sense. **GMP1.4** Explain that they will estimate to do this today.

Remind children that an **estimate** is an answer close to an exact answer. An estimate can also be used to get an idea ahead of time what a reasonable answer might be. This is true for number-story problems and for problems without stories, like those in the Math Message.

Ask children to make estimates for the problems below and explain how they arrived at them. Remind children that one way to estimate is to identify **close-but-easier numbers** and then add or subtract them. You may wish to model estimating the first sum.

Sample answers given.

- 42 + 89 40 + 90 = 130
- 74 − 27 75 − 30 = 45; 70 − 30 = 40
- 148 + 51 150 + 50 = 200
- 213 + 468 200 + 500 = 700; 210 + 470 = 680
- 63 − 35 60 − 35 = 25; 60 − 30 = 30; 60 − 40 = 20

Note that there is often more than one acceptable estimate. Ask: *Why might we have two different estimates for the same problem?* Sample answer: Because there can be more than one close-but-easier number to use. **GMP6.2**

As children explain their estimates, ask: *What close-but-easier numbers did you use?* Sample answer: I used 75 for 74 and 30 for 27. Close-but-easier numbers are often, but not always, multiples of 5 or 10. Encourage children to explain how their estimates differ from their classmates' estimates. As children discuss, model using constructive discussion language, such as: *That makes sense, but I used different close-but-easier numbers.* or *My estimate is different from yours because _____. Both of our estimates make sense.*

Professional Development

Rounding can help with estimation. This lesson introduces a common rounding method that involves rounding to the nearest 10 or 100. The traditional version of this algorithm involves rounding up if the digit to the right of the target place is 5 or greater, and rounding down if the digit is less than 5.

▶ Using Number Lines to Round

Math Journal 1, p. 6

| WHOLE CLASS | SMALL GROUP | PARTNER | INDEPENDENT |

One way to estimate sums and differences is to round the numbers that are involved in the calculations. Explain that when we **round** we can use numbers that are the closest multiples of 10 or 100. For example, to round the numbers to the nearest 10 in the expression 101 – 17, we round 101 to 100 and 17 to 20. The rounded numbers 100 and 20 are the closest multiple of 10 to each number and are easy to subtract mentally, so an estimated answer for 101 – 17 is about 80. The actual answer should be close to 80.

Remind children that in second grade, they used open number lines to represent addition and subtraction. An **open number line** is a line on which you can indicate points with tick marks and labels that are not spaced at regular intervals. Like number lines, there is an order and an implied origin, but unlike number lines, open number lines have no scale or unit intervals. Children can use open number lines to record their thinking as they solve problems.

Invite children to share what they remember about open number lines. Explain that they will use open number lines to round numbers to the nearest 10 or 100.

Model how to use an open number line to round 54 to the nearest 10:

1. Sketch a number line.

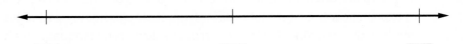

2. Have children use the Class Number Grid or Number Line, or skip count by 10s to decide which two multiples of 10 are closest to 54. 50 and 60 Record them on the number line.

Ask a volunteer to label the number that is halfway between the lower and higher numbers on the number line.

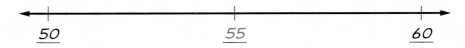

3. Invite another volunteer to estimate the location of 54 on the number line.

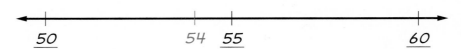

4. Ask: *Is 54 closer to 50 or 60?* 50 *Round 54 to the nearest 10.* 50

Next sketch another number line. Invite children to use it to round 168 to the nearest 10. Ask: *What digit is in the tens place?* 6 *What is its value?* 6 tens or 60 *Which two multiples of 10 are closest to 168?* 160 and 170 *How do you know?* Sample answer: I saw on the number grid that 60 and 70 are the closest multiples of 10 to 68, so I also know that the closest multiples to 168 are 160 and 170.

Have a volunteer label 160 and 170 and the number halfway between (165) on the number line. Then invite another volunteer to label the approximate location of 168 on the number line.

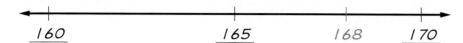

Ask: *Is 168 closer to 160 or 170?* 170 *Round 168 to the nearest 10.* 170

Next have children round 325 to the nearest 100. Ask: *What digit is in the hundreds place?* 3 *What is its value?* 3 hundreds or 300 Sketch an open number line and ask children to identify the two multiples of 100 that are closest to 325. 300 and 400 Label 300 and 400 on the number line. Ask: *What number is halfway between 300 and 400?* 350 Add 350 to the number line, and invite a volunteer to mark the approximate location of 325 on the number line.

Ask: *Is 325 closer to 300 or 400?* 300 *Round 325 to the nearest 100.* 300

Point out that when rounding to the nearest 10, most people look at the digit in the ones place. If that digit is 5 or greater, they round to the next higher multiple of 10. For example, 35 is rounded to 40 because the digit in the ones place is 5. Likewise, when rounding to the nearest 100, if the digit in the tens place is 5 or greater, they round to the next higher multiple of 100. For example, 350 is rounded to 400 because the digit in the tens place is 5.

Common Misconception

Differentiate Some children may think that the closest multiples of 100 to 325 are 200 and 300. Help them to realize that because 325 is greater than 300, the closest multiples are 300 and 400.

 Go Online Differentiation Support

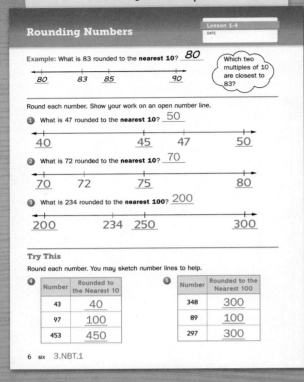
As needed, sketch open number lines and involve children in rounding a few more numbers to the nearest 10 or nearest 100. *Suggestions:*

Round to the nearest 10:
72 70
321 320
175 180
1,243 1,240

Round to the nearest 100:
67 100
289 300
450 500
1,512 1,500

When children seem comfortable with rounding, have them complete journal page 6.

✓ **Assessment Check-In**  CCSS 3.NBT.1

Math Journal 1, p. 6

Expect children to use open number lines to successfully identify the two multiples of 10 or 100 that are closest to the numbers they are rounding in Problems 1–3 on journal page 6. If children struggle, consider implementing the Readiness activity or the Common Misconception note. Many children will be able to round 2-digit numbers to the nearest 10 and 3-digit numbers to the nearest 100. Some children may be able to round 3-digit numbers to the nearest 10. Others may be able to round numbers without using an open number line.

✓ Assessment and Reporting   Go Online to record student progress and to see trajectories toward mastery for this standard.

▶ **Estimating Answers**

| WHOLE CLASS | SMALL GROUP | PARTNER | INDEPENDENT |

Refer the class back to the Math Message problem and work through an example of rounding numbers to make an estimate. Next to the unit box, show 27 + 56. Ask children to round each of the addends to the nearest 10. 30 and 60 Encourage them to sketch an open number line to help. Have children use the rounded addends to estimate the sum. 30 + 60 = 90 Then have them solve the problem. 27 + 56 = 83 Ask: *Is your answer reasonable? Explain your thinking.* GMP1.4 Sample answer: Yes. My answer is close, but it is a little less than my estimate because I rounded both addends to larger numbers.

As time allows, pose other addition and subtraction problems and have children estimate their sums and differences.

Summarize Ask: *How can rounding and estimating help you check whether your answers are reasonable?* GMP1.4

3 Practice 10–15 min Go Online ePresentations eToolkit Home Connections

▶ Minute Math+

Minute Math+, p. 80

To provide practice rounding numbers to the nearest 10 or nearest 100, see *Minute Math+*, page 80.

▶ Solving Calculator Puzzles

Math Masters, p. 12

| WHOLE CLASS | SMALL GROUP | PARTNER | INDEPENDENT |

Have children use their calculators to solve place-value puzzles on *Math Masters*, page 12. Children may use a number grid to help.

▶ Home Link 1-4

Math Masters, p. 13

Homework Children use an open number line to round numbers. Then they use the rounded numbers to make estimates.

Math Masters, p. 12

Calculator Puzzles Lesson 1-4

NAME   DATE

Solve the calculator puzzles. Add or subtract to find the "Change to" number. You may use a number grid to help. When you finish, compare answers with a partner. If you and your partner disagree on an answer, try the problem again.

Enter	Change to	How?
42	52	+ 10
61	51	− 10
80	40	− 40
58	78	+ 20
110	90	− 20
46	146	+ 100
238	538	+ 300
78	108	+ 30

✂ -

Solve the calculator puzzles. Add or subtract to find the "Change to" number. You may use a number grid to help. When you finish, compare answers with a partner. If you and your partner disagree on an answer, try the problem again.

Enter	Change to	How?
42	52	+ 10
61	51	− 10
80	40	− 40
58	78	+ 20
110	90	− 20
46	146	+ 100
238	538	+ 300
78	108	+ 30

12   3.NBT.2

Math Masters, p. 13

Rounding Numbers Home Link 1-4

NAME   DATE

Family Note Today your child used open number lines (see *Example*) to help round numbers to the nearest 10 and to the nearest 100. Rounding is one way to estimate calculations. For example, to estimate 83 − 37, your child can round 83 to 80 and 37 to 40, and then easily subtract 80 − 40 = 40, so an estimated answer for 83 − 37 is about 40. The actual answer, 46, is close to 40. Have your child explain how to use an open number line to round numbers.

Please return this Home Link to school tomorrow.

Example: What is 72 rounded to the **nearest 10**? _70_

Which two multiples of 10 are closest to 72?

70   72   75   80

Round each number. Show your work on an open number line.

① What is 87 rounded to the **nearest 10**? _90_

80   85   87   90

② What is 283 rounded to the **nearest 100**? _300_

200   250   283   300

③ Round the numbers in the problem below to the nearest 10. You may sketch an open number line to help.

Unit
books

Use the rounded numbers to estimate the answer. Then solve.

3 8
+ 5 6
———
94

Estimate: _40_ + _60_ = _100_

Is your answer reasonable? _Yes._ Explain. Sample answer: 94 is close to my estimate of 100, so my answer is reasonable.

3.NBT.1   13

Time

Overview Children tell time to the nearest minute and calculate elapsed time.

▶ **Vocabulary**
precise • elapsed time

CCSS **Common Core State Standards**

Focus Cluster
Solve problems involving measurement and estimation.

	Materials	
① Warm Up 5 min		
Mental Math and Fluency Children practice skip counting.	slate	**3.OA.7**

② Focus 45–50 min		
Math Message Children match times with analog clocks.	*Math Journal 1*, p. 7	**3.MD.1**
Reviewing Telling Time Children review reading clocks to the nearest 5 minutes.	*Math Journal 1*, p. 7; demonstration clock	**3.MD.1** **SMP1, SMP6**
Telling Time to the Nearest Minute Children tell and record time to the nearest minute.	*Math Journal 1*, p. 8; *Math Masters*, p. TA4 (optional); toolkit clocks; demonstration clock	**3.MD.1** **SMP5, SMP6**
✓ **Assessment Check-In** See page 45.	*Math Journal 1*, p. 8	**3.MD.1, SMP5, SMP6**
Introducing Elapsed Time Children are introduced to strategies for calculating elapsed time.	*Math Journal 1*, p. 8; *Student Reference Book*, pp. 184–186; toolkit clocks; demonstration clock	**3.MD.1** **SMP1, SMP5**

CCSS 3.MD.1 **Spiral Snapshot**

GMC Tell and write time.

1-3 Focus Practice	1-5 Focus Practice	1-6 Practice	1-8 Practice	1-10 Practice	1-11 Warm Up	1-13 Practice	2-1 Practice

▶ *Spiral Tracker* **Go Online** to see how mastery develops for all standards within the grade.

③ Practice 10–15 min		
Minute Math+ Children identify activities of varied lengths of time.	*Minute Math®+*, pp. 117–118	**3.MD.1**
Introducing the Math Boxes Routine Children are introduced to the Math Boxes routine.	*Math Journal 1*, p. 9; *Student Reference Book; Math Masters*, p. TA5 (optional)	See page 46.
Home Link 1-5 **Homework** Children practice telling time to the nearest minute.	*Math Masters*, p. 16	**3.MD.1** **SMP6**

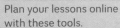
connectED.mcgraw-hill.com

Plan your lessons online with these tools.

 ePresentations

 Student Learning Center

 Facts Workshop Game

 eToolkit

 Professional Development

 Home Connections

 Spiral Tracker

 Assessment and Reporting

 English Learners Support

 Differentiation Support

Differentiation Options

RtI

CCSS 3.MD.1, SMP5

Readiness
10–15 min

Marking Five-Minute Intervals

WHOLE CLASS
SMALL GROUP
PARTNER
INDEPENDENT

Math Masters, p. 14; demonstration clock; scissors; brads; crayons

To review telling time, slowly move the minute hand around a demonstration clock starting from 12 o'clock as children count by 5s. Point out that the hour hand moved from 12 to 1. Repeat with various times as children call out: "three-oh-five, three-ten, three-fifteen," and so on. Have children record the five-minute intervals in a different color around the clock on *Math Masters,* page 14 and assemble the clock. Then show various times to the nearest five minutes on a digital display and have children show it on their clocks. GMP5.2

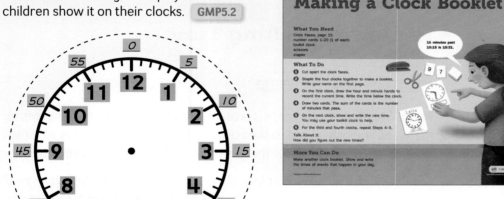

minute hand
x *Minute*

hour hand
x *Hour*

CCSS 3.MD.1, SMP5, SMP6

Enrichment
10–15 min

Making a Clock Booklet

WHOLE CLASS
SMALL GROUP
PARTNER
INDEPENDENT

Activity Card 7; *Math Masters,* p. 15; toolkit clock; scissors; stapler; number cards 1–20

To apply children's understanding of telling time and measuring elapsed time in one-minute intervals, have them make a clock booklet from *Math Masters,* page 15. Have children record a time on one clock, use number cards to determine the number of minutes that pass, and record the new time on the next clock. GMP5.2, GMP6.4 The clock booklet may be used as a portfolio item.

CCSS 3.MD.1, SMP6

Extra Practice
10–15 min

Telling and Writing Time to the Minute

WHOLE CLASS
SMALL GROUP
PARTNER
INDEPENDENT

Activity Card 8; *Math Masters,* p. 15; toolkit clock

For additional practice telling time, have partners tell and write time using their toolkit clocks. Have them explain their time-telling strategies. GMP6.1

English Language Learners Support

Beginning ELL Role-play to introduce the term *nearest,* connecting to *near* and *nearer* and contrasting with *far.* For example, place a book on a table and place four different-color crayons at different distances from the book. While placing each crayon, describe its placement using the terms *far from, near, nearer,* or *nearest.* For example, place a red crayon about 3 feet from the book. Gesture and say: *The red crayon is far from the book.* Model the terms with other objects and direct children to place objects near, nearer, and nearest to the book.

Go Online   ELL   English Learners Support

Standards and Goals for
Mathematical Practice

SMP1 **Make sense of problems and persevere in solving them.**
 GMP1.6 Compare the strategies you and others use.

SMP5 **Use appropriate tools strategically.**
 GMP5.2 Use tools effectively and make sense of your results.

SMP6 **Attend to precision.**
 GMP6.4 Think about accuracy and efficiency when you count, measure, and calculate.

① Warm Up   5 min

▶ Mental Math and Fluency

Have children skip count and record the next number in each series on their slates. *Leveled exercises:*

●○○ Skip count by 5s from 10 to 40. Stop and record the next number. 45

●●○ Skip count by 2s from 12 to 30. Stop and record the next number. 32

●●● Skip count by 2s from 34 to 48. Stop and record the next number. 50

② Focus   45–50 min

▶ Math Message

Math Journal 1, p. 7

Complete journal page 7. Be prepared to share how you matched the times with the correct clock.

▶ Reviewing Telling Time

Math Journal 1, p. 7

| WHOLE CLASS | SMALL GROUP | PARTNER | INDEPENDENT |

Math Message Follow-Up Have children compare their strategies for matching the given time to the correct clock. **GMP1.6** Discuss why the other clock does not show the given time. **GMP6.4** Review the following:

• Problem 1: Ask: *Which clock shows 1:30?* Clock a Remind children that the hour hand is the short hand and the minute hand is the long hand. Ask: *What time does clock b show?* 6:05 *How do you know it does not show 1:30?* Sample answer: Because the hour hand is on the 6 and the minute hand is on the 1.

• Problem 2: Ask: *Which clock shows 2:45?* Clock d *How do you know?* Sample answer: Because the hour hand is between the 2 and the 3. It is closer to the 3 because it is almost 3:00. Remind children that the hour hand is in a container for that hour. It moves from one clock number to the next as the minute hand moves around the clock. Ask: *What time does clock c show, with the hour hand a little before 2?* 1:45

Math Journal 1, p. 7

Telling Time   Lesson 1-5
 DATE

Math Message
Circle the clock that shows the time.

① Which clock shows 1:30?

a   b

② Which clock shows 2:45?

c   d

③ Which clock shows 4:55?

e   f

3.MD.1   seven 7

• **Problem 3:** Ask: *Which clock shows 4:55?* Clock e Have children compare the minute hands on the two clocks. Remind them that the minute hand moves 5 minutes from each clock number to the next. Model the movement of the minute hand on the demonstration clock, and count by 5s starting with 0 when the minute hand is at the 12. Continue until you reach 4:55. Ask: *What time does clock f show?* 4:50

Ask: *How many 1-minute marks are on each of the clocks? How do you know?* Sample answer: There are 60 one-minute marks. Between 12 and 1, there are 5 one-minute marks, so I counted by 5s all the way around the clock and got 60. *So how many minutes are in one hour?* 60 minutes *How many seconds are in a minute?* 60 seconds

Tell children that today they will practice telling time and calculating total minutes that pass from one time to another.

▶ Telling Time to the Nearest Minute

Math Journal 1, p. 8

| WHOLE CLASS | SMALL GROUP | PARTNER | INDEPENDENT |

Discuss situations in which children may need to tell time to the nearest minute. Some examples are: catching a bus or train, getting to a doctor's appointment, arriving at school on time, or knowing how long a movie is. Explain that telling time to the nearest minute is more **precise**, or exact, than telling time to the nearest 5 minutes, half hour, or hour. GMP6.4

Show 4:00 on a demonstration clock. Have children show the same time on their toolkit clocks. Ask:

• *What time does the clock show?* 4:00 Have children move the minute hand to the first minute mark past the 3. Starting at 12, chorally count the minutes by 5s while moving a finger from numbers 1, 2, and 3. Then count 1 minute more. 5, 10, 15, 16

• *What time is it now?* 4:16 Then have children move the minute hand 2 more minute marks.

• *What time is it now?* 4:18 Together count the minutes again by 5s and 1s. *Why did we not have to count all the minutes by 1s?*
  GMP5.2, GMP6.4 Sample answers: We can count by 5s from 0 to 3 and then by 1s to 18 minutes past. 5 minutes pass from each clock number to the next. We can count 2 minutes past 4:16 and get 4:18.

Differentiate | Adjusting the Activity

Have children who struggle to read clocks first tell a time to the hour. Then have them put their finger on the minute mark where the minute hand is pointing. Ask them to identify a familiar time that is close to this minute mark and count forward or backward from that time to tell the exact 5 minutes or minute.

Go Online 👥 Differentiation Support

• Explain that one way to read a clock to the nearest minute is to start with *familiar times,* or times we know without counting, such as those on the hour or half hour.

Academic Language Development

Explain *familiar time* to children as the clock times they know well, such as time to the hour and half hour. Note that when we say *we are familiar* with something, it means we know it very well. Provide examples and non-examples of things with which children might be familiar, such as friends, strangers on the bus, how to get to the cafeteria, and how to fly an airplane. Also connect the terms *family* and *familiar* by noting that they are very familiar with members of their family.

Professional Development

Beginning in *First* and *Second Grade Everyday Mathematics,* children move from reading hour-hand only clocks to telling time to the nearest half-hour, 5 minutes, and minute. Approximating time (a little past 6 o'clock, about halfway between 2 and 3 o'clock, a little before 7 o'clock, and so on) on hour-hand only clocks and reading times with the minute hand in all quadrants of the clock supports children's clock-reading ability as they read more precise times. They may also use familiar times, such as those on the hour and half hour, and count by minutes to the exact time.

Math Journal 1, p. 8

Reading Time to the Nearest Minute

Lesson 1-5
DATE •   TIME

Write the time shown on each clock.

① 2:15

② 2:40

③ 3:30

④ 3:37

⑤ 10:00

⑥ 10:13

Show 9:32. Ask: *What is the hour?* 9:00

Where would the minute hand be at exactly 9 o'clock? It would be on the 12. From this familiar time, have children count the minutes by 5s and then single minutes. 5, 10, 15, 20, 25, 30, 31, 32 Point out that the minute hand passed a group of 30 minutes plus two more minutes.

What time does the clock show? 9:32

What other familiar time could help you figure out 9:32? 9:30 *How?* **GMP5.2** Sample answer: I know that the time is 9:30 when the hour hand is halfway between 9 and 10 and the minute hand is on 6. So I count two more minutes to 9:32.

Next show 1:37 on the demonstration clock. Ask children to suggest a familiar time close to 1:37. Sample answers: 1:30; 1:15; 1:00 Have a volunteer show and explain how to use a familiar time to determine the time shown on the clock. Sample answer: I started at the familiar time 1:30. I counted by 5s to 1:35, and then by 1s: 36, 37. The time is 1:37. You may also wish to model counting back. For example, children may count back by 5s and 1s from 1:45 to 1:37 and say, 1:45, 1:40, 1:39, 1:38, 1:37.

Complete a few more examples to practice reading clocks to the nearest minute. Keep the hour the same and have children slightly adjust the hour hand as the minute hand moves into later quadrants of the clock. Invite children to share helpful familiar times and strategies for determining the exact time to the minute. Suggested times: 2:09; 2:21; 2:37; 2:49; 2:56.

Have children read the time to the nearest minute on the classroom clock and record it at the top of journal page 8. **GMP5.2** Invite them to share and compare the efficiency of their time-telling strategies. For example, using a familiar time might be faster than counting minutes all the way around the clock. **GMP6.4**

In subsequent lessons, children will tell and write the time at the top of each journal page. This routine provides daily practice for telling time.

Lesson 1-5

DATE 9/12/16   TIME 9:50

Have children complete Problems 1–6 by reading clocks to the nearest minute. Encourage children to use the clocks in Problems 3 and 5 to help them read time to the nearest minute in Problems 4 and 6. Invite volunteers to show how they solved each problem using the demonstration clock. **GMP5.2**

Assessment Check-In (CCSS) 3.MD.1

Math Journal 1, p. 8

Expect most children to tell time accurately to the nearest 5 minutes in Problems 1–3 and 5. GMP5.2, GMP6.4 However, do not expect all children to read time to the nearest minute in Problems 4 and 6, as this is the first exposure to telling time to the minute. Children will practice reading and writing time to the minute daily when they record the time on journal and *Math Masters* pages. For children who struggle with telling time to the nearest 5 minutes, consider implementing the Readiness activity and the Adjusting the Activity note in this lesson.

 Assessment and Reporting Go Online to record student progress and to see trajectories toward mastery for this standard.

▶ Introducing Elapsed Time

Math Journal 1, p. 8; *Student Reference Book*, pp. 184–186

| WHOLE CLASS | SMALL GROUP | PARTNER | INDEPENDENT |

Bring children together and have them share the times shown on the clocks for Problems 1 and 2. *2:15 and 2:40*

Pose this problem: *Michael's class started math centers at 2:15 and ended them at 2:40. How could we figure out the exact amount of time that passed while his class did math centers?* Sample answer: We could count the minutes that passed on our clocks. Explain that the difference between two times is called the **elapsed time.** Elapsed time is typically recorded in minutes and hours.

> **NOTE** This introduction to elapsed time will support children as they calculate elapsed time in the open response problem in Lesson 1-6.

Demonstrate the following strategies for determining the elapsed time from 2:15 to 2:40. Display a unit box labeled "minutes."

- Use a toolkit clock and count by 5s or other familiar blocks of time, such as 10 minutes or 15 minutes, until you reach the end time. (*See margin.*) Then add the total minutes. For example: $15 + 5 + 5 = 25$.
- Draw an open number line to represent the amounts of time that pass.

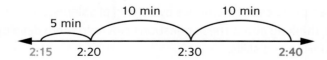

Show different ways of breaking down the elapsed time. Calculate the total time by adding. For example: $5 + 10 + 10 = 25$.

Use familiar blocks of time to help find the elapsed time.

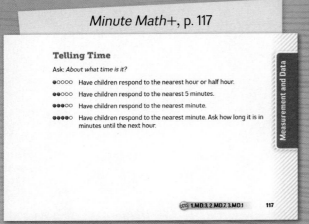

Telling Time

Ask: *About what time is it?*

●○○○○ Have children respond to the nearest hour or half hour.

●●○○○ Have children respond to the nearest 5 minutes.

●●●○○ Have children respond to the nearest minute.

●●●●○ Have children respond to the nearest minute. Ask how long it is in minutes until the next hour.

Measurement and Data

CCSS 1.MD.3, 2.MD.7, 3.MD.1   117

Have partners calculate the elapsed time between the times shown in Problems 5 and 6. Invite a few pairs to share their solution strategies. Compare strategies using an open number line and the clock.
GMP1.6, GMP5.2

Summarize Have partners read about telling time to the nearest minute on *Student Reference Book,* pages 184–186.

③ Practice 10–15 min

Go Online

ePresentations eToolkit Home Connections

▶ *Minute Math+*

Minute Math+, pp. 117–118

To provide practice identifying activities of varying lengths of time, see *Minute Math+,* page 117, levels 1 and 2. Also see page 118 for additional time-telling practice.

▶ Introducing the Math Boxes Routine

Math Journal 1, p. 9; *Student Reference Book*

| WHOLE CLASS | SMALL GROUP | PARTNER | INDEPENDENT |

Mixed Practice Math Boxes 1-5 are paired with Math Boxes 1-7.

Explain that Math Boxes are practice problems that children will complete on a regular basis. These pages are designed for independent work, but children may work in partnerships when appropriate.

Call children's attention to the *Student Reference Book* icons in the Math Boxes. Explain that these icons tell them which *Student Reference Book* pages to read or review if they need more information to complete the Math Boxes. You may want to demonstrate using a *Student Reference Book* page to help solve one of the Math Boxes problems.

As children work on Math Boxes throughout the year, encourage them to ask themselves questions such as: *What tools can I use to solve the problem?* GMP5.1 *How can I check my answer?* Explain that when children practice mathematics by solving problems, such as those in Math Boxes, thinking about these questions can help them develop stronger problem-solving skills.

Math Boxes

Lesson 1-5
DATE   TIME

① Write the numbers that are 10 less and 10 more.

10 less		10 more
28	38	48
235	245	255
357	367	377
809	819	829

② Use your calculator.

Enter	Change to	How?
31	41	+ 10
58	38	− 20
146	106	− 40
405	455	+ 50

③ Fill in the unit box. Add.

Unit

$3 + 7 = \underline{10}$

$12 = 5 + \underline{7}$

$\begin{array}{r} 9 \\ + 3 \\ \hline 1\ 2 \end{array}$ $\begin{array}{r} 9 \\ + 8 \\ \hline 1\ 7 \end{array}$

④ What time does the clock show?

7:15

⑤ **Writing/Reasoning** Explain how you found the numbers that were 10 more and 10 less in Problem 1.
Sample answers: I changed the digit in the tens place to 1 more or 1 less. I counted back by 10 and up by 10.

① 3.NBT.2 ② 3.NBT.2 ③ 3.NBT.2 ④ 3.MD.1
⑤ 3.NBT.2, SMP6

nine   9

Children will also have an opportunity to explain their thinking in Writing/ Reasoning prompts in Problem 5 within many Math Boxes. You may wish to model how to write a clear, complete response to set expectations for children's written work.

Math Masters, page TA5 is available for you to create your own Math Boxes page for practice or assessment purposes. Also see the online *Implementaion Guide* for suggestions about managing the Math Boxes routine.

► **Home Link 1-5**

Math Masters, p. 16

Homework Children practice telling time to the nearest minute. GMP6.2

Telling Time to the Nearest Minute

Home Link 1-5

NAME   DATE   TIME

Family Note Today your child practiced telling time to the nearest minute on analog clocks. Children used familiar times on the hour and half hour to help them read more precise times. For example, in Problem 1 the first clock shows 8:00. Children can use 8:00 as a familiar time to help them read the second clock as 8:06. They start at 8:00 and count by 5s to 8:05 and then 1 more to 8:06. As needed, help your child read and write each time.

Please return this Home Link to school tomorrow.

Write each time shown. Use the first clock to help you read the time on the second clock.

①

8:00   8:06

②

3:30   3:39

③

1:45   1:52

Talk about when you may need to tell time to the nearest minute.

16   3.MD.1

How Long Is a Morning?

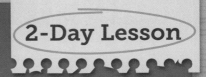

2-Day Lesson

Overview **Day 1:** Children use mathematical models to measure elapsed time. **Day 2:** Children share models and discuss strategies for calculating elapsed time, and then revise their work.

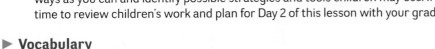

Day 1: Open Response

▶ **Before You Begin**

Children will calculate the length of their school morning. If the morning begins at 8:30 A.M. and ends at 11:30 A.M., you may wish to modify the times to present a more interesting problem, such as 8:15 A.M. to 11:20 A.M. Calculating elapsed time across noon is more challenging and will be practiced in the Length-of-Day Project (Lesson 1-11). Solve the open response problem yourself in as many ways as you can and identify possible strategies and tools children may use. If possible, schedule time to review children's work and plan for Day 2 of this lesson with your grade-level team.

▶ **Vocabulary**

strategy • mathematical model • elapsed time

Common Core State Standards

Focus Cluster
Solve problems involving measurement and estimation.

	Materials	
① Warm Up 5 min		
Mental Math and Fluency Children skip count using times.	demonstration clock	3.MD.1
②a Focus 55–65 min		
Math Message Children make sense of the solution to an elapsed-time problem that uses an open number line.	*Math Journal 1*, p. 10; toolkit clocks; demonstration clock	3.MD.1
Finding Elapsed Time Using a Number Line Children share their strategies for finding elapsed time using an open number line and toolkit clocks.	*Math Journal 1*, p. 10; *Student Reference Book*, pp. 187–188; toolkit clocks; demonstration clock (optional)	3.MD.1 SMP1, SMP4
Solving the Open Response Problem Children use a mathematical model to calculate elapsed time for the length of a school morning.	*Math Masters*, p. 17; toolkit clocks (optional)	3.MD.1 SMP4

Getting Ready for Day 2 →

Review children's work and plan discussion for reengagement.   *Math Masters*, p. TA6; children's work from Day 1

3.MD.1 **Spiral Snapshot**

GMC Solve number stories involving time intervals by adding or subtracting.

1-5 Focus	1-6 Focus Practice	1-9 Practice	1-10 Practice	1-11 Focus Practice	1-12 Practice	1-13 Practice	2-1 Practice

Spiral Tracker   Go Online   to see how mastery develops for all standards within the grade.

---

connectED.mcgraw-hill.com

Plan your lessons online with these tools.

 ePresentations   Student Learning Center   Facts Workshop Game   eToolkit   Professional Development   Home Connections   Spiral Tracker   Assessment and Reporting   ELL English Learners Support   Differentiation Support

48   Unit 1 | Math Tools, Time, and Multiplication

1 Warm Up   5 min   Go Online

ePresentations eToolkit

▶ Mental Math and Fluency

Have children skip count by minutes and hours. *Leveled exercises*:

● ○ ○ **Skip count forward by 5 minutes from 1:05 to 2:00.** 1:05, 1:10, 1:15, 1:20, 1:25, 1:30, 1:35, 1:40, 1:45, 1:50, 1:55, 2:00

● ● ○ **Skip count forward by 15 minutes from 1:00 to 3:00.** 1:00, 1:15, 1:30, 1:45, 2:00, 2:15, 2:30, 2:45, 3:00

● ● ● **Skip count by hours starting from 7:15 A.M. to 11:15 P.M.** 7:15 A.M., 8:15 A.M., 9:15 A.M., 10:15 A.M., 11:15 A.M., 12:15 P.M., 1:15 P.M., 2:15 P.M., 3:15 P.M., 4:15 P.M., 5:15 P.M., 6:15 P.M., 7:15 P.M., 8:15 P.M., 9:15 P.M., 10:15 P.M., 11:15 P.M.

2a Focus   55–65 min   Go Online

ePresentations eToolkit

▶ Math Message

Math Journal 1, p. 10

Complete journal page 10. You may use toolkit clocks or other tools to help you. Be ready to explain your thinking to a partner.

▶ Finding Elapsed Time Using a Number Line

Math Journal 1, p. 10; *Student Reference Book*, pp. 187–188

| WHOLE CLASS | SMALL GROUP | PARTNER | INDEPENDENT |

Math Message Follow-Up Have partners discuss their responses to the Math Message and their explanations of Sheena's **strategy.**
GMP1.6, GMP4.2 Provide sentence frames to help children get started, such as: "First Sheena _____. Then she _____. The hops on the number line start at _____. This hop shows _____."

Then bring the class together and ask the following:

• *What tool did Sheena use to solve the problem?* An open number line
• *How did Sheena start her number line?* Sample answer: She marked a starting time at 9:55.

Professional Development

Each Open Response and Reengagement lesson focuses on one Goal for Mathematical Practice (GMP). Through the focus GMPs, each of the CCSS Mathematical Practices will be addressed in the Open Response and Reengagement lessons in Grade 3. The focus of this lesson is GMP4.2. Telling time and measuring its duration offer rich opportunities for children to use mathematical models in answering everyday questions. In this lesson children use tools such as open number lines or toolkit clocks to model and measure elapsed time. For information on Mathematical Practices in this unit, see the Mathematical Background in the Unit Organizer.

Go Online to the *Implementation Guide* for more information about SMP4.

How Long is Math Class?

Lesson 1-6

DATE   TIME

Math Message

Sheena's math class began at 9:55 A.M. and ended at 11:10 A.M. She started to figure out how long the class lasted. She used a number line.

Use Sheena's number line to complete the problem. Tell the length of time in hours and minutes.

Math class lasted ___1___ hour and ___15___ minutes.

Explain Sheena's strategy to your partner.

10   ten   3.MD.1

Measurement and Data

You can also use an open number line to find the elapsed time for the length of day.

Example
What is the length of day?

Time of Sunrise	Time of Sunset
6:22 A.M.	7:29 P.M.

6 hours + 6 hours + 1 hour = 13 hours

The elapsed time from 6:22 A.M. to 7:29 P.M. is 13 hours and 7 minutes.

Check Your Understanding

1. How many hours pass from 7:00 A.M. to 7:00 P.M.? How many hours pass from 6:22 A.M. to 6:22 P.M.? How many hours have elapsed from 3:26 A.M. to 3:26 P.M.? Describe the pattern.

2. What is the longest possible time elapsed for an event if the time is within the same day?

Check your answers in the Answer Key.

SRB
188   one hundred eighty-eight

- *What does Sheena's first hop represent?* Sample answer: That it is 5 minutes from 9:55 to 10:00
- *What do the second and third hops represent?* Sample answer: That it is an hour from 10:00 to 11:00 and another 10 minutes to 11:10
- *What did Sheena write above the hops?* Sample answer: The length of time for each hop
- Review familiar times from Lesson 1-5. Ask: *What familiar times did Sheena use on her number line?* Sample answer: 10:00 and 11:00
- *How did you find the total time?* Sample answer: I added the hops together: 5 minutes + 1 hour + 10 minutes = 1 hour and 15 minutes.
- *Why are some hops smaller than others? Why is the middle hop the longest?* Sample answer: The length of time for each hop is different. The middle hop is the longest because it goes over more time than the other hops.

Explain that Sheena used an open number line as a **mathematical model** for calculating **elapsed time.** Have children turn to and read *Student Reference Book,* pages 187–188. Briefly discuss how mathematical models are used to solve problems and answer questions.

Ask: *What other tools could you use to solve this problem?* Sample answer: Toolkit clocks Have children use their toolkit clocks to solve Sheena's problem. Create a new model to show the length of Sheena's math class, such as a drawing of a clock. Ask: *How can you use a clock to solve the problem?* Sample answer: I set the clock to 9:55. Then I moved the minute hand all the way around and the hour hand from almost 10 to almost 11 to show 10:55. Then I moved the minute hand 15 more minutes and the hour hand to just after 11 to show 11:10, and that was 1 hour and 15 minutes. Ask: *Do you get the same answer using the toolkit clock as you did using the number line?* Yes.

Tell children that they will figure out how long the class's morning lasts using a model, such as an open number line or clock. GMP4.2

NOTE This is the first Open Response and Reengagement lesson in Grade 3. These two-day lessons appear in each unit to provide children consistent opportunities to engage in the mathematical practices as they solve problems. In these lessons, children solve an open response problem on the first day and reengage with the same problem on the second day to deepen their understanding of the content and practices.

Go Online to the *Implementation Guide* for more information about Open Response and Reengagement.

English Language Learners Support Prior to the lesson, use a classroom clock, toolkit clocks, or drawings to review the vocabulary for telling time with English language learners. Have children identify the *hour hand, minute hand, minute marks,* and *hour marks* on a clock face. Discuss the term *familiar times* and give examples such as 8:00, 8:15, and 8:30. Reviewing these terms will help you determine whether a child's difficulties with the open response problem are related to the mathematics or the language of the problems.

▶ Solving the Open Response Problem

Math Masters, p. 17

| WHOLE CLASS | SMALL GROUP | **PARTNER** | INDEPENDENT |

Distribute *Math Masters,* page 17 to each child. Display the start and end times for the problem and discuss them. See Before You Begin for suggestions on choosing start and end times for the morning.

Read the problem as a class and have partners discuss what the problem asks them to do. Note that they are only asked to solve the problem in one way, but they may choose to solve it a second way to check their answers. Partners may work together to share ideas about the task, but children should show how they solved the problem themselves.

As children work, note the tools they use and how they show their work. If they use an open number line, encourage them to clearly label the start and stop times of each hop and the length of the hops. If they use toolkit clocks, suggest that they use words or drawings to show their strategies.

Ask: *Is your work clear enough that someone else can use your strategy to solve the problem?* Answers vary.

Ask children who have difficulty getting started to draw a number line with the start and end times for the morning. Then ask whether they know any familiar times they can add to the number line.

Ask children who readily solve the problem and clearly show their work to choose a different strategy or tool and model it a second way. See the sample work in Getting Ready for Day 2 for examples of different strategies children may use. **GMP4.1, GMP4.2**

Summarize Ask: *How did you use your model to solve this problem?* **GMP4.2** Sample answer: I used a number line and added up the times on the hops to find out how long the morning lasts.

Collect children's work so you can evaluate it and prepare for Day 2. You may also want to make notes about children's strategies.

Getting Ready for Day 2

Math Masters, p. TA6

Planning a Follow-Up Discussion

Review children's work. Use the Reengagement Planning Form (*Math Masters,* page TA6) and the rubric on page 54 to plan ways to help children meet expectations for both the content and practice standards. Look for common errors, such as incorrect calculations of time, as well as interesting ways children modeled elapsed time and answered the question.

Math Masters, p. 17

How Long Is a Morning?

Lesson 1-6

NAME   DATE   TIME

Write the times:

We start at _____.

We go to lunch at _____.

Use at least one strategy to find how long you are in school in the morning. Show how you solve the problem.

How long was your morning? _____ hours and _____ minutes

Answers vary. See sample children's work on page 57 of the *Teacher's Lesson Guide.*

3.MD.1, SMP4   17

Common Misconception

Differentiate Watch for children who incorrectly count the total time. For example, when calculating the time from 8:45 to 11:30, some children may incorrectly think that 3 hours have passed from 8:00 to 11:00. Use an open number line or clock to help them recount and look for familiar times.

Sample child's work, Child A

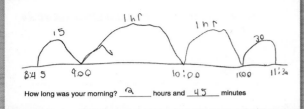

How long was your morning? ___2___ hours and __45__ minutes

Reengagement Planning Form

> **Common Core State Standard (CCSS):** *3.MD.1 . . . Solve word problems involving addition and subtraction of time intervals in minutes, e.g., by representing the problem on a number line diagram.*
>
> **Goal for Mathematical Practice (GMP):** *GMP4.2: Use mathematical models to solve problems and answer questions.*

Organize the discussion in one of the ways below or in another way you choose. If children's work is unclear or if you prefer to show work anonymously, rewrite the work for display.

Go Online for sample children's work that you can use in your discussion.

> **NOTE** The length of the morning in the sample work varies depending on the child's classroom.

1. Display a child's response that uses a number line to correctly model the elapsed time, as in Child A's work. Ask:
   * *What did this child use to model the total time?* **GMP4.1** The child used a number line.
   * *How did this child make the number line?* **GMP4.1** Sample answer: First the child put the start time of 8:45 on the number line, and then added the familiar times of 9:00, 10:00, 11:00, and 11:30.
   * *How did this child figure out how much time to write above each hop?* **GMP4.2** Sample answer: The child used the number line and counted up from 8:45 to 9:00 to get 15 minutes for the first hop. Then the 9:00 to 10:00 and 10:00 to 11:00 hops were each 1 hour and the last hop from 11:00 to 11:30 was 30 minutes.
   * *Explain how this child might have used this number line to find the length of the morning.* **GMP4.2** Sample answer: The child added up the hops. The 15-minute hop and the 30-minute hop add up to 45 minutes. There were two 1-hour hops. All the hops add up to 2 hours and 45 minutes.
   * *How could this child show his or her thinking more clearly?* **GMP4.2** Sample answers: The child could show adding up the hops. The child could have added the unit *minutes* to the hops labeled 15 and 30.

2. Display two different strategies using a number line, such as in Child A's and Child B's work. Ask:
   * *How is Child B's number line different from Child A's number line?* Sample answer: Child B's first hop is 2 hours, and Child A's first hop is 15 minutes. *Do they get the same answers?* Yes. *Which strategy do you think is easier to use?* **GMP1.6** Answers vary.

Sample child's work, Child B

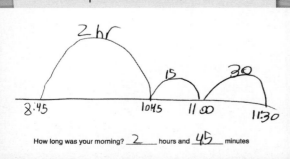

How long was your morning? __2__ hours and __45__ minutes

3. Display work that uses a number line and a clock, as in Child C's work. Ask questions similar to those on the previous page, and the following:
   - *Compare the solution that uses a number line to the one that uses a clock. How are they alike?* Sample answer: They both start and end at the same time. *How are they different?* GMP1.6 Answers vary.
   - *If we use different tools or strategies, should we get the same answer to this problem? Explain why or why not.* Sample answer: Yes. Since the starting time and the ending time are the same, the amount of time in the morning should stay the same.
   - *Explain how Child C used the clocks to find the elapsed time.* GMP4.2 Sample answer: The first clock shows 8:05, the next 9:05, then 10:05, and 11:05. That is 3 hours. The next clock shows 10 more minutes at 11:15, and the last clock adds 5 more minutes to get to 11:20. Those times add up to 3 hours and 15 minutes, just like on the number line.
   - *Which tool did you choose? Why?* Answers vary.

4. Display a child's response that shows a correct solution but does not clearly show the strategy, as in Child D's work. Ask:
   - *What do you notice about the hops on this number line?* GMP4.2 Sample answer: Some hops don't match the time written above them. The second hop goes from 8:10 to 9:00, but it says "5 min" above the hop.
   - *Did this child get the correct answer?* Yes.
   - *What could the child do to show his or her work more clearly?* GMP4.1 Sample answers: The child could mark the times on the number line more clearly. The child could make sure that each hop shows the right amount of time.

5. Display a child's response that does not provide a complete or correct answer. Ask:
   - *According to this child, how long is the morning?* Answers vary.
   - *Do you agree with this answer? Why or why not?* GMP1.6 Answers vary.
   - *Can you suggest ways to help this child complete or correct the work?* GMP4.2 Answers vary.

Planning for Revisions

Have copies of *Math Masters*, page 17 or extra paper available for children to use in revisions. You might want to ask children to use colored pencils so you can see what they revised.

Sample child's work, Child C

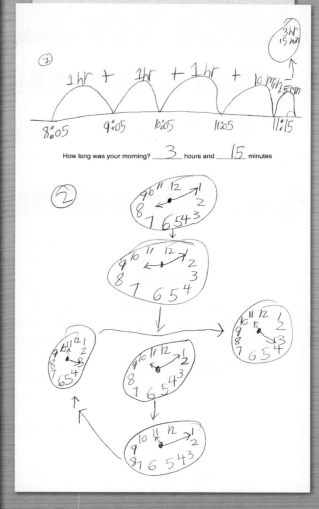

Sample child's work, Child D

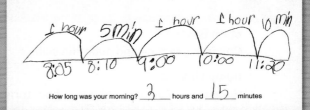

How Long Is a Morning?

Overview   **Day 2:** Children share models and discuss strategies for calculating elapsed time, and then revise their work.

Day 2: Reengagement

▶ **Before You Begin**
Have toolkit clocks and extra copies of *Math Masters,* page 17 available for children to revise their work.

Common Core State Standards

Focus Cluster
Solve problems involving measurement and estimation of intervals of time, liquid volumes, and masses of objects.

2b Focus — 50–55 min

	Materials	
Setting Expectations Children review the open response problem and discuss what a good response might include. They also review how to discuss others' work respectfully.	Class Data Pad or chart paper, Standards for Mathematical Practice Poster	**3.MD.1** **SMP4**
Reengaging in the Problem Children analyze sample work and discuss appropriate models and strategies for finding elapsed time.	selected samples of children's work, toolkit clock, demonstration clock	**3.MD.1** **SMP1, SMP4**
Revising Work Children revise their work from Day 1.	*Math Masters,* p. 17 (optional); colored pencils (optional); toolkit clocks; children's work from Day 1	**3.MD.1** **SMP4**

✓ **Assessment Check-In**   See page 56 and the rubric below.   **3.MD.1, SMP4**

Goal for Mathematical Practice **GMP4.2** Use mathematical models to solve problems and answer questions.	Not Meeting Expectations	Partially Meeting Expectations	Meeting Expectations	Exceeding Expectations
	Does not use a model to represent the elapsed time.	Uses a model to represent the elapsed time, but it is used incorrectly or the model lacks precision or clarity.	Uses a model to clearly represent and find the correct elapsed time.	Uses more than one model to clearly represent and find the correct elapsed time.

3 Practice — 10–15 min

Math Boxes 1-6 Children practice and maintain skills.	*Math Journal 1,* p. 11	See page 57.
Home Link 1-6 **Homework** Children solve number stories involving elapsed time using number lines.	*Math Masters,* p. 18	**3.MD.1** **SMP4**

50–55 min | Go Online

ePresentations eToolkit

> ## Setting Expectations

| **WHOLE CLASS** | SMALL GROUP | PARTNER | INDEPENDENT |

Establishing Guidelines for Reengagement

A significant part of the Day 2 reengagement portion of the lesson is a class discussion about children's strategies and explanations. To promote a cooperative environment, consider developing class guidelines for discussion on the Class Data Pad or chart paper. Solicit suggestions from the class and include items you feel are important. Add to the list throughout the year and refer to it during group discussions. (*See sample poster in the margin.*)

Consider modeling or having children role-play situations based on one or more of the guidelines on your poster. For example, model how you can learn from a mistake in your own work using a simple math problem as an example (such as $21 + 1 = 31$).

Point out that some children will think differently about the problem or change their minds during the discussion. Remind children that it is fine to change their minds, and that they should listen closely to each other to see whether they agree or disagree with what other children say. Use the following sentence frames as models and encourage children to use appropriate language when discussing other children's work:

- I like how you _____.
- Could you explain _____.
- I don't understand _____.
- I'd like to add _____.

Reviewing the Problem

Briefly review the open response problem from Day 1. Ask: *What were you asked to do?* Sample answer: Figure out how long our morning lasted *What do you think a response should include?* GMP4.2 Sample answer: It should have a model that could be used to figure out the length of the morning and work that shows how I found my answer.

Then tell children that they are going to look at other children's work to see whether they thought about the problem in the same way. Refer to GMP4.2 on the Standards for Mathematical Practice Poster. Explain that they will be trying to figure out how other children used models to solve the problem.

> ## Reengaging in the Problem

| **WHOLE CLASS** | SMALL GROUP | **PARTNER** | INDEPENDENT |

Children reengage in the problem by analyzing and critiquing other children's work in pairs and in a whole-group discussion. Have children discuss with partners before sharing with the whole group. Guide this discussion based on the decisions you made in Getting Ready for Day 2.
GMP1.6, GMP4.1, GMP4.2

NOTE These Day 2 activities will ideally take place within a few days of Day 1. Prior to beginning Day 2, see Planning a Follow-Up Discussion from Day 1.

Guidelines for Discussion

During our discussions, we can:
- ✔ Make mistakes and learn from them
- ✔ Share ideas and strategies respectfully
- ✔ Agree and disagree politely
- ✔ Change our minds about how to solve a problem
- ✔ Feel confused
- ✔ Ask questions of our teacher and classmates
- ✔ Listen closely to others' ideas
- ✔ Be patient

▶ Revising Work

| WHOLE CLASS | SMALL GROUP | **PARTNER** | **INDEPENDENT** |

Pass back children's work from Day 1. Before children revise anything, ask them to examine their responses and decide how they could be improved. Ask the following questions one at a time. Have partners discuss their responses and give a thumbs-up or thumbs-down based on their own work.

- *Did you make a model to solve the problem?* GMP4.1
- *Is your answer complete and correct?* GMP4.2

Tell children they now have a chance to revise their work. Children who wrote complete and correct explanations on Day 1 can find a new tool or strategy for solving the problem. Help children see that the explanations presented during the reengagement discussion are not the only correct ones. Tell children to add to their earlier work using colored pencils or to use another sheet of paper, instead of erasing their original work.

Summarize Have children reflect on their work. Ask: *Describe how you improved your strategy for figuring out how long your morning lasted.* GMP4.2 Answers vary.

✓ Assessment Check-In CCSS 3.MD.1

Collect and review children's revised work. Expect most children to improve their work based on the class discussion. For the content standard, expect most children to accurately calculate the elapsed time for the morning. You can use the rubric on page 54 to evaluate children's revised work for **GMP4.2**.

 Assessment and Reporting Go Online to record student progress and to see trajectories toward mastery for this standard.

Go Online for optional generic rubrics in the *Assessment Handbook* that can be used to assess any additional GMPs addressed in the lesson.

Sample Children's Work—Evaluated

See the sample in the margin. This work meets expectations for the content standard because the child correctly found that there were 3 hours and 15 minutes in the morning. The work meets expectations for the mathematical practice because the child drew a number line to model the elapsed time and used it to answer the question. The written description explains how the number line was used to find the total elapsed time of 3 hours and 15 minutes. **GMP4.2**

Go Online for other samples of evaluated children's work.

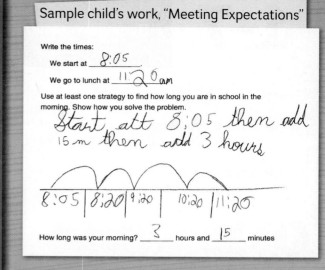
③ Practice   10–15 min   Go Online

ePresentations   eToolkit   Home Connections

▶ Math Boxes 1-6

Math Journal 1, p. 11

WHOLE CLASS | SMALL GROUP | PARTNER | INDEPENDENT

Mixed Practice Math Boxes 1-6 are paired with Math Boxes 1-8.

▶ Home Link 1-6

Math Masters, p. 18

Homework Children solve number stories involving elapsed time using number lines. **GMP4.2**

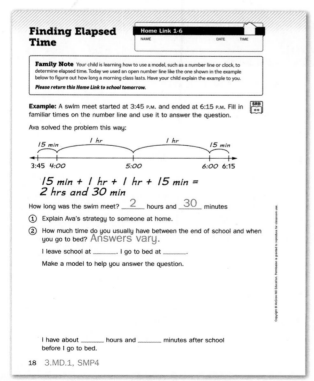

Math Masters, p. 18

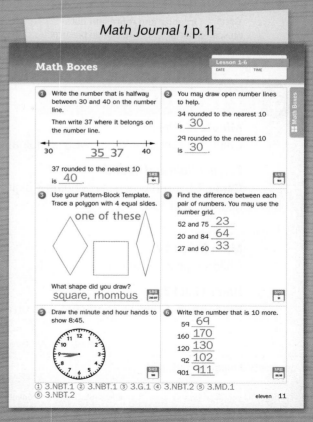

Math Journal 1, p. 11

Scaled Bar Graphs

Overview Children represent and interpret data on scaled bar graphs.

▶ **Before You Begin**
For Part 2, divide a page on the Class Data Pad into two columns labeled First Name and Last Name.

▶ **Vocabulary**
bar graph • data

CCSS Common Core State Standards

Focus Cluster
Represent and interpret data.

1 Warm Up   5 min

	Materials	
Mental Math and Fluency Children solve addition and subtraction facts.		3.NBT.2

2 Focus   40–50 min

	Materials	
Math Message Children record data and read about tally charts and bar graphs in their *Student Reference Book*.	*Math Journal 1*, p. 4; *Student Reference Book*, pp. 191–192; Class Data Pad	3.MD.3
Reviewing Tally Charts/Bar Graphs Children discuss tally charts and bar graphs.	*Student Reference Book*, pp. 191–192; Class Data Pad	3.MD.3 SMP2
Organizing and Representing Data Children organize and represent data in bar graphs.	*Math Journal 1*, pp. 12–13; *Math Masters*, p. TA7; Class Data Pad	3.MD.3 SMP2, SMP6
✓ **Assessment Check-In** See page 62.	*Math Journal 1*, pp. 12–13	3.MD.3, SMP6
Answering Questions about Data Children answer questions from scaled bar graphs.	*Math Journal 1*, p. 12 or *Math Masters*, p. TA7	3.MD.3 SMP2

CCSS 3.MD.3 **Spiral Snapshot**

GMC Organize and represent data on scaled bar graphs and scaled picture graphs.

| 1-7
Focus
Practice | 1-11
Focus | 3-7
Focus | 3-8
Focus | 3-10
Practice | 3-13
Practice | 4-2
Practice | 4-4
Practice |

Spiral Tracker   **Go Online** to see how mastery develops for all standards within the grade.

3 Practice   15–20 min

	Materials	
Minute Math+ Children practice addition with combinations of 10s.	*Minute Math®+*, p. 9	3.NBT.2
Playing *Spin and Round* **Game** Children practice rounding 3-digit numbers to the nearest 10 or 100.	*Student Reference Book*, pp. 258–259; *Math Masters*, pp. G4–G5; number cards 1–9 (4 of each); pencil; large paper clip	3.NBT.1
Math Boxes 1-7 Children practice and maintain skills.	*Math Journal 1*, p. 14	See page 63.
Home Link 1-7 **Homework** Children represent data on a scaled bar graph.	*Math Masters*, p. 21	3.MD.3

connectED.mcgraw-hill.com

Plan your lessons online
with these tools.

 ePresentations   **Student Learning Center**   **Facts Workshop Game**   **eToolkit**   **Professional Development**   **Home Connections**   **Spiral Tracker**   **Assessment and Reporting**   **ELL English Learners Support**   **Differentiation Support**

Differentiation Options

RtI

Readiness   5–10 min

| WHOLE CLASS |
| **SMALL GROUP** |
| PARTNER |
| INDEPENDENT |

Interpreting a Tally Chart

Math Masters, p. 19

To provide experience interpreting data on a tally chart, have children examine the tally chart on *Math Masters,* page 19. Ask: *What is the tally chart showing?* The favorite drink of some children *What are the favorite drinks listed on the tally chart?* Milk, lemonade, water, and juice *How many children picked milk as their favorite drink?* 6 children *How do you know?* **GMP2.2** There are 6 tally marks.

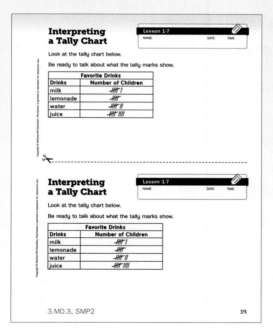

Enrichment   15–20 min

| WHOLE CLASS |
| SMALL GROUP |
| **PARTNER** |
| INDEPENDENT |

Conducting a Survey

Activity Card 9;
Math Masters, p. TA7

To extend understanding of collecting and representing data, have children choose a topic on which to conduct a survey. For example, they may ask others to name their favorite animal, color, subject, or food. Then have them record on a tally chart as others choose, represent the data in a scaled bar graph on *Math Masters,* page TA7, and write questions that can be answered from the graph. **GMP4.1, GMP4.2**

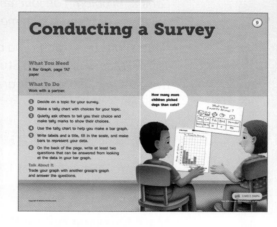

Extra Practice   5–10 min

| WHOLE CLASS |
| SMALL GROUP |
| **PARTNER** |
| **INDEPENDENT** |

Graphing Data

Math Masters, p. 20

To practice representing data on a scaled bar graph, have children complete *Math Masters,* page 20. **GMP2.1**

English Language Learners Support

Beginning ELL In some cultures, the last name, or family name, comes first. In other cultures, it is common to have one name. In many Spanish-speaking countries, the name order is given name, father's surname, and mother's surname, so the last name is the mother's surname. To make directions for Part 2 clear, you may want to refer to family names and given names.

[Go Online] [ELL] English Learners Support

Standards and Goals for
Mathematical Practice

SMP2 Reason abstractly and quantitatively.
GMP2.1 Create mathematical representations using numbers, words, pictures, symbols, gestures, tables, graphs, and concrete objects.

GMP2.2 Make sense of the representations you and others use.

SMP6 Attend to precision.
GMP6.3 Use clear labels, units, and mathematical language.

1 Warm Up 5 min

▶ Mental Math and Fluency

Ask children to solve each fact and briefly share their strategies.
Leveled exercises: Sample strategies given.

- ●○○ 6 + 7 I knew 6 and 6 made 12, so one more is 13.
  4 + 9 I thought of 9 + 4 and knew 10 + 4 = 14, so one less is 13.
- ●●○ 7 + 9 I knew 7 + 10 = 17, so one less is 16.
  9 − 4 I knew 10 − 4 = 6, so 9 − 4 is one less, which is 5.
- ●●● 8 + 6 I moved 2 to the 8 to make 10, and 10 and 4 is 14.
  15 − 7 I knew 14 − 7 = 7, so one more is 8.

2 Focus 40–50 min

▶ Math Message

Math Journal 1, p. 4; *Student Reference Book,* pp. 191–192

Look at Problem 1 on journal page 4. Write the number of letters in your partner's first and last names on the Class Data Pad.

Read about bar graphs and compare the Favorite Foods and Pull-Ups by Third Graders graphs on Student Reference Book, *pages 191–192. Use the data in one of the bar graphs to write a question for your partner to answer.*

▶ Reviewing Tally Charts/Bar Graphs

Student Reference Book, pp. 191–192

| WHOLE CLASS | SMALL GROUP | PARTNER | INDEPENDENT |

Math Message Follow-Up Make sure that all children have recorded their partners' first- and last-name data. Have partners ask each other and answer the questions they wrote about the graph. Afterward bring the class together and ask children to share what they notice about the **bar graphs** from their *Student Reference Book.* Point out the important parts of each, including the title and labels, axes, and the scales for numbering the axes. GMP2.2

Have children compare the vertical scales on the two bar graphs pictured on *Student Reference Book,* pages 191–192. Ask: *What differences do you notice?* Sample answer: The scale on the Favorite Foods of the Class graph is labeled by 2s, and the scale for the Pull-Ups by Third Graders graph is labeled by 1s. Discuss the bars that end halfway between the lines and those that end at the lines.

Student Reference Book, p. 191

Bar Graphs

A **bar graph** is a drawing that uses bars to represent data. Bar graphs can help you answer questions about the data. The example below is a **scaled bar graph.** The scale shows intervals of 2.

Example
The bar graph below shows how many children in a class chose certain foods as their favorites.

The title shows the subject of the graph.

Favorite Foods of the Class

The height of each bar shows how many children chose that food.

Each bar has a label.

How many children chose pizza?
The bar for pizza ends halfway between the line for 6 and the line for 8, so 7 children chose pizza as their favorite food.

How many more children chose tacos than spaghetti?
Eight children chose tacos as their favorite food, but only 3 children chose spaghetti. Five more children chose tacos than spaghetti.

Often, you choose the scale for a bar graph based on the data and the amount of available space for the graph. If the numbers in your data set are spread out, you will want to use larger intervals to create your bar graph.

one hundred ninety-one 191

Academic Language Development Children may be familiar with the term *scale* as in *fish scales, a musical scale,* and *scales for weighing.* Point to the scales for bar graph axes and ask children to consider which of the familiar meanings of the term is most like the use of *scales* on a bar graph. Sample answer: The scales for weighing because of the numbers Point out that this is an example of a word with many different meanings, even though they look and sound exactly alike.

Ask: *On the Favorite Foods of the Class bar graph, what does the bar that is halfway between 2 and 4 represent?* GMP2.2 3 children *How do you know?* Because 3 is halfway between 2 and 4 *What would the bars in the Favorite Foods of the Class graph look like if the scale showed spaces of 1?* The bars would be longer. *What would the bars in the Pull-Ups by Third Graders graph look like if the scale showed spaces of 2?* GMP2.2 The bars would be shorter. Explain that scales on bar graphs can show any size spaces. For example, a bar graph scale can show spaces, or intervals, of $\frac{1}{2}$ or 5 or 50. Generally the scale on a graph depends on the amount of available space for the graph.

Point out the tally chart on *Student Reference Book,* page 192. Compare the information shown in the tally chart with that shown in the bar graph on the same page.

▶ Organizing and Representing Data

Math Journal 1, pp. 12–13; *Math Masters,* p. TA7

| WHOLE CLASS | SMALL GROUP | PARTNER | INDEPENDENT |

Explain that there are different ways to collect information. We can count, ask questions, measure, or look at something and describe it. This information is called **data.**

Draw children's attention to the data on the Class Data Pad. Explain that the data will be organized in tally charts and represented on bar graphs.

Model how to organize the first names data in a tally chart. (*See margin.*) As a class, decide which numbers belong in the Number of Letters column and then tally how many children have first names with each number of letters. Display the completed tally chart for the remainder of the lesson.

Display *Math Masters,* page TA7. As a class, decide how to title and label the axes for a bar graph to represent the class data. GMP6.3 For example, use First Names for the title, label the vertical axis Number of Children and label the horizontal axis Number of Letters. Use the tally chart to fill numbers along the horizontal axis. Write intervals of 2 for the vertical axis scale. Fill a bar or two and discuss how to show data on the scaled graph. For example, if 4 children have first names that contain 5 letters, ask: *How far up must we shade in the bar for 5 letters?* to the 4 *How do you know?* Sample answer: Because there are 4 children in that group. Complete the graph as a class. GMP2.1

Next have partnerships complete a tally chart for the last names data on journal page 12 and use that to complete the scaled bar graph on page 13. GMP2.1

Student Reference Book, p. 192

Measurement and Data

After collecting data, you can organize it in a tally chart to help you make a bar graph.

Example
The children in Mr. Majumdar's class counted how many pull-ups each of them could do. Their results are shown in the tally chart.

Number of Pull-Ups	Number of Children
0	⁄⁄⁄⁄ /
1	⁄⁄⁄⁄
2	////
3	//
4	
5	///
6	/

The bar graph below shows the same information as the tally chart, but in a different way.

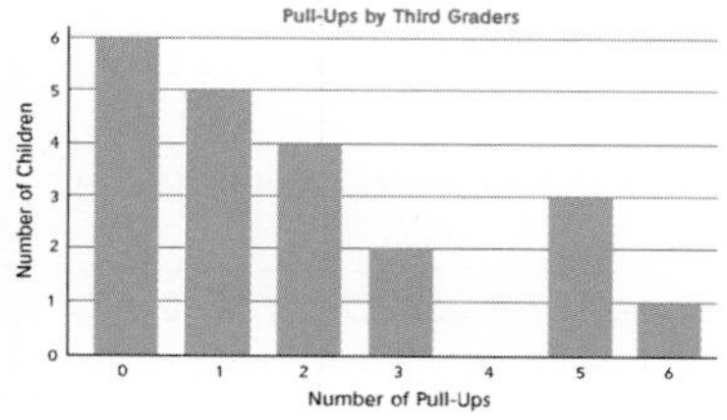

Pull-Ups by Third Graders

SRB 192 one hundred ninety-two

First Names	
Number of Letters	**Number of Children**
2	//
3	////
4	⁄⁄⁄⁄ /
5	⁄⁄⁄⁄ //
6	///
7	
8	/

Sample tally chart

Math Journal 1, p. 12

Displaying Data   Lesson 1-7
                                             DATE   TIME

① How many last names are there? __Answers vary.__

② Use the data you collected to make a tally chart for the last names in your class. Add rows as needed. __Answers vary.__

Last Names	
Number of Letters	Number of Children

③ Look at the data in your tally chart. Write at least three things you know from looking at the data.
__Sample answers: The longest name has 7__
__letters. The shortest name has 3 letters. No__
__one has a name with more than 8 letters.__

12 twelve   3.MD.3, SMP2, SMP6

Math Journal 1, p. 13

Displaying Data (continued)   Lesson 1-7
                                          DATE   TIME

④ Make a bar graph for your set of data. __Answers vary.__

Title: _____

(blank bar graph grid)

3.MD.3, SMP2, SMP6   thirteen 13

✓ Assessment Check-In CCSS 3.MD.3

Math Journal 1, pp. 12–13

Expect most children to accurately represent the last names data on a tally chart. Most children should also be able to set up their scaled bar graph to include an appropriate title and axis labels. GMP6.3 For those who struggle to represent the data on tally charts, consider implementing the Readiness activity. Some children may be able to represent the data on a scaled bar graph. Do not expect all children to do so, as this is their first exposure. Practice opportunities will occur in future lessons.

 Assessment and Reporting   (Go Online) to record student progress and to see trajectories toward mastery for this standard.

▶ Answering Questions about Data

Math Journal 1, p. 12 or *Math Masters*, p. TA7

| WHOLE CLASS | SMALL GROUP | PARTNER | INDEPENDENT |

Display the First Names bar graph completed in the previous activity and a Last Names bar graph. (You may use a child's completed graph or create your own completed graph on *Math Masters*, page TA7.)

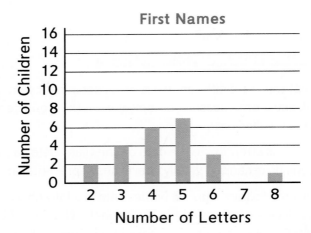

Have partnerships talk about what they notice about the data. GMP2.2 After a brief whole-class sharing session, pose questions similar to the following (note that answers below are based on the sample First Names bar graph):

- *How many letters are in the shortest first names?* 2 letters *Longest first names?* 8 letters *How many children have the shortest first names?* 2 children *Longest?* GMP2.2 1 child

- *How many letters do the most children have in their first names?* 7 children have 5 letters in their first names. *Last names?* GMP2.2 Answers vary.

Summarize Have partnerships discuss other data they can represent on bar graphs.

3 Practice 15–20 min | Go Online | ePresentations | eToolkit | Home Connections

▶ *Minute Math+*

Minute Math+, p. 9

To provide practice with combinations of 10s, see *Minute Math+,* page 9.

▶ Playing *Spin and Round*

Student Reference Book, pp. 258–259; *Math Masters,* pp. G4–G5

| WHOLE CLASS | SMALL GROUP | PARTNER | INDEPENDENT |

With the class, read the directions for *Spin and Round* on *Student Reference Book,* pages 258–259. Model a round or two before partners play on their own. Children may draw open number lines to help them round the numbers.

Observe

• Which children have difficulty identifying the closest two multiples of 10? Of 100?

• Which children draw open number lines to help?

Discuss

• *What strategies did you use to help you round?*

| Differentiate | Game Modifications | Go Online | Differentiation Support |

▶ Math Boxes 1-7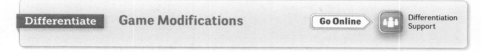

Math Journal 1, p. 14

| WHOLE CLASS | SMALL GROUP | PARTNER | INDEPENDENT |

Mixed Practice Math Boxes 1-7 are paired with Math Boxes 1-5.

▶ Home Link 1-7

Math Masters, p. 21

Homework Children represent data on a scaled bar graph.

Math Journal 1, p. 14

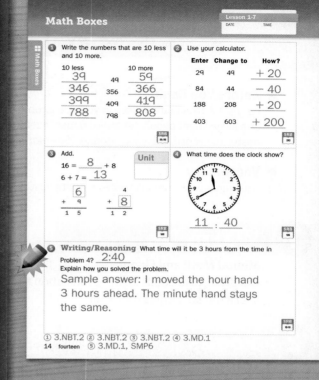

Math Masters, p. 21

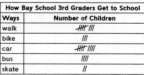

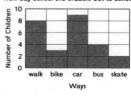

Multiplication Strategies

Overview Children use drawings and number models to represent and solve multiplication number stories.

▶ **Before You Begin**
For Part 2, designate a place in your classroom to post a Fact Strategy Wall. Title a bulletin board or a large sheet of bulletin-board paper "Fact Strategy Wall." Create a section at the start of the poster to record today's strategies. (*See margin on page 69.*)

▶ **Vocabulary**
equal groups • multiplication • multiplication symbol • array • row • column

 Common Core State Standards

Focus Clusters
• Represent and solve problems involving multiplication and division.
• Multiply and divide within 100.

1 Warm Up 5 min

Materials

Mental Math and Fluency
Children solve addition and subtraction facts and share the strategies they used.

3.NBT.2

2 Focus 45–55 min

Math Message Children solve a multiplication number story.	*Math Journal 1*, p. 15	3.OA.3
Sharing Strategies for Equal Groups and Arrays Children make sense of representations for equal-groups and array number stories.	*Math Journal 1*, p. 15	3.OA.1, 3.OA.3 SMP2, SMP4, SMP6
✓ **Assessment Check-In** See page 68.	*Math Journal 1*, p. 15	3.OA.3 SMP4
Starting a Fact Strategy Wall Children record multiplication strategies on the Fact Strategy Wall.	*Math Journal 1*, p. 15	3.OA.1, 3.OA.7 SMP2, SMP6
Writing Multiplication Number Stories Children write number stories to match number sentences.	*Math Journal 1*, p. 16	3.OA.1, 3.OA.3 SMP2

CCSS 3.OA.3 Spiral Snapshot

GMC Use multiplication and division to solve number stories.

| 1-2 Warm Up | 1-8 Focus Practice | 1-9 Focus Practice | 1-10 Practice | 2-1 through 2-4 Practice | 2-5 through 2-10 Warm Up Focus Practice |

 Spiral Tracker   **Go Online** to see how mastery develops for all standards within the grade.

3 Practice 10–15 min

Minute Math+ Children practice solving equal-groups problems.	*Minute Math®+*, p. 36	3.OA.3, 3.OA.7
Math Boxes 1-8 Children practice and maintain skills.	*Math Journal 1*, p. 17	See page 71.
Home Link 1-8 **Homework** Children solve multiplication number stories.	*Math Masters*, p. 22	3.OA.1, 3.OA.3 SMP4

connectED.mcgraw-hill.com

Plan your lessons online with these tools.

 ePresentations

 Student Learning Center

 Facts Workshop Game

 eToolkit

 Professional Development

 Home Connections

 Spiral Tracker

 Assessment and Reporting

ELL English Learners Support

Differentiation Support

Differentiation Options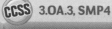

RtI

CCSS 3.OA.1, SMP2

Readiness
10–15 min

| WHOLE CLASS |
| SMALL GROUP |
| PARTNER |
| INDEPENDENT |

Designing Flags

Activity Card 10; 6-sided die; number cards 2–4 (4 of each); 24 counters; 4 quarter-sheets of paper; 1 full-sheet of paper

To provide practice concretely representing items in equal groups, have children design flags with stars. GMP2.1 Have children take turns drawing number cards to generate the number of flags and rolling a die to generate the number of stars on each flag.

CCSS 3.OA.3, SMP4

Enrichment
10–15 min

| WHOLE CLASS |
| SMALL GROUP |
| PARTNER |
| INDEPENDENT |

Writing Equal-Groups or Array Number Stories

Activity Card 11; *Math Masters,* p. TA8; 6-sided die

To provide practice with equal groups and arrays, have children create equal-groups or array number stories for their partner to solve. Have them record one of their stories and a multiplication number model that fits the story on *Math Masters,* page TA8. GMP4.1

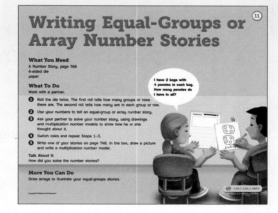

CCSS 3.OA.1, SMP2

Extra Practice
10–15 min

| WHOLE CLASS |
| SMALL GROUP |
| PARTNER |
| INDEPENDENT |

Representing Equal Groups and Arrays

Activity Card 12; 72 counters; 6-sided die; slate

To practice interpreting multiplication in terms of equal groups, have children create equal groups and arrays. They take turns rolling a die to generate the number of groups and counters in each group. One partner represents the combination as equal groups, while the other creates an array. GMP2.1 Have them compare their representations and write a matching number sentence. GMP2.2, GMP2.3

English Language Learners Support

Beginning ELL Prepare a vocabulary card illustrating *equal groups.* For example, draw four squares with three stars in each square. Below the four squares, write the term *equal groups.* Show children examples and non-examples of equal groups, and ask them to point to the equal groups or answer: *Is this an equal group?* Restate children's responses with simple statements, such as: *These are equal groups.* Encourage children to repeat your statements.

Go Online   **English Learners Support**

6 + 6 + 6 = 18

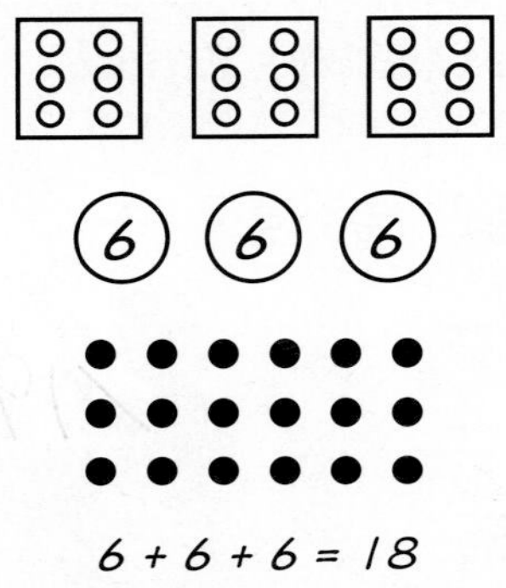

Sample pictures for the Math
Message problem

▶ **Mental Math and Fluency**

Ask children to solve each fact. Then have children briefly share their
strategies. Note that many children will be automatic with the facts.
Leveled exercises:

●○○ 9 + 7 16   5 + 8 13

●●○ 4 + 8 12   13 − 6 7

●●● 4 + 7 11   13 − 8 5

2 Focus   45–55 min   Go Online
ePresentations eToolkit

▶ **Math Message**

Math Journal 1, p. 15

Solve the Math Message problem on journal page 15.

▶ **Sharing Strategies for
Equal Groups and Arrays**

Math Journal 1, p. 15

| WHOLE CLASS | SMALL GROUP | PARTNER | INDEPENDENT |

Professional Development By the end of Grade 3, children are expected
to be automatic with products of whole numbers through 10 × 10. Units 1
and 2 build on children's intuitive, conceptual understanding of equal groups
to prepare them for fluent fact strategies developed in future units.

Math Message Follow-Up Ask children to share their pictures and
solution strategies. Expect a variety of representations, including pictures
of groups, arrays, and number models. (*See margin.*) Remind children that
it is not necessary to create an elaborate drawing to model the situation—
they should create a quick sketch that captures the mathematical ideas.

Strategies may include counting the objects in the picture by 1s, counting by 6s, adding 6s, or doubling 6 and then adding 6 more. Make sure the class understands each representation and agrees that it matches the context of the problem. GMP2.2, GMP4.1

Ask: *What do all these representations have in common?* GMP2.2 Sample answer: They all show 3 groups of 6. Tell children that groups with the same number of objects are called **equal groups.** Stories that involve finding the total number of objects in a set of equal groups are called equal-groups number stories. Invite volunteers to explain how their representations show the equal groups from the story. GMP4.1 Sample answers: My number model shows 6 added 3 times. I drew a square around each group of 6 stickers. The rows in my array are groups of 6.

Ask children to share number models that match the sketches in the margin. GMP2.2 Children may suggest $6 + 6 + 6 = 18$ and $3 \times 6 = 18$. Record both, and ask: *How do these number models match what is happening in our pictures?* GMP2.2 Sample answer: We are adding 6 three times because we have three equal groups of 6.

Explain that $3 \times 6 = 18$ is a multiplication number model. Describe **multiplication** as an operation that involves finding the number of objects in equal groups. The **multiplication symbol,** $\times$, is often read as "times." Since the meaning of "3 times 6" will likely have little meaning for children, refer instead to the idea of groups. Say: *3 times 6 means 3 groups of 6.* Children can then relate the numerical expression to the equal groups, which may help as they invent ways to solve these problems. GMP2.2

Next have the class solve Problem 1 on journal page 15 and share their ideas with their partners. As children sketch their representations and discuss their thinking, look for new representations and strategies, particularly sketches of arrays. Invite children to share their arrays. If no one uses an array, sketch one for the class and ask children to describe it. Sample answer: There are 4 groups of 5, and each group makes a row. Remind the class that a rectangular **array** is an arrangement of objects in **rows** and **columns.** Ask: *How do arrays show equal groups?* GMP2.2 Sample answer: The rows are like equal groups because there are 5 dots in each row.

Ask: *How did you figure out the total number of baseballs?* Sample answers: I counted each ball in my drawing. I skip counted by 5s. I added 5 and 5 to make 10, and then I added 10 and 10 to make 20. Help children recognize the efficiency of skip counting or repeated addition as opposed to counting by 1s, and encourage them to continue to apply efficient ways to find the totals throughout the rest of the lesson. GMP6.4

Ask: *What number models could we write for this story?* $5 + 5 + 5 + 5 = 20$; $4 \times 5 = 20$ *How could we read these number models?* GMP2.2, GMP4.1 Sample answer: 4 rows (or groups) of 5 is 20 all together

---

Math Journal 1, p. 15

Sharing Strategies for Equal Groups Lesson 1-8
DATE TIME

Math Message

Solve. Include sketches to show your thinking.

Ellie bought 3 packs of stickers. There are 6 stickers in each pack. How many stickers did Ellie buy in all?

___18___ stickers   Number model: $6 + 6 + 6 = 18$; $3 \times 6 = 18$

① Solve. Include sketches to show your thinking.

Max keeps his baseballs in a rectangular box. The box fits 4 rows of baseballs with 5 balls in each row. How many baseballs can Max fit into his box?

___20___ baseballs   Number model: $5 + 5 + 5 + 5 = 20$; $4 \times 5 = 20$

② For other number stories, draw sketches to show your solutions and write number models.

Story about: ___Answers vary.___   Story about: ___

Number model: Number model:

3.OA.1, 3.OA.3, SMP2, SMP4, SMP6   fifteen 15

Professional Development

Many situations can be represented by more than one number model relating the same numbers. For example, *If Sabrina has 3 packages of markers with 6 markers in each package, how many markers does she have in all?* could be modeled by $3 \times 6 = 18$, $6 \times 3 = 18$, $18 = 3 \times 6$, and $18 = 6 \times 3$. Usually only one number model is given as the answer for any problem. It is either the most common among children's work or the easiest to connect to the context. Accept any of these number models as correct, but help children understand the meanings of the factors and products. In this example, explain that the 3 represents the number of packages, the 6 is the number of markers in each package, and the 18 is the total number of markers.

Differentiate   **Adjusting the Activity**

To help children see why $5 + 5 + 5 + 5 = 20$ is a number model for the array, have them sketch the array, circle each row, and write the number 5 at the end of each row.

 Go Online   Differentiation Support

The baseball story is an example of an array number story. Array number stories are a kind of equal-groups story. Children are not expected to distinguish between equal-groups and array number stories, but they should have experience with both.

Have children solve additional number stories for Problem 2, sketching and writing number models on their journal page for each story. *Suggestions:*

- *There are 6 bicycles at the park. Each bicycle has 2 wheels. How many wheels are there in all?* 12 wheels; $2 + 2 + 2 + 2 + 2 + 2 = 12$; $6 \times 2 = 12$

- *There are 5 rows of cars in a parking lot. There are 5 cars in each row. How many cars are in the parking lot in all?* 25 cars; $5 + 5 + 5 + 5 + 5 = 25$; $5 \times 5 = 25$

 Assessment Check-In   **CCSS 3.OA.3**

Math Journal 1, p. 15

Expect most children to successfully solve the equal-groups number stories in Problems 1 and 2 on journal page 15 using drawings and a counting or addition strategy and to record an addition number model. **GMP4.1** If children struggle to interpret these number stories, consider implementing the Adjusting the Activity suggestion for Problem 1. Have children use a similar strategy for the additional number stories in Problem 2. As this is an initial exposure to modeling equal-groups number stories with multiplication, do not expect children to write multiplication number models. There will be many opportunities in later lessons to develop this skill.

 Assessment and Reporting   **Go Online**   to record student progress and to see trajectories toward mastery for this standard.

▶ **Starting a Fact Strategy Wall**

Math Journal 1, p. 15

| WHOLE CLASS | SMALL GROUP | PARTNER | INDEPENDENT |

Have partnerships review journal page 15 and discuss strategies for solving the multiplication number stories. GMP2.2 Bring the class together and introduce the Fact Strategy Wall as a place to record strategies for solving multiplication and division problems. Record children's suggestions on the Fact Strategy Wall under a heading for today's focus, such as "Strategies for Equal-Groups Problems." For example, draw pictures of equal groups, draw pictures of arrays, use addition, and use skip counting. You may also wish to post children's work directly on the Fact Strategy Wall. Encourage children to refer to the Fact Strategy Wall to help them choose efficient strategies as they complete the problems in the next activity. GMP6.4

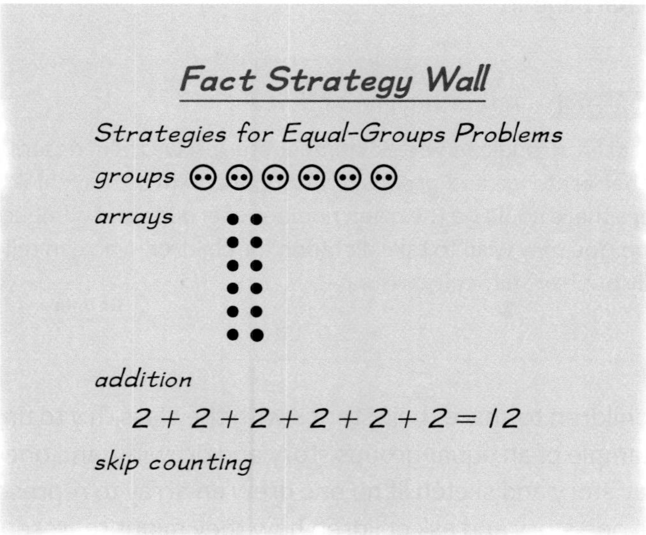

Fact Strategy Wall

Strategies for Equal-Groups Problems

groups ⊙ ⊙ ⊙ ⊙ ⊙ ⊙

arrays

addition

$$2 + 2 + 2 + 2 + 2 + 2 = 12$$

skip counting

The Fact Strategy Wall will be used extensively throughout third grade as children develop fluent strategies for multiplication and division facts. Display the Fact Strategy Wall throughout the year. You will continue to add new strategies, especially in Units 3 and 5.

Math Journal 1, p. 16

Writing Multiplication Number Stories

Lesson 1-8

DATE   TIME

Choose a number sentence from the bank. Tell a number story to match your number sentence.

Number Sentence Bank

$3 \times 4 = 12$	$2 \times 5 = 10$	$4 \times 2 = 8$
$5 \times 3 = 15$	$3 \times 6 = 18$	$4 \times 4 = 16$

My Number Sentence: __Answers vary.__

Write a number story to match your number sentence. Draw a picture of your story.

16   sixteen   3.OA.1, 3.OA.3, SMP2

▶ **Writing Multiplication Number Stories**

Math Journal, p. 16

WHOLE CLASS	SMALL GROUP	PARTNER	INDEPENDENT

Model creating a sample number story for the number sentence: $2 \times 3 = 6$. Ask: *What does $2 \times 3 = 6$ mean?* 2 groups of 3 Then tell a corresponding number story, such as: *There are 2 shelves with 3 toys on each shelf. How many toys are there in all?* Sketch a picture to match your number story. Ask: *Does my number story match $2 \times 3 = 6$?* Yes. *How do you know?* **GMP2.2** Sample answer: I see 2 groups with 3 toys in each group.

Have children take turns choosing a number sentence from the Number Sentence Bank on journal page 16. Then have them tell number stories to match while their partners create sketches on paper to represent the stories. **GMP2.2** Have each child choose one story to record and sketch on journal page 16.

Differentiate   **Adjusting the Activity**

If children struggle to write a number story, have them describe their number sentence as x *groups of* y. Support them as they think of a situation where there could be the given number of groups and number in each group. You may wish to take dictation for children who can tell a story orally but have difficulty writing it.

Go Online > | Differentiation Support

Invite children to share their stories with the class. Try to find at least one example of an equal-groups story and drawing, and one example of an array story and sketch. If no one drew an array to represent a story, choose one story and ask children how they might represent it with an array. *Sample stories:*

- Ben has 3 folders. There are 4 papers in each folder. How many papers does Ben have in all? He has 12 papers.
- On my desk there are 3 rows of coins. There are 4 coins in each row. How many coins are there all together? 12 coins

Summarize Have children share what was the same and what was different about the stories and sketches shared. Sample answer: They all showed equal groups, but in some the pictures were in separate groups, and in others they were in rows and columns.

3 Practice   10–15 min   Go Online

ePresentations eToolkit Home Connections

▶ Minute Math+

Minute Math+, p. 36

To provide practice solving equal-groups number stories, see *Minute Math+*, page 36.

▶ Math Boxes 1-8

Math Journal 1, p. 17

| WHOLE CLASS | SMALL GROUP | **PARTNER** | **INDEPENDENT** |

Mixed Practice Math Boxes 1-8 are paired with Math Boxes 1-6.

▶ Home Link 1-8

Math Masters, p. 22

Homework Children practice representing and solving equal-groups and array number stories. **GMP4.1** Children also look for examples of equal-groups or array situations at home and create a number story about one of them.

Planning Ahead

In Lesson 1-11 you will need sunrise and sunset data. Collect this data from local newspapers, newscasts, or the Internet (www.sunrisesunset.com). Fill in the times on the table on *Math Masters*, page TA10 to display during the lesson. Leave the Length-of-Day column blank. Also prepare the Length-of-Day Graph. (*See page 90.*)

Math Journal 1, p. 17

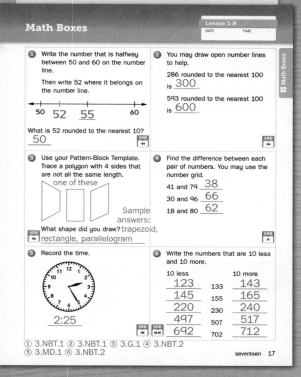

Math Masters, p. 22

Introducing Division

Overview Children are introduced to division as they solve division number stories.

▶ **Vocabulary**
equal sharing • division • equal grouping • division symbol

 Common Core State Standards

Focus Clusters
- Represent and solve problems involving multiplication and division.
- Understand properties of multiplication and the relationship between multiplication and division.
- Multiply and divide within 100.

1 Warm Up   5 min

Materials

Mental Math and Fluency Children practice skip counting by 2s, 5s, and 10s.		3.OA.7

2 Focus   40–45 min

Math Message Children solve a number story.	*Math Journal 1*, p. 18	3.OA.2, 3.OA.3
Exploring Division Children solve equal-shares and equal-groups number stories.	*Math Journal 1*, pp. 18–19	3.OA.2, 3.OA.3 SMP1
✓ **Assessment Check-In** See page 76.	*Math Journal 1*, p. 19	3.OA.2, 3.OA.3, SMP1
Introducing Division Number Models Children record division number models for number stories.	*Math Journal 1*, p. 19	3.OA.2, 3.OA.3, 3.OA.6 SMP4

CCSS 3.OA.2 Spiral Snapshot

GMC Interpret division in terms of equal shares or equal groups.

| 1-9
Focus
Practice | 2-7 through 2-10
Focus
Practice | 2-12
Practice | 3-1 through 3-3
Practice | 3-10
Warm Up
Practice | 4-1
Practice |

Spiral Tracker   **Go Online**   to see how mastery develops for all standards within the grade.

3 Practice   15–20 min

Minute Math+ Children use multiplication and division to solve number stories.	*Minute Math®+*, p. 58	3.OA.3, 3.NBT.3
Cutting Out Fact Triangles Children cut out Fact Triangles to prepare for Lesson 1-10.	*Math Journal 1*, Activity Sheets 1–3; scissors; envelopes or resealable plastic bags; paper clip	3.OA.7
Math Boxes 1-9 Children practice and maintain skills.	*Math Journal 1*, p. 20	See page 77.
Home Link 1-9 **Homework** Children solve division number stories.	*Math Masters*, p. 26	3.OA.2, 3.OA.3 SMP4

connectED.mcgraw-hill.com

Plan your lessons online with these tools.

 ePresentations   Student Learning Center   Facts Workshop Game   eToolkit   Professional Development   Home Connections   Spiral Tracker   Assessment and Reporting   ELL English Learners Support   Differentiation Support

Differentiation Options RtI

Readiness
10–15 min

WHOLE CLASS
SMALL GROUP
PARTNER
INDEPENDENT

Making Equal Groups of Cookies

Math Masters, p. 23

To explore equal-groups problems, read ***The Doorbell Rang*** by Pat Hutchins (Greenwillow Books, 1989). In this book, two children must figure out how to share 12 cookies equally as more friends come over. As children complete *Math Masters*, page 23 have them describe each situation using words such as *share, split, divide, equal,* and *same*. Discuss what changes about the equal groups. **GMP6.3**

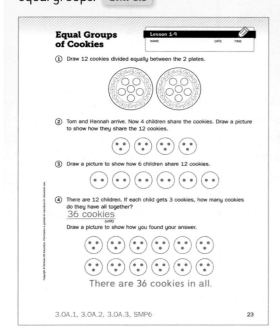

Enrichment
10–15 min

WHOLE CLASS
SMALL GROUP
PARTNER
INDEPENDENT

Exploring Remainders

Math Masters, p. 24

To extend children's experience with equal grouping, read ***A Remainder of One*** by Elinor J. Pinczes (HMH Books for Young Readers, 2002) and introduce them to the concept of a remainder. In this book, a group of 25 ants must create equal groups to please the queen. As they read the story, have children predict whether there will be a remainder each time the ants try a new grouping strategy. **GMP3.1** Have them complete *Math Masters*, page 24 and model each situation with an array.

Extra Practice
10–15 min

WHOLE CLASS
SMALL GROUP
PARTNER
INDEPENDENT

Exploring Equal Shares

Math Masters, p. 25; pennies or counters (optional)

To provide practice with equal sharing, have children model number stories on *Math Masters*, page 25. **GMP4.1**

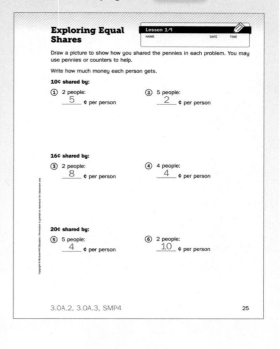

English Language Learners Support

Beginning ELL Think aloud with real objects to introduce the term *share* and help children understand equal-sharing number stories. For example, show three small plates and 15 counters. Demonstrate sharing the counters among the plates with statements such as: *I will share these 15 counters with you and my friend. One for you; one for my friend; one for me. One for you; one for my friend; one for me.* Follow with another example, directing children to share a given number of counters with two or three of their classmates, repeating the sentence, *One for you and one for me.*

Go Online **ELL** English Learners Support

Standards and Goals for
Mathematical Practice

SMP1 **Make sense of problems and persevere in solving them.**
  GMP1.1 Make sense of your problem.
  GMP1.2 Reflect on your thinking as you solve your problem.

SMP4 **Model with mathematics.**
  GMP4.1 Model real-world situations using graphs, drawings, tables, symbols, numbers, diagrams, and other representations.

Math Journal 1, p. 18

Equal Sharing and Equal Grouping

Lesson 1-9

DATE   TIME

Math Message

Solve. Sketch to show your thinking.

Ms. Smith has 20 scissors. She places scissors on 5 tables.
How many scissors can she place on each table? Sample answers:

○○○○○○○○○○
1 2 3 4 5 1 2 3 4 5
○○○○○○○○○○   ⊗ ⊗ ⊗ ⊗ ⊗
1 2 3 4 5 1 2 3 4 5

Answer: __4__ scissors

① Tomás is making snacks for his team. He has 15 strawberries and puts 3 strawberries in each teammate's bag. How many teammates does he have?

○ ○ ○
○ ○ ○
○ ○ ○
○ ○ ○
○ ○ ○ ○○○○○○○○○○○○○○○   ◌ ◌ ◌ ◌ ◌
                                   1 2 3 4 5

Answer: __5__ teammates

② Listen to each story. Show your work with sketches.

Story about _____   Story about _____

Answer: _____   Answer: _____
       (unit)   (unit)

18 eighteen   3.OA.2, 3.OA.3, SMP1

▶ Mental Math and Fluency

Have children practice skip counting. *Leveled exercises:*

- ●○○ Skip count by 10s from 50 to 150.
- ●●○ Skip count by 5s from 50 to 100.
- ●●● Skip count by 2s from 30 to 60.

---

2 **Focus** 40–45 min   Go Online   ePresentations   eToolkit

▶ Math Message

Math Journal 1, p. 18

Solve the Math Message problem on journal page 18.

▶ Exploring Division

Math Journal 1, pp. 18–19

| WHOLE CLASS | SMALL GROUP | PARTNER | INDEPENDENT |

Math Message Follow-Up Have children share their representations and solution strategies for the Math Message problem. Expect many of the strategies to involve distributing scissors one by one to the 5 groups. This is an example of an **equal-sharing** situation, where the number of groups and the total number of objects are known, but the number of objects in each group is to be found. Facilitate a discussion about making sense of the problem and reflecting on strategies by asking the following questions: **GMP1.1, GMP1.2**

- *What do you know from the problem?* Sample answer: There are 5 tables and 20 scissors in all to share.
- *How did you decide what to draw first?* Sample answer: I started by drawing the 5 tables in the story.
- *How did you know when to stop passing out the scissors?* Sample answer: I stopped when all 20 had been handed out.
- *How did you show your answer in your picture?* Sample answer: I showed 4 scissors in each of 5 groups.

Other strategies, such as relating to multiplication (*What do I need to multiply by 5 to get 20?*) or automaticity with division (knowing that 20 shared 5 ways is 4) might emerge. Focus the discussion on sharing, as that is likely the most natural strategy for children in this introductory lesson.

Pose this problem: *Three children share 21 pennies equally. How many pennies does each child get?* 7 pennies

Next ask: *What do we know from the problem?* GMP1.1 Sample answer: We know there are 21 pennies in all and 3 children to share them. Invite children to share solution strategies, emphasizing the 3 equal groups of pennies. Discuss similarities and differences between these number stories and the types of number stories in the previous lesson. Highlight that these stories start with the total and involve sharing, or dividing, that amount of objects equally.

Tell children that many sharing situations can be solved using **division** or multiplication, and that they will make sense of and solve problems like this in today's lesson.

Have the class solve Problem 1 on journal page 18. Give children time to sketch their representations and share their ideas with partners.

Note that this is an example of an **equal-grouping** situation: the total number of objects and number of objects per group are known, but children must solve for the number of groups. Children do not need to label number stories as equal sharing or equal grouping, but they need sufficient experience solving both types and reflecting on how their representations match the stories. Facilitate discussion by asking the following questions. GMP1.1, GMP1.2

- *What do you know from the problem?* There are 15 strawberries, and each teammate gets 3 strawberries.
- *How did you decide what to draw first?* Sample answer: The story says there are 3 strawberries in each bag, so I started by drawing the first bag.
- *How did you know when you were finished?* Sample answer: When I put all 15 strawberries into groups of 3.
- *How did you show your answer in your picture?* Sample answer: I showed 5 groups in all.

Pose more number stories and have children record their thinking in the spaces for Problem 2 on journal page 18. *Suggestions:*

- *Maisy divides 12 feet of rope into pieces that are each 4 feet long. How many pieces will Maisy have?* 3 pieces
- *Harrison passes out paintbrushes for art class. He has 16 brushes to share among 4 art tables. How many brushes does he place on each table?* 4 brushes per table

Remind children to include the units with their answers.

Adjusting the Activity

Differentiate Help children make sense of the stories by drawing the groups for equal-sharing situations or an initial group for equal-grouping situations. For example, draw 5 tables and have children distribute 20 counters among them, or draw the first group of 3 strawberries and have children draw the remaining groups until 15 strawberries are grouped.

 Go Online · Differentiation Support

Common Misconception

Differentiate Watch for children who misinterpret the known and missing quantities. For example, to solve Problem 1 on journal page 18 some children may create 3 groups of 5 instead of 5 groups of 3. Although the resulting answer is still 5, the interpretation is inconsistent with the context. Assist children by suggesting they first decide which is known: the number of groups or the number in each group.

 Go Online · Differentiation Support

Division Number Stories

Lesson 1-9

DATE   TIME

Draw pictures to help you solve each problem below.
Record your answer.
Wait until your teacher tells you to write the number models.

1 Kate wants to equally share 12 snap cubes among 3 friends.
How many cubes will each friend get?

Answer: ___4___ snap cubes
Number model: $12 \div 3 = 4$

2 Ms. Early is making sets of cubes to share. She has 25 total cubes, and she
puts them into sets of 5 cubes each. How many sets can she make?

Answer: ___5___ sets
Number model: $25 \div 5 = 5$

Try This

3 Manny wants to figure out the number of horses in a large stall. He can only
see the horses' legs. He counts 28 legs. How many horses are there?

Answer: ___7___ horses
Number model: $28 \div 4 = 7$

3.OA.2, 3.OA.3, SMP1   nineteen 19

Have partners continue solving and representing division number stories
on journal page 19. Ask children to wait until the next activity to write
number models for each story.

 Assessment Check-In  **CCSS** 3.OA.2, 3.OA.3

Math Journal 1, p. 19

Circulate and observe as children work on journal page 19. Expect most
children to make sense of and correctly solve Problems 1 and 2 by creating
drawings to represent each problem.   **GMP1.1**   Have children who
struggle to create representations use counters to physically act out the
situations, and then record their thinking with drawings. Make sure
children carefully count out the total number of counters before sharing
or grouping them.

✓ Assessment
and Reporting   **Go Online** ⟩ to record student progress and to see trajectories
toward mastery for these standards.

▶ Introducing Division Number Models

Math Journal 1, p. 19

| WHOLE CLASS | SMALL GROUP | PARTNER | INDEPENDENT |

When most children have completed journal page 19, ask those who
clearly represented the number stories with arrays or equal groups to
describe what they did. Encourage the rest of the class to make sense of
each strategy by asking questions and repeating the strategies in their
own words.

Invite children to suggest a multiplication number model to fit the context
of Problem 1. Record $3 \times ? = 12$. Help children see how this number model
represents knowing the number of groups and the total, but not knowing
how much goes into each group.   **GMP4.1**   Tell children that division
is related to multiplication in the same way that subtraction is related
to addition. Introduce the **division symbol,** ÷, explaining that it means
divided by. Ask: *What division number model could be used to represent
the story in Problem 1?*   **GMP4.1** $12 \div 3 = ?$ or $12 \div 3 = 4$

Have children suggest a division number model for Problem 2. At this
point, however, do not expect all children to easily generate a number
model.

Summarize Have partners describe situations when they had to
share equally with friends or family members. For example, children may
recall sharing a handful of treats with a sibling. Invite a few pairs to share
with the class.

3 Practice

15–20 min

Go Online

ePresentations eToolkit Home Connections

▶ *Minute Math+*

Minute Math+, p. 58

To provide practice with division and relating multiplication to division, see *Minute Math+*, page 58.

▶ Cutting Out Fact Triangles

Math Journal 1, Activity Sheets 1–3

| WHOLE CLASS | SMALL GROUP | **PARTNER** | **INDEPENDENT** |

In preparation for Lesson 1-10, have children carefully remove Activity Sheets 1–3 (Multiplication/Division Fact Triangles for 2s, 5s, and 10s facts) from the back of *Math Journal 1*. Have them cut out the triangles and write their initials in a corner on the back of each. Encourage partners to explore and discuss observations about their Fact Triangles. Children may notice that they are similar to addition and subtraction Fact Triangles from previous grades; the multiplication and division symbols are in the middle; and they show 2s, 5s, and 10s facts.

Have children clip the triangles together and store them in an envelope or resealable plastic bag and keep them in their toolkits. Tell children they will use the Fact Triangles in the next lesson.

▶ Math Boxes 1-9

Math Journal 1, p. 20

| WHOLE CLASS | **SMALL GROUP** | PARTNER | INDEPENDENT |

Mixed Practice Math Boxes 1-9 are paired with Math Boxes 1-12.

▶ Home Link 1-9

Math Masters, p. 26

Homework Children practice solving division number stories and representing their thinking. **GMP4.1**

Planning Ahead

In preparation for Lesson 1-13, gather objects of varying sizes and shapes that have masses of 1 gram to 1,000 grams, or 1 kilogram (a little over 2 pounds). You or the class can bring in unopened 1-liter bottles of water—at least 1 bottle per pair of children. There are notes on upcoming Home Links asking parents to send in 1-liter water bottles.

Math Journal 1, p. 20

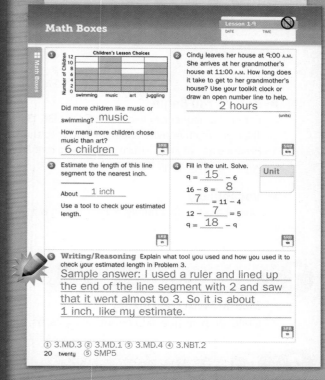

Math Masters, p. 26 23

Foundational Multiplication Facts

Overview Children develop strategies for 2s, 5s, and 10s facts.

▶ **Before You Begin**
For Part 2, sequence Quick Look Cards 136, 134, 132, 149, and 145. Make sure children cut out the Fact Triangles from Activity Sheets 1–3 prior to this lesson. (*See Lesson 1-9, Part 3.*) For the optional Extra Practice activity and future play, create one *Multiplication Draw* die per pair by labeling blank cubes with 2, 2, 5, 5, 10, and 10.

▶ **Vocabulary**
Quick Looks • fact family • Fact Triangle • product • factors

 Common Core State Standards

Focus Clusters
• Represent and solve problems involving multiplication and division.
• Understand properties of multiplication and the relationship between multiplication and division.
• Multiply and divide within 100.

---

① Warm Up 5 min

Materials

Mental Math and Fluency Children practice skip counting by 2s, 5s, and 10s.	slate	3.OA.7

---

② Focus 40–50 min

Math Message Children make sense of a dot pattern showing equal groups.	Quick Look Card 136	3.OA.1, 3.OA.7 SMP2
Introducing Quick Looks Children practice Quick Looks with patterns.	Quick Look Cards 132, 134, 136, 145, 149; slate or counters (optional)	3.OA.1, 3.OA.7 SMP2, SMP3
Multiplying by 2s, 5s, and 10s Children develop strategies for multiplying by 2s, 5s, and 10s.	*Math Journal 1*, p. 21; Quick Look Cards 132, 134, 149; Fact Strategy Wall; nickel; dime	3.OA.1, 3.OA.7, 3.NBT.2 SMP2, SMP8
✓ **Assessment Check-In** See page 82.	*Math Journal 1*, p. 21	3.OA.1, 3.OA.7, SMP2
Introducing ×/÷ Fact Triangles Children explore fact families and Fact Triangles.	*Math Masters*, p. TA9; 2s, 5s, and 10s Fact Triangles; slate	3.OA.6, 3.OA.7 SMP2

 3.OA.1 **Spiral Snapshot**

GMC Interpret multiplication in terms of equal groups.

| 1-8
Focus
Practice | 1-10
Focus | 1-12
Warm Up
Focus | 1-13
Warm Up
Practice | 2-6
Warm Up
Focus | 2-7
Warm Up
Focus
Practice | 3-9 through 3-12
Warm Up
Focus
Practice |

Spiral Tracker (**Go Online**) to see how mastery develops for all standards within the grade.

---

③ Practice 15–20 min

Minute Math+ Children solve number stories involving multiplication by 2.	*Minute Math®+*, p. 33	3.OA.3, 3.OA.7
Making Fact-Family Houses Children generate multiplication/division fact families.	scissors	3.OA.6, 3.OA.7 SMP7
Math Boxes 1-10 Children practice and maintain skills.	*Math Journal 1*, p. 22	See page 85.
Home Link 1-10 **Homework** Children solve fact families and Fact Triangles.	*Math Masters*, pp. 29–33	3.OA.6, 3.OA.7 SMP7

---

 connectED.mcgraw-hill.com

Plan your lessons online with these tools.

 ePresentations   Student Learning Center   Facts Workshop Game   eToolkit   Professional Development   Home Connections Spiral Tracker Assessment and Reporting   English Learners Support   Differentiation Support

Differentiation Options

 RtI

Readiness
5–10 min

WHOLE CLASS
SMALL GROUP
PARTNER
INDEPENDENT

Skip Counting on the Number Grid

Math Masters, p. 27

To prepare for work with 2s, 5s, and 10s multiplication facts, have children explore patterns in skip counting using *Math Masters,* page 27. Have them skip count by 2s and 5s, marking the 2s with Xs and the 5s with circles, and then record the numbers that are marked with both an X and a circle. Have children describe the pattern of numbers in both counts. **GMP7.1**

Sample answer: They are multiples of 10.

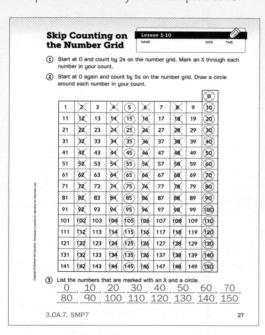

Enrichment
10–15 min

WHOLE CLASS
SMALL GROUP
PARTNER
INDEPENDENT

Noticing a Paper-Folding Pattern

Math Masters, p. 28

To apply children's understanding of doubling, have them predict the number of equal-size rectangles that result from folding paper. Encourage children to look for patterns and use them to predict the number of rectangles as the number of folds increases. **GMP7.1, GMP7.2**

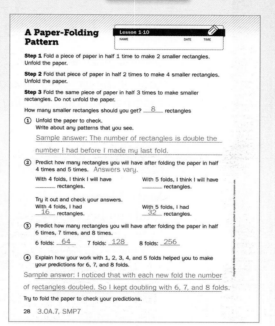

Extra Practice
10–15 min

WHOLE CLASS
SMALL GROUP
PARTNER
INDEPENDENT

Playing *Multiplication Draw*

Student Reference Book, p. 248; *Math Masters,* p. G6; die labeled 2, 2, 5, 5, 10, 10 (*See Before You Begin.*); number cards 1–10 (4 of each)

To provide additional practice with 2s, 5s, and 10s facts, have children play *Multiplication Draw* and use the record sheet on *Math Masters,* page G6. Game directions are on *Student Reference Book,* page 248. Encourage children to apply the strategies developed in the lesson to find the products efficiently. **GMP6.4**

English Language Learners Support

Beginning ELL To support children's understanding of Quick Looks, help them understand the word *quick* with demonstrations that contrast moving an object slowly and quickly. For example, move something slowly across a surface as you very slowly say the word *slow.* Then move the same object across the surface quickly as you very quickly say the word *quick.* Use Total Physical Response commands to direct children to carry out an action quickly or slowly, and say *quick* and *slow* as they do so.

Go Online ELL English Learners Support

Mathematical Practice

SMP2 Reason abstractly and quantitatively.
GMP2.2 Make sense of the representations you and others use.

SMP3 Construct viable arguments and critique the reasoning of others.
GMP3.2 Make sense of others' mathematical thinking.

SMP8 Look for and express regularity in reasoning.
GMP8.1 Create and justify rules, shortcuts, and generalizations.

Professional Development

Quick Looks lay a foundation for learning basic facts because they encourage children to subitize, or instantly recognize a small quantity without counting. Quick Looks will be used throughout the year to encourage children to make sense of array or equal-groups images and practice multiplication facts. Some children may be familiar with Quick Looks from *Second Grade Everyday Mathematics.* For more information on Quick Looks, see the *Implementation Guide.*

Go Online Professional Development

---

1 Warm Up 5 min
Go Online · ePresentations · eToolkit

▶ Mental Math and Fluency

On slates, have children record their first 10 skip counts. *Leveled exercises:*

◉○○ Skip count by 10s from 0. 0, 10, 20, 30, 40, 50, 60, 70, 80, 90
◉◉○ Skip count by 5s from 0. 0, 5, 10, 15, 20, 25, 30, 35, 40, 45
◉◉◉ Skip count by 2s from 0. 0, 2, 4, 6, 8, 10, 12, 14, 16, 18

2 Focus 40–50 min
Go Online   · ePresentations · eToolkit

▶ Math Message

Display Quick Look Card 136.

Look at the picture. How could you figure out how many dots there are all together without counting each dot? GMP2.2

▶ Introducing Quick Looks

| WHOLE CLASS | SMALL GROUP | PARTNER | INDEPENDENT |

Math Message Follow-Up Have children share strategies for finding the total number of dots, emphasizing seeing equal groups and skip counting by 5s. Have children share how they know each group has 5 dots. Some children may recognize the representation of 5 from the dot pattern on a 6-sided die. GMP2.2

Have children suggest number sentences that fit the image, eliciting and recording $3 \times 5 = 15$. Ask: *What does this number sentence mean?* 3 groups of 5

Introduce **Quick Looks.** Explain that children will see a group of dots, similar to what they saw in the Math Message, for only a few seconds. They should try to figure out how many dots they saw and think about how they saw them. Reassure them that you will always provide a second (or even third) look to ensure that everyone sees the image.

Show Quick Look Cards 134, 132, 149, and 145 in sequence for 2–3 seconds each. After each image, ask children to describe both *what* they saw and *how* they saw it. GMP2.2 Highlight examples in which children use equal groups or array structures to more easily make sense of the image.

Focus on helping children make sense of each other's thinking and strategies with prompts such as: **GMP3.2**

- *Did everyone understand Rebecca's strategy? Explain it in your own words.*
- *How could you try Rebecca's strategy on the next image?*

Tell children that Quick Looks are one way they will think about multiplication. Explain that today's images have something in common—they all represent multiplication situations involving 2s, 5s, or 10s. Children will work on these specific facts using Quick Looks and fact families.

▶ Multiplying by 2s, 5s, and 10s

Math Journal 1, p. 21

| WHOLE CLASS | SMALL GROUP | PARTNER | INDEPENDENT |

Display Quick Look Cards 134, 132, and 149 again, and ask children to write a number sentence to match each image. Record both multiplication and addition number sentences, as shown below:

$2 \times 4 = 8$ $4 + 4 = 8$

$2 \times 5 = 10$ $5 + 5 = 10$

$2 \times 6 = 12$ $6 + 6 = 12$

Support children in generalizing about the relationship between the addition and multiplication number sentences by asking: **GMP8.1**

- *What do you notice about the addition number sentences?*
  The number sentences show doubles facts.
- *Do you think this will always happen when we multiply by 2? Why?*
  Sample answer: Yes. When we multiply by 2, we have 2 equal groups and the addends in a double are equal.
- *What is another example that follows this rule?* Sample answer:
  $7 + 7 = 14$ and $2 \times 7 = 14$

Help children see that multiplying by 2 is the same as creating the addition double, or doubling the amount in each group. Add this idea to the Fact Strategy Wall. (*See margin.*)

Fact Strategy Wall

Strategies for multiplying by 2s, 5s, and 10s:

2s: Think of the addition double.

10s: Skip count by 10s; add 10 more each time.

5s: Skip count by 5s; add 5 more each time; find half of the same ×10 problem.

Math Journal 1, p. 21

Dimes and Nickels Totals

Lesson 1-10
DATE   TIME

1 Complete the table.

Number of dimes	Sketch	Multiplication number model
2 dimes	10¢ 10¢	2 × 10¢ = 20¢
4 dimes	10¢ 10¢ 10¢ 10¢	4 × 10¢ = 40¢
5 dimes	10¢ 10¢ 10¢ 10¢ 10¢	5 × 10¢ = 50¢
10 dimes	10¢ 10¢ 10¢ 10¢ 10¢ 10¢ 10¢ 10¢ 10¢ 10¢	10 × 10¢ = 100¢

2 Complete the table.

Number of nickels	Sketch	Multiplication number model
2 nickels	5¢ 5¢	2 × 5¢ = 10¢
4 nickels	5¢ 5¢ 5¢ 5¢	4 × 5¢ = 20¢
5 nickels	5¢ 5¢ 5¢ 5¢ 5¢	5 × 5¢ = 25¢
10 nickels	5¢ 5¢ 5¢ 5¢ 5¢ 5¢ 5¢ 5¢ 5¢ 5¢	10 × 5¢ = 50¢

3.OA.1, 3.OA.7, SMP2, SMP8

twenty-one   21

Adjusting the Activity

Differentiate Have children who are fluent with 2s, 5s, and 10s facts do further work to show that the product of a number and 5 is always half of the product of that same number and 10. For example, ask: *If you know that 5 × 4 = 20, how can you figure out what 10 × 4 is?* You can just double it because 5 is half of 10. Then have children generate more examples and explain why they think this rule always works.

Go Online | Differentiation Support

Have children get out their math journals. Then display a dime and ask: *What is the value of this coin?* 10 cents Have partners work on Problem 1 on journal page 21 to determine the values of 2 dimes, 4 dimes, 5 dimes, and 10 dimes. Ask children to record multiplication number models to help illustrate their thinking. Remind them to record the cents units.

Ask: *What do these number models have in common?* Sample answer: They all involve multiplying by 10. *Why?* Sample answer: Dimes are like groups of 10 cents. *How did you figure out each answer?* Sample answers: I skip counted by 10s. I added 10 more for each dime. Help children recognize that these are efficient strategies for multiplying by 10, and record them on the Fact Strategy Wall.

Display a nickel. Ask: *What is the value of this coin?* 5 cents Have partners complete Problem 2 on journal page 21. When they finish, elicit that this time we are multiplying by 5. Ask: *How did you figure out each answer?* Sample answers: I skip counted by 5s. I added 5 more for each nickel.

If no one mentions that 5s totals are always half of the corresponding 10s totals, have children compare the answers for corresponding amounts of dimes and nickels and discuss the repeating pattern. **GMP2.2** Children may notice that the value of the dimes is twice that for the same number of nickels. Support them in recognizing that the 5s product is always half of the 10s product. **GMP8.1** Add the strategies for multiplying by 5 to the Fact Strategy Wall.

The 2s, 5s, and 10s facts will be used in later lessons to derive other facts in efficient ways. Children will use them as "helper facts," so be sure children make sense of and practice effective strategies for solving them before additional fact work begins in Unit 3.

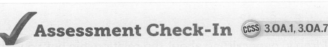

✓ **Assessment Check-In** CCSS 3.OA.1, 3.OA.7

Math Journal 1, p. 21

Expect most children to sketch equal groups of dimes and nickels for Problems 1 and 2 on journal page 21. Many children will record matching multiplication number models for each sketch and find the total by skip counting or doing repeated addition. Have children who struggle to make the sketches model and count with actual dimes and nickels. **GMP2.2** For children who are already fluent with their 2s, 5s, and 10s facts, consider the suggestions in the Adjusting the Activity note.

 Assessment and Reporting | **Go Online** to record student progress and to see trajectories toward mastery for these standards.

▶ Introducing ×/÷ Fact Triangles

Math Masters, p. TA9

| WHOLE CLASS | SMALL GROUP | PARTNER | INDEPENDENT |

Remind children of their work with addition and subtraction fact families in earlier grades. Explain that multiplication and division **fact families** include multiplication and division facts that relate the same sets of three numbers.

Display a blank **Fact Triangle** (*Math Masters*, page TA9). Record the multiplication fact $2 \times 5 = 10$, and write 2, 5, and 10 in the corresponding corners of the triangle. Be sure 10 is at the top, right below the large dot. Ask volunteers to name the multiplication and division facts in the fact family with these numbers. $2 \times 5 = 10$; $5 \times 2 = 10$; $10 \div 2 = 5$; $10 \div 5 = 2$ Write a few more sets of numbers in the triangle and have children record the fact families on their slates. Ask volunteers to read their number sentences as the others check their slates.

Have children take out the Fact Triangles they cut apart in Lesson 1-9. Introduce the terms **product** and **factors.** Explain that the product is the total when two factors are multiplied together. Emphasize that the dot is above the product on the Multiplication/Division Fact Triangles. Have children work with a partner to identify the product and two factors on one of their triangles. GMP2.2 Invite a few pairs to share.

Then have children find a Fact Triangle with factors that are the same. $2 \times 2, 5 \times 5, 10 \times 10$ Quickly record the fact families for at least two of these triangles. Ask: *What do you notice about the fact family when the factors are the same?* GMP8.1 There is only one multiplication fact and one division fact.

With a child as your partner, review the procedure for practicing multiplication facts with Fact Triangles as follows:

1. Cover the product (the number under the dot).
2. Have your partner say the multiplication fact with the product you are covering. For example, if you cover the 8 on a 2, 4, and 8 Fact Triangle, there are two possibilities: $2 \times 4 = 8$ and $4 \times 2 = 8$. GMP2.2
3. Switch roles.

For those who are ready, demonstrate division facts by covering one of the smaller numbers and having children name the corresponding division fact.

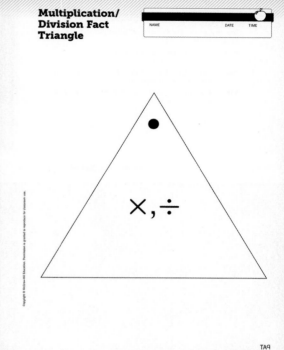

Math Masters, p. TA9

Multiplication/ Division Fact Triangle

NAME   DATE   TIME

×, ÷

TA9

Minute Math+, p. 33

Baby Penguin Meals Number Stories

Baby penguins eat almost all the time. Penguin parents feed a baby about 2 pounds of food every hour.

●○○○○ About how much does a baby penguin eat in 2 hours?
        (4 lb) In 5 hours? (10 lb)

●●○○○ A baby penguin has eaten about 10 pounds of food today. About
        how many hours have passed? (5 hr)

●●●○○ About how much does a baby penguin eat in 1 day (24 hours)?
        (48 lb) In 2 days? (96 lb)

Operations and Algebraic Thinking

ccss 1.OA.1, 1.OA.6, 2.OA.1, 3.OA.3, 3.OA.7   33

Circulate and assist as children work independently or in partnerships to practice with Fact Triangles. They may sort facts by those they know and those they need to practice. Encourage children to review Fact Triangles in spare moments. Remind them to return their Fact Triangles to their toolkits.

Summarize Have a few volunteers hold up Fact Triangles with facts they know and explain how they know them. GMP2.2

③ Practice 15–20 min   Go Online

ePresentations   eToolkit   Home Connections

▶ *Minute Math+*

Minute Math+, p. 33

To provide practice with number stories involving multiplication by 2, see *Minute Math+*, page 33, Level 1.

▶ **Making Fact-Family Houses**

| WHOLE CLASS | SMALL GROUP | **PARTNER** | **INDEPENDENT** |

To provide additional practice with fact families, guide children as they make a multiplication/division fact-family chain. Demonstrate how to make a chain of fact-family "houses":

- Fold an $8\frac{1}{2}$" by 11" sheet of paper in half so the two $8\frac{1}{2}$" sides touch.
- Fold again so the two $8\frac{1}{2}$" sides touch.
- Cut the corners off one of the shorter sides to form a triangular peak.
- Open the paper to show a chain of four fact-family houses.

Make a Fact Triangle in the triangular roof of one of the houses, and then use the numbers to write the fact family in the house. GMP7.2 Remind children to place a dot above the product and include the multiplication and division symbols in the middle. Explain that only facts containing the numbers belonging to the family can live in the house. Encourage children to make fact-family houses for 2s, 5s, and 10s facts they need to practice.

$2 \times 3 = 6$	$2 \times 5 = 10$	$5 \times 4 = 20$	$3 \times 10 = 30$
$3 \times 2 = 6$	$5 \times 2 = 10$	$4 \times 5 = 20$	$10 \times 3 = 30$
$6 \div 2 = 3$	$10 \div 2 = 5$	$20 \div 5 = 4$	$30 \div 10 = 3$
$6 \div 3 = 2$	$10 \div 5 = 2$	$20 \div 4 = 5$	$30 \div 3 = 10$

▶ ## Math Boxes 1-10

Math Journal 1, p. 22

| WHOLE CLASS | SMALL GROUP | PARTNER | INDEPENDENT |

Mixed Practice Math Boxes 1-10 are paired with Math Boxes 1-13.

▶ ## Home Link 1-10

Math Masters, pp. 29–33

Homework Children solve fact-family problems involving 2s, 5s, and 10s facts. Send home copies of 2s, 5s, and 10s Fact Triangles for children to practice with at home. GMP7.2

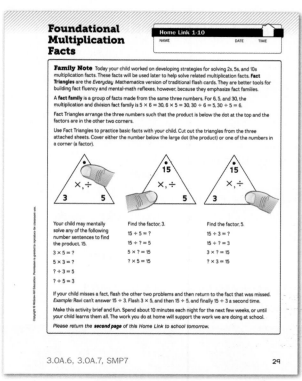

Math Masters, p. 29

Math Boxes   Lesson 1-10
                                  DATE   TIME

① There are __10__ shoes in all.
Write a number model.
$2 + 2 + 2 + 2 + 2$
$= 10; 5 \times 2 = 10$

② What time is it?

Fill in the circle next to the correct answer.
Ⓐ 6:45   Ⓑ 9:33
Ⓒ 10:35   Ⓓ 8:30

③ Add or subtract on your calculator to complete these problems.

Enter	Change to	How?
163	193	$+ 30$
603	803	$+ 200$
345	305	$- 40$
341	41	$- 300$

④ Write the numbers that are 100 less and 100 more.

100 less		100 more
313	413	513
402	502	602
632	732	832
791	891	991

⑤ Write the number that is halfway between 60 and 70 on the number line. Label 66 where it belongs.

60   65 66   70

66 rounded to the nearest ten is
__70__

⑥ Josh got to soccer practice at 3:10 P.M. He left at 3:55 P.M. How long was he at practice?
__45 minutes__
(unit)

① 3.OA.1, 3.OA.3 ② 3.MD.1 ③ 3.NBT.2 ④ 3.NBT.2 ⑤ 3.NBT.1
22 twenty-two ⑥ 3.MD.1

The Length-of-Day Project

Overview Children calculate elapsed time.

▶ **Before You Begin**
Find sunrise/sunset data for your location (www.sunrisesunset.com or your local newspaper) and record data for the current week, including today, on *Math Masters*, page TA10. Leave the Length-of-Day column blank. Display a prepared Length-of-Day Graph. (*See page 90.*)

▶ **Vocabulary**
elapsed time • length of day

Common Core State Standards

Focus Clusters
• Represent and interpret data.
• Solve problems involving measurement and estimation.

	Materials	
① Warm Up 5 min		
Mental Math and Fluency Children record clock times to the nearest minute.	demonstration clock, slate, marker	3.MD.1

② Focus 40–50 min		
Math Message Children calculate the length of a gym class.	toolkit clocks	3.MD.1 SMP4, SMP5
Reviewing Elapsed Time Children share strategies for calculating elapsed time.	toolkit clocks, demonstration clock	3.MD.1 SMP5
Finding the Length of Day Children analyze strategies for finding the length of day and calculate the elapsed time between sunrise and sunset.	*Student Reference Book*, pp. 187–188; *Math Masters*, p. TA10; toolkit clocks; demonstration clock	3.MD.1 SMP1, SMP4, SMP5
✔ **Assessment Check-In** See page 90.		3.MD.1, SMP1
Introducing the Length-of-Day Project Children discuss collecting data throughout the school year.	*Math Journal 1*, p. 23; *Math Masters*, p. TA10; Length-of-Day Graph	3.MD.1, 3.MD.3 SMP4

CCSS 3.MD.1 **Spiral Snapshot**

GMC Solve number stories involving time intervals by adding or subtracting.

1-5 Focus	1-6 Focus Practice	1-11 Focus Practice	1-12 Practice	1-13 Practice	2-1 Practice	2-3 Practice	2-5 Practice

Spiral Tracker **Go Online** to see how mastery develops for all standards within the grade.

③ Practice 15–20 min		
Minute Math+ Children mentally calculate elapsed time.	*Minute Math®+*, p. 122	3.MD.1
Practicing with Fact Triangles Children practice multiplication and division facts.	Fact Triangles	3.OA.7
Math Boxes 1-11: Preview for Unit 2 Children preview skills and concepts for Unit 2.	*Math Journal 1*, p. 24	See page 91.
Home Link 1-11 **Homework** Children solve elapsed-time problems.	*Math Masters*, p. 34	3.MD.1

connectED.mcgraw-hill.com

Plan your lessons online with these tools.

 ePresentations   **Student Learning Center**   **Facts Workshop Game**   **eToolkit**   **Professional Development**   **Home Connections**   **Spiral Tracker**   **Assessment and Reporting**   **English Learners Support**   **Differentiation Support**

86   Unit 1 | Math Tools, Time, and Multiplication

Differentiation Options

RtI

CCSS 3.MD.1, SMP5

Readiness
5–10 min

Counting Time on a Clock

WHOLE CLASS
SMALL GROUP
PARTNER
INDEPENDENT

toolkit clocks,
demonstration clock

Have children practice counting time on a clock by leading them through activities such as:

- *Show 12 o'clock. Use the minute hand to count 7 minutes more. What time is it now?* 12:07
- *Show 3:15. Count by 5-minute intervals until you reach 3:35.* 3:20, 3:25, 3:30, 3:35
- *Show 6:20. Use the minute hand to count on by 5-minute intervals and then by single minutes until you reach 6:47.* GMP5.2 6:25, 6:30, 6:35, 6:40, 6:45, 6:46, 6:47

CCSS 3.MD.1, SMP5, SMP6

Enrichment
10–15 min

Writing Elapsed-Time Number Stories

WHOLE CLASS
SMALL GROUP
PARTNER
INDEPENDENT

Activity Card 13, toolkit clocks, slate, markers

To extend work with finding elapsed time, have children write elapsed-time problems with a start and end time for an activity. Have partners solve each other's problems and explain their thinking. GMP6.1 Then have children discuss how they chose effective tools. GMP5.1, GMP5.2

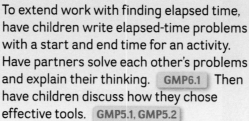

Writing Elapsed-Time Number Stories (13)

CCSS 3.MD.1, SMP5

Extra Practice
10–15 min

Finding Elapsed Time

WHOLE CLASS
SMALL GROUP
PARTNER
INDEPENDENT

Activity Card 14; *Math Masters,* pp. TA11–TA12; scissors; paper clip; envelope; toolkit clocks

To provide additional practice measuring time intervals in minutes, have partners cut apart one set of Elapsed Time Cards Deck A from *Math Masters,* page TA11. One partner sets a toolkit clock and reads the time. The other partner draws an Elapsed Time card to determine the change in time and sets a clock to the new time. GMP5.2 Advance to Deck B (*Math Masters,* page TA12) as children are ready.

Finding Elapsed Time (14)

English Language Learners Support

Beginning ELL Help children remember the meanings of *sunrise* and *sunset* by connecting *rise* and *set* with *up* and *down.* Use activities that involve restatements, gestures, and actions within classroom contexts. For example, gesture as you tell children to *stand up* or *rise* from their seats and to *put a book down* or *set a book down* on their desk. Use visual aids, such as pictures of sunrises and sunsets with arrows pointing up and down, to reinforce the differences between the terms.

 Go Online ELL English Learners Support

1 **Warm Up**   5 min   

▶ Mental Math and Fluency

Show times on the demonstration clock for children to read and record on slates. Ask children to identify familiar times they could use to help them determine the times you show. *Leveled exercises:* Sample familiar times given.

○●○○ **4:10; 6:40; 9:55**   4:00; 6:30; 9:45
●●○ **2:04; 5:33; 8:59**   2:00; 5:30; 9:00
●●● **1:11; 3:22; 10:48**   1:00; 3:15; 10:45

2 **Focus**   40–50 min   

▶ Math Message

Josie's class arrives at music at 10:06 A.M. Music is over at 10:55 A.M. Work with a partner to figure out the length of Josie's music class. 49 minutes *You may use your toolkit clock or an open number line.* **GMP4.1, GMP5.2**

▶ Reviewing Elapsed Time

WHOLE CLASS	SMALL GROUP	PARTNER	INDEPENDENT

Math Message Follow-Up Have children share how they used a toolkit clock or an open number line to calculate the length of Josie's music class. **GMP5.2** Highlight strategies for getting started, such as counting forward and backward by minutes to familiar times. *For example:*

- I set my toolkit clock to show 10:06. I counted back 1 minute to 10:05. Then I counted minutes by 5s until the minute hand was at the 11 to show 10:55. I counted 50 minutes. I subtracted 1 minute because I first moved the minute hand back from 10:06 to 10:05.

- I know that an hour passed from 10:00 to 11:00. One hour is 60 minutes. I subtracted 6 minutes from 60 because music starts at 10:06 (60 minutes − 6 minutes = 54 minutes). I subtracted 5 more minutes because it ends at 10:55 (54 minutes − 5 minutes = 49 minutes).

50 minutes − 1 minute = 49 minutes

- I drew an open number line and made four 1-minute hops to 10:10. Then I made one hop from 10:10 to 10:30. That was 20 minutes. I made another hop to 10:45. That was 15 more minutes. I made 2 five-minute hops to 10:50 and 10:55. That was 10 more minutes.

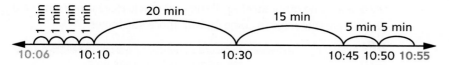

$$4 \text{ min} + 20 \text{ min} + 15 \text{ min} + 10 \text{ min} = 49 \text{ minutes}$$

Emphasize that these are just a few ways to solve the problem; there are many other ways to count intervals of time.

▶ Finding the Length of Day

Student Reference Book, pp. 187–188; *Math Masters,* p. TA10

WHOLE CLASS | **SMALL GROUP** | PARTNER | INDEPENDENT

Display the sunrise and sunset data collected on *Math Masters,* page TA10. Have children describe the data in the table. The data table shows the times at which the sun rose and set during the last few days. Explain that the **elapsed time,** or the total number of hours and minutes between sunrise and sunset, is the **length of day.** Ask:

- *How many hours are in a day?* 24 hours *What part of the day is the* A.M.? The time from 12:00 midnight to 11:59 A.M. *P.M.?* The time from 12:00 noon to 11:59 P.M.

- *Does the sun rise and set at the same time every day?* No.

Divide the class into small groups. Ask children to figure out the number of hours and minutes from sunrise to sunset for today in the Sunrise and Sunset Data table.

Encourage children to use toolkit clocks, open number lines, or other tools. They may refer to *Student Reference Book,* pages 187–188 for an example of a table in which to keep track of hours and minutes, and an example of calculating elapsed time with an open number line. As children work, circulate, assist, and ask questions such as: Answers vary.

- *How might you use a clock to help you? An open number line?*
  GMP4.1, GMP5.2

- *Will you count hours or minutes first? How?*

- *How will you keep track of the total minutes and hours?* GMP4.1

- *What could you try if you get stuck?* GMP1.3

Invite volunteers to share their solution strategies using the demonstration clock or an open number line. If no one kept track of hours and minutes in a table similar to the one on *Student Reference Book,* page 187, you may want to model doing so.

Record the answer on the Sunrise and Sunset Data table in the Length-of-Day column. Revisit this routine each week and encourage different children to share their strategies.

Math Masters, p. TA10

Sunrise and Sunset Data

NAME _____ DATE _____ TIME _____

Date	Time of Sunrise	Time of Sunset	Length of Day	
			hr	min
			hr	min
			hr	min
			hr	min
			hr	min
			hr	min
			hr	min
			hr	min
			hr	min
			hr	min
			hr	min
			hr	min
			hr	min
			hr	min
			hr	min
			hr	min
			hr	min
			hr	min
			hr	min
			hr	min

TA10

NOTE The content on *Math Masters,* page TA10, is identical to that on *Math Journal 1,* page 23.

Adjusting the Activity

Differentiate Help children who struggle to use an open number line to find elapsed times by having them choose familiar time increments using a clock. Note that many children will struggle to find the length of day at the beginning of the year, but will improve as they gain experience using strategies for finding elapsed time.

Go Online Differentiation Support

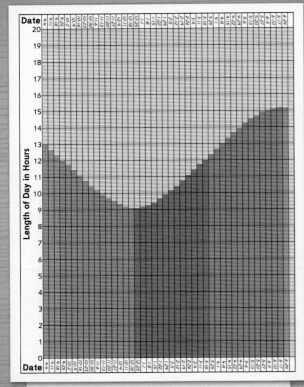

Length-of-Day Graph

NOTE You may want to collect data for another location to compare with yours, or if the length of day does not change much over the course of the year where you live. Use the same color throughout a season, and then change to a new color with the new season. If applicable, you may wish to note Daylight Saving Time on the graph.

✓ **Assessment Check-In** 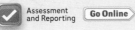 3.MD.1

This lesson introduces finding the length of day, so do not expect children to be successful with this skill at this time. Observe whether and how children persevere to find the elapsed time. **GMP1.3** Expect children to try at least one other strategy if they get stuck. Have those who struggle work in partnerships to come up with more strategies.

☑ **Assessment and Reporting** **Go Online** to record student progress and to see trajectories toward mastery for this standard.

▶ Introducing the Length-of-Day Project

Math Journal 1, p. 23; *Math Masters*, p. TA10

WHOLE CLASS | SMALL GROUP | PARTNER | INDEPENDENT

Explain that scientists predict the times for sunrise and sunset so people know them ahead of time. Tell children they will record sunrise and sunset data on journal page 23 once a week and, whenever possible, on the same day of the week. Demonstrate how to fill in the sunrise and sunset data table and Length-of-Day Graph:

Table Write today's date, the times for sunrise and sunset, and the total hours and minutes in the first row of the table. Use *Math Masters*, page TA10 if children need additional copies.

Graph Record the date at the top and bottom of the Length-of-Day Graph. Shade in the number of daytime hours and minutes to make a bar in the first column on the graph. Each hour interval is divided into 12 equal parts, so each part represents 5 minutes.

Discuss the Length-of-Day Graph. Ask: *What does the vertical axis represent?* The hours and minutes between sunrises and sunsets *What does the horizontal axis represent?* The dates for our data *What does the shaded portion represent?* The total number of daylight hours and minutes for the date *Why is this graph called the Length-of-Day Graph?* **GMP4.1** It shows the length of day, or total hours and minutes of daylight, throughout the year.

Explain your plan for collecting sunrise/sunset data, calculating the length of day, and recording it on the Length-of-Day Graph. If you assign class jobs, consider adding a Sunrise/Sunset job. Make sure all children enter sunrise and sunset data into their journals and practice calculating the length of day each week.

Summarize Have partnerships discuss what is easy and what is challenging about the Length-of-Day Project. Ask: *What tools might help make calculating the length of day easier?* Sample answers: Open number lines, tables, toolkit clocks

3 Practice 15–20 min [Go Online] ePresentations   eToolkit   Home Connections

▶ *Minute Math+*

Minute Math+, p. 122

Children solve elapsed-time problems mentally on *Minute Math+,* page 122.

▶ **Practicing with Fact Triangles**

| WHOLE CLASS | **SMALL GROUP** | **PARTNER** | INDEPENDENT |

Have children practice their 2s, 5s, and 10s facts using their Fact Triangles. See Lesson 1-10 for details. Knowing these facts fluently will help children develop more advanced fact strategies beginning in Unit 3.

▶ **Math Boxes 1-11:** Preview for Unit 2

Math Journal 1, p. 24

| WHOLE CLASS | **SMALL GROUP** | **PARTNER** | **INDEPENDENT** |

Mixed Practice Math Boxes 1-11 are paired with Math Boxes 1-14. These problems focus on skills and understandings that are prerequisite for Unit 2. You may want to use information from these Math Boxes to plan instruction and grouping in Unit 2.

▶ **Home Link 1-11**

Math Masters, p. 34

Homework Children solve elapsed-time problems.

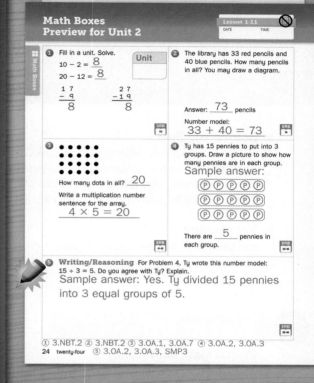

Math Journal 1, p. 24

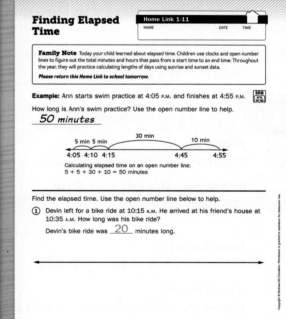

Math Masters, p. 34

Lesson 1-12
Explorations

Exploring Mass, Equal Shares, and Equal Groups

Overview Children compare masses and divide wholes and sets into equal shares.

▶ **Before You Begin**
For Part 1, select and sequence Quick Look Cards 130, 124, and 125. For the Math Message, display a pan balance with a heavier object in one pan and a lighter object in the other. For Exploration A, gather classroom objects that vary in size, shape, and mass, such as a calculator, scissors, tape, pencil, Pattern-Block Template, marker, and so on.

▶ **Vocabulary**
pan balance • mass • weight • zero • masses • equal shares

Common Core State Standards

Focus Clusters
- Represent and solve problems involving multiplication and division.
- Develop understanding of fractions as numbers.
- Solve problems involving measurement and estimation.
- Reason with shapes and their attributes.

---

1 Warm Up   5–10 min

	Materials	
Mental Math and Fluency Children practice Quick Looks with equal groups and arrays.	Quick Look Cards 124, 125, 130	3.OA.1, 3.OA.7 SMP2, SMP6

2 Focus   40–50 min

Math Message Children discuss how a pan balance works.	pan balance	3.MD.2
Introducing a Pan Balance Children are introduced to tools for comparing masses.	Everything Math Decks; pan balance; calculator; 2 standard masses; paper clips and tape (optional)	3.MD.2 SMP5
Exploration A: Comparing Masses Children estimate and compare masses of objects.	Activity Card 15; *Math Journal 1*, p. 25; pan balance; standard masses; objects	3.MD.2 SMP2, SMP5
Exploration B: Creating Equal Shares Children divide whole pancakes into equal shares.	Activity Card 16; *Math Journal 1*, p. 26; *Math Masters*, p. TA13; two 6-sided dice; scissors	3.NF.1, 3.G.2 SMP2, SMP4
Exploration C: Creating Equal Groups Children create equal groups.	Activity Card 17; 6-sided die; 36 counters	3.OA.1 SMP4

3 Practice   15–20 min

Minute Math+ Children solve number stories involving 1-half.	*Minute Math®+*, p. 97	3.NF.1, 3.MD.2
Introducing *Multiplication Draw* Children practice 2s, 5s, and 10s multiplication facts.	*Student Reference Book*, p. 248; *Math Masters*, p. G6; die labeled 2, 2, 5, 5, 10, 10; number cards 1–10 (4 of each)	3.OA.7 SMP7
Math Boxes 1-12 Children practice and maintain skills.	*Math Journal 1*, p. 27	See page 97.
Home Link 1-12 **Homework** Children find objects with similar masses.	*Math Masters*, p. 37	3.MD.2

Differentiation Options

RtI

CCSS 3.NF.1, SMP6

Readiness
5–10 min

Naming Fractional Parts

| WHOLE CLASS |
| SMALL GROUP |
| PARTNER |
| INDEPENDENT |

slate

To provide experience naming fractional parts, have children partition their slates into two equal-size parts. Brainstorm different ways to name each part, including: one-half, 1 half, and 1 out of 2 equal shares. Divide a slate into unequal-size parts and ask: *Did I divide the slate into halves? Why or why not?* Sample answers: No. The two parts are not the same size. They are not equal shares. One part is bigger than the other. Repeat the activity to practice partitioning and naming three and four equal parts of a slate. **GMP6.3**

CCSS 3.OA.1, SMP2

Enrichment
5–15 min

Solving Equal-Groups Riddles

| WHOLE CLASS |
| SMALL GROUP |
| PARTNER |
| INDEPENDENT |

Math Masters, p. 35; counters (optional)

To extend their work with equal groups, have children use *Math Masters,* page 35 to create and solve equal-groups riddles. Have them represent solutions with drawings. **GMP2.1**

Equal-Groups Riddles Lesson 1-12
NAME   DATE   TIME

What Number Am I?

① If you put me into 7 equal groups with 2 in each group, 5 are left over.
What number am I? __19__
Draw a picture.

Sample answer:

② I am between 20 and 30. When you put me into 5 equal groups, there is an odd number in each group and one is left over.
What number am I? __26__
Draw a picture.

Sample answer:

③ Write your own equal-groups riddle. Give it to a partner to solve.

_____

_____

_____

3.OA.1, SMP2   35

CCSS 3.OA.1, 3.NBT.2, SMP1

Extra Practice
5–15 min

Finding Totals for Equal Groups

| WHOLE CLASS |
| SMALL GROUP |
| PARTNER |
| INDEPENDENT |

Math Masters, p. 36; calculators

To practice solving equal-groups problems, have children use their calculators and repeated addition or multiplication to solve problems on Math Masters, page 36. Some children may want to program the calculator and skip count, while others may want to enter ⊕ repeatedly, or ⊗. Have children compare strategies and number models for the problems. **GMP1.6**

Finding Totals for Equal Groups Lesson 1-12
NAME   DATE   TIME

You may use your calculator to help you solve the problems. Compare the strategies you and others use. Answers vary.

① How many people are in my group? _____
How many hands do the people in my group have all together? _____
How many fingers do the people in my group have all together? _____
Write a number model to show how you figured out the total number of fingers. _____

② How many tables are in the classroom? _____
How many legs do the tables have all together? _____
Number model: _____

③ One flower has 5 petals.

How many petals do 6 flowers have? __30__
Number model: $5 \times 6 = 30$;
$5 + 5 + 5 + 5 + 5 + 5 = 30$

④ Make up your own problem like the ones above. Draw a picture to help someone solve your problem.

36   3.OA.1, 3.NBT.2, SMP1

English Language Learners Support

Beginning ELL Use the pictorial vocabulary card (recommended in English Language Learners Support for Lesson 1-8) to reintroduce the term *equal groups.* Add the term *equal shares* to the card to help children connect it to other terms they know. Give oral directions to make *equal groups* and *equal shares.* Encourage chidren to use the terms in simple sentences, such as: *4 people shared 12 eggs. Each person got a group of 3 eggs. Each person got an equal group. I cut a paper into 4 parts. Each part is the same size. Each part is an equal share.*

Go Online > **ELL** English Learners Support

1 Warm Up   5–10 min   Go Online
ePresentations   eToolkit

▶ Mental Math and Fluency

Show Quick Look Cards 130, 124, and 125, one at a time, for 2–3 seconds. Ask children to share both what they saw and how they saw it. GMP2.2, GMP6.1 Highlight strategies that recognize equal groups. Sample answers given.

Quick Look Card 130   I saw 4 groups of 2, and I know that $2 + 2 + 2 + 2 = 8$.
Quick Look Card 124   I saw 2 groups of 4, and I know 4 and 4 makes 8.
Quick Look Card 125   I saw 2 sets of 8, and $8 + 8 = 16$.

2 Focus   40–50 min   Go Online
ePresentations   eToolkit

▶ Math Message

Look at the pan balance. How do you think it works? Talk to a partner about your ideas.

▶ Introducing a Pan Balance

| WHOLE CLASS | SMALL GROUP | PARTNER | INDEPENDENT |

Math Message Follow-Up Discuss children's ideas about how a pan balance works. Responses may include that the pan holding the heavier object goes down, while the pan holding the lighter object goes up.

Explain that a **pan balance** is a tool used to compare and measure the masses of objects. Explain that **mass** is a measure of the amount of matter in an object. **Weight** is a measure of how heavy an object is. Have children hold an Everything Math Deck in one hand and a calculator in the other hand. Ask: *Which feels heavier?* Everything Math Deck Explain that they feel different weights because gravity is pulling on objects that have different masses.

Professional Development In everyday life, the terms *mass* and *weight* are used more or less interchangably. Roughly speaking, mass is a measure of the amount of matter in an object. Weight is a measure of the force of gravity acting on an object. Neil Armstrong's mass remained the same when he traveled to the moon, but his weight was much less on the moon than on Earth because the moon has less gravitational pull. Children will probably use the terms interchangeably, but that should not be a concern at this time. For more information on mass and weight, see the Unit 1 Mathematical Background in the Unit Organizer.

Demonstrate how to **zero** the pan balance, or make the pans level and balanced. It may be necessary to tape one or more paper clips to one pan to zero the balance. Then place a calculator in one pan and an Everything Math Deck in the other pan. The pan with the deck moves down because the deck has more mass than the calculator. Replace the calculator with another Everything Math Deck and guide children to understand that if two masses are equal, the pans balance. GMP5.2

Display a set of **masses,** or standard objects used in measuring mass and weight. Explain that we can compare masses of objects by placing them on different sides of a pan balance, but if we want to measure masses of objects, we must balance the object with a known amount of mass. Point out that the set of masses has 1-, 5-, 10-, 20-, 50-, and 100-gram masses and a 1-kilogram mass. Tell children that we use grams and kilograms to measure mass.

Demonstrate measuring the mass of an object using a pan balance and standard masses. Make sure the pan balance is zeroed. Then place an object, such as an Everything Math Deck, on one of the pans. Place as many masses as needed in the other pan to make the pans balance. The mass of the object is the sum of the masses in the other pan, which in this case is about 102 grams. GMP5.2

Explain and assign groups to each of the Explorations activities.

> **NOTE** In Explorations lessons, Exploration A often requires more explanation and guidance than Explorations B and C. Plan to spend most of your time with children working on Exploration A activities.

▶ **Exploration A:** Comparing Masses

Activity Card 15; *Math Journal 1*, p. 25

| WHOLE CLASS | **SMALL GROUP** | **PARTNER** | INDEPENDENT |

To explore with the pan balance and standard masses, have children place objects in one pan and standard masses in the other until the pans balance. GMP5.2 Have them follow directions on Activity Card 15 and record their work on journal page 25. GMP2.1 This activity prepares children for Lesson 1-13, Introducing Mass.

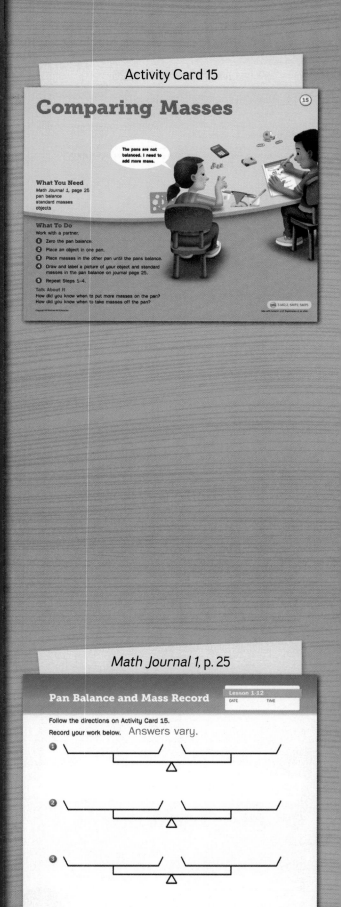

Activity Card 15

Comparing Masses

Math Journal 1, p. 25

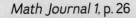

Equal Shares at a Pancake Breakfast

Lesson 1-12

DATE   TIME

Follow the directions on Activity Card 16.

1. Share 3 pancakes equally among 6 people. Draw a picture to show part of the 3 pancakes that each person gets. Write your answer next to your picture.
1-half of a pancake

Drawings vary.

2. Share 3 pancakes among 4 people. What part of the 3 pancakes does each person get? Draw a picture to show how you shared the pancakes. Write your answer next to your picture.

Sample answers: 1-half + 1-fourth of a pancake; 1-fourth + 1-fourth + 1-fourth of a pancake; or 3-fourths of a pancake

Drawings vary.

26   twenty-six   3.NF.1, 3.G.2, SMP2, SMP4

Activity Card 16

Creating Equal Shares

There are 3 people. Each person gets 1-half and 1-sixth of a pancake.

What You Need
Math Journal 1, page 26
Paper Pancakes, page TA13
scissors
two 6-sided dice
paper

What To Do
1. Carefully cut out the paper pancakes from page TA13.
2. Solve Problems 1 and 2 on journal page 26. You may fold and cut the paper pancakes to help you figure out the equal shares.
3. Find equal shares for more pancake problems:
   a. Roll two dice. Choose one number to represent the number of pancakes. The other number will represent the number of people sharing the pancakes.
   b. Draw or fold and cut paper pancakes to help you figure out the equal shares.
4. Record your problem and solution on paper.

Talk About It
What is another way to divide the pancakes so everyone gets equal shares?

3.NF.1, 3.G.2, SMP2, SMP4

Activity Card 17

Creating Equal Groups

There are 6 eggs in all.

What You Need
6-sided die
36 counters
6 quarter-sheets of paper
paper

What To Do
1. Use the quarter-sheets of paper as birds' nests and the counters as eggs.
2. Roll the die twice. The first roll tells how many nests to use. The second roll tells how many eggs to put in each nest.
3. Set up the nests and eggs for the numbers you rolled.
4. Figure out how many eggs there are in all.
5. Draw a picture showing the nests and eggs in each nest.
6. Write a number model below your drawing to show the total number of eggs.
7. Repeat Steps 1–6 three more times.

$3 \times 2 = 6$

Talk About It
Explain how you know that your number model fits your picture.

More You Can Do
Use the same numbers from your rolls, but use the first for the number of eggs in each nest and the second number for the number of nests.

3.OA.1, SMP4

▶ **Exploration B:** Creating Equal Shares

Activity Card 16; *Math Journal 1*, p. 26; *Math Masters*, p. TA13

| WHOLE CLASS | **SMALL GROUP** | PARTNER | INDEPENDENT |

Professional Development Children named fractional parts in *First and Second Grade Everyday Mathematics* using language such as 1-half and 1 out of 2 equal shares. Introducing standard notation for fractions ($\frac{1}{2}$ and $\frac{1}{4}$, for example) too early can promote misconceptions, such as thinking that $\frac{1}{4}$ is larger than $\frac{1}{2}$ because 4 is larger than 2. Although children may be familiar with standard fractional notation from everyday life, it will be introduced with length measurement in Unit 4 and covered in depth with fractions in Unit 5.

To explore dividing multiple wholes into **equal shares** and naming equal shares with unit fractions, have children follow directions on Activity Card 16. Have children cut out the circles from *Math Masters*, page TA13 to use as paper pancakes and record their representations on journal page 26. **GMP2.1, GMP4.1** Children may benefit from reviewing how to name fractional parts in the optional Readiness activity.

> **Differentiate**   **Adjusting the Activity**
>
> Watch for children who struggle to make equal groups and divide amounts into same-size shares. Ask them to show non-examples alongside correct examples in Explorations B and C. After each problem ask questions such as: *Does each person get an equal share of the pancake(s)?* or *Does each nest have the same number of eggs? How do you know they are equal?* Sample answers: I compared the sizes of the parts of the pancakes. I counted the eggs in each nest.
>
> **Go Online**   Differentiation Support

▶ **Exploration C:** Creating Equal Groups

Activity Card 17

| WHOLE CLASS | SMALL GROUP | **PARTNER** | INDEPENDENT |

Have partnerships follow directions on Activity Card 17. Have them make "nests" that hold the same number of "eggs" and write number models to represent their pictures. Some children may write an addition number model to represent the number of eggs. For example, for 4 nests with 3 eggs in each nest, they may write $3 + 3 + 3 + 3 = 12$. Others may record a multiplication number model, $4 \times 3 = 12$ or 4 [3s] is 12. Encourage children who use addition to also write a multiplication number model. **GMP4.1**

Summarize Have partners share something they learned from each Exploration.

(3) Practice   15–20 min   Go Online

ePresentations   eToolkit   Home Connections

▶ *Minute Math+*

Minute Math+, p. 97

To provide practice with number stories involving halves, see *Minute Math+,* p. 97.

▶ Introducing *Multiplication Draw*

Student Reference Book, p. 248; *Math Masters,* p. G6

| WHOLE CLASS | SMALL GROUP | **PARTNER** | INDEPENDENT |

To provide additional practice with 2s, 5s, and 10s facts, have children play *Multiplication Draw* and record rounds on *Math Masters,* page G6. As a class, read the directions on *Student Reference Book,* page 248. Play a round or two with children and then assign partnerships to play.

Observe

• What strategies do children use to multiply by 2s, 5s, and 10s?

• How do children compare their sums?

Discuss

• *What strategies do you use to solve the facts?*

• *What patterns do you notice in the products of 2s facts? 5s facts? 10s facts?* GMP7.1

| Differentiate | Game Modifications | Go Online | Differentiation Support |

▶ Math Boxes 1-12

Math Journal 1, p. 27

| WHOLE CLASS | **SMALL GROUP** | PARTNER | INDEPENDENT |

Mixed Practice Math Boxes 1-12 are paired with Math Boxes 1-9.

▶ Home Link 1-12

Math Masters, p. 37

Homework Children find objects at home that have about the same mass. They bring two of their objects to school to check their predictions.

Math Journal 1, p. 27

Math Boxes   Lesson 1-12
DATE   TIME

① [bar graph: Books Read — Jen, Mark, Inez, Lisa, Joe]

a. How many books did Jen and Mark read all together?
   25 books

b. How many more books did Joe read than Lisa?
   20 books

② Jacob went to his friend's house at 8:30 A.M. He stayed there until 10:00 A.M. How long was he at his friend's house? Use your toolkit clock or draw an open number line.

1 hour 30 minutes

③ Find the difference between 91 and 59.
   32

Which tool could help you check your answer?
Sample answer: Number grid

④ Fill in the unit. Solve.

$15 - 7 =$ **8**

8 $= 12 - 4$

$13 -$ **5** $= 8$

$7 =$ **14** $- 7$

Unit

⑤ **Writing/Reasoning** Explain how you used the graph to answer Problem 1a.
Sample answer: I found Jen and Mark's names on the bottom of the graph. I counted by 5s because each box stands for 5 books read.

① 3.MD.3 ② 3.MD.1 ③ 3.NBT.2 ④ 3.NBT.2
⑤ 3.MD.3, SMP4   twenty-seven 27

Math Masters, p. 37 (handwritten: 35)

Masses of Objects   Home Link 1-12
NAME   DATE   TIME

Family Note Today your child used a pan balance and grams and kilograms to compare and measure objects' masses or weights. In everyday life, mass and weight are hard to tell apart and *Everyday Mathematics* does not distinguish their differences. In later science classes your child will learn how scientists treat mass and weight.

Help your child find objects to compare at home. Below he or she will record the names of two objects that weigh about the same. Try to find objects that are different sizes or shapes.

Please remember to send an unopened 1-liter bottle of water to school with your child.

Our class is also collecting items for a Mass Museum. Help your child select an item that is 1 kilogram (2.2 pounds) or less to bring to school. Over the next several days, children will estimate and then measure the masses of objects in the museum.

Please return this Home Link to school tomorrow.

• Find objects that you can hold in one hand.

• Pick two objects and place one in each hand.

• Find two objects that feel like they have about the same mass or weight.

• Draw or write the names of the objects below.

• Tell someone how you know they have the same mass or weight.
Answers vary.

Ask someone at home if you can bring things to school for the Mass Museum.

3.MD.2   37

Measuring Mass

Overview Children estimate and measure masses of objects.

▶ **Before You Begin**

For Part 1, select and sequence Quick Look Cards 126, 127, and 128. For Part 2, start a Mass Museum. Use a pan balance and standard masses to determine and label a set of benchmark items with mass of 1 gram, 10 grams, 100 grams, and 500 grams, and 1 kilogram. See *Student Reference Book*, page 183 for examples of 1 gram and 1 kilogram items. Decide how children will rotate through the Mass Museum.

▶ **Vocabulary**

mass • gram • kilogram

Common Core State Standards

Focus Cluster
Solve problems involving measurement and estimation.

---

1 Warm Up   5-10 min

Materials

Mental Math and Fluency Children practice Quick Looks with equal groups and arrays.	Quick Look Cards 126, 127, and 128	3.OA.1, 3.OA.7 SMP2, SMP6

---

2 Focus   45-50 min

Math Message Children add objects to the class Mass Museum.		SMP5
Exploring Grams and Kilograms Children find objects that are about 1 gram and 1 kilogram.	*Math Journal 1*, p. 28; 1-liter bottles of water; large paper clips; pan balance; standard masses; Class Data Pad	3.MD.2 SMP5, SMP6
✓ **Assessment Check-In** See page 101.	*Math Journal 1*, p. 28	3.MD.2
Visiting the Mass Museum Children estimate and measure masses of objects in the Mass Museum.	*Math Masters*, p. 39; resealable plastic bag; 20 nickels; stick-on notes; objects; pan balance; standard masses; poster paper (optional)	3.MD.2 SMP1, SMP5
Solving Mass Number Stories Children solve number stories involving grams and kilograms.	*Math Journal 1*, p. 29; *Student Reference Book*, p. 271	3.MD.2

CCSS 3.MD.2 **Spiral Snapshot**

GMC Measure and estimate masses of objects using grams and kilograms.

1-12 Focus Practice	1-13 Focus	2-2 Practice	2-4 Practice	2-9 Practice	3-6 Practice	3-8 Practice	4-3 Focus

/// **Spiral Tracker**   **Go Online** to see how mastery develops for all standards within the grade.

---

3 Practice   10-15 min

Minute Math+ Children mentally solve number stories involving mass.	*Minute Math®+*, p. 124	3.MD.2
Playing *Spin and Round* **Game** Children practice rounding 3-digit numbers.	*Student Reference Book*, p. 258 ; *Math Masters*, pp. G4-G5; number cards 1-9 (4 of each); pencil and large paper clip	3.NBT.1
Math Boxes 1-13 Children practice and maintain skills.	*Math Journal 1*, p. 30	See page 103.
Home Link 1-13 **Homework** Children solve mass number stories.	*Math Masters*, p. 40	3.NBT.2, 3.MD.2

---

connectED.mcgraw-hill.com

Plan your lessons online with these tools.

 ePresentations

 Student Learning Center

 Facts Workshop Game

 eToolkit

 Professional Development

 Home Connections

 Spiral Tracker

 Assessment and Reporting

 English Learners Support

 Differentiation Support

Differentiation Options

RtI

Readiness 5–10 min

WHOLE CLASS
SMALL GROUP
PARTNER
INDEPENDENT

Ordering Objects

objects of varying weights and sizes

To provide access to measuring mass, have children hold pairs of objects to determine which is heavier. Then have partners place the objects in order from the least heavy to the heaviest.

Enrichment 5–10 min

WHOLE CLASS
SMALL GROUP
PARTNER
INDEPENDENT

Estimating with Grams and Kilograms

Math Masters, p. 38; benchmark objects and pan balance and masses (optional)

To explore estimating mass, have children estimate masses of the different objects listed on *Math Masters*, page 38. Have them discuss possibilities and decide which measure is the most reasonable for each object. GMP3.1 You may wish to provide some of the objects listed for children to measure using a pan balance.

Estimating with Grams and Kilograms

Lesson 1-13

NAME   DATE   TIME

A nickel has a mass of about 5 grams.
A liter of water has a mass of about 1,000 grams, or 1 kilogram.

In Problems 1–6, circle a reasonable mass for each object.

1. A dog might have a mass of about _____.
   (20 kilograms)   200 kilograms   2,000 kilograms

2. A can of soup might have a mass of about _____.
   4 grams   40 grams   (400 grams)

3. A newborn baby might have a mass of about _____.
   (3 kilograms)   30 kilograms   300 kilograms

4. A basketball might have a mass of about _____.
   6 grams   (600 grams)   6,000 grams

5. A pencil might have a mass of about _____.
   (5 grams)   50 grams   500 grams

6. A mouse might have a mass of about _____.
   (25 grams)   250 grams   2,500 grams

7. Choose one of the problems above. Explain why you chose your answer.
   Sample answer: For Problem 5, I thought a pencil might have the same mass as a nickel, so I circled 5 grams.

38   3.MD.2, SMP3

Extra Practice 5–10 min

WHOLE CLASS
SMALL GROUP
PARTNER
INDEPENDENT

Measuring Masses of Objects

Activity Card 18; *Math Masters*, p. 39; objects from the Mass Museum; pan balance; standard masses

To practice estimating and measuring masses of objects, have children use the labeled benchmark items from the Mass Museum to estimate the masses of objects, and a pan balance and standard masses to find the actual masses. Then have them discuss how they used benchmark items to help them estimate the masses of objects. GMP5.2

Measuring Masses of Objects

The hole punch is a little lighter than the base-10 bundle of longs. I think the hole punch has a mass of about 75 grams.

This hole punch has a mass of about 60 grams.

What You Need
Mass Museum Record Sheet, page 39
objects from the Mass Museum
pan balance
standard masses

What To Do
1. Choose an object from the Mass Museum.
2. Use benchmark objects to estimate your object's mass in grams or kilograms. Record your estimate on your Mass Museum Record Sheet.
3. Use a pan balance and standard masses to measure the mass of the object. Record the actual measure on your Mass Museum Record Sheet.
4. Repeat Steps 1–3.

Talk About It
How did you use the benchmark masses to help estimate the masses of other items?

More You Can Do
Estimate and then measure one of the objects a classmate measured. Check whether your measure is the same or different. If it is different, measure again.

English Language Learners Support

Beginning ELL Scaffold the comparative *-er* form of *heavy* and *light* to compare and order the weights of different objects, and to make the connection with the terms *more* and *less*. Think aloud while holding a heavy book and say: *This is heavy.* Then hold two copies of the same book and say: *These are heavier. They weigh more.* Repeat the process with other objects. Then compare light objects, such as a pencil, straw, and feather, using the terms *light* and *lighter.* Encourage children to repeat your statements.

Go Online   ELL   English Learners Support

SMP1 Make sense of problems and persevere in solving them.
GMP1.4 Check whether your answer makes sense.

SMP5 Use appropriate tools strategically.
GMP5.2 Use tools effectively and make sense of your results.

SMP6 Attend to precision.
GMP6.3 Use clear labels, units, and mathematical language.

1 Warm Up 5–10 min   Go Online
ePresentations eToolkit

▶ Mental Math and Fluency

Show Quick Look Cards 126, 127, and 128 one at a time for 2–3 seconds. Ask children to share what they saw and how they saw it. GMP2.2, GMP6.1 Highlight strategies that recognize equal groups. Sample answer given.

Quick Look Card 126 I saw 2 groups of 3, and I know $3 + 3 = 6$.
Quick Look Card 127 I saw 2 groups of 5, and I know $5 + 5 = 10$.
Quick Look Card 128 I saw 3 groups of 3, and I know $3 + 3 = 6$ and $6 + 3 = 9$.

2 Focus 45–50 min   Go Online
ePresentations eToolkit

▶ Math Message

Quietly visit the Mass Museum. Place the objects you brought from home into the museum. Talk with a partner about how you could find the mass of your objects. GMP5.2

▶ Exploring Grams and Kilograms

Math Journal 1, p. 28

| WHOLE CLASS | SMALL GROUP | PARTNER | INDEPENDENT |

Math Message Follow-Up Display a set of standard masses. Ask children what they know about these masses from Exploration A in Lesson 1-12. Expect responses to include that each **mass** is labeled with its amount of mass. For example, there are 1-, 5-, 10-, 20-, 50-, and 100-gram masses and a 1-kilogram mass.

Have children share their ideas for how to check the masses of their objects. You may wish to have volunteers check the mass of one or two objects from the Mass Museum using the standard masses and a pan balance. GMP5.2

Use masses and a pan balance to establish that a large paper clip has a mass of about 1 **gram** and that an unopened 1-liter bottle of water has a mass of about 1 **kilogram.** Tell children that 1 kilogram is equal to 1,000 grams. Record this equivalence on the Class Data Pad. Ask: *How many large paper clips balance the 1-kilogram mass?* GMP6.3 1,000 large paper clips

Remind children that in everyday life we can describe one object as having more or less mass than another. Encourage children to use language that precisely describes their measurements, such as *this paper clip has a mass of 1 gram.* GMP6.3

Provide each partnership with an unopened 1-liter bottle of water and a large paper clip. Explain that they are to hold the 1-liter bottle of water or 1 large paper clip in one hand and an object in the other hand to find objects that are also about 1 kilogram or 1 gram. Have children conduct a measurement hunt to test predictions about which classroom objects have masses of about 1 gram (roughly equivalent to the weight of a large paper clip) and about 1 kilogram (roughly equivalent to the weight of an unopened 1-liter bottle of water). They should also find objects with masses more than 1 gram, but less than 1 kilogram. Have children record their work on journal page 28.

Demonstrate measuring the mass of an object using a pan balance and standard masses. Remind children to make sure the pan balance is zeroed before using it to measure. Then place an object, such as a Pattern-Block Template, on one of the pans. Add masses to the other pan to make the pans balance. Explain that when the pans are level, the mass of the object is the sum of the standard masses—in this case about 20 grams. **GMP5.2** Over the next several days, invite small groups to check their Measurement Hunt estimates with a pan balance and masses.

Have children record their measurements on journal page 28. Remind children to record their masses as "about _____ grams."

 Assessment Check-In CCSS 3.MD.2

Math Journal 1, p. 28

Observe as children estimate masses. Expect children to "feel" the difference between 1-gram and 1-kilogram masses and tell whether objects are closer to 1 gram or 1 kilogram. For children who struggle to estimate, suggest that they close their eyes and hold their arms slack when they compare. This stance allows children to focus on their estimation with fewer external distractions.

 Assessment and Reporting ⬛ Go Online ▷ to record student progress and to see trajectories toward mastery for this standard.

Math Journal 1, p. 28

Measurement Hunt

Lesson 1-13
DATE   TIME

① Estimate the masses of objects. Record the names of objects in the columns below based on your estimates.

About 1 gram	More than 1 gram and less than 1 kilogram	About 1 kilogram

② Use a pan balance and standard masses to find the actual masses of your objects. Record your work in the table below. Write the unit.

Name of Object	Mass

28   twenty-eight   3.MD.2, SMP5, SMP6

Math Masters, p. 39

Mass Museum Record Sheet

Lesson 1-13
NAME   DATE   TIME

Use benchmark objects to estimate the mass of an object.

Then use a pan balance and masses to measure the mass of your object.

Record your work below. Answers vary.

Object	Estimated Mass	Measured Mass

① For which object was your estimate closest to your measurement?
_____

② For which object was your estimate farthest from your measurement?
_____

③ Which object has the least mass? _____
The greatest? _____

3.MD.2   39

Math Journal 1, p. 29

Mass Number Stories

Lesson 1-13

DATE TIME

Use mass measurements from *Student Reference Book*, page 271. Solve the number stories.

① One soccer ball has a mass of about __425__ grams. Dylan carries 2 soccer balls outside for gym class. What is the mass of 2 soccer balls together?

about __850__ grams

② One golf ball has a mass of about __43__ grams. Keisha can juggle 3 golf balls. If she drops one golf ball, what is the mass of the remaining balls?

about __86__ grams

③ Make up your own number story using the sports ball masses.
Answers vary.

④ Trade papers with a partner and solve Problem 3. Show your work.
Answers vary.

3.MD.2

twenty-nine 29

Student Reference Book, p. 271

Real-World Data

Masses of Sports Balls

Mr. Isaacs, the Lincoln School physical education teacher, had students in the school measure the mass of several balls from the gym. The table below lists the masses of the sports balls. Each mass is given in grams.

Masses of Sports Balls	
Ball	Mass (in grams)
Table tennis	$2\frac{1}{2}$ g
Squash	25 g
Golf	43 g
Tennis	57 g
Baseball	142 g
Cricket	156 g
Softball	184 g
Volleyball	270 g
Soccer	425 g
Water polo	425 g
Croquet	454 g
Basketball	625 g
Bowling	7,260 g

Note 1 kilogram equals 1,000 grams.
A wooden baseball bat has a mass of about 1 kilogram.

Check Your Understanding

1. Which sports balls have a mass that is 1 kilogram or more?
2. Which ball's mass is closest to 200 grams?
3. How much more mass does a basketball have than a volleyball?

Check your answers in the Answer Key.

two hundred seventy-one SRB 271

▶ **Visiting the Mass Museum**

Math Masters, p. 39

| WHOLE CLASS | SMALL GROUP | PARTNER | INDEPENDENT |

Turn children's attention to the Mass Museum. Hold up a few benchmark items that are labeled with their masses in grams or kilograms. (*See Before You Begin.*) Explain to children that over the next few weeks they will estimate the masses of objects in the museum and check their estimates with a pan balance and masses. Share the record sheet on *Math Masters,* page 39 and read through the directions. Demonstrate how to use benchmark items to estimate masses of other objects. For example, hold up a plastic bag with 20 nickels labeled "about 100 grams" in one hand and a pack of stick-on notes in the other. Say: *The bag of nickels feels heavier, so I know the stick-on notes have less mass. I estimate they are about 50 grams because it feels like it would take about twice as many packs of stick-on notes to balance the bag of nickels.* Have a child measure the mass of the stick-on notes with a pan balance and standard masses to check your estimate. **GMP1.4, GMP5.2** A pack of 3 inch-by-3 inch stick-on notes has a mass of about 45 grams.

Differentiate **Adjusting the Activity**

Support children as they estimate masses by using a visual representation of benchmarks. Have them write the name or draw a picture of an item on a stick-on note with the mass after they have measured it. Display the notes on a poster in order from the least to greatest mass. Place the poster in the Mass Museum.

Go Online | Differentiation Support

Consider having children sort the objects in the museum into categories, such as less than 100 grams, between 100 and 500 grams, between 500 and 1,000 grams, and more than 1,000 grams. You may want to remind them that 1,000 grams is the same as 1 kilogram. As children gain experience with estimating and measuring mass, encourage them to think of ways to refine their sorts.

Explain your procedure for how children will rotate through the Mass Museum over the next several weeks. Invite children to bring additional objects for the museum.

▶ **Solving Mass Number Stories**

Math Journal 1, p. 29; *Student Reference Book,* p. 271

| WHOLE CLASS | SMALL GROUP | PARTNER | INDEPENDENT |

Have partnerships use the data from *Student Reference Book,* page 271 to solve the number stories on journal page 29. Encourage children to make sense of the number stories by recalling the masses of benchmark objects they measured in class. Invite children to share their solution strategies.

Summarize Have partners share at least one thing they learned about mass.

③ **Practice** 10–15 min 〈Go Online〉 ePresentations eToolkit Home Connections

▶ *Minute Math+*

Minute Math+, p. 124

To provide practice with number stories involving grams and kilograms, see *Minute Math+*, page 124.

▶ *Playing Spin and Round*

Student Reference Book, p. 258; *Math Masters*, pp. G4–G5

| WHOLE CLASS | **SMALL GROUP** | **PARTNER** | INDEPENDENT |

Have children play *Spin and Round* to practice rounding numbers to the nearest 10 or 100. See Lesson 1-7 for details. Encourage children to draw open number lines to help them round the numbers.

Observe

- Which children identify the closest two multiples of 10? Of 100?
- Which children draw open number lines?

Discuss

- *What strategies did you use to help you round?*
- *What did you find challenging in this game? Easy?*

| **Differentiate** **Game Modifications** 〈Go Online〉 Differentiation Support |

▶ **Math Boxes 1-13**

Math Journal 1, p. 30

| WHOLE CLASS | **SMALL GROUP** | **PARTNER** | **INDEPENDENT** |

Mixed Practice Math Boxes 1-13 are paired with Math Boxes 1-10.

▶ **Home Link 1-13**

Math Masters, p. 40

Homework Children solve number stories relating grams and kilograms.

Math Journal 1, p. 30

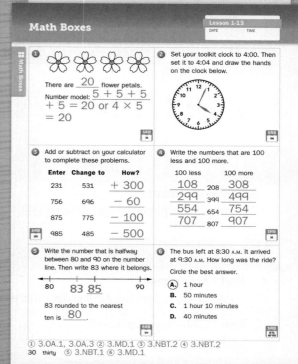

Math Boxes Lesson 1-13 DATE TIME

① There are __20__ flower petals.
Number model: $5 + 5 + 5 + 5 = 20$ or $4 \times 5 = 20$

② Set your toolkit clock to 4:00. Then set it to 4:04 and draw the hands on the clock below.

③ Add or subtract on your calculator to complete these problems.

Enter	Change to	How?
231	531	$+ 300$
756	696	$- 60$
875	775	$- 100$
985	485	$- 500$

④ Write the numbers that are 100 less and 100 more.

100 less		100 more
108	208	308
299	399	499
554	654	754
707	807	907

⑤ Write the number that is halfway between 80 and 90 on the number line. Then write 83 where it belongs.

80   83 85   90

83 rounded to the nearest ten is __80__.

⑥ The bus left at 8:30 A.M. It arrived at 9:30 A.M. How long was the ride?
Circle the best answer.

(A.) 1 hour
B. 50 minutes
C. 1 hour 10 minutes
D. 40 minutes

① 3.OA.1, 3.OA.3 ② 3.MD.1 ③ 3.NBT.2 ④ 3.NBT.2
30 thirty ⑤ 3.NBT.1 ⑥ 3.MD.1

Math Masters, p. 40

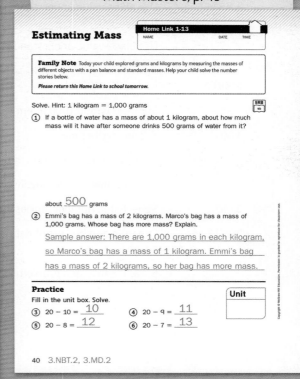

Estimating Mass Home Link 1-13 NAME DATE TIME

Family Note Today your child explored grams and kilograms by measuring the masses of different objects with a pan balance and standard masses. Help your child solve the number stories below.
Please return this Home Link to school tomorrow.

Solve. Hint: 1 kilogram = 1,000 grams

① If a bottle of water has a mass of about 1 kilogram, about how much mass will it have after someone drinks 500 grams of water from it?

about __500__ grams

② Emmi's bag has a mass of 2 kilograms. Marco's bag has a mass of 1,000 grams. Whose bag has more mass? Explain.

Sample answer: There are 1,000 grams in each kilogram, so Marco's bag has a mass of 1 kilogram. Emmi's bag has a mass of 2 kilograms, so her bag has more mass.

Practice
Fill in the unit box. Solve.

③ $20 - 10 = $ __10__
④ $20 - 9 = $ __11__
⑤ $20 - 8 = $ __12__
⑥ $20 - 7 = $ __13__

Unit

40 3.NBT.2, 3.MD.2

Unit 1 Progress Check

Overview **Day 1: Administer the Unit Assessments.**
Day 2: Administer the Open Response Assessment.

2-Day Lesson

 Student Learning Center
Students may take
assessments digitally.

 Assessment and Reporting
Record results and track
progress toward mastery.

Day 1: Unit Assessments

1 Warm Up   5–10 min

Materials

Self Assessment
Children complete the Self Assessment.

Assessment Handbook, p. 5

2a Assess   35–50 min

Unit 1 Assessment
These items reflect mastery expectations to this point.

Assessment Handbook, pp. 6–10

Unit 1 Challenge (Optional)
Children may demonstrate progress beyond expectations.

Assessment Handbook, pp. 11–12

CCSS Common Core State Standards	Goals for Mathematical Content (GMC)	Lessons	Self Assessment	Unit 1 Assessment	Unit 1 Challenge
3.OA.1	Interpret multiplication in terms of equal groups.	1-8, 1-10, 1-12		5a, 5b	1a–1c, 4b, 4c
3.OA.3	Use multiplication and division to solve number stories.	1-8, 1-9	6	5a, 5b	1a, 1c
	Model number stories involving multiplication and division.	1-8, 1-9		5a, 5b	1a, 1b
3.OA.7	Multiply within 100 fluently.	1-8, 1-10		4a–4f	4a–4c
	Know all products of 1-digit numbers × 1, × 2, × 5, and × 10 automatically.	1-10		4a–4f	4a–4c
3.NBT.1	Use place-value understanding to round whole numbers to the nearest 10.	1-4	3	7a, 7b	
	Use place-value understanding to round whole numbers to the nearest 100.	1-4	3	8a, 8b	
3.NBT.2	Add within 1,000 fluently.	1-1, 1-3, 1-4		5a, 5b	
	Subtract within 1,000 fluently.	1-1 to 1-4	1	1a, 1b	2
3.MD.1	Tell and write time.	1-3, 1-5	4	2a, 2b	
	Measure time intervals in minutes.	1-5, 1-6, 1-11			3
	Solve number stories involving time intervals by adding or subtracting.	1-5, 1-6, 1-11		6	3
3.MD.2	Solve 1-step number stories involving mass.	1-13		9	
3.MD.3	Organize and represent data on scaled bar graphs and scaled picture graphs.	1-7	5	3a	
	Solve 1- and 2-step problems using information in graphs.	1-7		3b, 3c	

Goals for Mathematical Practice (GMP)	Lessons	Self Assessment	Unit 1 Assessment	Unit 1 Challenge
SMP2 Create mathematical representations using numbers, words, pictures, symbols, gestures, tables, graphs, and concrete objects. **GMP2.1**	1-7, 1-12		3a	
Make sense of the representations you and others use. **GMP2.2**	1-7, 1-8, 1-10		3b, 3c, 7a, 7b, 8a, 8b	
SMP4 Model real-world situations using graphs, drawings, tables, symbols, numbers, diagrams, and other representations. **GMP4.1**	1-6, 1-8, 1-9, 1-11, 1-12		5a, 5b	1a, 1b
SMP5 Use tools effectively and make sense of your results. **GMP5.2**	1-2, 1-3, 1-5, 1-11 to 1-13	2	1a–1c	
SMP6 Explain your mathematical thinking clearly and precisely. **GMP6.1**	1-1, 1-2		1c, 4g	2
SMP7 Use structures to solve problems and answer questions. **GMP7.2**	1-1			4b, 4c

/// **Spiral Tracker** 〈 **Go Online** 〉 to see how mastery develops for all standards within the grade.

1 Warm Up 5–10 min

▶ Self Assessment

Assessment Handbook, p. 5

| WHOLE CLASS | SMALL GROUP | PARTNER | **INDEPENDENT** |

Children complete the Self Assessment to reflect on their progress in Unit 1.

Some children may benefit from recalling the types of problems cited in each row of the Self Assessment. Show children where these pointers appear on their Self Assessments. In Unit 2, children begin using these pointers themselves.

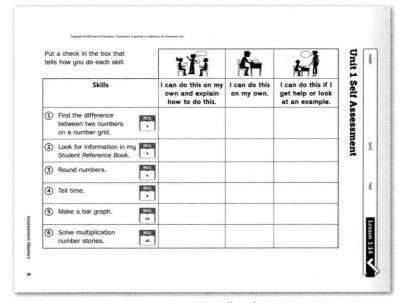

Assessment Handbook, p. 5

Unit 1 Assessment

① Use the number grid.

91	92	93	94	95	96	97	98	99	100
101	102	103	104	105	106	107	108	109	110
111	112	113	114	115	116	117	118	119	120
121	122	123	124	125	126	127	128	129	130

a. The difference between 95 and 127 is __32__.

b. The difference between 97 and 122 is __25__.

c. Explain how you used the number grid to solve Problem 1b.

Sample answer: I counted by 1s from 97 to 102 and got 5. Then I counted by 10s from 102 to 122 and got 20. So the difference is 25.

② Write the time shown on each clock.
You may use your toolkit clock to help you.

a.   b.

__6:50__   __12:35__

6 Assessment Handbook

Unit 1 Assessment (continued)

③ a. Use the tally chart to complete the bar graph.

Total Wins

Teams	Number of Wins
Team A	~~HHT~~ IIII
Team B	~~HHT~~ I
Team C	~~HHT~~
Team D	~~HHT~~ ~~HHT~~

Use the data in the bar graph to answer the questions below.

b. How many wins did the four teams have in all? __30__

c. How many fewer wins did Team C have than Team D? __5__

④ Solve each problem.

a. 2 × 5 = __10__   b. 2 × 8 = __16__

c. 5 × 3 = __15__   d. 4 × 5 = __20__

e. 10 × 2 = __20__   f. 3 × 10 = __30__

g. How did you solve 4 × 5?

Sample answers: I skip counted by 5s four times. I added 5 four times. I knew that two 5s make 10, so I added 10 two times.

Assessment Masters 7

► Unit 1 Assessment

Assessment Handbook, pp. 6–10

| WHOLE CLASS | SMALL GROUP | PARTNER | **INDEPENDENT** |

Children complete the Unit 1 Assessment to demonstrate their progress on the Common Core State Standards covered in this unit.

Generic rubrics in the *Assessment Handbook* appendix can be used to evaluate children's progress on the Mathematical Practices.

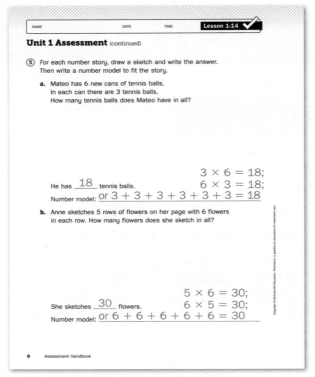

Unit 1 Assessment (continued)

⑤ For each number story, draw a sketch and write the answer. Then write a number model to fit the story.

a. Mateo has 6 new cans of tennis balls.
In each can there are 3 tennis balls.
How many tennis balls does Mateo have in all?

3 × 6 = 18;
6 × 3 = 18;
He has __18__ tennis balls.
Number model: or 3 + 3 + 3 + 3 + 3 + 3 = 18

b. Anne sketches 5 rows of flowers on her page with 6 flowers in each row. How many flowers does she sketch in all?

5 × 6 = 30;
6 × 5 = 30;
She sketches __30__ flowers.
Number model: or 6 + 6 + 6 + 6 + 6 = 30

8 Assessment Handbook

Assessment Handbook, p. 8

Written assessments are one way children can demonstrate what they know. The table below shows adjustments you can make to the Unit 1 Assessment to maximize opportunities for individual children or for your entire class.

Differentiate Adjusting the Assessment

Item(s)	Adjustments
1a, 1b	To extend Items 1a and 1b, have children find the differences without using the number grid.
1c	To scaffold Item 1c, have children gesture to show how they used their number grid.
2a, 2b	To scaffold Items 2a and 2b, provide a clock with labeled minute and hour hands.
3a	To scaffold Item 3a, include 1, 3, 5, 7, and 9 on the vertical axis.
3b, 3c	To scaffold Items 3b and 3c, have children use the bar graph to tell the number of wins for each team.
4	To scaffold Item 4, have children model problems with counter arrays.
5	To extend Item 5, have children write and solve their own number stories.
6	To extend Item 6, have children figure out what time Angela will get home if her travel time is 15 minutes.
7, 8	To scaffold Items 7 and 8, have children write the multiples of 10 to 100 and the multiples of 100 to 1,000 for reference.
9	To scaffold Item 9, have children use an actual pan balance and masses to act out the story.

Advice for Differentiation

Because this is the beginning of the school year, all of the content included on the Unit 1 Assessment was recently introduced and will be revisited in subsequent units.

Use the online assessment and reporting tools to track children's performance. Differentiation materials are available online to help you address children's needs.

NOTE See the Unit Organizer on pages 8–9 or the online Spiral Tracker for details on Unit 1 focus topics and the spiral.

Go Online for additional information in the *Implementation Guide* about assessment in *Everyday Mathematics*, including grading and differentiation.

Assessment Handbook, p. 9

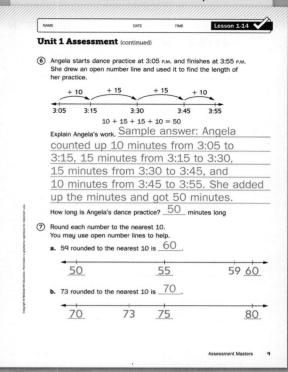

Assessment Handbook, p. 10

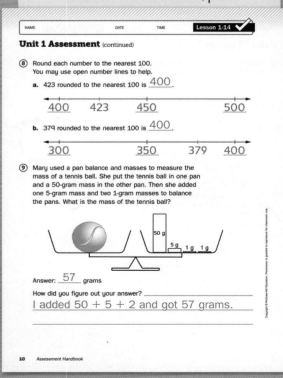

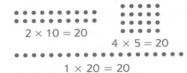
| NAME | DATE | TIME | Lesson 1-14 ✓ |

Unit 1 Challenge

① Marsha counts 20 blocks and arranges them in different arrays.

   a. Sketch all the possible arrays Marsha could make with the blocks.

$$2 \times 10 = 20$$

$$4 \times 5 = 20$$

$$1 \times 20 = 20$$

   b. Write multiplication number models for each of the arrays.

   c. Could Marsha make an array that has 3 rows? <u>No.</u>
      Explain. <u>Sample answer: She could put</u>
      <u>6 blocks in each row, but then there</u>
      <u>would be 2 left over. If she put 7 in each</u>
      <u>row, she would be missing 1.</u>

② Don and Molly played *Number-Grid Difference.*
   The object of the game is to have the lower sum of 5 scores.

   Don picked 3 and 5 and made the number 35.

   Molly picked 8 and 5. What number should Molly make? <u>58</u>
   Explain your answer. <u>Sample answer: She should</u>
<u>make 58 because the difference between 35</u>
<u>and 58 is less than the difference between 35</u>
<u>and 85.</u>

Assessment Masters **11**

| NAME | DATE | TIME | Lesson 1-14 ✓ |

Unit 1 Challenge (continued)

③ Solve. You may use your toolkit clock or an open number line
   to help you. Show your work.

   Evan starts basketball camp at 9:15 A.M.
   He finishes at 3:45 P.M.

   How many hours and minutes does Evan spend at camp?

   Evan spends <u>6</u> hours and <u>30</u> minutes at camp.

④ Manuel is working on his 10s and 5s facts.
   He knows most of his 10s facts, but he has trouble with his 5s facts.
   You can help him.

   a. Solve.

      $6 \times 10 = $ <u>60</u>

      6×10 means 6 equal groups of 10.

   b. Explain how Manuel can use his answer to 6×10
      to figure out what 6×5 would be.
   <u>Sample answer: 6 groups of 10 is 60. 5 is</u>
   <u>half of 10, so 6 groups of 5 is half of 60, or 30.</u>

   c. Explain another way that Manuel could solve 6×5.
      <u>Sample answers: He could skip count by</u>
      <u>5s six times. He could add 5 six times.</u>

12 Assessment Handbook

▶ **Unit 1 Challenge** (Optional)

Assessment Handbook, pp. 11–12

| WHOLE CLASS | SMALL GROUP | PARTNER | **INDEPENDENT** |

Children can complete the Unit 1 Challenge after they complete the Unit 1 Assessment. The Unit 1 Challenge offers children an opportunity to demonstrate a deeper understanding of the content and practices addressed so far this year. Do not expect all children to succeed at the Challenge problems. However, children's responses to these problems may help you choose appropriate interventions, including Enrichment activities.

Unit 1 Progress Check

Overview   **Day 2:** Administer the Open Response Assessment.

Day 2: Open Response Assessment

2b   Assess   50–55 min

Materials

Solving the Open Response Problem
After a brief introduction, children interpret a graph and use the graph to solve a problem.

Assessment Handbook, pp. 13–14;
Standards for Mathematical
Practice Poster

Discussing the Problem
Children share their observations from the graph and their solutions to the problem.

Assessment Handbook, pp. 13–14

CCSS   Common Core State Standards

	Goals for Mathematical Content (GMC)	Lessons
3.MD.1	Solve number stories involving time intervals by adding or subtracting.	1-5, 1-6, 1-11
3.MD.3	Solve 1- and 2-step problems using information in graphs.	1-7
	Goal for Mathematical Practice (GMP)	
SMP4	Use mathematical models to solve problems and answer questions. GMP4.2	1-6

III Spiral Tracker   **Go Online**   to see how mastery develops for all standards within the grade.

▶ **Evaluating Children's Responses**
Evaluate children's abilities to solve word problems using information presented in a graph and involving time intervals. Use the rubric below to evaluate their work based on **GMP4.2**.

Goal for Mathematical Practice GMP4.2 Use mathematical models to solve problems and answer questions.	Not Meeting Expectations	Partially Meeting Expectations	Meeting Expectations	Exceeding Expectations
	Provides inaccurate statements or statements not based on information in the graph for Problem 1. For Problem 2, does not provide an explanation of why Cheryl arrives first.	Provides fewer than five accurate statements based on information in the graph for Problem 1. For Problem 2, provides an incomplete explanation of why Cheryl arrives first.	Provides at least five accurate statements based on information in the graph for Problem 1. For Problem 2, provides a complete explanation of why Cheryl arrives first.	Provides at least five accurate statements, including some with comparisons for Problem 1. For Problem 2, provides a complete explanation of why Cheryl arrives first that includes the difference between the children's arrival times.

3   Look Ahead   10–15 min

Materials

Math Boxes 1-14: Preview for Unit 2
Children preview skills and concepts for Unit 2.

Math Journal 1, p. 31

Home Link 1-14
Children take home the Family Letter that introduces Unit 2.

Math Masters, pp. 41–44

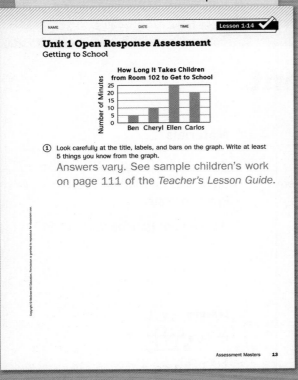
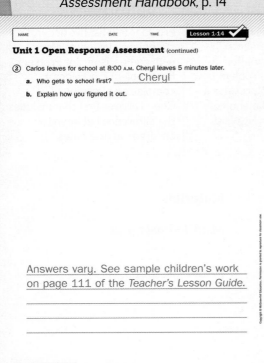
 **Assess**      50–55 min   **Go Online** ☑

Assessment
and Reporting

▶ Solving the Open Response Problem

Assessment Handbook, pp. 13–14

| WHOLE CLASS | SMALL GROUP | **PARTNER** | INDEPENDENT |

The open response problem requires children to interpret a graph and use the information to solve a problem. The focus of this task is **GMP4.2:** Use mathematical models to solve problems and answer questions.

Before starting the problem, tell children that today they will write true statements and answer questions based on information presented in a bar graph.

Distribute *Assessment Handbook,* pages 13–14. Read the directions aloud. Ask: *Where will you find the information that you need to solve Problems 1 and 2?* Sample answer: From the graph Refer children to **SMP4** and **GMP4.2** on the Standards for Mathematical Practice Poster. Point out that the model they will use in this problem is a graph. Tell children that they may solve Problem 2 before Problem 1 if they wish.

Circulate and observe children as they work. Look for children who are writing responses for Problem 1 that are overly similar (for example, Ben takes 5 minutes to get to school; Cheryl takes 10 minutes to get to school). Encourage these children to write comparisons or to be creative in making different types of statements.

> **Differentiate**   **Adjusting the Assessment**
>
> If children have difficulty writing statements about the graph on their own, have them talk with a partner about one thing they notice before having them work independently. As children construct their statements, they may benefit from labeling each bar with the appropriate number of minutes. Once children have worked on Problem 2, encourage them to go back to their list in Problem 1 to see if they have anything new to add.

▶ Discussing the Problem

Assessment Handbook, pp. 13–14

| **WHOLE CLASS** | SMALL GROUP | PARTNER | INDEPENDENT |

After children have had a chance to complete their work, invite individuals to share one thing they know from the graph. Encourage observations that go beyond determining the value of a single bar in the graph, such as, "It takes Ellen 5 minutes longer to get to school than Ben." Invite a few children to share their strategies for solving Problem 2.

Evaluating Children's Responses

CCSS 3.MD.1, 3.MD.3

Collect children's work. For the content standards, expect most children to solve Problem 2 correctly, using information from the graph to determine that Cheryl arrives at school first and adding minutes correctly. You can use the rubric on page 109 to evaluate children's work for **GMP4.2**.

See the sample in the margin. This work meets expectations for the content standards because the child used information from the bar graph to correctly solve Problem 2. The work meets expectations for the mathematical practice. For Problem 1, the child gave five accurate statements based on information from the graph. For Problem 2, the child provided a complete explanation of why Cheryl arrives at school first, including when Carlos and Cheryl leave and how many minutes Cheryl arrives before Carlos. **GMP4.2**

3 Look Ahead 10–15 min [Go Online]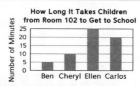

Home Connections

▶ Math Boxes 1-14: Preview for Unit 2 ✏️

Math Journal 1, p. 31

| WHOLE CLASS | SMALL GROUP | PARTNER | INDEPENDENT |

Mixed Practice Math Boxes 1-14 are paired with Math Boxes 1-11. These problems focus on skills and understandings that are prerequisite for Unit 2. You may want to use information from these Math Boxes to plan instruction and grouping in Unit 2.

▶ Home Link 1-14: Unit 2 Family Letter

Math Masters, pp. 41–44

Home Connection The Unit 2 Family Letter provides information and activities related to Unit 2 content.

Sample child's work, "Meeting Expectations"

How Long It Takes Children from Room 102 to Get to School

1. Carefully look at the title, labels, and bars on the graph. Write at least ⑤ things you know from the graph.

1 Ben takes 5 min.
2 Cheryl takes 10 min.
3 Ellen takes 25 min.
4 Carlos takes 20 min.
5 How long it takes children from Room 102 to get to school.

2. Carlos leaves for school at 8:00. Cheryl leaves five minutes later.

a. Who gets to school first? Cheryl

b. Explain how you figured it out.

I used a clock to figer it out. Well Carlos leves at 9:00. And Cheryl leves at 8:05. So Cheryl gets starts first. Cheryl is a First and it is 5 min. before him. 5 min. because she is

---

NOTE Additional samples of evaluated children's work can be found in the *Assessment Handbook* appendix.

Math Journal 1, p. 31

Math Boxes Preview for Unit 2 Lesson 1-14

① Fill in a unit. Solve.

$\underline{19} = 13 + 6$
$\underline{29} = 23 + 6$
$\underline{20} = 13 + 7$
$\underline{40} = 33 + 7$

Unit

② Claire had $40 in her bank. She spent $16. How much does she have left? You may draw a diagram.

Answer: ___$24___
(unit)

Number model:
$40 - 16 = 24$

③

How many dots in all? __25__

Write a multiplication number sentence.

$5 \times 5 = 25$

④ 4 children share 24 pennies equally. How many pennies does each child get? Use counters or draw a picture to help.

Answer: ___6 pennies___
(unit)

⑤ Writing/Reasoning Nicholas wrote $5 + 5 = 10$ as a number sentence for Problem 3. Do you agree? Explain your answer.

Sample answer: No. Nicholas is not correct because he needs to add 5 rows of 5 dots each to find the correct answer of 25.

① 3.NBT.2 ② 3.NBT.2 ③ 3.OA.1 ④ 3.OA.2, 3.OA.3
⑤ 3.OA.1, SMP3

thirty-one **31**

Unit 2 Organizer
Number Stories and Arrays

In this unit, children make sense of one- and two-step number stories involving all four arithmetic operations. They represent situations with diagrams, arrays, pictures, words, and number models. Through creating, sharing, comparing, and interpreting representations, children improve their problem-solving strategies and further their understanding that problems can be solved in more than one way.

CCSS Standards for Mathematical Content

Domain	Cluster
Operations and Algebraic Thinking	Represent and solve problems involving multiplication and division.
	Solve problems involving the four operations, and identify and explain patterns in arithmetic.
Number and Operations in Base Ten	Use place value understanding and properties of operations to perform multi-digit arithmetic.

Because the standards within each domain can be broad, *Everyday Mathematics* has unpacked each standard into Goals for Mathematical Content **GMC** . For a complete list of Standards and Goals, see page EM1.

For an overview of the CCSS domains, standards, and mastery expectations in this unit, see the **Spiral Trace** on pages 118–119. See the **Mathematical Background** (pages 120–122) for a discussion of the following key topics:

- Number Stories and Situation Diagrams
- Remainders
- Number Patterns
- Introducing Fractions

CCSS Standards for Mathematical Practice

SMP1	Make sense of problems and persevere in solving them.
SMP2	Reason abstractly and quantitatively.

For a discussion about how *Everyday Mathematics* develops these practices and a list of Goals for Mathematical Practice **GMP** , see page 123.

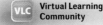
VLC Virtual Learning Community [Go Online] to **vlc.cemseprojects.org** to search for video clips on each practice.

McGraw-Hill Education

Go Digital with these tools at connectED.mcgraw-hill.com

 ePresentations

Student Learning Center

 Facts Workshop Game

 eToolkit

 Professional Development

 Home Connections

 Spiral Tracker

 Assessment and Reporting

 English Learners Support

Differentiation Support

Contents

* The standards listed here are addressed in the **Focus** of each lesson. For all the standards in a lesson, see the Lesson Opener.

Unit 2 Materials

VLC **Virtual Learning Community**

See how *Everyday Mathematics* teachers organize materials. Search "Classroom Tours" at **vlc.cemseprojects.org**.

Lesson	Math Masters	Activity Cards	Manipulative Kit	Other Materials
2-1	pp. 45–47; TA14		base-10 blocks (optional); toolkit clock	slate; calculator; number grid; Class Data Pad (optional); demonstration clock
2-2	pp. 48–49; TA8; TA15–TA16; G6	19	number cards 1–10 (4 of each); blank die	slate
2-3	pp. 50–51; TA2; TA8; TA15–TA16; G6 (optional)	20–21	number cards 1–10 (4 of each) (optional); die labeled 2, 2, 5, 5, 10, 10 (optional)	slate; Fact Triangles; calculator
2-4	pp. 52–54; TA2; TA15	22	number cards 0, 1, 2, 5, and 10 (4 of each)	slate
2-5	pp. 52; 55–56; G7	22	6-sided dice (2 per group); number cards 0, 1, 2, 5, and 10 (4 of each); counters; coins (optional)	slate
2-6	pp. 57–58; TA8; TA11; TA12 (optional); TA15	23	Quick Look Cards 123, 124, 129; toolkit clock; counters	slate; scissors; envelope; paper clip; container of objects (optional)
2-7	pp. 59–60; TA17–TA19; TA20 (optional); G8	24–26	Quick Look Cards 131, 132, 133; counters (optional); number cards 1–20; centimeter cubes; 6-sided die; 10-sided die	5″ by 7″ index cards labeled with 1, 2, and 5; Fact Triangles
2-8	pp. 61–62; TA6		counters	slate; marker; stick-on notes (optional); colored pencils (optional); Guidelines for Discussion Poster; selected samples of children's work; children's work from Day 1
2-9	pp. 39; 63–65; TA20 (optional)	27–28	counters; pan balance; standard masses; 6-sided die	slate; Mass Museum items; pennies; stick-on notes; paper
2-10	pp. 64; 66–67; G9	28–29	Quick Look Cards 151, 154, 156; counters; number cards 6–18; 6-sided die; base-10 blocks	slate (optional); full sheets of paper; quarter-sheets of paper
2-11	pp. 68–71; TA21	30–31	number cards 1–9 (4 of each)	slate
2-12	pp. 72–74; TA19; TA22; G9	32–33	Everything Math Decks including number cards 6–18; counters; 6-sided die; centimeter cubes; fraction circles; 1-liter beaker	slate; rectangular items of various sizes; tape (optional); assorted containers; paper towels; dishpan; pitcher; empty, transparent 1-liter bottle; water; food coloring (optional)
2-13	pp. 75–78; *Assessment Handbook*, pp. 15–24			

📖 **Literature Link**　　2-6　*Each Orange Had 8 Slices: A Counting Book*

Go Online for a complete literature list in Grade 3 and to download all Quick Look Cards.

Problem Solving  Professional Development

Everyday Mathematics emphasizes equally all three of the Common Core's dimensions of **rigor:**

- conceptual understanding
- procedural skill and fluency
- applications

Math Messages, other daily work, Explorations, and Open Response tasks provide many opportunities for children to apply what they know to solve problems.

▶ Math Message

Math Messages require children to solve a problem they have not been shown how to solve. Math Messages provide almost daily opportunities for problem solving.

▶ Daily Work

Journal pages, Home Links, Writing/Reasoning prompts, and Differentiation Options often require children to solve problems in mathematical contexts and real-life situations. **Minute Math+** offers number stories and a variety of other practice activities for transition times and spare moments throughout the day.

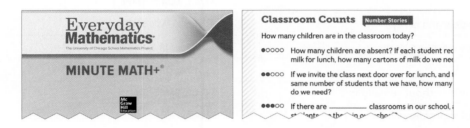

▶ Explorations

In Exploration A, children explore fraction circles. In Exploration B, children measure areas of rectangles by counting square inches and centimeters. In Exploration C, children compare liquid volumes of containers.

▶ Open Response and Reengagement

In Lesson 2-8, children use mathematical representations to solve division problems. They are encouraged to use pictures and words to show their reasoning. During the reengagement discussion on Day 2, children review the division problems, discuss their classmates' representations and solutions, and discuss what a good response might include. The focus practice for this lesson is creating mathematical representations using manipulatives, drawings, words, or number models. In discussion, they make sense of others' representations. GMP2.1

 **Virtual Learning Community** Go Online ⟩ to watch an Open Response and Reengagement lesson in action. Search "Open Response" at **vlc.cemseprojects.org.**

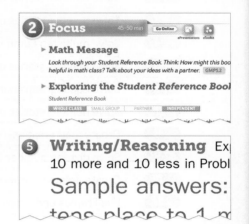

Look for GMP1.1–1.6 markers, which indicate opportunities for children to engage in SMP1: "Make sense of problems and persevere in solving them." Children also become better problem solvers as they engage in all of the CCSS Mathematical Practices. The yellow GMP markers throughout the lessons indicate places where you can emphasize the Mathematical Practices and develop children's problem-solving skills.

Assessment and Differentiation

 Assessment and Reporting

See pages xxii–xxv to learn about a comprehensive online system for recording, monitoring, and reporting children's progress using core program assessments.

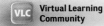 **Virtual Learning Community** **Go Online** to **vlc.cemseprojects.org** for tools and ideas related to assessment and differentiation from *Everyday Mathematics* teachers.

✔ Ongoing Assessment

In addition to frequent informal opportunities for "kid watching," every lesson (except Explorations) offers an **Assessment Check-In** to gauge children's performance on one or more of the standards addressed in that lesson.

Lesson	Task Description	**CCSS** Common Core State Standards
2-1	Use basic facts to solve fact extensions.	3.NBT.2, SMP7
2-2	Solve number stories using question marks for the unknown.	3.NBT.2, SMP1
2-3	Solve number stories using question marks for the unknown.	3.OA.8, 3.NBT.2, SMP1
2-4	Solve multistep number stories.	3.OA.8, SMP4
2-5	Solve number stories using representations.	3.OA.8, SMP4
2-6	Solve equal-groups number stories.	3.OA.1, 3.OA.3, SMP6
2-7	Solve number stories using number models and arrays.	3.OA.1, 3.OA.3, SMP2
2-8	Create mathematical representations to solve problems.	3.OA.2, 3.OA.3, SMP2
2-9	Solve division number stories.	3.OA.2, 3.OA.3, SMP2
2-10	Create arrays to practice division with and without remainders.	3.OA.2, SMP2, SMP7
2-11	Use Frames-and-Arrows diagrams to solve problems.	3.OA.7, 3.NBT.2, SMP7

▶ Periodic Assessment

Unit 2 Progress Check This assessment focuses on the CCSS domains of *Operations and Algebraic Thinking* and *Number and Operations in Base Ten*. It also contains a Cumulative Assessment to help monitor children's learning and retention of content that was the focus of Unit 1.

NOTE Odd-numbered units include an **Open Response Assessment.** Even-numbered units include a **Cumulative Assessment.**

► # Unit 2 Differentiation Activities **Differentiation Support** | **ELL** **English Learners Support**

Differentiation Options Every regular lesson provides Readiness, Enrichment, **Extra Practice,** and **Beginning English Language Learners Support** activities that address the Focus standards of that lesson.

Activity Card 20

CCSS 3.NBT.2		**CCSS** 3.NBT.2, SMP7		**CCSS** 3.NBT.2, SMP7	
Readiness	10–15 min	**Enrichment**	5–10 min	**Extra Practice**	5–10 min
Practicing Addition and Subtraction Facts with	WHOLE CLASS / SMALL GROUP / PARTNER	**Solving Fact Extensions Mentally**	WHOLE CLASS / SMALL GROUP / PARTNER	**Solving More Fact Extensions**	WHOLE CLASS / SMALL GROUP / PARTNER

Activity Cards These activities, written to the children, enable you to differentiate Part 2 of the lesson through small-group work.

English Language Learners Activities and point-of-use support help children at different levels of English language proficiency succeed.

Differentiation Support Two online pages for most lessons provide suggestions for game modifications, ways to scaffold lessons for children who need additional support, and language development suggestions for Beginning, Intermediate, and Advanced English language learners.

Differentiation Support online pages

Ongoing Practice **Differentiation Support**

► ## Embedded Facts Practice

Basic Facts Practice can be found in every part of the lesson. Look for activities or games labeled with CCSS 3.OA.7; or go online to the Spiral Tracker and search using CCSS 3.OA.7.

For **ongoing distributed practice,** see these activities:
- Mental Math and Fluency
- Differentiation Options: Extra Practice
- Part 3: Journal pages, Math Boxes, *Math Masters,* Home Links
- Print and online games

► ## Games

Games in *Everyday Mathematics* are an essential tool for practicing skills and developing strategic thinking.

Lesson	Game	Skills and Concepts	**CCSS** **Common Core State Standards**
2-1	*Addition Top-It*	Practicing addition facts	3.NBT.2
2-1	*Subtraction Top-It*	Practicing subtraction facts	3.NBT.2
2-1	*Salute!*	Practicing addition facts and finding missing addends	3.NBT.2
2-2	*Multiplication Draw*	Practicing 2s, 5s, and 10s facts	3.OA.7, SMP7
2-5	*Roll to 1,000*	Practicing mental addition with multiples of 10	3.OA.7, 3.NBT.2, SMP6
2-7	*Array Bingo*	Recognizing arrays as representations of multiplication facts	3.OA.1, 3.OA.7, SMP2
2-10 / 2-12	*Division Arrays*	Grouping counters equally to practice division with remainders	3.OA.2, 3.OA.7, SMP2, SMP7, SMP8

VLC **Virtual Learning Community** | **Go Online** to look for examples of *Everyday Mathematics* games at **vlc.cemseprojects.org**.

CCSS **Spiral Trace:** Skills, Concepts, and Applications

⭐ **Mastery Expectations** This Spiral Trace outlines instructional trajectories for key standards in Unit 2. For each standard, it highlights opportunities for Focus instruction, Warm Up and Practice activities, as well as formative and summative assessment. It describes the **degree of mastery**—as measured against the entire standard—expected at this point in the year.

Operations and Algebraic Thinking

3.OA.1 Interpret products of whole numbers, e.g., interpret 5 × 7 as the total number of objects in 5 groups of 7 objects each. *For example, describe a context in which a total number of objects can be expressed as 5 × 7.*

⭐ By the end of Unit 2, expect children to **interpret multiplication in terms of equal groups by drawing arrays or equal groups to match number stories.**

3.OA.2 Interpret whole-number quotients of whole numbers, e.g., interpret 56 ÷ 8 as the number of objects in each share when 56 objects are partitioned equally into 8 shares, or as a number of shares when 56 objects are partitioned into equal shares of 8 objects each. *For example, describe a context in which a number of shares or a number of groups can be expressed as 56 ÷ 8.*

⭐ By the end of Unit 2, expect children to **use drawings to interpret whole-number quotients of whole numbers.**

3.OA.3 Use multiplication and division within 100 to solve word problems in situations involving equal groups, arrays, and measurement quantities, e.g., by using drawings and equations with a symbol for the unknown number to represent the problem.

⭐ By the end of Unit 2, expect children to **solve word problems in situations involving equal groups and arrays by using drawings, repeated addition, or skip counting to represent the problem.**

Spiral Tracker

Go to **connectED.mcgraw-hill.com** for comprehensive trajectories that show how in-depth mastery develops across the grade.

3.OA.7 Fluently multiply and divide within 100, using strategies such as the relationship between multiplication and division (e.g., knowing that $8 \times 5 = 40$, one knows $40 \div 5 = 8$) or properties of operations. By the end of Grade 3, know from memory all products of two one-digit numbers.

| 1-12 Warm Up Practice | 1-14 Progress Check | 2-2 Practice | 2-3 Practice | 2-4 through 2-7 Warm Up Focus Practice | 2-8 Warm Up Practice | 2-10 Warm Up Focus Practice | 2-11 Warm Up Focus Practice | 2-12 Practice | 2-13 Progress Check | 3-1 Focus Practice |

By the end of Unit 2, expect children to **fluently multiply using strategies for all products of one-digit numbers and 1, 2, 5, and 10.**

3.OA.8 Solve two-step word problems using the four operations. Represent these problems using equations with a letter standing for the unknown quantity. Assess the reasonableness of answers using mental computation and estimation strategies including rounding.

| 2-2 through 2-5 Focus Practice | 2-10 Practice | 2-13 Progress Check | 3-2 through 3-6 Focus Practice | 3-8 Practice | 3-14 Progress Check | 4-1 Practice | 4-12 Focus | 5-4 Practice | 5-10 Focus |

By the end of Unit 2, expect children to **make sense of and represent two-step number stories involving addition and subtraction.**

Number and Operations in Base Ten

3.NBT.2 Fluently add and subtract within 1000 using strategies and algorithms based on place value, properties of operations, and/or the relationship between addition and subtraction.

| 1-7 Warm Up Practice | 1-8 Warm Up Practice | 1-14 Progress Check | 2-1 through 2-5 Warm Up Focus Practice | 2-6 Practice | 2-10 Practice | 2-11 Warm Up Focus Practice | 2-12 Warm Up Practice | 2-13 Progress Check | 3-1 through 3-6 Warm Up Focus Practice |

By the end of Unit 2, expect children to **add and subtract within 1000 using tools along with strategies based on place value and/or the relationship between addition and subtraction.**

Key ✓ = Assessment Check-In ✦ = Progress Check Lesson ▱ = Current Unit ▰ = Previous or Upcoming Lessons

Mathematical Background: Content

 The discussion below highlights major content areas and Common Core State Standards addressed in Unit 2. See the online Spiral Tracker for complete information about learning trajectories for all standards.

▶ Number Stories and Situation Diagrams
(Lessons 2-2 through 2-10)

Everyday Mathematics approaches the four basic operations of arithmetic by examining how they are used in various situations. Most of these situations can be sorted into a handful of categories called *use classes*. For each use class, *Everyday Mathematics* suggests a situation diagram to organize the information in simple one-step problems and help children write number models that represent the problems.

Children should be allowed to use problem-solving methods that best fit their needs. Not all will need situation diagrams to organize their problem solving. Keep in mind that more than one diagram may fit a given situation, and that most problems can be solved in more than one way. Some problems, however, may not easily fit into any diagram.

Addition and Subtraction Use Classes In *Everyday Mathematics*, there are three basic use classes for addition and subtraction: *parts and total, change,* and *comparison. (See margin.)* Each can be solved using either addition or subtraction, depending on the unknowns. **3.NBT.2** Children were introduced to corresponding situation diagrams in first and second grades and review them in Lessons 2-2 and 2-3.

Multiplication and Division Use Classes There are several multiplication and division use classes. In this unit, children solve *equal-groups* and *arrays* number story problems. Each type of situation can involve either multiplication or division, depending on the unknowns. As children first made sense of equal-groups and equal-sharing stories in Unit 1, they used a variety of representations and invented their own strategies to solve problems. **3.OA.1, 3.OA.2, 3.OA.3** In Unit 2, children examine those strategies and adopt more efficient strategies such as skip counting or repeated addition.

In an *equal-groups* situation, there are several groups of objects with the same number of objects in each group. When the numbers of groups and objects in each group are known, you can solve the problem by multiplying. **3.OA.1** Equal groups situations in which the total number of objects are known are called *equal-grouping* (unknown number of groups) and *equal-sharing* (unknown number of objects in each group) problems. You can solve an equal-grouping or equal-sharing problem by dividing or thinking of it as multiplication with an unknown factor. **3.OA.2, 3.OA.4**

 Standards and Goals for Mathematical Content

Because the standards within each domain can be broad, *Everyday Mathematics* has unpacked each standard into Goals for Mathematical Content **GMC**. For a complete list of Standards and Goals, see page EM1.

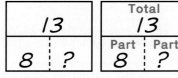
Parts-and-total diagrams
for 13 = 8 + ?

A change diagram for 14 − 5 = 9

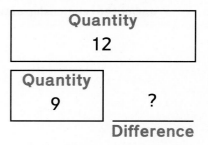
A comparison diagram
for 12 = 9 + ?

Unit 2 Vocabulary

area	equation	parts-and-total diagram
array	fact extensions	product
arrow rule	factors	quotient
change diagram	fraction	remainder
combinations of ten	fraction circles	representation
comparison diagram	frames	square centimeter (sq cm)
dividend	Frames and Arrows	square inch (sq in.)
division	liter	unknown
divisor	multiples	volume
efficient	number model	whole
equal groups	number sentence	

Number Stories and Situation Diagrams *Continued*

You share 12 blocks so that each friend gets 3 blocks. How many people get 3 blocks?

Equal-grouping Problem

12 blocks are shared among 3 friends so that each friend gets an equal number of blocks. How many blocks does each friend get?

Equal-sharing Problem

Array situations are equal-groups situations in which either factor can be thought of as the "number of groups" or the "number of objects in each group." **3.OA.1, 3.OA.2, 3.OA.3** If equal groups are arranged in rows and columns, they form a rectangular array. As with equal-groups situations, array problems can be solved using either multiplication or division.

Note that because of the Commutative Property of Multiplication, the factors in multiplication can be interchanged without affecting the product. For example, an array with 4 rows of 6 chairs has exactly the same number as an array of 6 rows with 4 chairs in each row. However, the difference may be important within the context of the number story. The convention is for the dimensions of an array to be named as "rows" by "columns," in that order. Reminding children of this convention will help the class communicate more effectively about how they solve array problems.

Exposing children to a wide variety of number-story situations, and changing which quantity within the stories is unknown, helps them learn to be flexible problem solvers. Children are not expected to distinguish between equal-grouping and equal-sharing situations; the classifications are a tool you can use to help ensure variety and present children with options.

Two-step or Multistep Number Stories The Common Core State Standards and *Everyday Mathematics* use the term *two-step number stories* as shorthand for number stories that can be solved by using two arithmetic operations. **3.OA.8** In Lessons 2-4 and 2-5, children solve number stories and model them with number sentences. The stories may be solved through direct modeling, counting, or by one or several calculations, and do not have to be solved in two steps. Some children will represent their strategies with one number model with several operations, while

Number Stories and Situation Diagrams *Continued*

others write a separate number model for each step. The Guide to Solving Number Stories provides support as they solve complex number stories without limiting children to a rigid set of problem-solving steps. Children will revisit two-step number stories throughout third grade. Through continued practice, children will make better sense of the problems they face and become more efficient at solving them.

Note that *Everyday Mathematics* uses the term *number model* specifically to mean number sentences, expressions, or equations that model number stories or other real-world situations. When number sentences are presented outside the contexts of number stories, they are not called number models. *Number sentence* (introduced in Lesson 2-7) and *equation* (introduced in Lesson 2-3) are also used, but children are not expected to distinguish the difference between these terms. Similarly, children do not need to understand the term *expression*.

▶ Remainders (Lessons 2-9 and 2-10)

In the equal-sharing number stories in Lesson 2-9, children are introduced to problems with remainders. **3.OA.2, 3.OA.3** They reason about the different ways to handle the "leftovers." Number stories that provide a real-world context for equal sharing of collections or objects help children develop a fundamental understanding of division. Most early exposures will be in contexts for which whole number remainders make sense. Number stories with contexts where it makes sense to further divide the remainders will be gradually introduced. This will support children as they learn fractions and apply their understanding of fractions and fraction notation later in the year. In Lesson 2-10 children learn to model division with and without remainders during the *Division Arrays* game. They identify even and odd number patterns in arithmetic and build their understanding of factors, remainders, and divisibility. **3.OA.9**

▶ Number Patterns (Lesson 2-11)

Everyday Mathematics uses Frames-and-Arrows diagrams across grades to represent number sequences. Each frame contains a number forming the sequence, and each arrow represents a rule (called an *arrow rule*) that may involve one or more arithmetic operations. **3.OA.7, 3.NBT.2** The rule determines which number goes in the next frame. (*See margin.*) Children apply rules to determine missing frames and interpret number patterns to figure out missing rules. **SMP7, SMP8** Frames-and-Arrows diagrams help develop children's abilities to determine patterns and rules and reinforce connections between operations.

▶ Introducing Fractions (Lesson 2-12)

Children use fraction circles to develop an understanding of the "whole" and of unit fractions as equal parts of that whole. **3.NF.1** Many children see the red circle as the only fraction circle that can be the "whole." To avoid this common misconception, Exploration A in Lesson 2-12 specifically has children using different shapes to represent the whole. While exploring relative sizes of shapes, children learn that the name of a fractional part is linked with the size of the whole, that is, the same physical object can be both one-quarter of a circle and also one-half of a semicircle. **3.NF.1**

Mathematical Background: Practices

 In Everyday Mathematics, *children learn the* **content** *of mathematics as they engage in the* **practices** *of mathematics. As such, the Standards for Mathematical Practice are embedded in children's everyday work, including hands-on activities, problem-solving tasks, discussions, and written work. Read here to see how Mathematical Practices 1 and 2 are emphasized in this unit.*

▶ Standard for Mathematical Practice 1

In *Everyday Mathematics*, problem solving is broadly conceived and permeates the entire curriculum. Children consider problems both in purely mathematical contexts and in real-world situations from the classroom and everyday life.

A key step in solving problems is to make sense of the problem. GMP1.1 To do this, children must have *number sense*, or a feeling for where numbers come from and what they mean. They must also have *operations sense*, or a feeling for what addition, subtraction, multiplication, and division do. Children use the Guide to Solving Number Stories, introduced in Lesson 2-2, as they work through complex problems. GMP1.2

Allow children time to makes sense of problems and persevere to find strategies that work best. They will develop a deeper understanding of various mathematical processes when asked to reflect and strategize rather than merely repeat the steps of a rigidly prescribed procedure. GMP1.2

Children develop a wider variety of problem-solving strategies when they are given the opportunity to share their ideas with their peers. Children should feel comfortable sharing their strategies, regardless whether their solutions are correct or incorrect, and their reasoning for why their solutions make sense. GMP1.4 Emphasize that everyone makes mistakes, and that we can learn from those mistakes. Encourage children to compare and contrast strategies and to find advantages and disadvantages of each. GMP1.6

▶ Standard for Mathematical Practice 2

When children "make sense of quantities and their relationships in problem situations," they are better able to create mathematical representations. GMP2.1 *Everyday Mathematics* focuses on four types of representations: concrete, verbal, pictorial, and symbolic. (*See margin.*) Double-headed arrows connect each kind of representation with each of the other kinds. Children and adults are likely to use all of these representations at one time or another, depending on the situation.

Representations are closely related to solution strategies; translating a problem into another representation is often a key to solving it. In the Open Response Problem in Lesson 2-8, children find ways to represent an equal-grouping problem. Some children will draw a picture or an array, some might use counters, and some may write a number model to represent the situation. As you discuss problems and solutions with children, compare their representations. Ask: *How are these representations similar? How are they different? Do both representations fit the story? Can we use another representation to solve this problem?* GMP2.2 Encouraging multiple representations and connecting them helps children develop into more powerful problem solvers.

 Standards and Goals for Mathematical Practice

SMP1 Make sense of problems and persevere in solving them.

GMP1.1 Make sense of your problem.

GMP1.2 Reflect on your thinking as you solve your problem.

GMP1.4 Check whether your answer makes sense.

GMP1.6 Compare the strategies you and others use.

SMP2 Reason abstractly and quantitatively.

GMP2.1 Create mathematical representations using numbers, words, pictures, symbols, gestures, tables, graphs, and concrete objects.

GMP2.2 Make sense of the representations you and others use.

Go Online to the *Implementation Guide* for more information about the Mathematical Practices.

For children's information on the Mathematical Practices, see *Student Reference Book*, pages 1–36.

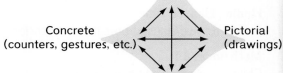

Four problem-solving representations

Extended Facts: Addition and Subtraction

Overview Children use basic addition and subtraction facts to solve problems with larger numbers.

▶ **Before You Begin**
Display sets of fact extensions without their sums or differences. See margin on page 127.

▶ **Vocabulary**
fact extensions • multiples • combinations of ten

 **Common Core State Standards**

Focus Cluster
Use place value understanding and properties of operations to perform multi-digit arithmetic.

1 Warm Up 5 min

	Materials	
Mental Math and Fluency Children use combinations of 10 to solve other basic facts.		3.NBT.2

2 Focus 40–50 min

Math Message Children use basic +/− facts to solve multidigit problems.	slate	3.NBT.2 SMP7
Extending Facts to Multiples of 10 Children look for patterns and solve fact extensions.	*Math Masters*, p. TA14 (optional); slate; base-10 blocks (optional)	3.NBT.2 SMP7
Extending to Higher Decades Children solve higher-decade fact extensions.	slate, number grid	3.NBT.2 SMP7
Extending Combinations of 10 Children use combinations of 10 to solve fact extensions.	*Math Journal 1*, p. 32; calculator; number grids; base-10 blocks (optional); Class Data Pad (optional)	3.NBT.2 SMP6, SMP7

✓ **Assessment Check-In** See page 129. | *Math Journal 1*, p. 32 | 3.NBT.2 , SMP7

CCSS 3.NBT.2 Spiral Snapshot

GMC Add within 1,000 fluently.

| 1-4 Focus Practice | 2-1 Warm Up Focus | 2-2 through 2-5 Warm Up Focus Practice | 2-6 Practice | 2-10 Practice | 2-11 Focus Practice | 2-12 Warm Up |

Spiral Tracker (Go Online) to see how mastery develops for all standards within the grade.

3 Practice 15–20 min

Minute Math+ Children solve teacher-selected problems from *Minute Math+*.	*Minute Math®+*	
Finding Elapsed Time Children solve elapsed-time number stories.	*Math Journal 1*, p. 33; toolkit clock; demonstration clock	3.MD.1
Math Boxes 2-1 Children practice and maintain skills.	*Math Journal 1*, p. 34	See page 129.
Home Link 2-1 **Homework** Children solve fact extension problems.	*Math Masters*, p. 47	3.NBT.2

connectED.mcgraw-hill.com

Plan your lessons online with these tools.

 ePresentations

 Student Learning Center

 Facts Workshop Game

 eToolkit

 Professional Development

 Home Connections

 Spiral Tracker

 Assessment and Reporting

 ELL English Learners Support

Differentiation Support

Differentiation Options RtI

CCSS 3.NBT.2

Readiness
10–15 min

| WHOLE CLASS |
| SMALL GROUP |
| PARTNER |
| INDEPENDENT |

Practicing Addition and Subtraction Facts with Games and Fact Triangles

Math Journal 1, Activity Sheets 4–5; *Student Reference Book,* pp. 255 and 261

To prepare children to solve fact extensions, have them play games that practice addition and subtraction facts. Children were introduced to *Addition Top-It* and *Subtraction Top-It* in *Kindergarten Everyday Mathematics,* and they played *Salute!* in first and second grades. Select one or more of the games. Directions can be found on *Student Reference Book,* pages 255 and 261. Play a few rounds with children. Observe which fact strategies they use, and encourage the use of efficient strategies. You may also wish to have children cut apart and practice the +/− Fact Triangles on Activity Sheets 4 and 5. Have children play the games and practice with the Fact Triangles at school and at home so they develop automaticity with these facts.

CCSS 3.NBT.2, SMP7

Enrichment
5–10 min

| WHOLE CLASS |
| SMALL GROUP |
| PARTNER |
| INDEPENDENT |

Solving Fact Extensions Mentally

Math Masters, p. 45

To extend work with fact extensions, have children solve higher-decade fact extensions mentally. Ask partners to take turns posing a basic addition or subtraction fact, followed by extensions with larger numbers. **GMP7.2** For example: *What is:* 8 + 7 ? 15; 18 + 7 ? 25; 58 + 7 ? 65 Then have partners discuss the patterns in the digits. **GMP7.1** Begin with 2-digit problems and progress to 3-digits.

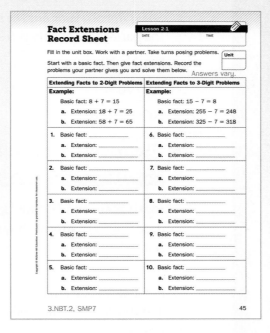

CCSS 3.NBT.2, SMP7

Extra Practice
5–10 min

| WHOLE CLASS |
| SMALL GROUP |
| PARTNER |
| INDEPENDENT |

Solving More Fact Extensions

Math Masters, p. 46; calculator; number grid (optional)

For practice with fact extensions, have children complete problems on *Math Masters,* page 46. Encourage them to think about what combinations of 10 could help them solve problems with larger numbers. **GMP7.2**

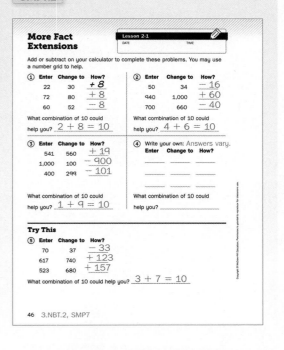

English Language Learners Support

Beginning ELL To support children's understanding of the term *extension* and to connect it to the base word *extend,* use a physical model to relate the terms to an everyday item, such as an extension cord. For example, say: *This electrical cord is not long enough. I need to add another cord to make it longer. I need to extend the cord. I need an extension cord.* Relate the idea of extending as you introduce fact extensions.

(Go Online) **ELL** English Learners Support

SMP6 **Attend to precision.**

GMP6.1 Explain your mathematical thinking clearly and precisely.

SMP7 **Look for and make use of structure.**

GMP7.1 Look for mathematical structures such as categories, patterns, and properties.

GMP7.2 Use structures to solve problems and answer questions.

Professional Development

Research suggests that mastering addition doubles ($1 + 1$, $2 + 2$, and so on) and combinations of 10 ($5 + 5$, $4 + 6$, and so on) helps children derive challenging addition and subtraction facts. Beginning in *Kindergarten Everyday Mathematics*, children work toward mastering these facts and develop strategies for deriving all other addition and subtraction facts. As children enter Grade 3, they should be automatic with addition facts within 20 and fluent with subtraction facts within 20.

---

1 Warm Up 5 min

Go Online
ePresentations eToolkit

▶ Mental Math and Fluency

Have children share how they can use the left pair of facts to help solve the right pair of facts. *Leveled exercises:*

◐○○ $5 + 5 = ?$ $5 + 6 = ?$ Add 1 more
     $9 + 1 = ?$ $9 + 3 = ?$ Add 2 more

◐◐○ $8 + 2 = ?$ $8 + 3 = ?$ Add 1 more
     $9 + 1 = ?$ $9 + 4 = ?$ Add 3 more

◐◐◐ $8 + 2 = ?$ $8 + 5 = ?$ Add 3 more
     $7 + 3 = ?$ $7 + 8 = ?$ Add 5 more

2 Focus 40–50 min

Go Online
ePresentations eToolkit

▶ Math Message

Solve. Record your answers on your slate. Think about the patterns that help you solve each set. **GMP7.1, GMP7.2**

$9 - 7 = ?$ 2	$? 16 = 7 + 9$
$90 - 70 = ?$ 20	$? 160 = 70 + 90$
$900 - 700 = ?$ 200	$? 1,600 = 700 + 900$

Unit
books

▶ Extending Facts to Multiples of 10

WHOLE CLASS	SMALL GROUP	PARTNER	INDEPENDENT

Math Message Follow-Up Have children share solution strategies and describe any patterns they noticed. Ask: *In each set, how are the problems related?* **GMP7.1** Sample answer: The numbers in the problems go from ones to tens to hundreds.

Remind children that another way to think of 90 is nine tens, or nine [10s], and 700 is seven hundreds, or seven [100s]. Model how to rewrite these problems:

$9 \text{ [1s]} - 7 \text{ [1s]} = 2 \text{ [1s]}$ $16 \text{ [1s]} = 7 \text{ [1s]} + 9 \text{ [1s]}$

$9 \text{ [10s]} - 7 \text{ [10s]} = 2 \text{ [10s]}$ $16 \text{ [10s]} = 7 \text{ [10s]} + 9 \text{ [10s]}$

$9 \text{ [100s]} - 7 \text{ [100s]} = 2 \text{ [100s]}$ $16 \text{ [100s]} = 7 \text{ [100s]} + 9 \text{ [100s]}$

Have children point out the basic fact in each problem set. Explain that the other problems in each set are called **fact extensions.** Children use their knowledge of basic facts to calculate with the larger numbers in fact extensions.

Explain **multiples** of 10 and 100 as products of counting numbers and 10 or 100. For example, 90 is a multiple of 10 because 90 is 9 groups of 10, or 9 × 10. And 900 is a multiple of 100 because 900 is 9 groups of 100, or 9 × 100. Ask: *How does knowing addition and subtraction facts help you add and subtract multiples of 10 and 100?* GMP7.2 Sample answer: They extend facts we already know. Explain that children will continue using basic facts to solve addition and subtraction fact extensions in this lesson.

Have children solve and briefly discuss more simple fact extensions.

> **Differentiate** **Adjusting the Activity**
>
> Have children who struggle to solve fact extensions involving multiples of 10 and 100 work with a 3-Digit Place-Value Mat (*Math Masters,* page TA14). Have them represent each problem with base-10 blocks. Help children connect the fact extensions and basic facts.
>
> Go Online Differentiation Support

▶ Extending to Higher Decades

| WHOLE CLASS | SMALL GROUP | PARTNER | INDEPENDENT |

Display higher-decade fact extensions and sums in a column:

$6 + 8 = 14$ $26 + 8 = 34$ $46 + 8 = 54$

Ask: *Which is the basic fact?* $6 + 8 = 14$ *What is the same about the addends in each problem?* Sample answer: 8 is one of the addends. There is a 6 in the ones place of the other. *What do you notice about the sums?* GMP7.1 Sample answers: The sums all have a 4 in the ones place. In each sum, the digit in the 10s place is 1 more than the tens place digit in the first addend. Explain and record each fact extension as the sum of $6 + 8$ and a multiple of 10. For example, in the second problem, $20 + 6 + 8$ or $2 [10s] + 6 + 8$.

Model how to use the number grid to relate fact extensions (*see margin*) and display more problems for children to solve. *Suggestions:*

$? 8 = 13 - 5$ $? 38 = 43 - 5$ $? 68 = 73 - 5$

$11 - 6 = ? 5$ $21 - 6 = ? 15$ $51 - 6 = ? 45$

Encourage children to use the number grid as needed. Have volunteers share their responses. Ask:

- *In each set, how are the problems related?* GMP7.1 Sample answers: The ones digit stays the same in all of them. In the differences, the tens digit changes, but the ones digit remains the same.
- *How does knowing basic facts help you add or subtract larger numbers?* GMP7.2 Sample answer: It helps me know the digit in the ones place.

$12 - 5 = 7$

$120 - 50 = 70$

$1,200 - 500 = 700$

$7 + 8 = 15$

$70 + 80 = 150$

$700 + 800 = 1,500$

Fact extensions involving multiples of 10 and 100

									0
1	2	3	4	5	⑥	7	8	9	10
11	12	13	⑭	15	16	17	18	19	20
21	22	23	24	25	㉖	27	28	29	30
31	32	33	㉞	35	36	37	38	39	40
41	42	43	44	45	㊻	47	48	49	50
51	52	53	㊾	55	56	57	58	59	60
61	62	63	64	65	㊻	67	68	69	70
71	72	73	㊸	75	76	77	78	79	80
81	82	83	84	85	㊏	87	88	89	90
91	92	93	㊼	95	96	97	98	99	100
101	102	103	104	105	106	107	108	109	110

$6 + 8 = 14$ $26 + 8 = 34$ $46 + 8 = 54$
$66 + 8 = 74$ $88 + 8 = 94$

Math Journal 1, p. 32

Using Basic Facts to Solve Fact Extensions   Lesson 2-1
DATE   TIME

Fill in the unit box. Complete the fact extensions.   Unit

① $\underline{\quad 5 \quad} = 12 - 7$
$\underline{\quad 50 \quad} = 120 - 70$
$\underline{\quad 500 \quad} = 1,200 - 700$

② $8 + 3 = \underline{\quad 11 \quad}$
$80 + 30 = \underline{\quad 110 \quad}$
$800 + 300 = \underline{1,100}$

Complete the fact extensions.

③ $\underline{\quad 14 \quad} = 6 + 8$
$\underline{\quad 24 \quad} = 16 + 8$
$\underline{\quad 64 \quad} = 56 + 8$

④ $14 - 9 = \underline{\quad 5 \quad}$
$24 - 9 = \underline{\quad 15 \quad}$
$54 - 9 = \underline{\quad 45 \quad}$

⑤ Explain how you used a basic fact to help you solve Problem 4.
Sample answer: $14 - 9 = 5$ helped me know that there are 5 ones in the differences for the next two problems.

Add or subtract to complete these problems on your calculator. You may also use a number grid or base-10 blocks.

⑥ Enter	Change to	How?	⑦ Enter	Change to	How?
33	40	$+ 7$	430	500	$+ 70$
80	73	$- 7$	700	640	$- 60$
80	23	$- 57$	1,000	400	$- 600$

⑧ What combination of 10 helped you solve Problem 6? Explain.
Sample answer: I used $3 + 7 = 10$. One number in each problem had a 3 in the ones place and the other had a 0 in the ones place. So the answers had to have a 7 in the ones place.

32 thirty-two 3.NBT.2, SMP6, SMP7

Enter	Change to	How?
4	10	+ 6
64	70	+ 6
80	73	− 7
640	632	− 8

Enter	Change to	How?
800	740	− 60
300	1,000	+ 700
570	800	+ 230

Math Journal 1, p. 33

Finding Elapsed Time

Lesson 2-1

DATE   TIME

Use a toolkit clock or an open number line to help you solve these problems. Show your work.

① Ava leaves to go swimming at 4:05 and returns at 4:57. How long has she been gone?

52 minutes

② Deven rides his bike 4 miles. He rides from 10:15 A.M. until 11:20 A.M. How long does it take him to ride 4 miles?

1 hour 5 minutes

Try This

③ LaToya leaves for school at the time shown on the first clock. She returns home at the time shown on the second clock. How long is LaToya away from home?

7 hours 55 minutes

Explain how you figured out the length of LaToya's school day.
Sample answer: I counted 40 minutes from 8:20 to 9:00.
Then I counted 7 hours from 9:00 to 4:00. Then there were
15 more minutes. So the total time was 7 hours and
55 minutes.

3.MD.1   thirty-three   33

▶ Extending Combinations of 10

Math Journal 1, p. 32

| WHOLE CLASS | SMALL GROUP | PARTNER | INDEPENDENT |

Remind children of their work in prior grades with **combinations of 10,** which are pairs of whole numbers that add to 10. Explain that these facts can help solve problems with larger numbers. You may wish to briefly review and record all combinations of 10 on the Class Data Pad ($0 + 10 = 10, 1 + 9 = 10, 2 + 8 = 10, 3 + 7 = 10$, and so on).

Display the following in a column:

$3 +$ ____ $= 10$ $33 +$ ____ $= 40$ $83 +$ ____ $= 90$

Ask: *What is the missing addend in these problems?* GMP7.1   7
How does knowing $3 + 7 = 10$ help you solve the last two problems?
GMP7.2   Sample answer: I know that 7 and a number with 3 in the ones place add to 10 or a multiple of 10.

Have children use calculators to solve problems involving extensions of combinations of 10. As children work, have them share their strategies and which combination of 10 may have been helpful. GMP6.1, GMP7.2

Display a table like the first one in the margin. Fill in the *Enter* and *Change to* numbers. Record children's answers in the *How?* column. For the first problem, have children enter 4 into their calculators and try to change it to 10. Ask: *Did you add or subtract? What number? Explain your strategy.* Sample answer: I need to add because the number gets larger. I add 6 to 4 to get to 10. Guide children through the remaining problems.

When children are comfortable with using combinations of 10 to solve extensions, move to more challenging problems. Highlight combinations of 10 for each problem. *Suggestions:*

- *Enter 46. Change it to 70. What did you do?* Added 24 *Explain your strategy.* Sample answer: I know $6 + 4 = 10$, so $46 + 4 = 50$. Since I know that $5 + 2 = 7, 50 + 20 = 70$. Finally, $4 + 20 = 24$.
- *Enter 80. Change it to 38. What did you do?* Subtracted 42 *Explain your strategy.* GMP6.1, GMP7.2   Sample answer: I can get from 80 to 40 by subtracting 4 [10s]. I know $2 + 8 = 10$, so $10 − 2 = 8$. I can take away 2 from 40 to get 38. So, $80 − 42 = 38$.

Next extend the problems to jumps by 10s and 100s as shown in the second table in the margin.

Differentiate   **Common Misconception**

If children struggle to jump from the *Enter* to the *Change to* number using multiples of 10 or 100, encourage them to repeatedly add or subtract 10 or 100. For example, to change from 800 to 740, a child could subtract 10 six times and record $−10, −10, −10, −10, −10, −10$ or $−60$, or $−6$ [10s] in the *How?* column.

Go Online   Differentiation Support

As children work on journal page 32, ask questions similar to those posed to the whole class. Encourage children to use a number grid.

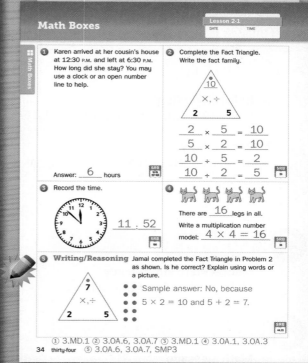

✓ **Assessment Check-In** CCSS 3.NBT.2

Math Journal 1, p. 32

Expect most children to correctly solve Problems 1–5 on journal page 32. **GMP7.2** Some children may use a number grid for Problems 3 and 4. Have children who struggle with basic facts play facts games and practice with +/− Fact Triangles (*Math Journal 1*, Activity Sheets 4–5) as suggested in the Readiness activity. For children who struggle to extend facts, implement the suggestion in the Adjusting the Activity note and encourage the use of the number grid.

☑ Assessment and Reporting **Go Online** to record student progress and to see trajectories toward mastery for this standard.

Summarize Have partners explain to each other how they used a basic fact to solve one of the problems on journal page 32. **GMP6.1, GMP7.2**

---

3 Practice 15–20 min **Go Online** ePresentations eToolkit Home Connections

▶ *Minute Math+*

Beginning in Unit 2, a reminder to use *Minute Math+* activities regularly appears in this part of the lesson. Choose any *Minute Math+* activity.

▶ **Finding Elapsed Time**

Math Journal 1, p. 33

| WHOLE CLASS | SMALL GROUP | PARTNER | INDEPENDENT |

Have children calculate elapsed times on journal page 33. Invite volunteers to share their solution strategies using a demonstration clock or an open number line.

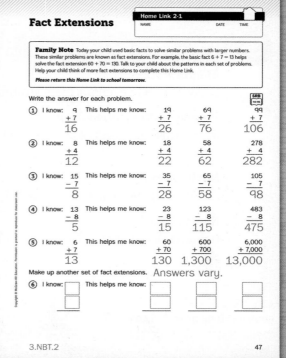

▶ **Math Boxes 2-1** ✏️

Math Journal 1, p. 34

| WHOLE CLASS | SMALL GROUP | PARTNER | INDEPENDENT |

Mixed Practice Math Boxes 2-1 are paired with Math Boxes 2-3.

▶ **Home Link 2-1**

Math Masters, p. 47

Homework Children practice fact extensions.

Number Stories

Overview Children use diagrams or pictures to help solve number stories.

▶ **Before You Begin**
For Part 3 Practice, write the numbers 2, 2, 5, 5, 10, 10 on each face of a blank die per partnership.

▶ **Vocabulary**
parts-and-total diagram • change diagram • comparison diagram • unknown • number model

 Common Core State Standards

Focus Clusters
- Solve problems involving the four operations, and identify and explain patterns in arithmetic.
- Use place value understanding and properties of operations to perform multi-digit arithmetic.

1 Warm Up 5 min

Materials

Mental Math and Fluency
Children solve fact extensions.

slate

3.NBT.2

2 Focus 40–50 min

Math Message
Children read about a nest of animal eggs called a *clutch*.

Student Reference Book, pp. 266–267

Using the Guide to Solving Number Stories
Children review parts-and-total, change, and comparison number stories.

Student Reference Book, pp. 30 and 266–267; *Math Masters,* pp. TA15–TA16

3.OA.8, 3.NBT.2
SMP1

Solving Number Stories
Children solve number stories and share strategies.

Math Journal 1, pp. 35–36; *Student Reference Book,* p. 30; *Math Masters,* p. TA16

3.OA.8, 3.NBT.2
SMP1

✓ **Assessment Check-In**   See page 135.

Math Journal 1, pp. 35–36

3.NBT.2, SMP1

CCSS 3.OA.8 **Spiral Snapshot**

GMC Assess the reasonableness of answers to problems.

| 2-2 Focus | 2-3 through 2-5 Focus | 3-2 through 3-6 Focus Practice | 3-7 through 3-10 Practice | 3-12 Practice |

 Spiral Tracker   Go Online to see how mastery develops for all standards within the grade.

3 Practice 15–20 min

Minute Math+
Children practice mental math strategies.

Minute Math®+

Playing *Multiplication Draw*
Game Children practice 2s, 5s, and 10s facts.

Student Reference Book, p. 248; *Math Masters,* p. G6; die labeled with 2, 2, 5, 5, 10, 10; number cards 1–10 (4 of each)

3.OA.7
SMP7

Math Boxes 2-2
Children practice and maintain skills.

Math Journal 1, p. 37

See page 135.

Home Link 2-2
Homework Children solve parts-and-total number stories.

Math Masters, p. 49

3.OA.8, 3.NBT.2

---

 connectED.mcgraw-hill.com

Plan your lessons online with these tools.

 ePresentations

 Student Learning Center

Facts Workshop Game

eToolkit

 Professional Development

Home Connections

 Spiral Tracker

 Assessment and Reporting

 English Learners Support

 Differentiation Support

Differentiation Options RtI

Readiness
5–10 min

Matching Number Sentences to Number Stories

| WHOLE CLASS |
| SMALL GROUP |
| PARTNER |
| INDEPENDENT |

To practice making sense of problems, have children match number sentences to number stories. Pose a number story such as: *I have 10 pencils. Some are yellow and 6 are red. How many yellow pencils do I have?* Display number sentences: $10 - ? = 6$, $6 + 10 = ?$, and $10 - 6 = ?$. Have children explain why each number sentence models or does not model the story. Sample answers: $10 - ? = 6$ and $10 - 6 = ?$ both fit the story because we know there are 6 red pencils and 10 pencils all together. So we are looking for the difference between red pencils and all the pencils to find the number of yellow pencils. $6 + 10 = ?$ doesn't match because there are only 10 pencils in all, not 16. Encourage children to draw pictures or use diagrams to help organize the information. **GMP1.1, GMP2.2**

Enrichment
10–15 min

Writing Two Number Models to Fit One Story

| WHOLE CLASS |
| SMALL GROUP |
| PARTNER |
| INDEPENDENT |

Activity Card 19; *Student Reference Book*, pp. 266–267; *Math Masters*, p. TA8

To apply children's understanding of number stories, have them write a number story for a partner to solve. Then have them write at least two number models that fit each story. Have children record their work on *Math Masters*, page TA8 and include diagrams or pictures to represent their stories. **GMP4.1, GMP4.2** When both stories are complete, have children compare the number models for each. **GMP1.6**

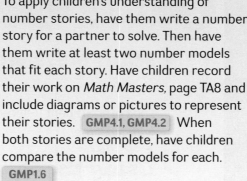

Writing Two Number Models to Fit One Story 19

What You Need
Student Reference Book, pages 266–267
A Number Story, page TA8

What To Do
Work with a partner.
1. Write a number story using information about the animals from *Student Reference Book*, pages 266–267.
2. Trade number stories with your partner.
3. Draw pictures, situation diagrams, or other representations of the story in the large box.
4. Write at least two number models that can be used to solve the problem.
5. Solve your partner's problem. Show your work.
6. Write the answer including the unit.
7. Check that your partner's number models fit your number story.

I have to think of one more number model.

Talk About It
Compare the number models for each story. How can each number model be used to solve the same problem?
How do the pictures, diagrams, or other representations fit the stories?

More You Can Do
Rewrite your number story for a different partner to solve. Compare how your two partners solved the number story.

Extra Practice
5–10 min

Writing Number Models and Solving Number Stories

| WHOLE CLASS |
| SMALL GROUP |
| PARTNER |
| INDEPENDENT |

Student Reference Book, p. 268; *Math Masters*, p. 48

To provide practice with number stories, have children use the information on *Student Reference Book*, page 268 to solve number stories on *Math Masters*, page 48. Children may draw diagrams to help organize the number story information. Have them write number models with a question mark to fit their stories. **GMP4.1**

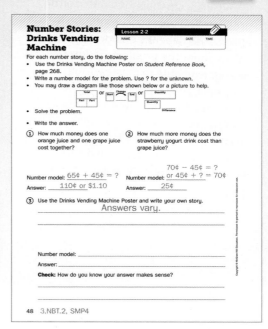

Number Stories: Drinks Vending Machine   Lesson 2-2

NAME   DATE   TIME

For each number story, do the following:
• Use the Drinks Vending Machine Poster on *Student Reference Book*, page 268.
• Write a number model for the problem. Use ? for the unknown.
• You may draw a diagram like those shown below or a picture to help.

Total / Part Part   Quantity / Start End   Quantity Quantity Difference

• Solve the problem.
• Write the answer.

1. How much money does one orange juice and one grape juice cost together?

2. How much more money does the strawberry yogurt drink cost than grape juice?

Number model: $65¢ + 45¢ = ?$
Answer: $110¢$ or $1.10

$70¢ - 45¢ = ?$
Number model: or $45¢ + ? = 70¢$
Answer: $25¢$

3. Use the Drinks Vending Machine Poster and write your own story.
Answers vary.

Number model: _____
Answer: _____
Check: How do you know your answer makes sense?
_____

48   3.NBT.2, SMP4

English Language Learners Support

Beginning ELL Use a think-aloud to introduce the prefix *un-* while demonstrating being able and unable to reach something. Use *un-* and *not* interchangeably, as in: *I am unable to reach the top shelf. I am not able to reach the top shelf.* Next show a complete number sentence, such as $20 + 7 = 27$. Point to the sum and say: *This is known.* Rewrite it with a question mark for the sum and say: *This is not known. It is unknown.* Repeat with other number sentences and change the position of the question marks.

Go Online > **ELL** English Learners Support

Standards and Goals for
Mathematical Practice

SMP1 **Make sense of problems and persevere in solving them.**
   GMP1.1 Make sense of your problem.
   GMP1.4 Check whether your answer makes sense.
   GMP1.6 Compare the strategies you and others use.

Professional Development

In Lessons 2-2 and 2-3, children review situation diagrams as one way to organize information and model number stories. There is not necessarily one kind of diagram that goes with a given problem. The best representation for a child to use depends on how the child thinks about the problem. Children are not expected to master using diagrams. They may choose to use diagrams, drawings, numbers, words, or other representations to make sense of and solve problems. For more information about situation diagrams, see Unit 2 Mathematical Background pages.

① Warm Up 5 min

▶ Mental Math and Fluency

Have children solve fact extensions and record their answers on slates. *Leveled exercises:*

● ○ ○   8 + 8 = ?   16   80 + 80 = ?   160   800 + 800 = ?   1,600

● ● ○   15 − 7 = ?   8   150 − 70 = ?   80   1,500 − 700 = ?   800

● ● ●   6 + 9 = ?   15   26 + 9 = ?   35   46 + 9 = ?   55

② Focus 40–50 min

▶ Math Message

Student Reference Book, pp. 266–267

Look over Student Reference Book, *pages 266–267. Share what you find with a partner.*

▶ Using the Guide to Solving Number Stories

Student Reference Book, pp. 30 and 266–267; *Math Masters,* pp. TA15–TA16

| WHOLE CLASS | SMALL GROUP | PARTNER | INDEPENDENT |

Math Message Follow-Up Have children share their observations about the animal clutches information in the *Student Reference Book.* Sample answers: All these animals lay eggs. A clutch is a nest of eggs. Animal clutches come in different sizes.

Tell children they will use data on animal clutches to solve a number story.

Display the Guide to Solving Number Stories from *Math Masters,* page TA15 or have children refer to *Student Reference Book,* page 30. To promote flexibility in children's problem solving, you may want to vary the order in which these guiding questions are asked. The questions are not a step-by-step procedure, but they provide children with ideas about what to do when they are stuck or checking to make sure they are finished.

Display a unit box with "eggs" as the label and pose the following:

Two pythons each laid a clutch of eggs. There were 59 eggs in all. One clutch had 36 eggs. How many eggs were in the other clutch?

Make sense of the problem.
   • *Think. What do you know from reading the story?* Two pythons laid a total of 59 eggs. One clutch had 36 eggs.
   • *What do you want to find out?* The number of eggs in the other clutch

Make a plan.

What do you have to do to find the number of eggs in the other clutch?
Sample answer: Find the difference between 59 and 36.

Children may suggest modeling the problem with counters or drawings,
or they may remember using diagrams from *First* and *Second Grade
Everyday Mathematics*. Display **parts-and-total, change,** and **comparison
diagrams** (*Math Masters,* page TA16) and explain that diagrams can help
organize information in the problem. Ask: *Which diagrams might fit the
story?* Sample answers: Parts-and-total, comparison Have children explain
how they make sense of the problem. GMP1.1

Parts-and-Total Children may reason that there is one known part, one
unknown part, and a known total. Have a volunteer complete the diagram.
Ask guiding questions such as: *Where might you write 59?* In the Total
box *36?* In a Part box Explain that we know these numbers from the story.
Write a question mark in the blank Part box to represent what we want to
find out, or the **unknown.**

Total	
59	
Part	Part
36	?

Comparison Children may wonder how many more eggs they need in
order to get from 36 to 59 eggs. Have a volunteer compare the quantities
of eggs and identify which is more and which is less, and then complete
the diagram. Ask: *Which number goes in the long Quantity box?* 59 *Why?*
Because it is the larger number. *Short Quantity box?* 36 *Where does the ?
go?* On the Difference line

Quantity
59

Quantity	
36	?

Difference

Remind children that **number models** are numbers and symbols that fit a
number story or situation. *What number models might we write for this
problem?* Sample answers: $? = 59 - 36$; $36 + ? = 59$ *What does the ?
represent?* The number of eggs in the other clutch

Solve the problem.

Have children solve the problem and share strategies. Some children may
record a strategy, while others may use mental computation. (*See margin.*)
Ask the following questions to help children make sense of and compare
each other's strategies. GMP1.6

• *How would you explain this child's strategy?*

• *How is your strategy similar to or different from this child's?*

Record the answer with units. There are 23 eggs in the other clutch.

Math Masters, p. TA15

**Guide to Solving
Number Stories**

NAME _____ DATE ___ TIME ___

Make sense of the problem.

• Read the problem. What do you understand?

• What do you know?

• What do you need to find out?

Make a plan.

What will you do?

• Add?	• Make a table?
• Subtract?	• Make a graph?
• Multiply?	• Write a number model?
• Divide?	• Use counters or base-10 blocks?
• Draw a picture?	• Make tallies?
• Draw a diagram?	• Use a number grid or number line?

Solve the problem.

• Show your work.

• Keep trying if you get stuck.

→ Reread the problem.

→ Think about the strategies you have already tried and try new
  strategies.

• Write your answer with the units.

Check.

Does your answer make sense? How do you know?

TA15

Mental computation:

Example: $59 - 36 = ?$

I know that $50 - 30$ is 20 and $9 - 6$ is 3,
so $59 - 36 = 23$.

Counting up:

Example: $36 + ? = 59$

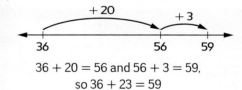

$36 + 20 = 56$ and $56 + 3 = 59$,
so $36 + 23 = 59$

Second Grade Everyday Mathematics
introduced children to counting up on open
number lines.

Sample Solution Strategies

Math Journal 1, p. 35

Number Stories

Lesson 2-2
DATE   TIME

For each number story:

• Write a number model. Use ? for the unknown.
• You may draw a diagram like those shown below or a picture to help.

• Solve the number story and write your answer.
• Explain how you know your answer makes sense.

① Two pythons each laid a clutch of eggs. One clutch had 47 eggs.
The other had 32 eggs. How many eggs were there in all?

Number model: ____47 + 32 = ?____

Answer the question: ____79 eggs____
(unit)

Check: How do you know your answer makes sense?
Sample answer: The total number of eggs has
to be larger than either of the clutches.

② An alligator clutch had 60 eggs. Only 12 hatched. How many eggs did
not hatch?

Number model: _60 − 12 = ? or 12 + ? = 60_

Answer the question: ____48 eggs____
(unit)

Check: How do you know your answer makes sense? Sample answer:
The number of unhatched eggs has to be less than the total.
I estimated 60 − 10 = 50, and 50 is close to 48.

3.OA.8, 3.NBT.2, SMP1   thirty-five   35

Math Journal 1, p. 36

Number Stories (continued)

Lesson 2-2
DATE   TIME

③ Ahmed had $22 in his bank account. For his birthday,
his grandmother deposited $25 for him. How much money
is in his bank account now?

Unit
dollars

Number model: ____22 + 25 = ?____

Answer the question: ____$47____

Check: How do you know your answer makes sense?
Sample answer: The end number has to be
greater than the start and change numbers.

④ Omar had $53 in his piggy bank. He used $16 to take his sister to the movies
and buy treats. How much money is left in his piggy bank?

Number model: _53 − 16 = ? or 16 + ? = 53_

Answer the question: ____$37____

Check: How do you know your answer makes sense?
Sample answer: The answer has to be less
than $53.

36   thirty-six   3.OA.8, 3.NBT.2, SMP1

Check.

Discuss strategies for checking answers. [GMP1.4] Sample answers given.

• *What strategies could you use to check your answer?* I could add 36
and 23 to see if I get 59.

• *Does your answer make sense? How do you know?* Yes. The number
of eggs in the clutch has to be smaller than the total number of eggs.
My answer makes the number model true.

Display a number model to summarize the story: 59 = 36 + 23.

Change the label in the unit box to "dollars." Pose another number story:
*José had $76. He spent some money. Now he has $47. How much did he
spend?* He spent $29.

Ask questions from the Guide for Solving Number Stories in a different
order to help children make sense of the problem. [GMP1.1]

Before children begin, ask: *Which diagrams might help you organize
the information in the story?* Sample answers: Change, comparison,
parts-and-total

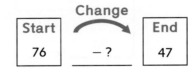

A change diagram. Because the end amount is less than
the start amount, this is a change-to-less diagram.
76 − ? = 47

Quantity
76

Quantity	
47	?

Difference

A comparison diagram
76 − 47 = ?

Total	
76	
Part	Part
47	?

A parts-and-total diagram
47 + ? = 76

Then have children solve the problem, share their solution strategies, and
write summary number models: 76 − 29 = 47, 76 − 47 = 29, 47 + 29 = 76.

▶ Solving Number Stories

Math Journal 1, pp. 35–36; Student Reference Book, p. 30; Math Masters, p. TA16

WHOLE CLASS	SMALL GROUP	PARTNER	INDEPENDENT

Have children solve the number stories on journal pages 35–36. Encourage
them to refer to the Guide to Solving Number Stories. Children may draw
diagrams or pictures to help solve the problems. When most children
have finished, bring them together to compare and contrast diagrams and
other representations for each number story and to share how they made
sense of the problems. [GMP1.1, GMP1.6]

Assessment Check-In (CCSS) 3.NBT.2

Math Journal 1, pp. 35–36

Expect most children to make sense of and solve Problems 1–4 and to write number models with question marks for the unknowns. For children who struggle to make sense of and solve the problems, ask the guiding questions from the lesson. If children struggle to write a number model, suggest that they use a situation diagram or draw a picture to help organize the information from the story. **GMP1.1**

☑ Assessment and Reporting | Go Online ⟩ to record student progress and to see trajectories toward mastery for this standard.

Summarize Ask: *How do you know your answer makes sense?*
GMP1.4 Sample answers: It should fit the number story. It should make my number model true.

3 Practice 15–20 min Go Online ⟩
ePresentations eToolkit Home Connections

▶ Minute Math+

To practice mental math strategies, select a *Minute Math+* activity.

▶ Playing *Multiplication Draw*

Student Reference Book, p. 248; *Math Masters*, p. G6

| WHOLE CLASS | SMALL GROUP | **PARTNER** | INDEPENDENT |

To provide additional fact practice, have children play *Multiplication Draw* and record their play on *Math Masters*, page G6. Directions are found on *Student Reference Book*, page 248.

Differentiate **Game Modifications** Go Online ⟩ Differentiation Support

▶ Math Boxes 2-2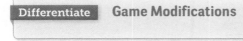

Math Journal 1, p. 37

| WHOLE CLASS | SMALL GROUP | PARTNER | INDEPENDENT |

Mixed Practice Math Boxes 2-2 are paired with Math Boxes 2-4.

▶ Home Link 2-2

Math Masters, p. 49

Homework Children solve number stories.

Math Journal 1, p. 37

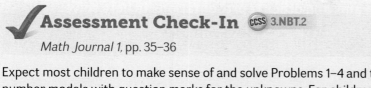

Math Boxes Lesson 2-2 DATE TIME

① Choose the best answer.
The mass of a centimeter cube is about
Ⓐ 1 gram.
Ⓑ 10 grams.
Ⓒ 50 grams.
Ⓓ 100 grams.

② Round each number to the nearest 10. You may draw open number lines to help.
68 _70_
83 _80_

③ Rachel has 3 packages of seeds. Each package has 10 seeds. How many seeds does she have in all?

Answer: _30_ seeds
Write a multiplication number model. $3 \times 10 = 30$

④ [bar graph: Books Read — Max, Li, Kay, Tim]
How many more books did Li read than Max? _15_ books
How many books did Kay and Tim read all together? _25_ books

⑤ **Writing/Reasoning** Write a number story to fit $2 \times 4 = 8$.
Sample answer: Mary has 2 pockets. She has 4 beads in each pocket. How many beads does she have in all? She has 8 beads.
Explain how your number story fits $2 \times 4 = 8$.
Sample answer: There are 2 groups of 4 beads, so $2 \times 4 = 8$.

① 3.MD.2 ② 3.NBT.1 ③ 3.OA.1, 3.OA.3 ④ 3.MD.3
⑤ 3.OA.1, 3.OA.3, SMP2   thirty-seven 37

Math Masters, p. 49

Number Stories Home Link 2-2 NAME DATE TIME

Family Note Today your child reviewed parts-and-total, change, and comparison diagrams. These diagrams help organize the information in a number story. For more information, see *Student Reference Book*, page 76. Remind your child to write the unit with the answer. For example, the problem below asks about the number of cans, so the answer should include cans as the unit.
Please return this Home Link to school tomorrow.

For the problem below:
• Write a number model. Use ? for the unknown.
• You may draw a diagram like the ones shown below or a picture to help.

[diagrams: Total/Part Part; Start Change End; Quantity Quantity Difference]

• Solve the problem and write your answer.
• Explain how you know your answer makes sense.

The second- and third-grade classes collected 750 cans to recycle. The second graders collected 300 cans. How many cans did the third graders collect?
Number model: Sample answers: $750 - 300 = ?$; $300 + ? = 750$

Answer the question: _450 cans_
(unit)

Check: How do you know your answer makes sense? Sample answer: The unknown has to be smaller than 750. I know $3 + 4 = 7$, so 3 [100s] + 4 [100s] is 7 [100s]. And 7 [100s] + 50 is 750.

3.OA.8, 3.NBT.2   49

More Number Stories

Overview Children use situation diagrams and other representations to help solve number stories.

▶ **Vocabulary**
equation

Common Core State Standards

Focus Clusters
- Solve problems involving the four operations, and identify and explain patterns in arithmetic.
- Use place value understanding and properties of operations to perform multi-digit arithmetic.

---

1 Warm Up 5 min

	Materials	
Mental Math and Fluency Children solve fact extensions.	slate	3.NBT.2

---

2 Focus 45–50 min

Math Message Children solve a number story.		3.NBT.2
Organizing Number Story Information Children share strategies to make sense of number stories.	*Student Reference Book,* p. 30; *Math Masters,* pp. TA15–TA16	3.OA.8, 3.NBT.2 SMP1
Solving More Number Stories Children solve number stories.	*Math Journal 1,* pp. 38–39	3.OA.8, 3.NBT.2 SMP1
✓ **Assessment Check-In** See page 140.	*Math Journal 1,* pp. 38–39	3.OA.8, 3.NBT.2, SMP1

CCSS 3.NBT.2 **Spiral Snapshot**

GMC Subtract within 1,000 fluently.

2-1 Warm Up Focus Practice	2-2 Warm Up Focus Practice	2-3 Warm Up Focus Practice	2-4 Warm Up Focus Practice	2-5 Focus Practice	2-10 Practice	2-11 Warm Up Focus Practice	2-12 Warm Up Practice

/// **Spiral Tracker** **Go Online** to see how mastery develops for all standards within the grade.

---

3 Practice 10–15 min

Minute Math+ Children practice mental math strategies.	*Minute Math®+*	
Sorting Fact Triangles Children practice 2s, 5s, and 10s facts with Fact Triangles.	*Student Reference Book,* p. 248 (optional); *Math Masters,* p. G6 (optional); Fact Triangles; die labeled 2, 2, 5, 5, 10, 10 (optional); number cards 1–10 (4 of each) (optional)	3.OA.7
Math Boxes 2-3 Children practice and maintain skills.	*Math Journal 1,* p. 40	See page 141.
Home Link 2-3 **Homework** Children solve a change number story.	*Math Masters,* p. 51	3.OA.8, 3.NBT.2

---

ePresentations Student Learning Center Facts Workshop Game eToolkit Professional Development Home Connections Spiral Tracker Assessment and Reporting English Learners Support Differentiation Support

Differentiation Options
RtI

Readiness — 10–15 min

Changing the Calculator Display

WHOLE CLASS
SMALL GROUP
PARTNER
INDEPENDENT

Math Masters, pp. 50 and TA2 (or inside front cover of *Math Journal 1*); calculator

To provide experience solving change number stories, have children complete the calculator puzzles on *Math Masters,* page 50. They may use a number grid to help and a calculator to check their answers.

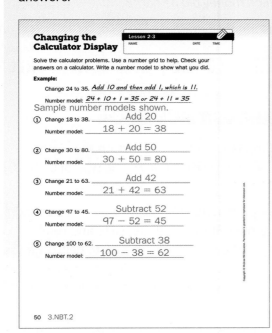

Enrichment — 10–15 min

Writing Number Stories to Match Diagrams

WHOLE CLASS
SMALL GROUP
PARTNER
INDEPENDENT

Activity Card 20; *Math Masters,* pp. TA8 and TA16

To apply children's understanding of number stories, have them write a number story to match their partner's situation diagram. **GMP1.1, GMP2.1** Children should work together to solve and discuss how they know their answers make sense. **GMP1.4, GMP2.2**

Extra Practice — 10–15 min

Writing and Solving Number Stories

WHOLE CLASS
SMALL GROUP
PARTNER
INDEPENDENT

Activity Card 21; *Student Reference Book,* pp. 268 and 269; *Math Masters,* p. TA8

To provide practice with number stories, have children write and solve number stories about costs of vending machine drinks and snacks (*Student Reference Book,* pages 268 and 269) and record their work on *Math Masters,* page TA8. **GMP2.1** Have partners check each other's work and discuss strategies. **GMP1.4, GMP2.2**

English Language Learners Support

Beginning ELL Since the "a" sounds in *equation* and *equal* are different, children may not hear or make the connection between the meanings of the two terms. Scaffold to make connections by displaying the two terms and directing children to use letter tiles to build them. Ask children to point to the letters the two words have in common. e-q-u-a Model the pronunciation of the two words for children to repeat, as you point to examples of equations and to the equal sign.

Go Online | **ELL** English Learners Support

SMP1 **Make sense of problems and persevere in
solving them.**

GMP1.1 Make sense of your problem.

GMP1.4 Check whether your answer makes
sense.

GMP1.6 Compare the strategies you and
others use.

Professional Development

When children continually hear the
same type of problem, they often stop
making sense of the problem and carry
out a rote operation with the numbers.
Exposing them to a variety of problem
types and positions of the unknown
quantity encourages them to attend to
the meaning of the story and develop
flexible thinking. Lessons 2-2 and 2-3
focus on parts-and-total, change-to-
more/less, and comparison problem
types. See Unit 2 Mathematical
Background pages for more on
different problem types.

---

① Warm Up   5 min   Go Online   ePresentations   eToolkit

▶ Mental Math and Fluency

Have children solve fact extensions and record their answers on slates.
Leveled exercises:

●○○ $2 + 9 = ?$ 11 $12 + 9 = ?$ 21 $42 + 9 = ?$ 51
●●○ $13 - 5 = ?$ 8 $33 - 5 = ?$ 28 $63 - 5 = ?$ 58
●●● $14 - 7 = ?$ 7 $44 - 7 = ?$ 37 $84 - 7 = ?$ 77

---

② Focus   45–50 min   Go Online   ePresentations   eToolkit

▶ Math Message

Unit

*Trung had $15 in his piggy bank. He earned money
by walking his neighbor's dogs for two weeks. Now
he has $60 in his bank. How much money did he earn?*

Fill in the unit box and solve the number story.

▶ Organizing Number Story Information

Student Reference Book, p. 30; *Math Masters*, pp. TA15–TA16

WHOLE CLASS   SMALL GROUP   PARTNER   INDEPENDENT

Math Message Follow-Up Circulate as children work on the Math
Message and identify children whose work includes some type of picture
or situation diagram.

Have children tell what label they put in the unit box. dollars or $ Remind
them of the Guide to Solving Number Stories and the parts-and-total,
change, and comparison diagrams they used in Lesson 2-2 to help organize
information from number stories. Tell children they will continue to
use the Guide to Solving Number Stories and diagrams as well as other
representations in today's lesson.

Ask children to describe what they know about the Math Message story.
GMP1.1 We know that Trung started with $15 and ended with $60. Ask:
What do we want to find out? How much money he earned *Did Trung
have more or less money after walking the dogs?* More

Invite children who used situation diagrams or other representations to
share how they organized the information from the story. GMP1.1

Invite volunteers to record their number models. Explain that these number sentences are called **equations** because they have equal signs. Ask: *What does the question mark represent in each number model?* It represents the amount of money Trung earned.

Possible equations:

$15 + ? = 60$	$60 = 15 + ?$	$\begin{array}{r} 15 \\ + \ ? \\ \hline 60 \end{array}$	$\begin{array}{r} 60 \\ - 15 \\ \hline ? \end{array}$
$60 - 15 = ?$	$? = 60 - 15$		

Tell children that they will see number sentences written horizontally and vertically. Explain that in horizontal equations it does not matter what is on the left or right of the equal sign as long as the left side has the same value as the right side. In vertical number sentences the bar acts as the equal sign, there is always something written above it, and the solution is usually written below the bar. Invite children to share their strategies.

Sample strategies:

Decomposing Numbers Some children may break 15 into 10 and 5 and think: "It is easier to subtract in pieces. So $60 - 10$ is 50 and $50 - 5$ is 45."

Compensation Others may use close-but-easier numbers and compensate: "I can subtract 20 from 60 to get 40. Since I only needed to subtract 15, I add 5 back to get 45."

Counting Up Other children may think: "What number added to 15 will give me 60? If I add 5 to 15, I'm at 20. From 20 to 60 is 40, so the answer is $40 + 5$ or 45."

Have children discuss how they can check their answers and whether their answers make sense. Ask: *Should your answer be more or less than $15? Why?* Sample answer: More, because it must add up to 60. $15 + 15$ is only 30. *Will it be more than $60?* No, because he ends with $60. *Does your answer make your number model true?* **GMP1.4** Yes. $15 + 45 = 60$

Record summary number models or equations.

$15 + 45 = 60$	$60 = 15 + 45$	$\begin{array}{r} 15 \\ + 45 \\ \hline 60 \end{array}$	$\begin{array}{r} 60 \\ - 15 \\ \hline 45 \end{array}$
$60 - 15 = 45$	$45 = 60 - 15$		

Two ways to represent the Math Message story

Start — $15   Change $+ ?$ End — 60

The End amount is more than the Start amount, so this is a change-to-more diagram.

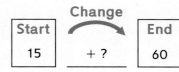

A comparison diagram

Math Journal 1, p. 38

More Number Stories

Lesson 2-3
DATE   TIME

For each number story:

• Write a number model. Use a ? for the unknown.

• You may draw a diagram like the ones below or a picture to help you solve.

| Total |
| Part | Part |

or

Change
| Start | ⌒ | End |

or

| Quantity |
| Quantity |
Difference

• Solve and write your answer with the unit.

• Explain how you know your answer makes sense.

① Cleo had $37. Then Jillian returned $9 that she borrowed. How much money does Cleo have now?
Number model: Sample answer: 37 + 9 = ?

Answer the question: _____ $46 _____
(unit)

Check: How do you know your answer makes sense? Sample answer: It's more than $37, since $9 was added.

② Audrey had $61 in her bank account. She took out $48. How much is left in her account? Sample answers:
Number model: ? = 61 − 48; 48 + ? = 61

Answer the question: _____ $13 _____
(unit)

Check: How do you know your answer makes sense? Sample answer: Audrey has $13 left from $61 because she withdrew $48.

38   thirty-eight   3.OA.8, 3.NBT.2, SMP1

Math Journal 1, p. 39

More Number Stories (continued)

Lesson 2-3
DATE   TIME

③ Pedro had 70¢. He bought grape juice and had 25¢ left. How much did the grape juice cost? Sample answers:
Number model: ? = 70 − 25; 25 + ? = 70

Answer the question: _____ 45¢ _____
(unit)

Check: How do you know your answer makes sense?
Sample answer: If I add 45¢ and 25¢, the answer is 70¢, so my answer makes sense.

④ Nikhil had $40 in his wallet when he went to the carnival. When he got home, he had $18. How much did he spend at the carnival? Sample answers:
Number model: ? = 40 − 18; 18 + ? = 40

Answer the question: _____ $22 _____
(unit)

Check: How do you know your answer makes sense?
Sample answer: Nikhil spent a little more than half of his money. $22 is about right.

3.OA.8, 3.NBT.2, SMP1   thirty-nine   39

Next pose this number story: *There are 43 children in the soccer club and 25 children in the science club. How many fewer children are in the science club?*

Ask: *What do we need to find out?* The difference between the number of children in each club *What should we write in the unit box?* Children

Have children make sense of the number story, plan their work, and solve independently or in partnerships. Encourage them to refer to the Guide to Solving Number Stories on *Student Reference Book,* page 30 and to use pictures or diagrams to help organize information from the story. Remind children to write a number model with a question mark for the unknown, to include a unit with their solution, and to write a summary number model. Circulate as children work and ask guiding questions such as:

• *How will you organize the information from the story?* **GMP1.1**
Sample answers: I will draw a comparison diagram. I will draw base-10 blocks to compare the quantities.

• *What do you know already?* **GMP1.1** There are 43 children in the soccer club and 25 children in the science club.

After a few minutes, bring the class together to share and compare their number models, strategies, and summary number models. Invite children to explain others' strategies based on their representations. **GMP1.6**

Number models with ?: $43 = 25 + ?$, $43 − 25 = ?$, $43 − ? = 25$

Summary number models: $43 = 25 + 18$, $43 − 25 = 18$, $43 − 18 = 25$

▶ Solving More Number Stories

Math Journal 1, pp. 38–39

| WHOLE CLASS | SMALL GROUP | PARTNER | INDEPENDENT |

Have children solve the number stories on journal pages 38–39.

 Assessment Check-In CCSS **3.OA.8, 3.NBT.2**

Math Journal 1, pp. 38–39

Expect most children to make sense of and solve Problems 1–4. Children should also write number models and explain why each answer makes sense. **GMP1.4** For those who struggle to make sense of and solve the problems, ask guiding questions based on the Guide to Solving Number Stories. If children have difficulty writing number models, suggest that they use a situation diagram or draw a picture to help organize the information from the story. If children struggle to check their answers and explain why they make sense, review the problem context and ask questions to help them make sense of their answers. Number stories practice will occur regularly in Math Boxes.

✓ Assessment and Reporting   **Go Online** to record student progress and to see trajectories toward mastery for these standards.

Bring the class together to review the problems. For example, model or have a child share different ways to make sense of Problem 4 with a picture or situation diagram. Ask: *How do you know your answer makes sense?* **GMP1.4, GMP1.6** Sample answers: My answer has to be less than 40 and is a little more than 18, so 22 makes sense. 22 makes 40 − ? = 18 true.

Summarize Have partners share strategies for deciding where they placed question marks for the unknowns in their number models on journal pages 38–39.

Practice   10–15 min

Go Online

ePresentations   eToolkit   Home Connections

▶ Minute Math+

To practice mental math strategies, select a *Minute Math+* activity.

▶ Sorting Fact Triangles

| WHOLE CLASS | **SMALL GROUP** | **PARTNER** | INDEPENDENT |

Have partners use Fact Triangles to practice facts with 2s, 5s, and 10s. Have them sort triangles into two piles—facts they know and facts they need to practice. Fluency with these facts will help children apply strategies introduced in Unit 3. Children already fluent in 2s, 5s, and 10s multiplication facts can either practice related division facts or play an advanced version of *Multiplication Draw*. See *Student Reference Book,* page 248.

▶ Math Boxes 2-3

Math Journal 1, p. 40

| WHOLE CLASS | **SMALL GROUP** | **PARTNER** | **INDEPENDENT** |

Mixed Practice Math Boxes 2-3 are paired with Math Boxes 2-1.

▶ Home Link 2-3

Math Masters, p. 51

Homework Children solve number stories.

Math Journal 1, p. 40

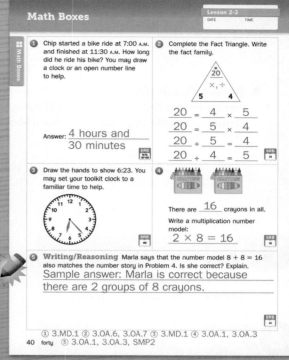

Math Masters, p. 51

Multistep Number Stories, Part 1

Overview Children make sense of and solve two-step number stories.

▶ **Before You Begin**
Familiarize yourself with the Snacks Vending Machine Poster on *Student Reference Book,* page 269. Consider possible solutions for the Math Message.

 Common Core State Standards

Focus Clusters
• Multiply and divide within 100.
• Solve problems involving the four operations, and identify and explain patterns in arithmetic.
• Use place value understanding and properties of operations to perform multi-digit arithmetic.

1 Warm Up 5 min

	Materials	
Mental Math and Fluency Children solve fact extensions.	slate	**3.NBT.2**

2 Focus 40–50 min

Math Message Children estimate the cost of snacks.	*Student Reference Book,* p. 269; slate	**3.OA.8, 3.NBT.2**
Estimating Costs Children estimate to solve number stories involving money.	*Student Reference Book,* p. 269; slate	**3.OA.8, 3.NBT.2** **SMP1, SMP6**
Exploring Multistep Stories Children model and solve two-step number stories.	*Student Reference Book,* pp. 30 and 269; *Math Masters,* p. TA15; slate	**3.OA.7, 3.OA.8, 3.NBT.2** **SMP1, SMP4**
Solving Multistep Stories Children solve multistep number stories.	*Math Journal 1,* p. 41; *Student Reference Book,* p. 30	**3.OA.7, 3.OA.8, 3.NBT.2** **SMP1, SMP4**
✓ **Assessment Check-In** See page 146.	*Math Journal 1,* p. 41	**3.OA.8, SMP4**

CCSS 3.OA.8 **Spiral Snapshot**

GMC Solve 2-step number stories involving two of the four operations.

2-4 Focus	2-5 Focus	2-10 Practice	3-2 Focus	3-8 Practice	4-1 Practice	4-12 Focus	5-4 Practice

Spiral Tracker **Go Online** to see how mastery develops for all standards within the grade.

3 Practice 15–20 min

Minute Math+ Children practice mental math strategies.	*Minute Math®+*	
Rounding Numbers Children practice rounding numbers.	*Math Journal 1,* p. 42	**3.NBT.1** **SMP2**
Math Boxes 2-4 Children practice and maintain skills.	*Math Journal 1,* p. 43	See page 147.
Home Link 2-4 **Homework** Children solve two-step number stories.	*Math Masters,* p. 53	**3.NBT.2** **SMP4**

connectED.mcgraw-hill.com

Plan your lessons online with these tools.

 ePresentations   Student Learning Center   Facts Workshop Game   eToolkit   Professional Development   Home Connections   Spiral Tracker   Assessment and Reporting   English Learners Support Differentiation Support

Differentiation Options

RtI

CCSS 3.NBT.2, SMP2

Readiness
5–10 min

	WHOLE CLASS
	SMALL GROUP
	PARTNER
	INDEPENDENT

Adding and Subtracting on a Number Grid

Math Masters, p. TA3; slate

To prepare children to solve number stories using two operations, have them add and subtract on a number grid. Give directions such as: *Begin at 19. Add 10. Subtract 6. Where did you land?* 23 Have children write two number models on their slates to represent their moves. **GMP2.1**
$19 + 10 = 29, 29 - 6 = 23$ Continue with similar problems.

Number Grid
NAME   DATE   TIME

-9	-8	-7	-6	-5	-4	-3	-2	-1	0
1	2	3	4	5	6	7	8	9	10
11	12	13	14	15	16	17	18	19	20
21	22	23	24	25	26	27	28	29	30
31	32	33	34	35	36	37	38	39	40
41	42	43	44	45	46	47	48	49	50
51	52	53	54	55	56	57	58	59	60
61	62	63	64	65	66	67	68	69	70
71	72	73	74	75	76	77	78	79	80
81	82	83	84	85	86	87	88	89	90
91	92	93	94	95	96	97	98	99	100
101	102	103	104	105	106	107	108	109	110
111	112	113	114	115	116	117	118	119	120

TA3

CCSS 3.OA.3, 3.OA.8, SMP1, SMP4

Enrichment
10–15 min

	WHOLE CLASS
	SMALL GROUP
	PARTNER
	INDEPENDENT

Solving a Multistep Number Story, Part 1

Student Reference Book, p. 269; *Math Masters,* p. 54

To provide experience solving number stories with two operations, have children find an alternative number-model pair that fits the number story on *Math Masters,* page 54. **GMP1.5, GMP4.1**

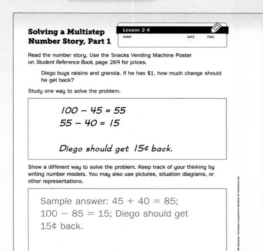

Solving a Multistep Number Story, Part 1
Lesson 2-4
NAME   DATE   TIME

Read the number story. Use the Snacks Vending Machine Poster on *Student Reference Book* page 269 for prices.

Diego buys raisins and granola. If he has $1, how much change should he get back?

Study one way to solve the problem.

$$100 - 45 = 55$$
$$55 - 40 = 15$$

Diego should get 15¢ back.

Show a different way to solve the problem. Keep track of your thinking by writing number models. You may also use pictures, situation diagrams, or other representations.

Sample answer: $45 + 40 = 85$;
$100 - 85 = 15$; Diego should get 15¢ back.

54   3.OA.3, 3.OA.8, SMP1, SMP4

CCSS 3.OA.3, 3.OA.8, SMP2

Extra Practice
10–15 min

	WHOLE CLASS
	SMALL GROUP
	PARTNER
	INDEPENDENT

Writing Sticker Stories

Activity Card 22; *Math Masters,* p. 52; number cards 0, 1, 2, 5, and 10 (4 of each)

To provide practice solving two-step number stories, have children fill in the numbers for a given story and then solve. Encourage them to show their work and write a number model for each step. **GMP2.1**

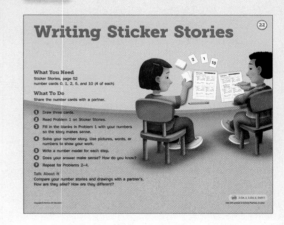

Writing Sticker Stories 22

What You Need
Sticker Stories, page 52
number cards 0, 1, 2, 5, and 10 (4 of each)

What To Do
Share the number cards with a partner.

1. Draw three cards.
2. Read Problem 1 on Sticker Stories.
3. Fill in the blanks in Problem 1 with your numbers so the story makes sense.
4. Solve your number story. Use pictures, words, or numbers to show your work.
5. Write a number model for each step.
6. Does your answer make sense? How do you know?
7. Repeat for Problems 2–4.

Talk About It
Compare your number stories and drawings with a partner's. How are they alike? How are they different?

English Language Learners Support

Beginning ELL Use visual aids and demonstrations to show children examples of *steps,* such as on stairs and steps we take as we walk. Demonstrate how we take a step one at a time to reach the top of a staircase and to get from one place to another. Count steps, saying, *step one, step two,* and so on. Extend the idea of counting steps to solving a problem in multiple steps, using statements such as *Step One is _____. The first step I took to solve was to _____.*

Go Online   **ELL** English Learners Support

Student Reference Book, p. 269

Snacks Vending Machine Poster

two hundred sixty-nine | SRB 269

1 Warm Up   5 min   Go Online

ePresentations   eToolkit

▶ Mental Math and Fluency

Pose fact extension problems for children to solve on their slates.
Leveled exercises:

◉○○ 3 + ? = 10 7   13 + ? = 20 7   43 + ? = 50 7
◉◉○ 4 + ? = 10 6   14 + ? = 30 16   24 + ? = 50 26
◉◉◉ 18 + ? = 20 2   38 + ? = 50 12   58 + ? = 100 42

2 Focus   40–50 min   Go Online

ePresentations   eToolkit

▶ Math Message

Student Reference Book, p. 269

Use the Snacks Vending Machine Poster on Student Reference Book,
page 269 to answer the questions below:

You have 80¢ in your pocket. Estimate. Do you have enough money to buy
two packages of the same snack? Which snack? Write your answer on
your slate.

▶ Estimating Costs

Student Reference Book, p. 269

| WHOLE CLASS | SMALL GROUP | PARTNER | INDEPENDENT |

Math Message Follow-Up Have children share the names of the snacks
they could buy. Crackers, granola, mints, and cheese sticks Ask: *How did*
you decide if you could buy two packages with 80¢? Sample answers: I
doubled the total cost to see if it was more or less than 80 cents. I added
the cost plus itself. I rounded the cost to the nearest 10 and doubled it.

If no one mentions it, model using 40¢ as a benchmark to estimate
whether 2 packs of a single snack will cost more or less than 80¢. Ask:
What is half of 80? 40 *If a snack costs less than 40¢, can you buy 2 of them*
for 80¢? How do you know? Sample answer: Yes. 40 + 40 (or 40 doubled)
is 80, so any snack less than 40¢ will be less than 80¢ together. Ask about
a snack that costs more than 40¢, for example: *Do you have enough to buy*
2 packs of pretzels? Why? Sample answer: No. 1 pack costs more than 40¢,
so 2 packs cost more than 80¢.

Help children recognize that estimating may be easier than calculating the
exact cost of two packages of each item. They can still solve the problem
using their estimates. GMP6.2

NOTE This lesson uses cents as the monetary unit. The Common Core State Standards recommend delaying work with decimals (which are included in dollars-and-cents notation) until Grade 4. If children are familiar with dollars-and-cents notation, however, allow them to use it when amounts exceed 1 dollar.

Ask: *How many cents are in 1 dollar?* 100¢ Tell children to imagine they have 100¢. Ask them to determine whether they have enough money for each of the following purchases. Have children share their reasoning.

- 1 bag of peanuts and 1 box of pretzels No. 50 + 50 = 100, and both cost more than 50¢, so the sum will be over 100¢.

- 1 package of mints and 1 package of granola Yes. Both are less than 50¢, so the sum will be less than 100¢.

- 1 package of raisins and 1 package of rice cakes Yes. One is 50¢ and the other is less than 50¢, so the sum will be less than 100¢.

Have children reflect on the usefulness of estimating by asking: *Why could we estimate the cost of the snacks instead of finding their exact cost?* `GMP1.2, GMP6.2` Sample answer: We didn't need to know the exact cost as long as we knew that one or both items were at or below 50¢. *How could estimation help you solve money problems?* Sample answers: Estimating helps me know quickly if I have enough money. I can do it in my head.

Encourage children to reflect on the reasonableness of their solutions as they solve multistep problems involving more complex purchasing situations.

▶ Exploring Multistep Stories

Student Reference Book, pp. 30 and 269; *Math Masters*, p. TA15

| **WHOLE CLASS** | SMALL GROUP | **PARTNER** | INDEPENDENT |

Have children refer to the Snacks Vending Machine Poster and solve the following number stories on their slates. For each problem, give them time to record their thinking and then share their strategies with the class. Remind children that they can use drawings, words, number models, situation diagrams, and other representations to help them organize the information in number stories and in their solutions. `GMP4.1`

As children share their thinking, model how to record their steps using a series of number models. (*See margin.*) Recording these number models will encourage children to keep track of and reflect on their thinking as they solve the problem. `GMP1.2` Continue to scaffold as necessary as children record their thinking with number models. `GMP4.1`

Problem 1: *You buy 2 packages of crackers and 1 package of sunflower seeds. How much money do you spend?* 120¢ or $1 and 20¢ or $1.20

As you discuss children's solutions, refer to the Guide to Solving Number Stories. Point out that the number story could be thought of as two problems and that both must be solved to find the answer.

- *What do you know from the story?* I buy 2 packages of crackers and 1 package of sunflower seeds.

Common Misconception

`Differentiate` Watch for children who mistakenly add all three quantities in multistep number stories or who add the first two numbers but do not know what to do with the third. Help them make sense of each part and choose the appropriate operation. Ask: *What happened first? Next?*

`Go Online` Differentiation Support

Recording Mental Steps with Number Models

Problem 1: Crackers and Sunflower Seeds

   30 + 30 = 60 or 2 × 30 = 60
   60 + 60 = 120

Problem 2: Mints and Cheese Sticks

   35 + 35 = 70 or 2 × 35 = 70
   25 + 25 + 25 = 75 or
   3 × 25 = 75
   75 − 70 = 5

Problem 3: Crackers

   5 × 2 = 10
   10 − 3 = 7

Multistep Number Stories, Part 1

Lesson 2-4
DATE   TIME

Solve each problem below. Use pictures, words, or numbers to keep track of your thinking. Write number models to show each of your steps.

A package of rice cakes contains 6 rice cakes.

① You buy 2 packages of rice cakes and then eat 4 rice cakes. How many rice cakes are left?

Number models: $6 + 6 = 12$ or $2 \times 6 = 12$
$12 - 4 = 8$

Answer: ___8___ rice cakes

② You buy 5 packages of rice cakes. You give 15 rice cakes away. How many rice cakes do you have now?

Number models: Sample answer: $5 \times 6 = 30$
$30 - 15 = 15$

Answer: __15__ rice cakes

Try This

③ For everyone in your class to have one rice cake, how many packages would you need? Answers vary.

_____ children _____ packages

Would there be any leftover rice cakes? _____

How many? _____ rice cakes

Number models: _____

3.OA.7, 3.OA.8, 3.NBT.2, SMP1, SMP4   forty-one **41**

Rounding Numbers

Lesson 2-4
DATE   TIME

Round the following numbers. Show your work on the open number lines.

① What is 64 rounded to the **nearest 10**? _60_

```
|———+————————+——+————————|
60          64  65         70
```

② What is 278 rounded to the **nearest 100**? _300_

```
|————————+————————+——+————|
200      250      278  300
```

Here is another way to think of rounding numbers.

Round 27 to the nearest 10.

What multiples of 10 are close to 27? _20_ and _30_

What number is halfway between 20 and 30? _25_

The halfway number is written at the top of the hill.

Would 27 be heading toward 20 or 30? _30_

27 rounded to the **nearest 10** is _30_

③ Fill in the "hill" to show how you would round 82 to the nearest 10.

82 rounded to the **nearest 10** is _80_.

④ Use either an open number line or hill to round 140 to the nearest 100.

140 rounded to the **nearest 100** is _100_.

Explain your work. Sample answer: My number line shows 100, 200, and 150. I marked 140 and saw that it was closer to 100 than 200.

42 forty-two   3.NBT.1, SMP2

- *What do you want to find out?* The total cost of those items
- *What is your plan?* I will figure out how much 2 packages of crackers cost and then add in the cost of 1 package of sunflower seeds.
- *Does your answer make sense? How do you know?* Sample answer: It makes sense because crackers are less than 50¢, and sunflower seeds are just a little more than 50¢. All three items should be a little more than 1 dollar.

In a similar manner, work through the following:

Problem 2: *What costs more: 2 packages of mints or 3 packages of cheese sticks? How much more?* 3 packages of cheese sticks; 5¢ more

Problem 3: *You buy 5 packs of crackers. There are 2 crackers in each pack. You eat 3 crackers. How many do you have left?* 7 crackers

▶ Solving Multistep Stories

Math Journal 1, p. 41; Student Reference Book, p. 30

| **WHOLE CLASS** | SMALL GROUP | **PARTNER** | INDEPENDENT |

Have partners read the directions on journal page 41. Make sure children understand that there are 6 rice cakes in each pack. Have them record their thinking and solve the number stories. Remind them to refer to the Guide for Solving Number Stories on *Student Reference Book*, page 30.

When solving number models involving a mixture of operations, the order of operations will affect the answer. Until grouping symbols are introduced in Unit 6, have children write a separate number model for each step in multistep stories. GMP4.1

✓ Assessment Check-In CCSS 3.OA.8

Math Journal 1, p. 41

Circulate and observe as children complete journal page 41. Expect most children to make sense of and use representations to solve Problems 1 and 2. GMP4.1 Some children may be able to write number models to record each step, but do not expect this of all children as this lesson introduces multistep number stories. For children who struggle to make sense of the stories, ask guiding questions similar to those in the lesson, and have them draw pictures or use concrete objects to model the stories.

 Assessment and Reporting | Go Online | to record student progress and to see trajectories toward mastery for this standard.

When most children have finished, bring the class together to share strategies and solutions.

Summarize Have children discuss why they think it is important to use representations, such as drawings or number models, when they solve number stories in more than one step. GMP1.2 Sample answers: So we can keep track of our steps to make sure we haven't forgotten anything. To help us avoid making silly mistakes and get reasonable answers

3 Practice 15–20 min

Go Online | ePresentations | eToolkit | Home Connections

▶ *Minute Math+*

To practice mental math strategies, select a *Minute Math+* activity.

▶ **Rounding Numbers**

Math Journal 1, p. 42

| WHOLE CLASS | **SMALL GROUP** | **PARTNER** | **INDEPENDENT** |

Have children round numbers using various representations. GMP2.2 Remind children to use the number grid or number line to help them choose multiples of 10 or 100.

▶ **Math Boxes 2-4**

Math Journal 1, p. 43

| WHOLE CLASS | **SMALL GROUP** | **PARTNER** | **INDEPENDENT** |

Mixed Practice Math Boxes 2-4 are paired with Math Boxes 2-2.

▶ **Home Link 2-4**

Math Masters, p. 53

Homework Children use pictures, words, or numbers to keep track of their thinking as they solve multistep number stories. GMP4.1

Planning Ahead

To prepare for *Array Bingo* in Lesson 2-7, cut out one set of *Array Bingo* Cards (*Math Masters*, page G8) per partnership.

Math Journal 1, p. 43

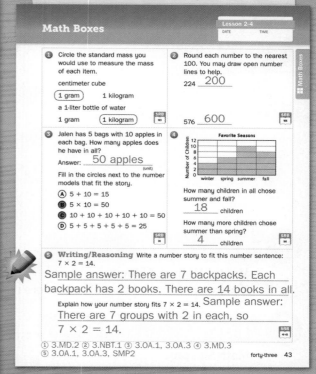

Math Masters, p. 53

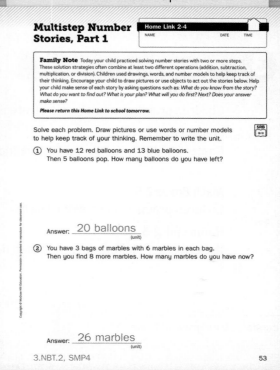

Multistep Number Stories, Part 2

Overview Children solve number stories using two operations.

**Common Core
State Standards**

Focus Clusters
- Represent and solve problems involving multiplication and division.
- Multiply and divide within 100.
- Solve problems involving the four operations, and identify and explain patterns in arithmetic.

1 Warm Up 5 min

	Materials	
Mental Math and Fluency Children practice adding three or more numbers.	slate	3.NBT.2

2 Focus 40–50 min

Math Message Children solve a multistep number story.	slate	3.OA.3, 3.OA.7, 3.OA.8, 3.NBT.2
Sharing Strategies Children explain and discuss their strategies and representations for a multistep number story.		3.OA.3, 3.OA.7, 3.OA.8, 3.NBT.2 SMP4
Using Number Models as Records Children record their thinking as they solve number stories.	*Student Reference Book*, pp. 30 and 269; coins (optional)	3.OA.3, 3.OA.7, 3.OA.8, 3.NBT.2 SMP1, SMP4
Writing Number Models Children solve number stories and record number models.	*Math Journal 1*, p. 44	3.OA.3, 3.OA.7, 3.OA.8, 3.NBT.2 SMP1, SMP4
✓ **Assessment Check-In** See page 152.	*Math Journal 1*, p. 44	3.OA.8, SMP4

CCSS 3.OA.8 **Spiral Snapshot**

GMC Solve 2-step number stories involving two of the four operations.

2-4 Focus	2-5 Focus	2-10 Practice	3-2 Focus	3-8 Practice	4-1 Practice	4-12 Focus	5-4 Practice

III Spiral Tracker 〈 **Go Online** 〉 to see how mastery develops for all standards within the grade.

3 Practice 15–20 min

Minute Math+ Children practice mental math strategies.	*Minute Math®+*	
Playing *Roll to 1,000* **Game** Children practice mental addition with multiples of 10.	*Student Reference Book*, pp. 253–254; *Math Masters*, p. G7; 6-sided dice (2 per group)	3.OA.7, 3.NBT.2 SMP6
Math Boxes 2-5 Children practice and maintain skills.	*Math Journal 1*, p. 45	See page 153.
Home Link 2-5 **Homework** Children solve multistep number stories.	*Math Masters*, p. 56	3.OA.3, 3.OA.7, 3.OA.8, 3.NBT.2 SMP4

connectED.mcgraw-hill.com

Plan your lessons online
with these tools.

ePresentations Student Learning Center Facts Workshop Game eToolkit Professional Development Home Connections Spiral Tracker Assessment and Reporting English Learners Support Differentiation Support

Differentiation Options

RtI

CCSS 3.NBT.2, SMP2

Readiness
5–10 min

Modeling Multiplication and Division

WHOLE CLASS
SMALL GROUP
PARTNER
INDEPENDENT

counters

To prepare children to solve number stories involving multiplication and division, have them use counters to model multiplication and equal sharing. Pose problems such as: *Show 2 groups of 3 counters. Give me 2 counters from 1 group. How many counters are left in that group?* **GMP2.1** 1 counter *Share 8 counters equally with a partner. Take 2 more counters. How many do you have now?* **GMP2.1** 6 counters Continue with similar problems.

CCSS 3.OA.3, 3.OA.8, SMP1, SMP4

Enrichment
10–15 min

Solving a Multistep Number Story, Part 2

WHOLE CLASS
SMALL GROUP
PARTNER
INDEPENDENT

Math Masters, p. 55

Challenge children to solve a number story with two operations in two different ways. Have them write two sets of number models that fit the number story on *Math Masters,* page 55. **GMP1.5, GMP4.1**

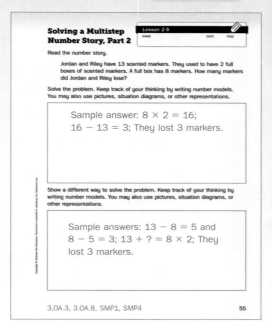

Solving a Multistep Number Story, Part 2 — Lesson 2-5

Read the number story.

Jordan and Riley have 13 scented markers. They used to have 2 full boxes of scented markers. A full box has 8 markers. How many markers did Jordan and Riley lose?

Solve the problem. Keep track of your thinking by writing number models. You may also use pictures, situation diagrams, or other representations.

> Sample answer: $8 \times 2 = 16$;
> $16 - 13 = 3$; They lost 3 markers.

Show a different way to solve the problem. Keep track of your thinking by writing number models. You may also use pictures, situation diagrams, or other representations.

> Sample answers: $13 - 8 = 5$ and
> $8 - 5 = 3$; $13 + ? = 8 \times 2$; They
> lost 3 markers.

3.OA.3, 3.OA.8, SMP1, SMP4   55

CCSS 3.OA.3, 3.OA.8, SMP2

Extra Practice
10–15 min

Writing Sticker Stories

WHOLE CLASS
SMALL GROUP
PARTNER
INDEPENDENT

Activity Card 22; *Math Masters,* p. 52; number cards 0, 1, 2, 5, and 10 (4 of each)

To practice solving number stories involving two operations, have children fill in the numbers for a given story and then solve. Encourage them to show their work and write a number model for each step. **GMP2.1**

Writing Sticker Stories

English Language Learners Support

Beginning ELL Help children connect the words in a number story to the symbols in a number model. Think aloud and demonstrate with objects to role-play a number story. Then retell the same number story, representing it with a number model. Pose other number stories using visual aids and actions and ask children to select the corresponding number model from a list of examples.

 Go Online **English Learners Support**

Standards and Goals for
Mathematical Practice

SMP1 **Make sense of problems and persevere in solving them.**

GMP1.2 Reflect on your thinking as you solve your problem.

GMP1.4 Check whether your answer makes sense.

SMP4 **Model with mathematics.**

GMP4.1 Model real-world situations using graphs, drawings, tables, symbols, numbers, diagrams, and other representations.

Sample representation:

⊠ ⊠ ⊠ ○ ○   ○ ○ ○ ○ ○
  James   **His Sister**

$$10 \div 2 = 5$$
$$5 - 3 = 2$$

Each number model represents one step in the solution strategy. James has 2 grapes left.

---

① Warm Up   5 min   Go Online

▶ Mental Math and Fluency

Display the following problems for children to solve on their slates. Encourage children to look for combinations that make adding easier. *Leveled exercises:*

● ○ ○ $6 + 9 + 1 = \underline{16}$; $5 + 8 + 5 = \underline{18}$; $6 + 2 + 4 + 8 = \underline{20}$

● ● ○ $13 + 15 + 7 = \underline{35}$; $17 + 3 + 6 = \underline{26}$; $19 + 2 + 28 + 11 = \underline{60}$

● ● ● $25 + 7 + 15 = \underline{47}$; $16 + 24 + 18 = \underline{58}$; $14 + 37 + 13 = \underline{64}$

② Focus   40–50 min   Go Online

▶ Math Message

James shares 10 grapes equally with his sister.
Then he eats 3 of his grapes.

How many grapes does James have left?

Use pictures, words, or numbers to show your work on your slate.

▶ Sharing Strategies

WHOLE CLASS   SMALL GROUP   **PARTNER**   INDEPENDENT

Math Message Follow-Up Circulate as children solve the Math Message and look for a variety of representations. Ask children to describe the steps involved in solving the problem. Sample answer: First I figured out how many grapes James and his sister each have. Then I figured how many grapes James has left after eating some.

Invite a few children to describe how their representations show the steps or calculations they did to answer the question. Children may distribute 10 grapes by 1s until James and his sister each have 5. Others may recognize 2 equal groups of 5 in 10. Help children connect division with equally sharing the grapes. Ask: *What operations can we use for each step or calculation?* Sample answer: Division and then subtraction Share sample number models with children as needed.

Tell children that today they will use number models to help make sense of and keep track of their steps while solving number stories. **GMP4.1**

▶ Using Number Models as Records

Student Reference Book, pp. 30 and 269

| WHOLE CLASS | SMALL GROUP | PARTNER | INDEPENDENT |

Have children refer to the Guide to Solving Number Stories and the Snacks Vending Machine Poster on *Student Reference Book,* pages 30 and 269. Explain that they can use number models to help keep track of their thinking as they solve number stories. Have them record number models that represent each step involved in solving this story:

You have 75¢. You buy a package of crackers and eat them. You are still hungry, so you buy a package of cheese sticks. How much money do you have left?

Ask guiding questions, such as:

- *What is your plan?* Sample answers: I will look at the poster to find the prices of crackers and cheese sticks. I will subtract the price of the 2 snacks from 75¢. I will figure out how much money I spent on the two snacks and see what's left over.

- *What will you do first?* Sample answers: I will find out how much money I have left after I bought the crackers. I will find how much money I spent on two snacks.

Have children write a number model for the first step. **GMP4.1** Sample answers: $75 - 30 = 45$; $30 + 25 = 55$

- *Are you finished? How do you know?* **GMP1.2** Sample answer: No. I still need to find out how much money is left from the original 75¢.

- *What will you do next?* Sample answers: I will subtract the cost of the cheese sticks. I will subtract the cost of the two snacks from 75¢.

Have children write a number model for the second step. **GMP4.1** Sample answers: $45 - 25 = 20$; $75 - 55 = 20$

- *Are you finished? How do you know?* **GMP1.2** Sample answer: Yes. I subtracted the cost of both items.

- *Does your answer make sense? Explain.* **GMP1.4** Sample answer: Yes. The answer has to be less than 75¢ because I spent money. I get 75¢ when I add the leftover money to the cost of both snacks: $20 + 30 + 25 = 75$.

In the same manner, guide children through this number story:

You buy 2 packages of granola and a package of mints. How much do you spend in all? 115¢; Sample number models: $2 \times 40 = 80$ and $80 + 35 = 115$; $40 + 40 = 80$ and $80 + 35 = 115$

Math Journal 1, p. 44

More Number Stories

Lesson 2-5
DATE   TIME

Solve each problem below. Show your work with pictures, numbers, or words.
Write number models to keep track of your thinking.

① Jill has 83¢. She buys 2 erasers for 25¢ each. How much money does she have left?

Number models:
$$2 \times 25 = 50 \text{ or}$$
$$25 + 25 = 50 \text{ or } 83 - 25 = 58$$
$$83 - 50 = 33 \text{ or } 58 - 25 = 33$$

Answer: __33__ ¢

② Each pack of pencils has 5 pencils. You have 4 packs of pencils. Then you give your friend 2 pencils. How many pencils do you have left?

Number models:
$$4 \times 5 = 20 \text{ or } 5 + 5 + 5 + 5 = 20$$
$$20 - 2 = 18$$

Answer: __18__ pencils

③ Three friends equally share 15 almonds. One friend eats 3 of her almonds. How many almonds does she have left?

Number models:
$$15 \div 3 = 5$$
$$5 - 3 = 2$$

Answer: __2__ almonds

44 forty-four   3.OA.3, 3.OA.7, 3.OA.8, 3.NBT.2, SMP1, SMP4

Student Reference Book, p. 253

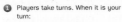

Games

Roll to 1,000

Materials	☐ 1 *Roll to 1,000* Record Sheet (*Math Masters*, p. G7)
	☐ 2 six-sided dice
Players	2 to 4
Skill	Adding multiples of 10
Object of the Game	To score at least 1,000.

Directions

Each dice roll represents a number of tens. For example, if you roll a 3 and a 4 for a total of 7, you have 7 tens, or 70.

① Players take turns. When it is your turn:
  • Roll the dice as many times as you want. Each roll tells you how many tens you have.
  • Mentally add the numbers you get for all of your dice rolls. Enter this as your score for the turn.
  • If you roll a 1, your turn is over. Enter 0 as your score for this turn.

③ Continue to add to your score each turn. If you roll a 1 at any time, your score for that turn is 0. The score you enter is the total from your previous turn. See the example on the next page.

④ The first player to score 1,000 or more wins the game.

Make 7 groups of 10, or 70.

Roll to 1,000 Record Sheet

two hundred fifty-three   SRB 253

▶ Writing Number Models

Math Journal 1, p. 44

| WHOLE CLASS | SMALL GROUP | PARTNER | INDEPENDENT |

Have children solve the number stories on journal page 44 and write number models to keep track of their thinking. **GMP1.2, GMP4.1** Remind children to write the number model for each step on a separate line.

 Assessment Check-In (CCSS) **3.OA.8**

Math Journal 1, page 44

Circulate and observe children's strategies as they complete journal page 44. Expect most children to make sense of and use representations to correctly solve Problems 1–3. Also expect children to attempt to write number models to show their thinking. **GMP4.1** For children who struggle to make sense of the stories, ask guiding questions and have them draw pictures or use concrete objects to act out the stories. For children who struggle with writing number models, consider the suggestion in the Adjusting the Activity note.

 Assessment and Reporting   (Go Online) to record student progress and to see trajectories toward mastery for this standard.

When most children are finished, have volunteers share their first step for solving Problem 1. As they share, record each strategy and the accompanying number models. Children may find the cost of two erasers ($25 + 25 = 50$ or $2 \times 25 = 50$), or subtract the cost of one eraser ($83 - 25 = 58$). Highlight that there may be more than one way to begin solving a multistep problem. Continue by having children explain the second step and their solution. As time permits, repeat with Problems 2 and 3.

Summarize Pose the following problem for children to act out as a class. Modify the numbers to fit your class as needed. *There are 20 children. The teacher tells them to make 2 teams with the same number on each team. If 3 more children join one team, how many children are on the larger team?* 13 Invite volunteers to record number models that fit the story. **GMP4.1** Sample answer: $20 \div 2 = 10$ and $10 + 3 = 13$

3 Practice 15–20 min Go Online ePresentations eToolkit Home Connections

▶ Minute Math+

To practice mental math strategies, select a *Minute Math+* activity.

▶ Playing *Roll to 1,000*

Student Reference Book, pp. 253–254; *Math Masters,* p. G7

WHOLE CLASS | **SMALL GROUP** | **PARTNER** | INDEPENDENT

Have children play *Roll to 1,000* to practice mental addition of multiples of 10. **GMP6.4** Together read the directions on *Student Reference Book,* page 253. Make sure children understand that:

- The number of dots on the die represents the number of tens, so rolling a die showing 2 dots means 20.
- They may roll as many times as they want on a given turn. If at any time they roll a 1, which counts as 10, their score for *that turn* is 0. They keep points scored on previous turns.

Before having partnerships play on their own, play a few rounds as a class. Stop to ask children how the scores are figured. For example: *If Player 1 rolls a 6 and a 3, what is the score so far?* The 6 gives us 60 and the 3 gives us 30, and $60 + 30 = 90$. Remind children that Player 1 could now choose to either roll again to try to increase the score or stop rolling and keep the 90 rather than risking rolling a 1 and losing all points for that round.

Observe

- Do children correctly interpret the dice rolls as multiples of 10?
- Do children add the multiples of 10 accurately? **GMP6.4**

Discuss

- *How did you figure out your score for this round?*
- *What helps you add multiples of 10 accurately?* **GMP6.4**

Differentiate **Game Modifications** Go Online Differentiation Support

▶ Math Boxes 2-5

Math Journal 1, p. 45

WHOLE CLASS | **SMALL GROUP** | **PARTNER** | **INDEPENDENT**

Mixed Practice Math Boxes 2-5 are paired with Math Boxes 2-7.

▶ Home Link 2-5

Math Masters, p. 56

Homework Children practice solving number stories and recording number models to show their steps. **GMP4.1**

Math Journal 1, p. 45

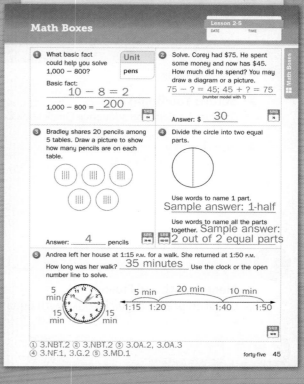

Math Boxes Lesson 2-5 DATE TIME

① What basic fact could help you solve $1,000 - 800$? Unit pens

Basic fact:
$$10 - 8 = 2$$
$$1,000 - 800 = \underline{200}$$

② Solve. Corey had $75. He spent some money and now has $45. How much did he spend? You may draw a diagram or a picture.

$75 - ? = 45; 45 + ? = 75$ (number model with ?)

Answer: $ ___30___

③ Bradley shares 20 pencils among 5 tables. Draw a picture to show how many pencils are on each table.

Answer: ___4___ pencils

④ Divide the circle into two equal parts.

Use words to name 1 part. Sample answer: 1-half

Use words to name all the parts together. Sample answer: 2 out of 2 equal parts

⑤ Andrea left her house at 1:15 P.M. for a walk. She returned at 1:50 P.M. How long was her walk? ___35 minutes___ Use the clock or the open number line to solve.

5 min   15 min

5 min 20 min 10 min
1:15 1:20   1:40 1:50

① 3.NBT.2 ② 3.NBT.2 ③ 3.OA.2, 3.OA.3
④ 3.NF.1, 3.G.2 ⑤ 3.MD.1 forty-five 45

Math Masters, p. 56

Multistep Number Stories, Part 2 Home Link 2-5 NAME DATE TIME

Family Note Today your child practiced solving additional number stories with two or more steps and writing number models for each step. Help your child make sense of the stories below by asking: *What do you know from the story? What do you want to find out? What is your plan? What will you do first? Next? Have you answered the question? Does your answer make sense?*
Please return this Home Link to school tomorrow.

Solve each problem. Show your work with pictures, words, or numbers. Write number models to keep track of your thinking. Remember to write the unit.

① Each basket in basketball is worth 2 points. Cathy makes 5 baskets and scores 6 more points with free throws. How many points did she score in all?

Number models:
$$5 \times 2 = 10 \text{ or}$$
$$2 + 2 + 2 + 2 + 2 = 10$$
$$10 + 6 = 16$$

Answer: ___16 points___ (unit)

② Elias reads 4 chapters. Each chapter has 10 pages. Then he reads 8 more pages. How many pages does Elias read in all?

Number models:
$$4 \times 10 = 40 \text{ or}$$
$$10 + 10 + 10 + 10 = 40$$
$$40 + 8 = 48$$

Answer: ___48 pages___ (unit)

56 3.OA.3, 3.OA.7, 3.OA.8, 3.NBT.2, SMP4

Equal Groups

Overview Children solve problems involving multiples of equal groups and make sense of multiplying by 0 and 1.

▶ **Before You Begin**
For Part 1, select and sequence Quick Look Cards 123, 124, and 129.

▶ **Vocabulary**
equal groups • efficient

 Common Core State Standards

Focus Clusters
- Represent and solve problems involving multiplication and division.
- Multiply and divide within 100.
- Solve problems involving the four operations, and identify and explain patterns in arithmetic.

① Warm Up 5–10 min

	Materials	
Mental Math and Fluency Children practice Quick Looks with equal groups and arrays.	Quick Look Cards 123, 124, and 129	**3.OA.1, 3.OA.7** **SMP2, SMP6**

② Focus 40–50 min

Math Message Children solve a number story.	slate	**3.OA.1, 3.OA.3**
Making Sense of Equal Groups Children solve equal-groups number stories and reflect on the efficiency of their strategies.	*Student Reference Book*, pp. 30 and 270; *Math Masters*, p. TA15; slate; container of objects (optional)	**3.OA.1, 3.OA.3, 3.OA.7** **SMP1, SMP6**
Multiplying by 0 and 1 Children make sense of multiplying by 0 and 1 in number story contexts.	*Student Reference Book*, pp. 30 and 270; *Math Masters*, p. TA15	**3.OA.1, 3.OA.3, 3.OA.5, 3.OA.7, 3.OA.9** **SMP8**
Solving Equal-Groups Stories Children practice solving equal-groups number stories.	*Math Journal 1*, p. 46; *Student Reference Book*, p. 270	**3.OA.1, 3.OA.3, 3.OA.7** **SMP6, SMP8**
✓ **Assessment Check-In** See page 158.	*Math Journal 1*, p. 46	**3.OA.1, 3.OA.3, SMP6**

CCSS 3.OA.1 Spiral Snapshot

GMC Interpret multiplication in terms of equal groups.

1-10 Focus Practice	1-12 Warm Up Focus	1-13 Warm Up Practice	2-6 Warm Up Focus Practice	2-7 Warm Up Focus Practice	3-9 through 3-12 Warm Up Focus Practice	3-13 Warm Up

 Spiral Tracker   **Go Online**   to see how mastery develops for all standards within the grade.

③ Practice 15–20 min

Minute Math+ Children practice mental math strategies.	*Minute Math®+*	
Finding Elapsed Time Children measure time intervals in minutes.	*Math Masters*, p. TA11, p. TA12 (optional); toolkit clock; scissors; envelope; paper clip	**3.MD.1** **SMP5**
Math Boxes 2-6 Children practice and maintain skills.	*Math Journal 1*, p. 47	See page 159.
Home Link 2-6 **Homework** Children solve equal-groups number stories.	*Math Masters*, p. 58	**3.OA.1, 3.OA.3, 3.OA.5, 3.OA.7, 3.OA.9, SMP6**

connectED.mcgraw-hill.com

Plan your lessons online
with these tools.

 ePresentations   **Student Learning Center**   **Facts Workshop Game**   **eToolkit**   **Professional Development**   **Home Connections**   **Spiral Tracker**   **Assessment and Reporting**   **ELL English Learners Support**   **Differentiation Support**

Differentiation Options
RtI

Readiness   5–10 min

| WHOLE CLASS |
| SMALL GROUP |
| PARTNER |
| INDEPENDENT |

Making Equal Groups

counters, slate

To provide experience modeling equal groups, pose a problem such as: *Count out 12 counters. Show 2 equal groups. How do you know they are equal?* Sample answer: There are the same number of counters in each group. Have children write a multiplication number model to represent the equal groups. **GMP2.1** $2 \times 6 = 12$ Then say: *Add another equal group. How many counters do you have now?* 18 *Write a new multiplication number model.* $3 \times 6 = 18$ Repeat with similar problems.

Enrichment   10–15 min

| WHOLE CLASS |
| SMALL GROUP |
| PARTNER |
| INDEPENDENT |

Patterns in Multiplying by 0 and 1

Math Masters, p. 57

To provide practice articulating the meaning of multiplying by 0 or 1, have children observe and explain patterns in multiplying by 0 and 1 on *Math Masters*, page 57. Then have them explain whether their pattern works for all numbers. **GMP7.1, GMP8.1**

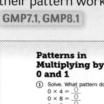

Patterns in Multiplying by 0 and 1   Lesson 2-6
NAME   DATE   TIME

① Solve. What pattern do you notice?   *Sample patterns and explanations given.*
$0 \times 4 = \underline{0}$
$0 \times 8 = \underline{0}$
$0 \times 5 = \underline{0}$
Pattern: The product is 0 for each problem.

Explain why your pattern makes sense.
You can think of each problem as 0 groups of the other number, and if you have 0 groups, you have nothing.

Do you think this is true for any number × 0? Explain.
Yes. 0 groups of any number of things is still going to be no things, so the product will still be 0.

② Solve. What pattern do you notice?
$1 \times 4 = \underline{4}$
$1 \times 8 = \underline{8}$
$1 \times 5 = \underline{5}$
Pattern: The product is the same as the number being multiplied by 1.

Explain why your pattern makes sense.
You can think of each problem as 1 group of the other number, which is just that number. So the answer is always the same as the number being multiplied by 1.

Do you think this is true for any number × 1? Explain.
Yes. 1 group of any number of things is still going to be that number of things, so the product will still be that number.

3.OA.1, 3.OA.5, 3.OA.7, 3.OA.9, SMP7, SMP8   57

Extra Practice   20–30 min

| WHOLE CLASS |
| SMALL GROUP |
| PARTNER |
| INDEPENDENT |

Writing Multiplication Stories

Activity Card 23; *Math Masters*, p. TA8; *Each Orange Had 8 Slices: A Counting Book*

To provide practice with equal groups, read ***Each Orange Had 8 Slices: A Counting Book*** by Paul Giganti, Jr. (Greenwillow Books, 1999). In this book, situations involving equal groups are shown and questions are posed about the total number of objects. Have partners write and illustrate their own multiplication number stories modeled after those in the book. **GMP4.1**

Writing Multiplication Stories (23)

What You Need
A Number Story, page TA8
Each Orange Had 8 Slices: A Counting Book by Paul Giganti, Jr.

What To Do
Work with a partner.
❶ Read a few pages of *Each Orange Had 8 Slices: A Counting Book*, and solve some of the number stories in the book.
❷ Make up your own number story like one in the book.
❸ Draw a picture for your number story.
❹ Trade papers with a partner. Solve your partner's number story.

Talk About It
Talk to your partner about how you solved the number story.

English Language Learners Support

Beginning ELL Children may have heard the term *package* in the context of boxes that come in the mail. Show children pictures or real examples of packages of different sizes and shapes. Then show packages packed with the same number of items in preparation for thinking about packages as sets of the same number of objects.

 Go Online   ELL **English Learners Support**

Standards and Goals for
Mathematical Practice

SMP1 **Make sense of problems and persevere in solving them.**
GMP1.6 Compare the strategies you and others use.

SMP6 **Attend to precision.**
GMP6.4 Think about accuracy and efficiency when you count, measure, and calculate.

SMP8 **Look for and express regularity in repeated reasoning.**
GMP8.1 Create and justify rules, shortcuts, and generalizations.

Academic Language Development

To help children connect *efficient* with *faster,* spill a container of objects on the floor. Place the container far from the objects and tell children you have to put the objects in it. Pick up one object at a time and walk to the container. Repeat twice. Ask: *What if I take two at a time? Would that be faster? More efficient? What if I take three? Four? What if I brought the container here and picked them all up at once?* Encourage children to use the sentence frame: *The most efficient way would be to _____.*

① Warm Up 5–10 min

▸ Mental Math and Fluency

Show Quick Look Cards 123, 124, and 129 one at a time for 2–3 seconds each. Ask children to share both what they saw and how they saw it. GMP2.2, GMP6.1 Highlight strategies involving equal groups.

Quick Look Card 123 Sample answer: I saw 2 columns of 5, and I know 5 and 5 makes 10.

Quick Look Card 124 Sample answer: I saw 2 groups of 4, and I know 4 and 4 makes 8.

Quick Look Card 129 Sample answer: I saw 4 groups of 4, and I know 2 groups of 4 makes 8 and $8 + 8 = 16$.

② Focus 40–50 min

▸ Math Message

Use your slate. Solve: You have 4 packages of pencils. There are 6 pencils in each package. How many pencils in all? Show your thinking with drawings, words, or number models. 24 pencils

▸ Making Sense of Equal Groups

Student Reference Book, pp. 30 and 270; *Math Masters,* p. TA15

WHOLE CLASS	SMALL GROUP	PARTNER	INDEPENDENT

Math Message Follow-Up Have children who used some of the following strategies share them with the class:

- drawing a picture and then counting by 1s
- skip counting by 6s
- drawing an array and skip counting by 4s
- repeatedly adding 6s or 4s

Ask: *What is similar about these strategies?* GMP1.6 Sample answer: They all involve equal groups. Remind children that groups with the same number of objects are called **equal groups.** Have children identify the equal groups within each strategy. For example, when repeatedly adding 6, each 6 represents another group of pencils. Next ask: *How are the strategies different from each other?* GMP1.6 Sample answers: Some count drawings by 1s, some count by equal groups, and others add the equal groups. Help children recognize that although the discussed strategies are all valid, some are more **efficient,** or faster and easier, than others. GMP6.4

Tell children that today they will continue with equal-groups problems, and they should think about the efficiency of their strategies.

Refer children to the Dollar Store Poster on *Student Reference Book*, page 270. Pose an equal-groups number story about multiples of a pictured item. For example: *There are 3 packages of party horns with 6 horns in each package. How many horns in all?* 18 horns

Have children find the total and share their strategies. Be sure to ask how they know their answer makes sense. Sample answer: Two groups of 6 are 12, and one more group of 6 is 18, so my answer makes sense. Then display a summary number model such as $3 \times 6 = 18$ or $6 + 6 + 6 = 18$.

Encourage children to refer to the Guide to Solving Number Stories as they plan, carry out, and reflect on efficient methods for solving more equal-groups number stories. The following are some suggestions for number stories using the Dollar Store Poster:

- If I buy 6 packages of chocolate-scented pens, how many pens will I have? 36 pens, $6 \times 6 = 36$; $6 + 6 = 12$ and $12 + 12 + 12 = 36$
- If I buy 4 packages of glitter stickers, will that be enough for everyone in our class to have 1 sticker? Why or why not? Sample answer: Yes. $4 \times 7 = 28$ stickers, and there are only 22 children in our class.

As children share their strategies and solutions, help them reflect on the efficiency of their strategies by asking questions such as:
GMP6.4 Answers vary.

- *How did he or she solve the problem?*
- *Does the strategy work for the problem? How do you know?*
- *Can you think of a faster and easier strategy?*

▶ Multiplying by 0 and 1

Student Reference Book, pp. 30 and 270; *Math Masters*, p. TA15

| WHOLE CLASS | SMALL GROUP | PARTNER | INDEPENDENT |

Next use equal-groups number stories to help children make sense of multiplying by 1 or 0. Help them generalize the following $\times 1$ and $\times 0$ problems by thinking of having 1 or 0 groups. **GMP8.1** You buy:

- 1 package of marbles. How many marbles do you have?
  $1 \times 45 = 45$; 45 marbles
- 1 package of file cards. How many file cards do you have?
  $1 \times 100 = 100$; 100 file cards

Math Journal 1, p. 46

Equal-Groups Number Stories   Lesson 2-6
DATE   TIME

Use the information on the Dollar Store Poster on *Student Reference Book*, page 270 to solve each number story. Use an efficient strategy. Show your work with drawings or words. Write number models to show your thinking.
Sample number models given.

1 Shanna buys 3 boxes of mini stock cars to share with her classmates. How many cars does she have all together?

Answer: **30 cars**
              (unit)
Number model: $3 \times 10 = 30; 10 + 10 + 10 = 30$

How much do 3 boxes of cars cost?

Answer: **$9**
              (unit)
Number model: $3 \times 3 = 9; 3 + 3 + 3 = 9$

2 A teacher buys 1 package of Value Pack pens and 0 packages of chocolate-scented pens. How many pens does she buy in all?

Answer: **10 pens**
              (unit)
Number models: $1 \times 10 = 10, 0 \times 6 = 0,$
$0 + 10 = 10$

46   forty-six   3.OA.1, 3.OA.3, 3.OA.7 SMP6, SMP8

Multiplying by 1 can be thought of as 1 group of something, which is that number of things.

- 0 packages of marbles. How many marbles do you have?
  $0 \times 45 = 0$; 0 marbles
- 0 bags of 9-inch balloons. How many balloons do you have?
  $0 \times 25 = 0$; 0 balloons

Multiplying by 0 can be thought of as 0 groups of something. Zero groups means nothing, so the answer is 0.

Display $1 \times 10 = 10$ and ask: *What number story could match this number model?* Sample answer: I buy 1 box of mini stock cars. How many cars do I have? I have 10 cars or 1 group of cars. Repeat with $0 \times 10 = 0$. Sample answer: I only have $1, so I cannot buy any groups of cars. I have zero cars because $0 \times 10 = 0$.

Have partnerships use the Dollar Store Poster to think of number stories that match the following number models:

- $1 \times 6 = 6$ Sample answer: You buy 1 package of party hats. How many party hats do you have? You have 6 party hats.
- $0 \times 8 = 0$ Sample answer: If you have 0 packages of pencils, you have 0 pencils.

Help children use the stories to explain the resulting products of their facts. As needed, provide additional stories using 1 and 0 groups.

▶ Solving Equal-Groups Stories

Math Journal 1, p. 46; Student Reference Book, p. 270

WHOLE CLASS   **SMALL GROUP**   PARTNER   **INDEPENDENT**

Have children solve the stories on journal page 46 using *Student Reference Book*, page 270.

✓ **Assessment Check-In** CCSS 3.OA.1, 3.OA.3

Math Journal 1, p. 46

Expect most children to solve the problems using skip counting, repeated addition, or known multiplication facts. Support children who count by 1s by referring them to the Fact Strategy Wall for more efficient strategies. (*See Lesson 1-10.*) **GMP6.4** For children who struggle to make sense of the problems, ask guiding questions similar to those in the Guide to Solving Number Stories.

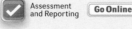 Assessment and Reporting **Go Online** to record student progress and to see trajectories toward mastery for these standards.

When most children finish, bring them together to discuss their solutions and number models. Help children reflect on the efficiency of their strategies and make sense of multiplying by 1 and 0. **GMP6.4**

Summarize Have children generalize how to multiply by 0 or 1 and add their ideas to the Fact Strategy Wall. Record ideas that demonstrate understanding of properties, such as "To multiply by 0, I think of 0 groups of something, which would be 0," and "To multiply by 1, I think of 1 group of something, which would give me that number of things." GMP8.1

3 Practice 15–20 min

Go Online — ePresentations · eToolkit · Home Connections

▶ Minute Math+

To practice mental math strategies, select a *Minute Math+* activity.

▶ Finding Elapsed Time

Math Masters, p. TA11

| WHOLE CLASS | SMALL GROUP | **PARTNER** | INDEPENDENT |

To provide additional practice measuring time intervals in minutes, have partners cut apart one set of Elapsed Time Cards Deck A from *Math Masters*, page TA11. Have one partner set a toolkit clock and read the time. The other partner should draw an Elapsed Time card to determine the change in time and set a clock to the new time. GMP5.2 Advance to Deck B (*Math Masters*, page TA12) as children are ready.

▶ Math Boxes 2-6

Math Journal 1, p. 47

| WHOLE CLASS | **SMALL GROUP** | **PARTNER** | **INDEPENDENT** |

Mixed Practice Math Boxes 2-6 are grouped with Math Boxes 2-8 and 2-11.

▶ Home Link 2-6

Math Masters, p. 58

Homework Children solve equal-groups number stories with efficient strategies. They also make sense of multiplying by 0 and 1. GMP6.4

Planning Ahead

If you do not already have ready-made fraction circle sets, carefully cut apart the fraction circle pieces on *Math Journal 1*, Activity Sheets 6–8, one set per child. Fraction circles are introduced in Lesson 2-12 and used throughout the year.

Math Journal 1, p. 47

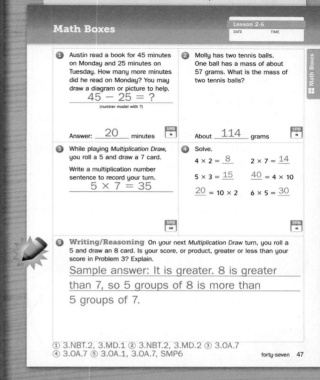

Math Boxes — Lesson 2-6

① Austin read a book for 45 minutes on Monday and 25 minutes on Tuesday. How many more minutes did he read on Monday? You may draw a diagram or picture to help.

$$45 - 25 = ?$$
(number model with ?)

Answer: __20__ minutes

② Molly has two tennis balls. One ball has a mass of about 57 grams. What is the mass of two tennis balls?

About __114__ grams

③ While playing *Multiplication Draw*, you roll a 5 and draw a 7 card. Write a multiplication number sentence to record your turn.

$$5 \times 7 = 35$$

④ Solve.

$4 \times 2 = 8$ $2 \times 7 = 14$
$5 \times 3 = 15$ $40 = 4 \times 10$
$20 = 10 \times 2$ $6 \times 5 = 30$

⑤ **Writing/Reasoning** On your next *Multiplication Draw* turn, you roll a 5 and draw an 8 card. Is your score, or product, greater or less than your score in Problem 3? Explain.

Sample answer: It is greater. 8 is greater than 7, so 5 groups of 8 is more than 5 groups of 7.

① 3.NBT.2, 3.MD.1 ② 3.NBT.2, 3.MD.2 ③ 3.OA.7
④ 3.OA.7 ⑤ 3.OA.1, 3.OA.7, SMP6   forty-seven 47

Math Masters, p. 58 51

Equal-Groups Number Stories — Home Link 2-6

NAME   DATE   TIME

Family Note Today your child practiced using efficient ways to solve equal-groups number stories, such as using repeated addition, skip counting, or using facts he or she knows. Children also talked about what multiplying by 0 or 1 means. Encourage your child to use the number stories to explain why multiplying by 0 equals 0 and multiplying by 1 equals the number in one group.

Please return this Home Link to school tomorrow.

Solve. Show your thinking using drawings, words, or number models.

A pack of Brilliant Color Markers contains 5 markers. Each pack costs $2.

① If you buy 6 packs, how many markers will you have?

Answer: __30 markers__
(unit)

② How much do 0 packs of Brilliant Color Markers cost?

Answer: __$0__
(unit)

Explain your answer. Sample answer: If I buy 0 packs of markers, I do not buy any markers, so my cost is $0.

③ Make up a number story to match the number sentence below:
$1 \times 5 = 5$
Sample answer: I have 1 hand with 5 fingers. How many fingers do I have in all? I have 5 fingers in all.

58   3.OA.1, 3.OA.3, 3.OA.5, 3.OA.7, 3.OA.9, 3.NBT.2, SMP6

Multiplication Arrays

Overview Children solve array problems and play *Array Bingo.*

▶ **Before You Begin**
For Part 1, select and sequence Quick Look Cards 131, 132, and 133. For Part 2 Math Message, display and label a 2-by-5 array to remind children what an array looks like. You will need one set each per partnership of *Array Bingo* Cards cut from *Math Masters,* page G8 (see Planning Ahead in Lesson 2-4) and number cards 1–20.

▶ **Vocabulary**
array • number sentence • factors • product

Common Core State Standards

Focus Clusters
• Represent and solve problems involving multiplication and division.
• Multiply and divide within 100.

---

1 Warm Up 5–10 min

Materials

Mental Math and Fluency
Children practice Quick Looks with equal groups and arrays.

Quick Look Cards 131, 132, and 133

3.OA.1, 3.OA.7
SMP2, SMP6

---

2 Focus 45–50 min

Math Message
Children find multiple arrays for 24.

Math Masters, p. TA17; counters (optional)

3.OA.2, 3.OA.3

Exploring Many Arrays, Same Total
Children discuss how to find all possible arrays for a product.

Math Masters, p. TA17; counters (optional)

3.OA.1, 3.OA.3
SMP3, SMP4

Representing Number Stories with Arrays
Children draw arrays to represent number stories.

Math Journal 1, p. 48; *Math Masters,* p. TA18 and p. TA20 (optional); counters (optional)

3.OA.1, 3.OA.3, 3.OA.4
SMP2, SMP4

✓ **Assessment Check-In**   See page 164.

Math Journal 1, p. 48

3.OA.1, 3.OA.3, SMP2

Introducing *Array Bingo*
Game Children practice multiplication with arrays and equal groups.

Student Reference Book, pp. 232 and 233; *Math Masters,* p. G8; number cards 1–20

3.OA.1, 3.OA.7
SMP2

CCSS 3.OA.3 **Spiral Snapshot**

GMC Use multiplication and division to solve number stories.

| 2-6 Focus Practice | 2-7 Focus Practice | 2-8 through 2-10 Warm Up Focus Practice | 2-11 Practice | 3-8 Practice | 3-10 through 3-12 Warm Up Focus Practice |

Spiral Tracker **Go Online** to see how mastery develops for all standards within the grade.

---

3 Practice 10–15 min

Minute Math+
Children practice mental math strategies.

Minute Math®+

Math Boxes 2-7
Children practice and maintain skills.

Math Journal 1, p. 49

See page 165.

Home Link 2-7
Homework Children practice representing array situations.

Math Masters, p. 60

3.OA.1, 3.OA.3
SMP4

---

connectED.mcgraw-hill.com

Plan your lessons online with these tools.

 ePresentations

 Student Learning Center

Facts Workshop Game

 eToolkit

Professional Development

 Home Connections

 Spiral Tracker

 Assessment and Reporting

 ELL English Learners Support

 Differentiation Support

Differentiation Options

CCSS 3.OA.1, SMP5

Readiness | 10–15 min

Building Arrays

WHOLE CLASS
SMALL GROUP
PARTNER
INDEPENDENT

Activity Card 24; *Math Masters,* pp. 59 and TA19; 6-sided die; centimeter cubes

To provide experience with multiplication, have children build arrays with centimeter cubes. Have partners record the arrays on *Math Masters,* page TA19 and fill in the Building Arrays Record Sheet on *Math Masters,* page 59. Then have children discuss how building arrays can help them learn multiplication facts. GMP5.2

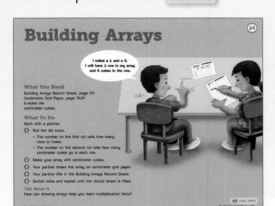

CCSS 3.OA.1, SMP7

Enrichment | 10–15 min

Building and Predicting with Arrays

WHOLE CLASS
SMALL GROUP
PARTNER
INDEPENDENT

Activity Card 25; centimeter cubes; 5" by 7" index cards labeled with 1, 2, and 5; 10-sided die

To further explore arrays, have children build arrays for 1s, 2s, or 5s facts with centimeter cubes. Have them write number models, look for patterns, and predict the next array. Then have children build additional arrays to check their predictions and discuss the patterns they notice. GMP7.1

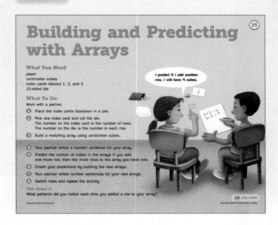

CCSS 3.OA.1, SMP2

Extra Practice | 5–15 min

Drawing Arrays for Fact Triangles

WHOLE CLASS
SMALL GROUP
PARTNER
INDEPENDENT

Activity Card 26; Fact Triangles; counters (optional)

To provide practice with multiplication, have children draw arrays for Fact Triangles. GMP2.1, GMP2.2 Have partners talk about how the arrays match each fact family and how the arrays could help them learn multiplication and division facts. GMP2.3

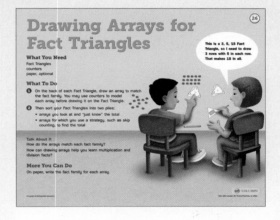

English Language Learners Support

Beginning ELL Help children describe nonverbally how they saw the dots on the Quick Look Cards. Show them how to use up-and-down gestures for *column,* side-to-side gestures for *row,* and their fingers to show how many dots they saw in each row or column. Verbalize children's nonverbal accounts with short statements, and then have them revoice your statements using *I* as they point to themselves. For example: *You saw three rows going across.* "I saw three rows going across." *You saw three dots in each row.* "I saw three dots in each row."

Go Online > | ELL | English Learners Support

SMP2 **Reason abstractly and quantitatively.**
GMP2.2 Make sense of the representations you and others use.

SMP3 **Construct viable arguments and critique the reasoning of others.**
GMP3.1 Make mathematical conjectures and arguments.

SMP4 **Model with mathematics.**
GMP4.1 Model real-world situations using graphs, drawings, tables, symbols, numbers, diagrams, and other representations.

1 Warm Up 5–10 min

Go Online | ePresentations | eToolkit

▶ Mental Math and Fluency

Show Quick Look Cards 131, 132, and 133 one at a time for 2–3 seconds. Ask children to share both what they saw and how they saw it.
GMP2.2, GMP6.1 Highlight strategies involving equal groups or arrays.

Quick Look Card 131 Sample answer: I saw 2 rows of 2, and that makes 4.
Quick Look Card 132 Sample answer: I saw 2 rows of 5, and $5 + 5 = 10$.
Quick Look Card 133 Sample answer: I saw 3 rows of 3, and I know $3 + 3 = 6$ and $6 + 3 = 9$.

2 Focus 45–50 min

Go Online | ePresentations | eToolkit

▶ Math Message

Math Masters, p. TA17

Suppose there are 24 trombone players in a big parade. Find at least 3 different ways the players could arrange themselves into an array to march. Shade or draw Xs in the squares on your grid paper to record each array.

▶ Exploring Many Arrays, Same Total

Math Masters, p. TA17

| WHOLE CLASS | SMALL GROUP | PARTNER | INDEPENDENT |

Math Message Follow-Up Remind children that a rectangular **array** is an arrangement of objects in rows and columns. Have children display their arrays until the class is sure all the possibilities have been shown. As each array is discussed, have children suggest number models to match. Record the number models with the arrays. **GMP4.1** The arrays are 4-by-6, 6-by-4, 3-by-8, 8-by-3, 2-by-12, 12-by-2, 1-by-24, and 24-by-1. The number models are $4 \times 6 = 24$, $6 \times 4 = 24$, $3 \times 8 = 24$, $8 \times 3 = 24$, $2 \times 12 = 24$, $12 \times 2 = 24$, $1 \times 24 = 24$, and $24 \times 1 = 24$.

Help children differentiate between the two possible arrays formed by a set of factors. For example, a 4-by-6 array would represent 4 rows of 6 players, while a 6-by-4 array would represent 6 rows of 4 players. (*See margin.*) Although both have the same number of players, these arrays would look different in a parade.

Remind children that the two numbers being multiplied together in each **number sentence** are called **factors,** and the resulting total is called the **product.** Support children in applying these ideas by asking the following:

- *What factors did we find for 24?* 1, 2, 3, 4, 6, 8, 12, 24 Point to them in the number models as you list them.
- *What are some numbers that we have not used as factors of 24?* Sample answers: 5; 7; 9
- *Could those numbers work as factors of 24? Explain.* **GMP3.1** Sample answer: No. I tried to use 5, but 5 rows of 4 gives me 20 with 4 left over. 5 rows of 5 is 25, so I would be one short.

Point out that if it is not possible to form a complete rectangle using a particular number of rows, then that number is not a factor of 24. Gesture to an array of 24 to emphasize the filled rows and columns, and trace around the rectangular border. Explain that today children will work with arrays to help them think about and solve multiplication problems.

▶ Representing Number Stories with Arrays

Math Journal 1, p. 48; *Math Masters,* p. TA18

| WHOLE CLASS | SMALL GROUP | PARTNER | INDEPENDENT |

Ask: *What have we used so far to show our arrays?* Sample answers: Dots, Xs, shading in squares on grid paper, counters Display the dot grids on *Math Masters,* page TA18 and model how to mark dots with an X to show the 3-by-8 array from the Math Message.

Pose the following number story: *3 boxes of crayons, 5 crayons in each box: how many crayons?* 15 crayons

As children follow along, use *Math Masters,* page TA18 to model representing the number story in Problem 1 on journal page 48.

- Write the topic for the story. For example: crayons.
- Record a number model using a question mark to represent the unknown quantity. For example: $3 \times 5 = ?$ or $? = 3 \times 5$. **GMP4.1**

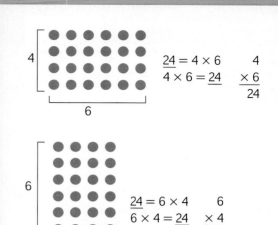

$$24 = 4 \times 6 \qquad \begin{array}{r} 4 \\ \times 6 \\ \hline 24 \end{array}$$
$$4 \times 6 = \underline{24}$$

$$24 = 6 \times 4 \qquad \begin{array}{r} 6 \\ \times 4 \\ \hline 24 \end{array}$$
$$6 \times 4 = \underline{24}$$

Academic Language Development

Have children work in partnerships to explain the meaning of the term *array* using the 4-Square Graphic Organizer (*Math Masters,* page TA20) with the headings Definition, Visual Representation/Picture, Non-Example, and Example. Challenge children to use the terms *factor* and *product* in their definitions.

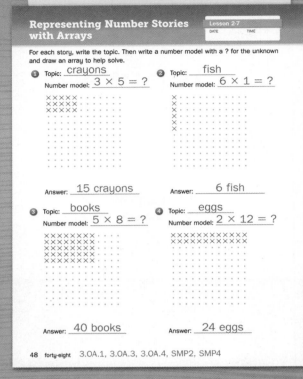

Representing Number Stories with Arrays

For each story, write the topic. Then write a number model with a ? for the unknown and draw an array to help solve.

① Topic: crayons
Number model: 3 × 5 = ?
Answer: 15 crayons

② Topic: fish
Number model: 6 × 1 = ?
Answer: 6 fish

③ Topic: books
Number model: 5 × 8 = ?
Answer: 40 books

④ Topic: eggs
Number model: 2 × 12 = ?
Answer: 24 eggs

48 forty-eight   3.OA.1, 3.OA.3, 3.OA.4, SMP2, SMP4

Games

Array Bingo

Materials ☐ 1 set of *Array Bingo* Cards for each player (Math Masters, p. G8)
☐ number cards 1–20 (1 of each)

Players   2 or 3

Skill   Modeling multiplication with arrays

Object of the Game   To have a row, column, or diagonal of cards facedown.

Directions

❶ Each player arranges his or her *Array Bingo* Cards faceup in a 4-by-4 array.

❷ Shuffle the number cards. Place them number-side down.

❸ Players take turns. When it is your turn, draw a number card. Look for any one of your array cards with that number of dots and turn it facedown. If there is no matching array card, your turn ends. Place your number card in a discard pile.

❹ The first player to turn a card facedown so that a row, column, or diagonal of cards is all facedown calls out "Bingo!" See example on the next page.

❺ If all the number cards are used before someone wins, shuffle the deck and continue playing.

- Draw an array on a dot grid to model the story with 3 rows and 5 Xs in each row. Ask: *What does our array show?* It shows 3 rows with 5 in each row. *How does it represent the story?* GMP2.2, GMP4.1 The 3 rows represent 3 boxes of crayons. The 5 Xs in each row show 5 crayons in each box.

- Solve the problem and share solution strategies, for example, counting the rows by 5s. Be sure to include the unit in the answer.

- Discuss the reasonableness of the answer and whether it makes the number model true.

In a similar manner, have children use arrays to model and solve the following stories using journal page 48. GMP2.2, GMP4.1

- 6 fishbowls, 1 fish per bowl: how many fish? 6 fish
- 5 shelves of books, 8 books per shelf: how many books? 40 books
- 2 cartons of eggs, 12 eggs per carton: how many eggs? 24 eggs

 Assessment Check-In CCSS 3.OA.1, 3.OA.3

Math Journal 1, page 48

Expect most children to create arrays and number models that fit the stories. If children have difficulty translating between equal groups and arrays, label the first row of the array as "group 1," the second row as "group 2," and so on. GMP2.2 If children have difficulty writing number models, remind them that the number of rows and the number of objects in each row in their arrays make up the factors. The total number of objects in their array is the product.

✓ Assessment and Reporting   Go Online   to record student progress and to see trajectories toward mastery for these standards.

Have children share their arrays, and help them recognize that arrays can represent equal-groups situations even when the real-life groups do not look like arrays. GMP2.2

▶ Introducing *Array Bingo*

Student Reference Book, pp. 232 and 233; *Math Masters,* p. G8

| WHOLE CLASS | SMALL GROUP | PARTNER | INDEPENDENT |

To practice recognizing arrays as representations for multiplication facts, have children play *Array Bingo.* GMP2.2 (*See Before You Begin.*) Read and discuss the rules on *Student Reference Book,* page 232 with the class. Play a few rounds together and have children share strategies for matching arrays and products. Refer them to the Fact Strategy Wall and discuss efficient strategies for figuring out the total number of dots in an array, such as skip counting, repeated addition, and recalling known multiplication facts.

Observe

- Do children correctly match products and arrays?
- Which arrays do children instantly recognize? Which are more difficult for them to match? **GMP2.2**

Discuss

- *Which arrays do you recognize easily, or "just know"?*
- *What strategies did you use to find the total dots in the arrays? Can you think of more efficient strategies you could use?*

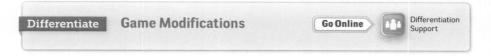

| Differentiate | Game Modifications | Go Online | Differentiation Support |

Summarize Have children share their strategies for finding the total number of dots in the arrays in *Array Bingo.* Add new strategies to the Fact Strategy Wall.

3 Practice   10–15 min   Go Online

ePresentations   eToolkit   Home Connections

▶ Minute Math+

To practice mental math strategies, select a *Minute Math+* activity.

▶ Math Boxes 2-7

Math Journal 1, p. 49

| WHOLE CLASS | SMALL GROUP | PARTNER | INDEPENDENT |

Mixed Practice Math Boxes 2-7 are paired with Math Boxes 2-5.

▶ Home Link 2-7

Math Masters, p. 60

Homework Children practice representing array situations, including finding several arrays for a given product. **GMP4.1**

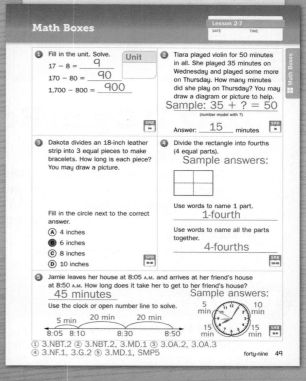

Math Journal 1, p. 49

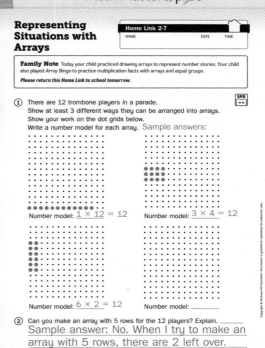

Math Masters, p. 60

Picturing Division

Overview **Day 1:** Children create mathematical representations for solving division problems. **Day 2:** Children discuss representations and solutions and then revise their work.

2-Day Lesson

Day 1: Open Response

▶ **Before You Begin**
Solve the open response problem and think about different ways children might represent their solutions. If possible, schedule time to review children's work and plan for Day 2 of this lesson with your grade-level team.

▶ **Vocabulary**
division • representation • remainder

 Common Core State Standards

Focus Cluster
Represent and solve problems involving multiplication and division.

1 Warm Up   5 min

	Materials	
Mental Math and Fluency Children do start-and-stop skip counting.	slate	3.OA.7

2a Focus   55–65 min

Math Message Children represent and solve an equal-sharing problem.	*Math Journal 1*, p. 50	**3.OA.2, 3.OA.3, 3.OA.4** **SMP2**
Comparing Mathematical Representations Children compare their representations.	*Math Journal 1*, p. 50	**3.OA.2, 3.OA.3, 3.OA.4** **SMP1, SMP2**
Solving the Open Response Problem Children use representations to solve division problems.	*Math Masters*, p. 61; counters; slate and marker; stick-on notes (optional)	**3.OA.2, 3.OA.3, 3.OA.4** **SMP1, SMP2**

Getting Ready for Day 2 →

Review children's work and plan discussion for reengagement. *Math Masters*, p. TA6; children's work from Day 1

CCSS 3.OA.2 **Spiral Snapshot**

GMC Interpret division in terms of equal shares or equal groups.

| 2-7
Focus
Practice | 2-8
Focus | 2-9
Focus | 2-10
Focus | 2-12
Focus
Practice | 3-1 through 3-3
Practice | 3-10
Warm Up
Practice |

/// Spiral Tracker **Go Online** to see how mastery develops for all standards within the grade.

connectED.mcgraw-hill.com

Plan your lessons online
with these tools.

 ePresentations
 Student Learning Center
 Facts Workshop Game
 eToolkit
 Professional Development
 Home Connections
 Spiral Tracker
Assessment and Reporting
ELL English Learners Support
 Differentiation Support

166 Unit 2 | Number Stories and Arrays

1 Warm Up

5 min

Go Online

ePresentations eToolkit

▶ Mental Math and Fluency

To support multiplication, have children do start-and-stop skip counting and record the next number on their slates. *Leveled exercises:*

● ○ ○ Skip count forward by 5s from 25 to 55. 60 Skip count back by 10s from 70 to 20. 10

● ● ○ Skip count forward by 2s from 20 to 48. 50 Skip count back by 5s from 60 to 20. 15

● ● ● Skip count forward by 2s from 46 to 66. 68 Skip count back by 2s from 46 to 28. 26

2a Focus

55–65 min

Go Online

ePresentations eToolkit

▶ Math Message

Math Journal 1, p. 50

Complete journal page 50. Share your drawing with a partner. **GMP2.1**

▶ Comparing Mathematical Representations

Math Journal 1, p. 50

| **WHOLE CLASS** | SMALL GROUP | PARTNER | INDEPENDENT |

Math Message Follow-Up Children's strategies for solving the problem may include counting by 1s or 2s to equally share the pennies (for example, one for you and one for me). They may recognize that 14 has 2 equal parts of 7, or they may think of the multiplication or division fact and determine the missing factor (for example, 2 times what number is 14). Children's representations of their strategies may vary as well. Have a few children with different representations draw and display them. **GMP2.1** Then have children make sense of and compare the different strategies and their representations. Representations may include:

• two groups of 7 tally marks

• an addition number model ($7 + 7 = ?$ or $7 + 7 = 14$), multiplication number model ($2 \times ? = 14$ or $2 \times 7 = 14$), or **division** number model ($14 \div 2 = ?$ or $14 \div 2 = 7$)

Standards and Goals for Mathematical Practice

SMP1 **Make sense of problems and persevere in solving them.**
  GMP1.6 Compare the strategies you and others use.

SMP2 **Reason abstractly and quantitatively.**
  GMP2.1 Create mathematical representations using numbers, words, pictures, symbols, gestures, tables, graphs, and concrete objects.
  GMP2.2 Make sense of the representations you and others use.

Professional Development

The focus of this lesson is **GMP2.1**. Children represent number stories involving equal shares or equal groups using manipulatives, drawings, words, or number models. Then they make sense of others' representations. For more information on **GMP2.1**, see the Mathematical Background section in the Unit Organizer.

Go Online to the *Implementation Guide* for more information about **SMP2**.

Math Journal 1, p. 50

Sharing Pennies

Lesson 2-8

DATE   TIME

Solve the problem below.
Use drawings, numbers, and words to show your thinking.

Leah and Matthew share 14 pennies equally.
How many pennies does each child get?

Sample answer:

Ⓟ Ⓟ Ⓟ Ⓟ Ⓟ Ⓟ Ⓟ   Ⓟ Ⓟ Ⓟ Ⓟ Ⓟ Ⓟ Ⓟ
Leah   Matthew
$14 \div 2 = 7$

Answer: ___7___ pennies

50 fifty   3.OA.2, 3.OA.3, 3.OA.4, SMP2

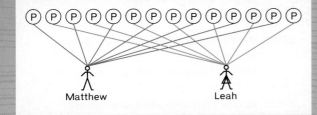

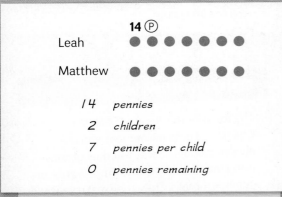

14 Ⓟ

Leah ● ● ● ● ● ● ●

Matthew ● ● ● ● ● ● ●

14   pennies
2   children
7   pennies per child
0   pennies remaining

Leah and Matthew share 14 pennies equally.

- drawings such as two circles with 7 pennies in each or 14 pennies in a row with lines drawn to Leah and Matthew to show 7 pennies each, as shown in the margin
- an array with two equal rows of 7 dots or Xs, as shown in the margin

If an array is not among the representations shown, model an array as described above.

As a class, compare the different representations and make connections among them. **GMP1.6** Ask:

- *How is this picture or representation of the problem similar to another child's? How is it different?* Answers vary.
- *How did you use the drawing (array, number model) to help you solve the problem?* Sample answer: For my array, I made a row of dots for Matthew and a row for Leah. I took turns putting a dot in Matthew's row and then Leah's row until I counted 14 in all. There were 7 dots in each row.
- *Does this representation match the problem?* **GMP2.2** *How do you know?* Sample answer: It shows two children and 14 pennies shared fairly between them, so it matches.
- *How does this picture show that the pennies are shared equally?* Sample answers: Leah and Matthew each have 7 pennies. The pennies are divided into two groups of 7.

Have children explain their equal-sharing strategies and encourage them to ask questions when they are unsure about others' strategies.

English Language Learners Support Prior to the lesson, use counters to preview the vocabulary for situations involving sharing. Give Total Physical Response commands and ask short questions, such as: *Pick up 8 counters. Divide the counters to share them equally between 2 people. How many did each person get?* 4 counters *Share the counters equally between 4 people. How many did each person get?* 2 counters *Pick up 7 counters. Divide the counters to share equally between 3 people. How many did each person get?* 2 counters *How many are left over?* 1 counter

Explain that a **representation** includes the pictures, numbers, and words they use to solve the problem and communicate their thinking. Point to the representations displayed. Tell children they will continue to work on representing number story solutions.

NOTE The Math Message problem is an example of an equal-sharing problem. The number of groups and the total number of objects are known, and the number of objects in each group is to be found. The open response problem is an equal-grouping problem, which is another type of problem that can be solved using division. The number of objects per group and the total number of objects are known. The number of equal groups is to be found. It is important that children have experience with both types of problems, but they do not need to be able to distinguish between them.

▶ Solving the Open Response Problem

Math Masters, p. 61

| WHOLE CLASS | SMALL GROUP | **PARTNER** | INDEPENDENT |

Distribute *Math Masters*, page 61. Read each problem with the class and ask partners to briefly discuss what they know from each problem and what they need to find out. Emphasize that children should use representations to show how they solve the problems so someone else can understand their thinking. **GMP2.1** Make slates, markers, and counters available so children can act out the problem, but remind them to record drawings and words that describe their thinking on paper.

As children work, observe their strategies and ask them to explain the meaning of their drawings and words, even if it is clear to you. For children who finish quickly, encourage them to solve the problems using different strategies or representations, such as arrays or number models. **GMP2.1**

Strategies for Problem 2 may be similar to those used for Problem 1. Note how children interpret the **remainder** in this problem. Some children may recognize that they need a fourth table for the remaining 2 children even though it is not full. Other children may choose to seat 5 children at each of the 4 tables. Ask children to be sure their drawings show how many children are at each table. If children suggest that only 3 tables are needed, ask them to explain their thinking and whether all 20 children will have seats at tables.

Math Masters, p. 61

Picturing Division

Lesson 2-8
NAME · DATE · TIME

Solve each problem.
Use pictures and words to show your thinking.

① There are 20 children in art class. If 4 children can sit at each table, how many tables do they need?

Answers vary. See sample children's work on page 175 of the *Teacher's Lesson Guide*.

_____ tables

② There are 20 children in music class. If 6 children can sit at each table, how many tables do they need?

Answers vary. See sample children's work on page 175 of the *Teacher's Lesson Guide*.

_____ tables

3.OA.2, 3.OA.3, 3.OA.4, SMP1, SMP2 · 61

Common Misconception

Differentiate Some children may think of 4 as the number of children in each group, rather than the number of tables (groups). Have them review the context of the problem and ask whether their strategies make sense. These children may benefit from using counters to represent children and stick-on notes to represent tables. With these manipulatives, children can create a representation that reflects the number of children at each table to help them determine the total number of tables needed.

1. There are 20 children in art class. If 4 children can sit at each table, how many tables do they need?

_5_ tables

2. There are 20 children in music class. If 6 children can sit at each table, how many tables do they need?

_4_ tables

1. There are 20 children in art class. If 4 children can sit at each table, how many tables do they need?

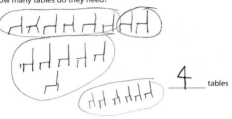

_5_ tables

2. There are 20 children in music class. If 6 children can sit at each table, how many tables do they need?

$20 \div 5 = 4$

_4_ tables

Summarize Ask: *How was your solution for Problem 2 different from your solution for Problem 1?* GMP1.6 Sample answer: In Problem 1, all the tables were full and the groups came out even. In Problem 2, I put only 2 children at the last table.

Collect children's work so that you can evaluate it and prepare for Day 2.

Getting Ready for Day 2

Math Masters, p. TA6

Planning a Follow-Up Discussion

Review children's work. Use the Reengagement Planning Form (*Math Masters*, page TA6) and the rubric on page 172 to plan ways to help children meet expectations for both the content and practice standards. Look for common misconceptions, such as interpreting the remainder in Problem 2 incorrectly, as well as interesting and varied representations of the solutions including drawings, arrays, and number models.

Reengagement Planning Form

Common Core State Standard (CCSS): *3.OA.2 Interpret whole-number quotients of whole numbers . . . as the number of objects in each share. . . . 3.OA.3 Use multiplication and division within 100 to solve word problems in situations involving equal groups, arrays, and measurement quantities. . . .*
Goal for Mathematical Practice (GMP): *GMP2.1: Create mathematical representations using numbers, words, pictures, symbols, gestures, tables, graphs, and concrete objects.*

Organize the discussion in one of the ways below or in another way you choose. If children's work is unclear or if you prefer to show work anonymously, rewrite the work for display.

Go Online for sample children's work that you can use in your discussion.

1. Display two different strategies with correct responses for Problem 1, such as Child A's work and Child B's work. Have children compare and contrast the two strategies. Ask:
   - *After looking at their pictures, what can you tell about how these children solved the problem?* Answers vary.
   - *How are their representations different?* Sample answer: Child A drew pictures of tables and children, and Child B did not.
   - *How did Child B represent the tables and children in the picture?* Sample answer: The child drew an array. The child drew a circle for each child and put 4 circles in a row to show 4 children can sit at 1 table. There are 5 rows, so that shows you need 5 tables.

- *How are the strategies similar?* `GMP1.6, GMP2.2` Sample answer: Both children knew they had 20 children and could only have 4 children at each table.

2. Display two different strategies with correct responses for Problem 2. For example, Child A's work shows 3 tables with 6 children and 1 table with 2 children, and Child B's work shows 4 tables with 5 children each. Ask:
   - *How are the strategies of Child A and Child B similar in Problem 2?* Sample answer: They both showed 4 tables were needed for the children.
   - *How are their representations different?* Sample answer: Child A has 6 children at 3 tables and 2 children at 1 table. Child B has 5 children at 4 tables.
   - *Are both representations correct?* `GMP1.6, GMP2.2` Sample answer: Yes. They are both correct because the problem doesn't say that you have to put 6 children at each table.

3. Display a child's response that indicates a misconception or incorrect interpretation of what to do with the remainder in Problem 2, such as Child C's work. Ask:
   - *Explain the strategy this child used to find the number of tables needed in Problem 2.* Sample answer: The child put 6 children at 3 tables and put the last 2 on the rug.
   - *Do you agree that the number of tables needed is 3? Why or why not?* `GMP2.1, GMP2.2` Sample answers: I agree that they only need 3 tables because that is all they can fill up; I disagree and think they need 4 tables because it would not be fair for 2 children to sit on the rug.
   - *Do you think the number sentence accurately represents the problem? Is the number sentence a true number sentence?* Sample answer: No. 6 × 3 doesn't equal 18 + 2, so I don't think you should write it like that. *What would you tell this child to improve the number model?* Sample answer: You should write two separate number models like this: 6 × 3 = 18 and then 18 + 2 = 20. *Are the number models true statements now?* Yes.

Planning for Revisions

Have copies of *Math Masters*, page 61 or extra paper available for children to use in revisions. You might want to ask children to use colored pencils so you can see what they revised.

Sample child's work, Child C

2. There are 20 children in music class. If 6 children can sit at each table, how many tables do they need?

$6 \times 3 = 18 + 2 = 20$

KEY
□ = person
— = table
◯ = rug

▦▦▦ ▦▦▦ ▦▦▦ ___3___ tables + 2 people left over can sit on the rug

⬭ (□ □)

Picturing Division

Day 2: Reengagement

▶ **Before You Begin**
Have extra copies of *Math Masters*, page 61 for children to revise their work.

CCSS Common Core State Standards

Focus Cluster
Represent and solve problems involving multiplication and division.

2b Focus   50–55 min

Setting Expectations Children review the open response problem and discuss what a good response might include. They review how to discuss others' work respectfully.	Guidelines for Discussion Poster	SMP2
Reengaging in the Problem Children discuss other children's representations and solutions.	selected samples of children's work	3.OA.2, 3.OA.3, 3.OA.4 SMP1, SMP2
Revising Work Children revise their work from Day 1.	*Math Masters*, p. 61 (optional); counters; colored pencils (optional)	3.OA.2, 3.OA.3, 3.OA.4 SMP1, SMP2
✓ **Assessment Check-In** See page 174 and rubric below.		3.OA.2, 3.OA.3 SMP2

Goal for Mathematical Practice **GMP2.1** Create mathematical representations using numbers, words, pictures, symbols, gestures, tables, graphs, and concrete objects.	Not Meeting Expectations	Partially Meeting Expectations	Meeting Expectations	Exceeding Expectations
	Does not provide representations for either Problem 1 or Problem 2, or both representations are incomplete or unclear.	Provides a representation for one of the problems, but not both, that is complete and clearly communicates an equal-grouping strategy.	Provides representations for both Problems 1 and 2 that are complete and clearly communicate equal-grouping strategies and solutions.	Meets expectations and provides a second representation for one of the problems that shows a different strategy.

3 Practice   10–15 min

Math Boxes 2-8 Children practice and maintain skills.	*Math Journal 1*, p. 51	See page 175.
Home Link 2-8 **Homework** Children solve division problems and represent their work with drawings, words, and number models.	*Math Masters*, p. 62	3.OA.2, 3.OA.3, 3.OA.4 SMP2

2b) Focus — 50–55 min

ePresentations   eToolkit

NOTE These Day 2 activities will ideally take place within a few days of Day 1. Prior to beginning Day 2, see Planning a Follow-Up Discussion from Day 1.

▶ Setting Expectations

WHOLE CLASS | SMALL GROUP | PARTNER | INDEPENDENT

Revisiting Guidelines for Reengagement

To promote a cooperative environment, consider revisiting the class guidelines for discussion that you developed in Unit 1. Review the guidelines and have children reflect on how well they are following them. Solicit additional guidelines from the class. Your revised list might look like the one in the margin. You may wish to focus on a particular guideline in today's discussion, such as listening to others' ideas or asking questions.

Model some of the sentence frames to show children appropriate language for discussing other children's work:

- I like how you _____.
- I'd like to add _____.
- Could you explain _____?
- I wonder why _____.
- I agree/disagree with that because _____.

Reviewing the Problem

Briefly review the open response problem from Day 1. Remind children that their tasks were to solve both of the problems and to use pictures, numbers, and written explanations to show their thinking. Ask: *What do you think a complete response needs to include?* GMP2.1 Sample answer: It should include representations for both problems that show how that child solved them.

Then tell children that they are going to look at other children's work and think about their different representations and strategies.

▶ Reengaging in the Problem

WHOLE CLASS | SMALL GROUP | **PARTNER** | INDEPENDENT

Children reengage in the problem by analyzing and critiquing other children's work in pairs and in a whole-group discussion. Have children discuss with partners before sharing with the whole group. Guide this discussion based on the decisions you made in Getting Ready for Day 2.
GMP1.6, GMP2.1, GMP2.2

Guidelines for Discussion

During our discussions, we can:

✓ *Make mistakes and learn from them*

✓ *Share ideas and strategies respectfully*

✓ *Agree and disagree politely*

✓ *Change our minds about how to solve a problem*

✓ *Feel confused*

✓ *Ask questions of our teacher and classmates*

✓ *Listen closely to others' ideas*

✓ *Be patient*

✓ *Take time to think about someone else's solution without rushing*

✓ *Use tools to help explain our thinking*

▶ Revising Work

WHOLE CLASS | SMALL GROUP | **PARTNER** | **INDEPENDENT**

Pass back children's work from Day 1. Before children revise anything, ask them to examine their drawings and explanations and decide how to improve them. Ask the following questions one at a time. Have partners discuss their responses and give a thumbs-up or thumbs-down based on their own work.

- *Did you show all of your work using drawings, words, or numbers so someone else can understand your thinking?* GMP1.6
- *Do you still agree with your original answers?* GMP2.1
- *Does your partner's work make sense to you?* GMP2.2

Tell children they now have a chance to revise their work. Make counters available, but remind children they need to represent their strategies on their papers. Help children see that the strategies shown in the reengagement discussion are not the only strategies they may use. If children produced clear representations on Day 1, encourage them to try new strategies and show their work using pictures and words. Tell children to add to their earlier work using colored pencils or to use another sheet of paper, instead of erasing their original work.

Summarize Have children reflect on their work. Ask: *How did you improve your representations?* GMP2.1 Answers vary. *What did you learn from other children's strategies and representations?* GMP1.6 Answers vary.

✔ Assessment Check-In CCSS 3.OA.2, 3.OA.3

Collect and review children's revised work. Expect children to improve their work based on the class discussion. For the content standards, expect most children to correctly solve Problem 1 in terms of equal groups. Some may struggle more with Problem 2, especially if they chose to put 6 children at 3 tables and needed to decide what to do with the remaining 2 children. Do not expect all children to correctly interpret the remainder at this point. You can use the rubric on page 172 to evaluate children's revised work for **GMP2.1**.

 Assessment and Reporting Go Online to record student progress and to see trajectories toward mastery for these standards.

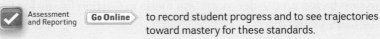 Go Online for optional generic rubrics in the *Assessment Handbook* that can be used to assess any additional GMPs addressed in the lesson.

Sample Children's Work—Evaluated

See the sample in the margin. This work meets expectations for the content standards because the child correctly solved Problem 1, interpreting the number story as an equal-grouping problem. The work meets expectations for the mathematical practice because the drawings for Problems 1 and 2 clearly show the equal-grouping strategy the child used. **GMP2.1**

Go Online for other samples of evaluated children's work.

3 Practice 10–15 min

ePresentations eToolkit Home Connections

▶ Math Boxes 2-8

Math Journal 1, p. 51

| WHOLE CLASS | SMALL GROUP | PARTNER | INDEPENDENT |

Mixed Practice Math Boxes 2-8 are grouped with Math Boxes 2-6 and 2-11.

▶ Home Link 2-8

Math Masters, p. 62

Homework Children solve division problems and represent their work with drawings, words, and number models. **GMP2.1**

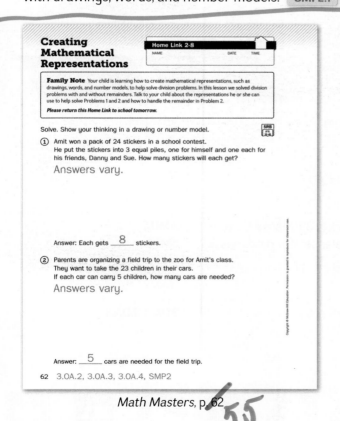

Math Masters, p. 62

Sample child's work, "Meeting Expectations"

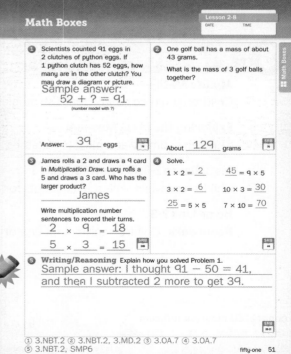

Math Journal 1, p. 51

Modeling Division

Overview Children solve division number stories and learn about remainders.

▶ **Before You Begin**
For Part 3, have a pan balance and standard masses along with items from the Mass Museum available for children to explore.

▶ **Vocabulary**
remainder • dividend • divisor • quotient

CCSS **Common Core State Standards**

Focus Clusters
• Represent and solve problems involving multiplication and division.
• Develop understanding of fractions as numbers.

1 **Warm Up** 5 min	**Materials**	
Mental Math and Fluency Children solve division number stories.	slate	3.OA.3

2 **Focus** 40–50 min		
Math Message Children solve an equal-sharing problem.	slate	3.OA.3, 3.NF.1, 3.G.2 SMP2
Exploring Sharing Problems Children discuss equal-sharing representations.	*Math Masters*, p. TA20 (optional); slate	3.OA.3, 3.NF.1, 3.G.2 SMP1, SMP2, SMP3
Modeling with Division Children divide to solve number stories and learn about remainders.	*Student Reference Book*, p. 30 (optional); slate; counters (optional)	3.OA.2, 3.OA.3 SMP2
Dividing to Solve Number Stories Children represent and solve division number stories.	*Math Journal 1*, p. 52; counters (optional)	3.OA.2, 3.OA.3, 3.OA.7 SMP2
✓ **Assessment Check-In** See page 181.	*Math Journal 1*, p. 52	3.OA.2, 3.OA.3, SMP2

CCSS 3.OA.3 **Spiral Snapshot**

GMC Model number stories involving multiplication and division.

| 1-9
Focus
Practice | 2-5 through 2-7
Focus
Practice | 2-9
Focus
Practice | 2-10
Focus
Practice | 2-11
Practice | 3-5 through 3-8
Practice |

III Spiral Tracker (**Go Online**) to see how mastery develops for all standards within the grade.

3 **Practice** 15–20 min		
Minute Math+ Children practice mental math strategies.	*Minute Math*®+	
Exploring the Mass Museum Children estimate and measure masses.	*Math Masters*, p. 39; Mass Museum items; pan balance; standard masses	3.MD.2 SMP5
Math Boxes 2-9: Preview for Unit 3 Children preview skills and concepts for Unit 3.	*Math Journal 1*, p. 53	See page 181.
Home Link 2-9 **Homework** Children solve number stories with remainders.	*Math Masters*, p. 65	3.OA.2, 3.OA.3

 ePresentations
 Student Learning Center
 Facts Workshop Game
 eToolkit
 Professional Development
 Home Connections
 Spiral Tracker
 Assessment and Reporting
 English Learners Support
 Differentiation Support

Differentiation Options RtI

Readiness
5–10 min

Making Equal Shares with Pennies

WHOLE CLASS
SMALL GROUP
PARTNER
INDEPENDENT

Activity Card 27, pennies, stick-on notes, paper

To provide concrete experience with equal-grouping situations, have children share pennies equally with a partner. Point out that some penny amounts can be shared equally between two people and others cannot, so there may be leftovers. Have partners discuss what they notice about the different amounts. **GMP7.1** Sample answer: Even amounts can be shared equally between 2 people, and odd amounts always have one penny left over.

Enrichment
10–15 min

Dividing Strips

Math Masters, p. 63

WHOLE CLASS
SMALL GROUP
PARTNER
INDEPENDENT

To apply children's understanding of division, have them find two ways to divide rectangular fruit strips into equal amounts. Have them explain how both ways show equal amounts. **GMP2.3**

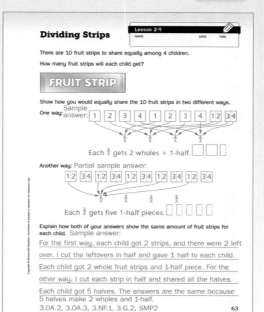

Extra Practice
10–15 min

Sharing Equally

WHOLE CLASS
SMALL GROUP
PARTNER
INDEPENDENT

Activity Card 28;
Math Masters, p. 64;
6-sided die; counters

To provide division practice, have children share counters equally among different numbers of people. Have them record the shares, remainders, and number models on *Math Masters,* page 64 and then discuss the results and why there might be leftovers. **GMP7.1**

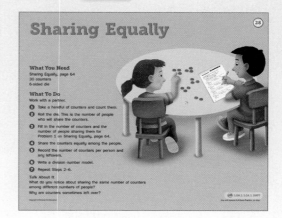

English Language Learners Support

Beginning ELL Help children understand the Mental Math and Fluency and the Math Message number story contexts by using visual aids, short questions, and role play. Count and think aloud while equally distributing 15 sheets of paper, one at a time, among 5 groups of children. For example: *How many papers does this group of children get? This group? And this group? Think. How many for each group?*

Go Online **ELL** English Learners Support

Professional Development

Research suggests that equal-sharing problems resulting in fractional shares, such as the one in the Math Message, are an important way to introduce children to fractions. Children shared fractional parts of pancakes in Lesson 1-12. When given contexts that involve sharing familiar objects, children will use intuitive notions about sharing to divide multiple wholes equally.

---

1 Warm Up 5 min [Go Online] ePresentations eToolkit

▶ Mental Math and Fluency

Pose number stories for children to solve on slates. *Leveled exercises:*

● ○ ○ You have 16 stickers to share equally between yourself and a friend. How many stickers will you each get? 8 stickers

● ● ○ You have a string that is 40 cm long, and you cut it into pieces 10 cm long. How many pieces do you have? 4 pieces

● ● ● You have 15 papers to hand out to 5 groups in your class. How many papers will each group receive? 3 papers

2 Focus 40–50 min [Go Online] ePresentations eToolkit

▶ Math Message

4 friends equally share 6 granola bars. How many granola bars will each friend get? Use sketches to show your thinking. GMP2.1

▶ Exploring Sharing Problems

| WHOLE CLASS | SMALL GROUP | PARTNER | INDEPENDENT |

Math Message Follow-Up Look for sharing strategies, such as those pictured below and on the next page. Children may record a variety of combinations of whole, half, and quarter granola bars because there are many ways to share them equally. GMP2.1 Some children may share wholes and divide the remaining granola bars into halves or fourths to share. Others may divide all the bars into halves or fourths to share. Encourage children to compare and make sense of the different representations using questions such as: GMP1.6, GMP3.2 Answers vary.

• *How did this child share the granola bars?*
• *Does that method work? How do you know?*
• *What is the same and what is different about this strategy and your strategy?*

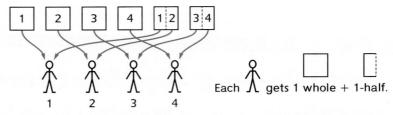

Each 👤 gets 1 whole + 1-half.

Sketch A: First distributing the largest piece of granola bar possible to each friend, and then the next largest piece

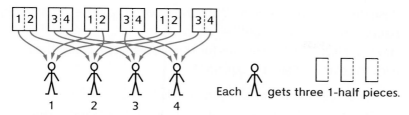

Each 🚶 gets three 1-half pieces.

Sketch B: Dividing each granola bar in half and sharing the halves

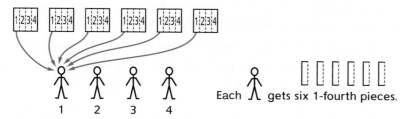

Each 🚶 gets six 1-fourth pieces.

Sketch C: Dividing each granola bar into 4 pieces and giving one piece of each bar to one friend. Repeat the process for the other friends.

Display or provide a strategy similar to Sketch A, and ask children to interpret it. Help the class recognize that whole granola bars must be broken apart to share all 6 bars equally. Show examples of dividing the remaining 2 granola bars into halves and fourths so those pieces could be shared equally. Explain that this is an example of a division problem. They divided whole granola bars and could also share the leftovers, or remainders.

Tell children they will continue to solve division number stories involving equal shares and groups, and they will learn what to do with leftovers that cannot be shared.

▶ Modeling with Division

| **WHOLE CLASS** | **SMALL GROUP** | PARTNER | INDEPENDENT |

Ask children to imagine sharing 6 pennies, instead of granola bars, with 4 friends. *How would it be different? What would your answer be?* Sample answer: You cannot split a penny, so each friend would get 1 penny. There would be 2 pennies left over. Explain that these leftovers are called the **remainder.** The remainder is the quantity left over when a set of objects is shared equally or separated into equal groups. Point out that in the previous problem the remainder would have been 2 granola bars, but they could be divided into smaller pieces and shared equally. We cannot do that with pennies. Each friend receives 1 penny and the remainder is 2 pennies.

Model writing the division number model with a remainder: $6 \div 4 \rightarrow 1$ remainder 2, or 1 R 2. Explain that we use an arrow instead of the equal sign when there is a remainder. This arrow is read as *leads to, gives, results in,* or a similar expression.

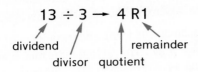

$$13 \div 3 \longrightarrow 4 \text{ R1}$$

dividend   remainder
divisor quotient

Math Journal 1, p. 52

Equal-Sharing Number Stories

Lesson 2-9
DATE   TIME

Solve each number story and draw a sketch to show your thinking. Write a division number model for each story.

① A class of 30 children wants to play ball. How many teams can be made with exactly 6 children on each team?

Answer: ___5___ teams
How many children are left over? ___0___ children
Number model: ___30 ÷ 6 = 5___

② For another game, the same class of 30 children wants to have exactly 4 children on each team. How many teams can be made?

Answer: ___7___ teams
How many children are left over? ___2___ children
Number model: ___30 ÷ 4 → 7 R 2___

③ Roberto has 25 pencils to share equally among 3 pencil boxes. How many pencils does he put in each box?

Answer: ___8___ pencils
How many pencils are left over? ___1___ pencil
Number model: ___25 ÷ 8 → 3 R 1___

52 fifty-two   3.OA.2, 3.OA.3, 3.OA.7, SMP2

Pose the following problem: *3 children share 13 pennies. How many pennies will each child get?* 4 pennies with 1 remainder, or 4 pennies R 1. Have children create sketches for the problem and share their solutions with the class. GMP2.1 Explain that:

- A number model for this problem is 13 ÷ 3 → 4 R 1.
- The **dividend** is the total before dividing. Ask: *What is the dividend in this problem?* 13
- The **divisor** can be the number of equal shares or the number in each equal share. Ask: *What is the divisor in this problem?* 3
- The **quotient** is the result of the division, or what you get after you divide. Ask: *What is the quotient in this problem?* 4 *What is the remainder?* 1

Although it is beneficial to use the vocabulary terms when discussing division number stories, do not insist that children use them.

Have children solve more equal-sharing number stories, representing each with a division number model. GMP2.1 Include problems with and without remainders. As needed, refer to the Guide to Solving Number Stories (*Student Reference Book,* page 30). Consider distributing counters for children to use to act out the stories. *Suggestions:*

- *21 candles are arranged with 3 in each row. How many rows are there?* 7 rows; 21 ÷ 3 = 7 *How many candles are leftover?* none; 0 candles
- *Each player is dealt 4 cards. There are 18 cards in all. How many players are there?* 4 players *How many cards are left over?* 2 cards; 18 ÷ 4 → 4 R 2
- *18 markers are shared equally among 6 children. How many markers does each child get?* 3 markers; 18 ÷ 6 = 3 *How many markers are left over?* none; 0 markers
- *15 yards of cloth are cut into smaller pieces for dresses. Each dress needs 2 yards. How many dresses can be made?* 7 dresses *How many yards of cloth are left over?* 1 yard; 15 ÷ 2 → 7 R 1

Discuss children's solutions. Model using the inverse relationship between multiplication and division to check their answers. For example, children can check that 14 yards of cloth is used to make 7 dresses with 2 yards each (7 × 2 = 14). Adding the 1 extra yard (the remainder) gives a total of 15 yards of cloth—the original dividend.

▶ Dividing to Solve Number Stories

Math Journal 1, p. 52

| WHOLE CLASS | SMALL GROUP | PARTNER | INDEPENDENT |

Have children solve division number stories on journal page 52 and record number models that fit. Children may use counters, but be sure to tell them to sketch what they did. GMP2.1 Remind children to multiply and add the remainder, if any, to check their answers.

Assessment Check-In (CCSS) 3.OA.2, 3.OA.3

Math Journal 1, p. 52

Expect children to solve each number story using sketches. (GMP2.1)
As this is their first exposure, do not expect all children to represent the
problems with division number models with remainders. Continue to model
problems using the arrow symbol and the R to familiarize children with the
notation. If children struggle to make sense of and solve the number stories,
have them use counters to act out each situation.

☑ Assessment and Reporting (Go Online) to record student progress and to see trajectories toward mastery for these standards.

Summarize Name different real-world objects and have children
reason whether or not the remainders could be shared equally. Have
children stand if the remainder can be shared (pancakes, orange slices,
play dough) or sit if the leftovers cannot be shared (sports balls, barrettes,
toy cars).

3 Practice 15–20 min (Go Online) ePresentations eToolkit Home Connections

▶ *Minute Math+*

To practice mental math strategies, select a *Minute Math+* activity.

▶ **Exploring the Mass Museum**

Math Masters, p. 39

| WHOLE CLASS | **SMALL GROUP** | **PARTNER** | INDEPENDENT |

Have children estimate and measure the masses of objects in the Mass
Museum using the pan balance and masses. Have them record their work
on *Math Masters*, page 39. (GMP5.2) For details, see Lesson 1-13.

▶ **Math Boxes 2-9:** Preview for Unit 3

Math Journal 1, p. 53

| WHOLE CLASS | **SMALL GROUP** | **PARTNER** | **INDEPENDENT** |

Mixed Practice Math Boxes 2-9 are paired with Math Boxes 2-13. These
problems focus on skills and understandings that are prerequisite for
Unit 3. You may want to use information from these Math Boxes to plan
instruction and grouping in Unit 3.

▶ **Home Link 2-9**

Math Masters, p. 65

Homework Children solve number stories with remainders.

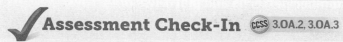

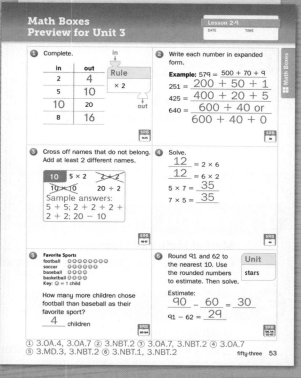

Math Journal 1, p. 53

Math Masters, p. 65

Playing *Division Arrays*

Overview Children explore even and odd number patterns and play *Division Arrays*.

▶ **Before You Begin**
For Part 1, select and sequence Quick Look Cards 156, 154, and 151.

 Common Core State Standards

Focus Clusters
- Represent and solve problems involving multiplication and division.
- Multiply and divide with 100.

① **Warm Up** 5–10 min

	Materials	
Mental Math and Fluency Children practice Quick Looks with equal groups and arrays.	Quick Look Cards 151, 154, 156	3.OA.1, 3.OA.7 SMP2, SMP6

② **Focus** 40–45 min

Math Message Children use arrays to solve number stories.	*Math Journal 1,* p. 54; counters (optional)	3.OA.2, 3.OA.3
Exploring Even and Odd with Arrays Children explore even and odd number patterns.	*Math Journal 1,* p. 54; counters (optional)	3.OA.2 SMP7, SMP8
Introducing *Division Arrays* **Game** Children group counters equally to practice division.	*Student Reference Book,* pp. 238 and 239; *Math Masters,* p. G9; number cards 6–18 (1 of each); counters; 6-sided die, slate (optional)	3.OA.2, 3.OA.7 SMP2, SMP7, SMP8
✓ **Assessment Check-In** See page 186.	*Math Masters,* p. G9	3.OA.2 SMP2, SMP7

CCSS 3.OA.2 **Spiral Snapshot**

GMC Interpret division in terms of equal shares or equal groups.

2-7 through 2-9 Focus Practice	2-10 Focus	3-10 Warm Up Practice	4-1 Practice	4-10 Warm Up	5-10 Focus

Spiral Tracker **Go Online** to see how mastery develops for all standards within the grade.

③ **Practice** 15–20 min

Minute Math+ Children practice mental math strategies.	Minute Math®+	
Solving More Multistep Number Stories Children solve number stories with more than one operation.	*Math Journal 1,* p. 55; *Student Reference Book,* p. 270	3.OA.3, 3.OA.7, 3.OA.8, 3.NBT.2
Math Boxes 2-10 Children practice and maintain skills.	*Math Journal 1,* p. 56	See page 187.
Home Link 2-10 **Homework** Children represent division with arrays.	*Math Masters,* p. 67	3.OA.2, 3.OA.7

connectED.mcgraw-hill.com

Plan your lessons online with these tools.

 ePresentations
 Student Learning Center
 Facts Workshop Game
 eToolkit
 Professional Development
 Home Connections
 Spiral Tracker
 Assessment and Reporting
 English Learners Support
Differentiation Support

Differentiation Options RtI

CCSS 3.OA.2, 3.OA.3, SMP4

Readiness   10–15 min

WHOLE CLASS
SMALL GROUP
PARTNER
INDEPENDENT

Exploring Equal Shares

Math Masters, p. 66; counters;
quarter-sheets of paper

To provide concrete experience with
division, have children model equal-sharing
stories with counters. **GMP4.1** Provide
each child with 8 quarter-sheets of paper
and 20 counters to use in solving the
problems on *Math Masters,* page 66.

Exploring Equal Shares | Lesson 2-10

NAME   DATE   TIME

Use counters and quarter-sheets of paper to solve each problem.
Record your work in the rectangles.

Example:

Nomi had 8 crayons. She gave the crayons to 4 of her friends. Each
friend got the same number of crayons. Draw the number of crayons
each friend got.

| | | | | | | | | | | |

① Latrell shares 10 marbles with his best friend. Draw the number
of marbles each child has.

② Melissa has 6 bags of treats for her birthday party. She has a total
of 12 treats in her bags. Draw the number of treats in each bag.

③ Make up your own problem. Draw your solution.

66   3.OA.2, 3.OA.3, SMP4

CCSS 3.OA.2, SMP4, SMP6

Enrichment   15–20 min

WHOLE CLASS
SMALL GROUP
PARTNER
INDEPENDENT

Modeling Division with Base-10 Blocks

Activity Card 29;
base-10 blocks; paper

To further explore the concept of division,
have children model equal-sharing
problems with base-10 blocks and use base-
10 shorthand to record their solutions.
GMP4.1 163 paper clips per box with 1
paper clip left over Observe as children
predict whether there will be a remainder
and discuss how they divided the base-10
blocks. **GMP6.1**

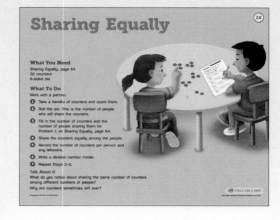

Modeling Division with Base-10 Blocks (29)

What You Need
base-10 blocks
4 sheets of paper
1 half-sheet of paper

What To Do
Work with a partner.
① Read this number story.
   You need to divide 653 paper clips into four boxes.
   How many paper clips will be in each box?
② Predict whether you will have a remainder.
③ Solve. Use four pieces of paper to represent the boxes.
④ Use base-10 blocks to represent the paper clips.
⑤ Share the blocks equally on the pieces of paper.
   When needed, trade longs for flats and cubes for longs.
⑥ Write your answer on paper.

Talk About It
Tell someone how you divided the blocks. Is there a remainder?

More You Can Do
Use base-10 blocks to divide. Predict if there will be a remainder.
• 244 paper clips into three boxes
• 455 paper clips into five boxes
• 840 paper clips into six boxes

CCSS 3.OA.2, 3.OA.3, SMP7

Extra Practice   10–15 min

WHOLE CLASS
SMALL GROUP
PARTNER
INDEPENDENT

Sharing Equally

Activity Card 28;
Math Masters, p. 64;
6-sided die; counters

To provide practice with division, children
share counters equally among different
numbers of people. **GMP7.1** See the
Extra Practice activity in Lesson 2-9.

Sharing Equally (28)

What You Need
Sharing Equally, page 64
30 counters
6-sided die

What To Do
Work with a partner.
① Take a handful of counters and count them.
② Roll the die. This is the number of people
   who will share the counters.
③ Fill in the number of counters and the
   number of people sharing them for
   Problem 1 on Sharing Equally, page 64.
④ Share the counters equally among the people.
⑤ Record the number of counters per person and
   any leftovers.
⑥ Write a division number model.
⑦ Repeat Steps 2–6.

Talk About It
What do you notice about sharing the same number of counters
among different numbers of people?
Why are counters sometimes left over?

English Language Learners Support

Beginning ELL Help children associate *row* with *going across* by gesturing across rows in
an array while saying *side to side.* Encourage children to move their fingers across a row in
an array as they repeat: *side to side.* Provide opportunities for children to hear and practice
using the term *row.* Have them count the number of rows in different arrays and use the
sentence frame: *There are _____ rows.*

(Go Online) **ELL** English Learners Support

Standards and Goals for
Mathematical Practice

SMP2 **Reason abstractly and quantitatively.**
GMP2.2 Make sense of the representations you and others use.

SMP7 **Look for and make use of structure.**
GMP7.2 Use structures to solve problems and answer questions.

SMP8 **Look for and express regularity in repeated reasoning.**
GMP8.1 Create and justify rules, shortcuts, and generalizations.

---

① Warm Up

5–10 min

Mental Math and Fluency

Show Quick Look Cards 156, 154, and 151 one at a time for 2–3 seconds. Ask children to share both what they saw and how they saw it. **GMP2.2, GMP6.1** Highlight strategies involving equal groups or arrays.

Quick Look Card 156 Sample answer: I saw 2 groups of 4, and I know 4 and 4 makes 8.

Quick Look Card 154 Sample answer: I saw 3 groups of 3, and I know $3 + 3 = 6$ and $6 + 3 = 9$.

Quick Look Card 151 Sample answer: I saw 4 groups of 5, and I know 2 groups of 5 makes 10 and $10 + 10 = 20$.

---

② Focus

40–45 min

▶ Math Message

Math Journal 1, p. 54

Solve the Math Message problem on journal page 54. You may use counters.

▶ Exploring Even and Odd with Arrays

Math Journal 1, p. 54

| WHOLE CLASS | SMALL GROUP | PARTNER | INDEPENDENT |

Math Message Follow-Up Have children share their answers and corresponding arrays on journal page 54. Discuss what they noticed about equal groups based on the arrays. Guide children to make generalizations based on these patterns by asking questions such as:

- *What do you notice about the numbers that could make arrays with two equal rows?* **GMP8.1** They are even numbers. *The numbers that could not make 2-row arrays?* **GMP8.1** They are odd numbers.
- *What happens when you cannot make an array?* Sample answer: There is one plant left over.
- *Predict what would happen with 25 tomato plants. Explain your prediction.* **GMP7.2** 25 could not be in 2 equal rows because it is an odd number. *30 tomato plants?* 30 could be in 2 rows because it is an even number.
- *Explain the patterns you see in making 2-row arrays with even numbers and with odd numbers.* **GMP8.1** Sample answers: Even numbers of plants can be made into 2-row arrays, but odd numbers of plants cannot because there will be one plant left over. Even numbers can be divided by 2 with no leftovers, but odd numbers cannot.

Math Journal 1, p. 54

Exploring Even and Odd Patterns with Arrays

Lesson 2-10

DATE   TIME

Math Message

Amanda wants 2 rows of tomato plants in her garden. Make sketches to show your thinking.

Can Amanda make an array with 2 equal rows if she has:

9 tomato plants? No.

12 tomato plants? Yes.

14 tomato plants? Yes.

15 tomato plants? No.

What do you notice about the numbers of plants that could be planted in arrays with 2 equal rows? What do you notice about the numbers of plants that could *not* be planted in arrays with 2 equal rows?

Sample answer: The numbers that made equal rows were even numbers. The numbers that did not make equal rows were odd numbers.

54 fifty-four   3.OA.2, 3.OA.3, SMP7, SMP8

Remind children that the leftovers they have when dividing odd numbers by 2 are called remainders. Tell them that they will continue using arrays to model division with and without remainders as they learn a new game called *Division Arrays.*

▶ Introducing *Division Arrays*

Student Reference Book, pp. 238 and 239; *Math Masters,* p. G9

| WHOLE CLASS | SMALL GROUP | PARTNER | INDEPENDENT |

With the class, read the directions on *Student Reference Book,* page 238. Together play a few sample rounds that involve division with and without remainders. For example, draw a 10 card and roll a 3. Ask the following questions to help children understand how to form the array and keep score:

- *How do you make the array?* I make 3 rows because we rolled a 3. I use 10 counters to make equal rows because we drew a 10 card.
- *Is there a remainder? How do you know?* Yes. There are 3 rows with 3 in each row, which makes 9 and 1 left over.
- *How do you figure out the score?* Since there is a remainder, the score is the number of counters in one row, 3.
- *What division number sentence could represent this array?* **GMP2.2** 10 ÷ 3 → 3 R 1

Make sure children understand that they double the number in one row to find their score when there is no remainder. For example, drawing an 18 card and rolling a 3 would result in an array with three equal rows of 6 and a score of 12. Model recording a round or two on *Math Masters,* page G9.

Student Reference Book, p. 238

Games

Division Arrays

Materials	☐ number cards 6–18 (1 of each)
	☐ 1 six-sided die
	☐ 18 counters
	☐ 1 *Division Arrays* Record Sheet for each player (*Math Masters,* p. G9)
Players	2 to 4
Skill	Modeling division with and without remainders
Object of the Game	To have the highest total score.

Directions

1. Shuffle the cards. Place the deck number-side down on the table.
2. Players take turns. When it is your turn, draw a card and take the number of counters shown on the card. You will use the counters to make an array.
   - Roll the die. The number on the die is the number of equal rows you must have in your array.
   - Make an array with the counters.
   - Your score is the number of counters in one row. If there are no leftover counters, your score is double the number of counters in one row. See the example on the next page.
3. Players keep track of their scores. The player with the highest total score at the end of 5 rounds wins.

SRB
238   two hundred thirty-eight

When children seem comfortable with the rules, have them play in partnerships or in small groups and record their play on *Math Masters*, page G9.

Observe

- Do children build their arrays correctly?
- Do children calculate their score correctly when there is and is not a remainder? **GMP2.2**

Discuss

- *How do you figure out the number of counters to put in each row?* **GMP2.2**
- *How do you know if there are leftover counters? What numbers have leftover counters more often than others?*

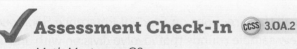

Differentiate   **Game Modifications**   **Go Online**   Differentiation Support

---

✓ **Assessment Check-In** **CCSS** 3.OA.2

Math Masters, p. G9

Circulate and observe as children play *Division Arrays* and record their work on *Math Masters*, page G9. Expect most children to create the arrays by distributing their counters among the given number of rows, particularly in the case of no remainders. **GMP2.2** For children who struggle with making arrays, consider implementing the suggestion in the Adjusting the Activity note. Encourage children who excel at the game to predict whether there will be leftovers before they construct the arrays. **GMP7.2**

 Assessment and Reporting   **Go Online**   to record student progress and to see trajectories toward mastery for this standard.

Summarize Tell children to imagine they are playing *Division Arrays* and that they rolled a 2 and drew a card with an even number on it. Have them talk with a partner about whether there will be leftover counters. No. Highlight that even numbers can be divided into 2 equal groups. **GMP8.1**

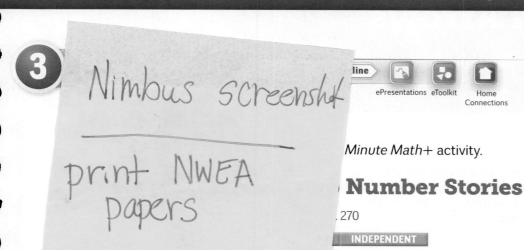

Nimbus screenshot

print NWEA papers

3

ePresentations eToolkit Home Connections

Minute Math+ activity.

Number Stories

. 270

INDEPENDENT

n *Student Reference Book,*
s on journal page 55.

▶ ### Math Boxes 2-10

Math Journal 1, p. 56

| WHOLE CLASS | SMALL GROUP | PARTNER | INDEPENDENT |

Mixed Practice Math Boxes 2-10 are paired with Math Boxes 2-12.

▶ ## Home Link 2-10

Math Masters, p. 67

Homework Children use arrays to represent division problems with and without remainders. They also think of household items they could share with family members that might have remainders.

Math Journal 1, p. 56

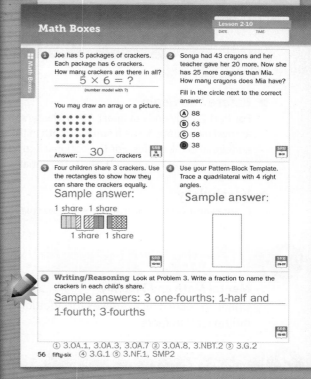

Math Boxes

Lesson 2-10
DATE   TIME

① Joe has 5 packages of crackers. Each package has 6 crackers. How many crackers are there in all?

$5 \times 6 = ?$
(number model with ?)

You may draw an array or a picture.

Answer: __30__ crackers

② Sonya had 43 crayons and her teacher gave her 20 more. Now she has 25 more crayons than Mia. How many crayons does Mia have?
Fill in the circle next to the correct answer.
Ⓐ 88
Ⓑ 63
Ⓒ 58
Ⓓ 38

③ Four children share 3 crackers. Use the rectangles to show how they can share the crackers equally.
Sample answer:
1 share 1 share
1 share 1 share

④ Use your Pattern-Block Template. Trace a quadrilateral with 4 right angles.
Sample answer:

⑤ **Writing/Reasoning** Look at Problem 3. Write a fraction to name the crackers in each child's share.
Sample answers: 3 one-fourths; 1-half and 1-fourth; 3-fourths

① 3.OA.1, 3.OA.3, 3.OA.7 ② 3.OA.8, 3.NBT.2 ③ 3.G.2
56 fifty-six ④ 3.G.1 ⑤ 3.NF.1, SMP2

Math Masters, p. 67

Division with Arrays

Home Link 2-10
NAME   DATE   TIME

Family Note Today your child practiced using arrays to model problems and show division with and without remainders. Children also learned a new game called *Division Arrays.*
Please return this Home Link to school tomorrow.

Use arrays to represent each division problem. If there is a remainder, show it in the Leftovers column.

	Problem	Sketch of Array Formed	Leftovers
Example	23 ÷ 6		● ● ● ● ●
1.	15 ÷ 3		0
2.	32 ÷ 5		● ●

③ List household items you could share with your family members that might have leftovers, for example, spoons, plates, and cups.
Sample answers: A package of markers, all the pillows in the house

Practice
④ 5 × 5 = __25__
⑤ 40 = 5 × __8__
⑥ 20 ÷ 5 = __4__
⑦ 45 ÷ __9__ = 5

3.OA.2, 3.OA.7   67

Lesson 2-11

Frames and Arrows

Overview Children review Frames-and-Arrows diagrams and solve problems using the four operations.

▶ **Before You Begin**
For Part 2, copy and cut apart *Math Masters*, page 69. For the optional Enrichment activity, fill in the arrow rules, some of the frames, or both in the first two problems on *Math Masters*, page 69. Make additional blank copies. For the optional Extra Practice activity, you may want to fill in rules or frames on *Math Masters*, page TA21. See Differentiation Options for details.

▶ **Vocabulary**
Frames and Arrows • frames • arrow rule

Common Core State Standards

Focus Clusters
• Multiply and divide within 100.
• Use place value understanding and properties of operations to perform multi-digit arithmetic.

1 Warm Up 5–10 min

Materials

Mental Math and Fluency
Children record fact families for addition and multiplication facts.

slate

3.OA.7, 3.NBT.2

2 Focus 40–45 min

Math Message
Children solve problems involving arithmetic patterns.

Math Masters, p. 69

3.OA.7, 3.NBT.2
SMP7

Reviewing Frames and Arrows
Children solve Frames-and-Arrows problems.

Math Masters, pp. 69–70

3.OA.7, 3.NBT.2
SMP7

Solving Frames and Arrows
Children share strategies for solving Frames-and-Arrows problems.

Math Journal 1, p. 57; *Math Masters*, pp. 70 and TA21 (optional)

3.OA.7, 3.NBT.2
SMP3, SMP7

✓ **Assessment Check-In**   See page 192.

Math Journal 1, p. 57

3.OA.7, 3.NBT.2
SMP7

CCSS 3.OA.7 **Spiral Snapshot**
GMC Multiply within 1,000 fluently.

| 2-2 Practice | 2-4 through 2-7 Warm Up Focus Practice | 2-8 Warm Up Practice | 2-10 Warm Up Practice | 2-11 Warm Up Focus Practice | 3-1 Focus Practice | 3-5 Practice |

Spiral Tracker   **Go Online**   to see how mastery develops for all standards within the grade.

3 Practice 15–20 min

Minute Math+
Children practice mental math strategies.

Minute Math®+

Representing Number Stories
Children multiply to solve number stories.

Math Journal 1, p. 58

3.OA.3, 3.OA.7
SMP4

Math Boxes 2-11
Children practice and maintain skills.

Math Journal 1, p. 59

See page 193.

Home Link 2-11
Homework Children solve Frames-and-Arrows problems.

Student Reference Book, pp. 72–73; *Math Masters*, p. 71

3.OA.7, 3.NBT.2

connectED.mcgraw-hill.com

Plan your lessons online with these tools.

 ePresentations   Student Learning Center   Facts Workshop Game   eToolkit   Professional Development   Home Connections   Spiral Tracker   Assessment and Reporting   English Learners Support   Differentiation Support

188   Unit 2 | Number Stories and Arrays

Differentiation Options  RtI

Readiness   5–10 min

Writing Fact Families for Different Operations

WHOLE CLASS
SMALL GROUP
PARTNER
INDEPENDENT

number cards 1–9 (4 of each)

To provide experience with different operations, have children draw two number cards and write an appropriate fact family either for addition/subtraction or multiplication/division. Have children compare their fact families.

Enrichment   10–15 min

Solving Two-Rule Frames and Arrows

WHOLE CLASS
SMALL GROUP
PARTNER
INDEPENDENT

Activity Card 30;
Math Masters, p. 68

To extend children's understanding of patterns and rules, have them apply two rules in Frames-and-Arrows problems. Fill in the arrow rules, some of the frames, or both in the first two problems. Leave the last two blank. Have children look for helpful patterns as they solve problems.
GMP7.1

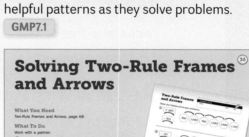

Extra Practice   10–15 min

Solving Frames-and-Arrows Problems

WHOLE CLASS
SMALL GROUP
PARTNER
INDEPENDENT

Activity Card 31;
Math Masters, p. TA21

To apply children's ability to solve problems using number patterns, have them make up and share their own Frames-and-Arrows problems. GMP7.2 You may adjust the activity by filling in the arrow rules, some of the frames, or both in some of the problems.

English Language Learners Support

Beginning ELL Scaffold the term *frame.* Utilize outlining gestures to show that a frame surrounds something and that frames can have different shapes. Show a variety of frames, such as a picture, a window, a door, and eyeglass frames. Label several examples with the term so children generalize that the term names different objects, but in each case, it surrounds something.

Go Online   ELL   English Learners Support

1 Warm Up 5–10 min

▶ Mental Math and Fluency

Pose each basic fact without an answer. Have children write out the rest of the fact family, including the answers, on their slates. *Leveled exercises:*

●○○ $6 + 4$ $6 + 4 = 10; 4 + 6 = 10; 10 - 6 = 4; 10 - 4 = 6$
    2×8 $2 \times 8 = 16; 8 \times 2 = 16; 16 \div 2 = 8; 16 \div 8 = 2$
●●○ $8 + 5$ $8 + 5 = 13; 5 + 8 = 13; 13 - 5 = 8; 13 - 8 = 5$
    5×4 $5 \times 4 = 20; 4 \times 5 = 20; 20 \div 4 = 5; 20 \div 5 = 4$
●●● $9 + 7$ $9 + 7 = 16; 7 + 9 = 16; 16 - 9 = 7; 16 - 7 = 9$
    5×9 $5 \times 9 = 45; 9 \times 5 = 45; 45 \div 9 = 5; 45 \div 5 = 9$

2 Focus 40–45 min

▶ Math Message

Math Masters, p. 69

Find and use patterns to solve the Math Message problems. **GMP7.1, GMP7.2**

▶ Reviewing Frames and Arrows

Math Masters, pp. 69–70

WHOLE CLASS	SMALL GROUP	PARTNER	INDEPENDENT

Math Message Follow-Up Ask children to describe the patterns they saw and how they used them to find the missing numbers. **GMP7.1, GMP7.2**

- Problem 1: Add 3 each time.
- Problem 2: Subtract 2 each time.
- Problem 3: Double, or multiply by 2 each time.
- Problem 4: Subtract 3 each time.

For Problem 3, emphasize that doubling and multiplying by 2 have the same result. If children have difficulty with problems in which the *first* numbers are missing, ask someone to explain how to work backward.

Differentiate **Common Misconception**

Some children may have attempted to apply addition rules to all four problems in the Math Message. Ask questions such as: *How do the numbers change? Do they get larger? Smaller? By how much?*

Go Online Differentiation Support

Math Masters, p. 69

Number Patterns Lesson 2-11
NAME DATE TIME

Math Message

For each problem, find the pattern and use it to find the missing numbers.
① 37, 40, 43, <u>46</u>, <u>49</u>, <u>52</u>
② 27, 25, <u>23</u>, 21, <u>19</u>, <u>17</u>
③ 1, 2, 4, 8, <u>16</u>, <u>32</u>
④ <u>42</u>, <u>39</u>, 36, 33, <u>30</u>, 27

Number Patterns Lesson 2-11
NAME DATE TIME

Math Message

For each problem, find the pattern and use it to find the missing numbers.
① 37, 40, 43, <u>46</u>, <u>49</u>, <u>52</u>
② 27, 25, <u>23</u>, 21, <u>19</u>, <u>17</u>
③ 1, 2, 4, 8, <u>16</u>, <u>32</u>
④ <u>42</u>, <u>39</u>, 36, 33, <u>30</u>, 27

3.OA.7, 3.NBT.2, SMP7   69

Remind children that in *First* and *Second Grade Everyday Mathematics* they explored patterns using **Frames-and-Arrows** diagrams. Display *Math Masters*, page 70 and review how to complete Frames and Arrows. Point to the first arrow rule and set of frames with the numbers from Math Message Problem 3, and ask: *What is our rule?* Multiply by 2 *What does the rule tell us to do?* GMP7.2 Sample answer: Multiply each number by 2 to get the next number.

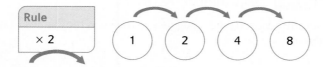

Tell children that the circles are called **frames** and that numbers are written in these frames. Explain that the frames do not always need to be circles—they might be squares, rectangles, or any other shape that can hold a number. (Avoid using triangles because it is difficult to write numbers in them.)

Explain that the arrows stand for the **arrow rule** shown in the box. The rule describes how to get from the number in one frame to the next. In the example, you can multiply each number by 2 to get the next number. Ask: *What number comes after 8, or equals 8 multiplied by 2?* 16 *What are the next two numbers?* 32, 64 *How do you know?* Sample answer: $16 \times 2 = 32$; $32 + 32 = 64$

▶ **Solving Frames and Arrows**

Math Journal 1, p. 57; *Math Masters*, p. 70

WHOLE CLASS	SMALL GROUP	PARTNER	INDEPENDENT

With the class, work through the remaining Frames-and-Arrows problems on *Math Masters*, page 70. Note that in some Frames-and-Arrows diagrams, missing numbers may occur in the first frame(s). Invite volunteers to explain how to work backward to fill in these numbers. Also the arrow rule may be missing, so children might need to look for a pattern before they can find the missing numbers. GMP7.1 To help children identify a missing rule, model the following steps:

• Look for a pattern in the numbers. Think: *What do you notice about how the numbers change?*

• Decide which operation is being used. Think: *Is a number being added, subtracted, multiplied, or divided?*

• Figure out what number is being added, subtracted, multiplied, or divided.

• Test your rule with each frame. If it does not fit all the frames, try other rules. Think: *If my rule does not work, how could it help me come up with a new rule?*

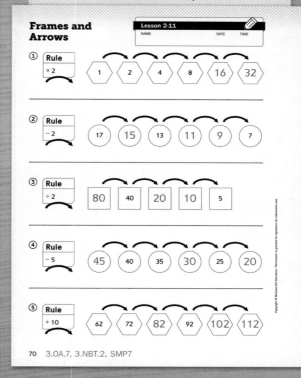

Math Masters, p. 70

Frames and Arrows

Lesson 2-11

NAME   DATE   TIME

① Rule × 2   1 2 4 8 16 32

② Rule − 2   17 15 13 11 9 7

③ Rule ÷ 2   80 40 20 10 5

④ Rule − 5   45 40 35 30 25 20

⑤ Rule + 10   62 72 82 92 102 112

70   3.OA.7, 3.NBT.2, SMP7

Academic Language Development

Encourage children to ask questions about each other's strategies by providing written question starters, such as: *Why did you _____? Did you think about _____? Why didn't you _____? What made you use the _____ strategy? What was good about the _____ strategy?*

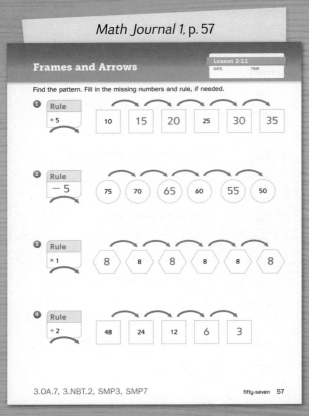

Math Journal 1, p. 57

Frames and Arrows

Lesson 2-11
DATE   TIME

Find the pattern. Fill in the missing numbers and rule, if needed.

① Rule
+ 5

10   15   20   25   30   35

② Rule
− 5

75   70   65   60   55   50

③ Rule
× 1

8   8   8   8   8   8

④ Rule
÷ 2

48   24   12   6   3

3.OA.7, 3.NBT.2, SMP3, SMP7   fifty-seven   57

Math Journal 1, p. 58

More Number Stories

Lesson 2-11
DATE   TIME

For each number story:
• Write a multiplication number model. Use ? to show the unknown.
• Make an array on the dot grid to match the story.
• Solve. Write the unit with your answer.

① Mrs. Kwan has 4 boxes of scented markers. Each box has 10 markers.
How many markers does she have?

Number model: $4 \times 10 = ?$

Answer: 40 markers
          (unit)

② Monica keeps her doll collection in a case with 5 shelves. On each shelf
there are 7 dolls. How many dolls are in Monica's collection?

Number model: $5 \times 7 = ?$

Answer: 35 dolls
          (unit)

③ During the summer, Jack mows lawns. He can mow 5 lawns per day.
How many lawns can he mow in 9 days?

Number model: $5 \times 9 = ?$

Answer: 45 lawns
          (unit)

58   fifty-eight   3.OA.3, 3.OA.7, SMP4

Observe which problems children find easy or difficult and tailor instruction accordingly. You may wish to use *Math Masters*, page TA21 to modify problems based on the needs of your class.

When most children seem ready, have them work in partnerships to complete the problems on journal page 57.

> **Differentiate**   **Adjusting the Activity**
>
> Encourage children who struggle with filling in the frames to write the rule above each arrow.
>
> **Go Online** ▷   Differentiation Support

As children work, circulate and ask questions such as: **GMP7.1, GMP7.2**
Answers vary.

• *How did you use the rule to figure out the number in this frame?*
• *How were you able to find the number that comes before this one?*
• *What pattern could help you figure out the missing rule?*

Select children to share both effective and ineffective strategies during the follow-up discussion. Encourage the class to repeat the strategies in their own words and to ask questions to help them make sense of others' strategies. You may wish to provide children with sentence stems, such as: *I noticed . . . I wonder . . . How did you . . . Why did you . . .*   **GMP3.2**

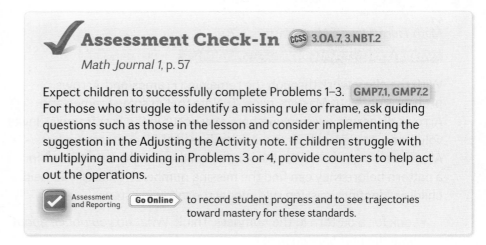

> ✔ **Assessment Check-In**   (CCSS) **3.OA.7, 3.NBT.2**
>
> *Math Journal 1*, p. 57
>
> Expect children to successfully complete Problems 1–3.   **GMP7.1, GMP7.2**
> For those who struggle to identify a missing rule or frame, ask guiding questions such as those in the lesson and consider implementing the suggestion in the Adjusting the Activity note. If children struggle with multiplying and dividing in Problems 3 or 4, provide counters to help act out the operations.
>
> ☑ Assessment and Reporting   **Go Online** ▷   to record student progress and to see trajectories toward mastery for these standards.

Summarize   Have children share the thinking they used to help them solve Frames-and-Arrows problems.   **GMP7.1**

3 Practice 15–20 min Go Online ePresentations eToolkit Home Connections

▶ *Minute Math+*

To practice mental math strategies, choose a *Minute Math+* activity.

▶ Representing Number Stories

Math Journal 1, p. 58

| WHOLE CLASS | SMALL GROUP | **PARTNER** | **INDEPENDENT** |

Have children represent number stories using multiplication number models and arrays. Then have them solve the number stories, attempting to use efficient strategies. GMP4.1

▶ Math Boxes 2-11

Math Journal 1, p. 59

| WHOLE CLASS | **SMALL GROUP** | PARTNER | INDEPENDENT |

Mixed Practice Math Boxes 2-11 are grouped with Math Boxes 2-6 and 2-8.

▶ Home Link 2-11

Math Masters, p. 71

Homework Children practice solving Frames-and-Arrows problems involving several different operations.

> **NOTE** The Family Notes frequently mention the *Student Reference Book.* Consider sending this book home on a daily basis as a resource for parents.

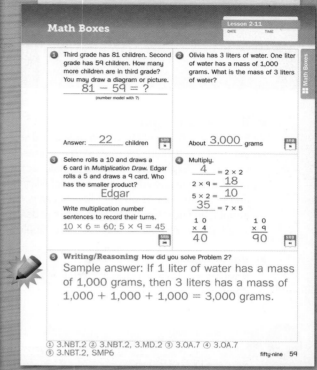

Math Journal 1, p. 59

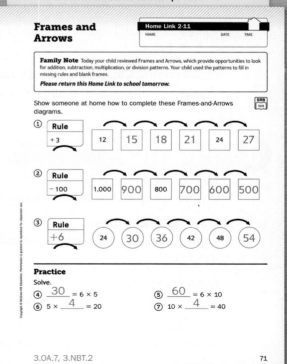

Math Masters, p. 71

Exploring Fraction Circles, Liquid Volume, and Area

Overview Children explore fraction circles, area measures, and liquid volume in liters.

▶ **Before You Begin**

Exploration A: Decide how to manage and store the fraction circles. If you do not have fraction circle sets, cut apart *Math Journal 1,* Activity Sheets 6–8, one set per child. See the Planning Ahead note in Lesson 2-6. Exploration B: Gather small, rectangular items, such as calculators, crayon boxes, and so on. Make available additional copies of *Math Masters,* pages TA19 and TA22. Exploration C: Mark 1-liter and 1-half liter points on the 1-liter beakers. Gather containers of different sizes and shapes that hold about a half liter (soup can), a liter (large deli container), and less than a half liter (yogurt cup). Each small group will need one of each size, labeled Containers A, B, and C.

▶ **Vocabulary**

fraction • whole • fraction circles • area • square inch (sq in.) • square centimeter (sq cm) • volume • liter

Common Core State Standards

Focus Clusters
• Develop understanding of fractions as numbers.
• Solve problems involving measurement and estimation of intervals of time, liquid volumes, and masses of objects.
• Geometric measurement: understand concepts of area and relate area to multiplication and to addition.

① Warm Up 5 min

	Materials	
Mental Math and Fluency Children solve fact extensions.	slate	3.NBT.2

② Focus 40–50 min

Math Message Children examine fraction circles.	fraction circles (*See Before You Begin.*)	SMP6
Introducing Fraction Circles Children name unit fractions.	fraction circles	3.NF.1
Exploration A: Exploring Fraction Circles Children explore fraction circles.	*Math Journal 1,* p. 60; fraction circles	3.NF.1 SMP3
Exploration B: Measuring Area Children measure areas of rectangles by counting square inches and square centimeters.	Activity Card 32; *Math Journal 1,* p. 61; *Math Masters,* pp. TA19 and TA22; Everything Math Decks; rectangular items of various sizes; tape (optional)	3.MD.5, 3.MD.5a, 3.MD.5b, 3.MD.6 SMP6
Exploration C: Comparing Liquid Volume Children compare liquid volumes of containers.	Activity Card 33; *Math Journal 1,* p. 62; assorted containers; 1-liter beaker; paper towels; dishpan; pitcher of water	3.MD.2 SMP5

③ Practice 15–20 min

Minute Math+ Children practice mental math strategies.	*Minute Math®+*	
Playing *Division Arrays* **Game** Children group counters equally to practice division.	*Student Reference Book,* pp. 238 and 239; *Math Masters,* p. G9; number cards 6–18 (one of each); counters; 6-sided die	3.OA.2, 3.OA.7 SMP2, SMP7
Math Boxes 2-12 Children practice and maintain skills.	*Math Journal 1,* p. 63	See page 199.
Home Link 2-12 **Homework** Children explore liquid volume and areas.	*Math Masters,* p. 74	3.OA.7, 3.MD.2, 3.MD.5, 3.MD.5a, 3.MD.5b, 3.MD.6

Differentiation Options

CCSS 3.MD.2

CCSS 3.MD.5, 3.MD.5a, 3.MD.5b, 3.MD.6, 3.MD.7, 3.MD.7a, SMP6

CCSS 3.MD.5, 3.MD.5a, 3.MD.5b, 3.MD.6

Readiness
5–10 min

Describing Volume

	WHOLE CLASS
	SMALL GROUP
	PARTNER
	INDEPENDENT

empty, transparent 1-liter bottle; water; container for pouring; food coloring (optional)

To provide experience with liquid volume, show children an empty bottle. Ask: *How much liquid is inside?* None. It is empty. Fill the bottle halfway with water and have children describe how full it is. Sample answers: Half full; half empty; partially full You may want to tint the water with food coloring for visibility. Continue to add and pour out water, having children describe amounts such as *less than half full* and *completely full*. Point out that the container does not have to be completely full to describe it as *almost full, more than halfway full,* and so on.

Enrichment
10–15 min

Estimating Area

	WHOLE CLASS
	SMALL GROUP
	PARTNER
	INDEPENDENT

Math Masters, p. 72; centimeter cubes

To extend their understanding of area measures and square units, have children estimate the number of centimeter cubes it takes to cover a 5-by-5 centimeter square and an 8-by-8 centimeter square. Have children check their estimates by completely covering the squares with centimeter cubes and explain how they counted the squares. **GMP6.1**

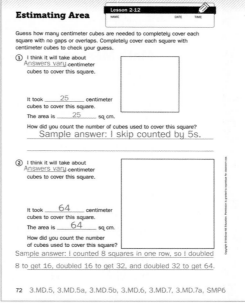

Extra Practice
5–10 min

Finding Letter Areas

	WHOLE CLASS
	SMALL GROUP
	PARTNER
	INDEPENDENT

Math Masters, p. 73; centimeter cubes

To provide practice measuring area, have children count the numbers of square centimeters it takes to cover the areas of block letters on *Math Masters,* page 73.

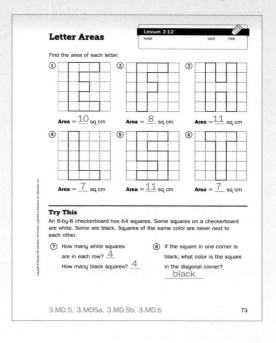

English Language Learners Support

Beginning ELL Demonstrate the meaning of *cover* by showing examples of items that cover each other exactly, such as two playing cards. Demonstrate that you cannot see the covered card hidden below. Show a non-example, such as a small book on top of a larger notebook, asking: *Does the book completely cover the notebook?* No. Extend the idea of covering to Exploration B by asking: *Do the squares completely cover the traced area? Does the _____ you traced cover a large area?*

Go Online **ELL** English Learners Support

1 Warm Up 5 min

ePresentations eToolkit

▶ Mental Math and Fluency

Have children solve fact extension problems mentally and record their answers on slates. Encourage them to think about combinations of 10. *Leveled exercises:*

●○○ 70 + ? = 100 30 20 + ? = 100 80 40 + ? = 100 60

●●○ 72 + ? = 80 8 134 + ? = 140 6 230 − ? = 223 7

●●● 1,000 − ? = 800 200 1,010 − ? = 990 20 1,250 − ? = 1,160 90

2 Focus 40–50 min

ePresentations eToolkit

▶ Math Message

Take a set of fraction circles. Examine the pieces and use math language to describe them with a partner. GMP6.3

▶ Introducing Fraction Circles

| WHOLE CLASS | SMALL GROUP | PARTNER | INDEPENDENT |

Math Message Follow-Up Have children share their observations about the fraction circles. Sample answers: The pink pieces are each half of the red circle. Pieces that are the same color are the same size. Same-color pieces cover the red circle. Remind children that a **fraction** names equal parts of a **whole.** Explain that the **fraction circle** pieces can be used to show fractional parts of a whole. Connect this to their experience dividing pancakes into equal shares in Lesson 1-12 Explorations.

Discuss the total number of pieces for each color. For example, ask: *How many light blue pieces are there?* 6 Emphasize that for each color the pieces are the same size.

Display a pink piece and a yellow piece. Tell children the pink piece is the whole. Ask: *How many yellow pieces does it take to cover the entire pink piece?* 2 Place the yellow piece on the pink piece. Ask: *What part or fraction of the whole is one yellow piece?* One out of two parts; 1-half

Explain the Exploration activities and assign groups to each. Plan to spend more of your time with children working on Exploration A.

Academic Language Development Display, say, and have children repeat the word *whole.* Contrast it with other words that start with *wh,* such as *what, which,* and *when,* noting that the "w" in *whole* is silent. Display *hole* and discuss the different meanings of these homophones.

Math Journal 1, p. 60

**Exploration A:
Fraction Circles**

Lesson 2-12

DATE   TIME

Use your fraction circles to answer the questions.

The red circle is the whole.

1. How many yellow pieces cover the red circle? **4**

2. How many dark blue pieces cover the red circle? **8**

3. How many pink pieces cover the red circle? **2**

What fraction or part of the red circle is one pink piece?
1-half; 1 out of 2 equal parts

The pink piece is the whole.

4. How many yellow pieces cover one pink piece? **2**

5. How many light blue pieces cover one pink piece? **3**

What fraction or part of the pink piece is one light blue piece?
1-third; 1 out of 3 equal parts

The orange piece is the whole.

6. How many light blue pieces cover one orange piece? **2**

What fraction or part of the orange piece is one light blue piece?
1-half; 1 out of 2 equal parts

The yellow piece is the whole.

7. How many dark blue pieces cover one yellow piece? **2**

What fraction or part of the yellow piece is one dark blue piece?
1-half; 1 out of 2 equal parts

60 sixty 3.NF.1, SMP3

▶ Exploration A: Exploring Fraction Circles

Math Journal 1, p. 60

| WHOLE CLASS | SMALL GROUP | **PARTNER** | INDEPENDENT |

Explain your routine for managing and putting away the fraction circles.
To encourage children to think flexibly about the whole, have them
follow directions on journal page 60. Have them count the number of
same-size pieces that cover different wholes and name unit fractions.
Encourage children to make and confirm predictions about
part-whole relationships between different fraction circle pieces. Ask:
*What fraction of a _____ piece is a _____ piece? How do you
know?* GMP3.1 For example, a yellow piece is 1-fourth of the red circle.
More formal instruction with fractions will begin in Unit 5.

Differentiate **Adjusting the Activity**

To help children keep track of a particular *whole* when comparing different
fraction circle pieces, provide a sentence frame: __2__ __yellow__ pieces
cover one whole __pink__ *piece*. Model and have children repeat the
statements. Then add the fraction names to the description. *One yellow
piece is 1-half of a pink piece.*

Go Online ▸ Differentiation Support

▶ Exploration B: Measuring Area

Activity Card 32; *Math Journal 1*, p. 61; *Math Masters*, pp. TA19 and TA22

| WHOLE CLASS | **SMALL GROUP** | **PARTNER** | **INDEPENDENT** |

Professional Development Help children connect the discrete view
of area (counting unit squares) with a more continuous view of area by
sweeping your hand across the surface of objects from boundary to
boundary. More formal instruction on area will begin in Unit 4.

Have children follow directions on Activity Card 32 to measure and record
the areas of different rectangular objects. Explain that the amount of
surface inside the borders, or boundary, of each object is called the **area.**
Model tracing around an object on *Math Masters*, page TA22 and sweeping
your hand across the space inside. Then count the squares inside the
tracing. Tell children that the number of squares inside the borders is a
measurement of the area in **square inches.** When using *Math Masters*,
page TA19 the measurement of the area is in **square centimeters.**

As a reference, display *Math Masters*, page TA19 and label it "Square
Centimeters" and *Math Masters*, page TA22 and label it "Square Inches."
You may also display abbreviations for both units (sq in. and sq cm).

Activity Card 32

Measuring Area 1

What You Need
Math Journal 1, page 61
Centimeter Grid Paper, page TA19
One-Inch Grid Paper, page TA22
Everything Math Deck
small rectangular objects
tape and larger rectangular objects (optional)

What To Do
1. Trace around an Everything Math Deck on the Centimeter Grid Paper.
2. Count the number of square centimeters inside the border.
   • If more than half of a square is inside the border, count
     the whole square.
   • If less than half of a square is inside the border, do not
     count the square at all.
3. Record the number of square centimeters on journal page 61.
   This is your measurement of the area.
4. Repeat Steps 1–3 using one-inch grid paper.
5. Choose other rectangular objects. Measure their areas, and record your work.

Talk About It
Compare your measurements in square centimeters and square inches.
What do you notice?
What is a faster way to find the area than counting the squares by 1s?

More You Can Do
Tape square centimeter paper together. Trace the areas of larger rectangular objects.
Count the number of square centimeters.

3.MD.5, 3.MD.5a, 3.MD.5b, 3.MD.6, SMP6

1, 2, 3, 4, ...

Math Journal 1, p. 61

Exploration B:
Measuring Area

Lesson 2-12
DATE   TIME

Follow the directions on Activity Card 32.
1. a. I traced *the Everything Math Deck*
   b. It has an area of about _____ square centimeters.
   c. It has an area of about _____ square inches.

2. a. I traced _____.
   b. It has an area of about _____ square centimeters.
   c. It has an area of about _____ square inches.

3. a. I traced _____.
   b. It has an area of about _____ square centimeters.
   c. It has an area of about _____ square inches.

4. a. I traced _____.
   b. It has an area of about _____ square centimeters.
   c. It has an area of about _____ square inches.

Compare your square centimeters and square inches measurements.
What do you notice?
Sample answer: The number of square
centimeters in an area is larger because a
square centimeter is smaller than a square
inch.

3.MD.5, 3.MD.5a, 3.MD.5b, 3.MD.6, SMP6   sixty-one 61

Comparing Liquid Volume 33

What You Need
Math Journal 1, page 62
containers A, B, and C
pitcher of water
dishpan
paper towels
1-liter beaker

What To Do
Work with a partner or small group.
Record each step on journal page 62.
1 Draw Containers A, B, and C.
2 Predict: Which container will hold the most water?
  Circle that container.
3 Using the water from the pitcher, carefully fill Container
  A with water while holding it over the dishpan.
4 Pour the water from Container A into the 1-liter beaker.
  Shade that amount of water on the picture of the 1-liter
  beaker on journal page 62.
5 Pour the water back into the pitcher.
6 Repeat Steps 3–5 for Containers B and C.

Talk About It
How does the 1-liter beaker help you compare the liquid
volumes for Containers A, B, and C?

More You Can Do
Repeat the activity with three different containers.

Math Journal 1, p. 62

Exploration C:
Comparing Liquid Volumes

Lesson 2-12
DATE   TIME

• Draw containers A, B, and C.
• Circle the container in the top row that you think will hold the most water.
• Below each drawing, show the liquid volume that your container can hold
  by shading in the 1-liter beaker. Sample answers given.

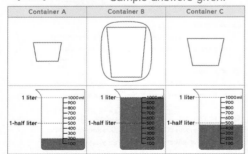

Which container holds the most water? Answers vary.

Write at least two things you notice about the different liquid volumes.

Container A holds less than 1-half liter of water.
Container B holds about 1 liter of water. Container
B holds the most water even though Container C
is wider.

62 sixty-two   3.MD.2, SMP5

To support children as they find area measures, suggest marking a dot
or X inside each square to help keep track of their counts.

Discuss what children notice about the areas of each object in square
centimeters and in square inches. Ask: *Why is it important to include units
in area measures?* **GMP6.3** Sample answers: So we know whether the
area is in square centimeters or square inches. So we know they are areas
and not lengths.

▶ **Exploration C:** Comparing
Liquid Volume

Activity Card 33; *Math Journal 1*, p. 62

| WHOLE CLASS | **SMALL GROUP** | **PARTNER** | INDEPENDENT |

Explain that liquid **volume** is the amount of liquid in a container and that a
liter is a unit of volume.

Briefly introduce the 1-liter beaker, pointing out the marks you made that
show 1-half liter (500 mL) and 1 liter (1,000 mL). (*See Before You Begin.*)
Explain that the markings on the beaker's scale show milliliters, a smaller
unit of liquid volume.

   NOTE Volume measures in milliliters are explored further in Unit 7. Children
   estimate volume relative to 1 liter in this Exploration.

Emphasize that when the 1-liter beaker is filled to the top line, the volume
of the liquid inside is 1 liter. Using a smaller container, gradually fill a 1-liter
beaker to show different volumes, such as *less than half a liter, about 1-half
liter,* and *about 1 liter.* Encourage children to describe the changing volume
as you fill the beaker.

Have children follow directions on Activity Card 33 and explain how the
1-liter beaker helps them compare the liquid volume different containers
can hold. **GMP5.2**

Summarize Have children share their favorite Exploration activity
and describe the math they learned or practiced.

3 Practice

15–20 min

Go Online ePresentations eToolkit Home Connections

▶ *Minute Math+*

To practice mental math strategies, select a *Minute Math+* activity.

▶ Playing *Division Arrays*

Student Reference Book, pp. 238 and 239; *Math Masters,* p. G9

| WHOLE CLASS | **SMALL GROUP** | **PARTNER** | INDEPENDENT |

Have children play *Division Arrays* to practice division as equal grouping. Refer to Lesson 2-10 and *Student Reference Book,* page 238 for detailed instructions.

Observe

- Do children build their arrays correctly?
- Do children find the correct score with and without remainders? **GMP2.2**

Discuss

- *How do you know if there are leftover counters? Do certain numbers have leftover counters more often than others?* **GMP7.1**

Differentiate **Game Modifications** **Go Online** Differentiation Support

---

▶ Math Boxes 2-12

Math Journal 1, p. 63

| WHOLE CLASS | **SMALL GROUP** | **PARTNER** | **INDEPENDENT** |

Mixed Practice Math Boxes 2-12 are paired with Math Boxes 2-10.

▶ Home Link 1-12

Math Masters, p. 74

Homework Children explore volume and count squares to find areas.

Math Journal 1, p. 63

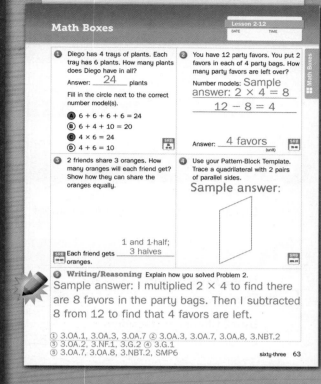

Math Boxes

Lesson 2-12
DATE TIME

① Diego has 4 trays of plants. Each tray has 6 plants. How many plants does Diego have in all?

Answer: __24__ plants

Fill in the circle next to the correct number model(s).

Ⓐ 6 + 6 + 6 + 6 = 24
Ⓑ 6 + 4 + 10 = 20
Ⓒ 4 × 6 = 24
Ⓓ 4 + 6 = 10

② You have 12 party favors. You put 2 favors in each of 4 party bags. How many party favors are left over?

Number models: Sample answer: $2 \times 4 = 8$
$12 - 8 = 4$

Answer: __4 favors__ (unit)

③ 2 friends share 3 oranges. How many oranges will each friend get? Show how they can share the oranges equally.

Each friend gets __1 and 1-half; 3 halves__ oranges.

④ Use your Pattern-Block Template. Trace a quadrilateral with 2 pairs of parallel sides.

Sample answer:

⑤ **Writing/Reasoning** Explain how you solved Problem 2.
Sample answer: I multiplied 2×4 to find there are 8 favors in the party bags. Then I subtracted 8 from 12 to find that 4 favors are left.

① 3.OA.1, 3.OA.3, 3.OA.7 ② 3.OA.3, 3.OA.7, 3.OA.8, 3.NBT.2
③ 3.OA.2, 3.NF.1, 3.G.2 ④ 3.G.1
⑤ 3.OA.7, 3.OA.8, 3.NBT.2, SMP6

sixty-three 63

Math Masters, p. 74

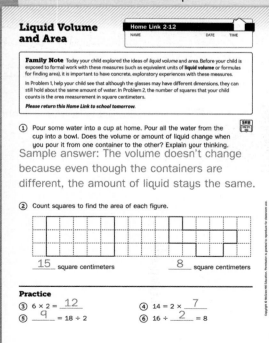

Liquid Volume and Area

Home Link 2-12
NAME DATE TIME

Family Note Today your child explored the ideas of *liquid volume* and area. Before your child is exposed to formal work with these measures (such as equivalent units of **liquid volume** or formulas for finding area), it is important to have concrete, exploratory experiences with these measures.

In Problem 1, help your child see that although the glasses may have different dimensions, they can still hold about the same amount of water. In Problem 2, the number of squares that your child counts is the area measurement in square centimeters.

Please return this Home Link to school tomorrow.

① Pour some water into a cup at home. Pour all the water from the cup into a bowl. Does the volume or amount of liquid change when you pour it from one container to the other? Explain your thinking.
Sample answer: The volume doesn't change because even though the containers are different, the amount of liquid stays the same.

② Count squares to find the area of each figure.

__15__ square centimeters   __8__ square centimeters

Practice

③ $6 \times 2 =$ __12__
④ $14 = 2 \times$ __7__
⑤ __9__ $= 18 \div 2$
⑥ $16 \div$ __2__ $= 8$

74 3.OA.7, 3.MD.2, 3.MD.5, 3.MD.5a, 3.MD.5b, 3.MD.6

Unit 2 Progress Check

Overview **Day 1:** Administer the Unit Assessments.
Day 2: Administer the Cumulative Assessment.

2-Day Lesson

 Student Learning Center
Students may take assessments digitally.

 Assessment and Reporting
Record results and track progress toward mastery.

Day 1: Unit Assessments

1 Warm Up 5–10 min

Materials

Self Assessment
Children complete the Self Assessment.

Assessment Handbook, p. 15

2a Assess 35–50 min

Unit 2 Assessment
These items reflect mastery expectations to this point.

Assessment Handbook, pp. 16–19

Unit 2 Challenge (Optional)
Children may demonstrate progress beyond expectations.

Assessment Handbook, pp. 20–21

CCSS Common Core State Standards	Goals for Mathematical Content (GMC)	Lessons	Self Assessment	Unit 2 Assessment	Unit 2 Challenge
3.OA.1	Interpret multiplication in terms of equal groups.	2-6, 2-7	4	8a, 9a, 9b	3a, 3b
3.OA.2	Interpret division in terms of equal shares or equal groups.	2-7 to 2-10	5	10	
3.OA.3	Use multiplication and division to solve number stories.	2-5 to 2-10	4, 5	8a, 9b, 10	3a
	Model number stories involving multiplication and division.	2-5 to 2-7, 2-9, 2-10	4, 5	8a, 9a, 9b, 10	3a, 3b
3.OA.7	Multiply within 100 fluently.	2-4 to 2-7, 2-9, 2-11	6	8a	4
	Know all products of 1-digit numbers × 1, × 2, × 5, and × 10 automatically.	2-6, 2-11		4, 9b	
	Divide within 100 fluently.	2-5, 2-10			2
3.OA.8	Solve 2-step number stories involving two of the four operations.	2-4, 2-5		7	2
3.NBT.2	Add within 1,000 fluently.	2-1 to 2-5, 2-11	1, 2, 6	1a–1c, 5, 6	1, 2, 4
	Subtract within 1,000 fluently.	2-1 to 2-5, 2-11	1, 2, 6	2a–2c, 3, 5, 6	1

Goals for Mathematical Practice (GMP)		Lessons	Self Assessment	Unit 2 Assessment	Unit 2 Challenge
SMP1	Check whether your answer makes sense. GMP1.4	2-2, 2-3, 2-5	3	5, 6	
SMP2	Make sense of the representations you and others use. GMP2.2	2-4, 2-7, 2-8, 2-10		7	2, 3a, 3b
SMP4	Model real-world situations using graphs, drawings, tables, symbols, numbers, diagrams, and other representations. GMP4.1	2-4, 2-5, 2-7, 2-9		9a, 9b, 10	
SMP6	Explain your mathematical thinking clearly and precisely. GMP6.1	2-1		7, 8b	1, 3b
	Think about accuracy and efficiency when you count, measure, and calculate. GMP6.4	2-6		7, 8a	
SMP7	Look for mathematical structures such as categories, patterns, and properties. GMP7.1	2-1, 2-11		3, 4	
	Use structures to solve problems and answer questions. GMP7.2	2-1, 2-10, 2-11		1a–1c, 2a–2c	1
SMP8	Create and justify rules, shortcuts, and generalizations. GMP8.1	2-6, 2-10		3, 4	4

III **Spiral Tracker** ⟨ **Go Online** ⟩ to see how mastery develops for all standards within the grade.

1 Warm Up 5–10 min

▶ Self Assessment

Assessment Handbook, p. 15

| WHOLE CLASS | SMALL GROUP | PARTNER | **INDEPENDENT** |

Children complete the Self Assessment to reflect on their progress in Unit 2.

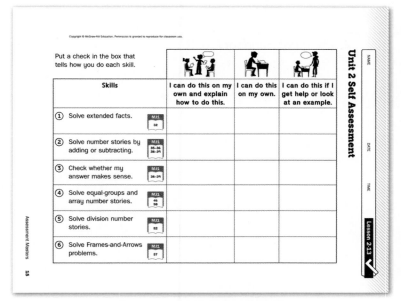

Assessment Handbook, p. 15

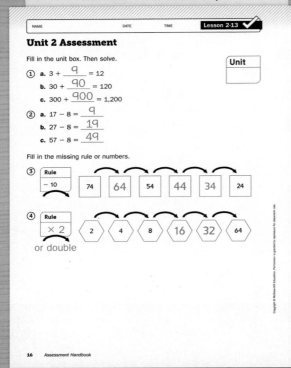

Unit 2 Assessment

Fill in the unit box. Then solve.

Unit

① **a.** 3 + _9_ = 12
b. 30 + _90_ = 120
c. 300 + _900_ = 1,200

② **a.** 17 − 8 = _9_
b. 27 − 8 = _19_
c. 57 − 8 = _49_

Fill in the missing rule or numbers.

③ Rule − 10
| 74 | 64 | 54 | 44 | 34 | 24 |

④ Rule × 2 or double
2 4 8 16 32 64

2a Assess   35–50 min   Go Online ✓

Assessment and Reporting   Differentiation Support

▶ Unit 2 Assessment

Assessment Handbook, pp. 16–19

| WHOLE CLASS | SMALL GROUP | PARTNER | **INDEPENDENT** |

Children complete the Unit 2 Assessment to demonstrate their progress on the Common Core State Standards covered in this unit.

Generic rubrics in the *Assessment Handbook* appendix can be used to evaluate children's progress on the Mathematical Practices.

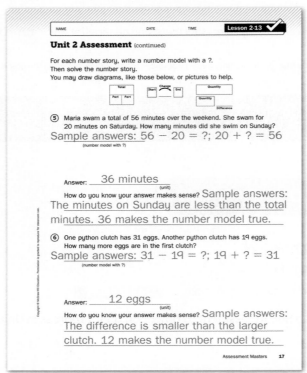

Unit 2 Assessment (continued)

For each number story, write a number model with a ?.
Then solve the number story.
You may draw diagrams, like those below, or pictures to help.

⑤ Maria swam a total of 56 minutes over the weekend. She swam for 20 minutes on Saturday. How many minutes did she swim on Sunday?
Sample answers: 56 − 20 = ?; 20 + ? = 56
(number model with ?)

Answer: _36 minutes_
(unit)
How do you know your answer makes sense? Sample answers: The minutes on Sunday are less than the total minutes. 36 makes the number model true.

⑥ One python clutch has 31 eggs. Another python clutch has 19 eggs. How many more eggs are in the first clutch?
Sample answers: 31 − 19 = ?; 19 + ? = 31
(number model with ?)

Answer: _12 eggs_
(unit)
How do you know your answer makes sense? Sample answers: The difference is smaller than the larger clutch. 12 makes the number model true.

Assessment Masters   17

Assessment Handbook, p. 17

Differentiate **Adjusting the Assessment**

Item(s)	Adjustments
1, 2	To extend Items 1 and 2, have children describe patterns in the fact extensions.
3	To scaffold Item 3, have children use a number grid.
4	To scaffold Item 4, have children use counters to model each frame and then describe how the numbers change. To extend Item 4, have children make up their own Frames-and-Arrows problems.
5	To scaffold Item 5, have children draw a parts-and-total diagram to help organize the story information. Discuss what is known and unknown.
6	To scaffold Item 6, have children draw comparison diagrams to help organize the story information. Discuss what is known and unknown.
7, 8	To scaffold Items 7 and 8, provide squares of paper to represent the packs and counters to represent the pencils and balloons.
9	To scaffold Item 9, have children build the array using counters.
10	To scaffold Item 10, have children model sharing marbles with counters.

Advice for Differentiation

Because this is the beginning of the school year, all of the content included on the Unit 2 Assessment was recently introduced and will be revisited in subsequent units.

Use the online assessment and reporting tools to track children's performance. Differentiation materials are available online to help you address children's needs.

NOTE See the Unit Organizer on pages 118–119 or the online Spiral Tracker for details on Unit 2 focus topics and the spiral.

Assessment Handbook, p. 18

NAME　　　　　DATE　　　　TIME　　　Lesson 2-13

Unit 2 Assessment (continued)

⑦ Jeremiah read the number story below. Then he drew a picture and wrote two number models to help keep track of his thinking.

> Mr. Riley has 2 packs of pencils with 5 pencils in each pack. He gives 4 of the pencils to his students. How many pencils does he still have?

$2 \times 5 = 10$
$10 - 4 = 6$

Do Jeremiah's number models fit the number story? Explain your answer.
Yes. Sample explanation: They fit because Mr. Riley had 2 packs of 5 pencils each, and that is $2 \times 5 = 10$. Then he gave 4 of them away, and that is $10 - 4 = 6$. So he has 6 pencils left.

⑧ There are 5 giant balloons in a pack.
　a. How many balloons are in 5 packs? You may draw a picture to help you solve.

　　Circle the number model that fits the story.
　　$5 + 5 = ?$　　($5 \times 5 = ?$)
　　Answer: 25 balloons
　　　　　　　(unit)
　b. Explain how you solved Problem 8a. Sample answer:
　　I skip counted by 5s and got 25.

18　Assessment Handbook

Assessment Handbook, p. 19

NAME　　　　　DATE　　　　TIME　　　Lesson 2-13

Unit 2 Assessment (continued)

⑨ You have 2 rows of chairs with 9 chairs in each row. How many chairs do you have in all?
　a. Draw an array on the dot grid to match the story.

　b. Circle the number model that fits the story.
　　($2 \times 9 = ?$)　$2 + 9 = ?$
　　There are 18 chairs in all.
　　　　　　　　　　(unit)

⑩ Share 20 marbles equally among 5 friends. Draw a picture to show how you shared the marbles.
Drawings vary.

Each friend gets 4 marbles
　　　　　　　　　(unit)
There are 0 marbles left over.
　　　　　　(unit)

Assessment Masters　19

Unit 2 Challenge

① Lila says that knowing 3 + 7 = 10 helps her solve this problem on her calculator:

Enter 423. Change it to 480. How? **+ 57**

Explain how Lila might use the basic fact. **Sample answer: Knowing 3 + 7 can help because 7 ones added to 3 ones gets to the next ten. Lila can add 423 + 7 to get 430 and then add 50 to get to 480. So 423 + 57 = 480.**

② Read the number story and circle the pair of number models that fit the story. Then solve.

Mrs. Ball equally shared 30 markers among 3 groups. Mike's group found 6 more markers. How many markers does Mike's group have now? You may draw a picture to help.

Circle the pair of number models that best fit the story.

A 30 ÷ 3 = 10
   10 + 6 = 16

B 30 × 3 = 90
   90 + 6 = 96

C 30 + 3 = 33
   33 + 6 = 39

D 30 − 3 = 27
   27 + 6 = 33

Mike's group now has __16__ markers.

20   Assessment Handbook

▶ **Unit 2 Challenge** (Optional)

Assessment Handbook, pp. 20–21

| WHOLE CLASS | SMALL GROUP | PARTNER | **INDEPENDENT** |

Children can complete the Unit 2 Challenge after they complete the Unit 2 Assessment.

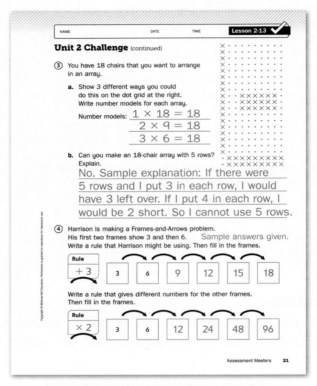

Assessment Handbook, p. 21

Unit 2 Progress Check ✔

Day 2: Cumulative Assessment

2b Assess   35–50 min

Cumulative Assessment
These items reflect mastery expectations to this point.

Materials

Assessment Handbook, pp. 22–24

Common Core State Standards	Goals for Mathematical Content (GMC)	Cumulative Assessment
3.OA.7	Multiply within 100 fluently.	3a–3f
	Know all products of 1-digit numbers × 1, × 2, × 5, and × 10 automatically.	3a–3f
3.NBT.1	Use place-value understanding to round whole numbers to the nearest 10.	4a, 4b
	Use place-value understanding to round whole numbers to the nearest 100.	5a, 5b
3.NBT.2	Add within 1,000 fluently.	6a, 6c
	Subtract within 1,000 fluently.	6b
3.MD.1	Tell and write time.	1a–1c, 2a, 2b
3.MD.3	Solve 1- and 2-step problems using information in graphs.	6a–6d
	Goal for Mathematical Practice (GMP)	
SMP6	Explain your mathematical thinking clearly and precisely. GMP6.1	3g, 4c, 6d

Spiral Tracker **Go Online** to see how mastery develops for all standards within the grade.

3 Look Ahead   15–20 min

Math Boxes 2-13: Preview for Unit 3
Children preview skills and concepts for Unit 3.

Math Journal 1, p. 64

Home Link 2-13
Children take home the Family Letter that introduces Unit 3.

Math Masters, pp. 75–78

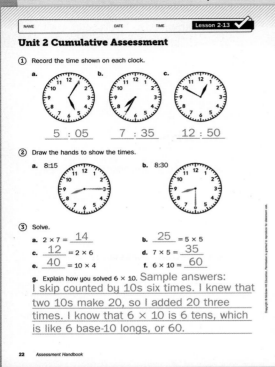

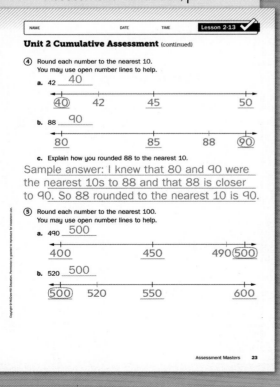

2b Assess

35–50 min | Go Online

Assessment and Reporting | Differentiation Support

▶ Cumulative Assessment

Assessment Handbook, pp. 22–24

| WHOLE CLASS | SMALL GROUP | PARTNER | **INDEPENDENT** |

Children complete the Cumulative Assessment. The items in the Cumulative Assessment address content from Unit 1. It can help you monitor learning and retention of some (but not all) of the content and practices that were the focus of that unit, as detailed in the Cumulative Assessment table on page 205. Successful responses to these items indicate adequate progress at this point in the year.

Monitor children's progress on the Common Core State Standards using the online assessment and reporting tools.

Generic rubrics in the *Assessment Handbook* appendix can be used to evaluate children's progress on the Mathematical Practices.

Written assessments are one way children can demonstrate what they know. The table below shows adjustments you can make to the Cumulative Assessment to maximize opportunities for individual children or for your entire class.

Differentiate — Adjusting the Assessment

Item(s)	Adjustments
1	To scaffold Item 1, have children match their toolkit clocks to the times shown, determine the hour, and then count the minutes after the hour.
2	To extend Item 2, have children continue to show times on their toolkit clocks in 15-minute increments and then discuss the placement of the clock hands for each increment.
3	To extend Item 3, have children multiply one of the factors in each problem by 10 and then figure out the product. For example, 2×7 becomes 20×7.
4	To scaffold Item 4, have children list the multiples of 10 from 0 to 100.
5	To scaffold Item 5, have children list the multiples of 100 from 0 to 1,000.
6	To extend Item 6, have children gather data about the books in the class library. Then have them represent that data on a scaled bar graph and ask and answer questions about the data.

Advice for Differentiation

Because this is the beginning of the school year, all of the content included on the Cumulative Assessment was recently introduced and will be revisited in subsequent units.

Use the online assessment and reporting tools to track children's performance. Differentiation materials are available online to help you address children's needs.

3 Look Ahead 10–15 min

Go Online ▸ 🏠 Home Connections

▶ ## Math Boxes 2-13: Preview for Unit 3

Math Journal 1, p. 64

| WHOLE CLASS | SMALL GROUP | **PARTNER** | **INDEPENDENT** |

Mixed Practice Math Boxes 2-13 are paired with Math Boxes 2-9. These problems focus on skills and understandings that are prerequisite for Unit 3. You may want to use information from these Math Boxes to plan instruction and grouping in Unit 3.

▶ ## Home Link 2-13: Unit 3 Family Letter

Math Masters, pp. 75–78

Home Connection The Unit 3 Family Letter provides information and activities related to Unit 3 content.

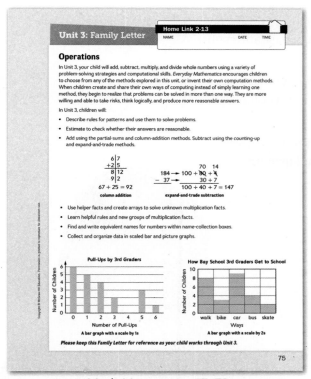

Math Masters, pp. 75–78

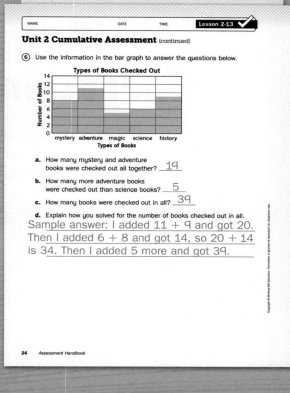

Math Journal 1, p. 64

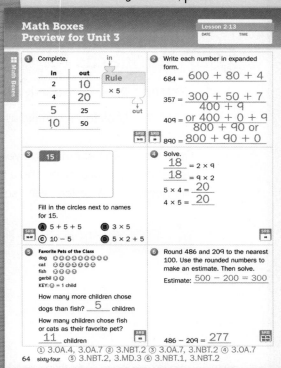

Unit 3 Organizer
Operations

In this unit, children use place value to develop and practice strategies for addition and subtraction of 2- and 3-digit numbers. They represent multiplication using arrays, and use these representations to develop strategies for solving multiplication facts.

CCSS Standards for Mathematical Content

Domain	Cluster
Operations and Algebraic Thinking	Represent and solve problems involving multiplication and division.
	Multiply and divide within 100.
	Solve problems involving the four operations, and identify and explain patterns in arithmetic.
Number and Operations in Base Ten	Use place value understanding and properties of operations to perform multi-digit arithmetic.

Because the standards within each domain can be broad, *Everyday Mathematics* has unpacked each standard into Goals for Mathematical Content GMC. For a complete list of Standards and Goals, see page EM1.

For an overview of the CCSS domains, standards, and mastery expectations in this unit, see the **Spiral Trace** on pages 214–215. See the **Mathematical Background** (pages 216–218) for a discussion of the following key topics:

- Adding and Subtracting Multidigit Numbers
- Explorations
- Practicing Operations and Equivalence
- Multiplication Fact Strategies

CCSS Standards for Mathematical Practice

SMP2	Reason abstractly and quantitatively.
SMP7	Look for and make use of structure.

For a discussion about how *Everyday Mathematics* develops these practices and a list of Goals for Mathematical Practice GMP, see page 219.

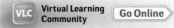 **Virtual Learning Community** Go Online to **vlc.cemseprojects.org** to search for video clips on each practice.

McGraw-Hill Education

Go Digital with these tools at **connectED.mcgraw-hill.com**

 ePresentations

 Student Learning Center

 Facts Workshop Game

 eToolkit

 Professional Development

Home Connections

Spiral Tracker

 Assessment and Reporting

 English Learners Support

 Differentiation Support

Contents

*The standards listed here are addressed in the **Focus** of each lesson. For all the standards in a lesson, see the Lesson Opener.

Unit 3 Materials

 **Virtual Learning Community**

See how *Everyday Mathematics* teachers organize materials. Search "Classroom Tours" at **vlc.cemseprojects.org**.

Lesson	Math Masters	Activity Cards	Manipulative Kit	Other Materials
3-1	pp. 79; TA23–TA24; G7	34–35	counters (optional); two 6-sided dice; Class Number Line (optional)	slate; box (optional); calculator (optional)
3-2	pp. 80–83; TA6			Standards for Mathematical Practice Poster; Guidelines for Discussion Poster; colored pencils (optional); selected samples of children's work; children's work from Day 1
3-3	pp. 84; TA14; G10–G11	36	number cards 0–9 (4 of each); base-10 blocks	slate; half-sheet of paper
3-4	pp. 85–87; TA14 (optional)	37	number cards 1–9 (4 of each); base-10 blocks	slate
3-5	pp. 88–89; TA3; *Assessment Handbook*, pp. 54–56 and 60	38	number cards 1–9 (4 of each); Class Number Line	slate; number grid (optional); Fact Triangles
3-6	pp. 90; TA3; TA14	39–40	number cards 0–9 (4 of each); base-10 blocks	slate; large poster paper; markers; scissors; tape
3-7	pp. 91–96; TA7 (optional); G10	41–42	pattern blocks; 25 centimeter cubes; number cards 1–9 (4 of each)	slate; 1-foot square cardboard templates; colored paper; scissors; straightedge (optional); masking tape (optional); collection of objects (optional)
3-8	pp. 97–99; TA25	43		calculator; slate (optional)
3-9	pp. 100–102; TA19–TA20 (optional); TA22 (optional)	44–46	10-sided die; per partnership: 100 centimeter cubes	slate; half-sheet of paper; tape; Class Data Pad; scissors; paper clips; Fact Triangles; crayons and markers
3-10	pp. 103–105; TA18; TA20 (optional); TA26–TA27		6-sided die; dominoes	slate; scissors
3-11	pp. 106–107; G6	47	Quick Look Cards 134, 135, 136; counters; 6-sided die; number cards 1–10 (4 of each); number cards 0–10	half-sheet of paper; colored pencils; Fact Triangles; large poster paper; markers or crayons; Class Data Pad
3-12	pp. 108–110	48	counters; number cards 0–10	slate; half-sheet of paper; Class Data Pad; scissors; 2s, 5s, and 10s Fact Triangles; large poster paper; markers or crayons
3-13	pp. 111–113; TA28–TA29; G12	49–50	Quick Look Cards 11, 15, 16; base-10 blocks; counters (optional); number cards 0–10 (4 of each); number cards 11–20	slate; blank name-collection box for the number 14 and filled-in name-collection box for the number 18
3-14	pp. 114–117; *Assessment Handbook*, pp. 25–32		base-10 blocks	Standards for Mathematical Practice Poster (optional)

📖 **Literature Link** 3-9 *Sea Squares*

Go Online for a complete literature list for Grade 3 and to download all Quick Look Cards.

Problem Solving  Professional Development

Everyday Mathematics emphasizes equally all three of the Common Core's dimensions of **rigor:**

- conceptual understanding
- procedural skill and fluency
- applications

Math Messages, other daily work, Explorations, and Open Response tasks provide many opportunities for children to apply what they know to solve problems.

▶ Math Message

Math Messages require children to solve a problem they have not been shown how to solve. Math Messages provide almost daily opportunities for problem solving.

▶ Daily Work

Journal pages, Home Links, Writing/Reasoning prompts, and Differentiation Options often require children to solve problems in mathematical contexts and real-life situations. **Minute Math+** offers number stories and a variety of other practice activities for transition times and spare moments throughout the day.

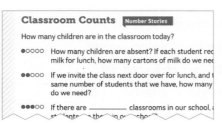

▶ Explorations

In Exploration A, children create a scaled bar graph. In Exploration B, children measure area using 1-foot squares. In Exploration C, children partition rectangles, divide shapes into squares, and count squares to find the area.

▶ Open Response and Reengagement

In Lesson 3-2 children make estimates for problems they solve using mental math. In estimating costs, children discuss estimation strategies, including close-but-easier numbers, that can be used to check the reasonableness of a sum. During the reengagement discussion on Day 2, children examine each other's explanations using a rubric as a guide, and then revise their work. Explaining mathematical thinking clearly and precisely is the focus practice for the lesson. GMP6.1

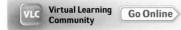 **Virtual Learning Community** **Go Online** to watch an Open Response and Reengagement lesson in action. Search "Open Response" at **vlc.cemseprojects.org**.

▶ Open Response Assessment

In Progress Check Lesson 3-14 children make sense of a subtraction problem to identify an error and use place value to explain their thinking. They discuss and make sense of each other's mathematical thinking. GMP3.2

Look for GMP1.1–1.6 markers, which indicate opportunities for children to engage in **SMP1:** "Make sense of problems and persevere in solving them." Children also become better problem solvers as they engage in all of the CCSS Mathematical Practices. The yellow GMP markers throughout the lessons indicate places where you can emphasize the Mathematical Practices and develop children's problem-solving skills.

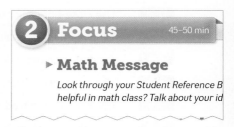

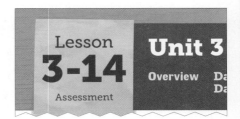

Assessment and Differentiation  Assessment and Reporting

See pages xxii–xxv to learn about a comprehensive online system for recording, monitoring, and reporting children's progress using core program assessments.

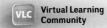 **Virtual Learning Community** **Go Online** to **vlc.cemseprojects.org** for tools and ideas related to assessment and differentiation from *Everyday Mathematics* teachers.

✓ Ongoing Assessment

In addition to frequent informal opportunities for "kid watching," every lesson (except Explorations) offers an **Assessment Check-In** to gauge children's performance on one or more of the standards addressed in that lesson.

Lesson	Task Description	**CCSS** Common Core State Standards
3-1	Find inputs, outputs, and rules in "What's My Rule?" tables.	3.OA.4, 3.NBT.2, SMP7
3-2	Use close-but-easier numbers and mental math.	3.OA.8, SMP6
3-3	Estimate and use partial-sums addition to solve problems.	3.NBT.2
3-4	Estimate and use column addition to solve problems.	3.OA.8, 3.NBT.2
3-5	Use multiples of 100s, 10s, and 1s to count up.	3.OA.8, 3.NBT.2, SMP2
3-6	Use expand-and-trade subtraction.	3.NBT.1, 3.NBT.2
3-8	Complete a picture graph with symbols representing the data.	3.MD.3, SMP4
3-9	Create arrays and determine products for multiplication squares.	3.OA.1, 3.OA.7
3-10	Generate pairs of facts that demonstrate the turn-around rule.	3.OA.5
3-11	Use adding-a-group strategy to solve multiplication facts.	3.OA.1, 3.OA.5, 3.OA.7
3-12	Use subtracting-a-group strategy to solve multiplication facts.	3.OA.1, 3.OA.5, 3.OA.7
3-13	Write equivalent names using addition, subtraction, and multiplication.	3.OA.7, 3.NBT.2

▶ Periodic Assessment

Unit 3 Progress Check This assessment focuses on the CCSS domains of *Operations and Algebraic Thinking* and *Number and Operations in Base Ten*. It also contains an Open Response Assessment to assess children's ability to identify an error in a subtraction problem and use place value to explain their thinking. GMP3.2

NOTE Odd-numbered units include an **Open Response Assessment.** Even-numbered units include a **Cumulative Assessment.**

► Unit 3 Differentiation Activities

 Differentiation Support   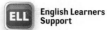 **English Learners Support**

Differentiation Options Every regular lesson provides **Readiness, Enrichment, Extra Practice,** and **Beginning English Language Learners Support** activities that address the Focus standards of that lesson.

CCSS 3.OA.4, 3.NBT.2, SMP8	CCSS 3.OA.4, 3.OA.7, SMP7, SMP8	CCSS 3.OA.4, 3.OA.7, 3.NBT.2, SMP7, SMP8
Readiness 5–10 min	**Enrichment** 10–15 min	**Extra Practice** 10–15 min
WHOLE CLASS / SMALL GROUP / PARTNER	WHOLE CLASS / SMALL GROUP / PARTNER	WHOLE CLASS / SMALL GROUP / PARTNER
Identifying a Mystery Rule number line (optional);	**Creating "What's My Rule?" Problems**	**Practicing "What's My Rule?" Problems**

Activity Cards These activities, written to the children, enable you to differentiate Part 2 of the lesson through small-group work.

English Language Learners Activities and point-of-use support help children at different levels of English language proficiency succeed.

Differentiation Support Two online pages for most lessons provide suggestions for game modifications, ways to scaffold lessons for children who need additional support, and language development suggestions for Beginning, Intermediate, and Advanced English language learners.

Activity Card 44

Differentiation Support online pages

Ongoing Practice **Differentiation Support**

► Embedded Facts Practice

Basic Facts Practice can be found in every part of the lesson. Look for activities or games labeled with CCSS 3.OA.7; or go online to the Spiral Tracker and search using CCSS 3.OA.7.

► Games

Games in *Everyday Mathematics* are an essential tool for practicing skills and developing strategic thinking.

> For **ongoing distributed practice,** see these activities:
> • Mental Math and Fluency
> • Differentiation Options: Extra Practice
> • Part 3: Journal pages, Math Boxes, *Math Masters,* Home Links
> • Print and online games

Lesson	Game	Skills and Concepts	CCSS Common Core State Standards
3-1	*Roll to 1,000*	Practicing mental addition with multiples of 10	3.OA.7, 3.NBT.2, SMP6, SMP7
3-3 / 3-7	*Shuffle to 100*	Estimating and making combinations that have a sum close to 100	3.NBT.1, 3.NBT.2, SMP1, SMP6
3-3	*Shuffle to 1,000*	Estimating and making combinations that have a sum close to 1,000	3.NBT.1, 3.NBT.2
3-10	*Array Bingo*	Matching arrays with multiplication facts	3.OA.1, 3.OA.7, SMP2, SMP6
3-11	*Multiplication Draw*	Practicing multiplication facts	3.OA.7, SMP7
3-13	*Name That Number*	Using different operations to name a number	3.OA.7, 3.NBT.2, SMP2

VLC Virtual Learning Community **Go Online** to look for examples of *Everyday Mathematics* games at **vlc.cemseprojects.org.**

Ⓒ CCSS Spiral Trace: Skills, Concepts, and Applications

⭐ **Mastery Expectations** This Spiral Trace outlines instructional trajectories for key standards in Unit 3. For each standard, it highlights opportunities for Focus instruction, Warm Up and Practice activities, as well as formative and summative assessment. It describes the **degree of mastery**—as measured against the entire standard—expected at this point in the year.

Operations and Algebraic Thinking

3.OA.1 Interpret products of whole numbers, e.g., interpret 5 × 7 as the total number of objects in 5 groups of 7 objects each. *For example, describe a context in which a total number of objects can be expressed as 5 × 7.*

| 2-6 Warm Up Focus Practice | 2-7 Warm Up Focus Practice | 2-13 Progress Check ✓ | 3-9 through 3-12 Warm Up Focus Practice ✓ | 3-13 Warm Up | 3-14 Progress Check ✓ | 4-2 Warm Up Practice | 4-5 Warm Up Practice | 4-9 Warm Up Practice | 4-13 Progress Check ✓ |

⭐ By the end of Unit 3, expect children to **interpret multiplication in terms of equal groups by drawing arrays or equal groups and writing number models.**

3.OA.5 Apply properties of operations as strategies to multiply and divide. *Examples: If 6 × 4 = 24 is known, then 4 × 6 = 24 is also known. (Commutative property of multiplication.) 3 × 5 × 2 can be found by 3 × 5 = 15, then 15 × 2 = 30, or by 5 × 2 = 10, then 3 × 10 = 30. (Associative property of multiplication.) Knowing that 8 × 5 = 40 and 8 × 2 = 16, one can find 8 × 7 as 8 × (5 + 2) = (8 × 5) + (8 × 2) = 40 + 16 = 56. (Distributive property.)*

| 3-10 through 3-12 Focus ✓ | 3-14 Progress Check ✓ | 4-1 through 4-5 Practice | 5-4 through 5-6 Warm Up Focus Practice ✓ | 5-9 Focus | 5-11 Focus | 5-12 Progress Check ✓ | 6-3 Focus ✓ | 6-7 Warm Up Focus |

⭐ By the end of Unit 3, expect children to **use the turn-around rule (commutative property) as a strategy to solve problems.**

3.OA.7 Fluently multiply and divide within 100, using strategies such as the relationship between multiplication and division (e.g., knowing that 8 × 5 = 40, one knows 40 ÷ 5 = 8) or properties of operations. By the end of Grade 3, know from memory all products of two one-digit numbers.

| 2-11 Warm Up Focus Practice ✓ | 2-12 Practice | 2-13 Progress Check ✓ | 3-1 Focus Practice | 3-5 Practice | 3-8 Warm Up Practice | 3-9 through 3-13 Warm Up Focus Practice ✓ | 3-14 Progress Check ✓ | 4-1 Warm Up Practice | 4-3 through 4-5 Warm Up Practice |

⭐ By the end of Unit 3, expect children to **fluently multiply using strategies for all products of 1-digit numbers and 1, 2, 5, and 10, and recognize the relationship between multiplication and division.**

Spiral Tracker

Go to **connectED.mcgraw-hill.com** for comprehensive trajectories that show how in-depth mastery develops across the grade.

3.OA.8 Solve two-step word problems using the four operations. Represent these problems using equations with a letter standing for the unknown quantity. Assess the reasonableness of answers using mental computation and estimation strategies including rounding.

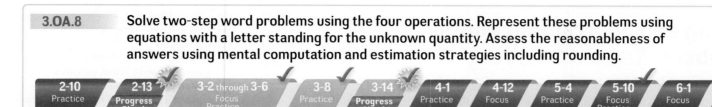

| 2-10 Practice | 2-13 Progress Check | 3-2 through 3-6 Focus Practice | 3-8 Practice | 3-14 Progress Check | 4-1 Practice | 4-12 Focus | 5-4 Practice | 5-10 Focus Practice | 6-1 Focus | 6-7 Focus Practice |

⭐ By the end of Unit 3, expect children to **represent and solve 2-step number stories involving addition and subtraction, and assess the reasonableness of answers using estimation, including rounding.**

Number and Operations in Base Ten

3.NBT.2 Fluently add and subtract within 1000 using strategies and algorithms based on place value, properties of operations, and/or the relationship between addition and subtraction.

| 2-13 Progress Check | 3-1 through 3-6 Warm Up Focus Practice | 3-7 Focus Practice | 3-8 Focus Practice | 3-13 Focus Practice | 3-14 Progress Check | 4-1 through 4-5 Practice | 4-6 Warm Up Practice | 4-7 Warm Up Practice | 4-9 Practice |

⭐ By the end of Unit 3, expect children to **add and subtract within 1000 using partial-sum addition, and counting-up and expand-and-trade subtraction, or other strategies.**

Measurement and Data

3.MD.3 Draw a scaled picture graph and a scaled bar graph to represent a data set with several categories. Solve one- and two-step "how many more" and "how many less" problems using information presented in scaled bar graphs. *For example, draw a bar graph in which each square in the bar graph might represent 5 pets.*

| 1-7 Focus | 1-11 Focus | 1-14 Progress Check | 2-4 Practice | 2-13 Progress Check | 3-6 Practice | 3-7 Focus | 3-8 Focus | 3-14 Progress Check | 4-2 Practice | 4-4 Practice | 4-13 Progress Check |

⭐ By the end of Unit 3, expect children to **represent a data set with several categories on a given scaled bar graph and use the information presented in the graph to solve one-step "how many more" and "how many less" problems.**

Key ✓ = Assessment Check-In   ✓ = Progress Check Lesson   ▰ = Current Unit   ▰ = Previous or Upcoming Lessons

Mathematical Background: Content

 The discussion below highlights major content areas and the Common Core State Standards addressed in Unit 3. See the online Spiral Tracker for complete information about learning trajectories for all standards.

▶ Adding and Subtracting Multidigit Numbers (Lessons 3-3 through 3-6)

In this unit, children build on their understanding of place value to develop and compare methods for adding and subtracting 2- and 3-digit numbers. **3.NBT.2**

Addition Methods Lessons 3-3 and 3-4 focus on two different addition methods: *partial-sums addition* and *column addition*.

Partial-sums addition was introduced in *Second Grade Everyday Mathematics* as a strategy for adding 2- and 3-digit numbers. In third grade, children review and use this method to add 3-digit numbers. **3.NBT.2** As the name suggests, this method involves calculating partial sums, and then adding all partial sums to find the total.

Children write the addends in expanded form, then find partial sums by adding the components from corresponding digits together, and finally add all partial sums together to find the total. Partial sums can be calculated in any order, but working from left to right allows children to compare their answer with their estimate throughout the addition process. Also, children tend to focus on larger quantities first—just as most children combine the largest blocks first when performing addition with base-10 blocks.

Column addition is similar to partial-sums addition in that it relies on place-value understanding, but column addition also involves trading between ones and tens, and tens and hundreds. Column addition retains the explicit connection to the place value of the digits in the addends. Trading between place-value columns is reminiscent of children's experiences trading base-10 blocks.

Children begin by writing the digits of the addends in columns. They draw vertical lines to separate ones, tens, hundreds, and so on. Once columns have been created, the usual place-value convention that each place must have only one digit can be broken without confusion. If desired, children can label the columns "1s," "10s," and so on. Then children add the digits in each column. If the sum of any column is a 2-digit number, they trade 10 ones for a ten (or 10 tens for a hundred, and so on) and move the resulting ten (or hundred) to its appropriate column. After all of these trades have been made so that each column contains a single digit, the resulting digits can be written in their appropriate places to form the sum of the original addends.

 Standards and Goals for Mathematical Content

Because the standards within each domain can be broad, *Everyday Mathematics* has unpacked each standard into Goals for Mathematical Content **GMC**. For a complete list of Standards and Goals, see page EM1.

Solving $137 + 65 = ?$

Partial sums:

First write addends in expanded form.	$137 = 100 + 30 + 7$ $65 = 60 + 5$
Then find the partial sums.	$100 + 0 = 100$ $30 + 60 = 90$ $7 + 5 = 12$
Then add the partial sums to find the total.	$100 + 90 + 12 = 202$

Column addition:

		100s	10s	1s
Add the numbers in each column.		1	3	7
	+		6	5
Trade 10 ones for 1 ten and 10 tens for 1 hundred, until there is only one digit in each column.		1	9̶	1̶2̶
		1	1̶0̶	2
$137 + 65 = 202$		2	0	2

Unit 3 Vocabulary

adding a group
area
close-but-easier numbers
column addition
counting up
equivalent
estimate
expand-and-trade
    subtraction
expanded form
expression
factors
facts table

function machine
helper fact
input
key
Multiplication/Division Facts
    Table
multiplication squares
name-collection box
open number line
output
partial-sums addition
partition
picture graph

precisely
reasonable
rubric
rule
scaled bar graph
scaled picture graph
square product
square units
subtracting a group
tile
turn-around rule
"What's My Rule?"

Adding and Subtracting Multidigit Numbers *Continued*

Subtraction Methods In Lesson 3-5 children review counting-up subtraction on open number lines. **3.NBT.2** In this method, children represent the minuend and subtrahend as points on an open number line, and represent finding the difference as a series of "jumps" by multiples of 1, 10, and 100 beginning with the smaller number and ending at the larger. (*See margin.*) Children may also represent these differences with a series of number sentences.

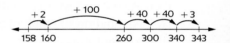

counting-up subtraction

$$2 + 100 + 40 + 40 + 3 = 185$$
$$343 - 158 = 185$$

In Lesson 3-6 children review expand-and-trade subtraction. **3.NBT.2** They begin by writing the subtrahend and the minuend in expanded form. For each place value, children compare the two numbers and determine whether subtracting the subtrahend from the minuend yields a difference that is nonnegative (greater than or equal to zero). If not, children trade from the next-larger place value and continue this process until they have adjusted the hundreds, tens, and ones so that the subtraction of each place-value pair will yield a nonnegative number. (*See margin.*)

$$
\begin{array}{r}
100 \\
300 \quad 110 \quad 15 \\
415 \longrightarrow 400 + 10 + 5 \\
-129 \longrightarrow 100 + 20 + 9 \\
\hline
200 + 80 + 6 = 286
\end{array}
$$

expand-and-trade subtraction

Performing expand-and-trade subtraction with 3-digit numbers adds several complexities. If children subtract a 2-digit number from a 3-digit number, they must carefully align the tens digits from both numbers. In this case, some children may benefit from writing the 2-digit number as if it were a 3-digit number with a zero in the hundreds place, for example, $74 = 0 + 70 + 4$. Likewise, if there is a zero in the tens place of either number, children must carefully align the hundreds digits and ones digits, leaving a space for the tens digit in that number, for example $302 = 300 + 0 + 2$. Finally note that the trades can be made either from left to right or right to left without affecting the outcome. Once the trading has been completed, subtraction can be performed in any order.

Exposure to a variety of computation methods, such as partial-sums and column addition, and counting-up and expand-and-trade subtraction, encourages flexibility and allows children to choose the method that works best for them. Comparing different strategies also helps to develop a more robust understanding of the operations.

▶ **Explorations** (Lesson 3-7)

In Lesson 3-7 children represent data in scaled bar graphs, measure area of surfaces in the classroom using 1-foot squares, and tile rectangles using unit squares and then partition rectangles into rows and columns. **3.MD.3, 3.MD.5, 3.MD.6, 3.MD.7**

▶ **Multiplication Fact Strategies**
(Lessons 3-9 through 3-12)

In *Third Grade Everyday Mathematics,* children develop mastery of basic multiplication facts by building a rich understanding of the meanings and representations for the operation of multiplication. **3.OA.1, 3.OA.5, 3.OA.7**

In Lesson 3-9 children build and explore arrays with equal factors and classify these as multiplication squares. Multiplication squares, like doubles in addition, tend to be easier to retain for many children. **3.OA.7**

In Lesson 3-10 children use array representations to explore the Commutative Property of Multiplication. Arrays are used to connect to multiplication facts by representing $r \times c$ as an array with r rows and c columns. By physically turning their arrays so that the rows and columns switch, children notice that the same array can be used to represent two different multiplication facts, $r \times c$ and $c \times r$. (*See margin.*) By investigating the multiplication facts table, children come to realize the power of the Commutative Property of Multiplication: for every fact that they already know, there is a fact related by the turn-around rule that they do not have to memorize.

$8 \times 5 = 5 \times 8$

Commutative Property of Multiplication

In Lessons 3-11 and 3-12, children are introduced to adding- and subtracting-a-group strategies for deriving new facts from familiar multiplication facts, such as multiplication squares and 2s, 5s, and 10s facts. Such facts are called "helper facts." Children use helper facts, together with the equal groups meaning of multiplication, to derive other multiplication facts. **3.OA.5** In the adding-a-group strategy, children derive an unknown multiplication fact by adding a group to a helper fact. The groups are often represented as arrays. The subtracting-a-group strategy is similar. Children begin with a helper fact and find the unknown multiplication fact by taking one group away from the helper fact. **3.OA.7** (*See margin.*)

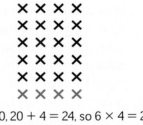

$5 \times 4 = 20, 20 + 4 = 24,$ so $6 \times 4 = 24$

adding a group

These strategies are a major focus of Unit 3. Learning these strategies can help children figure out and remember facts they do not automatically know.

▶ **Practicing Operations and Equivalence**
(Lesson 3-13)

Name-collection boxes are used throughout *Everyday Mathematics* to help children develop flexible ways of thinking about numbers and understanding numeric equivalence. The name-collection boxes in Lesson 3-13 set up a routine for practicing adding, subtracting, multiplying, and dividing. **3.OA.7, 3.NBT.2, 3.NBT.3, 3.OA.7** They also explicitly show children that numbers can be represented in a variety of ways and still be equivalent. Allowing children time to internalize equivalence with whole numbers will help them better understand it in the specific case of fractions in Unit 5.

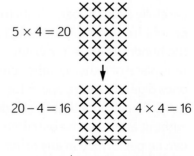

$5 \times 4 = 20$

$20 - 4 = 16$ $4 \times 4 = 16$

subtracting a group

Mathematical Background: Practices

 In Everyday Mathematics, *children learn the **content** of mathematics as they engage in the **practices** of mathematics. As such, the Standards for Mathematical Practice are embedded in children's everyday work, including hands-on activities, problem-solving tasks, discussions, and written work. Read here to see how Mathematical Practices 2 and 7 are emphasized in this unit.*

▶ Standard for Mathematical Practice 2

An important component of Mathematical Practice 2 is the interplay between the complementary processes of *decontextualizing* and *contextualizing*. When working with representations to solve mathematical problems, children learn that at times it is more effective to manipulate the symbols without referring back to their meaning: to decontextualize. At other times, it is important to return attention to the meaning of the symbols: to contextualize. Mathematically proficient children move fluently back and forth between these two ways of relating to representations.

In Lesson 3-4 children practice this back-and-forth between decontextualizing and contextualizing when working with column addition. When adding the digits in columns, children decontextualize—they add the digits without relating back to place value or the expanded form of the number. GMP2.1 Once the addition in each column is complete, children contextualize to find the total sum (especially when the sum in a column is a 2-digit number, requiring them to trade) and also to make sense of their results. GMP2.2

Another important aspect of SMP2 is the notion of connecting different representations for the same concept. GMP2.3 In Lesson 3-5 children represent counting-up subtraction as a series of "jumps" on open number lines and with a string of number sentences. They make connections between these two representations. In Lessons 3-9 through 3-12, children represent multiplication facts as arrays. When working to derive multiplication facts, children connect number models with the array representation.

Providing opportunities to make connections among different representations can enable children to make sense of an unfamiliar representation by explicitly relating it to familiar ones.

▶ Standard for Mathematical Practice 7

In the words of Mathematical Practice 7, "Mathematically proficient children look closely to discern a pattern or structure." In Lesson 3-1 children describe rules and patterns in "What's My Rule?" tables, while in Lesson 3-13 they solve and create their own Frames-and-Arrows problems. In Lesson 3-9 they build and explore arrays for products with equal factors and classify these as multiplication squares. GMP7.1 In Lesson 3-10 children explore their array representations of multiplication facts to discover the Commutative Property of Multiplication (the turn-around rule). Later in this lesson, children look for patterns in the multiplication facts table, and connect these patterns with square numbers and facts related by the turn-around rule. GMP7.1 In later lessons, children will use the Commutative Property when developing strategies for deriving unknown multiplication facts. GMP7.2

 Standards and Goals for Mathematical Practice

SMP2 **Reason abstractly and quantitatively.**

GMP2.1 Create mathematical representations using numbers, words, pictures, symbols, gestures, tables, graphs, and concrete objects.

GMP2.2 Make sense of the representations you and others use.

GMP2.3 Make connections between representations.

SMP7 **Look for and make use of structure.**

GMP7.1 Look for mathematical structures such as categories, patterns, and properties.

GMP7.2 Use structures to solve problems and answer questions.

Go Online to the *Implementation Guide* for more information about the Mathematical Practices.

For children's information on the Mathematical Practices, see *Student Reference Book*, pages 1–36.

"What's My Rule?"

Overview Children find missing numbers and rules in "What's My Rule?" tables.

▶ **Before You Begin**

For Part 2, fill out the What's My Rule? tables and rules on *Math Masters,* page TA24 to match those shown in the margin on page 223.

For the optional Extra Practice activity, fill in rules and numbers that meet children's needs in Problems 1 through 5 on *Math Masters,* page TA24.

▶ **Vocabulary**

"What's My Rule?" • function machine • input • rule • output

CCSS

Common Core State Standards

Focus Clusters
- Represent and solve problems involving multiplication and division.
- Multiply and divide within 100.
- Use place value understanding and properties of operations to perform multi-digit arithmetic.

---

1 Warm Up 5 min

	Materials	
Mental Math and Fluency Children write numbers in expanded form.	slate	3.NBT.2

---

2 Focus 45–55 min

Math Message Children apply a multiplication rule to complete a table.	slate	3.OA.7, 3.NBT.2 SMP7
Reviewing "What's My Rule?" Tables Children describe patterns in "What's My Rule?" tables.	*Math Masters,* p. TA23	3.OA.4, 3.OA.7, 3.NBT.2 SMP7, SMP8
Reviewing "What's My Rule?" Variations Children discuss types of "What's My Rule?" problems.	*Math Masters,* p. TA24	3.OA.4, 3.OA.7, 3.NBT.2 SMP7, SMP8
Completing "What's My Rule?" Problems Children solve "What's My Rule?" problems.	*Math Journal 1,* p. 65; *Student Reference Book,* pp. 74–75; *Math Masters,* p. TA24; box and counters (optional)	3.OA.4, 3.OA.7, 3.NBT.2 SMP7, SMP8
✓ **Assessment Check-In** See page 224.	*Math Journal 1,* p. 65	3.OA.4, 3.NBT.2, SMP7

CCSS 3.NBT.2 **Spiral Snapshot**

GMC Add within 1,000 fluently.

| 2-12
Warm Up
Practice | 3-1
Warm Up
Focus
Practice | 3-2 through 3-6
Warm Up
Focus
Practice | 3-7
Practice | 3-8
Focus
Practice | 3-13
Focus
Practice | 4-3
Practice |

III Spiral Tracker (**Go Online**) to see how mastery develops for all standards within the grade.

---

3 Practice 15–20 min

Minute Math+ Children practice mental math strategies.	*Minute Math®+*	
Playing *Roll to 1,000* **Game** Children practice mental addition with multiples of 10.	*Student Reference Book,* p. 253; *Math Masters,* p. G7; two 6-sided dice	3.OA.7, 3.NBT.2 SMP6, SMP7
Math Boxes 3-1 Children practice and maintain skills.	*Math Journal 1,* p. 66	See page 225.
Home Link 3-1 **Homework** Children solve "What's My Rule?" problems.	*Math Masters,* p. 79	3.OA.4, 3.OA.7, 3.NBT.2 SMP7

---

connectED.mcgraw-hill.com

Plan your lessons online with these tools.

| ePresentations | Student Learning Center | Facts Workshop Game | eToolkit | Professional Development | Home Connections | Spiral Tracker | Assessment and Reporting | English Learners Support | Differentiation Support |

Differentiation Options

RtI

CCSS 3.OA.4, 3.NBT.2, SMP8

Readiness
5–10 min

	WHOLE CLASS
	SMALL GROUP
	PARTNER
	INDEPENDENT

Identifying a Mystery Rule

number line (optional);
counters (optional)

To practice using patterns to determine rules, have children identify a mystery rule after it is applied to a series of numbers. Ask a child to say a number between 1 and 10. Mentally add an amount to the given number and "give back" the result. Repeat several times, always applying the same rule to the given number. Then have a volunteer identify the rule. **GMP8.1** For example: A child says 7. You mentally add 2 and give back 9. You repeat this several times. A child guesses the rule Add 2. To provide visuals, you may wish to point to the given number and the "give back" number on the number line or model with counters and record the number pairs. The activity can also be used with subtraction, multiplication, and division.

CCSS 3.OA.4, 3.OA.7, SMP7, SMP8

Enrichment
10–15 min

	WHOLE CLASS
	SMALL GROUP
	PARTNER
	INDEPENDENT

Creating "What's My Rule?" Problems

Activity Card 34;
Math Masters, p. TA24;
calculator (optional)

To extend applying rules, have children make up and solve "What's My Rule?" problems on *Math Masters*, page TA24. Have partners solve each other's problems and discuss strategies for completing the tables. **GMP7.1, GMP7.2, GMP8.1** For example, suggest that children verbalize the corresponding equations. You may want to provide calculators for children to use if they work with large or negative numbers and as they check their answers.

CCSS 3.OA.4, 3.OA.7, 3.NBT.2, SMP7, SMP8

Extra Practice
10–15 min

	WHOLE CLASS
	SMALL GROUP
	PARTNER
	INDEPENDENT

Practicing "What's My Rule?" Problems

Activity Card 35;
Math Masters, p. TA24

To practice solving "What's My Rule?" problems, fill in the rule, some *in* and *out* numbers, or both for Problems 1 through 5 on *Math Masters*, page TA24. Choose numbers according to children's needs. Leave the last problem blank so children can make up their own problem to share with a partner. Encourage children to think of corresponding equations to help them fill in missing numbers. **GMP7.1, GMP7.2, GMP8.1**

English Language Learners Support

Beginning ELL To scaffold the terms *input* and *output*, build on children's understanding of the words *in* and *out*. Use Total Physical Response prompts to have children either come in and go out of a room or put an object in and take it out of their desks to reinforce the opposite meanings. Have children point to where numbers go in (input) and come out (output) on the large function machine.

Go Online | **ELL** English Learners Support

Standards and Goals for
Mathematical Practice

SMP7 **Look for and make use of structure.**
   GMP7.1 Look for mathematical structures such as categories, patterns, and properties.
   GMP7.2 Use structures to solve problems and answer questions.

SMP8 **Look for and express regularity in repeated reasoning.**
   GMP8.1 Create and justify rules, shortcuts, and generalizations.

1 Warm Up 5 min

Go Online

ePresentations   eToolkit

▶ Mental Math and Fluency

Have children write numbers in expanded form on their slates.
Leveled exercises:

●○○ **58** 50 + 8 **136** 100 + 30 + 6

●●○ **807** 800 + 7 or 800 + 0 + 7 **760** 700 + 60 or 700 + 60 + 0

●●● **1,001** 1,000 + 1 or 1,000 + 0 + 0 + 1 **2,030** 2,000 + 30 or 2,000 + 0 + 30 + 0

2 Focus 45–55 min

Go Online

ePresentations eToolkit

▶ Math Message

Some bacteria double in number every 20 minutes.
Use this information to complete this table on your slate. GMP7.2

Now	20 min later
8	16
50	100
200	400
75	150
150	300

Unit
bacteria

▶ Reviewing "What's My Rule?" Tables

Math Masters, p. TA23

WHOLE CLASS   **SMALL GROUP**   **PARTNER**   INDEPENDENT

Math Message Follow-Up Display a function machine and **"What's My Rule?"** table (*Math Masters,* page TA23). Remind children that they use a "What's My Rule?" table to keep track of how a **function machine** changes numbers:

- A number (the **input**) is dropped into the machine.
- The machine changes the number according to a **rule.**
- A new number (the **output**) comes out the other end.

Ask: *What is the rule for the Math Message problem?* GMP8.1 Multiply by 2, or double. *How did you use this rule to determine the* out *numbers?* GMP7.2 Sample answer: I multiplied the *in* numbers by 2.

in	out
8	16
50	100
200	400
75	150
150	300

in ↓
Rule
Multiply by 2
↓ **out**

Write the rule in the function machine and fill in the table with the first pair of numbers from the Math Message. Explain that numbers in the *in* column represent the number of bacteria now. Corresponding numbers in the *out* column represent the number of bacteria 20 minutes from now.

Review the answers to the Math Message problem by asking: *If 50 is dropped into the function machine, what number will come out?* **GMP7.2** 100 Encourage children to think, "50 doubled is what number?" or "50 × 2 is what number?" Invite children to enter the appropriate numbers in the *in* and *out* columns in the display.

Academic Language Development Help children understand the term *function* as *what something does* or *how it works*. For example, show a pencil sharpener and ask: *What is the function of this machine? What does it do?* It sharpens pencils by taking off part of the wood. Extend to "What's My Rule?" tables by asking: *What is the function of this machine?* It takes numbers and doubles them to make new numbers.

▶ ## Reviewing "What's My Rule?" Variations

Math Masters, p. TA24

WHOLE CLASS	SMALL GROUP	PARTNER	INDEPENDENT

Display each type of "What's My Rule?" problem on *Math Masters,* page TA24. (*See margin.*) As a class, discuss and solve each problem. Note that the "types" are to organize discussion only. Children do not need to learn or use these labels.

- **Type 1: Missing output numbers** Support children in applying a rule to each *in* number. **GMP7.2** Think aloud and then have children verbalize the process: *13 goes in. I subtract 9, and 4 comes out.*
- **Type 2: Missing input numbers** Help children determine and apply the inverse rule. **GMP7.2** *If 12 comes out, I think ___ + 5 = 12 or 12 − 5 = ___.*
- **Type 3: Missing rule** Encourage children to look for patterns in the relationships between given pairs. Ask: *Do the outputs increase or decrease? By how much? Could the new rule involve addition, subtraction, multiplication, or division? How do you know?* **GMP7.1, GMP8.1** Sample answer: I think the new rule involves multiplication because to get from 2 to 10 and from 3 to 15, I multiply by 5. Encourage children to think: *2 times what number is 10?*
- **Type 4: Missing rule and missing *in* and *out* numbers** Guide children to find patterns in pairs of numbers to determine the rule and apply it to missing numbers. **GMP7.1, GMP7.2, GMP8.1**

Encourage children to check their work by reading the number sentence formed by the *in* number, the rule, and the *out* number. For each problem type, have children suggest an additional *in* and *out* number pair that fits the rule. **GMP8.1**

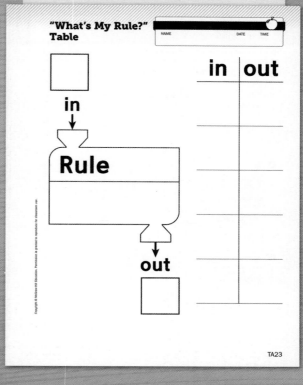

Math Masters, p. TA23

"What's My Rule?" Table

in | out

TA23

Type 1

Rule	
Subtract 9	

in	out
13	4
10	1
17	8
18	9

Type 2

Rule	
Add 5	

in	out
7	12
10	15
21	26
45	50

Type 3

Rule	
Multiply by 5	

in	out
2	10
3	15
4	20
5	25

Type 4

Rule	
Subtract 20	

in	out
45	25
30	10
100	80
52	32

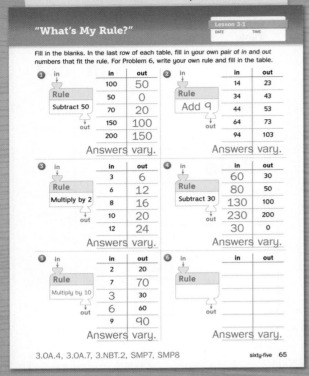

"What's My Rule?" Lesson 3-1
DATE   TIME

Fill in the blanks. In the last row of each table, fill in your own pair of *in* and *out* numbers that fit the rule. For Problem 6, write your own rule and fill in the table.

① in
Rule: Subtract 50
out

in	out
100	50
50	0
70	20
150	100
200	150

Answers vary.

② in
Rule: Add 9
out

in	out
14	23
34	43
44	53
64	73
94	103

Answers vary.

③ in
Rule: Multiply by 2
out

in	out
3	6
6	12
8	16
10	20
12	24

Answers vary.

④ in
Rule: Subtract 30
out

in	out
60	30
80	50
130	100
230	200
30	0

Answers vary.

⑤ in
Rule: Multiply by 10
out

in	out
2	20
7	70
3	30
6	60
9	90

Answers vary.

⑥ in
Rule:
out

in	out

Answers vary.

3.OA.4, 3.OA.7, 3.NBT.2, SMP7, SMP8   sixty-five 65

Differentiate **Common Misconception**

Watch for children who assume that missing rules always involve addition or subtraction. For example, after seeing a 4 in the *in* column and an 8 in the *out* column, some children may immediately assume the rule is + 4 when it may actually be × 2. Remind children to check that the rule works with all the given number pairs.

Go Online Differentiation Support

▶ Completing "What's My Rule?" Problems

Math Journal 1, p. 65; *Student Reference Book*, pp. 74–75; *Math Masters*, p. TA24

| WHOLE CLASS | SMALL GROUP | **PARTNER** | **INDEPENDENT** |

Have children complete "What's My Rule?" problems by finding inputs, outputs, rules, or a combination on journal page 65. **GMP7.1, GMP7.2, GMP8.1** Remind children to write their own pair of *in* and *out* numbers that fit the rule. For Problem 6, have children write interesting rules, and challenge them to stretch their thinking when selecting input values.

As children are ready, invite them to create situations that match their completed "What's My Rule?" problems. For example, Problem 1 fits this situation: *I read 50 pages every evening. The input is the number of pages I start with and the output is the number I have left after I've read 50 pages.* Use *Math Masters,* page TA24 to provide additional practice with "What's My Rule?" tables.

 Assessment Check-In CCSS 3.OA.4, 3.NBT.2

Math Journal 1, p. 65

Expect most children to successfully find the missing inputs, outputs, or rules in Problems 1 through 4 on journal page 65. **GMP7.1, GMP7.2** Some children may be able to find both the missing rule and missing numbers in Problem 5. Encourage children who struggle to find the missing inputs, outputs, and rules to think of the corresponding equation. For example, in Problem 3, think, "3 × 2 is what number?" You may also consider implementing the Readiness activity or the suggestion in the Adjusting the Activity note.

Assessment and Reporting **Go Online** to record student progress and to see trajectories toward mastery for these standards.

When most children have finished, have them share strategies for finding and applying rules on journal page 65. **GMP7.2**

Summarize Have partnerships read and discuss *Student Reference Book*, pages 74–75.

Adjusting the Activity

Differentiate If children have difficulty completing the "What's My Rule?" tables, provide a concrete model. Draw a picture of an *Everyday Mathematics* function machine on the side of a box without a lid. Place at least 15 counters inside the box. To begin, put 3 counters into the machine and then take 6 counters out. Record 3 and 6 as *in* and *out* numbers on a table. Repeat with additional counters (4 and 8; 5 and 10). Ask: *What is the rule? How is the machine changing the number of counters each time?* It is multiplying by 2, or doubling, each time. Repeat with other rules, and have children take turns as the rule maker.

Go Online Differentiation Support

③ Practice 15–20 min

Go Online

ePresentations   eToolkit   Home Connections

▶ Minute Math+

To practice mental math strategies, select a *Minute Math+* activity.

▶ Playing *Roll to 1,000*

Student Reference Book, p. 253; *Math Masters*, p. G7

| WHOLE CLASS | **SMALL GROUP** | **PARTNER** | INDEPENDENT |

Have children play *Roll to 1,000* to develop fluency with mental addition of fact extensions. For more details, see Lesson 2-5. You may wish to briefly review the scoring rules, reminding children that if they roll a 1 (10), their score for the round is 0, but they keep their score from prior rounds.

Observe

- Do children interpret the dice rolls as multiples of 10?
- Do children add the fact extensions accurately? GMP6.4

Discuss

- *What helps you add two multiples of 10?* GMP7.2
- *How do you keep track of your score when you roll more than once?*

Differentiate   **Game Modifications**   Go Online   Differentiation Support

▶ Math Boxes 3-1

Math Journal 1, p. 66

| WHOLE CLASS | **SMALL GROUP** | **PARTNER** | **INDEPENDENT** |

Mixed Practice Math Boxes 3-1 are paired with Math Boxes 3-3.

▶ Home Link 3-1

Math Masters, p. 79

Homework Children solve "What's My Rule?" problems involving several operations and explain to someone at home how the function machine works. GMP7.1, GMP7.2

Math Journal 1, p. 66

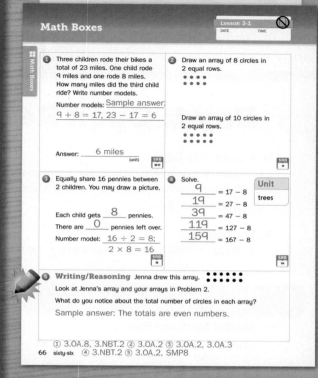

Math Masters, p. 79

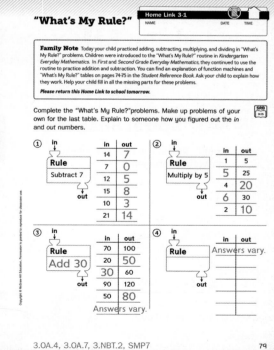

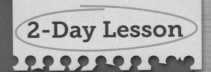

Lesson 3-2

Open Response and Reengagement

Estimating Costs

2-Day Lesson

Overview **Day 1:** Children make estimates for problems they solve using mental math. **Day 2:** Children examine others' explanations using a rubric as a guide, and then revise their work.

Day 1: Open Response

▶ **Before You Begin**
Solve the open response problem and consider which estimation strategies children may use. If possible, schedule time to review children's work and plan for Day 2 of this lesson with your grade-level team.

▶ **Vocabulary**
estimate • close-but-easier numbers • reasonable • precisely • rubric

 Common Core State Standards

Focus Clusters
• Solve problems involving the four operations, and identify and explain patterns in arithmetic.
• Use place value understanding and properties of operations to perform multi-digit arithmetic.

	Materials	
1 Warm Up 5 min		**3.NBT.1**
Mental Math and Fluency Children find the closest multiple of 10.		
2a Focus 55–70 min		
Math Message Children make sense of an estimation strategy used to check whether an answer to an addition problem is reasonable.	*Math Journal 1*, p. 67	**3.OA.8, 3.NBT.1, 3.NBT.2 SMP1, SMP6**
Estimating Costs Children discuss estimation strategies that can be used to check the reasonableness of a sum.	*Math Journal 1*, p. 67	**3.OA.8, 3.NBT.1, 3.NBT.2 SMP1, SMP6**
Solving the Open Response Problem Children make estimates for a two-step number story and explain their thinking.	*Math Masters*, pp. 80–81	**3.OA.8, 3.NBT.1, 3.NBT.2 SMP1, SMP6**

Getting Ready for Day 2 →

Review children's work and plan discussion for reengagement. *Math Masters*, pp. TA6 and 82; children's work from Day 1

3.OA.8 **Spiral Snapshot**

GMC Assess the reasonableness of answers to problems.

| 2-2 through 2-5 Focus Practice | 3-2 Focus Practice | 3-3 through 3-6 Focus Practice | 3-7 through 3-10 Practice | 5-10 Focus |

 Spiral Tracker | **Go Online** | to see how mastery develops for all standards within the grade.

connectED.mcgraw-hill.com

Plan your lessons online with these tools.

ePresentations | Student Learning Center | Facts Workshop Game | eToolkit | Professional Development | Home Connections | Spiral Tracker | Assessment and Reporting | English Learners Support | Differentiation Support

226 Unit 3 | Operations

1 Warm Up 5 min Go Online ePresentations eToolkit

▶ Mental Math and Fluency

Have children answer the following questions. *Leveled exercises:*

● ○ ○ Is 18 closer to 10 or 20? 20
    Is 21 closer to 20 or 30? 20

● ● ○ Is 188 closer to 180 or 190? 190
    Is 105 closer to 100 or 110? Same distance away

● ● ● Is 2,777 closer to 2,770 or 2,780? 2,780
    Is 2,850 closer to 2,800 or 2,900? Same distance away

2a Focus 55–70 min Go Online ePresentations eToolkit

▶ Math Message

Math Journal 1, p. 67

Complete journal page 67. Explain Rosa's thinking to your partner.
GMP1.4, GMP6.1, GMP6.2

▶ Estimating Costs

Math Journal 1, p. 67

| WHOLE CLASS | SMALL GROUP | PARTNER | INDEPENDENT |

Math Message Follow-Up Ask children to explain the idea of an **estimate** to their partners. Ask: *When might you use an estimate?*
GMP1.4, GMP6.2 Sample answers: When I need to solve problems in my head; when I do not need an exact answer; to check whether an answer to an addition or subtraction problem makes sense

Have children explain Rosa's estimation strategy. Highlight the **close-but-easier numbers** she used, explaining that they are close enough to the numbers in the addition problem to come up with a reasonable estimate, but they are easier to add in our heads. Children may notice that Rosa rounded the numbers to the nearest ten.

CCSS Standards and Goals for
Mathematical Practice

SMP1 Make sense of problems and persevere in solving them.
  GMP1.4 Check whether your answer makes sense.

SMP6 Attend to precision.
  GMP6.1 Explain your mathematical thinking clearly and precisely.
  GMP6.2 Use an appropriate level of precision for your problem.

Professional Development

The focus mathematical practice for this lesson is GMP6.1. Children are asked to show the thinking they do in their heads to solve a two-step number story. To explain their thinking clearly and precisely, children need to show both the close-but-easier numbers and the mental computations they used.

Go Online to the *Implementation Guide* for more information about SMP6.

Math Journal 1, p. 67

Strategies for Estimation Lesson 3-2 DATE TIME

Rosa makes an estimate for the addition problem below. She uses numbers that are **close** to the numbers in the problem but are **easier** to use.

$$322 + 487 = ?$$

Unit
$

$$320 + 490 = 810$$

① Explain Rosa's thinking to a partner.

② Make a different estimate. What **close-but-easier** numbers could you use? Write a number sentence in the thought bubble to show your thinking.

Sample answer:

$$300 + 500 = 800$$

3.OA.8, 3.NBT.1, 3.NBT.2, SMP1, SMP6 sixty-seven 67

Math Masters, p. 80

Estimating Costs

Lesson 3-2

NAME   DATE   TIME

Ann and her friend are walking home from school. Ann shows her friend this homework problem and her answer.

Name _____ *Ann* _____

The art club has **$100** to spend on materials. They bought watercolor paints for $38 and brushes for $19.

$38 $19

How much money does the club have left over?

$67

① Suppose that you are Ann's friend and you do not have a pencil or a calculator with you.

In your head, make an estimate for how much money the club has left over. Write your answers on the next page.

80   3.OA.8, 3.NBT.1, 3.NBT.2, SMP1, SMP6

Ask: *What are some other close-but-easier numbers you could use?* Sample answer: 300 + 500 *How is this estimate different from Rosa's?* GMP6.2 Sample answers: The numbers are rounded to the nearest hundred instead of the nearest ten. Rosa's estimate was 810, and my estimate was 800.

Briefly discuss how both estimates are **reasonable.** Explain that the close-but-easier numbers you choose depend on how you add in your head or how close you want the estimate to be. Sometimes the strategy you choose depends on the situation in the problem. GMP6.1, GMP6.2 Ask: *Which of the estimates we discussed was easier to do in your head? Why?* Sample answer: Rounding to the nearest hundred was easier because I didn't have to do any trades. *Which of the estimates are close enough to decide whether the answer was reasonable? Why?* Sample answer: Both are close enough because they are only 10 apart.

Tell children that today they will make an estimate in their heads to check whether an answer is reasonable, and they will then show or explain their thinking clearly enough so others can solve the problem using the same strategy. GMP1.4, GMP6.1, GMP6.2

▶ Solving the Open Response Problem

Math Masters, pp. 80–81

| WHOLE CLASS | SMALL GROUP | **PARTNER** | INDEPENDENT |

Distribute *Math Masters,* page 80 and read the problem with the class. Have partners discuss what they understand from the problem. Invite volunteers to explain the task, asking questions such as: *What did Ann need to figure out? What do you need to figure out?* Make sure children understand the steps in Ann's math problem and that they must decide whether Ann's answer makes sense.

Tell children to put their pencils away, and ask them to pretend they are walking home from school with Ann without a pencil or calculator. Ask:

- *How could you help Ann?* Sample answer: I can make an estimate in my head to figure out about how much money the art club has left over.

- *Do you need an exact answer to decide whether the answer makes sense?* GMP6.2 No.

- *How could you use your estimate to decide whether Ann's answer is reasonable?* GMP1.4 Sample answer: I can compare my estimate with Ann's answer to see if they are close.

Remind children to complete this part of the problem in their heads. Once they have a solution, distribute *Math Masters,* page 81 and tell them to record their estimate for the leftover money and write *yes* or *no* for whether Ann's answer is reasonable. In the thought bubble, children should show their mental math strategies and write a clear explanation of their thinking. GMP1.4, GMP6.1, GMP6.2

Allow children time to complete the page. Partners can talk together about the task, but each child should write an explanation.

Circulate and assist. If children try to find an exact answer using paper and pencil, ask: *How can you use close-but-easier numbers in your head to help you decide whether Ann's answer is reasonable?* GMP1.4, GMP6.2 Sample answer: I can subtract them from 100 to estimate the amount of leftover money. Ann's answer is reasonable if it's close to my estimate. If children find an exact answer mentally, have them explain their thinking. Encourage them to check their answer with an estimate and show their estimation strategy in the thought bubble.

Summarize Ask: *When is it helpful to estimate instead of finding an exact answer?* GMP6.2 Sample answers: When I don't have a pencil or calculator and I just want to see whether an answer is reasonable; when I need to solve a problem in my head

Collect children's work so that you can evaluate it and prepare for Day 2.

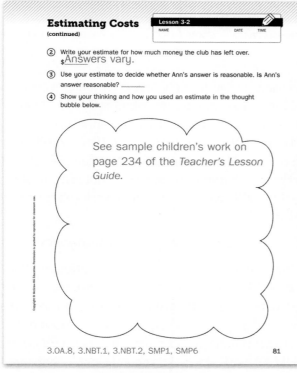

Math Masters, p. 81

Adjusting the Activity

Differentiate   If children have trouble understanding the problem, consider using the following questions as needed: *About how much money did the art club spend? What else do you know about the situation? What do you need to find out?*

Rubric for Estimating Costs

Lesson 3-2

NAME   DATE   TIME

Goal: Explain your mathematical thinking clearly and precisely.

Meets Expectations	Child 1	Child 2	Child 3	
Shows the close-but-easier numbers used to make estimates.				
Shows how to make an estimate of how much money the art club has left over.				
Exceeds Expectations				
Explains that Ann's answer of $67 is NOT reasonable because it is not close to an estimated leftover amount of $40.				

82

Getting Ready for Day 2

Math Masters, pp. TA6 and 82

Planning a Follow-Up Discussion

Review children's work. Use the Reengagement Planning Form (*Math Masters*, page TA6) and the rubric on page 232 to plan ways to help children meet expectations for both the content and practice standards. Look for estimation strategies using different close-but-easier numbers and common misconceptions, such as only completing some of the calculations needed to answer the question, or not keeping track of what the calculations mean in the context of the number story.

Reengagement Planning Form

Common Core State Standard (CCSS): *3.OA.8 Solve two-step word problems using the four operations. . . . Assess the reasonableness of answers using mental computation and estimation strategies including rounding.*

Goal for Mathematical Practice (GMP): *GMP6.1 Explain your mathematical thinking clearly and precisely.*

This lesson introduces using a child-friendly rubric. Organize a peer discussion using a child-friendly rubric as described in Option 1 below. Or, facilitate a class discussion using a child-friendly rubric as described in Options 2 through 4 or in another way you choose. If many children did not successfully solve the problem, discuss one or two samples of children's work to first establish that Ann's answer is not reasonable. If children's work is unclear or if you prefer to show work anonymously, rewrite the work for display.

Go Online for sample children's work that you can use in your discussion.

1. Have partners review and discuss other children's work using the child-friendly rubric on *Math Masters,* page 82. Choose sample work from three children who all agree that Ann's answer is not reasonable but who show a range of strategies or explanations. Choose one sample that meets expectations because the child met both criteria in the rubric, as in Child A's work. Choose a second sample that partially meets expectations because the child met one of the criteria, but not both, as in Child B's work. The third sample can meet or partially meet expectations, but it should show the thinking in a different way, as in Child C's work. Label the three samples as Child 1, Child 2, and Child 3, or print them on different colored paper. Make enough copies so children can review all three samples in partnerships. Plan to model how to use the rubric with Child 1's work, and for partners to work together to review the work of Child 2 and Child 3. See the Reengaging in the Problem section in Day 2 for more information. GMP1.4, GMP 6.1

Sample child's work, Child A

2. Write your estimate for how much money the club has left over. $ __40__

3. Use your estimate to decide if Ann's answer is reasonable. Is Ann's answer reasonable? __not reasonabl__

4. Show your thinking and how you used an estimate in the thought bubble below.

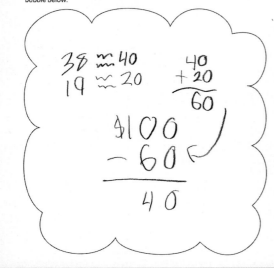

For a whole class discussion, distribute or display the child-friendly rubric on *Math Masters*, page 82. Use discussion questions similar to those below.

2. Display work that shows close-but-easier numbers and both of the calculations used to estimate how much money the club has left, such as in Child A's work. Ask:
   - *What are the close-but-easier numbers Child A used, and how were they found?* Sample answer: Child A used 40 because it is close to 38 and 20 because it is close to 19. Point out that Child A met the first criterion on the child-friendly rubric by showing all the close-but-easier numbers.
   - *What other thinking do you see in the bubble?* Sample answer: I see 40 plus 20 is 60, and I see 100 minus 60 is 40.
   - *Is $40 the answer? Explain your thinking.* GMP6.2 Sample answer: No. $40 is an estimate of how much money is left. Note that because Child A showed how the estimate was made, the work meets expectations for the second criterion on the child-friendly rubric.
   - *How can Child A's estimate help decide whether Ann's answer is reasonable?* Sample answer: $40 is not very close to $67, so Child A said that Ann's answer is not reasonable.

3. Display work that shows close-but-easier numbers but does not show the calculations used to estimate how much money the club has left, such as in Child B's work. Ask:
   - *Do you agree with the answer to Problem 3 and the reasoning? Explain your thinking.* Sample answer: I agree with the answer, but the reasoning is wrong. Adding to get $60 gives you an estimate of how much they spent, but we need to know how much is left.
   - *What is missing in this work?* GMP6.1 Sample answer: The work does not show subtracting $60 from $100 to get $40 to estimate how much money is left. Discuss that since Child B showed the close-but-easier numbers but did not show how to estimate how much money is left over, the work meets expectations for the first criterion but not the second on the child-friendly rubric.

4. Display work that does not show close-but-easier numbers, such as in Child C's work. Ask:
   - *What is missing in this work?* Sample answer: The work does not show how the child used close-but-easier numbers to get $60.
   - *What do you think about this child's reasoning?* GMP6.1 Sample answer: I think this child made a good estimate of how much money the club has left, which is $40. But I don't agree with the child that Ann's answer was reasonable because $67 is not close to $40. Discuss that since Child C did not show all the close-but-easier numbers but did show how to make the estimate, the work does not meet expectations for the first criterion but does for the second.

Planning for Revisions

Have copies of *Math Masters,* pages 80–81 or extra paper available for children to use in revisions. You might want to ask children to use colored pencils so you can see what they revise.

Sample child's work, Child B

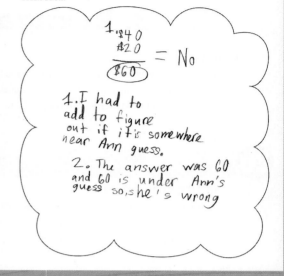

Sample child's work, Child C

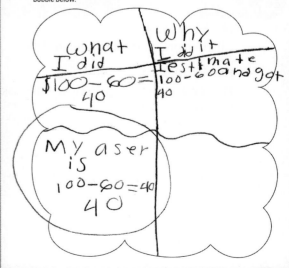

Estimating Costs

Overview **Day 2:** Children examine others' explanations using a rubric as a guide and then revise their work.

Day 2: Reengagement

▶ **Before You Begin**
Have extra copies of *Math Masters,* pages 80–81 available for children to revise their work. See Option 1 in Planning a Follow-Up Discussion on page 230 for information on preparing for a peer review using a child-friendly rubric.

Common Core State Standards

Focus Clusters
- Solve problems involving the four operations, and identify and explain patterns in arithmetic.
- Use place value understanding and properties of operations to perform multi-digit arithmetic.

2b Focus 50–55 min

	Materials	
Setting Expectations Children review the open response problem and discuss what a good explanation would include. They review how to respectfully talk about others' work.	Standards for Mathematical Practice Poster; Guidelines for Discussions Poster; *Student Reference Book,* pp. 20–21 (optional)	SMP6
Reengaging in the Problem Children examine others' representations and explanations of the mental math used to solve the open response problem.	*Math Masters,* p. 82; selected samples of children's work	3.OA.8, 3.NBT.1, 3.NBT.2 SMP1, SMP6
Revising Work Children revise their work from Day 1.	*Math Masters,* pp. 80–81 (optional), p. 82; colored pencils (optional); children's work from Day 1	3.OA.8, 3.NBT.1, 3.NBT.2 SMP1, SMP6
✓ **Assessment Check-In** See page 234 and rubric below.		3.OA.8 SMP6

Goal for Mathematical Practice **GMP6.1** Explain your mathematical thinking clearly and precisely.	**Not Meeting Expectations**	**Partially Meeting Expectations**	**Meeting Expectations**	**Exceeding Expectations**
	Shows neither the close-but-easier numbers nor the calculations for an estimate of how much money the club has left.	Shows the close-but-easier numbers **or** shows both of the calculations used to estimate how much money the club has left.	Shows the close-but-easier numbers **and** both of the calculations used to estimate how much money the club has left.	Meets expectations and clearly explains the thinking used to decide whether the answer is reasonable.

3 Practice 10–15 min

Math Boxes 3-2 Children practice and maintain skills.	*Math Journal 1,* p. 68	See page 235.
Home Link 3-2 **Homework** Children use close-but-easier numbers to make estimates.	*Math Masters,* p. 83	3.OA.8, 3.NBT.1, 3.NBT.2

2b Focus

50–55 min | Go Online | ePresentations | eToolkit

NOTE These Day 2 activities will ideally take place within a few days of Day 1. Prior to beginning Day 2, see Planning a Follow-Up Discussion from Day 1.

▶ Setting Expectations

| WHOLE CLASS | SMALL GROUP | PARTNER | INDEPENDENT |

Briefly review the open response problem from Day 1. Remind children that their task was to decide whether Ann's answer was reasonable using an estimate, and to explain how they decided. Ask: *What do you think a good explanation would include?* Sample answer: A good explanation would show the close-but-easier numbers and calculations used to make an estimate and tell why Ann's estimate is reasonable or not. Remind children that a goal in solving this problem is to explain their thinking clearly and **precisely.** Refer to the Standards for Mathematical Practice Poster for **GMP6.1.** Discuss the word *precisely.* Explain that a precise explanation is one that gives details and is accurate and complete.
GMP6.1 You may want to have children read *Student Reference Book,* pages 20–21 to see what it means to write clear and precise explanations.

Remind children that if they find that someone else's work is unclear or incomplete, they should still be respectful when they explain why they think so. Refer to your list of discussion guidelines from Units 1 and 2, and encourage children to use sentence frames such as:

- I think this is a clear and complete explanation because _____.
- I think this explanation needs to include _____.

▶ Reengaging in the Problem

Math Masters, p. 82

| WHOLE CLASS | SMALL GROUP | PARTNER | INDEPENDENT |

Children reengage in the problem by analyzing and critiquing other children's work in pairs and in a whole-group discussion. Have children discuss with partners before sharing with the whole group. Guide this discussion based on the decisions you made in Getting Ready for Day 2. Include a discussion in which the class comes to a consensus that Ann's answer to her homework problem is not reasonable.
GMP1.4, GMP6.1, GMP6.2

If you planned to facilitate a peer review using a child-friendly rubric, use *Math Masters,* page 82 to structure children's analysis of sample work. Distribute copies of the sample work you chose for Child 1, Child 2, and Child 3 and the rubric to each partnership. Tell children that a **rubric** is a guide for evaluating others' work. Briefly discuss **GMP6.1,** which is written at the top of the child-friendly rubric. Model reviewing Child 1's work with the class. Point out that to meet expectations, the work must clearly show that the child did both of the things listed in the rubric. Ask children to explain how the work meets or does not meet each of the criteria and write "Yes" or "No" in the appropriate boxes. Ask: *What would work look like that exceeds, or goes beyond, expectations?* Sample answer: The work would explain that Ann's answer is not reasonable because $67 is not close to $40.

Student Reference Book, p. 20

Standards for Mathematical Practice

Be Precise and Accurate

Mr. Lopez's class is recording the number of pages they read each week. Each child's goal is to read at least 500 pages in four weeks.

Martin and Bella are keeping track of the number of pages they read.

Martin		Bella	
Week	Number of Pages	Week	Number of Pages
1	147	1	157
2	203	2	149
3	198	3	191
4		4	

After three weeks, Mr. Lopez asks Martin and Bella, "Have you each met the goal of 500 pages yet? If not, how many more pages do you need to read?"

How would you figure out if Martin and Bella have each read 500 pages after three weeks?

I know I read at least 500. I add 1 + 2 + 1 and that's 4. Then I look at the other places.

Martin

Mr. Lopez asks Martin to explain his thinking more clearly using place-value language and units.

Martin thinks about what he wants to say and explains his thinking this way: "First, I add the hundreds digits of my numbers: 1 + 2 + 1 = 4, so that means I read at least 400 pages. Just by looking at the numbers in the tens and the ones places, I know they add up to more than 100 pages. So I've already read more than 500 pages."

SRB
20 twenty

Have partners work together to review and come to a decision on where Child 2's and Child 3's work fall on the rubric. Conclude by discussing their choices for each child's work. Ask children to support their choices by showing how each child met or did not meet each of the criteria.
GMP1.6, GMP6.4

► # Revising Work

Math Masters, p. 82

| WHOLE CLASS | SMALL GROUP | **PARTNER** | **INDEPENDENT** |

Pass back children's work from Day 1. Before children revise anything, ask them to examine their responses and decide how to improve them. They can use the child-friendly rubric to decide whether their work meets expectations for Problem 4. Have children add their names to the last column of the rubric and write "Yes" or "No" in the boxes for their own work. **GMP1.4, GMP6.1**

Tell children they now have a chance to revise their work so it meets the two criteria in the rubric or exceeds expectations. Help children see that the explanations presented during the discussion are not the only correct ones. Tell children to add to their earlier work using colored pencils or to use another sheet of paper, instead of erasing their original work.
GMP1.4, GMP6.1

Summarize Ask children to reflect on their work and revisions. Ask: *What did you learn from other children's explanations?* **GMP1.4** *How did you make your explanations more clear and precise?* **GMP6.1** Answers vary.

✓ ## Assessment Check-In CCSS 3.OA.8

Collect and review children's revised work. For the content standard, expect most children to correctly use close-but-easier numbers and mental math in both steps of the problem to conclude that Ann's answer is not reasonable. You can use the rubric on page 232 to evaluate children's revised work for **GMP6.1**.

☑ Assessment and Reporting **Go Online** to record student progress and to see trajectories toward mastery for this standard.

Go Online for optional generic rubrics in the *Assessment Handbook* that can be used to assess any additional GMPs addressed in the lesson.

Sample Children's Work—Evaluated

See the sample in the margin. This work meets expectations for the content standard because the child used close-but-easier numbers to find that Ann's answer was not reasonable. The work meets expectations for the mathematical practice because the child clearly showed the close-but-easier numbers and the calculations used in both steps of the problem $(40 + 20 = 60$ and $100 - 60 = 40)$ to find an estimate. **GMP6.1**

Go Online for other samples of evaluated children's work.

Sample child's work, "Meeting Expectations"

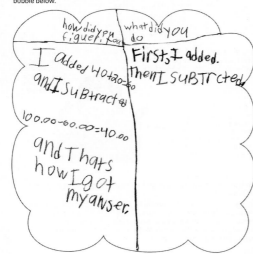

2. Write your estimate for how much money the club has left over.

3. Use your estimate to decide if Ann's answer is reasonable. Is Ann's answer reasonable? no

4. Show your thinking and how you used an estimate in the thought bubble below.

3 **Practice** 10–15min | **Go Online** | ePresentations eToolkit Home Connections

▶ **Math Boxes 3-2**

Math Journal 1, p. 68

| WHOLE CLASS | SMALL GROUP | PARTNER | INDEPENDENT |

Mixed Practice Math Boxes 3-2 are paired with Math Boxes 3-4.

▶ **Home Link 3-2**

Math Masters, p. 83

Homework Children use close-but-easier numbers to make estimates.

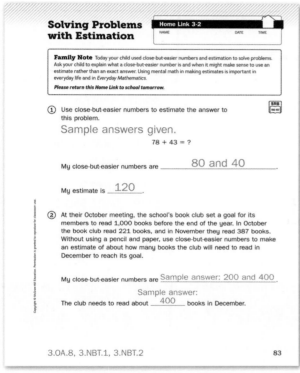

Math Masters, p. 83

Math Journal 1, p. 68

Math Boxes

Lesson 3-2
DATE   TIME

① Jocelyn shares a fruit strip equally among herself and 3 friends. How much does each child get? Use the rectangle below to show the equal shares.

Each child gets ___1-fourth___ of a fruit strip.

② You have exactly enough money to buy two grape juice boxes for 45 cents each.

How much money do you have? You may draw a diagram or a picture.

Sample answer:
(number model with ?)
? = 45 + 45

Answer: ___90 cents___ (unit)

③ There are 12 chairs in an array. Which are possible ways to set up the chairs? Fill in the circles next to the best answers.

- (A) 6 rows of 2 chairs
- (B) 3 rows of 4 chairs
- (C) 12 rows of 1 chair
- (D) 7 rows of 5 chairs

④ **November Weather**

How many days were not rainy?
___26 days___ (unit)

⑤ Fill in the empty frames.

Rule
+ 25

| 50 | 75 | 100 | 125 | 150 | 175 |

① 3.NF.1, 3.G.2 ② 3.NBT.2 ③ 3.OA.1, 3.OA.2
68 sixty-eight ④ 3.MD.3 ⑤ 3.NBT.2

Partial-Sums Addition

Overview Children use partial-sums addition to add 2- and 3-digit numbers.

▶ **Vocabulary**
partial-sums addition • expanded form

 CCSS **Common Core State Standards**

Focus Clusters
- Solve problems involving the four operations, and identify and explain patterns in arithmetic.
- Use place value understanding and properties of operations to perform multi-digit operations.

1 Warm Up 5 min

	Materials	
Mental Math and Fluency Children write numbers in expanded form.	slate	3.NBT. 2

2 Focus 40–50 min

Math Message Children add and use estimates to check their sums.	slate	3.NBT.1, 3.NBT.2
Discussing Estimates Children share estimation and addition strategies.	slate	3.OA.8, 3.NBT.1, 3.NBT.2 SMP1, SMP6
Adding with Partial Sums Children review and practice partial-sums addition to add 3-digit numbers.	*Math Journal 1*, p. 69; base-10 blocks (optional)	3.OA.8, 3.NBT.2 SMP1, SMP2, SMP6
✓ **Assessment Check-In** See page 240.	*Math Journal 1*, p. 69; base-10 blocks (optional)	3.NBT.2

CCSS 3.NBT.2 **Spiral Snapshot**

GMC Add within 1,000 fluently.

3-1 Warm Up Focus Practice	3-2 Focus Practice	3-3 Warm Up Focus Practice	3-4 through 3-6 Warm Up Focus Practice	3-7 Practice	3-8 Focus Practice	3-13 Focus Practice

▦ **Spiral Tracker** **Go Online** ▸ to see how mastery develops for all standards within the grade.

3 Practice 15–20 min

Minute Math+ Children practice mental math strategies.	*Minute Math®+*	
Introducing *Shuffle to 100* **Game** Children estimate and make addends with a sum close to 100.	*Student Reference Book*, pp. 256–257; *Math Masters*, p. G10; number cards 1–9 (4 of each)	3.NBT.1, 3.NBT.2 SMP6
Math Boxes 3-3 Children practice and maintain skills.	*Math Journal 1*, p. 70	See page 241.
Home Link 3-3 **Homework** Children make estimates and add 3-digit numbers.	*Math Masters*, p. 84	3.NBT.1, 3.NBT.2

connectED.mcgraw-hill.com

Plan your lessons online with these tools.

 ePresentations   **Student Learning Center**   **Facts Workshop Game**   **eToolkit**   **Professional Development**   **Home Connections**   **Spiral Tracker**   **Assessment and Reporting**   **ELL English Learners Support** **Differentiation Support**

Differentiation Options

RtI

CCSS **3.NBT.2, SMP2**

Readiness
10–15 min

WHOLE CLASS
SMALL GROUP
PARTNER
INDEPENDENT

Modeling with Base-10 Blocks

Math Masters, p. TA14; base-10 blocks; number cards 0–9 (4 of each); half-sheet of paper

To review place value concretely, have children build numbers with base-10 blocks. Have them draw two or three number cards and place them on *Math Masters*, page TA14. Next have children use the appropriate columns on the place-value mat to represent hundreds with flats, tens with longs, and ones with cubes. **GMP2.1** Have children write the number in standard notation, expanded form, and base-10 shorthand (□ | .) to show what they did and make connections between representations. **GMP2.3**

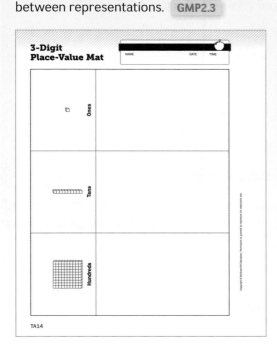

3-Digit Place-Value Mat

Ones

Tens

Hundreds

TA14

CCSS **3.NBT.1, 3.NBT.2**

Enrichment
10–15 min

WHOLE CLASS
SMALL GROUP
PARTNER
INDEPENDENT

Playing *Shuffle to 1,000*

Student Reference Book, p. 257; *Math Masters*, p. G11

To extend children's understanding of estimation and multidigit addition, have them play *Shuffle to 1,000* by following the directions for the variation on *Student Reference Book*, page 257.

Shuffle to 1,000 Record Sheet

Record your combinations and scores while playing *Shuffle to 1,000*.

Score

Round 1: _____ + _____ = _____

Round 2: _____ + _____ = _____

Round 3: _____ + _____ = _____

Round 4: _____ + _____ = _____

Total Score: _____

Shuffle to 1,000 Record Sheet

Record your combinations and scores while playing *Shuffle to 1,000*.

Score

Round 1: _____ + _____ = _____

Round 2: _____ + _____ = _____

Round 3: _____ + _____ = _____

Round 4: _____ + _____ = _____

Total Score: _____

G11

CCSS **3.OA.8, 3.NBT.1, 3.NBT.2, SMP1**

Extra Practice
5–15 min

WHOLE CLASS
SMALL GROUP
PARTNER
INDEPENDENT

Estimating with Partial Sums

Activity Card 36; *Student Reference Book*, pp. 116–117; number cards 1–9 (4 of each); paper or slate

Have children practice rounding and making mental estimates to check their exact answers to partial-sums addition problems. **GMP1.4**

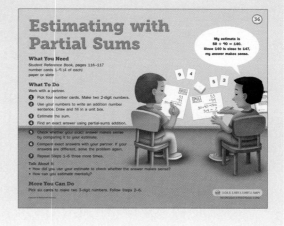

English Language Learners Support

Beginning ELL Use simple jigsaw puzzles to build background knowledge for understanding the term *partial*. As you show the puzzle pieces, make statements such as: *This is a part of the puzzle. This is a partial section of the puzzle.* Use Total Physical Response commands, such as: *Show me one part. Count all the parts. Use the parts to make the whole. Put the partial sections together.*

Go Online ELL English Learners Support

Professional Development

Partial-sums addition was introduced in *Second Grade Everyday Mathematics.* As the name suggests, this method involves calculating partial sums, working one place-value column at a time, and then adding all the partial sums to find the total. The partial sums can be found in any order, but working from left to right allows children to compare their answer with their estimate throughout the addition process. For example, if they estimate a sum of 120 for 44 + 77 and then add the tens, 40 + 70 = 110, children can see that this partial sum makes sense because it is close to their estimate.

---

① Warm Up 5 min

▶ Mental Math and Fluency

Have children write numbers in expanded form on their slates.
Leveled exercises:

● ○ ○ **189** 100 + 80 + 9 **325** 300 + 20 + 5
● ● ○ **603** 600 + 3 or 600 + 0 + 3 **991** 900 + 90 + 1
● ● ● **2,050** 2,000 + 50 or 2,000 + 0 + 50 + 0 **4,002** 4,000 + 2 or 4,000 + 0 + 0 + 2

② Focus 40–50 min

▶ Math Message

For each problem, round or use close-but-easier numbers to make an estimate. Then solve. Use your estimate to check whether your answer is reasonable.

Unit
keys

Sample estimate: 40 + 80 = 120

44 + 77 = ? 121

Sample estimate: 60 + 100 = 160

58 + 96 = ? 154

▶ Discussing Estimates

| WHOLE CLASS | SMALL GROUP | **PARTNER** | INDEPENDENT |

Math Message Follow-Up Have children share how they estimated and whether their answers make sense. GMP1.4, GMP6.1 Estimation strategies may include:

• Rounding each of the addends to the nearest 10. 40 + 80 = 120; 60 + 100 = 160
• Adding close-but-easier numbers. Sample answer: 45 + 80 = 125; 60 + 95 = 155

Next have children explain how they calculated the exact answer for 44 + 77 = ?. GMP6.1

Sample Strategies
• Take 4 ones from 44 (that makes 40). Think of the 4 ones as 3 + 1. Add 3 to 77 to make 80; then 40 + 80 = 120. Add the extra 1 to make 121.
• Think 44 = 40 + 4; 77 + 40 = 117; 117 + 4 = 121.
• Start at 77 and count by 10s four times, and then by 1s four times: 77, 87, 97, 107, 117, 118, 119, 120, 121.

• Think of 44 and 77 as their tens and ones. Add the tens: $40 + 70 = 110$; add the ones: $4 + 7 = 11$; then add the tens to the ones: $110 + 11 = 121$. This strategy uses **partial-sums addition,** which children will review in this lesson.

If no one shares partial-sums addition, model it for the class and record the steps: *I can add the tens and ones in any order, so I'm going to start with the tens. 40 + 70 = 110. Now I'll add the ones. 4 + 7 = 11. Now I'll add the partial sums: 110 + 11 = 121.*

In a similar manner, review $58 + 96 = ?$, highlighting a variety of strategies.

Remind children that in *Second Grade Everyday Mathematics* they used partial-sums addition. Explain that today they will use this method to add 3-digit addends.

▶ Adding with Partial Sums

Math Journal 1, p. 69

WHOLE CLASS	SMALL GROUP	PARTNER	INDEPENDENT

Display $145 + 322$ in vertical form.

Ask: *What is the **expanded form** of each addend?* $145 = 100 + 40 + 5$; $322 = 300 + 20 + 2$ As you model how to solve the problem using partial sums, remind children to think of each addend in its expanded form. GMP2.3 You may want to write the expanded forms next to each addend. Then record the partial sums as shown.

- Add the hundreds: $100 + 300 = 400$
- Add the tens: $40 + 20 = 60$
- Add the ones: $5 + 2 = 7$
- Add the partial sums: $400 + 60 + 7 = 467$.

Differentiate **Adjusting the Activity**

Have children who struggle with place value represent each addend with base-10 blocks or base-10 shorthand. To add, they gather the flats together, then the longs, then the cubes, and count the total number of hundreds, tens, and ones. (*See margin.*)

Go Online Differentiation Support

Some children may benefit from seeing or writing each step:

$$
\begin{array}{r}
145 \\
+ \ 322 \\
\end{array}
$$

$$
\begin{array}{rcl}
100 + 300 & \rightarrow & 400 \\
40 + \ 20 & \rightarrow & 60 \\
5 + \ \ 2 & \rightarrow & 7 \\
\end{array}
$$

$$400 + 60 + 7 = 467$$

$$145 + 322 = 467$$

Have children estimate to check whether the answer is reasonable, and invite them to share their estimation strategies. GMP1.4, GMP6.1

Sample answers: Add close-but-easier numbers: $150 + 300 = 450$. Round addends to 10s: $150 + 320 = 470$. Round addends to 100s: $100 + 300 = 400$.

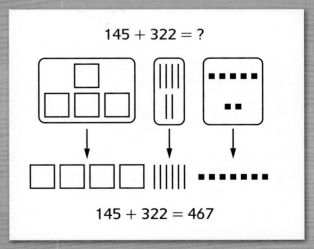

One way to record partial sums:

$$
\begin{array}{r}
145 \\
+ \ 322 \\
\hline
400 \\
60 \\
7 \\
\hline
467 \\
\end{array}
$$

$145 + 322 = ?$

$145 + 322 = 467$

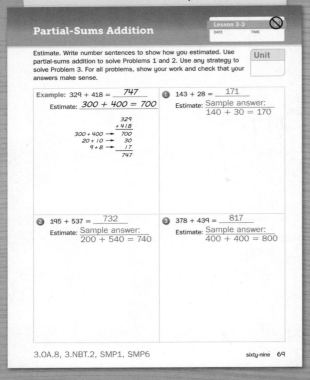

Partial-Sums Addition

Lesson 3-3
DATE   TIME

Estimate. Write number sentences to show how you estimated. Use partial-sums addition to solve Problems 1 and 2. Use any strategy to solve Problem 3. For all problems, show your work and check that your answers make sense.

Unit

Example: 329 + 418 = **747**
Estimate: *300 + 400 = 700*

```
              329
             +418
  300 + 400 →  700
   20 + 10 →   30
    9 + 8  →   17
              747
```

① 143 + 28 = **171**
Estimate: Sample answer:
140 + 30 = 170

② 195 + 537 = **732**
Estimate: Sample answer:
200 + 540 = 740

③ 378 + 439 = **817**
Estimate: Sample answer:
400 + 400 = 800

3.OA.8, 3.NBT.2, SMP1, SMP6   sixty-nine 69

Games

Shuffle to 100

Materials	☐ number cards 1–9 (4 of each)
	☐ 1 Shuffle to 100 Record Sheet for each player (Math Masters, p. G10)
Players	2 or 3
Skill	Estimating sums and making combinations close to 100
Object of the Game	To have the lowest score.

Directions

① Take turns being the dealer. The dealer shuffles the cards and deals 5 number cards to each player number-side up.

② Players think about two 2-digit numbers they can make with their cards. For example, the cards 3 and 4 could make either 34 or 43.

③ Players estimate to decide which of their possible 2-digit numbers will add up to a sum closest to 100. After choosing four cards to use, each player discards the extra card.

④ Players add their two 2-digit numbers to find an exact answer.

⑤ Players record their 2-digit numbers and sums on their Shuffle to 100 Record Sheet.

⑥ Each player finds his or her score by finding the difference between their sum and 100.

⑦ Players discard the cards they used. When all of the cards have been used, the dealer shuffles the discarded cards to make a new deck to finish the game.

Shuffle to 100 Record Sheet

⑧ The next dealer deals 5 new cards to each player. Players make new combinations that will add to a sum closest to 100.

⑨ Players add their scores after 4 rounds. The player with the LOWEST total score wins.

SRB
256 two hundred fifty-six

Ask: *Does 467 seem like a reasonable answer? Does it make sense? Explain.* Sample answers: Yes. My estimate of 450 is only 17 less than 467. In rounding to the nearest 100, I got 400, which is about 65 less than the actual answer.

Have partnerships solve 269 + 475 = ? using partial sums. 744 Remind children that they can use the expanded form of the numbers to make the calculations easier. For example,

- Mentally picture or write the expanded form for each addend: 200 + 60 + 9 and 400 + 70 + 5.
- Calculate the partial sums: 200 + 400 = 600; 60 + 70 = 130; 9 + 5 = 14
- Add the partial sums to find the total sum: 600 + 130 + 14 = 744, so 269 + 475 = 744.

Discuss strategies for finding and adding the partial sums. GMP6.1 Encourage children to estimate to check whether their answers make sense. GMP1.4 Pose additional 3-digit addition problems as needed.

When children seem comfortable, have them complete journal page 69.

✓ **Assessment Check-In** CCSS 3.NBT.2

Math Journal 1, p. 69

Expect children to be familiar with partial-sums addition from *Second Grade Everyday Mathematics* and successfully complete Problems 1–3 on journal page 69. If children have difficulty with the calculations, consider the suggestion in the Adjusting the Activity note.

☑ Assessment and Reporting   Go Online ⟩ to record student progress and to see trajectories toward mastery for this standard.

Summarize Have partners explain how they know their answers on journal page 69 make sense. GMP6.1

3 Practice 15–20 min Go Online

ePresentations eToolkit Home Connections

▶ Minute Math+

To practice mental math strategies, select a *Minute Math+* activity.

▶ Introducing *Shuffle to 100*

Student Reference Book, pp. 256–257; *Math Masters*, p. G10

WHOLE CLASS	**SMALL GROUP**	**PARTNER**	INDEPENDENT

With the class, read and discuss the directions on *Student Reference Book*, page 256. Model a few rounds and discuss making 2-digit addends whose sum is closest to 100.

Observe

• How do children choose combinations close to 100? GMP6.4

Discuss

• *How did you decide which combinations would get you closest to 100?*
• *How did you calculate your score for this turn?* GMP6.1

Differentiate   **Game Modifications**   Go Online   Differentiation Support

▶ Math Boxes 3-3 ✎

Math Journal 1, p. 70

| WHOLE CLASS | SMALL GROUP | PARTNER | INDEPENDENT |

Mixed Practice Math Boxes 3-3 are paired with Math Boxes 3-1.

▶ Home Link 3-3

Math Masters, p. 84

Homework Children make estimates and add 3-digit numbers.

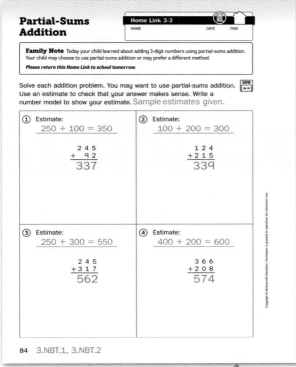

Math Masters, p. 84

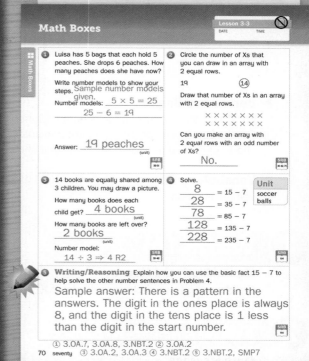

Math Journal 1, p. 70

Math Boxes   Lesson 3-3   DATE   TIME

① Luisa has 5 bags that each hold 5 peaches. She drops 6 peaches. How many peaches does she have now?

Write number models to show your steps. Sample number models given.
Number models: $5 \times 5 = 25$
       $25 - 6 = 19$

Answer: __19 peaches__ (unit)

② Circle the number of Xs that you can draw in an array with 2 equal rows.

19   ⑭

Draw that number of Xs in an array with 2 equal rows.

× × × × × × ×
× × × × × × ×

Can you make an array with 2 equal rows with an odd number of Xs?

__No.__

③ 14 books are equally shared among 3 children. You may draw a picture.

How many books does each child get? __4 books__

How many books are left over?
__2 books__

Number model:
$14 \div 3 \Rightarrow 4 \text{ R2}$

④ Solve.
$\underline{8} = 15 - 7$
$\underline{28} = 35 - 7$
$\underline{78} = 85 - 7$
$\underline{128} = 135 - 7$
$\underline{228} = 235 - 7$

Unit
soccer balls

⑤ **Writing/Reasoning** Explain how you can use the basic fact $15 - 7$ to help solve the other number sentences in Problem 4.

Sample answer: There is a pattern in the answers. The digit in the ones place is always 8, and the digit in the tens place is 1 less than the digit in the start number.

① 3.OA.7, 3.OA.8, 3.NBT.2 ② 3.OA.2
70   seventy   ③ 3.OA.2, 3.OA.3 ④ 3.NBT.2 ⑤ 3.NBT.2, SMP7

Column Addition

Overview Children are introduced to column addition.

▶ **Before You Begin**
For Part 2, display the column addition solution for 89 + 47 (see page 246) on the Class Data Pad. For the Summarize portion, prepare two posters for 283 + 37 (or a problem of your choice)—one that shows partial-sums addition and one that shows column addition.

▶ **Vocabulary**
column addition

 Common Core State Standards

Focus Clusters
• Solve problems involving the four operations, and identify and explain patterns in arithmetic.
• Use place value understanding and properties of operations to perform multi-digit arithmetic.

1 Warm Up 5 min

Materials

Mental Math and Fluency
Children find the closest multiple of 10.

3.NBT.1

2 Focus 40–50 min

Math Message
Children use partial sums to solve addition problems.

slate

3.NBT.2

Introducing Column Addition
Children learn column addition and compare it to partial-sums addition.

base-10 blocks (optional)

3.OA.8, 3.NBT.2
SMP2, SMP3

Practicing Column Addition
Children use column addition with multidigit numbers.

Math Journal 1, p. 71;
Math Masters, p. TA14 (optional);
base-10 blocks (optional)

3.OA.8, 3.NBT.2
SMP2, SMP3

✓ **Assessment Check-In**   See page 247.

Math Journal 1, p. 71

3.OA.8, 3.NBT.2

CCSS 3.NBT.2 **Spiral Snapshot**

GMC Add within 1,000 fluently.

| 3-1 through 3-3 Warm Up Focus Practice | 3-4 Focus Practice | 3-5 Warm Up Focus Practice | 3-6 Warm Up Focus | 3-7 Practice | 3-8 Focus Practice | 3-13 Focus Practice |

/// Spiral Tracker   Go Online   to see how mastery develops for all standards within the grade.

3 Practice 15–20 min

Minute Math+
Children practice mental math strategies.

Minute Math®+

Adding to Solve Number Stories
Children add mileage data to solve number stories.

Student Reference Book, p. 272;
Math Masters, p. 86

3.NBT.2

Math Boxes 3-4
Children practice and maintain skills.

Math Journal 1, p. 72

See page 247.

Home Link 3-4
Homework Children make sense of and use column addition.

Student Reference Book, p. 118;
Math Masters, p. 87

3.NBT.2, 3.OA.8
SMP2

connectED.mcgraw-hill.com

Plan your lessons online with these tools.

 ePresentations
 Student Learning Center
 Facts Workshop Game
 eToolkit
 Professional Development
 Home Connections
 Spiral Tracker
 Assessment and Reporting
 English Learners Support
 Differentiation Support

Differentiation Options

RtI

CCSS 3.NBT.2, SMP2

Readiness   5–10 min

Making Trades with Base-10 Blocks

WHOLE CLASS
SMALL GROUP
PARTNER
INDEPENDENT

base-10 blocks

To prepare children to add based on place value, have them represent numbers and make trades with base-10 blocks. **GMP2.1** Ask them to count out 12 cubes and then show 12 with the fewest possible base-10 blocks. 1 long and 2 cubes Ask: *What did you trade?* I traded 10 cubes for 1 long because 10 cubes is the same as 1 ten. Next have children count 15 longs. Ask: *What is their value?* 150 *How can you trade to show 150 with the fewest possible blocks?* 1 flat and 5 longs *Explain.* I traded 10 longs for 1 flat because 10 tens is the same as 1 hundred. Continue with other 2- and 3-digit numbers. Help children identify when to trade a group of 10 ones for 1 ten, and 10 tens for 1 hundred.

CCSS 3.NBT.1, 3.NBT.2, SMP3

Enrichment   10–15 min

Using Addition Strategies

WHOLE CLASS
SMALL GROUP
PARTNER
INDEPENDENT

Math Masters, p. 85

To extend children's understanding of multidigit addition, have them make sense of and discuss George and Tina's addition strategies presented on *Math Masters,* page 85. **GMP3.2** George's strategy: George broke 243 into 200 + 40 + 3. First he added the hundreds to 138, then the tens, and then the ones. Tina's strategy: Tina changed 138 into an easier number. She added 2 to 138 and got 140. She added 140 and 243 and got 383. Then she subtracted the extra 2 and got 381. Have children apply one or both strategies to two other problems on the page.

Using Addition Strategies

Lesson 3-4
NAME   DATE   TIME

George and Tina used different strategies to solve 138 + 243.
See if you can figure out how they each solved the problem.

George's Strategy
138 + 243 = ?
138 + 200 = 338
338 + 40 = 378
378 + 3 = 381
138 + 243 = 381

Tina's Strategy
138 + 243 = ?
138 + 2 = 140
140 + 243 = 383
383 − 2 = 381
138 + 243 = 381

Talk to your partner about how George's strategy works.
Then talk about how Tina's strategy works.

Use either George's or Tina's strategy to solve the problems below.
Sample answers given.

255 + 139 = ?	127 + 367 = ?
Estimate: 300 + 100 = 400	Estimate: 130 + 370 = 500
George's Strategy 255 + 100 = 355 355 + 30 = 385 385 + 9 = 394 255 + 139 = 394	Tina's Strategy 127 + 3 = 130 130 + 367 = 497 497 − 3 = 494 127 + 367 = 494

3.NBT.1, 3.NBT.2, SMP3   85

CCSS 3.OA.8, 3.NBT.1, 3.NBT.2, SMP1

Extra Practice   10–15 min

Adding with Column Addition

WHOLE CLASS
SMALL GROUP
PARTNER
INDEPENDENT

Activity Card 37;
Student Reference Book, p. 118;
number cards 1–9 (4 of each)

Have children practice estimating sums and finding exact answers using column addition. Then have children use their estimates to check whether their answers make sense. **GMP1.4**

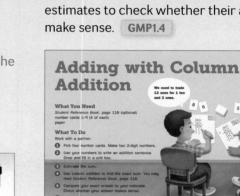

English Language Learners Support

Beginning ELL Use pictures or video clips to provide children with visual examples of columns found in large buildings. Have children trace or "air draw" the columns from top to bottom with their fingers as they repeat the word *column* and the sentence: *Columns go up and down.*

 Go Online ELL **English Learners Support**

SMP2 **Reason abstractly and quantitatively.**

GMP2.1 Create mathematical representations using numbers, words, pictures, symbols, gestures, tables, graphs, and concrete objects.

GMP2.2 Make sense of the representations you and others use.

SMP3 **Construct viable arguments and critique the reasoning of others.**

GMP3.2 Make sense of other's mathematical thinking.

Professional Development

Column addition emphasizes place-value understanding through trades between ones and tens, and tens and hundreds. Exposure to different computation methods, such as partial sums and column addition, encourages flexibility and allows children to choose the method that works best for them. For more information about column addition, see the Mathematical Background in the Unit Organizer.

---

1 Warm Up   5 min

ePresentations   eToolkit

▶ Mental Math and Fluency

Have children answer the following questions. *Leveled exercises:*

- ●○○ Is 42 closer to 40 or 50? 40
  Is 56 closer to 50 or 60? 60
- ●●○ Is 210 closer to 200 or 300? 200
  Is 998 closer to 900 or 1,000? 1,000
- ●●● Is 2,068 closer to 2,000 or 2,100? 2,100
  Is 3,243 closer to 3,240 or 3,250? 3,240

2 Focus   40–50 min

ePresentations   eToolkit

▶ Math Message

Fill in the unit. Use partial sums to add. Show your work.

Unit

$47 + 68 = ?$

$248 + 187 = ?$

▶ Introducing Column Addition

WHOLE CLASS	SMALL GROUP	PARTNER	INDEPENDENT

Math Message Follow-Up Invite volunteers to model and record their work for the class. GMP2.1

$$
\begin{array}{r}
47 \\
+ 68 \\
\end{array}
$$

$40 + 60 \longrightarrow 100$
$7 + 8 \longrightarrow 15$
_____
115

$$
\begin{array}{r}
248 \\
+ 187 \\
\end{array}
$$

$200 + 100 \longrightarrow 300$
$40 + 80 \longrightarrow 120$
$8 + 7 \longrightarrow 15$
_____
435

Ask: *Does 115 make sense? 435? Explain.* Yes. I can round the addends to the nearest 10 and get 120, which is close to 115. Yes. I can round the addends to the nearest 100 and get 400, which is close to 435.

Tell children they will continue to use estimates to check answers as they learn another method for adding numbers, called **column addition.**

Explain that in column addition, columns are made by drawing vertical lines between the digits in the addends. The digits are separated into ones, tens, hundreds, and so on, and labeled as shown on the following page.

Display 47 + 68 = ? vertically.

Add each column of numbers. (*See below.*) Point out that there are now 10 tens and 15 ones. Explain that the answer can only have one digit in each place. If there are multiple digits in a place, we need to make trades. **GMP2.2** You may wish to model making trades with base-10 blocks.

Ask: *How can we trade so there is only one digit in the ones place?* Trade 10 ones for 1 ten. *How many ones are left?* 5 ones Explain that because we need to move 1 ten to the 10s column, we add 1 ten to 10 tens to get 11 tens.

Ask: *How can we trade so there is only one digit in the tens place?* Trade 10 tens for 1 hundred. *How many tens are left?* 1 ten Explain that we need to move 1 hundred into the 100s column, so we add 1 hundred to 0 hundreds to get 1 hundred.

Tell children that since each column has only one digit, there are no more trades to make. The sum of 47 + 68 is 1 hundred, 1 ten, and 5 ones, or 115. Record a summary number sentence.

	100s	10s	1s
		4	7
Add each column of numbers.	+	6	8
Trade 10 ones for 1 ten and move the 1 ten to the tens column.		10	15
Trade 10 tens for 1 hundred and move the 1 hundred to the hundreds column.		11	5
47 + 68 = 115	1	1	5

Ask: *Does 115 make sense? Explain.* Yes. It matches the answer we got using partial sums.

With the class, use column addition to solve the 3-digit problem from the Math Message.

Display 248 + 187 = ? vertically. Invite volunteers to add and record each column of numbers.

Ask: *Do we need to make trades?* Yes. Have children explain the appropriate trades as you record them. **GMP2.1, GMP2.2**

	100s	10s	1s
	2	4	8
	+ 1	8	7
Trade 10 ones for 1 ten and add 1 ten to the 12 tens in the tens column.	3	12	15
Trade 10 tens for 1 hundred and add the 1 hundred to the 3 hundreds in the hundreds column.	3	13	5
248 + 187 = 435	4	3	5

Ask: *Does 435 make sense?* Yes. It matches the answer we got with partial sums.

Common Misconception

Differentiate Watch for children who do not trade and write incorrect sums that combine all the digits. For example, a child might say the sum in the problem below is 31,215 instead of 435.

	100s	10s	1s
	2	4	8
+	1	8	7
	3	12	15

Encourage children to estimate to check whether their answers make sense. Provide base-10 blocks and a place-value mat (*Math Masters*, page TA14) to model the ones, tens, and hundreds and make appropriate trades.

Go Online Differentiation Support

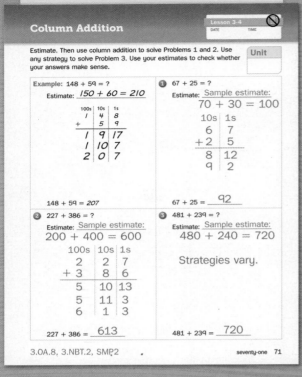
Compare partial-sums addition and column addition by asking:

- *How are partial-sums addition and column addition alike?* Sample answers: They both involve adding hundreds, tens, and ones. They both end up with the same answer.
- *How are they different?* Sample answer: For partial sums, you add the values in each place and then add the partial sums to find the total. For column addition, you add the digits in each place and trade to larger places to find the total.

Next display 89 + 47 = ? and the solution shown with column addition. (*See Before You Begin.*) Have partnerships work together to make sense of each step. GMP2.2   After several minutes, invite children to share their partner's thinking. GMP3.2   Expect responses similar to the following:

100s	10s	1s
	8	9
+	4	7
	12	16
	13	6
1	3	6

- First the numbers in each column were added to get 12 tens and 16 ones.
- Next 10 ones were traded for 1 ten, leaving 6 ones and 13 tens.
- Then 10 tens were traded for 1 hundred, leaving 3 tens and 1 hundred.
- The sum of 89 + 47 is 1 hundred, 3 tens, and 6 ones, or 136.

With the class, solve additional problems using column addition. Have children use estimates to check whether their answers make sense. *Suggestions:*

78 + 65 = ? 143   439 + 171 = ? 610

In the second problem, note the 0 in the ones place after the ten is traded. Explain that zero serves as a placeholder in the final sum 610.

▶ Practicing Column Addition

Math Journal 1, p. 71

| WHOLE CLASS | SMALL GROUP | **PARTNER** | **INDEPENDENT** |

Have children work independently or with a partner using column addition to complete Problems 1–2 on journal page 71. GMP2.1, GMP2.2   Tell children that they may choose any method to solve Problem 3.

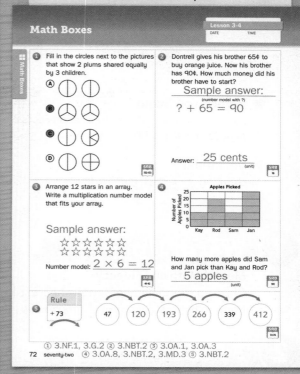

Math Journal 1, p. 72

✓ Assessment Check-In CCSS 3.OA.8, 3.NBT.2

Math Journal 1, p. 71

Expect most children to make reasonable estimates for Problems 1 through 3 and to solve Problem 3. This lesson introduces column addition, so do not expect children to use this method to find exact answers to Problems 1 and 2. Have children who struggle with estimating reasonable answers use number lines to identify close-but-easier numbers. Have children who struggle with using a strategy to solve Problem 3 act out the problem with base-10 blocks.

✓ Assessment and Reporting 〈 Go Online 〉 to record student progress and to see trajectories toward mastery for these standards.

Have children trade journals and make sense of their partner's work on Problem 3. Invite volunteers to share how their partner solved the problem. **GMP3.2**

Summarize Display two methods, partial-sums and column addition, for solving 283 + 459 (or another problem) in two different areas of the classroom. (*See Before You Begin.*) Have children stand by the addition strategy they prefer and discuss the reasons for their choices.

3 Practice 15–20 min 〈 Go Online 〉

ePresentations   eToolkit   Home Connections

▶ Minute Math+

To practice mental math strategies, select a *Minute Math+* activity.

▶ Adding to Solve Number Stories

Student Reference Book, p. 272; *Math Masters*, p. 86

| WHOLE CLASS | SMALL GROUP | PARTNER | INDEPENDENT |

Have children use road mileage data on *Student Reference Book*, page 272 to solve number stories.

▶ Math Boxes 3-4

Math Journal 1, p. 72

| WHOLE CLASS | SMALL GROUP | PARTNER | INDEPENDENT |

Mixed Practice Math Boxes 3-4 are paired with Math Boxes 3-2.

▶ Home Link 3-4

Student Reference Book, p. 118; *Math Masters,* p. 87

Homework Children make sense of and use column addition. **GMP2.2**

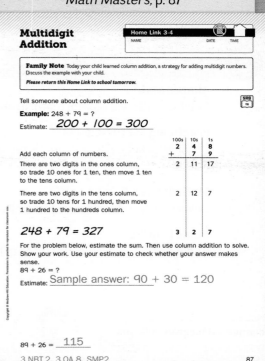

Math Masters, p. 87

Counting-Up Subtraction

Overview Children review counting-up subtraction.

▶ **Before You Begin**
For Part 3, prepare the Multiplication Facts Assessment Tool on *Assessment Handbook*, pages 136–138 and 142.

▶ **Vocabulary**
counting up • open number line

CCSS **Common Core State Standards**

Focus Clusters
• Solve problems involving the four operations, and identify and explain patterns in arithmetic.
• Use place value understanding and properties of operations to perform multi-digit arithmetic.

1 Warm Up 5 min

	Materials	
Mental Math and Fluency Children round numbers to the nearest 10 and use them to estimate sums and differences.	slate	3.NBT.1, 3.NBT.2

2 Focus 40–50 min

Math Message Children subtract 2-digit numbers.	slate (optional)	3.NBT.2 SMP2
Counting Up to Subtract Children count up on open number lines.	slate	3.OA.8, 3.NBT.2 SMP1, SMP2
Representing Counting Up Children represent counting-up subtraction with open number lines or number sentences.	*Math Journal 1*, p. 73; slate; number grid (optional)	3.OA.8, 3.NBT.2 SMP1, SMP2
✓ **Assessment Check-In** See page 252.	*Math Journal 1*, p. 73	3.OA.8, 3.NBT.2 , SMP2

CCSS 3.NBT.2 **Spiral Snapshot**

GMC Subtract within 1,000 fluently.

| 2-12
Warm Up
Practice | 3-1
Focus
Practice | 3-5
Warm Up
Focus | 3-6
Focus | 3-7
Warm Up
Practice | 3-8
Focus
Practice | 3-13
Focus
Practice | 4-1
Practice |

III **Spiral Tracker**   **Go Online** to see how mastery develops for all standards within the grade.

3 Practice 15–20 min

Minute Math+ Children practice mental math strategies.	*Minute Math®+*	
Practicing Fact Triangles Children practice 2s, 5s, and 10s multiplication facts.	*Assessment Handbook*, pp. 136–138 and 142; *Student Reference Book*, p. 248 (optional); Fact Triangles	3.OA.7
Math Boxes 3-5 Children practice and maintain skills.	*Math Journal 1*, p. 74	See page 253.
Home Link 3-5 **Homework** Children count up to subtract.	*Math Masters*, p. 89	3.OA.8, 3.NBT.2

---

connectED.mcgraw-hill.com

Plan your lessons online with these tools.

 ePresentations

 Student Learning Center

Facts Workshop Game

 eToolkit

Professional Development

 Home Connections

 III Spiral Tracker

Assessment and Reporting

 ELL English Learners Support

 Differentiation Support

Differentiation Options RtI

Readiness
5–10 min

Finding Multiples of 10

WHOLE CLASS
SMALL GROUP
PARTNER
INDEPENDENT

Math Masters, p. TA3;
Class Number Line

To prepare children for counting-up subtraction, have them use the Class Number Line or a number grid (*Math Masters*, page TA3) to find multiples of 10. Point to 16 and ask: *What is the next multiple of 10, or number with zero in the ones place, past 16?* 20 *What is the distance from 16 to 20?* 4 *How do you know?*
GMP7.2 Sample answers: I counted up. I know that 6 is 4 away from 10, so 16 is 4 away from 20. Continue with other 2-digit numbers. When children are comfortable, have them find the next multiples of 10 and 100 for 3-digit numbers.

Enrichment
10–15 min

Counting Up Efficiently

WHOLE CLASS
SMALL GROUP
PARTNER
INDEPENDENT

Activity Card 38; *Student Reference Book*, pp. 122–123; number cards 1–9 (4 of each)

To encourage efficient counting-up strategies, have partners count up to solve 3-digit subtraction problems using the fewest steps possible. **GMP6.4**

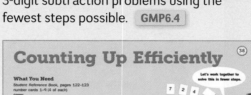

Extra Practice
10–15 min

Subtracting on an Open Number Line

WHOLE CLASS
SMALL GROUP
PARTNER
INDEPENDENT

Math Masters, p. 88

For additional practice counting up, have children solve subtraction problems and show their work on open number lines.
GMP2.1

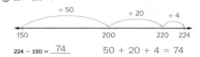

English Language Learners Support

Beginning ELL Display a number line vertically, with the smaller numbers at the bottom. Demonstrate *counting up* as you move your hand up along the number line. Orally and with gestures, direct children to count up on a number line. For example, say, *Count up from 25*, gesturing to 25, then 26, 27, 28, and so on as children count. Once children can count up as you gesture, point to a number and have them count up without gestures. Provide for oral practice by asking children short-response questions, such as: *How will you count?* Sample answers: Up. I will count up.

Go Online   ELL   English Learners Support

Standards and Goals for
Mathematical Practice

SMP1 **Make sense of problems and persevere in solving them.**

GMP1.2 Reflect on your thinking as you solve your problem.

GMP1.3 Keep trying when your problem is hard.

SMP2 **Reason abstractly and quantitatively.**

GMP2.1 Create mathematical representations using numbers, words, pictures, symbols, gestures, tables, graphs, and concrete objects.

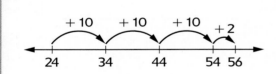

$$10 + 10 + 10 + 2 = 32$$
$$56 - 24 = 32$$

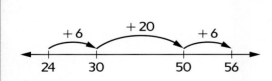

$$6 + 20 + 6 = 32$$
$$56 - 24 = 32$$

---

1 Warm Up   5 min    Go Online   ePresentations   eToolkit

▶ Mental Math and Fluency

On slates, have children round each number to the nearest 10 and estimate sums and differences. *Leveled exercises:*

● ○ ○ $99 + 49$ $100 + 50 = 150$
       $76 + 24$ $80 + 20 = 100$
       $49 - 21$ $50 - 20 = 30$

● ● ○ $249 - 103$ $250 - 100 = 150$
       $347 - 253$ $350 - 250 = 100$
       $584 + 121$ $580 + 120 = 700$

● ● ● $421 - 296$ $420 - 300 = 120$
       $338 + 79$ $340 + 80 = 420$
       $537 + 186$ $540 + 190 = 730$

2 Focus   40–50 min    Go Online   ePresentations   eToolkit

▶ Math Message

Fill in the unit box. Subtract. Show your work and explain it to a partner. **GMP2.1**

$56 - 24 = ?$ 32

Unit

▶ Counting Up to Subtract

| WHOLE CLASS | SMALL GROUP | PARTNER | INDEPENDENT |

Math Message Follow-Up Have children share their subtraction strategies. These may include using number grids or number lines, open number lines, mental calculations, or expand-and-trade subtraction (reviewed in Lesson 3-6). Note that *Second Grade Everyday Mathematics* introduced all of these strategies.

Highlight **counting up** on an **open number line** by inviting volunteers to model their work. **GMP2.1** Draw attention to representations that show counting up by 1s and 10s to multiples of 10 or other close-but-easier numbers. (*See margin.*)

- I started at 24 and made jumps of 10 to 34, 44, and 54. I made one jump of 2 to 56, so $10 + 10 + 10 + 2 = 32$.

- I started at 24 and made a jump of 6 to 30. I made a jump of 20 to 50 and another jump of 6 to 56, so $6 + 20 + 6 = 32$.

Ask: *Why do we add the jumps to find the answer?* Sample answer: Adding the jumps gives us the total distance, or difference, between the numbers.

Pose $53 - 39 = ?$. 14 Ask children to try visualizing an open number line to solve the problem mentally. Encourage them to picture their jumps and keep track of the differences either mentally or by jotting them down.
GMP1.3 After giving children time to count up mentally, invite them to share their strategies. Sample answer: I started at 39 and jumped 1 to 40, then 10 to 50, and then 3 more to 53. I added in my head: $1 + 10 + 3 = 14$.

Explain that recording or mentally visualizing jumps on open number lines may help children subtract larger numbers. Tell them they will use counting up to subtract 3-digit numbers using both open number lines and number sentences.

▶ Representing Counting Up

Math Journal 1, p. 73

| WHOLE CLASS | SMALL GROUP | PARTNER | INDEPENDENT |

Display $343 - 158 = ?$. 185 Remind children that they can make jumps by 10s or 100s to solve 3-digit subtraction problems. Have partnerships solve the problem on open number lines.

As children work and share counting-up strategies, note whether they make jumps of 10s and 100s and count to easy numbers strategically. If children make many jumps of 10, for example, encourage them to try to count up in fewer steps by combining 10s or counting by a multiple of 10. Ask questions such as: Sample answers given.

- *What is your first jump? Why did you make that jump?* **GMP1.2**
  I jumped from 158 to 160 by 2 because 160 is an easy number. I jumped from 158 to 258 because it's easy to add 100 to a number.
- *What helps you choose the size of your jumps?* **GMP1.2** I might take a small jump to get to an easy number. I can make bigger jumps by 10s or 100s.
- *What could you try if you are not sure what to do next?* **GMP1.3**
  I could try making jumps of 10 or 100 and check whether I need to keep going. I could use the number grid to find a close-but-easier number to count up to.

Some possible strategies:

- I started at 158 and jumped 2 to the easier number 160. I jumped 100 from 160 to 260, and then jumped 40 more to 300. I jumped another 40 and 3 more to 343. $2 + 100 + 40 + 40 + 3 = 185$
- I started at 158 and jumped 100 to 258. To get to an easier number, I jumped 2 to 260. I jumped 40 to 300 and another 40 to 340. Then I jumped 3 to 343. $100 + 2 + 40 + 40 + 3 = 185$

Record a summary number sentence: $343 - 158 = 185$

Have children make an estimate to check whether this exact answer is reasonable. Sample estimate: $350 - 150 = 200$; since 185 is close to 200, the answer is reasonable.

Discuss using addition to check the exact answer. Explain that 343, 158, and 185 form a number family. To check whether $343 - 158 = 185$, add $158 + 185$. Since the sum is 343, the answer is correct.

Math Journal 1, p. 73

Counting-Up Subtraction
Lesson 3-5
DATE   TIME

Fill in the unit box. For each problem, make an estimate. Count up to solve Problems 1–3. Use open number lines or number sentences. Use any strategy to solve Problem 4. Show your work. Use your estimates to check whether your answers make sense.

Unit

① $67 - 37 = ?$ Sample estimates given.
Estimate: ___$70 - 40 = 30$___

$67 - 37 = $ ___30___

② $? = 91 - 46$
Estimate: ___$40 = 90 - 50$___

___45___ $= 91 - 46$

③ $? = 283 - 256$
Estimate: ___$20 = 280 - 260$___

___27___ $= 283 - 256$

④ $752 - 487 = ?$
Estimate: ___$750 - 500 = 250$___

$752 - 487 = $ ___265___

3.OA.8, 3.NBT.2, SMP1, SMP2   seventy-three 73

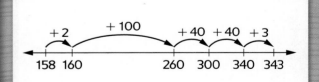

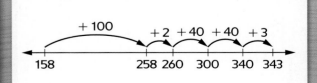

Assessment Handbook, p. 136

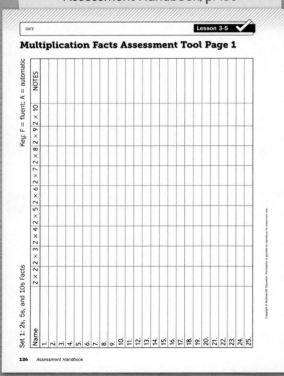

Next model another way to record counting-up subtraction to solve 343 − 158.

$$158 + 2 = 160$$
$$160 + 40 = 200$$
$$200 + 100 = 300$$
$$300 + 40 = 340$$
$$340 + 3 = 343$$

$$2 + 40 + 100 + 40 + 3 = 185$$
$$343 - 158 = 185$$

Discuss how this representation with number sentences and the open number line representation are similar and different. Sample answers: This is a list of number sentences, while the open number line shows what is added by jumps. In both, you count up by multiples of 10 or 100 to easier numbers and find the total of your differences.

Pose 261 − 146 = ?. 115 Have partners count up to solve and show their work with representations of their choice. **GMP2.1** As children work, ask questions such as: *How did you decide what to add (jump) first? Why did you choose an open number line? Number sentences? What could you do if you are not sure how to count up?* **GMP1.2, GMP1.3** Invite partnerships to share their strategies. Encourage children to check and justify their answers based on their estimates as they share.

When most children seem comfortable, have them complete Problems 1 through 4 on journal page 73. **GMP2.1**

✓ Assessment Check-In   CCSS 3.OA.8, 3.NBT.2

Math Journal 1, p. 73

Expect children to use counting-up subtraction to solve Problems 1 through 3 and show their work on open number lines or with number sentences. **GMP2.1** Some children may be able to combine multiples of 10 or 100 to count up more efficiently. For children who struggle to identify easier numbers to count to, such as nearby multiples of 10 and 100, consider implementing the suggestion in the Adjusting the Activity note.

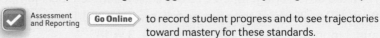 ✓ Assessment and Reporting **Go Online** to record student progress and to see trajectories toward mastery for these standards.

Bring the class together and encourage children to ask questions to make sense of each other's representations and strategies.

Summarize Have partnerships talk about whether they prefer recording their calculations on open number lines or with number sentences, or if they like counting up mentally.

3 Practice 15–20 min

Go Online

ePresentations · eToolkit · Home Connections

▶ Minute Math+

To practice mental math strategies, select a *Minute Math+* activity.

▶ Practicing Fact Triangles

Assessment Handbook, pp. 136–138 and 142

| WHOLE CLASS | **SMALL GROUP** | **PARTNER** | INDEPENDENT |

Have children practice with Fact Triangles. Begin assessing individuals or small groups for fluency with 2s, 5s, and 10s multiplication facts and with their understanding of ×0 and ×1 facts using the Multiplication Facts Assessment Tool (*Assessment Handbook*, pages 136–138 and 142). Do not expect to assess many children or many facts at one time. Assess a few children on a few facts each time children play fact games or use their Fact Triangles.

Observe and record children's ease with solving particular facts, and ask questions to assess their strategies:

- Record an *F* for *fluent* if a child uses an efficient and appropriate strategy but takes a few seconds to do so.
- Record an *A* for *automatic* if a child generates the answer with great efficiency, either by instinctively applying a strategy or just "knowing" the fact.
- If a child does not know a fact, leave the cell blank.

See the Unit 6 Mathematical Background in the Unit Organizer for more information about fluency and automaticity.

The foundation for upcoming multiplication fact strategies are the 2s, 5s, and 10s facts. Children who are not yet fluent with 2s, 5s, and 10s facts may benefit from playing *Multiplication Draw*. Directions for this game are on *Student Reference Book*, page 248.

▶ Math Boxes 3-5

Math Journal 1, p. 74

| WHOLE CLASS | SMALL GROUP | PARTNER | **INDEPENDENT** |

Mixed Practice Math Boxes 3-5 are paired with Math Boxes 3-7.

▶ Home Link 3-5

Math Masters, p. 89

Homework Children count up to subtract. They show their work on open number lines or with number sentences.

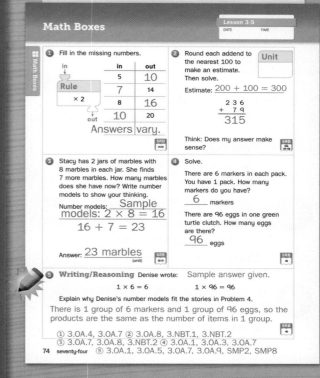

Math Journal 1, p. 74

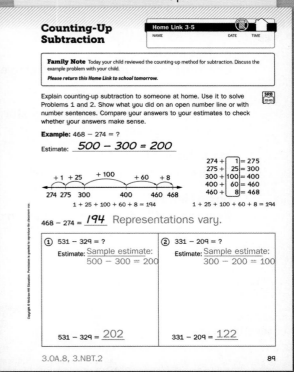

Math Masters, p. 89

Expand-and-Trade Subtraction

Overview Children use expand and trade to solve subtraction problems.

▶ **Before You Begin**
For Part 1, provide 7 base-10 longs and 20 base-10 cubes for each child or partnership.

▶ **Vocabulary**
expand-and-trade subtraction

CCSS **Common Core State Standards**

Focus Cluster
Use place value understanding and properties of operations to perform multi-digit arithmetic.

---

1 Warm Up 5 min

	Materials	
Mental Math and Fluency Children estimate sums.	slate	3.NBT.1, 3.NBT.2

---

2 Focus 45–55 min

Math Message Children solve a subtraction problem.	base-10 blocks	3.NBT.2 SMP5
Reviewing Expand-and-Trade Subtraction Children review expand-and-trade subtraction.	base-10 blocks	3.NBT.2 SMP2, SMP5
Practicing Expand-and-Trade Subtraction Children use expand-and-trade subtraction.	*Math Journal 1*, p. 75	3.OA.8, 3.NBT.1, 3.NBT.2 SMP1, SMP2
✓ **Assessment Check-In** See page 258.	*Math Journal 1*, p. 75; *Math Masters*, p. TA14 (optional); base-10 blocks (optional)	3.NBT.1, 3.NBT.2

CCSS 3.NBT.2 **Spiral Snapshot**

GMC Subtract within 1,000 fluently.

| 2-12
Warm Up
Practice | 3-1
Focus
Practice | 3-5
Warm Up
Focus | 3-6
Focus | 3-7
Warm Up
Practice | 3-8
Focus
Practice | 3-13
Focus
Practice | 4-1
Practice |

III Spiral Tracker **Go Online** to see how mastery develops for all standards within the grade.

---

3 Practice 10–15 min

Minute Math+ Children practice mental math strategies.	*Minute Math®+*	
Comparing Data in a Bar Graph Children solve comparison number stories using a scaled bar graph.	*Math Journal 1*, p. 76	3.OA.8, 3.MD.3
Math Boxes 3-6 Children practice and maintain skills.	*Math Journal 1*, p. 77	See page 259.
Home Link 3-6 **Homework** Children solve subtraction problems.	*Math Masters*, p. 90	3.OA.8, 3.NBT.1, 3.NBT.2

---

connectED.mcgraw-hill.com

Plan your lessons online with these tools.

 ePresentations

 Student Learning Center

 Facts Workshop Game

 eToolkit

 Professional Development

 Home Connections

 Spiral Tracker

 Assessment and Reporting

 English Learners Support

Differentiation Support

Differentiation Options

RtI

CCSS 3.NBT.2, SMP2

Readiness
5–10 min

Trading with Base-10 Blocks

Math Masters, p. TA14;
base-10 blocks

| WHOLE CLASS |
| **SMALL GROUP** |
| PARTNER |
| INDEPENDENT |

To practice place-value trades using a concrete model, have children represent the same number in different ways with base-10 blocks. Have children display 4 flats, 9 longs, and 8 cubes on a place-value mat (*Math Masters,* page TA14). Ask: *What number do these blocks represent?* 498 Trade 1 long for 10 cubes, and ask: *How do these blocks represent the same number?* **GMP2.2** Sample answer: One long is the same as 10 cubes, so 4 flats, 8 longs, and 18 cubes also show 498. Verify this by counting the blocks. Ask: *Are there other trades we could make and still show 498?* Sample answers: Trade another long for 10 cubes; trade a flat for 10 longs. As children suggest other exchanges, make the exchanges and count to show that the blocks still represent 498.

CCSS 3.NBT.2, SMP1

Enrichment
10–15 min

Exploring Subtraction Strategies

Activity Card 39; *Student Reference Book,* pp. 119–123; *Math Masters,* p. TA3; base-10 blocks (optional); large poster paper; markers; scissors; tape

| WHOLE CLASS |
| **SMALL GROUP** |
| PARTNER |
| INDEPENDENT |

To further explore subtraction strategies, have children write 2- or 3-digit subtraction problems and find the difference in multiple ways and compare strategies. **GMP1.5, GMP1.6**

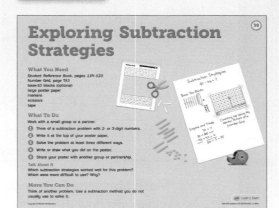

CCSS 3.OA.8, 3.NBT.2, SMP1

Extra Practice
10–15 min

Practicing Expand-and-Trade Subtraction

Activity Card 40; *Student Reference Book,* p. 119; number cards 0–9 (4 of each); base-10 blocks (optional)

| WHOLE CLASS |
| SMALL GROUP |
| **PARTNER** |
| INDEPENDENT |

For additional practice with 3-digit subtraction, have partners estimate differences and use expand-and-trade subtraction to solve problems. They may use base-10 blocks, base-10 shorthand, or drawings. Partners compare their exact answers with their estimates. **GMP1.4**

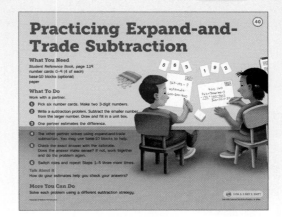

English Language Learners Support

Beginning ELL Scaffold the term *trade* by role-playing familiar, everyday situations. For example, role-play trading an apple for an orange: *I have an apple. You have an orange. We both have a piece of fruit. We could trade. You give me your orange. I will give you my apple.* Provide practice opportunities for using the term *trade* with other objects and sentence frames such as: *I have a _____. You have a _____. We both have a _____. Can we trade?*

 Go Online ELL **English Learners Support**

Standards and Goals for
Mathematical Practice

SMP1 Make sense of problems and persevere in solving them.
GMP1.6 Compare the strategies you and others use.

SMP2 Reason abstractly and quantitatively.
GMP2.3 Make connections between representations.

SMP5 Use appropriate tools strategically.
GMP5.2 Use tools effectively and make sense of your results.

Professional Development

This lesson reviews expand-and-trade subtraction, which was introduced late in *Second Grade Everyday Mathematics*. Expand-and-trade subtraction relies on place-value understanding. Exposing children to multiple strategies allows them to think flexibly and choose the most efficient strategy for them. By the end of third grade, children are expected to fluently subtract within 1,000 using strategies based on place-value, properties of operations, and/or the relationship between addition and subtraction. See the Mathematical Background in the Unit Organizer for more information about expand-and-trade subtraction.

---

1 Warm Up · 5 min

▶ Mental Math and Fluency

Display each set of problems. Have children estimate the sums and write the appropriate problem on their slates. Then have them share how they estimated. *Leveled exercises:*

●○○ *Which of these has a sum of about 200?*
(153 + 52)   75 + 63   198 + 71

●●○ *Which of these has a sum less than 500?*
(145 + 188)   396 + 285   403 + 112

●●● *Which of these has a sum less than 600?*
189 + 432   451 + 154   (252 + 342)

2 Focus · 40–50 min

▶ Math Message

Fill in the unit box. Solve using base-10 blocks. Be ready to show and explain what you did. GMP5.2

Unit

$71 - 46 = ?$ 25

▶ Reviewing Expand-and-Trade Subtraction

WHOLE CLASS	SMALL GROUP	PARTNER	INDEPENDENT

Math Message Follow-Up Have volunteers share their units and explain and model how they subtracted with base-10 blocks. GMP5.2 *A possible strategy:*

- I couldn't take away 6 cubes from 1 cube, so I traded 1 long for 10 cubes.
- Then I had 6 longs and 11 cubes and could subtract the 4 longs and 6 cubes.
- 2 longs and 5 cubes were left, which is 25.

Ask children to compare representations of 71 before and after the trade. GMP2.3 Sample answer: We started by showing 71 with 7 longs and 1 cube. After the trade we had 6 longs and 11 cubes, but that also makes 71.

Have children solve additional 2- and 3-digit subtraction problems using base-10 blocks. $53 - 27 = ?$ 26; $66 - 48 = ?$ 18; $? = 241 - 125$ 116

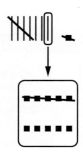

$71 - 46 = 25$

Next review **expand-and-trade subtraction.**

Display 71 − 46 vertically.

Rewrite or have a volunteer rewrite both numbers in expanded form.
70 + 1; 40 + 6 Make sure the place values are aligned. (*See margin.*)

Point out how expanded form shows tens and ones, similar to how base-10 blocks show tens and ones. Guide children through the solution process.

1. Decide whether trades are needed. Ask: *Is 70 greater than (or equal to) 40?* Yes. *Is 1 greater than (or equal to) 6?* No. *Then we need to make a trade so there are more than 6 ones. What trade can we make?* Break apart 1 ten into 10 ones to add to the 1 one to make 11 ones.

2. Represent the trade. Cross out the 70 and write 60 above it, and then cross out the 1 and write 11 above it. (*See margin.*) Ask: *Is 60 + 11 another name for 71? Explain.* **GMP2.3** Yes, because 6 tens and 11 ones is 71.

3. Subtract either the tens or ones first. Record 20 and 5 below the tens and ones places. Explain that after taking 46 from 71, there are 2 tens and 5 ones left. Record 20 + 5, or 25; 71 − 46 = 25.

Next display 353 − 168 vertically.

In a similar manner, have children rewrite each number in expanded form and record the problem in columns according to place value. Then work through the solution process.

$$353 \longrightarrow 300 + 50 + 3$$
$$- \ 168 \longrightarrow 100 + 60 + 8$$

1. Decide whether trades are needed. Ask: *Is 300 greater than (or equal to) 100?* Yes. *Is 50 at least as large as 60?* No. *Is 3 greater than (or equal to) 8?* No. *We need to make some trades.*

2. Represent the trades. Trades can be carried out from left to right or right to left, so interim steps may differ, although the results should be the same. (*See below.*) The following describes trades from left to right:
   • *How can I get more tens so I can subtract the 60?* Trade 1 hundred to get 10 tens.
   • *How can I get more ones so I can subtract the 3?* Trade 1 ten to get 10 ones.
   • *Is 200 + 140 + 13 a name for 353? How do you know?* **GMP2.3** Yes, because when I add 200 to 140, I get 340 and 13 more is 353.

3. Carry out the subtraction in any order and record the answer:
   100 + 80 + 5, or 185; 353 − 168 = 185.

$$\begin{array}{c}
\quad\quad\quad 140 \\
200 \quad \cancel{150} \quad 13 \\
353 \longrightarrow \cancel{300} + \cancel{50} + \cancel{3} \\
- \ 168 \longrightarrow 100 + 60 + 8 \\
\hline
100 + 80 + 5 = 185
\end{array}$$

Making trades from left to right

$$\begin{array}{c}
\quad\quad\quad 140 \\
200 \quad \cancel{40} \quad 13 \\
353 \longrightarrow \cancel{300} + \cancel{50} + \cancel{3} \\
- \ 168 \longrightarrow 100 + 60 + 8 \\
\hline
100 + 80 + 5 = 185
\end{array}$$

Making trades from right to left

$$71 \longrightarrow 70 + 1$$
$$- \ 46 \longrightarrow 40 + 6$$

$$\begin{array}{c}
\quad\quad\quad 60 \quad\ 11 \\
71 \longrightarrow \cancel{70} + \cancel{1} \\
- \ 46 \longrightarrow 40 + 6 \\
\hline
\quad\quad\quad 20 + 5 = 25
\end{array}$$

Common Misconception

Differentiate Watch for children who interpret the addition symbols in the expanded forms of each number as signals to add rather than subtract the subtrahend and minuend. Have them circle the subtraction symbol in the problem as a reminder. Point out that the expanded forms help to illustrate the place value before making trades and subtracting—they do not change the directions for the problem.

  Differentiation Support

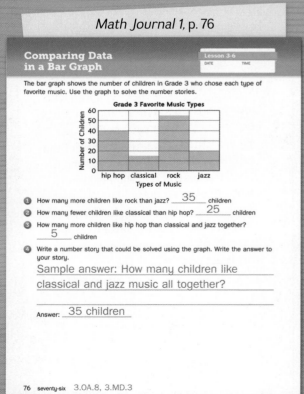

Expand-and-Trade Subtraction — Lesson 3-6

Fill in the unit box. For each problem, write a number sentence for your estimate. Write each number in expanded form. Solve using expand-and-trade subtraction. Compare your answer to your estimate. Does your answer make sense? Sample estimates given.

Example: 247 − 186 = ?
Estimate: 250 − 200 = 50

247 − 186 = **61**

① 65 − 47 = ?
Estimate: 70 − 50 = 20

65 − 47 = **18**

② 182 − 56 = ?
Estimate: 180 − 60 = 120

182 − 56 = **126**

③ 341 − 225 = ?
Estimate: 340 − 230 = 110

341 − 225 = **116**

3.OA.8, 3.NBT.1, 3.NBT.2, SMP1, SMP2   seventy-five   75

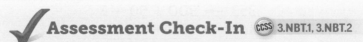

$$104 \rightarrow 100 + 0 + 4 \rightarrow 90 + 10 + 14$$
$$- 37 \rightarrow 30 + 7$$
$$60 + 7 = 67$$

Comparing Data in a Bar Graph — Lesson 3-6

The bar graph shows the number of children in Grade 3 who chose each type of favorite music. Use the graph to solve the number stories.

Grade 3 Favorite Music Types

① How many more children like rock than jazz? **35** children
② How many fewer children like classical than hip hop? **25** children
③ How many more children like hip hop than classical and jazz together? **5** children
④ Write a number story that could be solved using the graph. Write the answer to your story.
Sample answer: How many children like classical and jazz music all together?

Answer: **35 children**

76 seventy-six   3.OA.8, 3.MD.3

Pose additional problems as needed. Remind children to write the expanded notation for each number in columns according to place value.

Suggestions:

104 − 37 = ? 67 (*See margin.*)

? = 437 − 248 189

524 − 432 = ? 92

▶ Practicing Expand-and-Trade Subtraction

Math Journal 1, p. 75

| WHOLE CLASS | SMALL GROUP | **PARTNER** | **INDEPENDENT** |

Have children solve the problems on journal page 75 independently. As they finish, have them share their answers with partners. If partnerships disagree, encourage them to discuss their strategies and work together until they agree on an answer.

Then have children share and compare their strategies with the class. **GMP1.6** Help them recognize how their work may look different based on the order in which they made their trades. **GMP2.3**

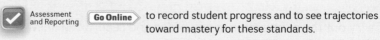

✓ Assessment Check-In   CCSS 3.NBT.1, 3.NBT.2

Math Journal 1, p. 75

Expect most children to make reasonable estimates and to write the numbers in Problems 1 through 3 in expanded form. Expand-and-trade subtraction was introduced late in *Second Grade Everyday Mathematics,* so children have had few opportunities to practice. At this time, do not expect many children to solve Problems 1 through 3 using this method. If children struggle with making reasonable estimates, briefly review identifying close-but-easier numbers or rounding to the nearest 10 or 100. If children struggle with writing numbers in expanded form, have them represent each number with base-10 blocks on place-value mats (*Math Masters,* page TA14). Encourage those who struggle with expand-and-trade subtraction to solve each problem with a different method and then to try expand and trade again.

✓ Assessment and Reporting   **Go Online** to record student progress and to see trajectories toward mastery for these standards.

Summarize Invite children to compare and contrast the counting-up and expand-and-trade strategies. Ask: *Which method would take less time, or be more efficient, for a problem such as 1,000 − 996? Why?* **GMP1.6** Sample answer: Counting up is more efficient because I can count up 4 from 996 to 1,000 instead of making three trades.

3 Practice 10–15 min

Go Online

ePresentations eToolkit Home Connections

▶ *Minute Math+*

To practice mental math strategies, select a *Minute Math+* activity.

▶ Comparing Data in a Bar Graph

Math Journal 1, p. 76

| WHOLE CLASS | SMALL GROUP | PARTNER | INDEPENDENT |

Have children solve comparison problems using information presented in a scaled bar graph on journal page 76.

▶ Math Boxes 3-6

Math Journal 1, p. 77

| WHOLE CLASS | SMALL GROUP | PARTNER | INDEPENDENT |

Mixed Practice Math Boxes 3-6 are paired with Math Boxes 3-8.

▶ Home Link 3-6

Math Masters, p. 90

Homework Children solve subtraction problems using strategies of their choice.

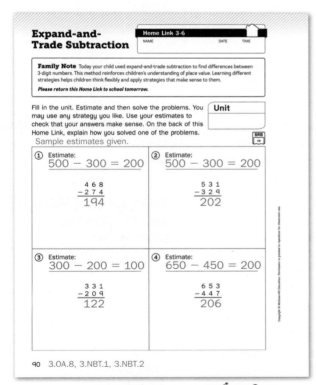

Math Masters, p. 90 *79*

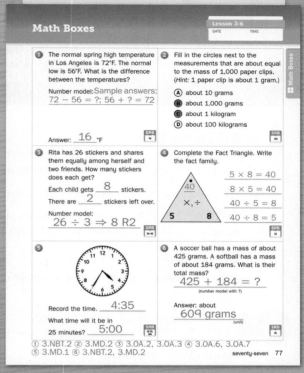

Math Journal 1, p. 77

Exploring Bar Graphs, Area, and Partitioning Rectangles

Overview Children explore different ways to measure area, partition rectangles, and represent data on a scaled bar graph.

▶ **Before You Begin**

For Exploration A: Prepare sets of pattern blocks with 14 triangles, 12 wide rhombuses, 6 hexagons, 10 narrow rhombuses, and 8 trapezoids for each small group.

For Exploration B: Make several 1-foot square templates from cardstock or disassembled cereal boxes.

For Exploration C: Prepare sets of 1 square pattern block and at least 25 centimeter cubes per child or partnership. Make additional copies of *Math Masters*, page 95.

▶ **Vocabulary**

scale • scaled bar graph • area • square units • tile • partition

Common Core State Standards

Focus Clusters
• Represent and interpret data.
• Geometric measurement: understand concepts of area and relate area to multiplication and to addition.
• Reason with shapes and their attributes.

① **Warm Up** 5 min	**Materials**	
Mental Math and Fluency Children estimate differences between 3-digit numbers.	slate	3.NBT.2

② **Focus** 45–50 min		
Math Message Children discuss setting up a bar graph.	*Math Journal 1*, p. 78	3.MD.3
Discussing a Scale for a Data Set Children discuss a scale for a data set.	*Math Journal 1*, p. 78; *Math Masters*, p. TA7	3.MD.3 SMP2, SMP6
Exploration A: Creating a Scaled Bar Graph Children graph pattern-block sorts.	Activity Card 41; *Math Journal 1*, p. 79; *Math Masters*, p. TA7 (optional); pattern blocks; collection of other objects (optional)	3.MD.3 SMP6
Exploration B: Measuring Area Children measure surfaces in square feet.	Activity Card 42; 1-foot square cardboard templates; colored paper; scissors; masking tape, square pattern blocks or centimeter cubes (optional)	3.MD.5, 3.MD.5a, 3.MD.5b, 3.MD.6, 3.MD.7, 3.MD.7a SMP6
Exploration C: Partitioning Rectangles Children connect tiling and partitioning.	*Math Masters*, pp. 94–95; 25 centimeter cubes; square pattern block	3.MD.5, 3.MD.5a, 3.MD.5b, 3.MD.6, 3.MD.7, 3.MD.7a, 3.G.2 SMP2, SMP6

③ **Practice** 10–15 min		
Minute Math+ Children practice mental math strategies.	*Minute Math®+*	
Playing *Shuffle to 100* **Game** Children estimate and make combinations that have a sum close to 100.	*Student Reference Book*, pp. 256–257; *Math Masters*, p. G10; number cards 1–9 (4 of each)	3.NBT.2 SMP1, SMP6
Math Boxes 3-7 Children practice and maintain skills.	*Math Journal 1*, p. 80	See page 265.
Home Link 3-7 **Homework** Children solve scaled bar-graph problems.	*Math Masters*, p. 96	3.MD.3 SMP4

Differentiation Options RtI

CCSS 3.MD.3, SMP2

CCSS 3.MD.5, 3.MD.5a, 3.MD.5b, 3.MD.6, 3.G.2, SMP6

CCSS 3.MD.5, 3.MD.5a, 3.MD.5b, 3.MD.6, SMP6

Readiness   10–15 min

| WHOLE CLASS |
| SMALL GROUP |
| PARTNER |
| INDEPENDENT |

Making a Scaled Bar Graph

Math Masters, p. 91

To provide experience with scaled bar graphs, have children represent data on *Math Masters,* page 91. **GMP2.1** Ask: *How should you show the data that is between the numbers on the scale?* Shade up to somewhere between two numbers. Then have children solve simple comparison problems using information in the bar graph.

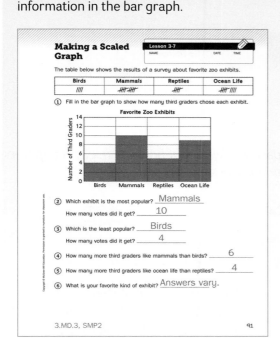

Enrichment   10–15 min

| WHOLE CLASS |
| SMALL GROUP |
| PARTNER |
| INDEPENDENT |

Partitioning Polygons

Math Masters, pp. 92–93; straightedge (optional)

To extend children's understanding of partitioning, have them partition polygons into rectangles and then into same-size squares on *Math Masters,* pages 92–93. **GMP6.4**

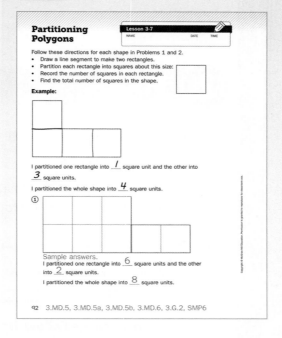

Extra Practice   5–15 min

| WHOLE CLASS |
| SMALL GROUP |
| PARTNER |
| INDEPENDENT |

Measuring Different Areas with 1-Foot Squares

1-foot squares (from Exploration B)

For additional practice measuring area, have children continue to use 1-foot squares to cover surfaces throughout the classroom or school, and compare the areas of the surfaces they measure. Remind children to measure area without gaps or overlaps between squares. **GMP6.4**

English Language Learners Support

Beginning ELL Introduce children to multiple uses of the word *scale* using a pictorial 4-Square Graphic Organizer (*Math Masters,* page TA20). In the first three quadrants, show highlighted fish scales, musical scales, and scales for weighing. In the last, show a scaled bar graph. Point to the scale along the axis and then to the weighing scales to connect the use of numbers. Note that the numbers along the bar graph are the same distance apart. Point to each quadrant, then to the term, and have children repeat *scale* to help them understand that this is a word with many different meanings.

Go Online   ELL   English Learners Support

1 Warm Up　5 min　Go Online　ePresentations　eToolkit

▶ Mental Math and Fluency

Display each set of problems. Have children estimate the differences and write the appropriate problem on their slates. Have children share how they estimated. *Leveled exercises:*

● ○ ○ *Which has a difference of about 100?*
　　115 — 49　(362 — 258)　329 — 111

● ● ○ *Which has a difference less than 200?*
　　598 — 105　382 — 113　(899 — 782)

● ● ● *Which has a difference more than 300?*
　　417 — 195　(674 — 182)　529 — 499

2 Focus　45–50 min　Go Online　ePresentations　eToolkit

▶ Math Message

Math Journal 1, p. 78

Read journal page 78 with a partner. Talk about how you might set up the graph. Be ready to share your ideas about what scale to use.

▶ Discussing a Scale for a Data Set

Math Journal 1, p. 78; *Math Masters,* p. TA7

| WHOLE CLASS | SMALL GROUP | PARTNER | INDEPENDENT |

Math Message Follow-Up Have children share what they learned from looking at Jasmine's table and graph. Ask: *What is the greatest number of minutes Jasmine spent on homework?* 45 minutes *On which day?* Monday *Least?* 17 minutes on Friday

Discuss the parts of the graph that are already labeled, including the title and the horizontal and vertical axes. Ask: *What else does Jasmine need to set up before she can graph her data?* Sample answers: the numbers along the vertical axis; the scale

Remind children that the **scale** for bar length can show any size interval. For example, it may show intervals of 1, 5, 50, or 100, depending on the data and size of the graph.

Support children as they share ideas for the scale of this bar graph. Ask: *What is the largest number we need to graph?* 45 minutes *If the scale showed intervals of 1, would our data fit on this graph? Explain.*
GMP6.2 No. The largest number would be 5, and we need to graph data up to 45 minutes.

Math Journal 1, p. 78

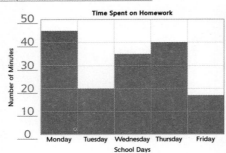

Scale for a Data Set　Lesson 3-7　DATE　TIME

Math Message

Jasmine kept a record of the number of minutes she did homework each school day.

Monday	Tuesday	Wednesday	Thursday	Friday
45	20	35	40	17

She wants to use the bar graph below to show her data. Talk with a partner about how Jasmine could set up her graph. What scale could she use for Number of Minutes?
Sample answer: Intervals of 10

Time Spent on Homework

78 seventy-eight　3.MD.3, SMP2, SMP6

If no one mentions it, suggest using a scale with intervals of 10 and record 0, 10, 20, 30, 40, and 50 along the vertical axis on *Math Masters*, page TA7 as children follow along on journal page 78.

Ask children how to use a scale of 10 to graph: GMP2.1

- **45 minutes.** Sample answer: Shade up to halfway between 40 and 50.
- **17 minutes.** Sample answer: Shade up to a little more than halfway between 10 and 20.

Have children complete the bar graph. Briefly check to make sure they used the scale to correctly shade the bars.

Tell children they will create another **scaled bar graph** based on sorting pattern blocks in an Exploration activity.

After explaining the Explorations activities, assign groups to each. Plan to spend more of your time working with children on Exploration A.

▶ Exploration A: Creating a Scaled Bar Graph

Activity Card 41; *Math Journal 1*, p. 79

| WHOLE CLASS | **SMALL GROUP** | PARTNER | INDEPENDENT |

> **NOTE** See Before You Begin and Adjusting the Activity (below) about preparing sets of pattern blocks.

Have children sort their set of pattern blocks by shape and create a scaled bar graph to show their data. If needed, support them in choosing an appropriate scale for their data. GMP2.1, GMP6.2

Children will need their data and completed graphs on journal page 79 for Lesson 3-8.

Differentiate **Adjusting the Activity**

Consider either limiting or increasing the types and number of pattern blocks. For children who struggle to graph scaled data, provide them with 2 hexagons, 8 trapezoids, and 10 triangles. Guide children to scale by 2s and construct the graph to reflect their data. For children who are ready for a challenge, provide them with large quantities of blocks to sort and graph.

Go Online   Differentiation Support

▶ Exploration B: Measuring Area

Activity Card 42

| WHOLE CLASS | SMALL GROUP | **PARTNER** | **INDEPENDENT** |

Provide 1-foot square templates and colored paper. (*See Before You Begin.*) Have children trace and cut out their own 1-foot squares.

Activity Card 41

Creating a Scaled Bar Graph
⁴¹

What You Need
Math Journal 1, page 79
A Bar Graph, page TA7 (optional)
pattern blocks
collection of objects (optional)

What To Do
Work with a small group.
1 Sort the pattern blocks by shape.
2 Record the number of pattern blocks in each group on journal page 79.
3 Choose a scale for your graph based on your data.
4 Complete your bar graph.

Talk About It
Compare your bar graph with others in your group. How are they alike? How are they different?

More You Can Do
Repeat the activity using a different collection of objects and represent the data on A Bar Graph, page TA7.

Activity Card 42

Measuring Area 2
⁴²

What You Need
1-foot square
desk, table, rug, or other rectangular surface
paper
square pattern blocks or centimeter cubes (optional)

What To Do
Work with a partner or small group.
1 Measure the area of a rectangular surface. The number of 1-foot squares it takes to completely cover the surface is the area of that surface. On paper, record your measure in square units.
2 Measure and record the area of a different rectangular surface.

Talk About It
Compare the areas of all the surfaces you measured. Which had the greatest area? Which had the smallest area?

More You Can Do
- Use square pattern blocks or centimeter cubes to measure the areas of smaller surfaces.
- Try using one block or cube to measure the area of a surface.

There are two ways to use your squares to measure area by tiling:

tiling with multiple 1-foot squares

tiling by repeatedly laying down the same 1-foot square

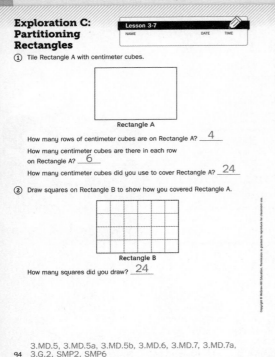
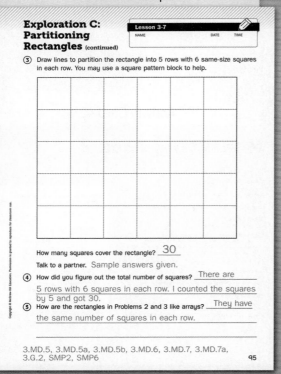
Before children complete Activity Card 42, remind them that the amount of surface inside the boundaries of a 2-dimensional shape is called the **area.** The number of squares that cover the surface is a measurement of the area in **square units.** Explain that in this exploration, they will use 1-foot squares to **tile,** or completely cover, surfaces. Model the two strategies for measuring area shown on the Activity Card.

Explain that there may be leftover space within the boundary of the surface. Ask children to think about how to estimate that space. For example, if space about the size of 2 half-squares remains, they could add 1 square foot to the area measure. Remind children that their area measures should be reported as "about ___ square feet." GMP6.4

Differentiate **Common Misconception**

Watch for children who leave gaps or overlaps between squares. Help them line up their squares end to end (provide masking tape for marking the endpoints of squares), and discuss why gaps and overlaps lead to errors in measurement.

Go Online | Differentiation Support

Store children's 1-foot squares for use in Lessons 4-7 and 4-8.

▶ **Exploration C:** Partitioning Rectangles

Math Masters, pp. 94–95

WHOLE CLASS | SMALL GROUP | **PARTNER** | **INDEPENDENT**

Children partitioned rectangles in *Second Grade Everyday Mathematics.* Remind them that to **partition** something is to divide it into smaller parts. Explain that we can find the area of a shape by dividing, or partitioning, it into equal parts.

Have children follow the directions on *Math Masters,* pages 94–95 to practice partitioning rectangles and measuring area. GMP6.4

Expect to see strategies such as tracing the square block multiple times, drawing rows or columns of squares, or drawing squares along the edge of the rectangle and then extending lines to form squares throughout the shape. GMP2.1

Summarize Ask children how the activities in Exploration B and Exploration C are similar. Sample answer: We measured the areas of shapes. In Exploration B, we put squares together to find the area. In Exploration C, we partitioned shapes into squares and counted them to find the area.

3 Practice   10–15 min   Go Online   ePresentations eToolkit Home Connections

▶ *Minute Math+*

To practice mental math strategies, select a *Minute Math+* activity.

▶ Playing *Shuffle to 100*

Student Reference Book, pp. 256–257; *Math Masters*, p. G10

| WHOLE CLASS | **SMALL GROUP** | **PARTNER** | INDEPENDENT |

Review directions for *Shuffle to 100* on *Student Reference Book*, page 256. As needed, play a round or two to remind children of the rules and share mental estimation strategies.

Observe

• How do children choose combinations that get them closest to 100? GMP6.4

Discuss

• How do you estimate the sums?

• How did you calculate your score for this turn? GMP6.1

| Differentiate | Game Modifications | Go Online | Differentiation Support |

▶ Math Boxes 3-7

Math Journal 1, p. 80

| WHOLE CLASS | SMALL GROUP | PARTNER | INDEPENDENT |

Mixed Practice Math Boxes 3-7 are paired with Math Boxes 3-5.

▶ Home Link 3-7

Math Masters, p. 96

Homework Children solve problems using a scaled bar graph. GMP4.2

Math Journal 1, p. 80

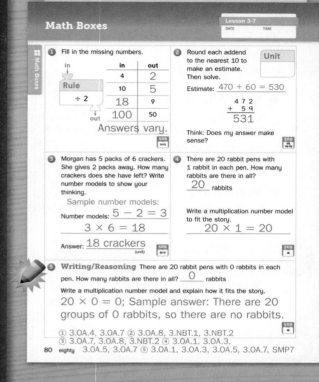

Math Boxes   Lesson 3-7   DATE   TIME

1. Fill in the missing numbers.

   Rule ÷ 2

in	out
4	2
10	5
18	9
100	50

   Answers vary.

2. Round each addend to the nearest 10 to make an estimate. Then solve.   Unit

   Estimate: 470 + 60 = 530

   ```
     4 7 2
   +   5 9
   ───────
     5 3 1
   ```

   Think: Does my answer make sense?

3. Morgan has 5 packs of 6 crackers. She gives 2 packs away. How many crackers does she have left? Write number models to show your thinking.

   Sample number models:

   Number models: 5 − 2 = 3

   3 × 6 = 18

   Answer: 18 crackers

4. There are 20 rabbit pens with 1 rabbit in each pen. How many rabbits are there in all?

   20 rabbits

   Write a multiplication number model to fit the story.

   20 × 1 = 20

5. **Writing/Reasoning** There are 20 rabbit pens with 0 rabbits in each pen. How many rabbits are there in all? 0 rabbits

   Write a multiplication number model and explain how it fits the story.

   20 × 0 = 0; Sample answer: There are 20 groups of 0 rabbits, so there are no rabbits.

① 3.OA.4, 3.OA.7 ② 3.OA.8, 3.NBT.1, 3.NBT.2
③ 3.OA.7, 3.OA.8, 3.NBT.2 ④ 3.OA.1, 3.OA.3,
80 eighty 3.OA.5, 3.OA.7 ⑤ 3.OA.1, 3.OA.3, 3.OA.5, 3.OA.7, SMP7

Math Masters, p. 96

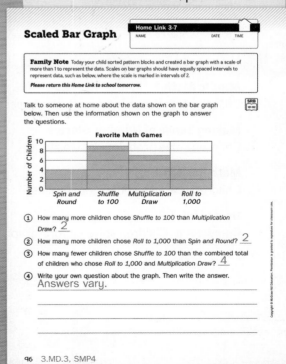

Scaled Bar Graph   Home Link 3-7   NAME   DATE   TIME

Family Note Today your child sorted pattern blocks and created a bar graph with a scale of more than 1 to represent the data. Scales on bar graphs should have equally spaced intervals to represent data, such as below, where the scale is marked in intervals of 2.

Please return this Home Link to school tomorrow.

Talk to someone at home about the data shown on the bar graph below. Then use the information shown on the graph to answer the questions.

Favorite Math Games

(bar graph with y-axis "Number of Children" marked 0, 2, 4, 6, 8, 10; x-axis: Spin and Round, Shuffle to 100, Multiplication Draw, Roll to 1,000)

① How many more children chose *Shuffle to 100* than *Multiplication Draw*? 2

② How many more children chose *Roll to 1,000* than *Spin and Round*? 2

③ How many fewer children chose *Shuffle to 100* than the combined total of children who chose *Roll to 1,000* and *Multiplication Draw*? 4

④ Write your own question about the graph. Then write the answer.
   Answers vary.

96 3.MD.3, SMP4

Scaled Picture Graphs

Overview Children create scaled picture graphs.

▶ **Before You Begin**
Children learned to skip count on calculators in *Grade 2 Everyday Mathematics*. For Part 1, if needed, refer to pages 294–295 in the *Student Reference Book*. For Part 2, children need their completed pattern-block bar graphs from Lesson 3-7. Partner those who did not complete this graph with a child who did, or provide alternative pattern-block data represented on a scaled bar graph.

▶ **Vocabulary**
scale • picture graph • key • scaled picture graph

**Common Core
State Standards**

Focus Clusters
• Use place value understanding and properties of operations to perform multi-digit arithmetic.
• Represent and interpret data.

	Materials	
1 **Warm Up** 5–10 min		
Mental Math and Fluency Children skip count using calculators.	calculator	3.OA.7

2 **Focus** 40–50 min		
Math Message Children write questions about their scaled bar graphs.	*Math Journal 1*, pp. 79 and 81; slate (optional)	3.MD.3
Exploring Scaled Bar and Picture Graphs Children ask and answer questions about their scaled bar graphs and read about picture graphs.	*Math Journal 1*, pp. 79 and 81; *Student Reference Book*, pp. 193–194; *Math Masters*, p. TA25	3.NBT.2, 3.MD.3 SMP4, SMP6
Drawing a Scaled Picture Graph Children graph given data with a scale.	*Math Journal 1*, p. 82; *Student Reference Book*, pp. 193–194 (optional)	3.NBT.2, 3.MD.3 SMP4
✓ **Assessment Check-In** See page 270.	*Math Journal 1*, p. 82	3.MD.3, SMP4

CCSS 3.MD.3 **Spiral Snapshot**

GMC Solve 1-step and 2-step problems using information in graphs.

2-9 Practice	3-2 Practice	3-4 Practice	3-6 Practice	3-8 Focus	4-2 Practice	5-5 through 5-6 Practice

 Spiral Tracker (**Go Online**) to see how mastery develops for all standards within the grade.

3 **Practice** 15–20 min		
Minute Math+ Children practice mental math strategies.	*Minute Math®+*	
Making Sense of Number Stories Children solve problems in two steps.	*Math Journal 1*, pp. 84–85	3.OA.3, 3.OA.7, 3.OA.8, 3.NBT.2 SMP1
Math Boxes 3-8 Children practice and maintain skills.	*Math Journal 1*, p. 83	See page 271.
Home Link 3-8 **Homework** Children solve picture-graph problems.	*Math Masters*, p. 99	3.MD.3, SMP4

connectED.mcgraw-hill.com

Plan your lessons online with these tools.

 ePresentations
 Student Learning Center
 Facts Workshop Game
 eToolkit
 Professional Development
 Home Connections
 Spiral Tracker
 Assessment and Reporting
 English Learners Support
 Differentiation Support

Differentiation Options RtI

CCSS 3.MD.3, SMP4

Readiness
5–10 min

WHOLE CLASS
SMALL GROUP
PARTNER
INDEPENDENT

Completing a Picture Graph

Math Masters, p. 97

To practice representing data on picture graphs, have children complete *Math Masters,* page 97. **GMP4.1** Then have them write and answer a question about the information in the graph. **GMP4.2**

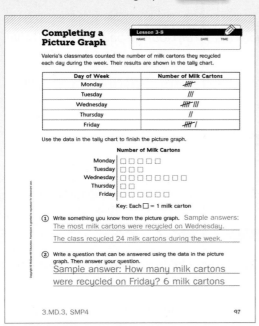

CCSS 3.MD.3, SMP4

Enrichment
15–20 min

WHOLE CLASS
SMALL GROUP
PARTNER
INDEPENDENT

Collecting and Representing Data

Activity Card 43;
Math Masters, p. TA25

To challenge children to collect and represent scaled data, have them pose a survey question and then represent the data on a scaled picture graph. **GMP4.1**

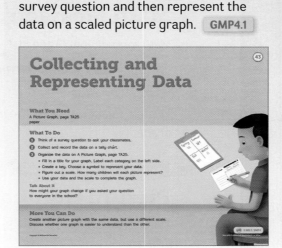

CCSS 3.MD.3, SMP4

Extra Practice
10–15 min

WHOLE CLASS
SMALL GROUP
PARTNER
INDEPENDENT

Drawing a Scaled Picture Graph

Math Masters, p. 98

For additional practice representing data, have children draw a scaled picture graph on *Math Masters,* page 98. **GMP4.1** Then have them write and answer questions about the graph. **GMP4.2**

English Language Learners Support

Beginning ELL Introduce children to the multiple uses of the word *key* by preparing a pictorial 4-Square Graphic Organizer (*Math Masters,* page TA20). In the first three quadrants, show images of a set of keys, keys on a calculator, and keys on a computer keyboard. In the last quadrant, show a picture graph and its corresponding key. Tell children that the key to a picture graph tells what each symbol means on the graph. Point to each quadrant, then to the term, and have children repeat *key* to help them understand that this is a word with many different meanings.

Go Online | **ELL** English Learners Support

1 Warm Up 5–10 min

▶ Mental Math and Fluency

To support multiplication, have children skip count using calculators. *Leveled exercises:*

● ○ ○ Count by 10s from 50 to 120. Count back by 5s from 120 to 90.

● ● ○ Count by 20s from 0 to 100. Count back by 10s from 100 to 0.

● ● ● Count by 25s from 100 up to 300. Count back by 50s from 300 to 0.

2 Focus 40–50 min

▶ Math Message

Math Journal 1, pp. 79 and 81

Carefully copy your pattern-block data from journal page 79 to the table on journal page 81.

Write a question about the information in your Pattern-Block Sort bar graph.

▶ Exploring Scaled Bar and Picture Graphs

Math Journal 1, pp. 79 and 81; *Student Reference Book,* pp. 193–194; *Math Masters,* p. TA25

| WHOLE CLASS | SMALL GROUP | PARTNER | INDEPENDENT |

Math Message Follow-Up Check that children transferred their data to use later in the lesson.

Invite a few children to display their bar graphs and pose their questions for the class to answer. **GMP4.2** If children struggle to generate questions, pose examples, such as: *How many hexagons were in this child's sort? How many rhombuses were there in all? Were there more triangles or trapezoids?*

Next ask: *Why is it important to pay attention to the **scale** on the bar graph when answering questions?* **GMP6.3** Sample answers: You have to know what the scale is before you can tell how many there are of each shape. A scale by 1s is different from a scale by 2s or 10s.

Math Journal 1, p. 81

Creating a Scaled Picture Graph

Lesson 3-8

DATE   TIME

Math Message   Answers

Copy your pattern-block data from journal page 79 into the table below. vary.

Triangle	Wide Rhombus	Narrow Rhombus	Hexagon	Trapezoid

Title: _____

_____

_____

_____

_____

_____

Key: Each ___ = _____ pattern blocks

3.NBT.2, 3.MD.3, SMP4, SMP6   eighty-one **81**

Explain that a **picture graph** uses pictures or symbols to represent data, while a bar graph uses the lengths of bars. Review picture graphs by discussing the "Favorite Foods of the Class" graph on *Student Reference Book,* page 193.

Point out the title and categories on the graph and have a child explain the **key.** GMP6.3 Each symbol means 1 child. Remind children to check the key before reading picture graphs.

As children examine the "Number of Children in Each Grade" graph on *Student Reference Book,* page 194, ask:

- *What does the key tell you?* Each smiley face means 10 children.
- *How many smiley faces are next to 3rd Grade?* 9
- *How can you figure out the number of children in 3rd Grade?* GMP4.2 Sample answers: I can count by 10s: 10, 20, 30 . . . 90. I can multiply 9 × 10 and get 90 children.

Have partners figure out the number of children in Grade 4 and Grade 5. GMP4.2 70 children and 80 children

Tell children that the "Number of Children in Each Grade" graph is an example of a **scaled picture graph** because the key tells us that each picture stands for more than one child.

Discuss the "Number of Children Who Ride a Bicycle to School" graph on *Student Reference Book,* page 194 and work through the Check Your Understanding problems with the class. Focus on using the key to determine the scale of the graph and the value of a half symbol.

Next explain that children will create a scaled picture graph using their pattern-block sort data from Lesson 3-7. Display *Math Masters,* page TA25. Have volunteers model how to fill in the title and labels for the picture graph as the other children follow along on journal page 81. GMP6.3 With the class, decide on a symbol for the key. Choose a symbol that does not resemble the shapes of the individual blocks, such as an X or a circle.

An appropriate scale for the picture graph depends on the data collected. Facilitate a discussion about the scale, such as the following. Sample discussion questions and answers match the picture graph in the margin.

Ask: *What number is the greatest in the data set?* 14 *If we used one symbol to show each block, how many symbols would we need?* 14 for the triangles, 12 for the wide rhombuses, 6 for the hexagons, 10 for the narrow rhombuses, and 8 for the trapezoids *Is there room on our graph to show this?* No.

Suggest using a scale of 2 and model representing the 14 triangles accordingly: *We need 7 symbols to show 14 triangles because 7 × 2 = 14.* Invite children to share how they determine the number of symbols needed for the other blocks. 6 × 2 = 12, so 6 symbols for the wide rhombuses; 3 × 2 = 6, so 3 symbols for the hexagons; 5 × 2 = 10, so 5 symbols for the narrow rhombuses; and 4 × 2 = 8, so 4 symbols for the trapezoids. Ask: *Will a scale of 2 work?* Yes.

Student Reference Book, 193

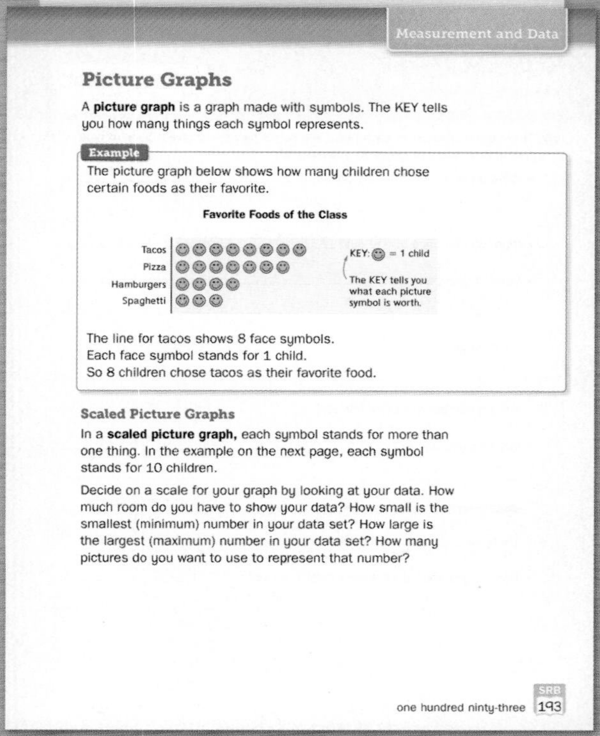

Measurement and Data

Picture Graphs

A **picture graph** is a graph made with symbols. The KEY tells you how many things each symbol represents.

Example

The picture graph below shows how many children chose certain foods as their favorite.

Favorite Foods of the Class

Tacos ☺☺☺☺☺☺☺☺
Pizza ☺☺☺☺☺☺
Hamburgers ☺☺☺☺
Spaghetti ☺☺☺

KEY: ☺ = 1 child

The KEY tells you what each picture symbol is worth.

The line for tacos shows 8 face symbols.
Each face symbol stands for 1 child.
So 8 children chose tacos as their favorite food.

Scaled Picture Graphs

In a **scaled picture graph,** each symbol stands for more than one thing. In the example on the next page, each symbol stands for 10 children.

Decide on a scale for your graph by looking at your data. How much room do you have to show your data? How small is the smallest (minimum) number in your data set? How large is the largest (maximum) number in your data set? How many pictures do you want to use to represent that number?

one hundred ninty-three SRB 193

Title: **Pattern-Block Sort**

triangle	X X X X X X X
wide rhombus	X X X X X X
hexagon	X X X
narrow rhombus	X X X X X
trapezoid	X X X X

Key: Each X = ___2___ pattern blocks

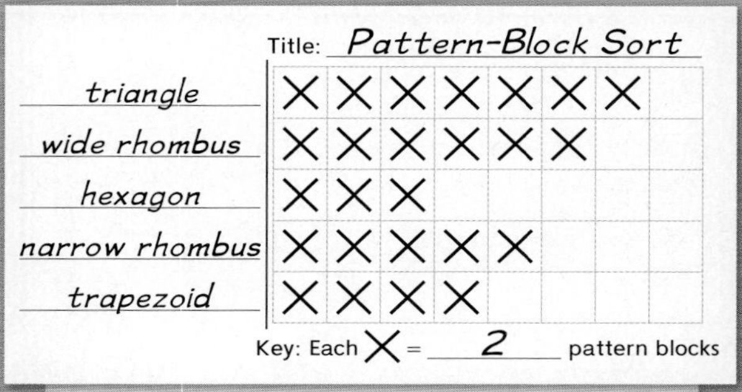

Sample pattern-block sort picture graph

Math Journal 1, p. 82

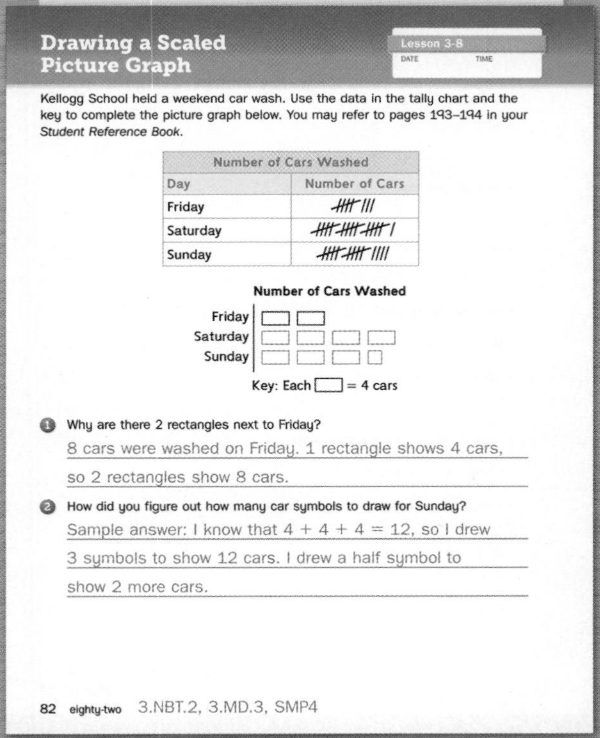

Drawing a Scaled Picture Graph

Lesson 3-8
DATE   TIME

Kellogg School held a weekend car wash. Use the data in the tally chart and the key to complete the picture graph below. You may refer to pages 193–194 in your *Student Reference Book.*

Number of Cars Washed

Day	Number of Cars
Friday	⁄⁄⁄⁄ ⁄⁄⁄
Saturday	⁄⁄⁄⁄ ⁄⁄⁄⁄ ⁄⁄⁄⁄ ⁄
Sunday	⁄⁄⁄⁄ ⁄⁄⁄⁄ ⁄⁄⁄⁄

Number of Cars Washed

Friday □ □
Saturday □ □ □ □
Sunday □ □ □ □

Key: Each □ = 4 cars

① Why are there 2 rectangles next to Friday?
8 cars were washed on Friday. 1 rectangle shows 4 cars,
so 2 rectangles show 8 cars.

② How did you figure out how many car symbols to draw for Sunday?
Sample answer: I know that 4 + 4 + 4 = 12, so I drew
3 symbols to show 12 cars. I drew a half symbol to
show 2 more cars.

82 eighty-two   3.NBT.2, 3.MD.3, SMP4

Math Journal 1, p. 84

Making Sense of Number Stories

Lesson 3-8
DATE   TIME

① There are 4 crackers in each pack. You buy 3 packs and give 1 pack to your friend. How many crackers do you have left?

• What do you know from the problem? Sample answer: I buy
3 packs of crackers with 4 in each pack. I give 1 pack
to a friend and keep the rest.

• What do you need to find out? the number of crackers I have left

• What is your plan? Sample answer: I will multiply 3 × 4 to
figure out the number of crackers in 3 packs, and then I will
subtract 4 crackers for the 1 pack I give away.

• What do you do first? Sample answer: I will find out how many
crackers are in 3 packs.

Write a number model for this step: Sample answers:
3 × 4 = 12; 4 + 4 + 4 = 12

• What do you do next? Sample answer: I still need to subtract
the 4 crackers I give away to find the number left.

Write a number model for the second step: Sample answer:
12 − 4 = 8

There are __8__ crackers left.

• How do you know your answer makes sense? Sample answers:
I have less than the total number of crackers left. I have
more than there are in 1 pack.

84 eighty-four   3.OA.3, 3.OA.7, 3.OA.8, 3.NBT.2, SMP1

Math Journal 1, p. 85

Making Sense of Number Stories (continued)

Lesson 3-8
DATE   TIME

② Each pack of crackers costs 30¢. You have $1 (100¢). How much change will you get after you buy 3 packs?

• What do you know from the problem? Sample answer: I buy 3 packs
for 30¢ each and pay with $1.

• What do you need to find out? how much change I will have
left over

• What is your plan? Sample answer: I could figure out the
amount of money spent and subtract that from $1.

• What do you do first? Sample answer: I will multiply 3 by 30¢.

Write a number model for this step: Sample answers: 3 × 30 = 90,
or 30 + 30 + 30 = 90

• What could you do next? Sample answer: I could subtract 90¢
from 100¢ to figure out my change.

Write a number model for this step: 100 − 90 = 10, or
90 + 10 = 100

I have __10__ ¢ left.

• How do you know your answer makes sense? Sample answer: I made
an estimate and figured that I would spend a little less
than $1.

3.OA.3, 3.OA.7, 3.OA.8, 3.NBT.2, SMP1   eighty-five 85

Discuss the possibility of using one symbol to show 3 blocks. Note that children would need to show part of a symbol or round to the nearest multiple of 3, so encourage them to use a scale that works better with their data.

Think aloud and invite children to test whether a scale of 4 would work. triangles: 3 and 1-half symbols; wide rhombuses: 3 symbols; hexagons: 1 and 1-half symbols; narrow rhombuses: 2 and 1-half symbols; trapezoids: 2 symbols

Continue with attempts for other scales, or have the class choose a scale of 2 or 4. Complete the key and draw symbols to represent the data on *Math Masters,* page TA25 as children complete their keys and represent their own data on journal page 81. **GMP4.1** Discuss any half symbols that are used.

Differentiate   **Adjusting the Activity**

If children struggle to interpret symbols representing more than 1 on a scaled picture graph, have them write the value above each symbol on their graph. They can skip count or add the values to find the total. Watch for children who need additional support interpreting and calculating with a half symbol. Remind them to include that value in the total.

Go Online   Differentiation Support

▶ Drawing a Scaled Picture Graph

Math Journal 1, p. 82

| WHOLE CLASS | SMALL GROUP | **PARTNER** | **INDEPENDENT** |

Have children represent given data in a scaled picture graph. Then have them make up and answer questions using information from the graph. **GMP4.1, GMP4.2** They may use *Student Reference Book,* pages 193–194 for support.

✓ **Assessment Check-In** CCSS 3.MD.3

Math Journal 1, p. 82

Children will be familiar with picture graphs from second grade, but scaled picture graphs are new to third graders. Expect children to complete Problem 1 and explain that the 2 rectangles represent the 8 cars washed on Friday. **GMP4.2**   Some children may complete the picture graph and answer Problem 2 correctly. **GMP4.1**   If children struggle, consider implementing the suggestion in the Adjusting the Activity note.

 Assessment and Reporting   **Go Online**   to record student progress and to see trajectories toward mastery for this standard.

Summarize Display one (or more) scaled bar graphs of the pattern-block data in one part of the room and scaled picture graphs of the same data in another area. Ask children to stand by the type of graph they prefer. Have the two groups explain their preference.

3 Practice

15–20 min | Go Online

ePresentations · eToolkit · Home Connections

▶ Minute Math+

To practice mental math strategies, select a *Minute Math+* activity.

▶ Making Sense of Number Stories

Math Journal 1, pp. 84–85

| WHOLE CLASS | SMALL GROUP | **PARTNER** | **INDEPENDENT** |

Have children make sense of and solve number stories involving two operations. **GMP1.1** Children may draw pictures to help. Highlight the importance of communicating their thinking about the process, not just finding a solution. **GMP6.1** You may wish to have children explain their thinking to a partner.

▶ Math Boxes 3-8

Math Journal 1, p. 83

| WHOLE CLASS | SMALL GROUP | PARTNER | INDEPENDENT |

Mixed Practice Math B_____ with Math Boxes 3-6.

_____ture graph.

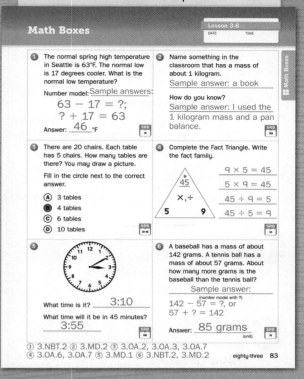

Math Journal 1, p. 83

Math Boxes — Lesson 3-8

DATE · TIME

1. The normal spring high temperature in Seattle is 63°F. The normal low is 17 degrees cooler. What is the normal low temperature?
Number model: Sample answers:
$$63 - 17 = ?;$$
$$? + 17 = 63$$
Answer: __46__ °F

2. Name something in the classroom that has a mass of about 1 kilogram.
Sample answer: a book
How do you know?
Sample answer: I used the 1 kilogram mass and a pan balance.

3. There are 20 chairs. Each table has 5 chairs. How many tables are there? You may draw a picture.
Fill in the circle next to the correct answer.
(A) 3 tables
(B) 4 tables
(C) 6 tables
(D) 10 tables

4. Complete the Fact Triangle. Write the fact family.
45, 5, 9
×,÷
$$9 \times 5 = 45$$
$$5 \times 9 = 45$$
$$45 \div 9 = 5$$
$$45 \div 5 = 9$$

5. What time is it? __3:10__
What time will it be in 45 minutes? __3:55__

6. A baseball has a mass of about 142 grams. A tennis ball has a mass of about 57 grams. About how many more grams is the baseball than the tennis ball?
Sample answer: (number model with ?)
$$142 - 57 = ?,\text{ or}$$
$$57 + ? = 142$$
Answer: __85 grams__ (unit)

① 3.NBT.2 ② 3.MD.2 ③ 3.OA.2, 3.OA.3, 3.OA.7
④ 3.OA.6, 3.OA.7 ⑤ 3.MD.1 ⑥ 3.NBT.2, 3.MD.2
eighty-three 83

Math Masters, p. 99

Interpreting a Picture Graph — Home Link 3-8

NAME · DATE · TIME

Family Note Today your child learned to read and draw picture graphs with a scale of more than one. The key on a picture graph shows a symbol that represents the scale.
Please return this Home Link to school tomorrow.

The picture graph shows how many fish each child caught on a fishing trip.

Number of Fish Caught at Clear Lake

Key: 🐟 = 2 fish

Use the graph to answer the questions.

1. How many fish did Amy catch? __2__ fish
2. How many fish did Chen catch? __8__ fish
3. How many more fish did Bill catch than Maria? __6__ fish
4. Maria catches 3 more fish. Now how many has she caught in all? __7__ fish

Revise the picture graph to show the number of fish Maria caught in all.

5. Did Chen and Max or Beth and Bill catch more fish? How many more? Explain your answer. Sample answer: Beth and Bill caught more fish than Max and Chen. Max and Chen caught 7 and 8, or 15 fish. Beth and Bill caught 11 and 10, or 21 fish. Beth and Bill caught 6 more fish.

3.MD.3, SMP4   99

Exploring Multiplication Squares

Overview Children discover the multiplication squares and begin a fact strategy journal.

▶ **Before You Begin**
For Part 2, prepare sets of 100 centimeter cubes for each partnership, and display a T-chart labeled "array" and "number sentence" on the Class Data Pad. Make sure your Fact Strategy Wall is up to date. (*See Lessons 1-8, 1-10, and 2-6.*)

▶ **Vocabulary**
factors • multiplication squares • square product

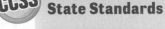
Common Core State Standards

Focus Clusters
• Represent and solve problems involving multiplication and division.
• Multiply and divide within 100.

---

1 Warm Up 5 min

Mental Math and Fluency
Children multiply to solve number stories.

Materials	
slate	3.OA.1, 3.OA.3

---

2 Focus 45–55 min

Math Message
Children sketch equal-factor arrays.
half-sheet of paper — 3.OA.1

Exploring Multiplication Squares
Children build and explore equal-factor arrays.
Math Journal 1, p. 86; *Math Masters*, p. TA19, p. TA22 (optional); centimeter cubes (100 per pair); tape; Class Data Pad — 3.OA.1, 3.OA.7 / SMP6, SMP7

✓ **Assessment Check-In**   See page 275.
Math Journal 1, p. 86 — 3.OA.1, 3.OA.7

Rolling and Recording Squares
Children solve multiplication squares and record products.
Math Masters, p. 100, p. TA20 (optional); 10-sided die — 3.OA.7 / SMP6

Introducing Multiplication Facts Strategy Logs
Children revisit the Fact Strategy Wall and record examples on My Multiplication Facts Strategy Logs.
Math Journal 1, pp. 135–140 — 3.OA.7 / SMP6, SMP7

3.OA.7 Spiral Snapshot

GMC Know all square products of 1-digit numbers automatically.

3-8 Warm Up	3-9 Focus Practice	3-10 Focus	5-1 Practice	5-8 Practice	5-9 Warm Up Focus Practice	6-2 through 6-4 Focus Practice

Spiral Tracker   **Go Online**   to see how mastery develops for all standards within the grade.

---

3 Practice 10–15 min

Minute Math+
Children practice mental math strategies.
Minute Math®+

Practicing with Fact Triangles
Children practice multiplication squares.
Math Journal 1, Activity Sheet 9; scissors; paper clips — 3.OA.7

Math Boxes 3-9
Children practice and maintain skills.
Math Journal 1, p. 87 — See page 277.

Home Link 3-9
Homework Children practice multiplication squares.
Math Masters, pp. 101–102 — 3.OA.7, 3.OA.8, 3.NBT.2

---

connectED.mcgraw-hill.com

Plan your lessons online with these tools.

 ePresentations   Student Learning Center   Facts Workshop Game   eToolkit   Professional Development   Home Connections   Spiral Tracker   Assessment and Reporting   English Learners Support   Differentiation Support

Differentiation Options RtI

CCSS 3.OA.1, 3.OA.7, SMP2

Readiness   10–15min

| WHOLE CLASS |
| SMALL GROUP |
| PARTNER |
| INDEPENDENT |

Building Arrays for Facts

Activity Card 44, centimeter cubes, Fact Triangles

To review representing multiplication facts with arrays, have children build arrays for the facts on their Fact Triangles. **GMP2.1** If children have not already sketched arrays on the backs of their Fact Triangles, they may complete that prior to or instead of this activity. (See Activity Card 44.)

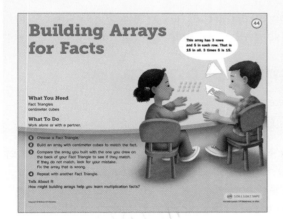

CCSS 3.OA.1, 3.OA.3, 3.OA.7, SMP7

Enrichment   15–20 min

| WHOLE CLASS |
| SMALL GROUP |
| PARTNER |
| INDEPENDENT |

Writing Multiplication-Squares Number Stories

Activity Card 45, *Sea Squares* by Joy N. Hulme, crayons and markers

To extend their understanding of square numbers, have children read **Sea Squares** by Joy N. Hulme (Hyperion Books, 1999) and write and illustrate similar number stories involving squares. This rhyming book about sea animals provides visual representations of squaring numbers one to ten. Encourage children to look for patterns in the book and their own illustrations. **GMP7.1**

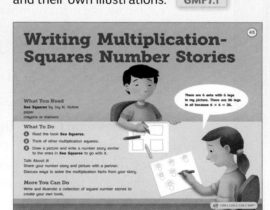

CCSS 3.OA.7

Extra Practice   5–10 min

| WHOLE CLASS |
| SMALL GROUP |
| PARTNER |
| INDEPENDENT |

Rolling and Recording Squares

Activity Card 46; *Math Masters*, p. 100; 10-sided die

For additional practice recognizing multiplication squares, have children do the Rolling and Recording Squares activity and record their work on *Math Masters*, page 100.

English Language Learners Support

Beginning ELL To scaffold the term *array*, prepare a T-chart with the headings Examples and Non-Examples. Populate the chart with images of common objects that are organized in arrays, such as egg cartons, muffin pans, or ice cube trays, and common objects that are lined up but not in arrays, such as bowling pins and stars on the U.S. flag. Provide other images for children to place on the chart. Encourage them to move their fingers across each row and up and down in each column as they say *array*.

Go Online ⟩   **ELL**   **English Learners Support**

Standards and Goals for
Mathematical Practice

SMP6 Attend to precision.
  GMP6.4 Think about accuracy and efficiency when you count, measure, and calculate.

SMP7 Look for and make use of structure.
  GMP7.1 Look for mathematical structures such as categories, patterns, and properties.
  GMP7.2 Use structures to solve problems and answer questions.

Professional Development

The multiplication squares, like the doubles in addition, tend to be easier to remember. This lesson lays a foundation for a series of fact-strategy lessons later in this unit and in Unit 5, during which children use facts they know, such as multiplication squares, to derive unknown facts by adding or subtracting a group.

Adjusting the Activity

Differentiate Some children may benefit from using inch grid paper (*Math Masters*, page TA22) to create and explore multiplication squares. Larger squares and arrays may enable them to see the patterns. Have children cut out the square arrays so they can touch, turn, and compare them.

 Go Online ▸ **Differentiation Support**

---

1 Warm Up 5 min

Go Online ▸ ePresentations eToolkit

▸ Mental Math and Fluency

Have children solve number stories on slates and share their solutions. *Leveled exercises:*

● ○ ○ You have 2 homework pages each school day. How many homework pages do you have in a 5-day school week?
10 homework pages

● ● ○ A cook places 10 grapes in each of 7 fruit cups. How many grapes are there in all? 70 grapes

● ● ● Kara has 5 stickers on each page of her journal. Her journal has 8 pages in it. How many stickers does Kara have? 40 stickers

2 Focus 45–55 min

Go Online ▸ ePresentations eToolkit

▸ Math Message

On a half-sheet of paper, draw an array that has 3 rows of Xs with 3 Xs in each row. Record a number sentence that matches your array.

▸ Exploring Multiplication Squares

Math Journal 1, p. 86; *Math Masters*, p. TA19

| WHOLE CLASS | SMALL GROUP | PARTNER | INDEPENDENT |

Math Message Follow-Up Have children share their arrays and number sentences. Ask: *What do you notice about the two **factors**, the numbers being multiplied, in the number sentence 3 × 3 = 9?* They are both 3. Tell children that today they will create and explore more arrays with equal factors.

Distribute *Math Masters*, page TA19 (Centimeter Grid Paper) and read the directions on journal page 86. Have partnerships work together to build and record arrays. Circulate and ask questions such as the following: Sample answers given.

• *How does this number sentence match this array?* The factors are the same as the number of rows and columns. The product is the same as the total number of dots in the array.

• *How are your arrays alike?* GMP7.1 They are all squares.

• *Why are they all square?* GMP7.1 They have the same number of rows and columns; the sides are the same length.

• *How did you figure out the product?* GMP7.2 I skip counted by columns. I knew part of the product and added the rest.

Support children who count by 1s by modeling how to skip count by the number of Xs in each row or to count half of the array and double to find the total. GMP6.4

✓ **Assessment Check-In** CCSS 3.OA.1, 3.OA.7

Math Journal 1, p. 86

Expect most children to create arrays and determine products for familiar multiplication squares (1 × 1, 2 × 2, 5 × 5, 10 × 10) and to notice that the arrays are squares. Encourage children who struggle to see their arrays as square to build the arrays on grid paper and trace around their perimeters.

☑ Assessment and Reporting   **Go Online** to record student progress and to see trajectories toward mastery for these standards.

Bring the class together to record the number sentences in order, 1 × 1 = 1 through 10 × 10 = 100, and the corresponding arrays on the Class Data Pad. (*See Before You Begin.*) Have children share strategies for finding products, highlighting efficient strategies such as skip counting or repeated addition. GMP6.4 Discuss children's answers to Problem 4, eliciting that every array is a square when there are the same number of columns as there are rows. GMP7.1

Explain that these facts are examples of **multiplication squares**—facts in which both factors are the same—which have **square products.** Tell children they will practice recognizing multiplication squares in the next activity.

▶ **Rolling and Recording Squares**

Math Masters, p. 100

| WHOLE CLASS | SMALL GROUP | PARTNER | INDEPENDENT |

Have children practice multiplication squares as they complete the Rolling and Recording Squares activity. Working with a volunteer, model the following steps for the class:

- Roll a 10-sided die and use the number as both factors in a multiplication-square fact. Use a strategy from the Fact Strategy Wall, such as skip counting, to find the square product efficiently and report it to your partner.

- Have your partner record the square product on *Math Masters,* page 100 by shading in the first open box in the column above that multiplication square.

- Switch roles and repeat.

Math Journal 1, p. 86

Exploring Arrays with Equal Factors   Lesson 3-9   DATE   TIME

Work with a partner.

Materials ☐ Centimeter Grid Paper (*Math Masters,* page TA19)
☐ centimeter cubes
☐ tape

Directions

① Choose a number 1 through 10. Use centimeter cubes to build an array with that number of rows and that same number of columns.

② Record the array on centimeter grid paper. Use Xs or color in each square. Write a multiplication number sentence below each array. Example:

3 × 3 = 9

③ Repeat Steps 1 and 2 with at least two other numbers. You may need to tape pieces of grid paper together for the larger arrays.

④ Look at the arrays you made. How are they similar? How are they different?

Sample answers: Each array is a square. Each one has the same number of columns as there are rows. Each number sentence has two of the same factor. When the factors are larger, the square arrays are larger. Smaller square products have smaller arrays.

86 eighty-six   3.OA.1, 3.OA.7, SMP6, SMP7

Academic Language Development

Have partnerships complete a 4-Square Graphic Organizer (*Math Masters,* page TA20) for the term *multiplication squares* showing a definition, mathematical example, non-example, and visual representation. Challenge children to use the terms *factor* and *product* in their definitions.

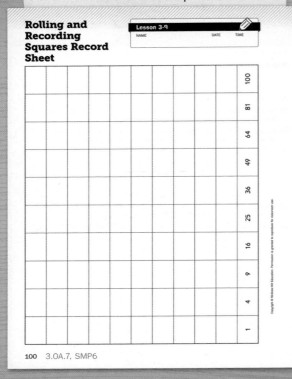

Rolling and Recording Squares Record Sheet

Lesson 3-9

NAME   DATE   TIME

100   3.OA.7, SMP6

My Multiplication Facts Strategy Log 3

DATE   TIME

Strategies for Squares

Example:

I can sketch a 4-by-4 square array and skip count by 4 to solve 4×4.

4, 8, 12, 16

so $4 \times 4 = 16$

Sketch:

× × × ×
× × × ×
× × × ×
× × × ×

My examples:

3.OA.7   one hundred thirty-seven   137

For example, if you roll a 4, think aloud: *4 × 4 = what number? I can count by 4s: 4, 8, 12, 16. 4 × 4 = 16.* Tell your partner to shade in the first open box in the column for 16. Encourage children to use square products on the record sheet and known facts to help them recognize unknown multiplication squares. For example, a child may use $9 \times 10 = 90$ to recognize 81 as the product of 9×9.

During the activity, note which multiplication squares children know and the strategies they use to solve for unknown square products

▶ Introducing Multiplication Facts Strategy Logs

Math Journal 1, pp. 135–140

| WHOLE CLASS | SMALL GROUP | PARTNER | INDEPENDENT |

Tell children that multiplication squares are just one of several groups of multiplication facts they have learned so far this year. Point out the Fact Strategy Wall and have children flip through their My Multiplication Facts Strategy Logs in the back of *Math Journal 1*, on pages 135–140. Explain to children that they will record strategies that help them learn and retain multiplication facts in their My Multiplication Facts Strategy Logs.

> **NOTE** Children will need the information from their *Math Journal 1* strategy logs when they switch to *Math Journal 2* after Unit 4.

Remind children of their work with the 0s, 1s, 2s, 5s, and 10s facts. Look at the Example strategies provided on My Multiplication Facts Strategy Log 1 and 2, journal pages 135–136. Ask children to make sense of strategies and suggest others that they could use if they forget one of these facts. Have children record the strategies and specific applications to 0s, 1s, 2s, 5s, or 10s facts. Children may also reference the Fact Strategy Wall.

Next, have children look at the Example and apply a strategy to solve another example of a multiplication square in My Multiplication Facts Strategy Log 3 on journal page 137 while you add examples to the Fact Strategy Wall. Ask: *How might you figure out square products that you do not know?* GMP7.2 Sample answers: I can skip count. I can sketch a square array and find the total number of Xs.

Tell children that 2s, 5s, and 10s facts and multiplication squares will be helpful in figuring out other facts. In spare moments, have children continue adding examples and more efficient strategies to their first three logs. GMP6.4

Summarize Ask: *What would an array for 20 × 20 look like? How do you know?* Sample answers: It would be a square. It would have 20 rows and 20 columns. I know because the factors are the same as the numbers of rows and columns.

3 Practice

10–15 min   **Go Online**   ePresentations   eToolkit   Home Connections

▶ *Minute Math+*

To practice mental math strategies, select a *Minute Math+* activity.

▶ **Practicing with Fact Triangles**

Math Journal 1, Activity Sheet 9

| WHOLE CLASS | SMALL GROUP | **PARTNER** | **INDEPENDENT** |

Have children cut out the ×,÷ Fact Triangles: Multiplication Squares from *Math Journal 1,* Activity Sheet 9. Remind them to write their initials in a corner on the backs of their triangles.

Have children find the multiplication squares among their 2s, 5s, and 10s Fact Triangles (2×2, 5×5, and 10×10). Review the procedure for using Fact Triangles, and have children focus on practicing multiplication squares. They might observe that there are only two facts in the fact family for multiplication squares, which connects to work on the Commutative Property of Multiplication in Lesson 3-10.

When time is up, remind children to clip their Fact Triangles together and store them in their toolkits.

▶ **Math Boxes 3-9**

Math Journal 1, p. 87

| WHOLE CLASS | **SMALL GROUP** | PARTNER | INDEPENDENT |

Mixed Practice Math Boxes 3-9 are paired with Math Boxes 3-12.

▶ **Home Link 3-9**

Math Masters, pp. 101–102

Homework Children cut out and practice multiplication squares Fact Triangles and repeat the Rolling and Recording Squares activity.

Math Journal 1, p. 87

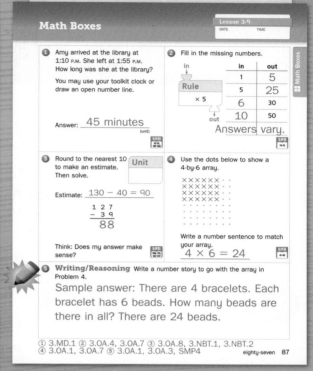

Math Masters, p. 101

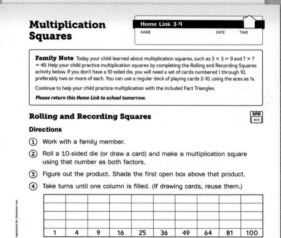

The Commutative Property of Multiplication

Overview Children learn about the turn-around rule for multiplication.

▶ **Before You Begin**
Decide where to add an example of the turn-around rule (Commutative Property of Multiplication) to your Fact Strategy Wall.

▶ **Vocabulary**
turn-around rule • Multiplication/Division Facts Table • facts table

 Common Core State Standards

Focus Clusters
• Represent and solve problems involving multiplication and division.
• Understand properties of multiplication and the relationship between multiplication and division.
• Multiply and divide within 100.
• Solve problems involving the four operations, and identify and explain patterns in arithmetic.

1 Warm Up 5–10 min

	Materials	
Mental Math and Fluency Children solve equal-grouping number stories.	slate	3.OA.2, 3.OA.3, 3.OA.7

2 Focus 40–45 min

Math Message Children represent a product with arrays.		3.OA.1, 3.OA.3
Introducing the Turn-Around Rule for Multiplication Children develop the turn-around rule for multiplication.	*Math Journal 1*, p. 88; 6-sided dice	3.OA.5, 3.OA.7 SMP8
✓ **Assessment Check-In** See page 281.	*Math Journal 1*, p. 88	3.OA.5
Introducing the Multiplication/Division Facts Table Children recognize the turn-around rule.	*Math Journal 1*, p. 138; *Math Masters*, p. TA26	3.OA.5, 3.OA.7, 3.OA.9 SMP6, SMP7, SMP8
Taking Inventory of Known Facts Children complete part of the Multiplication Facts Inventory.	*Math Journal 1*, p. 141; *Math Masters*, p. TA20 (optional)	3.OA.7 SMP6

CCSS 3.OA.5 **Spiral Snapshot**

GMC Apply properties of operations to multiply and divide.

2-6 Focus	3-10 Focus Practice	3-11 Focus Practice	3-12 Focus Practice	4-1 through 4-5 Practice	4-7 Practice	5-4 through 5-6 Warm Up Focus Practice

Spiral Tracker   **Go Online**   to see how mastery develops for all standards within the grade.

3 Practice 15–20 min

Minute Math + Children practice mental math strategies.	*Minute Math®+*	
Playing *Array Bingo* **Game** Children match arrays with multiplication facts.	*Student Reference Book*, pp. 232–233; *Math Masters*, p. TA18	3.OA.1, 3.OA.7 SMP2, SMP6
Math Boxes 3-10 Children practice and maintain skills.	*Math Journal 1*, p. 89	See page 283.
Home Link 3-10 **Homework** Children apply and explain the turn-around rule for multiplication.	*Math Masters*, p. 105	3.OA.5, 3.OA.7 SMP8

connectED.mcgraw-hill.com

Plan your lessons online with these tools.

  ePresentations   Student Learning Center   Facts Workshop Game   eToolkit   Professional Development   Home Connections   Spiral Tracker   Assessment and Reporting   English Learners Support   Differentiation Support

Differentiation Options

 RtI

CCSS 3.OA.9, 3.NBT.2, SMP7, SMP8

Readiness
5–10 min

| WHOLE CLASS |
| SMALL GROUP |
| PARTNER |
| INDEPENDENT |

Writing Facts with Dominoes

Math Masters, p. TA27 or dominoes

To prepare children for learning the turn-around rule for multiplication, have them review the turn-around rule for addition using dominoes or cutouts from *Math Masters,* page TA27. Have them choose dominoes and write corresponding addition number sentences. Then have children rotate their dominoes and write the number sentences with addends switched. Ask: *What do you notice about the number sentences?* **GMP7.1** Sample answers: The addends are the same, just turned around. The sum is the same for both. Ask children to generate additional pairs of addition facts and explain how they used the turn-around rule. **GMP8.1**

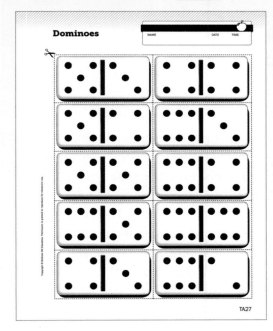

CCSS 3.OA.5, 3.OA.9, SMP3, SMP8

Enrichment
10–15 min

| WHOLE CLASS |
| SMALL GROUP |
| PARTNER |
| INDEPENDENT |

Exploring the Turn-Around Rule

Math Masters, p. 103

To extend children's understanding of the turn-around rule, challenge them to justify why the turn-around rule does not apply to division on *Math Masters,* page 103.
GMP3.1, GMP8.1

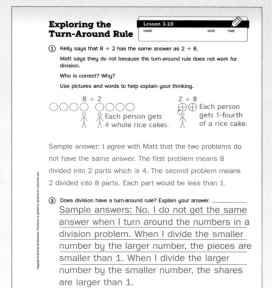

CCSS 3.OA.5, 3.OA.9, SMP7

Extra Practice
10–15 min

| WHOLE CLASS |
| SMALL GROUP |
| PARTNER |
| INDEPENDENT |

Showing the Turn-Around Rule on a Facts Table

Math Masters, p. 104; scissors

To demonstrate the turn-around rule, have children cut out and fold the Multiplication/Division Facts Table diagonally along the darker shaded squares and point out that equal factors and products fold onto themselves. Encourage children to discuss visual patterns they see on the table. The same factors appear along the top row as going down the first column. The products of two factors are the same even if you turn them around. Then have children use this pattern and the turn-around rule to help them fill in missing products and factors in the table. **GMP7.2**

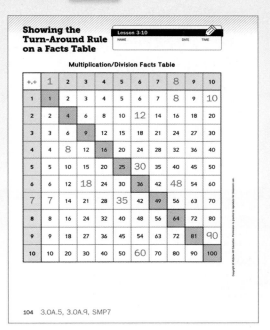

English Language Learners Support

Beginning ELL Children may understand the phrase *turn around,* as in *Turn around to face the person behind you.* To teach children that *turn around* can also mean switching or exchanging places, have pairs role-play, either by exchanging seats or moving around to stand on the opposite side. Use Total Physical Response prompts to guide children as they turn around pairs of objects so they exchange places.

Go Online **ELL** English Learners Support

SMP6 Attend to precision.
 GMP6.4 Think about accuracy and efficiency when you count, measure, and calculate.

SMP7 Look for and make use of structure.
 GMP7.2 Use structures to solve problems and answer questions.

SMP8 Look for and express regularity in repeated reasoning.
 GMP8.1 Create and justify rules, shortcuts, and generalizations.

---

① Warm Up 5–10 min
ePresentations eToolkit

▶ Mental Math and Fluency

Have children solve number stories on slates and share their solutions. *Leveled exercises:*

- ●○○ You divide 25 rulers equally among 5 groups. How many rulers does each group get? 5 rulers
- ●●○ You use 100 paper clips to make chains with 10 paper clips each. How many chains do you have? 10 chains
- ●●● You have 50 marbles and put 5 in each bag. How many bags do you need? 10 bags

---

② Focus 40–45 min
ePresentations eToolkit

▶ Math Message

You have 8 apples for sale and want to display them in an array. How many different ways can you arrange them? Make sketches on paper to show your thinking.

▶ Introducing the Turn-Around Rule for Multiplication

Math Journal 1, p. 88

| WHOLE CLASS | SMALL GROUP | PARTNER | INDEPENDENT |

Math Message Follow-Up Have children share their sketches, and acknowledge all correct arrays. 4-by-2, 2-by-4, 8-by-1, and 1-by-8 Display 4-by-2 and 2-by-4 sketches created by children. Ask: *How are the 2-by-4 array and the 4-by-2 array different?* The 2-by-4 array has 2 rows and 4 columns. The 4-by-2 array has 4 rows and 2 columns. Have children suggest number sentences to represent the arrangements and the total number of apples. Record $4 \times 2 = 8$ and $2 \times 4 = 8$ below the corresponding pictures, and ask: *What do these number sentences mean?* Sample answer: 4 rows with 2 in each row, and 2 rows with 4 in each row. *What do you notice about them?* GMP7.2 Sample answer: Both have the same product, 8, even though the factors are reversed. Tell children that they will work with similar examples to develop a rule for multiplication.

> **Professional Development** The Commutative Property of Multiplication states that for any two numbers a and b, $a \times b = b \times a$. In other words, multiplying two numbers in either order results in the same product. Third graders are expected to apply this property, but they are not expected to know the formal name or definition. In the early grades, *Everyday Mathematics* uses *turn-around rule for multiplication* as a less formal name for the Commutative Property of Multiplication.

Math Journal 1, p. 88

A Multiplication Rule Lesson 3-10
DATE   TIME

Roll a die twice to get 2 factors. Sketch an array using those 2 factors and record a number sentence to match. Switch the factors and record an array and number sentence to match.

Example: I roll a 3 and a 4:

First Array
●●●● ●●●● $3 \times 4 = 12$
●●●● ●●●●
●●●●

Second Array
●●● ●●● $4 \times 3 = 12$
●●● ●●●
●●● ●●●

① Factors I am using: _____ and _____
   First Array   Second Array

   Number sentence: Number sentence:
   _____   _____

② Factors I am using: _____ and _____
   First Array   Second Array

   Number sentence: Number sentence:
   _____   _____

What do you notice about each pair of arrays? ___Sample answers: They look the same, only turned. They both show the same product, or number of Xs.

88 eighty-eight 3.OA.5, 3.OA.7, SMP8

Discuss the example on journal page 88. Then distribute dice and have children complete the page.

✓ Assessment Check-In **CCSS** 3.OA.5

Math Journal 1, p. 88

Expect most children to generate pairs of facts and arrays that demonstrate the turn-around rule. For children who struggle, record a simple number sentence and array, such as $2 \times 3 = 6$, and then help them rotate their journals to see the turn-around rule applied: $3 \times 2 = 6$.

 Assessment and Reporting (Go Online) to record student progress and to see trajectories toward mastery for this standard.

Bring the class together to share their examples. Demonstrate or have a child turn an array pair for the class to see. Ask: *What do you notice when you turn the arrays?* Sample answers: The rows and columns switch. Turning the first array makes it look like the second array. Point to the number sentences and ask: *If you switch the factors, will you always get the same product? Explain.* **GMP8.1** Sample answer: Yes. It will always be the same because switching the factors is like turning the array—the product doesn't change, even though the rows and columns switch. Explain that this can be called the **turn-around rule** for multiplication because the factors are turned around. Record a pair of multiplication facts and remind children of the turn-around rule for addition by also displaying a pair of addition facts.

► Introducing the Multiplication/ Division Facts Table

Math Journal 1, p. 138; *Math Masters*, p. TA26

| WHOLE CLASS | SMALL GROUP | PARTNER | INDEPENDENT |

Distribute the **Multiplication/Division Facts Table** on *Math Masters,* page TA26 to each child. Point out the factors along the outer edges and have children run their finger along the row and column of factors. Explain that the products make up the inner rows and columns of the table. Help children make sense of the **facts table** by modeling how to find products. Children may highlight the facts with a sheet of paper as shown in the margin.

Have children examine the products in the shaded diagonal on the table and elicit that these products are multiplication squares. For the square fact 3×3, have children find the factor 3 along the 3-row. Go across the 3-row to the 3-column. Point out that they meet at the number 9, showing that $3 \times 3 = 9$. Ask: *What is special about the factors for a multiplication square?* They are the same. Use this idea to help children find factors for other multiplication squares in their table. **GMP7.2**

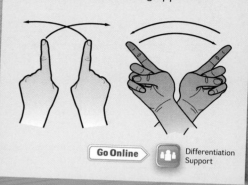
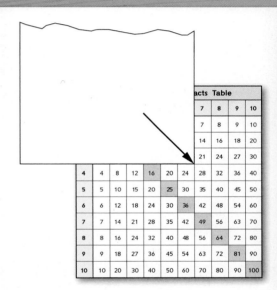

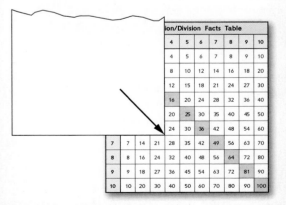

The guide may be positioned either way to show $4 \times 7 = 28$ and $7 \times 4 = 28$ or $28 \div 4 = 7$ and $28 \div 7 = 4$.

My Multiplication Facts Inventory Part 1

DATE   TIME

Multiplication Fact	Know It	Don't Know It	How I Can Figure It Out . . .
2 × 2			
10 × 5			
3 × 2			
2 × 7			
5 × 5			
9 × 2			
3 × 10			
2 × 5			
2 × 8			
5 × 4			
6 × 2			
3 × 5			
10 × 2			
2 × 4			
10 × 10			

3.OA.7, SMP6

one hundred forty-one   141

Academic Language Development

Have partnerships complete a 4-Square Graphic Organizer (*Math Masters*, page TA20) for the term *inventory* before and after the activity, with the following labels: *What We Think It Means (before), What It Actually Means, How It's Used in Math*, and *Picture Reminder*.

Next help children recognize how the two sides of the table across the diagonal are alike. Guide children in finding 4 × 7 on their table, and have them circle the factors and the product. Have them find and circle the factors and product for 7 × 4. Repeat this process with 6 × 5 and 9 × 3.

Connect children's observations to the turn-around rule by asking:

- *What do you notice about the products of each pair of facts?* They are on opposite sides of the square products. *Do you think this is true for every pair of facts with different factors? Explain.* **GMP8.1** Yes, because the factors switch but the product stays the same, so we find the product on both sides of the table.

- *How could the turn-around rule help us figure out more facts?* Sample answer: We can switch the factors of facts we know to solve more facts. Emphasize that switching the factors can make an unknown fact easier to solve. For example, it's easier to think of 7 groups of 5 and skip count by 5s than 5 groups of 7 and skip count by 7s. Tell children that the turn-around rule can help them solve multiplication facts more efficiently. **GMP6.4**

- *How would you explain the rule to someone who did not know it?* **GMP8.1** Sample answer: When we switch around the factors, the product is still the same because we have just turned the array.

Record children's strategies for applying the turn-around rule to solve facts on the Fact Strategy Wall. Have children add the turn-around rule, with examples to illustrate it, to their My Multiplication Facts Strategy Log 4 on journal page 138.

▶ Taking Inventory of Known Facts

Math Journal 1, p. 141

| WHOLE CLASS | SMALL GROUP | PARTNER | INDEPENDENT |

Introduce the My Multiplication Facts Inventory as a tool for keeping track of which facts children know. Have them mark (with a ✔ or ✗) whether they know the fact without having to think about how to solve it, or whether they still need to work on it. For the latter, have them record an efficient strategy for solving the fact. **GMP6.4** Model this for 5 × 8 by thinking aloud: *I do not know 5 × 8, but I can turn the fact around to 8 × 5 and skip count by 5 eight times to get 40.*

Have children complete only the My Multiplication Facts Inventory, Part 1 (journal page 141, behind the strategy logs). Encourage children to work slowly and thoughtfully and to be sure to read and think carefully about each fact. If children mark all the facts as known, have them practice recording helpful strategies for two or three facts of their choice. Tell children not to record products so they can try solving them again later.

Summarize Ask: *What do you notice about using the turn-around rule for 4 × 4?* Sample answers: The fact looks exactly the same. When I turn the square array, it still has 4 rows and 4 columns. 4 × 4 only appears once in the Multiplication/Division Facts Table. *Name other examples of facts that look the same after applying the turn-around rule.* Any multiplication square

3 **Practice** 15–20 min

Go Online

ePresentations ｜ eToolkit ｜ Home Connections

▶ *Minute Math+*

To practice mental math strategies, select a *Minute Math+* activity.

▶ **Playing *Array Bingo***

Student Reference Book, pp. 232–233; *Math Masters,* p. TA18

| WHOLE CLASS | **SMALL GROUP** | **PARTNER** | INDEPENDENT |

As needed, review the directions for *Array Bingo.* See Lesson 2-7 for details. As children play, refer them to the Fact Strategy Wall to help them find totals on the arrays.

Observe

- Which arrays do children instantly recognize?
- Which arrays are more difficult for them to match? GMP2.2

Discuss

- *Which arrays do you recognize easily or "just know"?*
- *Can you think of more efficient strategies you could use?* GMP6.4

Differentiate **Game Modifications** Go Online Differentiation Support

▶ **Math Boxes 3-10**

Math Journal 1, p. 89

| WHOLE CLASS | **SMALL GROUP** | **PARTNER** | **INDEPENDENT** |

Mixed Practice Math Boxes 3-10 are paired with Math Boxes 3-13.

▶ **Home Link 3-10**

Math Masters, p. 105

Homework Children practice applying and explaining the turn-around rule for multiplication. GMP8.1 They also record a strategy for a fact they need to practice.

Math Journal 1, p. 89

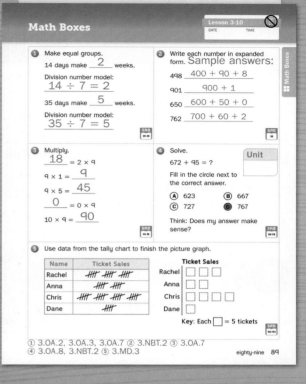

Math Boxes

Lesson 3-10

1 Make equal groups.
14 days make __2__ weeks.
Division number model:
14 ÷ 7 = 2
35 days make __5__ weeks.
Division number model:
35 ÷ 7 = 5

2 Write each number in expanded form. Sample answers:
498 __400 + 90 + 8__
901 __900 + 1__
650 __600 + 50 + 0__
762 __700 + 60 + 2__

3 Multiply.
__18__ = 2 × 9
9 × 1 = __9__
9 × 5 = __45__
__0__ = 0 × 9
10 × 9 = __90__

4 Solve.
672 + 95 = ?
Fill in the circle next to the correct answer.
(A) 623 (B) 667
(C) 727 (D) 767
Think: Does my answer make sense?

Unit

5 Use data from the tally chart to finish the picture graph.

Name	Ticket Sales
Rachel	‖‖‖ ‖‖‖ ‖‖‖
Anna	‖‖‖ ‖‖‖
Chris	‖‖‖ ‖‖‖ ‖‖‖ ‖‖‖
Dane	‖‖‖

Ticket Sales

Rachel	☐☐☐
Anna	☐☐
Chris	☐☐☐☐
Dane	☐

Key: Each ☐ = 5 tickets

① 3.OA.2, 3.OA.3, 3.OA.7 ② 3.NBT.2 ③ 3.OA.7
④ 3.OA.8, 3.NBT.2 ⑤ 3.MD.3

eighty-nine 89

Math Masters, p. 105

The Turn-Around Rule for Multiplication

Home Link 3-10

NAME DATE TIME

Family Note Today your child explored the *turn-around rule for multiplication,* which says two numbers may be multiplied in either order and the product will remain the same. *For example:* 2 × 5 = 10 and 5 × 2 = 10. Knowing this rule can help children multiply more easily. Children also took inventory of the facts they solve quickly and easily and those they still need to practice.

Please return this Home Link to school tomorrow.

Sketch an array to match each fact. Then sketch that array turned around. Record a number sentence to match the second array.

① 2 × 6 = 12 Number sentence: __6 × 2 = 12__

② 5 × 3 = 15 Number sentence: __3 × 5 = 15__

③ Use Problems 1 and 2 to tell someone why the turn-around rule works.

④ Choose a multiplication fact you need to practice. Write a strategy you can use to figure it out. Answers vary.

My fact: _____ × _____ = _____

Strategy: _____

3.OA.5, 3.OA.7, SMP8 105

Adding a Group

Overview Children develop the adding-a-group strategy for solving unknown multiplication facts.

▶ **Before You Begin**

For Part 1, select and sequence Quick Look Cards 134, 135, and 136.

For Part 2, prepare a 2-by-7 array on the Class Data Pad. Plan to add Problem 2 from journal page 91 to your Fact Strategy Wall as an example of the adding-a-group strategy.

▶ **Vocabulary**

helper fact • adding a group

Common Core State Standards

Focus Clusters
- Represent and solve problems involving multiplication and division.
- Understand properties of multiplication and the relationship between multiplication and division.
- Multiply and divide within 100.

1 Warm Up   5–10 min

	Materials	
Mental Math and Fluency Children practice Quick Looks with equal groups and arrays.	Quick Look Cards 134, 135, and 136	3.OA.1, 3.OA.7 SMP2, SMP6

2 Focus   45–55 min

Math Message Children sketch an array and solve a number story.	half-sheet of paper	3.OA.1, 3.OA.3
Exploring Adding a Group Children use helper facts to solve other multiplication facts.	*Math Journal 1,* p. 141; colored pencils; counters (optional)	3.OA.1, 3.OA.3, 3.OA.5, 3.OA.7 SMP2, SMP7
Practicing Adding a Group Children add groups to helper facts.	*Math Journal 1,* pp. 90–91 and 139; Class Data Pad; colored pencils	3.OA.1, 3.OA.3, 3.OA.5, 3.OA.7 SMP2, SMP3, SMP7
✓ **Assessment Check-In** See page 289.	*Math Journal 1,* pp. 90–91	3.OA.1, 3.OA.5, 3.OA.7

CCSS 3.OA.1   **Spiral Snapshot**

GMC Interpret multiplication in terms of equal groups.

2-6 Warm Up Focus Practice	2-7 Warm Up Focus Practice	3-9 Warm Up Focus Practice	3-10 Focus Practice	3-11 Warm Up Focus Practice	3-12 Focus Practice	3-13 Warm Up	4-2 Warm Up

III Spiral Tracker   **Go Online** to see how mastery develops for all standards within the grade.

3 Practice   10–15 min

Minute Math+ Children practice mental math strategies.	*Minute Math®+*	
Playing *Multiplication Draw* **Game** Children practice multiplication facts.	*Student Reference Book,* p. 248; *Math Masters,* p. G6; 6-sided die; number cards 1–10 (4 of each)	3.OA.7 SMP7
Math Boxes 3-11: Preview for Unit 4 Children preview skills and concepts for Unit 4.	*Math Journal 1,* p. 92	See page 291.
Home Link 3-11 **Homework** Children practice the adding-a-group strategy.	*Math Masters,* p. 107	3.OA.1, 3.OA.3, 3.OA.5, 3.OA.7 SMP7

connectED.mcgraw-hill.com

Plan your lessons online with these tools.

ePresentations   Student Learning Center   Facts Workshop Game   eToolkit   Professional Development   Home Connections   Spiral Tracker   Assessment and Reporting   English Learners Support   Differentiation Support

Differentiation Options

RtI

CCSS 3.OA.1, 3.OA.5, SMP2

Readiness
5–10 min

Adding Another Group

WHOLE CLASS
SMALL GROUP
PARTNER
INDEPENDENT

counters

To practice representing equal groups, have children build arrays with counters. Tell them to make an array with 2 rows and 3 columns. Ask: *How many rows are there?* 2 *How many columns?* 3 *How many counters in all?* 6 Have children add another row of counters to the array and ask: *How many counters did you add?* 3 *How many counters in all?* 9 Continue by having children add a group to different arrays and describe the changes. GMP2.1

CCSS 3.OA.1, 3.OA.5, 3.OA.7, SMP6

Enrichment
15–20 min

Adding a Group to Helper Facts

WHOLE CLASS
SMALL GROUP
PARTNER
INDEPENDENT

Activity Card 47, Fact Triangles, large poster paper, markers or crayons

To further apply adding a group to multiply, challenge children to make reference posters for the class that illustrate the strategy. Then have them clearly explain their work to classmates. GMP6.1

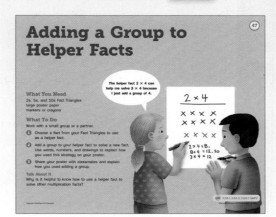

CCSS 3.OA.1, 3.OA.5, 3.OA.7, SMP7

Extra Practice
10–15 min

Solving Problems by Adding a Group

WHOLE CLASS
SMALL GROUP
PARTNER
INDEPENDENT

Math Masters, p. 106; number cards 0–10

For additional practice adding a group, have children apply the strategy to solve multiplication number stories. GMP7.2

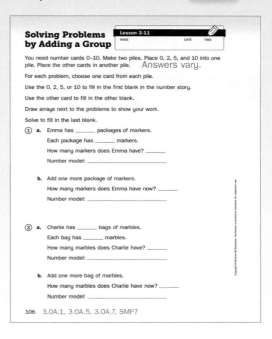

English Language Learners Support

Beginning ELL Build on children's experiences as classroom helpers to scaffold the term *helper facts*. Display *help* and *helper*. If there is a Classroom Helper chart, point to the appropriate task and ask questions, such as: *Who is this week's helper for cleaning up?* Model the use of *helper* by dropping a few items on the floor and thinking aloud: *I need help picking these up. Can you help me? Will you be my helper?* Point to the displayed words as you say them. Connect this to helper facts making it easier to multiply.

Go Online **English Learners Support**

Professional Development

Adding a group to a known product is an application of the Distributive Property of Multiplication over Addition. (See CCSS 3.OA.5.) In Unit 5, children will be introduced to the Distributive Property more formally. Implicitly using properties of multiplication is a focus of third grade. This lesson and the next will help children use familiar facts (2s, 5s, and 10s) as helper facts to determine nearby 3s, 6s, and 9s facts. Helper facts will be revisited in Unit 5 after children have had opportunities to practice adding and subtracting groups.

1 Warm Up 5–10 min Go Online ePresentations eToolkit

▶ Mental Math and Fluency

Show Quick Look Cards 134, 135, and 136 one at a time for 2–3 seconds. Ask children to share both what they saw and how they saw it. **GMP2.2, GMP6.1** Highlight strategies involving equal groups or arrays.

Quick Look Card 134 Sample answer: I saw 2 groups of 4, and I know 4 and 4 makes 8.

Quick Look Card 135 Sample answer: I saw 2 groups (or rows) of 4, and I know 4 and 4 together make 8.

Quick Look Card 136 Sample answer: I saw 3 groups of 5, and I skip counted by 5s: 5, 10, 15.

2 Focus 45–55 min Go Online ePresentations eToolkit

▶ Math Message

Suppose you are arranging chairs for a class show. On a half-sheet of paper, sketch 5 rows with 4 chairs in each row. Write a number model that shows the total number of chairs.

NOTE Review *sketches* as basic representations. Briefly discuss a quick way to represent objects, such as with Xs or circles.

▶ Exploring Adding a Group

Math Journal 1, p. 141

| WHOLE CLASS | SMALL GROUP | PARTNER | INDEPENDENT |

Math Message Follow-Up Have children share their arrays and number models.

Display an array and number model that match the Math Message. Highlight that the array and number model, $5 \times 4 = 20$, represent 5 equal groups of 4 chairs. Point to each row, saying: *Here is one group of 4, two groups of 4, three groups of 4, four groups of 4, and five groups of 4.*

Explain that another row of chairs needs to be added because more people are coming to the show. As you model doing so on your array, have children do the same on their sketch in colored pencil. Ask them to describe the new array. 6 rows with 4 chairs in each row Have them think about how to use a sketch and number model for 5 rows of 4 chairs to figure out the new total number of chairs. **GMP7.2**

Facilitate a discussion with the following questions:

- *How many rows of chairs did you add?* 1 *How many chairs are in that 1 row?* 4
- *How is this array different from the 5-by-4 array?* `GMP2.3` Sample answers: It has 6 rows of 4. It has one more row of 4 chairs.
- *What is a multiplication number model for your new array?* $6 \times 4 = 24$
- *How is this number model different from the first number model?* Sample answer: 6×4 has one more group of 4 than 5×4.

Invite children to share how the first fact, 5×4, can help them determine the product of the related fact, 6×4. `GMP7.2` If no one mentions it, connect the facts by thinking aloud: *We started with 5 groups of 4 chairs, and then we added another group of 4 chairs. So there are now 6 rows of 4 chairs, or 6 × 4 chairs, which is 4 more than 5 × 4 chairs.* Have a few children express this idea in their own words. Record $20 + 4 = 24$ as the intermediate step to help children connect $6 \times 4 = 24$ to 4 more than $5 \times 4 = 20$. Visually connect each number model with the appropriate array. `GMP2.3`

Explain to children that 5×4 is a **helper fact** because it helped them figure out 6×4. Tell children that they will use helper facts, or facts they know, to help them figure out facts they may not know. The My Multiplication Facts Inventory Part 1 (journal page 141), introduced in Lesson 3-10, is helpful for identifying helper facts such as 2s, 5s, and 10s.

Explain that today children will continue to use helper facts and sketches to practice the strategy called **adding a group.** Ask: *Why can we call using 5 × 4 to solve 6 × 4 adding a group?* Sample answer: Because we added one more group of 4.

Pose the following problem: *Javon has 2 boxes of crayons with 8 crayons in each box. How many crayons does he have all together?* 16 crayons

Have children make sketches and share a number model to fit the story. $2 \times 8 = 16$ Next have partnerships use their sketches and solutions to figure out the number of crayons in 3 boxes. `GMP7.2` 24 crayons Emphasize that they should add to their sketch showing 2 groups of 8 rather than drawing a new sketch of 3 groups of 8.

Have children share their ideas and connect it to adding a group:

- *How many crayons are in the box we are adding?* 8 crayons
- *How did you use your first sketch to show the additional box of crayons?* Sample answers: I drew a third box with 8 lines. I drew another row of 8.
- *How could you use your first product to find the new total number of crayons?* Sample answer: I could add 8 to 16 to get 24.
- *What number model fits your sketch now?* $3 \times 8 = 24$

Explain that children added a group of 8 to the helper fact 2×8 to solve 3×8.

$5 \times 4 = 20$ and $20 + 4 = 24$, so $6 \times 4 = 24$

Common Misconception

Differentiate If children start from their first product and add 1 (rather than one group), remind them of the problem's context. Have them act it out with counters or explain their drawings. Encourage children to think about what *adding a row* or *group of objects* means.

`Go Online` Differentiation Support

$2 \times 8 = 16, 16 + 8 = 24$, so $3 \times 8 = 24$

Math Journal 1, p. 90

Adding a Group

Lesson 3-11
DATE   TIME

1. Sketch a picture to show 2 rows of jars with 7 jars in each row. How many jars are there in all?

```
x x x x x x x
x x x x x x x
o o o o o o o
```

Multiplication number model: __2__ × __7__ = __14__

Use a colored pencil to add another row of jars to show **3 rows** of 7 jars in each row.

I added one group of __7__ jars.

Write a number model to describe your new picture.
3 × 7 = 21; 2 × 7 + 7 = 21 or 14 + 7 = 21

How did knowing 2 × 7 help you figure out 3 × 7?
Sample answer: I know that 2 × 7 is 14, so I can add 1 more group of 7 to get 3 rows of 7. So I add 14 + 7, which is 21.

90 ninety   3.OA.1, 3.OA.3, 3.OA.5, 3.OA.7, SMP2, SMP3, SMP7

Math Journal 1, p. 91

Adding a Group (continued)

Lesson 3-11
DATE   TIME

2. Suppose you do not know the answer to 6 × 3 = ?.
Helper fact: 5 × 3 = __15__

Use pictures, numbers, or words to show how you can use 5 × 3 to help you figure out 6 × 3. Solve.
Sample answer:

```
x x x
x x x
x x x
x x x
x x x
o o o
```

5 × 3 = 15, 15 + 3 = 18, so 6 × 3 = 18

6 × 3 = __18__

Try This

Write a fact you do not know. Then write a helper fact that can help you solve it.
Fact: _____ × _____ = ?

Helper Fact: _____ × _____ = _____

Use pictures, numbers, or words to show how you can use your helper fact to solve a new fact. Solve.

Answers vary.
_____ × _____ = _____

3.OA.1, 3.OA.3, 3.OA.5, 3.OA.7, SMP2, SMP3, SMP7   ninety-one 91

Differentiate **Adjusting the Activity**

To act out adding a group, have 16 volunteers arrange themselves into 2 groups of 8, or a 2-by-8 array. (You may prefer smaller facts, depending on class size.) Ask children to describe what they see. Sample answers: I see 2 groups of 8 children. I see 16 children in two equal groups. Add a group of children to make 3 groups of 8. Ask: *What do you see now?* Sample answers: Now there are 3 groups of 8. We added one group of 8 to 16, so now there are 24 children. Highlight that a group was added to 2 × 8 to solve 3 × 8.

Go Online ▸   Differentiation Support

In the next activity, children will practice adding a group to a helper fact to find a new product. Although some children may already know some of the new facts, it is important that they learn the adding-a-group strategy. This strategy can help them figure out and remember other facts they do not know.

▶ **Practicing Adding a Group**

Math Journal 1, pp. 90–91 and 139

| WHOLE CLASS | SMALL GROUP | PARTNER | INDEPENDENT |

Have partnerships practice the adding-a-group strategy on journal pages 90–91. Before children begin work, read each problem with the class and discuss possible solution strategies. Emphasize that children should use helper facts and sketches to figure out the related facts. GMP7.2 As you circulate, ask questions such as:

- *For Problem 1, how many groups of 7 did you start with?* 2 *How many jars are there in all?* 14

- *How many groups of 7 did you add?* 1 *How many jars are there now?* Sample answers: 21; 2 × 7 + 7; 14 + 7

- *How could you use 2 × 7 to help you figure out 3 × 7? How might you make your array show this?* GMP2.3, GMP7.2 Sample answer: I add one more group of 7 to my first total of 14. I add one more row of 7 to my array.

Differentiate **Common Misconception**

Watch for children who add on to the wrong factor. For example, to use 2 × 7 to help with 3 × 7, they might add a column of 2 to their array, or 14 + 2. Redirect children by asking: *What does 2 × 7 mean here?* 2 rows of 7 *What does 3 × 7 mean?* 3 rows of 7 *So what do you need to add?* Another row of 7

Go Online ▸   Differentiation Support

- *For Problem 2, what is 5 × 3?* 15 *What does 5 × 3 mean?* 5 groups of 3

- *If 5 × 3 (5 groups of 3) is 15, what is 6 × 3 (6 groups of 3)?* 18 *How do you know?* GMP7.2 Sample answer: I added one group of 3 to 15, and 15 + 3 = 18.

✓ **Assessment Check-In** (CCSS) **3.OA.1, 3.OA.5, 3.OA.7**

Math Journal 1, pp. 90–91

Expect most children to know the products for the helper facts and solve the related multiplication facts using arrays or other representations for Problems 1 and 2. If children do not know the products of helper facts, encourage them to use strategies such as skip counting or repeated addition. To support children with making arrays, restate the helper facts as _____ *groups of* _____. Because this is their first exposure to this strategy, children may struggle to add a group to helper facts to derive new facts.

✓ Assessment and Reporting ⟨ **Go Online** ⟩ to record student progress and to see trajectories toward mastery for these standards.

When most children are finished, have them share strategies for using 2 × 7 to help solve 3 × 7 in Problem 1. Invite a child to use a different-color marker to model adding another group of 7 to the 2-by-7 array on the Class Data Pad. (*See Before You Begin.*) Ask: *Why didn't your classmate draw a new 3-by-7 array?* GMP2.3, GMP3.2, GMP7.2 Sample answers: It is faster to add a row to the 2-by-7 array. You can add 7 to 14 to figure out that 3 × 7 is 21. You can add 7 to 14 in your head.

Have children share their number models with the class, or model recording an intermediate step for the problem, such as 2 × 7 = 14, 14 + 7 = 21, so 3 × 7 = 21. Recording thinking with number models will be addressed again in Unit 5.

Next guide children in recording Problem 2 (5 × 3 helps with 6 × 3) to show the adding-a-group strategy in their My Multiplication Facts Strategy Log 5, journal page 139 while you add it to the Fact Strategy Wall. Remind children to also use the example problem as a guide and include additional facts as time permits. Children may also add more examples in spare moments.

Adding a Group
Fact: 6 × 3 = ?
Helper Fact: 5 × 3 = 15

× × ×
× × ×
× × ×   *I add one group of 3.*
× × ×   *15 + 3 = 18*
× × ×   *6 × 3 = 18*
× × ×

Adding a Group on the Fact Strategy Wall

Summarize Ask: *How do you know whether a fact is a helper fact for you?* Sample answers: I can answer it quickly. It is easy. I know it. Remind children that they can use facts they marked as "I know it" on the My Multiplication Facts Inventory pages as helper facts.

Math Journal 1, p. 139

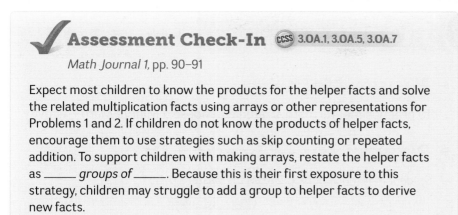

My Multiplication Facts Strategy Log 5

DATE   TIME

Strategy: Adding a Group

Example: 3 × 8 = ?   Sketch:

Helper fact: 2 × 8 = 16

I start with 2 groups of 8.

I add 1 group of 8 to find 3 groups of 8.

16 + 8 = 24, so 3 × 8 = 24.

My examples: Sketch:
  Fact: _____ × _____ = _____
  Helper Fact: _____ × _____ = _____

                                              Sketch:
  Fact: _____ × _____ = _____
  Helper Fact: _____ × _____ = _____

3.OA.7   one hundred thirty-nine   139

3 Practice   10–15 min   Go Online

ePresentations   eToolkit   Home Connections

▶ Minute Math+

To practice mental math strategies, choose a *Minute Math+* activity.

▶ Playing *Multiplication Draw*

Student Reference Book, p. 248; *Math Masters*, p. G6

| WHOLE CLASS | SMALL GROUP | **PARTNER** | INDEPENDENT |

To provide facts practice, have children play an advanced version of *Multiplication Draw* by rolling a regular 6-sided die and drawing a number card to generate a fact. Have children record their results on *Math Masters*, page G6. See Lesson 1-10 for details.

Observe

- What strategies do children use to solve multiplication facts?
- Which facts do children solve fluently?

Discuss

- *Did you use the adding-a-group strategy? For which fact? What other strategies could you use?*   GMP7.2

| Differentiate | Game Modifications | Go Online | Differentiation Support |

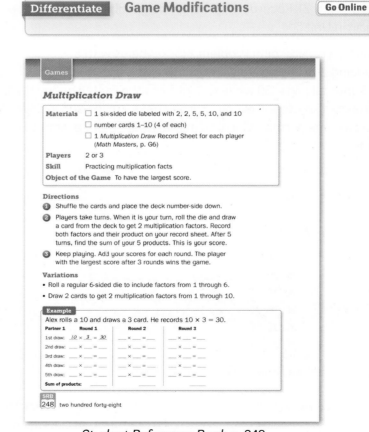

Student Reference Book, p. 248

▶ **Math Boxes 3-11:** Preview for Unit 4

Math Journal 1, p. 92

| WHOLE CLASS | SMALL GROUP | PARTNER | INDEPENDENT |

Mixed Practice Math Boxes 3-11 are paired with Preview Math Boxes 3-14. These problems focus on skills and understandings that are prerequisite for Unit 4. You may want to use information from these Math Boxes to plan instruction and grouping in Unit 4.

▶ **Home Link 3-11**

Math Masters, p. 107

Homework Children practice the adding-a-group strategy. `GMP7.2`

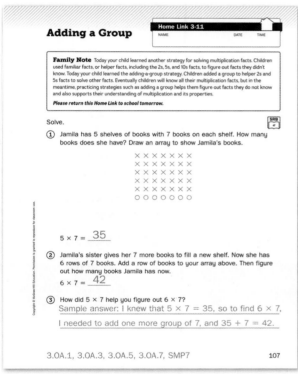

Math Masters, p. 107

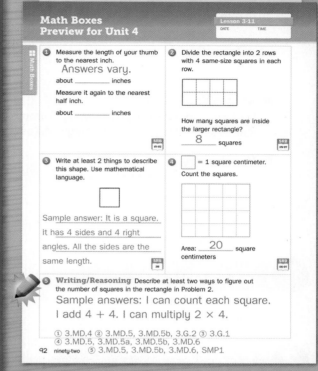

Math Journal 1, p. 92

Subtracting a Group

Overview Children develop the subtracting-a-group strategy.

▶ **Before You Begin**
For Part 2, prepare a display showing 10 groups of 4 on the Class Data Pad. Plan to add Problem 2 on journal page 94 to your Fact Strategy Wall as an example of the subtracting-a-group strategy.

▶ **Vocabulary**
helper fact • subtracting a group

 Common Core State Standards

Focus Clusters
• Represent and solve problems involving multiplication and division.
• Understand properties of multiplication and the relationship between multiplication and division.
• Multiply and divide within 100.

---

1 Warm Up 5 min

	Materials	
Mental Math and Fluency Children solve 2s, 5s, and 10s facts.	slate	3.OA.4, 3.OA.7

---

2 Focus 45–55 min

Math Message Children sketch an array and solve a number story.	half-sheet of paper	3.OA.1, 3.OA.3
Exploring Subtracting a Group Children use helper facts to solve other multiplication facts.		3.OA.1, 3.OA.3, 3.OA.5, 3.OA.7 SMP2, SMP7
Practicing Subtracting a Group Children subtract groups from helper facts.	*Math Journal 1*, pp. 93–94 and 140; Class Data Pad	3.OA.1, 3.OA.3, 3.OA.5, 3.OA.7 SMP2, SMP7
✓ **Assessment Check-In** See page 296.	*Math Journal 1*, pp. 93–94	3.OA.1, 3.OA.5, 3.OA.7

CCSS 3.OA.7 Spiral Snapshot

GMC Know all the products of 1-digit numbers ×1, ×2, ×5, ×10 automatically.

2-11 Focus Practice	3-1 Focus Practice	3-5 Practice	3-10 Warm Up	3-11 Warm Up Focus Practice	3-12 Warm Up Focus Practice	3-13 Warm Up Focus Practice	4-1 Warm Up Practice

Spiral Tracker (**Go Online**) to see how mastery develops for all standards within the grade.

---

3 Practice 10–15 min

Minute Math+ Children practice mental math strategies.	*Minute Math®+*	
Practicing with Fact Triangles Children sketch arrays on the 3s and 9s Fact Triangles.	*Math Journal 1*, Activity Sheet 10; scissors; counters (optional)	3.OA.1, 3.OA.7 SMP2
Math Boxes 3-12 Children practice and maintain skills.	*Math Journal 1*, p. 95	See page 297.
Home Link 3-12 **Homework** Children practice the subtracting-a-group strategy.	*Math Masters*, pp. 109–110	3.OA.1, 3.OA.5, 3.OA.7 SMP7

---

connectED.mcgraw-hill.com

Plan your lessons online with these tools.

 ePresentations
 Student Learning Center
 Facts Workshop Game
 eToolkit
 Professional Development
 Home Connections
 Spiral Tracker
 Assessment and Reporting
 English Learners Support
 Differentiation Support

Differentiation Options RtI

CCSS 3.OA.1, 3.OA.5, SMP2

Readiness   5–10 min

Subtracting Another Group

WHOLE CLASS
SMALL GROUP
PARTNER
INDEPENDENT

counters

To practice representing equal groups, have children make an array with 3 rows and 5 columns. Ask: *How many rows are there?* 3 *How many columns?* 5 *How many counters in all?* 15 Have children remove a row of counters from the array and ask: *How many counters did you subtract?* 5 *How many counters are there now?* 10 Continue by having children subtract a group from different arrays and describe the changes. GMP2.1

CCSS 3.OA.1, 3.OA.5, 3.OA.7, SMP6

Enrichment   15–20 min

Subtracting a Group from Helper Facts

WHOLE CLASS
SMALL GROUP
PARTNER
INDEPENDENT

Activity Card 48; 2s, 5s, and 10s Fact Triangles; large poster paper, markers or crayons

To further apply subtracting a group in order to multiply, challenge children to make reference posters that illustrate the strategy. Then have them clearly explain their work to classmates. GMP6.1

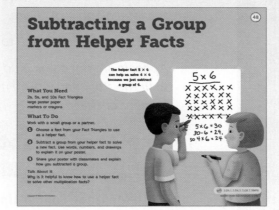

CCSS 3.OA.1, 3.OA.5, 3.OA.7, SMP7

Extra Practice   10–15 min

Solving Problems by Subtracting a Group

WHOLE CLASS
SMALL GROUP
PARTNER
INDEPENDENT

Math Masters, p. 108; number cards 0–10

For additional practice subtracting a group, have children apply the strategy to solve multiplication number stories. GMP7.2

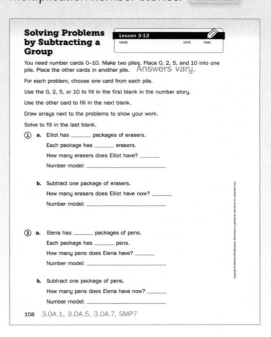

English Language Learners Support

Beginning ELL Think aloud while displaying a pair of objects that are equal but not identical, such as a dime and 10 pennies. Say: *I have 1 dime and 10 pennies. They look different but are the same amount.* Then replace one of the amounts with one that is noticeably different, like a dollar bill. Say: *This one is not like the other. This one is different. The amounts do not match. They don't go together.* Build on the term *match* to explain arrays and number models that go together because they are different ways of representing the same number. Have children point to the number model and array and say: *The number model and array match.* _____ × _____ *goes with this array.*

Go Online   ELL   English Learners Support

SMP2 **Reason abstractly and quantitatively.**
GMP2.1 Create mathematical representations using numbers, words, pictures, symbols, gestures, tables, graphs, and concrete objects.

GMP2.3 Make connections between representations.

SMP7 **Look for and make use of structure.**
GMP7.2 Use structures to solve problems and answer questions.

Professional Development

The adding- and subtracting-a-group strategies for deriving solutions to unknown facts are introduced with visual representations, such as arrays. Allow children to move away from using visual support for these strategies at their own pace, connecting the strategies to number models as they are ready. Given opportunities for meaningful practice with facts, children will apply strategies more efficiently over time. For more information about adding- and subtracting-a-group strategies, see the Mathematical Background in the Unit Organizer.

$5 \times 4 = 20$

$20 - 4 = 16$ $4 \times 4 = 16$

---

① Warm Up   5 min   [Go Online]
    ePresentations   eToolkit

▶ Mental Math and Fluency

Pose the following facts. Have children record the products on slates.
Leveled exercises:

●○○ $2 \times 5 = ?$ 10 $2 \times 6 = ?$ 12 $2 \times 7 = ?$ 14

●●○ $10 \times 3 = ?$ 30 $10 \times 4 = ?$ 40 $10 \times 5 = ?$ 50

●●● $4 \times 5 = ?$ 20 $5 \times 5 = ?$ 25 $6 \times 5 = ?$ 30

② Focus   45–55 min   [Go Online]
    ePresentations   eToolkit

▶ Math Message

On a half-sheet of paper, sketch an array like you made for the last lesson:

There are 5 rows of 4 chairs for a class show. Write a number model for the total number of chairs.

Then change your sketch to fit this situation—do not draw a new sketch:

4 people are not coming, so you need 4 fewer chairs. Change your sketch to fit the story and write a number model that shows the new total number of chairs.

▶ Exploring Subtracting a Group

| WHOLE CLASS | SMALL GROUP | PARTNER | INDEPENDENT |

Math Message Follow-Up Have children share how they changed their sketches to show that 4 fewer chairs are needed. Sample answer: I crossed out a row of 4 chairs. (*See margin.*) If children struggle to make sense of the new situation, ask:

- *How many rows of chairs did you take away?* 1 *How many chairs were in that row?* 4
- *How is this array different from the 5-by-4 array?* **GMP2.3, GMP7.2** Sample answers: It has 4 rows of 4. It has one fewer row.
- *What is a multiplication number model for your new array?* $4 \times 4 = 16$
- *How is this number model different from the first number model?* **GMP7.2** Sample answer: 4×4 has one fewer group of 4 than 5×4.

Invite children to share how 5 × 4 helped them determine the product of the related fact 4 × 4. **GMP7.2** Connect the facts by thinking aloud: *We started with 5 groups of 4 chairs. Then we subtracted a group of 4 chairs. So there are now 4 rows of 4 chairs, or 4 × 4 chairs, which is 4 less than 5 × 4 chairs.* Have a few children express this idea in their own words. Record 20 − 4 = 16 as the intermediate step to help children connect 4 × 4 = 16 to 4 less than 5 × 4 = 20. Visually connect each number model with the appropriate array. **GMP2.3, GMP7.2**

Explain to children that 5 × 4 is a **helper fact** because it helped them figure out 4 × 4. Tell them that this strategy is called **subtracting a group.** Remind children that in the previous lesson, 5 × 4 helped them to figure out 6 × 4 when a group was added, so helper facts can be used to solve multiple related facts.

Ask children to create a sketch to show how they could solve the following:

Danielle has 10 toy tricycles that each have 3 wheels. How many wheels are there all together?

Allow children time to figure out the total number of wheels, and then invite a few children to share their sketches. Ask: *What number model fits this story?* Sample answer: 10 × 3 = 30 Explain that they can use this helper fact to solve the next part of the number story.

Danielle lost 1 tricycle. How many total wheels are there now? 27 Discuss strategies by asking questions such as:

- *How can the helper fact, 10 × 3 = 30, help us find the number of wheels in 9 tricycles?* **GMP7.2** We need to take away 1 group of 3 wheels from 30 total wheels.

- *Why do you need to take away 3 wheels?* Sample answer: Tricycles have 3 wheels. There were 10 tricycles and then Danielle lost 1, so I need to take away 1 group of 3 wheels.

- *How many wheels are on 9 tricycles?* 27 wheels *What multiplication number model can represent this?* 9 × 3 = 27

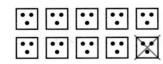

$$10 \times 3 = 30$$
$$30 - 3 = 27$$
$$so\ 9 \times 3 = 27$$

Adjusting the Activity

Differentiate If children start over with a new array or picture when moving from the helper fact to the unknown fact, help them connect their sketches. For example, some children may draw one picture to show 10 × 3 and draw another picture to show 9 × 3. Guide them to start with the sketch of the helper fact and change it to reflect one less group, modeling as needed. Emphasize that changing one sketch is easier than drawing two different sketches.

 Go Online Differentiation Support

Subtracting a Group

① Sketch a picture to show 10 toy cars with 4 wheels on each car.
How many wheels are there in all?

Multiplication number model: __10__ × __4__ = __40__

Use a colored pencil to change your picture to show the number of wheels on
9 toy cars with 4 wheels on each car.

Explain what you did.
Sample answer: Each group shows the wheels on one car.
I crossed out one group of wheels because there is one
less car.

Write a number model to describe your new picture. Sample answers:
9 × 4 = 36; 10 × 4 − 4 = 36 or 40 − 4 = 36

How did knowing 10 × 4 help you figure out 9 × 4?
Sample answer: I know 10 × 4 = 40, and 9 × 4 is one
less group of 4, so I subtract 4 from 40 to get 36.
So 9 × 4 = 36.

3.OA.1, 3.OA.3, 3.OA.5, 3.OA.7, SMP2, SMP7   ninety-three   93

Subtracting a Group (continued)

② Suppose you do not know the answer to 4 × 7 = ?.
Helper fact: 5 × 7 = __35__

Use pictures, numbers, or words to show how
you can use 5 × 7 to help figure out 4 × 7. Solve.

Sample answer:

5 × 7 = 35, 35 − 7 = 28, so 4 × 7 = 28.

4 × 7 = __28__

Try This

Write a fact you do not know. Then write a helper fact you can use to help solve it.

Fact: ___ × ___

Helper fact: ___ × ___ = ___

Use pictures, numbers, or words to show how you can use your helper fact to solve
an unknown fact. Solve.

Answers vary.

___ × ___ = ___

94   ninety-four   3.OA.1, 3.OA.3, 3.OA.5, 3.OA.7, SMP2, SMP7

▶ Practicing Subtracting a Group

Math Journal 1, pp. 93–94 and 140

| WHOLE CLASS | **SMALL GROUP** | **PARTNER** | INDEPENDENT |

Have partners practice the subtracting-a-group strategy by solving
Problems 1 and 2 on journal pages 93–94. Before children begin work,
read each problem with the class and discuss possible solution strategies.
As children work, help them connect the helper fact to the related fact.
Encourage children who start new sketches to work from their original
sketch.

Circulate and ask questions, such as:

- *What helper fact does your first sketch show?* 10 × 4 = 40
- *How does your sketch show this fact?* Sample answer: It shows
  10 groups of 4 toy cars each.
- *How did you change your sketch to show 9 groups of toy cars?*
  Sample answer: I crossed off one group of 4.
- *What is the number model for the new sketch?* 9 × 4 = 36

 Assessment Check-In **CCSS** 3.OA.1, 3.OA.5, 3.OA.7

Math Journal 1, pp. 93–94

Expect most children to know the products of the helper facts and to solve
the related multiplication facts using arrays or other representations in
Problems 1 and 2. If children do not know the products of helper facts,
encourage them to use strategies such as skip counting or repeated
addition. To support children with making arrays, restate the helper facts
as _____ *groups of* _____. Because this is their first exposure to this
strategy, children may struggle to subtract a group from helper facts to
derive new facts.

 Assessment and Reporting   **Go Online** ▷ to record student progress and to see trajectories
toward mastery for these standards.

When most children have finished, discuss their strategies for Problem 1.
Ask: *How can you use 10 × 4 = 40 to figure out 9 × 4?* **GMP7.2** Sample
answer: I can subtract one group of 4 from 40. 40 − 4 = 36. So 9 × 4 = 36.
Invite a child to demonstrate this process using the sketch on the Class
Data Pad. (*See Before You Begin.*) Have children share their number
models with the class, or model recording an intermediate step in the
problem, such as 10 × 4 = 40, 40 − 4 = 36, so 9 × 4 = 36.

Next guide children in recording Problem 2 (5 × 7 helps with 4 × 7) as an
example of the subtracting-a-group strategy on journal page 140 while you
add it to the Fact Strategy Wall. Remind children to also use the example
problem as a guide and include additional facts as time permits. Children
may also add more examples in spare moments.

Summarize Ask: *If you wanted to solve 4 × 8 using the subtracting-a-
group strategy, what helper fact could you use? How would you do it?*
Sample answer: I could start with the helper fact 5 × 8 and subtract one
group of 8, so 40 − 8 = 32.

③ Practice   10–15 min   Go Online

ePresentations   eToolkit   Home Connections

▶ Minute Math+

To practice mental math strategies, choose a *Minute Math+* activity.

▶ Practicing with Fact Triangles

Math Journal 1, Activity Sheet 10

| WHOLE CLASS | SMALL GROUP | **PARTNER** | **INDEPENDENT** |

Have children cut out the 3s and 9s ×,÷ Fact Triangles (*Math Journal 1,* Activity Sheet 10). Remind children to write their initials in one of the corners on the backs of their triangles.

Over the next few days, have children sketch arrays that match each of the facts on the backs of their Fact Triangles. GMP2.1, GMP2.3 If children struggle to draw arrays, you may want them to first build arrays with counters.

▶ Math Boxes 3-12

Math Journal 1, p. 95

| WHOLE CLASS | **SMALL GROUP** | **PARTNER** | **INDEPENDENT** |

Mixed Practice Math Boxes 3-12 are paired with Math Boxes 3-9.

▶ Home Link 3-12

Math Masters, pp. 109–110

Homework Children continue to practice the subtracting-a-group strategy and cut out a new set of Fact Triangles. GMP7.2

Math Journal 1, p. 95

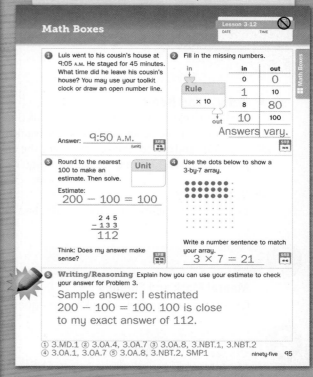

Math Masters, p. 109

Equivalent Names

Overview Children use all four operations to generate equivalent names for numbers.

▶ **Before You Begin**
For Part 1, select and sequence Quick Look Cards 137, 133, and 138. For Part 2, be prepared to display three large name-collection boxes: one blank for 14; one filled for 18 with errors (*See margin on page 301.*); and one for the summary. For the optional Extra Practice activity, you may want to target practice by filling in some numbers and equivalent names on *Math Masters,* page TA28.

▶ **Vocabulary**
expression • equivalent • name-collection box

 **Common Core
State Standards**

Focus Clusters
• Multiply and divide within 100.
• Use place value understanding and properties of operations to perform multi-digit arithmetic.

---

1 Warm Up 5–10 min

Materials

Mental Math and Fluency Children practice Quick Looks with equal groups and arrays.	Quick Look Cards 133, 137, 138	**3.OA.1, 3.OA.7** **SMP2, SMP6**

2 Focus 40–50 min

Math Message Children find equivalent names.	slate	**3.NBT.2**
Finding Equivalent Names Children find equivalent names with name-collection boxes.	blank name-collection box for 14 and filled-in name collection box for 18 (*See Before You Begin.*)	**3.OA.7, 3.NBT.2** **SMP1, SMP2**
Completing Name-Collection Boxes Children solve name-collection problems.	*Math Journal 1,* p. 96; *Student Reference Book,* pp. 96–97	**3.OA.7, 3.NBT.2** **SMP1, SMP2**
✓ **Assessment Check-In** See page 302.	*Math Journal 1,* p. 96; base-10 blocks or counters (optional)	**3.OA.7, 3.NBT.2**
Introducing *Name That Number* **Game** Children use different operations to name a number.	*Student Reference Book,* pp. 249–250; *Math Masters,* p. G12; number cards 0–10 (4 of each) and 11–20 (1 of each)	**3.OA.7, 3.NBT.2** **SMP2**

CCSS 3.NBT.2 Spiral Snapshot
GMC Subtract within 1,000 fluently.

◁ | 3-6 Focus | 3-7 Warm Up Practice | 3-8 Focus Practice | **3-13 Focus Practice** | 4-1 Practice Practice | 4-5 | 4-7 Practice | 4-9 Practice | ▷

/// Spiral Tracker (Go Online) to see how mastery develops for all standards within the grade.

3 Practice 15–20 min

Minute Math+ Children practice mental math strategies.	*Minute Math®+*	
Practicing Frames and Arrows Children solve double-rule Frames and Arrows.	*Math Masters,* p. 112, p. TA20 (optional)	**3.OA.7, 3.NBT.2** **SMP7**
Math Boxes 3-13 Children practice and maintain skills.	*Math Journal 1,* p. 97	See page 303.
Home Link 3-13 **Homework** Children find equivalent names for numbers.	*Math Masters,* p. 113	**3.OA.7, 3.NBT.2** **SMP1**

---

connectED.mcgraw-hill.com ▷

Plan your lessons online
with these tools.

 ePresentations   **Student Learning Center**   **Facts Workshop Game**   **eToolkit**   **Professional Development**   **Home Connections**   **Spiral Tracker**   **Assessment and Reporting**   **ELL English Learners Support**   **Differentiation Support**

Differentiation Options RtI

Readiness

CCSS 3.NBT.2, SMP1, SMP2

5–10 min

WHOLE CLASS
SMALL GROUP
PARTNER
INDEPENDENT

Representing Equivalent Names

Activity Card 49; base-10 blocks; number cards 0–9 (4 of each)

To review equivalent names, have children use base-10 blocks to represent 2- and 3-digit numbers in two different ways. **GMP1.5, GMP2.1** Have children explain how their representations show the same number. **GMP2.3**

Enrichment

CCSS 3.OA.7, 3.NBT.2, SMP2

5–10 min

WHOLE CLASS
SMALL GROUP
PARTNER
INDEPENDENT

Writing Equivalent Names

Math Masters, p. 111

To further explore equivalent numbers, have children evaluate expressions to determine whether they are equivalent. Then have them write equivalent names using the four operations. **GMP2.1**

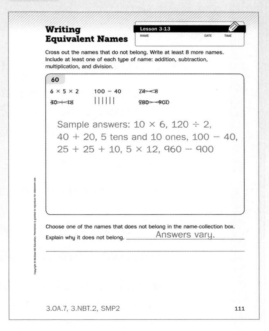

3.OA.7, 3.NBT.2, SMP2   111

Extra Practice

CCSS 3.OA.7, 3.NBT.2, SMP2

10–15 min

WHOLE CLASS
SMALL GROUP
PARTNER
INDEPENDENT

Creating Name-Collection Boxes

Activity Card 50;
Math Masters, p. TA28

To provide practice writing equivalent names for numbers, have partners create their own name-collection boxes on *Math Masters*, page TA28. **GMP2.1** You may also wish to create name-collection box problems for targeted practice.

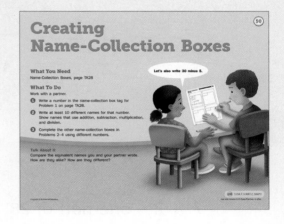

English Language Learners Support

Beginning ELL Write "Mom" in the tag of a name-collection box. Discuss names for moms, such as *mama, mother*, a picture of a mom, and so on. Children might share the word from their native language. Point out that this box contains a collection of names for the same person, so it is a name-collection box. Talk about different names children are called—full name, nickname, son/daughter, and so on—and discuss what might go in children's own name-collection boxes. Connect this to numbers and how they can be represented in many different ways.

Go Online   **ELL** English Learners Support

Standards and Goals for Mathematical Practice

SMP1 **Make sense of problems and persevere in solving them.**
    GMP1.5 Solve problems in more than one way.

SMP2 **Reason abstractly and quantitatively.**
    GMP2.1 Create mathematical representations using numbers, words, pictures, symbols, gestures, tables, graphs, and concrete objects.
    GMP2.3 Make connections between representations.

14

$$2 + 12 \qquad 7 + 7$$

$$7 \times 2 \quad \text{one-half of } 28$$

$$24 - 10$$

$$1 \text{ dozen and 2 more}$$

$$6 + 6 + 2$$

Name-collection box

▶ Mental Math and Fluency

Show Quick Look Cards 137, 133, and 138 one at a time for 2–3 seconds. Ask children to share both what they saw and how they saw it. **GMP2.2, GMP6.1** Highlight strategies involving equal groups or arrays.

Quick Look Card 137   Sample answer: I saw 2 rows of 3, and I know 3 and 3 makes 6.

Quick Look Card 133   Sample answer: I saw 3 rows of 3. I know $3 + 3 = 6$, and 3 more makes 9.

Quick Look Card 138   Sample answer: I know 2 rows of 3 makes 6, and there are 2 groups of 6, which makes 12.

2 **Focus**   40–50 min   Go Online   ePresentations   eToolkit

▶ Math Message

What is the same about all of these problems?
Write your answer on your slate.

$$2 + 12 \qquad 7 \times 2 \qquad 15 - 1$$

$$24 - 10 \qquad 1 \text{ dozen and 2 more}$$

Write another problem that belongs with these.

Unit
eggs

▶ Finding Equivalent Names

WHOLE CLASS	SMALL GROUP	PARTNER	INDEPENDENT

Math Message Follow-Up Explain that in mathematics an **expression** is made up of numbers and symbols but has no $>$, $<$, or $=$. The problems in the Math Message are expressions.

Have children share their Math Message responses. Expect many children to realize that all the expressions are equal to 14. **GMP2.3** As needed, have volunteers explain the meaning of *dozen* and share things that are sold in dozens, such as eggs, roses, and bagels. Explain that $2 + 12$, 7×2, $15 - 1$, $24 - 10$, and 1 dozen and 2 more are all **equivalent,** or equal, names for 14. Next have children check that the expressions they wrote are equivalent to 14.

Display the large blank name-collection box for the number 14. (*See Before You Begin and margin.*) Explain that today you will discuss how to find equivalent names for numbers and that a **name-collection box** is a way to show several equivalent names at once.

Write all the Math Message names and those the children wrote for 14 in the box. Ask: *Can you think of other equivalent names for 14?* GMP1.5

Sample answers: ⊬⊬⊬ ⊬⊬⊬ ////, one-half of 28, 10 + 4, 2 × 7,

28 ÷ 2, Write them in the name-collection box. GMP2.1

Display the 18 name-collection box as shown in the margin. (*See Before You Begin.*) Have children carefully review the names and share what they notice. Some may benefit from solving each expression to help them keep track of their thinking. Ask children to find the names that do not belong and to share their reasoning with their partners. Then discuss as a class. GMP2.3 These do not show 18: 3 + 3 + 3 = 9, 2 + 9 = 11, 20 − 8 = 12, 1 ten and 6 ones, 1 long and 6 cubes, 2 dozen Ask: *How could we revise these names to make them equivalent to 18?* GMP2.1 3 + 3 + 3 + 3 + 3 + 3 or 6 + 6 + 6; 2 + 16; 20 − 2; 1 long and 8 cubes; 1 ten and 8 ones; 2 dozen − 6

Tell children that they will use name-collection boxes in this lesson and throughout the year to think about equivalent names for numbers and to practice writing and solving addition, subtraction, multiplication, and division expressions.

▶ **Completing Name-Collection Boxes**

Math Journal 1, p. 96; *Student Reference Book*, pp. 96–97

WHOLE CLASS | **SMALL GROUP** | **PARTNER** | **INDEPENDENT**

Before children begin work on the journal page, have them find the pages on name-collection boxes in their *Student Reference Book*. Remind them to use the index. Read the essay with children and discuss any questions that arise.

Next have children complete Problems 1 and 2 in partnerships and Problems 3 and 4 independently on journal page 96. GMP1.5, GMP2.1 Encourage children to create a variety of representations and try to use all four operations in their names.

Differentiate | **Adjusting the Activity**

Encourage children to refer to the different types of expressions in the displayed 14 and 18 name-collection boxes and use similar types for their boxes.

Go Online Differentiation Support

Math Journal 1, p. 96

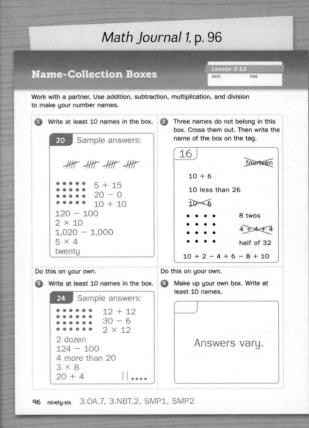

Student Reference Book, p. 249

Name That Number

Materials	☐ number cards 0–20 (4 of each card 0–10, and 1 of each card 11–20)
Players	2 to 4 (The game is more interesting when played by 3 or 4 players.)
Skill	Finding equivalent names for numbers
Object of the Game	To collect the most cards.

Directions

❶ Shuffle the deck and place 5 cards number-side up on the table. Leave the rest of the deck number-side down. Then turn over the top card of the deck and lay it down next to the deck. The number on this card is the number to be named. This is the *target number*.

❷ Players take turns. When it is your turn:
- Try to name the target number. You can name the target number by adding, subtracting, multiplying, or dividing the numbers on 2 or more of the 5 cards that are number-side up. A card may be used only once for each turn.
- If you can name the target number, take the cards you used to name it. Also take the target-number card. Then replace all the cards you took by drawing from the top of the deck. See the example on the next page.
- If you cannot name the target number, your turn is over. Turn over a new card from the top of the deck and lay it down on the target-number pile. The number on this card becomes the new target number to be named.

❸ Play continues until all of the cards in the deck have been turned over. The player who has taken the most cards wins.

two hundred forty-nine **SRB 249**

Math Masters, p. 112

Frames and Arrows

Lesson 3-13

NAME · DATE · TIME

Fill in the missing numbers and rule. For Problem 2, create your own rule and fill in the diagram with the number pattern that fits your rule. Sample answer:

① Rule
$\times 2$

4 → 8 → 16 → 32 → 64 → 128

② Rule

◇ ◇ ◇ ◇ ◇

Answers vary.

Use two rules to fill in the empty frames.

③ Add 100 · Subtract 50

40 → 140 → 90 → 190 → 140 → 240

④ Double · − 10

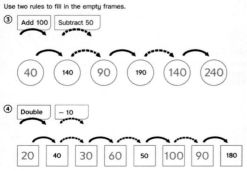

20 → 40 → 30 → 60 → 50 → 100 → 90 → 180

112 3.OA.7, 3.NBT.2, SMP7

✓ Assessment Check-In CCSS 3.OA.7, 3.NBT.2

Math Journal 1, p. 96

Expect most children to write at least 10 equivalent names using addition, subtraction, and multiplication for Problems 3 and 4, as well as name the box in Problem 4. Some children may be able to write equivalent names using division. If children struggle, consider implementing the Adjusting the Activity suggestion. Some children may benefit from using base-10 blocks or counters to represent the number in the name-collection box tag.

☑ **Assessment and Reporting** **Go Online** to record student progress and to see trajectories toward mastery for these standards.

When most children have completed the page, have children share some of the names they generated in Problems 1 and 2. Ask: *Why might your name-collection box for 24 look different from someone else's?* **GMP1.5**
Sample answer: There are lots of different names for each number.

▶ Introducing *Name That Number*

Student Reference Book, pp. 249–250; *Math Masters,* p. G12

WHOLE CLASS	**SMALL GROUP**	**PARTNER**	INDEPENDENT

Remind children that they played *Name That Number* in *Second Grade Everyday Mathematics.* Review the rules on *Student Reference Book,* pages 249–250. Play a few rounds with the class and share strategies for using multiple cards to make the target number. Encourage children to try to use all four arithmetic operations. Model how to record each step in a turn with a number sentence. Have children record one round of their play on *Math Masters,* page G12.

Observe

- Which children use one operation in their solution? Which children use more than one?
- Which children perform the computations accurately? Efficiently?

Discuss

- *What mathematics did you use in this game?*
- *How are your number representations in name-collection boxes and in* Name That Number *alike or different?* **GMP2.3**

Differentiate **Game Modifications** **Go Online** Differentiation Support

Summarize Post a large, blank name-collection box somewhere in the classroom and label the tag with a number of your choice. Have partners share ideas for equivalent names. Record a few suggestions and invite children to add names in spare moments over the next few days. You may wish to continue this as an ongoing routine with different numbers.

 **Practice** 15–20 min

Go Online

ePresentations eToolkit Home Connections

▶ Minute Math+

To practice mental math strategies, select a *Minute Math+* activity.

▶ Practicing Frames and Arrows

Math Masters, p. 112

| WHOLE CLASS | SMALL GROUP | **PARTNER** | **INDEPENDENT** |

Have children practice solving and creating Frames-and-Arrows problems. Point out that Problems 3 and 4 involve solving problems with two rules. Remind children that they may keep track of the rules by writing them above the arrows. If children finish quickly, or in other spare moments, encourage them to create more problems involving different operations, including missing frames and missing rules on *Math Masters*, page TA29.
GMP7.1, GMP7.2

▶ Math Boxes 3-13

Math Journal 1, p. 97

| WHOLE CLASS | SMALL GROUP | PARTNER | INDEPENDENT |

Mixed Practice Math Boxes 3-13 are paired with Math Boxes 3-10.

▶ Home Link 3-13

Math Masters, p. 113

Homework Children identify and write equivalent names for numbers in name-collection boxes. **GMP1.5**

▶ Planning Ahead

For Lesson 4-3, collect items that have a mass of about 1 gram (paper clip, centimeter cube), 50 grams (golf ball, 20 pennies), 100 grams (a box of 100 paper clips, 4 AA batteries), 500 grams (paperback book, loaf of bread) and 1,000 grams (liter of water, a pineapple).

For Lesson 4-4, in *What's My Polygon Rule?*, each small group will need a set of cards cut from *Math Masters*, pages TA32 and G13. You may want to laminate the cards for durability.

Math Journal 1, p. 97

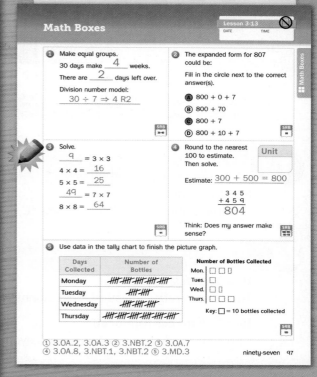

Math Masters, p. 113

Unit 3 Progress Check

Overview   Day 1: Administer the Unit Assessments.
Day 2: Administer the Open Response Assessment.

2-Day Lesson

 Student Learning Center
Students may take
assessments digitally.

 Assessment and Reporting
Record results and track
progress toward mastery.

Day 1: Unit Assessments

1 Warm Up   5–10 min

Self Assessment
Children complete the Self Assessment.

Materials

Assessment Handbook, p. 25

2a Assess   35–50 min

Unit 3 Assessment
These items reflect mastery expectations to this point.

Assessment Handbook, pp. 26–29

Unit 3 Challenge (Optional)
Children may demonstrate progress beyond expectations.

Assessment Handbook, pp. 30–31

CCSS Common Core State Standards	**Goals for Mathematical Content (GMC)**	**Lessons**	**Self Assessment**	**Unit 3 Assessment**	**Unit 3 Challenge**
3.OA.1	Interpret multiplication in terms of equal groups.	3-9 to 3-12		8a, 8b, 10	1a, 1c, 2a, 2b
3.OA.4	Determine the unknown in multiplication and division equations.	3-1	1	8a, 8b	2b
3.OA.5	Apply properties of operations to multiply or divide.	3-10 to 3-12	5, 6	8a–8c, 10	1b, 1c, 2b
3.OA.7	Multiply within 100 fluently.	3-1, 3-9 to 3-13	1, 4–6	8a, 8b, 9a, 9b, 10	1c, 2b
	Know all products of 1-digit numbers × 1, × 2, × 5, and × 10 automatically.	3-1, 3-11 to 3-13		8a, 8b, 9a, 9b	1c
	Know all square products of 1-digit numbers automatically.	3-9, 3-10		9b, 9c	
	Know all products of 1-digit numbers × 4, × 6, × 7, and × 8 automatically.	3-11, 3-12		10	2b
	Divide within 100 fluently.	3-13	1, 4		
3.OA.8	Assess the reasonableness of answers to problems.	3-2 to 3-6		4c, 5c	
3.NBT.1	Use place-value understanding to round numbers to the nearest 10.	3-2, 3-3, 3-6		3a, 4a, 5a, 6a	
	Use place-value understanding to round numbers to the nearest 100.	3-3, 3-6		3a, 5a, 6a	
3.NBT.2	Add within 1,000 fluently.	3-1 to 3-6, 3-8, 3-13	1, 2, 4	1, 2, 3b, 5b	
	Subtract within 1,000 fluently.	3-1, 3-5, 3-6, 3-8, 3-13	1, 3, 4	1, 2, 4b, 6b	
3.MD.3	Organize and represent data on scaled bar graphs and scaled picture graphs.	3-7, 3-8		7	

	Goals for Mathematical Practice (GMP)	Lessons	Self Assessment	Unit 3 Assessment	Unit 3 Challenge
SMP1	Check whether your answer makes sense. GMP1.4	3-2, 3-3		4c, 5c	
SMP2	Create mathematical representations using numbers, words, pictures, symbols, gestures, tables, graphs, and concrete objects. GMP2.1	3-4, 3-5, 3-7, 3-12, 3-13		8a, 8b	
	Make sense of the representations you and others use. GMP2.2	3-4		8a–8c, 9a–9c, 10	
SMP4	Model real-world situations using graphs, drawings, tables, symbols, numbers, diagrams, and other representations. GMP4.1	3-8		7	
SMP6	Explain your mathematical thinking clearly and precisely. GMP6.1	3-2, 3-3		4c, 5c, 9c, 10	1c, 2b
SMP7	Look for mathematical structures such as categories, patterns, and properties. GMP7.1	3-1, 3-9			1c
	Use structures to solve problems and answer questions. GMP7.2	3-1, 3-9 to 3-12	1	1, 10	1c
SMP8	Create and justify rules, shortcuts, and generalizations. GMP8.1	3-1, 3-10	1	2	

/// Spiral Tracker   Go Online   to see how mastery develops for all standards within the grade.

1 Warm Up   5–10 min

▶ Self Assessment

Assessment Handbook, p. 25

| WHOLE CLASS | SMALL GROUP | PARTNER | **INDEPENDENT** |

Children complete the Self Assessment to reflect on their progress in Unit 3.

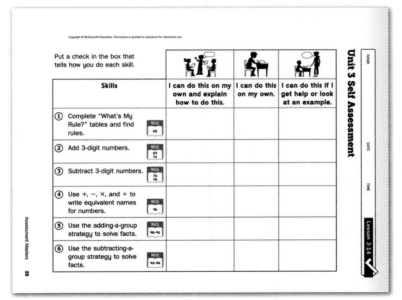

Assessment Handbook, p. 25

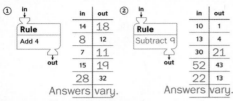

Unit 3 Assessment

Complete the tables. Write your own number pair in the last row of each table.

① in → **Rule** Add 4 → out

in	out
14	18
8	12
7	11
15	19
28	32

Answers vary.

② in → **Rule** Subtract 9 → out

in	out
10	1
13	4
30	21
52	43
22	13

Answers vary.

For each problem, use rounding to estimate and then solve.
Use your estimate to check whether your answer makes sense.
Show your work.

③ a. Estimate: Sample answer: 170 + 30 = 200

b.
$$\begin{array}{r} 169 \\ +\ 28 \\ \hline 197 \end{array}$$

④ a. Estimate: Sample answer: 80 − 40 = 40

b.
$$\begin{array}{r} 82 \\ -36 \\ \hline 46 \end{array}$$

c. Does your answer make sense? Explain. Sample answers:
Yes, because my estimate is 40 and my answer is 46.
Yes, because I added 46 to 36 and got 82.

26   Assessment Handbook

②ª Assess   35–50 min   Go Online

 Assessment and Reporting   Differentiation Support

▶ Unit 3 Assessment

Assessment Handbook, pp. 26–29

| WHOLE CLASS | SMALL GROUP | PARTNER | **INDEPENDENT** |

Children complete the Unit 3 Assessment to demonstrate their progress on the Common Core State Standards covered in this unit.

Generic rubrics in the *Assessment Handbook* appendix can be used to evaluate children's progress on the Mathematical Practices.

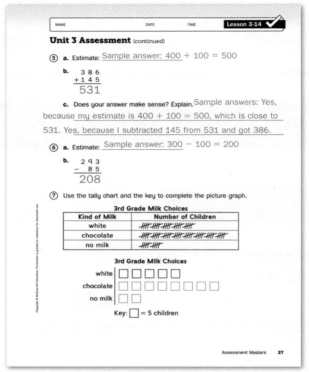

| NAME | DATE | TIME | Lesson 3-14 ✓ |

Unit 3 Assessment (continued)

⑤ a. Estimate: Sample answer: 400 + 100 = 500

b.
$$\begin{array}{r} 386 \\ +145 \\ \hline 531 \end{array}$$

c. Does your answer make sense? Explain. Sample answers: Yes, because my estimate is 400 + 100 = 500, which is close to 531. Yes, because I subtracted 145 from 531 and got 386.

⑥ a. Estimate: Sample answer: 300 − 100 = 200

b.
$$\begin{array}{r} 293 \\ -\ 85 \\ \hline 208 \end{array}$$

⑦ Use the tally chart and the key to complete the picture graph.

3rd Grade Milk Choices

Kind of Milk	Number of Children
white	///// ///// ///// ///// /////
chocolate	///// ///// ///// ///// ///// ///// ///// /////
no milk	///// /////

3rd Grade Milk Choices

white □ □ □ □ □
chocolate □ □ □ □ □ □ □ □
no milk □ □

Key: □ = 5 children

Assessment Masters   27

Assessment Handbook, p. 27

Differentiate | Adjusting the Assessment

Item(s)	Adjustments
1, 2	To scaffold Items 1 and 2, have children write the rules between each pair of numbers and check whether their answers makes sense.
3a, 4a, 5a, 6a	To scaffold Items 3a, 4a, 5a, and 6a, have children change the numbers to close-but-easier numbers to estimate.
3b, 4b, 5b, 6b	To extend Items 3b, 4b, 5b, and 6b, have children show other ways to solve.
4c, 5c, 8c	To scaffold Items 4c, 5c, and 8c, have children verbalize their answers to someone else.
7	To extend Item 7, have children draw a new picture graph showing the same data and then change the key so 1 square represents 10 children.
8a, 8b, 9a, 9b	To scaffold Items 8a, 8b, 9a, and 9b, have children describe each array in terms of equal groups.
8a, 8b	To extend Items 8a and 8b, have children write additional pairs of facts and draw arrays to match.
9c	To extend Item 9c, have children draw other examples and non-examples of multiplication squares and write number sentences to match.
10	To extend Item 10, have children record number sentences to match Li's strategy.

Advice for Differentiation

Because this is the beginning of the school year, all of the content included on the Unit 3 Assessment was recently introduced and will be revisited in subsequent units.

Use the online assessment and reporting tools to track children's performance. Differentiation materials are available online to help you address children's needs.

NOTE See the Unit Organizer on pages 214–215 or the online Spiral Tracker for details on Unit 3 focus topics and the spiral.

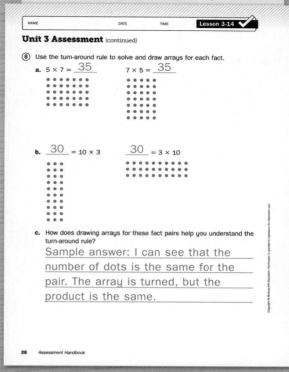

Assessment Handbook, p. 28

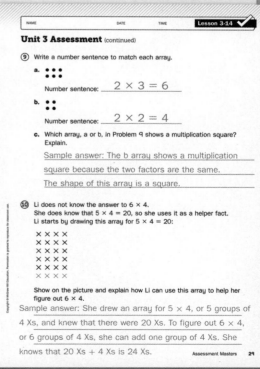

Assessment Handbook, p. 29

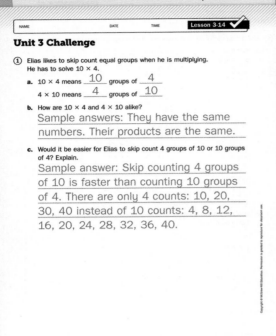

▶ Unit 3 Challenge (Optional)

Assessment Handbook, pp. 30–31

WHOLE CLASS	SMALL GROUP	PARTNER	**INDEPENDENT**

Children can complete the Unit 3 Challenge after they complete the Unit 3 Assessment.

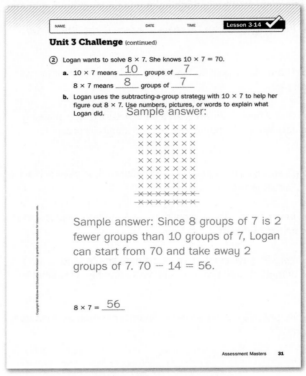

Assessment Handbook, p. 31

Unit 3 Progress Check ✓

Day 2: Open Response Assessment

2b Assess   50–55 min

Solving the Open Response Problem
After a brief introduction, children make sense of a subtraction problem
to identify an error and use place value to explain their thinking.

Discussing the Problem
Children share their thinking and explanations.

Materials

Assessment Handbook, p. 32; base-10
blocks; Standards for Mathematical
Practice Poster (optional)

Assessment Handbook, p. 32

CCSS Common Core State Standards

Standards	Goal for Mathematical Content (GMC)	Lessons
3.NBT.2	Subtract within 1,000 fluently.	3-1, 3-5, 3-6, 3-8, 3-13
	Goal for Mathematical Practice (GMP)	
SMP3	Make sense of others' mathematical thinking. GMP3.2	3-4, 3-11

/// Spiral Tracker   Go Online ⟩   to see how mastery develops for all standards within the grade.

▶ **Evaluating Children's Responses**
Evaluate children's abilities to use strategies to subtract. Use the rubric below to evaluate their work
based on **GMP3.2**.

Goal for Mathematical Practice GMP3.2 Make sense of others' mathematical thinking.	Not Meeting Expectations	Partially Meeting Expectations	Meeting Expectations	Exceeding Expectations
	Does not identify the location of the error as in the hundreds place **and** does not address the need to compensate (maintain the value of the minuend).	Explains or shows only that the error occurred in the hundreds place **or** provides an incomplete or incorrect explanation.	Explains or shows that not changing 500 to 400 is an error because the increase in the value of the tens place must be compensated by a decrease in the value of the hundreds place.	Meets expectations and clearly explains that the value of the minuend must be maintained (i.e., regrouping the hundreds and tens renames the 'top' number without changing its value).

3 Look Ahead   10–15 min

Math Boxes 3-14
Children preview skills and concepts for Unit 4.

Home Link 3-14
Children take home the Family Letter that introduces Unit 4.

Materials

Math Journal 1, p. 98

Math Masters, pp. 114–117

Unit 3 Open Response Assessment
Finding a Mistake in a Subtraction Problem

Mia wants to solve this problem: 552 − 153 = ?
She begins by making an estimate.

Estimate: 550 − 150 = 400

Then she uses expand-and-trade subtraction to find an exact answer,
but her answer is not close to her estimate. This is her work:

$$\begin{array}{r} 140 \\ 40\ \ 12 \\ 552 \to 500 + 50 + 2 \\ -\ 153 \to 100 + 50 + 3 \\ \hline 400 + 90 + 9 = 499 \end{array}$$

"Oops," said Mia, "I didn't cross out 500 and write 400."
Explain **why** not changing 500 to 400 is a mistake.

(Hint: Use what you know about place value in your answer.)

Answers vary. See sample children's work on
page 310 of the *Teacher's Lesson Guide.*

32   Assessment Handbook

Sample child's work, "Meeting Expectations"

$$\begin{array}{r} 140 \\ 40\ \ 12 \\ 552 \to 500 + 50 + 2 \\ -\ 153 \to 100 + 50 + 3 \\ \hline 400 + 90 + 9 = 499 \end{array}$$

"Oops," said Mia, "I didn't cross out 500 and write 400."
Explain **why** not changing 500 to 400 is a mistake.

(Hint: Use what you know about place value in your answer.)

She needed to cross of 500
and write 400 because she
took away a hundred and
put it in the 40 so she got
140.

NOTE Additional samples of evaluated
children's work can be found in the
Assessment Handbook appendix.

2b Assess   50–55 min   Go Online

Assessment
and Reporting

▶ Solving the Open Response Problem

Assessment Handbook, p. 32

| WHOLE CLASS | SMALL GROUP | PARTNER | **INDEPENDENT** |

This open response problem requires children to apply skills and concepts
from Unit 3 to find a mistake in a subtraction problem. The focus of this
task is **GMP3.2**: Make sense of others' mathematical thinking.

Before starting the problem, tell children that they will make sense of
another child's work on a subtraction problem and find and explain a
mistake.

Distribute *Assessment Handbook,* page 32. Read the directions together.
Remind children that they should find and explain Mia's mistake using what
they know about place value. Make base-10 blocks available. These
directions reflect an emphasis on **GMP3.2.** You may wish to refer to the
Standards for Mathematical Practice Poster and discuss the mathematical
practice with children.

> **Differentiate** **Adjusting the Assessment**
>
> For children who have difficulty, work together to use base-10 blocks to
> model the subtraction problem and then have children describe in words
> what they did.

▶ Discussing the Problem

Assessment Handbook, p. 32

| **WHOLE CLASS** | SMALL GROUP | **PARTNER** | INDEPENDENT |

After children complete their work, invite a few children to explain Mia's
mistake. Remind them to use what they know about place value in their
explanation. Discuss how Mia used an estimate to catch her mistake.

Evaluating Children's Responses   CCSS 3.NBT.2

Collect children's work. For the content standard, expect most children to
show an understanding of how to use expand-and-trade subtraction. You can
use the rubric on page 309 to evaluate children's work for **GMP3.2.**

See the sample in the margin. This work meets expectations for the content
standard because the child's explanation of Mia's mistake shows an
understanding of how to use expand-and-trade subtraction. The work meets
expectations for the mathematical practice because the child makes
appropriate use of place-value concepts in making sense of Mia's mistake. The
child explains that "she needed to cross out 500 and write 400 because she
took away a hundred and put it in the 40 so she got 140." **GMP3.2**

Go Online Assessment
and Reporting

Math Journal 1, p. 98

3 Look Ahead 10–15 min Go Online

Home Connections

▶ **Math Boxes 3-14:** Preview for Unit 4 ✏

Math Journal 1, p. 98

| WHOLE CLASS | **SMALL GROUP** | **PARTNER** | INDEPENDENT |

Mixed Practice Math Boxes 3-14 are paired with Math Boxes 3-11. These problems focus on skills and understandings that are prerequisite for Unit 4. You may want to use information from these Math Boxes to plan instruction and grouping in Unit 4.

▶ **Home Link 3-14:** Unit 4 Family Letter

Math Masters, pp. 114–117

Home Connection The Unit 4 Family Letter provides information and activities related to the Unit 4 content.

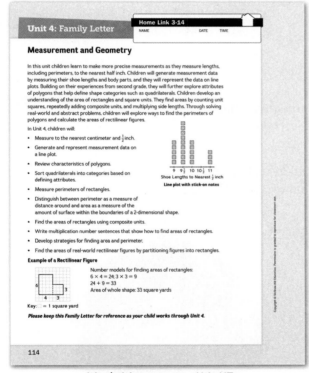

Math Masters, pp. 114–117

Math Boxes
Preview for Unit 4

Lesson 3-14
DATE   TIME

① Measure the length of your calculator to the nearest half-inch.
Answers vary.

about _____ inches

about _____ centimeters

② Partition the rectangle into 3 rows with 4 same-size squares in each row.

How many squares are inside the larger rectangle?
____12____ squares

③ Write at least 2 things to describe this shape. Use mathematical language.

Sample answers: It has
6 sides. There are no right
angles. All the sides are
the same length. It is a
hexagon.

④ Each ☐ = 1 square centimeter

Count the squares to find the area.

Area: ____21____ square centimeters

⑤ **Writing/Reasoning** In Problem 3, Allie said the shape is a quadrilateral. Do you agree? Explain.

Sample answer: No. Quadrilaterals have 4 sides, and this shape has 6 sides.

① 3.MD.4 ② 3.MD.5, 3.MD.5b, 3.G.2 ③ 3.G.1 ④ 3.MD.5,
98 ninety-eight   3.MD.5a, 3.MD.5b, 3.MD.6 ⑤ 3.G.1, SMP3

Unit 4 Organizer
Measurement and Geometry

In this unit, children measure to the nearest half inch. Then they generate measurement data and represent it on a scaled line plot. After children explore geometric attributes of polygons and classify quadrilaterals into categories based on their attributes, they identify and measure the perimeters of polygons, and distinguish between perimeter and area. They develop multiple strategies to determine the areas of rectangles and extend those ideas to determine the areas of rectilinear shapes.

CCSS Standards for Mathematical Content

Domain	Cluster
Measurement and Data	Solve problems involving measurement and estimation.
	Represent and interpret data.
	Geometric measurement: understand concepts of area and relate area to multiplication and to addition.
	Geometric measurement: recognize perimeter.
Geometry	Reason with shapes and their attributes.

Because the standards within each domain can be broad, *Everyday Mathematics* has unpacked each standard into Goals for Mathematical Content **GMC**. For a complete list of Standards and Goals, see page EM1.

For an overview of the CCSS domains, standards, and mastery expectations in this unit, see the **Spiral Trace** on pages 318–319. See the **Mathematical Background** (pages 320–322) for a discussion of the following key topics:

- Measuring Length
- Measuring Perimeter and Area
- Classifying Geometric Shapes

CCSS Standards for Mathematical Practice

SMP6	Attend to precision.
SMP7	Look for and make use of structure.

For a discussion about how *Everyday Mathematics* develops these practices and a list of Goals for Mathematical Practice **GMP**, see page 323.

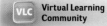 **VLC Virtual Learning Community** **Go Online** to **vlc.cemseprojects.org** to search for video clips on each practice.

McGraw-Hill Education

Go Digital with these tools at **connectED.mcgraw-hill.com**

 ePresentations

 Student Learning Center

 Facts Workshop Game

 eToolkit

 Professional Development

 Home Connections

 Spiral Tracker

 Assessment and Reporting

English Learners Support

 Differentiation Support

Contents

*The standards listed here are addressed in the **Focus** of each lesson. For all the standards in a lesson, see the Lesson Opener.

Unit 4 Materials

 **Virtual Learning Community** See how *Everyday Mathematics* teachers organize materials. Search "Classroom Tours" at **vlc.cemseprojects.org**.

Lesson	Math Masters	Activity Cards	Manipulative Kit	Other Materials
4-1	pp. 118–120; TA30	51	toolkit ruler; toolkit tape measure; six or more 1-inch-square pattern blocks; centimeter cubes	slate; 15 and 16 cm-long pencils; scissors; small classroom objects such as calculators, crayons, erasers, and markers; classroom objects such as tissue boxes and small books
4-2	pp. 121–123; TA20 (optional)	52–53	measuring tools such as a ruler or tape measure	slate (optional); paper; stick-on notes; small objects
4-3	pp. 124–126; TA30; G12	54–55	Quick Look Cards 133, 139, 140; toolkit ruler; tape measure; yardstick; pattern-block triangles; dice; pan balance; set of standard masses; number cards 0–10 (4 of each) and number cards 11–20	string; objects of selected masses; colored pencils; scissors; bags (optional); stick-on notes
4-4	pp. 127; TA31–TA32; G6; G13–G14	56–57	ruler; geoboard; rubber bands; die labeled 2, 2, 5, 5, 10, 10; number cards 1–10 (4 of each) and number cards 4–8 (4 of each); straws	slate; Class Data Pad; paper; small bags; Two-Dimensional Shapes Poster; straightedge; scissors; twist ties; shape cards (optional)
4-5	pp. 128–129; TA33; G13; G15	58	pattern blocks	slate; Class Data Pad; Fact Triangles; *Math Journal 1*, Activity Sheets 11–12 (Quadrilateral Cutouts)
4-6	pp. 130–132; TA19; TA30		pattern blocks; measurement tools including toolkit ruler	slate; small boxes; quadrilateral cutouts from Lesson 4-5; opaque bags or boxes; small classroom objects
4-7	pp. 133; TA19	59	measurement tools including toolkit ruler; number cards 0–20 (4 of each) and number cards 0–10; square pattern blocks; per partnership: 32 base-10 cubes	slate; 1-foot squares; 1-yard square; Class Data Pad; various rectangular prisms
4-8	pp. 134–137		tape measure	slate; 1-foot squares; tape; colored pencils
4-9	pp. 138–140; TA19; TA34; TA35 (optional)	60	Quick Look Cards 134, 136, 146; geoboard; rubber bands; number cards 6–20	half-sheet of paper (optional); pennies; tape
4-10	pp. 141–142; TA35; G16		square pattern blocks; inch ruler	slate; Perimeter and Area T Chart from Lesson 4-7; Fact Triangles; various rectangular prisms; red and blue crayons; scissors; half-sheet of paper (optional)
4-11	pp. 143–145; TA6; TA19; TA42 (optional)			slate; Standards for Mathematical Practice Poster; Guidelines for Discussion Poster; Class Data Pad or chart paper (optional); colored pencils (optional); selected samples of children's work; children's work from Day 1
4-12	pp. 146–148; TA20 (optional); TA22; TA34	61	Quick Look Cards 138, 144, 145	scissors; tape
4-13	pp. 149–152; *Assessment Handbook*, pp. 33–43			

📖 **Literature Link** **4-5** *Grandfather Tang's Story* **4-7** *Spaghetti and Meatballs for All!*

Go Online for a complete literature list for Grade 3 and to download all Quick Look Cards.

Problem Solving  **Professional Development**

Everyday Mathematics emphasizes equally all three of the Common Core's dimensions of **rigor:**

- conceptual understanding
- procedural skill and fluency
- applications

Math Messages, other daily work, Explorations, and Open Response tasks provide many opportunities for children to apply what they know to solve problems.

▶ Math Message

Math Messages require children to solve a problem they have not been shown how to solve. Math Messages provide almost daily opportunities for problem solving.

▶ Daily Work

Journal pages, Home Links, Writing/Reasoning prompts, and Differentiation Options often require children to solve problems in mathematical contexts and real-life situations. *Minute Math+* offers number stories and a variety of other practice activities for transition times and spare moments throughout the day.

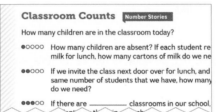

▶ Explorations

In Exploration A, children measure distances around objects to the nearest half inch. In Exploration B, children compare masses of objects to standard masses to determine benchmarks. In Exploration C, children create and compare a variety of triangles on geoboards.

▶ Open Response and Reengagement

In Lesson 4-11 children use models of a rabbit pen to identify possible side lengths of rectangles with a perimeter of 24 feet. During the reengagement discussion on Day 2, children compare and discuss their models and offer explanations for the model they chose. The focus practice for this lesson is "model with mathematics." By creating drawings of a rabbit pen, and then using the models to determine area and decide which pen is the best, children use mathematical ideas to represent real-world situations. `GMP4.1`

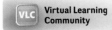 **Virtual Learning Community** `Go Online` to watch an Open Response and Reengagement lesson in action. Search "Open Response" at **vlc.cemseprojects.org**.

Look for `GMP1.1–1.6` markers, which indicate opportunities for children to engage in **SMP1**: "Make sense of problems and persevere in solving them." Children also become better problem solvers as they engage in all of the CCSS Mathematical Practices. The yellow GMP markers throughout the lessons indicate places where you can emphasize the Mathematical Practices and develop children's problem-solving skills.

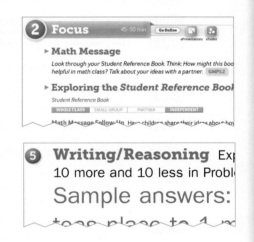

Assessment and Differentiation

See pages xxii–xxv to learn about a comprehensive online system for recording, monitoring, and reporting children's progress using core program assessments.

 to **vlc.cemseprojects.org** for tools and ideas related to assessment and differentiation from *Everyday Mathematics* teachers.

✓ Ongoing Assessment

In addition to frequent informal opportunities for "kid watching," every lesson (except Explorations) offers an **Assessment Check-In** to gauge children's performance on one or more of the standards addressed in that lesson.

Lesson	Task Description	CCSS Common Core State Standards
4-1	Measure line segments to the nearest inch and centimeter.	3.MD.4, SMP5
4-2	Use scaled line plots with fractions of inches.	3.MD.4, SMP4
4-4	Represent triangles and quadrilaterals with equal side lengths and right angles.	3.G.1, SMP7
4-5	Recognize and describe similarities between quadrilaterals.	3.G.1, SMP7
4-6	Measure side lengths of a rectangle to the nearest $\frac{1}{2}$ inch and write number models for the perimeter.	3.MD.4, 3.MD.8, SMP5
4-7	Count unit squares to find the area of rectangles.	3.MD.5, 3.MD.5a, 3.MD.5b, 3.MD.6
4-8	Find the area of rectangles.	3.MD.5, 3.MD.5a, 3.MD.5b, 3.MD.6, 3.MD.7, 3.MD.7a, SMP7
4-9	Determine side lengths of a rectangle and write a number sentence for its area.	3.MD.7, 3.MD.7a, 3.MD.7b, SMP7
4-10	Calculate the area and perimeter of rectangles.	3.MD.6, 3.MD.8
4-11	Draw at least two rectangular pens with different areas and a perimeter of 24 feet, and discuss strategies.	3.MD.8, SMP4
4-12	Decompose rectilinear figures into rectangles.	3.MD.7, 3.MD.7d

▶ Periodic Assessment

Unit 4 Progress Check This assessment focuses on the CCSS domains of *Measurement and Data* and *Geometry*. It also contains a Cumulative Assessment to help monitor children's learning and retention of content that was the focus of previous units.

Mid-Year Assessment This benchmark test checks children's mastery of some of the concepts and skills that are important for success in *Third Grade Everyday Mathematics*. See the *Assessment Handbook*.

NOTE Odd-numbered units include an **Open Response Assessment.** Even-numbered units include a **Cumulative Assessment.**

Differentiation Options Every regular lesson provides **Readiness**, **Enrichment**, **Extra Practice**, and **Beginning English Language Learners Support** activities that address the Focus standards of that lesson.

Activity Card 53

CCSS 3.NF.2, 3.NF.2a, 3.MD.4, SMP2, SMP5	CCSS 3.MD.2, SMP5	CCSS 3.MD.8
Readiness 10–15 min	**Enrichment** 10–15 min	**Extra Practice** 10–15 min
Counting Half Inches Math Masters, p. TA30; WHOLE CLASS SMALL GROUP PARTNER	**Finding More Benchmarks** pan balance; standard masses; WHOLE CLASS SMALL GROUP PARTNER	**Measuring Distances Around Objects** WHOLE CLASS SMALL GROUP PARTNER

Making a Line Plot

Activity Cards These activities, written to the children, enable you to differentiate Part 2 of the lesson through small-group work.

English Language Learners Activities and point-of-use support help children at different levels of English language proficiency succeed.

Differentiation Support online pages

Differentiation Support Two online pages for most lessons provide suggestions for game modifications, ways to scaffold lessons for children who need additional support, and language development suggestions for Beginning, Intermediate, and Advanced English language learners.

Ongoing Practice Differentiation Support

> **Embedded Facts Practice**

Basic Facts Practice can be found in every part of the lesson. Look for activities or games labeled with CCSS 3.OA.7; or go online to the Spiral Tracker and search using CCSS 3.OA.7.

For **ongoing distributed practice,** see these activities:
- Mental Math and Fluency
- Differentiation Options: Extra Practice
- Part 3: Journal pages, Math Boxes, *Math Masters*, Home Links
- Print and online games

> **Games**

Games in *Everyday Mathematics* are an essential tool for practicing skills and developing strategic thinking.

Lesson	Game	Skills and Concepts	CCSS Common Core State Standards
4-3 4-7	*Name That Number*	Using various operations to find a given number	3.OA.7, 3.NBT.2, 3.NBT.3, SMP2
4-4	*What's My Polygon Rule?*	Classifying polygons by similarities and differences	3.G.1, SMP7, SMP8
4-4	*Multiplication Draw*	Practicing 2s, 5s, and 10s multiplication facts	3.OA.7
4-5	*Shading Shapes*	Practicing with properties of quadrilaterals	3.G.1, SMP7
4-10	*The Area and Perimeter Game*	Calculating the area and perimeter of rectangles	3.MD.5, 3.MD.5a, 3.MD.5b, 3.MD.6, 3.MD.7, 3.MD.7b, 3.MD.8, SMP6, SMP7

VLC Virtual Learning Community **Go Online** ▷ to look for examples of *Everyday Mathematics* games at **vlc.cemseprojects.org.**

(CCSS) Spiral Trace: Skills, Concepts, and Applications

⭐ **Mastery Expectations** This Spiral Trace outlines instructional trajectories for key standards in Unit 4. For each standard, it highlights opportunities for Focus instruction, Warm Up and Practice activities, as well as formative and summative assessment. It describes the **degree of mastery**—as measured against the entire standard—expected at this point in the year.

Measurement and Data

3.MD.4 Generate measurement data by measuring lengths using rulers marked with halves and fourths of an inch. Show the data by making a line plot, where the horizontal scale is marked off in appropriate units—whole numbers, halves, or quarters.

⭐ By the end of Unit 4, expect children to **measure lengths to the nearest half-inch and represent the data on a line plot where the horizontal scale is marked off in whole numbers and halves.**

3.MD.5 Recognize area as an attribute of plane figures and understand concepts of area measurement.

    a. A square with side length 1 unit, called "a unit square," is said to have "one square unit" of area, and can be used to measure area.

    b. A plane figure which can be covered without gaps or overlaps by *n* unit squares is said to have an area of *n* square units.

⭐ By the end of Unit 4, expect children to **recognize area as an attribute of plane figures.**

3.MD.6 Measure areas by counting unit squares (square cm, square m, square in, square ft, and improvised units).

⭐ By the end of Unit 4, expect children to **measure areas by counting unit squares.**

Go to **connectED.mcgraw-hill.com** for comprehensive trajectories
that show how in-depth mastery develops across the grade.

3.MD.7 Relate area to the operations of multiplication and addition.

  a. Find the area of a rectangle with whole-number side lengths by tiling it, and show that the area is
     the same as would be found by multiplying the side lengths.

  b. Multiply side lengths to find areas of rectangles with whole-number side lengths in the context
     of solving real world and mathematical problems, and represent whole-number products as
     rectangular areas in mathematical reasoning.

  c. Use tiling to show in a concrete case that the area of a rectangle with whole-number side lengths
     a and $b + c$ is the sum of $a \times b$ and $a \times c$. Use area models to represent the distributive property in
     mathematical reasoning.

  d. Recognize area as additive. Find areas of rectilinear figures by decomposing them into
     non-overlapping rectangles and adding the areas of the non-overlapping parts, applying this
     technique to solve real world problems.

| 3-7 Focus | 4-7 through 4-12 Focus Practice | 4-13 Progress Check | 5-1 Warm Up Practice | 5-2 through 5-4 Practice | 5-5 Focus Practice | 5-6 Focus Practice | 5-11 Focus Practice | 6-1 through 6-4 Practice |

⭐ By the end of Unit 4, expect children to **find the area of a rectangle with whole-number side lengths by tiling.**

3.MD.8 Solve real world and mathematical problems involving perimeters of polygons, including finding
the perimeter given the side lengths, finding an unknown side length, and exhibiting rectangles
with the same perimeter and different areas or with the same area and different perimeters.

| 4-3 Focus | 4-6 through 4-8 Focus Practice | 4-10 Focus Practice | 4-11 Focus Practice | 4-12 Practice | 4-13 Progress Check | 5-1 Warm Up Focus Practice | 5-11 Practice | 6-5 Warm Up Focus Practice | 7-10 Practice | 9-1 Practice |

⭐ By the end of Unit 4, expect children to **solve problems involving perimeters of polygons.**

Geometry

3.G.1 Understand that shapes in different categories (e.g., rhombuses, rectangles, and others) may
share attributes (e.g., having four sides), and that the shared attributes can define a larger category
(e.g., quadrilaterals). Recognize rhombuses, rectangles, and squares as examples of quadrilaterals,
and draw examples of quadrilaterals that do not belong to any of these subcategories.

| 1-3 Focus | 4-4 Focus Practice | 4-5 Focus Practice | 4-6 Focus Practice | 4-13 Progress Check | 6-5 Focus Practice | 6-8 Practice | 6-12 Progress Check | 8-8 Focus Practice | 9-4 Focus |

⭐ By the end of Unit 4, expect children to **understand that shapes in different categories may share attributes.**

Key ✓ = Assessment Check-In   ⭐ = Progress Check Lesson   ▱ = Current Unit   ▰ = Previous or Upcoming Lessons

Mathematical Background: Content

 The discussion below highlights major content areas and Common Core State Standards addressed in Unit 4. See the online Spiral Tracker for complete information about learning trajectories for all standards.

▶ Measuring Length (Lessons 4-1, 4-2)

Lesson 4-1 focuses on measuring with rulers and tape measures. Children measure pencils to the nearest inch and nearest centimeter, and compare their results. They realize that when measuring with whole units, two pencils can have the same measurement even though one is clearly longer than the other. This activity leads to a discussion about precision in measurement and the need for fractional units. Children then examine inch rulers marked with $\frac{1}{4}$-inch increments and use the quarter-inch marks to measure to the nearest half inch. They also examine centimeter rulers and use the half-centimeter mark to measure to the nearest whole centimeter. **3.MD.4**

After measuring with standard rulers, children consider unusual rulers. (*See margin.*) This activity helps children develop the following important concepts about measurement.

- Measurement requires identical units. Children realize that the ruler with unequal markings cannot be used as a measuring tool because the unequal units cannot be used to accurately communicate length. Rulers with evenly spaced units are suitable measurement tools.

- Measuring is more than simply reading off a number from a ruler. Children also must carefully consider how many units lie between the endpoints of the object or path. For example, they can use a "broken" ruler to measure, even though its markings do not begin at zero, by counting the units spanned by the object.

In Lesson 4-2 children measure their shoe lengths and represent this measurement data in line plots. Then they use line plots to interpret data and answer questions in real-life scenarios about ordering gym shoes. **3.MD.4**

▶ Classifying Geometric Shapes (Lessons 4-4, 4-5)

Children have been sorting shapes into categories since Kindergarten, developing increasingly sophisticated classification systems as their understanding of geometry and their mathematical vocabulary grow. In this unit, children review the geometric properties of polygons and identify and sketch common polygons. Children also explore attributes of quadrilaterals, using mathematical language such as *parallel sides* and *right angles*, and classify quadrilaterals into categories and subcategories based on their properties. They extend this reasoning to explore the relationships between categories of quadrilaterals. **3.G.1**

 Standards and Goals for Mathematical Content

Because the standards within each domain can be broad, *Everyday Mathematics* **has unpacked each standard into Goals for Mathematical Content GMC. For a complete list of Standards and Goals, see page EM1.**

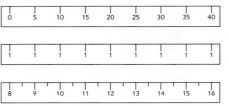

These rulers are suitable for measuring because they each have same-size units.

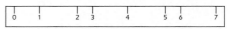

This ruler is not suitable for measuring because it has unequal units.

Unit 4 Vocabulary

angle	length	rectangle
approximate	line plot	rectilinear figure
area	mass	rhombus
array	mathematical model	right angle
attributes	maximum	scale
benchmark	minimum	side
composite unit	parallel	square
data	parallelogram	square unit
decompose	perimeter	trapezoid
face	polygon	vertex
kilogram	precise	
kite	quadrilateral	

▶ Measuring Perimeter and Area
(Lessons 4-6 through 4-12)

In Lesson 4-6 children draw on their experiences with measuring lengths to develop strategies for determining perimeter. They measure distances around the faces of boxes, and then measure perimeters of rectangles and other polygons to the nearest half inch. **3.MD.8** Lesson 4-7 focuses on distinguishing perimeter from area. Children use 1-foot square units to measure first the perimeter and then the area of a 1-yard square. They use the edge of the square unit to measure perimeter and tile the interior of the shape with square units to measure area. **3.MD.5, 3.MD.5b, 3.MD.6, 3.MD.8**

Lesson 4-8 introduces the concept of grouping units to form a larger composite unit. Measuring with composite units helps to connect the strategy of skip counting groups of units with the concept of area as space covered.

In Lesson 4-9 children draw explicit connections between counting units of area and their earlier work with arrays and multiplication. They recognize that the square units inside their rectangles form arrays. Rather than counting individual units or skip counting by rows, children learn they can multiply rows and columns of square units to find area. They discover there is a one-to-one correspondence between the dimensions of the array and the lengths of the sides of the rectangle. The length of one pair of sides of a rectangle is the same as the number of square units in a row, and the length of the adjacent sides of that rectangle is the same as the number of columns in the array of square units. **3.MD.7, 3.MD.7a, 3.MD.7b** This realization sets the stage for the development of the standard formula of the area of rectangles in *Fourth Grade Everyday Mathematics*.

Measuring Perimeter and Area *Continued*

In Lesson 4-10 children play *The Area and Perimeter Game*. The object of the game is to determine whether the areas or the perimeters of given rectangles are greater. The distinction between area and perimeter is key to winning the game. Children also learn that areas and perimeters of rectangles do not have a linear relationship. That is, as areas get larger, perimeters do not necessarily grow. **3.MD.8**

In Lesson 4-11 children engage in an open response task that involves creating models of a rabbit pen. They draw at least 2 different rectangles with the same perimeter, but different areas. **3.MD.8** Then they use their models to determine the best pen for the rabbit.

In Lesson 4-12 children extend their strategies for finding areas of rectilinear figures—polygons whose sides meet to form right angles—by decomposing them into multiple, nonoverlapping rectangles. Adding the areas of the decomposed parts to find the total area helps children learn that area is additive. **3.MD.7, 3.MD.7d**

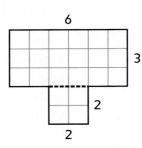

$6 \times 3 = 18$ and $2 \times 2 = 4$.
$18 + 4 = 22$
The area of this shape is 22 square units.

Mathematical Background: Practices

 In Everyday Mathematics, *children learn the **content** of mathematics as they engage in the **practices** of mathematics. As such, the Standards for Mathematical Practice are embedded in children's everyday work, including hands-on activities, problem-solving tasks, discussions, and written work. Read here to see how Mathematical Practices 6 and 7 are emphasized in this unit.*

► Standard for Mathematical Practice 6

Mathematical Practice 6 focuses on precision in the context of clear communication and of measurement. Throughout *Everyday Mathematics,* children are encouraged to use vocabulary that makes sense to them, but are also expected to develop a precise academic vocabulary that enables them to clearly communicate and differentiate related mathematical ideas. **GMP6.1**

Children learn about recording length measurements to appropriate degrees of precision in Lesson 4-1. **GMP6.4** They learn that all measurement is inexact and that the most precise measurement they can obtain depends on the size of the units marked on their measuring tool. **GMP6.2** When greater precision is needed, the measurer needs smaller units. This understanding is also necessary when choosing the most appropriate unit of measure for a given task. **GMP6.3**

In Lesson 4-5 children sort quadrilaterals into categories based on attributes. Children use informal language to describe the properties that pertain to each shape. Then the teacher introduces formal vocabulary and definitions that provide children with a means to clearly distinguish these quadrilaterals. **GMP6.1**

Many children confuse the related concepts of area and perimeter; when asked to find the area of a shape, children often add the lengths of its sides. Lessons 4-6 through 4-12 were designed to address this confusion by grounding the understanding of formal vocabulary with experiences of physically measuring both perimeter and area of shapes, and focusing children's attention on the difference between the two measurements for given rectangles. **GMP6.3**

► Standard for Mathematical Practice 7

Mathematical Practice 7 focuses on discerning and making use of structure. In this unit, two important skills of mathematical structure are developed: exploring the complex relationships among categories and subcategories of quadrilaterals, and arranging square units in meaningful ways to measure the space enclosed by a rectangle. **GMP7.1** When exploring types of quadrilaterals, children are able to make use of the structured relationships among categories to make logical inferences about properties of shapes. For example, knowing that a mystery shape does not fit the category of parallelograms, they can conclude that the shape is not a rectangle, square, or rhombus without any further information about that shape's attributes. **GMP7.1, GMP7.2** When measuring area, children place square units within a shape's boundary so there are no gaps or overlaps, and count the total number of units that cover the space. Children organize this collection of square units into arrays, and connect the measurement of area to skip counting and then to multiplication. **GMP7.1, GMP7.2**

 Standards and Goals for Mathematical Practice

SMP6 Attend to precision.

GMP6.1 Explain your mathematical thinking clearly and precisely.

GMP6.2 Use an appropriate level of precision for your problem.

GMP6.3 Use clear labels, units, and mathematical language.

GMP6.4 Think about accuracy and efficiency when you count, measure, and calculate.

SMP7 Look for and make use of structure.

GMP7.1 Look for mathematical structures such as categories, patterns, and properties.

GMP7.2 Use structures to solve problems and answer questions.

Go Online ▷ to the *Implementation Guide* for more information about the Mathematical Practices.

For children's information on the Mathematical Practices, see *Student Reference Book,* pages 1–36.

Lesson 4-1

Measuring with a Ruler

Overview Children measure to the nearest half inch and centimeter.

▶ **Before You Begin**

For Part 2, plan how to store and keep track of toolkit tape measures. Find two pencils whose lengths differ by about 1 cm but round to the same nearest inch. For example, they may be about 15 cm and 16 cm long, or about 6 in. long. Prepare to display Rulers A, C, and D (*Math Masters*, page TA30).

▶ **Vocabulary**

precise • approximate

Common Core State Standards

Focus Cluster
Represent and interpret data.

---

1 · Warm Up 5 min

	Materials	
Mental Math and Fluency Children use helper facts to solve multiplication facts.	slate	3.OA.7

---

2 · Focus 40–50 min

Math Message Children measure their pencils to the nearest inch and centimeter.	toolkit ruler, toolkit tape measure, pencil	3.MD.4 SMP5
Examining Different Rulers Children discuss how to measure more precisely.	*Math Masters*, p. TA30; toolkit ruler; toolkit tape measure; 15 and 16 cm-long pencils; scissors	3.MD.4 SMP5, SMP6
Measuring to the Nearest $\frac{1}{2}$ Inch and Centimeter Children measure to the nearest $\frac{1}{2}$ inch and centimeter.	*Math Journal 1*, p. 99; *Math Masters*, p. TA30; scissors	3.MD.4 SMP5
✓ **Assessment Check-In** See page 328.	*Math Journal 1*, p. 99	3.MD.4, SMP5
Exploring Unusual Rulers Children make sense of non-standard rulers.	*Math Journal 1*, p. 100; *Math Masters*, p. TA30	3.MD.4 SMP5, SMP6

CCSS 3.MD.4 Spiral Snapshot

GMC Measure lengths to the nearest $\frac{1}{2}$ inch, $\frac{1}{4}$ inch, or whole centimeter.

| 1-3 Focus Practice | 4-1 Focus | 4-2 Focus | 4-3 Focus | 4-6 Focus Practice | 4-7 Focus Practice | 4-8 Practice | 6-5 Focus |

▶

Spiral Tracker   **Go Online** ▷ to see how mastery develops for all standards within the grade.

---

3 · Practice 15–20 min

Minute Math+ Children practice mental math strategies.	*Minute Math®+*	
Solving Length Number Stories Children solve two-step number stories involving lengths.	*Math Journal 1*, p. 101; *Student Reference Book*, p. 30	3.OA.2, 3.OA.3, 3.OA.8, 3.OA.7, 3.NBT.2 SMP1
Math Boxes 4-1 Children practice and maintain skills.	*Math Journal 1*, p. 102	See page 329.
Home Link 4-1 **Homework** Children measure to the nearest $\frac{1}{2}$ inch.	*Math Masters*, p. 120	3.NBT.2 , 3.MD.4

---

connectED.mcgraw-hill.com

Plan your lessons online with these tools.

ePresentations | Student Learning Center | Facts Workshop Game | eToolkit | Professional Development | Home Connections | Spiral Tracker | Assessment and Reporting | English Learners Support | Differentiation Support

Differentiation Options

RtI

Readiness
10–15 min

WHOLE CLASS
SMALL GROUP
PARTNER
INDEPENDENT

Measuring Length

small classroom objects
such as calculators, crayons,
markers, scissors, and so on;
six or more 1-inch square pattern blocks;
centimeter cubes; ruler

To practice measuring length, have children
use square pattern blocks to measure small
objects. Have children carefully line up
the blocks end to end along each object's
edge, count to find the total length, and
record the measure on paper as "about
_____ square pattern blocks long." Ask:
*Which part of the pattern block do we
use to measure length?* The edges Then
have children carefully measure the same
object with the inch side of their ruler and
record the measure on paper as "about
_____ inches." **GMP6.4** Ask: *What do you
notice about the two measures?* They are
the same. Note that each side of a square
pattern block is 1 inch long. Have children
repeat the activity with centimeter cubes
and the centimeter side of their ruler.

Enrichment
5–10 min

WHOLE CLASS
SMALL GROUP
PARTNER
INDEPENDENT

Measuring with Different Rulers

Math Masters, p. 118

To extend children's understanding of
measurement, have them determine which
rulers on *Math Masters,* page 118 can be
used to measure accurately. Have children
provide arguments for why they think the
rulers do or do not work. **GMP3.1**

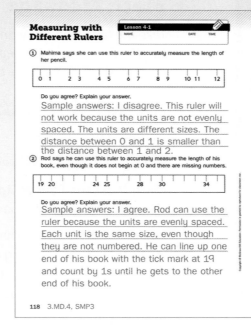

Extra Practice
10–15 min

WHOLE CLASS
SMALL GROUP
PARTNER
INDEPENDENT

Measuring Objects

Activity Card 51;
Math Masters, pp. 119 and TA30;
classroom objects such as
markers, tissue box, eraser, small books,
and so on

For additional practice measuring to the
nearest half inch, have children measure
the lengths of different objects in the
classroom using Rulers A and C from
Math Masters, page TA30. **GMP6.4** Have
them record their measurements on *Math
Masters,* page 119 and compare them.

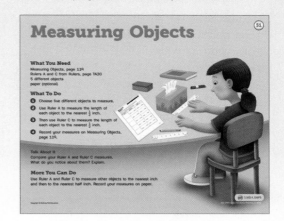

English Language Learners Support

Beginning ELL Use role play to introduce the term *nearest,* connecting it to *near/nearer*
and contrasting with *far away.* Have children stand around the room at various distances
from you. Use sentence frames such as: _____ *is near to me.* _____ *is nearer to me.* _____ *is
nearest to me.* _____ *is far away from me.* Model the terms with other objects while directing
the children to place objects near, nearer, and nearest to a point of reference.

 Go Online ELL **English Learners
Support**

Professional Development

Measuring to the nearest half inch is more precise than measuring to the nearest inch. Because smaller units yield more precise measures, a ruler with $\frac{1}{8}$-inch markings can give a more precise measurement than a ruler with $\frac{1}{2}$-inch markings. Children attend to precision as they choose the most appropriate unit of measure, or level of precision, for a given measurement task or tool.

Math Masters, p. TA30

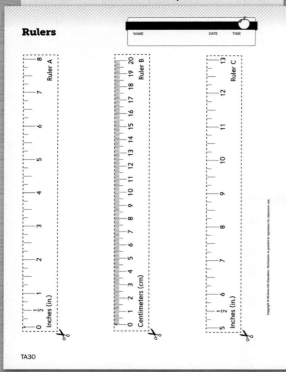

1 Warm Up 5 min `Go Online` ePresentations eToolkit

▶ Mental Math and Fluency

Have children solve each pair of facts on their slates and share their strategies. Highlight strategies that use the first fact to solve the second by adding or subtracting a group.

Leveled exercises:

● ○ ○ **Set 1:** $2 \times 6 = ?$ 12 $3 \times 6 = ?$ 18 **Set 2:** $2 \times 8 = ?$ 16 $3 \times 8 = ?$ 24
● ● ○ **Set 1:** $5 \times 3 = ?$ 15 $6 \times 3 = ?$ 18 **Set 2:** $5 \times 8 = ?$ 40 $6 \times 8 = ?$ 48
● ● ● **Set 1:** $10 \times 4 = ?$ 40 $9 \times 4 = ?$ 36 **Set 2:** $10 \times 7 = ?$ 70 $9 \times 7 = ?$ 63

2 Focus 40–50 min `Go Online` ePresentations eToolkit

▶ Math Message

Take the tape measure with your toolkit number. Use it to measure the length of a pencil to the nearest inch and nearest centimeter. Discuss what you notice about the two measurements with a partner. GMP5.2

▶ Examining Different Rulers

Math Masters, p. TA30

| WHOLE CLASS | SMALL GROUP | PARTNER | INDEPENDENT |

Math Message Follow-Up In *Second Grade Everyday Mathematics,* children used a toolkit tape measure. Briefly review how to rewind it.

Invite children to share what they noticed about their measurements. Support them in explaining that centimeter measures are larger numbers because centimeters are smaller than inches, and vice versa.

Show two pencils that differ in length by about a centimeter but whose measures in inches are about the same. (*See Before You Begin.*) Have volunteers verify that the pencils measure about the same in inches. Then place the pencils side by side to show that they are not exactly the same length. Ask: *How can the pencils measure about the same number of inches?* Sample answer: One pencil could be a little less than 6 inches long and one could be a little more. *What unit could we use to measure them more exactly? Explain.* Sample answer: We can use centimeters because they are smaller than inches. Remind the class that smaller units give us more **precise,** or exact, measurements. GMP6.2 Have volunteers verify that the lengths measured in centimeters are different.

Explain that measuring to the nearest half inch is another way to measure more precisely. Tell children that today they will measure more precisely by using half inches and centimeters as their measurement units.

Have children cut Rulers A, B, and C from *Math Masters,* page TA30 and put Ruler C aside for the next activity. Display each ruler and have children follow along.

Ruler A: Draw attention to the fraction notation $\frac{1}{2}$ on the ruler. Point out that $\frac{1}{2}$ is another way to write *1 half* or *1 out of 2 equal parts.* Remind children that they wrote *1-half* in numbers and words in second grade. In third grade, they can write $\frac{1}{2}$ in fraction, or standard, notation. Have children write $\frac{1}{2}$ in the air with their fingers, saying *1-half.*

Have children identify the half-inch marks between the whole numbers. Emphasize that a half inch is 1 of 2 equal parts of an inch, so from 0 to $\frac{1}{2}$ is a half inch and from $\frac{1}{2}$ to 1 is another half inch, so there are two half inches in each inch. Together, count the sixteen $\frac{1}{2}$-inch units on the ruler. GMP5.2 Tell children that another way to say *8 inches* is *sixteen half inches.*

Point out the marks halfway between the half-inch marks. Ask: *What do these marks do?* Sample answer: They divide the inch into 4 equal parts. Tell children that 1 of the 4 parts is called *1-fourth inch,* and that fourth inches can help when measuring to the nearest half inch. Display $\frac{1}{4}$ and have children use their fingers to practice writing $\frac{1}{4}$ in the air, saying *1-fourth.* If the end of an object is to the right of the fourth-inch mark, you round the measure to the next greater half inch. If the end of an object is to the left of the fourth-inch mark, you round the measure to the next smaller half inch. Emphasize that the nearest half-inch measures may be whole numbers. You may wish to model this using illustrations like those below or by measuring real objects.

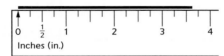

This line segment is about $3\frac{1}{2}$ inches long.

This line segment is about 2 inches long.

Ask: *How might you use the arrow on Ruler A to help with measuring lengths?* Sample answer: I can line up one end of an object with the 0 and see how many inches long it is.

Ruler B: Ask: *How is Ruler B different from Ruler A?* GMP6.3 Sample answers: Ruler B shows centimeters and Ruler A shows inches. There are more units labeled on Ruler B than on Ruler A. Point out that children can use the half-centimeter marks to help measure to the nearest centimeter like they used the quarter-inch marks to measure to the nearest half inch.

Emphasize that measurements can be only as precise as the smallest unit the ruler shows. If children use a ruler with only inch marks, the most precise measurements they can make are to the nearest inch. Smaller units, such as half inches, allow for more precise measures. Remind children that all measurements are **approximate,** or close, but not exact. We can learn to measure more precisely, but there is a limit to what people can observe and what tools can measure.

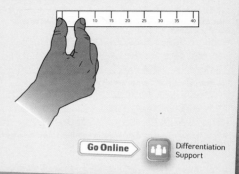
Math Journal 1, p. 99

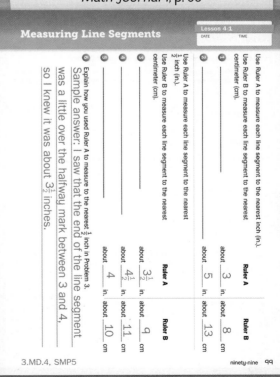

3.MD.4, SMP5

ninety-nine   99

NOTE The unconventional rulers used in this lesson were created by the NSF-supported STEM Project at Michigan State University.

▶ Measuring to the Nearest $\frac{1}{2}$ Inch and Centimeter

Math Journal 1, p. 99; Math Masters, p. TA30

| WHOLE CLASS | **SMALL GROUP** | **PARTNER** | INDEPENDENT |

Have children use Ruler A to measure the line segments on journal page 99 to the nearest inch or half inch, and Ruler B to measure them to the nearest centimeter.

> ✔ **Assessment Check-In**   **CCSS** **3.MD.4**
>
> *Math Journal 1, p. 99*
>
> Expect most children to accurately measure line segments to the nearest inch and centimeter for Problems 1 and 2. For children who struggle, consider implementing the Readiness activity. Many children will be able to accurately measure line segments to the nearest half inch for Problems 3 through 6. **GMP5.2** To support children with measuring to the nearest half inch, have them shade the fourth-inch spaces on Ruler A in alternating colors. The colors can help them determine the nearest half inch to the end of the line segment.
>
> ✔ Assessment and Reporting   **Go Online** to record student progress and to see trajectories toward mastery for this standard.

▶ Exploring Unusual Rulers

Math Journal 1, p. 100; Math Masters, p. TA30

| WHOLE CLASS | SMALL GROUP | **PARTNER** | INDEPENDENT |

Ruler C: Ask children to compare Ruler C with Rulers A and B from *Math Masters*, page TA30 and invite them to share what they notice. If no child mentions it, point out that Ruler C does not start with zero. Have children discuss whether you can use this ruler to measure. Ask questions to guide their thinking:

- *Can you use Ruler C to measure in inches or centimeters?* Inches
- *How many inches does Ruler C show? How do you know?* **GMP6.3**
  Ruler C shows 8 inches because there are eight 1-inch spaces between 5 and 13.
- *How could you measure to the nearest inch with Ruler C?* **GMP5.2**
  Sample answers: I could count the inch spaces and ignore the numbers. I could line up one end of an object with the 5, look at the number at the other end, and subtract 5 since the ruler starts at 5.

Next have partnerships examine the unusual rulers on journal page 100 and answer the questions. After most children finish, invite partners to share their answers with the class. Elicit that Rulers 1, 2, and 3 can all be used to measure accurately because they have same-size units, so we can report our measurements as "about _____ units." **GMP6.3** Point out that Ruler 4 does not have same-size units. Since each interval is a different size, this ruler could not be used to measure accurately.

Summarize Have partnerships discuss what they learned today about the units on rulers. Sample answers: Units on rulers need to be the same size. Smaller units give more precise measures.

3 Practice   15–20 min   Go Online   ePresentations   eToolkit   Home Connections

▶ Minute Math+

To practice mental math strategies, select a *Minute Math+* activity.

▶ Solving Length Number Stories

Math Journal 1, p. 101; *Student Reference Book,* p. 30

| WHOLE CLASS | **SMALL GROUP** | **PARTNER** | **INDEPENDENT** |

Have children make sense of and solve length number stories using more than one step. Encourage children to use the Guide to Solving Number Stories on *Student Reference Book,* page 30 to help make a plan for solving each problem. **GMP1.1**

▶ Math Boxes 4-1 ✦

Math Journal 1, p. 102

| WHOLE CLASS | **SMALL GROUP** | **PARTNER** | **INDEPENDENT** |

Mixed Practice Math Boxes 4-1 are paired with Math Boxes 4-3.

▶ Home Link 4-1

Math Masters, p. 120

Homework Children measure themselves to the nearest $\frac{1}{2}$ inch.

Math Journal 1, p. 102

Math Boxes   Lesson 4-1
DATE   TIME

① The third-grade class starts lunch at 10:55 A.M. They have 40 minutes to eat. What time is lunch over?

   11:35 A.M.

② Fill in the missing numbers.

   in → Rule ÷ 5 → out

in	out
5	1
10	2
25	5
30	6
45	9

   Answers vary.

③ An alligator clutch had 82 eggs. 19 eggs did not hatch. How many eggs did hatch? Sample answer:

   82 − 19 = ?
   (number model with ?)

   Answer: **63 eggs**
   (unit)

④ Use this array to show how 5 × 3 can help you figure out 6 × 3.

   × × ×
   × × ×
   × × ×
   × × ×
   × × ×
   × × ×

   Helper fact: 5 × 3 = 15
   6 × 3 = **18**

⑤ **Writing/Reasoning** What strategy could you use to check your answer to Problem 3?
Sample answer: I could add 19 and 63 to see if I get 82 eggs in all. I could estimate 80 − 20 = 60 and compare it with my answer.

102   one hundred two
① 3.MD.1 ② 3.OA.4, 3.OA.6, 3.OA.7 ③ 3.NBT.2 ④ 3.OA.1, 3.OA.5, 3.OA.7 ⑤ 3.OA.8, 3.NBT.2, SMP1

Math Masters, p. 120

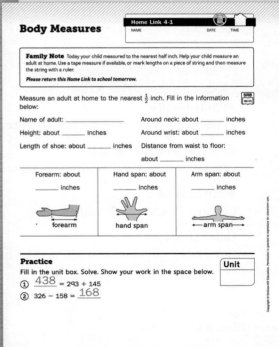

Body Measures   Home Link 4-1
NAME   DATE   TIME

Family Note Today your child measured to the nearest half inch. Help your child measure an adult at home. Use a tape measure if available, or mark lengths on a piece of string and then measure the string with a ruler.
Please return this Home Link to school tomorrow.

Measure an adult at home to the nearest $\frac{1}{2}$ inch. Fill in the information below:

Name of adult: _____   Around neck: about _____ inches

Height: about _____ inches   Around wrist: about _____ inches

Length of shoe: about _____ inches   Distance from waist to floor:
   about _____ inches

Forearm: about	Hand span: about	Arm span: about
_____ inches	_____ inches	_____ inches

forearm   hand span   ←arm span→

Practice
Fill in the unit box. Solve. Show your work in the space below.

   Unit

① **438** = 293 + 145

② 326 − 158 = **168**

120   3.NBT.2, 3.MD.4

Lesson 4-2

Application: Line Plots

Overview Children generate measurement data and represent the data on a line plot.

▶ **Before You Begin**

For Part 2, distribute a stick-on note to each child. Decide where children should display their stick-on notes so everyone can see the measures. (*See page 333.*) For the optional Extra Practice activity, collect a variety of small objects that range in length from about 2 inches to 4 or 5 inches. Some of the objects can be the same lengths.

▶ **Vocabulary**

data • line plot • scale • maximum • minimum

Common Core State Standards

Focus Cluster
Represent and interpret data.

---

1 Warm Up 5 min

Materials

Mental Math and Fluency
Children solve number stories involving multiplication.

slate (optional)

3.OA.1

---

2 Focus 40–50 min

Math Message Children measure their shoe lengths and display the data.	stick-on notes, measuring tools	3.MD.4 SMP4
Organizing Measurement Data Children organize shoe-length data on a line plot.	*Math Journal 1*, p. 103; *Math Masters*, p. TA20 (optional)	3.MD.4 SMP4, SMP6
✓ **Assessment Check-In** See page 333.	*Math Journal 1*, p. 103	3.MD.4, SMP4
Ordering Gym Shoes Children discuss data in a line plot.	*Math Journal 1*, p. 103	3.MD.4 SMP4
Analyzing Line Plot Data Children solve number stories based on a line plot.	*Math Journal 1*, p. 104	3.MD.4 SMP4, SMP6

CCSS 3.MD.4 **Spiral Snapshot**

GMC Collect, organize, and represent data on line plots.

4-2 Focus Practice	5-6 Practice	5-10 Practice	6-5 Focus	8-2 Practice

Spiral Tracker **Go Online** to see how mastery develops for all standards within the grade.

---

3 Practice 15–20 min

Minute Math+ Children practice mental math strategies.	*Minute Math®+*	
Creating a Picture Graph Children create a picture graph using provided data.	*Math Journal 1*, p. 105	3.MD.3 SMP4
Math Boxes 4-2 Children practice and maintain skills.	*Math Journal 1*, p. 106	See page 335.
Home Link 4-2 **Homework** Children create a line plot using a data set.	*Math Masters*, p. 123	3.OA.7, 3.MD.4 SMP4

---

connectED.mcgraw-hill.com

Plan your lessons online with these tools.

 ePresentations
 Student Learning Center
 Facts Workshop Game
 eToolkit
 Professional Development
 Home Connections
 Spiral Tracker
 Assessment and Reporting
 English Learners Support
ÅÅÅ Differentiation Support

330 Unit 4 | Measurement and Geometry

Differentiation Options
RtI

Readiness
10–15 min

WHOLE CLASS	
SMALL GROUP	
PARTNER	
INDEPENDENT	

Plotting Plant Heights

Math Masters, p. 121

To provide experience representing data, have children use a given data set to complete a line plot on *Math Masters,* page 121.

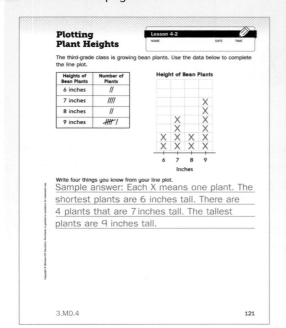

Enrichment
25–30 min

WHOLE CLASS	
SMALL GROUP	
PARTNER	
INDEPENDENT	

Making a Line Plot of Hand Spans

Activity Card 52;
Student Reference Book, p. 196
(optional); paper; stick-on notes; tape measure

To apply their knowledge of representing and interpreting data, have children collect, organize, and represent hand-span measurements to the nearest half inch on a line plot. **GMP4.1** Then have them discuss what they notice about their data. **GMP4.2**

Extra Practice
25–30 min

WHOLE CLASS	
SMALL GROUP	
PARTNER	
INDEPENDENT	

Making a Line Plot

Activity Card 53;
Student Reference Book, p. 196
(optional); *Math Masters,* p. 122;
small objects; ruler or tape measure

For additional experience collecting, gathering, and organizing data, have children measure objects (*See Before You Begin*) to the nearest half inch, record the measures, and order their data from shortest to longest lengths on *Math Masters,* page 122. **GMP4.1** Then have children represent their measures on a line plot.

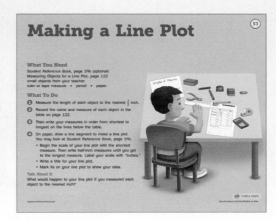

English Language Learners Support

Beginning ELL To help children understand different meanings of the word *order,* use visual aids and role play. For example, role-play placing an order in a restaurant, following orders to do something, or lining up children by height order from shortest to tallest. Provide visuals for each scenario, and describe the scenes so children come to understand the word *order* in different contexts.

> **Go Online** **ELL** English Learners Support

CCSS

Standards and Goals for
Mathematical Practice

SMP4 **Model with mathematics.**
  GMP4.1 Model real-world situations using graphs, drawings, tables, symbols, numbers, diagrams, and other representations.
  GMP4.2 Use mathematical models to solve problems and answer questions.

SMP6 **Attend to precision.**
  GMP6.3 Use clear labels, units, and mathematical language.

Math Journal 1, p. 103

Shoe-Length Data

Lesson 4-2
DATE   TIME

Look at the measurements on the stick-on notes. Sample answers given.

1. What is the shortest shoe length in your class? ___9 inches___
2. What is the longest shoe length in your class? ___11 inches___

Use the class shoe-length data to complete the line plot.

Class Shoe Lengths

	X			
	X			
	X	X		
X	X	X		
X	X	X	X	
X	X	X	X	X
X	X	X	X	X

9   9½   10   10½   11
Inches

3. If you were buying gym shoes for your class, which sizes should you buy the most of? Why?
   I would buy 9½ and 10 inches because those numbers occurred the most in our data set.

3.MD.4, SMP4, SMP6   one hundred three   **103**

---

1 Warm Up   5 min

Go Online

ePresentations   eToolkit

▶ Mental Math and Fluency

Pose number stories for children to solve.
Leveled exercises:

● ○ ○   There are 5 rows of chairs and 5 chairs in each row.
How many chairs are there in all?   25 chairs

● ● ○   A pencil box has 4 rows of pencils and 4 pencils in each row.
How many pencils does it hold in all?   16 pencils

● ● ●   A patio has 8 rows of bricks and 8 bricks in each row.
How many bricks are there in the patio?   64 bricks

2 Focus   40–50 min

Go Online

ePresentations   eToolkit

▶ Math Message

Measure your shoe length to the nearest $\frac{1}{2}$ inch. Write your measurement on a stick-on note. Write large so others can see your writing. Do not write your name on the stick-on note. Your teacher will tell you where to place it.

Talk to a partner about how to organize the stick-on notes so we know how many children have the same length shoes.

▶ Organizing Measurement Data

Math Journal 1, p. 103

| WHOLE CLASS | SMALL GROUP | PARTNER | INDEPENDENT |

Math Message Follow-Up Invite children to share ideas about organizing the class **data,** or information, about shoe lengths. **GMP4.1** Expect a variety of ideas to emerge, but highlight ordering the numbers from either shortest to longest or longest to shortest. Have volunteers help you order the stick-on notes.

Remind children that one way to organize data is to create a **line plot.** Sketch a line plot similar to the one on journal page 103 and title it Class Shoe Lengths. Below the scale, write the label Inches. Point out to children that the line plot is a number line, and they can use the number line to organize numerical data like their shoe lengths. **GMP4.1** Have children follow along and label the line plot on journal page 103. If needed, have children extend the number line for additional data.

Have children answer Problems 1 and 2 on journal page 103 to help determine the starting number and **scale,** or interval size, for the line plot. Invite children to share their answers, checking that they have correctly identified the shortest and longest shoe length. **GMP6.3**

Remind them that all the class data must be shown on the line plot. Discuss what the start number on the line should be. If children suggest zero, prompt them to explain their reasoning. Ask: *What is the smallest number we need to show on our line plot?* Sample answer: The smallest shoe length Help children see that since no one in the class has a shoe length of zero inches, zero does not need to be included. If nobody mentions it, point out that the numbers on the line should begin near the smallest number in the data set. When there is limited space, it is easiest to start the scale with the smallest number. Record this number on the line plot as children record it on journal page 103.

Help children understand that since the shoe-length measurements are to the nearest $\frac{1}{2}$ inch, the scale should use $\frac{1}{2}$-inch increments and the line should go up to at least the longest shoe-length measure in the class. (*See margin.*)

Invite children to move their shoe measurements above the corresponding numbers on the line-plot display. Emphasize that each stick-on note represents one child. Then have children draw an X to represent each measurement on their line plots. GMP4.1

✔ **Assessment Check-In** ⒸⒸⓈⓈ 3.MD.4

Math Journal 1, p. 103

Because this is the first exposure to scaled line plots with fractions of inches, do not expect all children to determine the scale and represent the class shoe-length data correctly on the line plot. GMP4.1 Opportunities to collect, organize, and represent data on scaled line plots will occur through ongoing practice.

✔ Assessment and Reporting ⟨ Go Online ⟩ to record student progress and to see trajectories toward mastery for this standard.

When everyone has plotted the data, ask children how to figure out whether the graph shows everyone's data. GMP4.2 We can count the number of stick-on notes. There should be one note for every child in the class.
Count together to verify that all data have been collected.

Have children make sense of and use the graph to answer questions. GMP4.2 Answers given below are based on the line plot in the margin.

- *What do you notice about the shape of the graph?* There are more stick-on notes above the numbers in the middle than the numbers at the ends.
- *Which measurement occurs most often?* $9\frac{1}{2}$ inches
- Point to a gap in the data. *What does this gap mean?* No one has a shoe length of $10\frac{1}{2}$ inches.
- *What is the longest shoe length in the class?* 11 inches *This is the* **maximum** *of our data set.*
- *What is the shortest shoe length in the class?* 9 inches *This is the* **minimum** *of our data set.*

Common Misconception

Differentiate Watch for children who skip numbers on the scale because no data were collected for that number. Support children in understanding that if no data were collected, the space above that number is simply left blank so you can see the gap in sizes on the graph.

⟨ Go Online ⟩ Differentiation Support

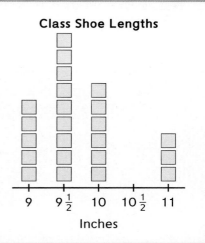

Line plot with stick-on notes

Academic Language Development

Have children work in small groups to deepen their understanding of the terms *maximum and minimum.* Assign partnerships within each group to complete a 4-Square Graphic Organizer (*Math Masters*, page TA20) for one of the two words, using the headings *Picture* or *Illustration*, *Example*, *Non-Example*, and *Synonym* or *Words with the Same Meaning*. To provide oral language practice, direct children to explain their organizers to their group members.

Math Journal 1, p. 104

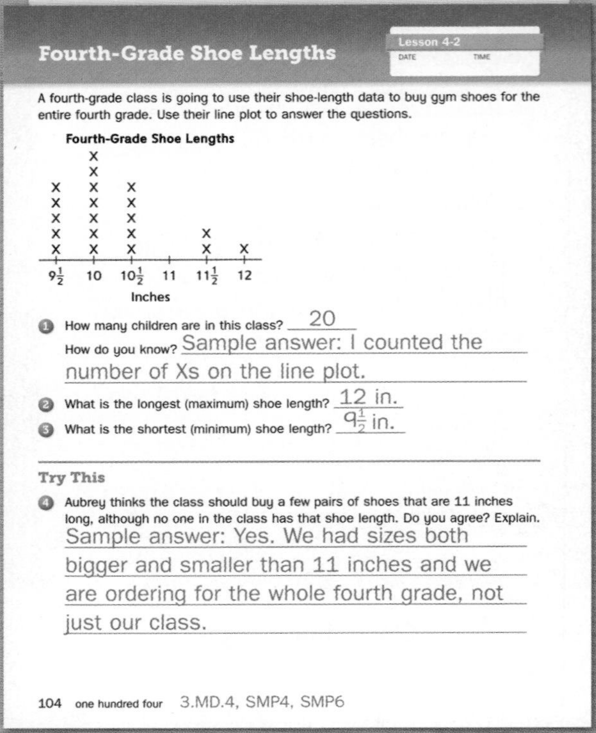

Fourth-Grade Shoe Lengths

Lesson 4-2
DATE   TIME

A fourth-grade class is going to use their shoe-length data to buy gym shoes for the entire fourth grade. Use their line plot to answer the questions.

Fourth-Grade Shoe Lengths

```
    X
    X
X   X   X
X   X   X
X   X   X            X
X   X   X        X
X   X   X        X   X
+---+---+---+---+---+
9½  10  10½ 11  11½ 12
        Inches
```

① How many children are in this class? __20__
How do you know? Sample answer: I counted the number of Xs on the line plot.

② What is the longest (maximum) shoe length? __12 in.__

③ What is the shortest (minimum) shoe length? __9½ in.__

Try This

④ Aubrey thinks the class should buy a few pairs of shoes that are 11 inches long, although no one in the class has that shoe length. Do you agree? Explain.
Sample answer: Yes. We had sizes both bigger and smaller than 11 inches and we are ordering for the whole fourth grade, not just our class.

104   one hundred four   3.MD.4, SMP4, SMP6

Math Journal 1, p. 105

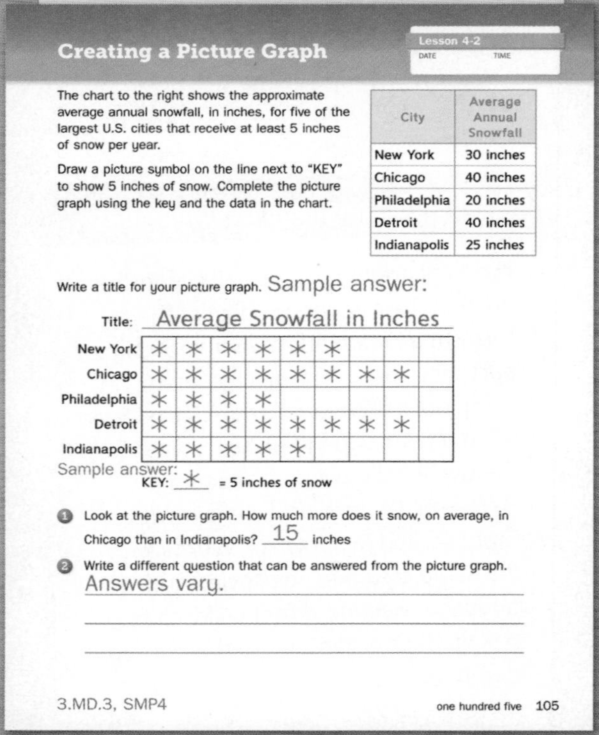

Creating a Picture Graph

Lesson 4-2
DATE   TIME

The chart to the right shows the approximate average annual snowfall, in inches, for five of the largest U.S. cities that receive at least 5 inches of snow per year.

Draw a picture symbol on the line next to "KEY" to show 5 inches of snow. Complete the picture graph using the key and the data in the chart.

City	Average Annual Snowfall
New York	30 inches
Chicago	40 inches
Philadelphia	20 inches
Detroit	40 inches
Indianapolis	25 inches

Write a title for your picture graph. Sample answer:

Title: __Average Snowfall in Inches__

New York	✳	✳	✳	✳	✳	✳	
Chicago	✳	✳	✳	✳	✳	✳	✳	✳
Philadelphia	✳	✳	✳	✳			
Detroit	✳	✳	✳	✳	✳	✳	✳	✳
Indianapolis	✳	✳	✳	✳	✳		

Sample answer:
KEY: ✳ = 5 inches of snow

① Look at the picture graph. How much more does it snow, on average, in Chicago than in Indianapolis? __15__ inches

② Write a different question that can be answered from the picture graph.
Answers vary.

3.MD.3, SMP4   one hundred five   105

▶ Ordering Gym Shoes

Math Journal 1, p. 103

WHOLE CLASS   **SMALL GROUP**   **PARTNER**   INDEPENDENT

Pose the following situation: *Suppose we were buying gym shoes for the entire third grade. How might our class data help us?* GMP4.2 Have partners discuss and then share their ideas with the class. Highlight that organizing the data in a line plot helps us see that some measurements occur more often than others. Ask:

- *Do we know the shoe length of every third grader? Explain.* No. We only collected data for our class.
- *Do you think data from other third-grade classes would be similar to ours? Explain.* Sample answer: Yes, because we are all about the same age and our feet are probably about the same size.
- *Should we buy the same number of shoes in each size? Explain.* GMP4.2 Sample answer: No. Since $9\frac{1}{2}$ inches and 10 inches were the most common, we should buy more of these sizes than others. Since only 2 people have 11-inch shoe lengths, we should buy fewer of that size.

Have partnerships answer Problem 3 on journal page 103. Invite them to share their answers with the class.

Professional Development Data-collection activities are usually more meaningful to children if they come from questions about situations that children really care about. You may wish to further explore real-life problems based on the interests of your class.

▶ Analyzing Line Plot Data

Math Journal 1, p. 104

WHOLE CLASS   **SMALL GROUP**   **PARTNER**   INDEPENDENT

Have partnerships analyze the line plot and answer the questions on journal page 104. GMP4.2

Invite children to share their answers to Problem 4. If children struggle to understand why the class should buy some 11-inch shoes, remind them that this is the data for one fourth-grade class and that they will need to buy shoes for the entire fourth grade. Ask: *Why would it make sense to buy some 11-inch shoes, even though no one in this class had 11-inch shoes?* GMP6.3 Sample answer: Some kids had shoe lengths of $10\frac{1}{2}$ and $11\frac{1}{2}$ inches, so other fourth graders might have an 11-inch shoe length because it is between those two.

Summarize Ask: *What are some things you learned about shoe lengths in our class by organizing our data on a line plot?* GMP4.2 Sample answers: Most of us have a shoe length of $9\frac{1}{2}$ inches. No one in our class has a shoe length greater than 11 inches. If a number on the scale has no data, the number still has to be on the scale.

3 Practice   15–20 min   Go Online

ePresentations eToolkit Home Connections

▶ **Minute Math+**

To practice mental math strategies, select a *Minute Math+* activity.

▶ **Creating a Picture Graph**

Math Journal 1, p. 105

| WHOLE CLASS | **SMALL GROUP** | PARTNER | INDEPENDENT |

Have children represent data on scaled picture graphs and answer questions. Support them in choosing a picture symbol and recognizing that each picture stands for 5 inches. Some children may benefit from writing 5 above or on top of their picture symbols. GMP4.1, GMP4.2

▶ **Math Boxes 4-2**

Math Journal 1, p. 106

| WHOLE CLASS | **SMALL GROUP** | PARTNER | INDEPENDENT |

Mixed Practice Math Boxes 4-2 are paired with Math Boxes 4-4.

▶ **Home Link 4-2**

Math Masters, p. 123

Homework Children create a line plot using a set of data and then use their graph to answer questions. GMP4.1, GMP4.2

Planning

...for each small group by ...you may want to laminate

...e quadrilaterals from

Kate
gr. 3
I have her
Baptismal info.

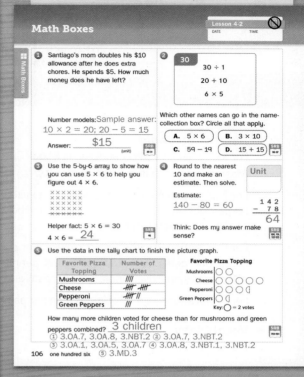

Math Journal 1, p. 106

Math Masters, p. 123

Exploring Measures of Distance and Comparisons of Mass

Overview Children measure distances around objects to the nearest $\frac{1}{2}$ inch, compare masses, and determine distances in half-inch increments.

► Before You Begin

For Part 1, select and sequence Quick Look Cards 133, 139, and 140. For the Math Message, cut *Math Masters*, page 125 into quarter sheets.

For Exploration A and the optional Extra Practice activity, the variety of small and large objects may respectively include markers, books, lunch boxes, and water bottles, and rectangular area rugs, bookcases, bulletin boards, or tables.

For Exploration B, gather various objects or collections that have a mass of about 1 gram (paper clip, centimeter cube), 50 grams (golf ball, 20 pennies), 100 grams (box of paper clips, four AA batteries), 500 grams (paperback book, loaf of bread), and 1,000 grams (liter of water, pineapple).

For Exploration C, set up stations (one per partnership) by taping rulers on a table.

► Vocabulary

mass • kilogram • benchmark

Common Core State Standards

Focus Clusters
- Solve problems involving measurement and estimation.
- Represent and interpret data.
- Geometric measurement: recognize perimeter.
- Develop understanding of fractions as numbers.

---

1 Warm Up 5–10 min

	Materials	
Mental Math and Fluency Children practice Quick Looks with equal groups and arrays.	Quick Look Cards 133, 139, 140	**3.OA.1, 3.OA.7** SMP2, SMP6

2 Focus 40–50 min

Math Message Children measure distances around their heads and wrists.	*Math Masters*, p. 125; tape measure; string; toolkit ruler; yardstick	**3.MD.4, 3.MD.8** SMP5
Measuring Around Objects Children choose tools for measuring distances.		**3.MD.4, 3.MD.8** SMP5
Exploration A: Measuring Distances Around Objects Children measure distances to the nearest $\frac{1}{2}$ inch.	*Math Journal 1*, p. 107; tape measure; toolkit ruler; yardstick; string	**3.MD.4, 3.MD.8** SMP5
Exploration B: Comparing Masses Children compare masses of objects to standard masses to determine benchmarks.	Activity Card 54; *Math Journal 1*, p. 108; pan balance; set of standard masses; objects of selected masses	**3.MD.2** SMP5
Exploration C: Traveling Along a Ruler Children determine the number of half inches a pattern-block triangle moves on a ruler.	Activity Card 55; *Math Masters*, p. 124; pattern-block triangles; rulers; dice; yardstick (optional)	**3.NF.2, 3.NF.2a, 3.MD.4** SMP5

3 Practice 15–20 min

Minute Math+ Children practice mental math strategies.	*Minute Math*®+	
Playing *Name That Number* **Game** Children use different operations to name a number.	*Student Reference Book*, pp. 249–250; *Math Masters*, p. G12; number cards 0–10 (4 of each); number cards 11–20	**3.OA.7, 3.NBT.2**
Math Boxes 4-3 Children practice and maintain skills.	*Math Journal 1*, p. 109	See page 341.
Home Link 4-3 **Homework** Children measure perimeters to the nearest $\frac{1}{2}$ inch.	*Math Masters*, p. 126	**3.MD.4, 3.OA.7** SMP5

Differentiation Options

RtI

Readiness
10–15 min

Counting Half Inches

WHOLE CLASS
SMALL GROUP
PARTNER
INDEPENDENT

Math Masters, p. TA30;
colored pencils; scissors

To practice recognizing half-inch
increments on a ruler, have children cut out
Ruler A from *Math Masters,* page TA30 and
shade the half-inch spaces with alternating
colors. Ask them to count the total number
of half inches on the ruler. **GMP5.2**
16 half inches Have children do the same
on Ruler C. Highlight that the total number
of half inches are the same on both rulers,
even though the inch marks are labeled
differently. **GMP2.2**

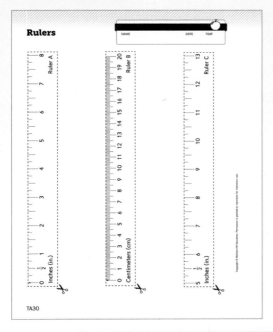

TA30

Enrichment
10–15 min

Finding More Benchmarks

WHOLE CLASS
SMALL GROUP
PARTNER
INDEPENDENT

pan balance; standard masses;
classroom objects; bags
(optional); stick-on notes

To extend children's skills with estimating
and measuring mass, have them add to the
collection of benchmarks used to estimate
mass. Have children use a pan balance and
standard masses to identify objects or
collections of objects with masses of about
25 grams and 250 grams. **GMP5.2** Provide
bags for the collections and have children
label the masses with stick-on notes. Store
the benchmark items for later use.

Extra Practice
10–15 min

Measuring Distances Around Objects

WHOLE CLASS
SMALL GROUP
PARTNER
INDEPENDENT

various objects,
ruler or tape measure

For additional practice measuring length
to the nearest half inch, have children
measure the distances around classroom
objects. Have them write a description or
draw a sketch of each object and record on
paper the distance around to the nearest
half inch.

English Language Learners Support

Beginning ELL Label and display a yardstick, meterstick, ruler, and tape measure. Use Total
Physical Response (TPR) prompts to model naming the different tools. For example, say: *This
is a yardstick.* Have children repeat the statement in response to: *What is this called?* Repeat
with each tool. After all the items have been introduced, use TPR prompts such as: *Point to
the meterstick. Put the yardstick on your desk. Bring me the tape measure.* Point to each tool
and ask: *What is this called?*

Go Online   ELL **English Learners Support**

Professional Development

In Grade 3, children are expected to find perimeters of polygons. To understand perimeter as the distance around a 2-dimensional figure, children should first explore measuring the distances, or lengths of paths, around concrete 3-dimensional objects. Then children can move more naturally to the concept of measuring the perimeter of 2-dimensional figures. They can also come to understand the perimeter of a polygon as the sum of the lengths of its sides.

1 Warm Up   5–10 min   Go Online   ePresentations   eToolkit

▶ Mental Math and Fluency

Show Quick Look Cards 133, 139, and 140 one at a time for 2–3 seconds. Ask children to share both what they saw and how they saw it. **GMP2.2, GMP6.1** Highlight equal-group and array strategies.

Quick Look Card 133 Sample answer: I saw 3 rows of 3, and I know $3 + 3 = 6$ and $6 + 3 = 9$.

Quick Look Card 139 Sample answer: I remembered the last one was 9, so I had 2 groups of 9, and $9 + 9 = 18$.

Quick Look Card 140 Sample answer: I saw 3 groups of 4, and I know $4 + 4 = 8$ and $8 + 4 = 12$.

2 Focus   40–50 min   Go Online   ePresentations   eToolkit

▶ Math Message

Math Masters, p. 125

Work with a partner. Choose a measuring tool, and measure around your head and wrist. **GMP5.1** *Record your measures on your record sheet.*

▶ Measuring Around Objects

| WHOLE CLASS | SMALL GROUP | PARTNER | INDEPENDENT |

Math Message Follow-Up Have children compare their measurements with a partner and think about whether they make sense. Invite volunteers to share how they measured and how they know whether their measures make sense. **GMP5.2** Expect responses to include that the distance aound someone's head is more than the distance around someone's wrist because a head is bigger around than a wrist.

Ask: *Which measuring tool did you choose and why?* **GMP5.1** Sample answer: I chose a tape measure because it bends, so it is easier to use to measure around something. *When might it be useful to know these measurements?* Sample answer: When buying a fitted baseball cap or making a bracelet

Have children use a finger to trace a path around the outside edge of their journals. Explain that they are tracing the distance, or length of the path, around the edges of their journal.

Ask: *How could you use a tape measure to measure the distance around your journal?* Sample answer: I would wrap my tape measure all the way around the edges of my journal. *How could we measure the distance around the journal if we had a ruler?* Sample answers: We could measure the length of each of the 4 sides and add them together. We could wrap string around the outside edge and measure the length of the string.

Tell children they will choose measuring tools and use them to find the distance around different objects in an Exploration activity.

After explaining each of the Explorations activities, assign groups to each. Plan to spend more of your time with children working on Exploration A.

▶ **Exploration A: Measuring Distances Around Objects**

Math Journal 1, p. 107

| WHOLE CLASS | SMALL GROUP | PARTNER | INDEPENDENT |

Provide a variety of measuring tools, and have partnerships use them to measure distances around small and large objects. (*See Before You Begin.*) Support children as they measure to the nearest $\frac{1}{2}$ inch and record their measurements on journal page 107.

Have children share their results and what they did to measure each distance. Circulate as children work and ask the following questions:

• *What helped you decide which tool to choose?* GMP5.1 Sample answers: Measuring tools that cannot bend do not work well for measuring curved surfaces. A yardstick is easier to use than a toolkit ruler when measuring a longer distance.

• *How did you use your tape measure to measure around a curved object? A flat object?* GMP5.2 Sample answers: For curved objects, I wrapped my tape measure all the way around to find the distance around. For flat objects, I measured the length of each edge and added the measurements to find the total distance.

▶ **Exploration B: Comparing Masses**

Activity Card 54; *Math Journal 1*, p. 108

| WHOLE CLASS | SMALL GROUP | PARTNER | INDEPENDENT |

Have children follow the directions on Activity Card 54 to explore objects that have **masses** of 1 gram, 50 grams, 100 grams, 500 grams, and 1,000 grams. GMP5.2 Tell children that another name for 1,000 grams is a **kilogram.**

Explain that sometimes we may not have access to measuring tools such as pan balances. In this situation, we can estimate masses of objects by comparing them to masses of familiar objects, or **benchmarks.** For example, a liter bottle of water is a benchmark for 1,000 grams, or 1 kilogram. Through this exploration, children will explore objects to use as benchmarks for mass.

Math Journal 1, p. 107

Measuring Distances Around Objects   Lesson 4-3

Measure the distances around some small objects and some large objects to the nearest $\frac{1}{2}$ inch. Answers vary.

1 Object: _____ Measurement: about _____ inches
2 Object: _____ Measurement: about _____ inches
3 Object: _____ Measurement: about _____ inches
4 Object: _____ Measurement: about _____ inches
5 Object: _____ Measurement: about _____ inches
6 Object: _____ Measurement: about _____ inches

7 How would you measure the distance around a real sign that looks like the one in the picture below?

Sample answers: I would use a tape measure to measure the distance around the sign. I would use a ruler to measure the length of each side and add the lengths of the sides together.

3.MD.4, 3.MD.8, SMP5   one hundred seven 107

Activity Card 54

Exploration B: Comparing Masses

I wonder what has a mass of about 1 gram?

What You Need
Math Journal 1, page 108
pan balance
1-gram, 50-gram, 100-gram, 500-gram, and 1,000-gram (1-kilogram) masses
classroom objects

What To Do
1 Zero the pan balance.
2 Place a 1-gram mass in one pan of the pan balance.
3 Place an object in the other pan that you think has about the same mass as 1-gram.
4 Keep trying with other objects until you find an object that has about the same mass.
5 Record the object on journal page 108.
6 Repeat Steps 1–5 with the other masses.

Talk About It
When might you use benchmark masses to estimate the mass of an object?

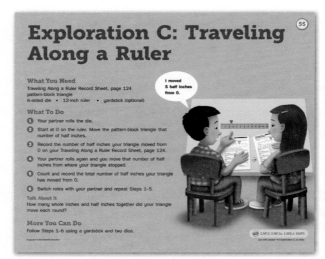
► Exploration C: Traveling Along a Ruler

Activity Card 55; *Math Masters*, p. 124

| WHOLE CLASS | SMALL GROUP | **PARTNER** | INDEPENDENT |

Have children follow the directions on Activity Card 55 to travel distances in half-inch increments along a ruler (representing fractions on a number line). Children should roll a die and move a pattern-block triangle that number of half inches from 0. As a class, study and discuss the example round on *Math Masters*, page 124. Emphasize that for each round children should record the total distance the triangle has moved from 0. If needed, model two rounds. For example, roll a 4 and move your triangle 4 half inches from 0 to 2 inches. Point and count each half-inch space as you move. Then roll a 5 and move your triangle 5 more half inches to $4\frac{1}{2}$ inches. Ask: *Now how many half inches is my triangle from 0?* 9 half inches *How many inches is it from 0?* GMP5.2 $4\frac{1}{2}$ inches

---

Differentiate   **Adjusting the Activity**

Encourage children who recognize equivalents, such as $4\frac{1}{2}$ inches and 9 half inches, to record equivalent measures for each roll.

Go Online   Differentiation Support

Summarize   Ask: *Which Exploration activity would you like to do again with someone at home? Why? What do you think it would teach your family about math?*

Exploration C: Traveling Along a Ruler

Activity Card 55

3 Practice

15–20 min | Go Online

ePresentations eToolkit Home Connections

▶ ## Minute Math+

To practice mental math strategies, select a *Minute Math+* activity.

▶ ## Playing *Name That Number*

Student Reference Book, pp. 249–250; *Math Masters,* p. G12

| WHOLE CLASS | **SMALL GROUP** | **PARTNER** | INDEPENDENT |

To practice naming equivalent names for numbers, have children play *Name That Number*. If needed, revisit *Student Reference Book,* pages 249–250 for game directions. Have children record their number sentences on *Math Masters,* page G12. Encourage them to use multiplication and division, as well as addition and subtraction, to make the target number.

Observe

• What operations do children use to name the target number?
• Do children find the target number using more than one step?

Discuss

• *How did your group check one another's solutions?*
• *How could you make the target number using more than one operation?*

| **Differentiate** | **Game Modifications** | **Go Online** | Differentiation Support |

▶ ## Math Boxes 4-3

Math Journal 1, p. 109

| WHOLE CLASS | **SMALL GROUP** | **PARTNER** | **INDEPENDENT** |

Mixed Practice Math Boxes 4-3 are paired with Math Boxes 4-1.

▶ ## Home Link 4-3

Math Masters, p. 126

Homework Children talk about how to measure the distances around objects. Then they find the distances around two objects in their home.
GMP5.1

Math Journal 1, p. 109

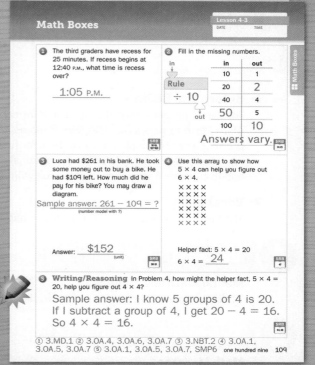

Math Masters, p. 126

Polygon Review

Overview Children review characteristics of polygons.

▶ **Before You Begin**

For Part 2, prepare a set of shape cards for each small group by cutting out, or having children cut out, *Math Masters*, pages G13–G14. (*See Planning Ahead, Lessons 3-13 and 4-2.*) You may want to laminate the shape cards and plan to store them for future use. Create a sample gameboard with a large circle for *What's My Polygon Rule?* For the optional Extra Practice activity, each child will need 18 twist ties and 18 straws—6 straws each of the following lengths: 2 in., 4 in., and 6 in.

▶ **Vocabulary**

attributes • polygon • side • vertex • angle • right angle • parallel • quadrilateral

**Common Core
State Standards**

Focus Cluster

Reason with shapes and their attributes.

---

1 Warm Up 5 min

	Materials	
Mental Math and Fluency Children solve related pairs of multiplication facts.	slate	3.OA.7

---

2 Focus 40–50 min

Math Message Children identify figures that are not polygons.	*Math Journal 1*, p. 110	3.G.1 SMP7
Reviewing Polygons Children compare and classify polygons based on numbers of sides.	*Math Journal 1*, p. 110; *Student Reference Book*, pp. 210–211; Class Data Pad	3.G.1 SMP7
Introducing *What's My Polygon Rule?* **Game** Children classify polygons based on other similarities and differences.	*Student Reference Book*, p. 262 (optional); *Math Masters*, pp. G13–G14; Class Data Pad; ruler; small bags	3.G.1 SMP7, SMP8
Representing Polygons Children represent polygons on geoboards.	*Math Masters*, p. TA31 (optional); geoboard; rubber bands; Two-Dimensional Shapes poster	3.G.1 SMP7
✓ **Assessment Check-In** See page 346.	shape cards (optional)	3.G.1, SMP7

 3.G.1 Spiral Snapshot

GMC Understand that shapes in different categories may share attributes that can define a larger category.

1-3 Focus	2-10 Practice	4-4 Focus Practice	4-5 Focus Practice	4-6 Practice	6-5 Focus Practice	6-8 Practice	8-8 Focus Practice

Spiral Tracker   **Go Online** to see how mastery develops for all standards within the grade.

---

3 Practice 15–20 min

Minute Math+ Children practice mental math strategies.	*Minute Math®+*	
Playing *Multiplication Draw* **Game** Children practice 2s, 5s, and 10s multiplication facts.	*Student Reference Book*, p. 248; *Math Masters*, p. G6; die labeled 2, 2, 5, 5, 10, 10; number cards 1–10 (4 of each)	3.OA.7
Math Boxes 4-4 Children practice and maintain skills.	*Math Journal 1*, p. 111	See page 347.
Home Link 4-4 **Homework** Children identify polygons and their attributes.	*Math Masters*, p. 127	3.G.1, SMP7

---

connectED.mcgraw-hill.com

Plan your lessons online
with these tools.

 ePresentations

 Student Learning Center

 Facts Workshop Game

 eToolkit

 Professional Development

 Home Connections

 Spiral Tracker

 Assessment and Reporting

 English Learners Support

 Differentiation Support

Differentiation Options

RtI

CCSS 3.G.1, SMP7

Readiness
5–10 min

Identifying Parallel Lines

WHOLE CLASS
SMALL GROUP
PARTNER
INDEPENDENT

straightedge

To practice recognizing parallel line segments, have children identify them using a concrete model. On blank paper, have children place a straightedge and draw line segments along its top and bottom edges. Explain that the two line segments are parallel because they are the same distance apart. Next have children take a straight object, such as a pencil, and align it on top of one of the line segments. Tell children to slowly slide the pencil, without turning it at all, toward the other line segment to "see" if their pencil can slide on top of the other line segment. Explain that if one line segment can be lined up with the other without turning their pencils, the lines are parallel. **GMP7.1** Discuss where things are parallel in the real world. Give examples such as railroad tracks, shelves in a bookcase, and so on.

CCSS 3.G.1, SMP2

Enrichment
10–15 min

Exploring Polygon Attributes

WHOLE CLASS
SMALL GROUP
PARTNER
INDEPENDENT

Activity Card 56;
Math Masters, p. TA32;
geoboard; rubber bands; scissors

To further explore shapes and their attributes, have children create polygons with a variety of attributes using geoboards and Shape Attribute Cards cut from *Math Masters*, page TA32. **GMP2.1**

CCSS 3.G.1, SMP2

Extra Practice
10–15 min

Constructing Polygons with Straws and Twist Ties

WHOLE CLASS
SMALL GROUP
PARTNER
INDEPENDENT

Activity Card 57;
number cards 4–8 (4 of each);
straws; twist ties (*See Before You Begin.*)

For additional practice with shape attributes, have children construct polygons with straws and twist ties. **GMP2.1** Then have them compare and describe their polygons. If needed, demonstrate how to join two straws by inserting opposite ends of a twist tie into each of the straws.

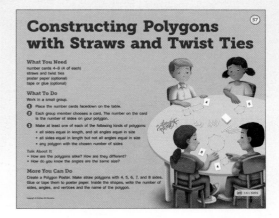

English Language Learners Support

Beginning ELL Scaffold terms used in the lesson, such as *curved, straight, line segment, vertex, connect, closed, open,* and *side* by providing children with individual vocabulary cards showing each term and corresponding illustrations. Use Total Physical Response prompts to model and direct children to find examples of the terms around the classroom.

Go Online **ELL** English Learners Support

Standards and Goals for
Mathematical Practice

SMP7 Look for and make use of structure.

   GMP7.1 Look for mathematical structures such as categories, patterns, and properties.

   GMP7.2 Use structures to solve problems and answer questions.

SMP8 Look for and express regularity in repeated reasoning.

   GMP8.1 Create and justify rules, shortcuts, and generalizations.

Math Journal 1, p. 110

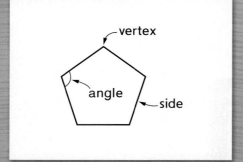

vertex · angle · side

1 Warm Up   5 min   Go Online

ePresentations   eToolkit

▶ Mental Math and Fluency

Have children solve each pair of facts on their slates. Highlight strategies that use the first fact to solve the second by adding or subtracting a group. *Leveled exercises:*

◉○○ **Set 1:** $2 \times 4 = ?$ 8 $3 \times 4 = ?$ 12 **Set 2:** $2 \times 7 = ?$ 14 $3 \times 7 = ?$ 21

◉◉○ **Set 1:** $2 \times 8 = ?$ 16 $3 \times 8 = ?$ 24 **Set 2:** $5 \times 7 = ?$ 35 $6 \times 7 = ?$ 42

◉◉◉ **Set 1:** $10 \times 6 = ?$ 60 $9 \times 6 = ?$ 54 **Set 2:** $10 \times 8 = ?$ 80 $9 \times 8 = ?$ 72

2 Focus   40–50 min   Go Online

ePresentations   eToolkit

▶ Math Message

Math Journal 1, p. 110

Look for patterns to complete the Math Message problems on journal page 110. **GMP7.1**

▶ Reviewing Polygons

Math Journal 1, p. 110; *Student Reference Book*, pp. 210–211

WHOLE CLASS	SMALL GROUP	PARTNER	INDEPENDENT

Math Message Follow-Up Have children explain which shapes do not belong. **GMP7.1**

Highlight that in Problem 1, one figure is open and has a curved side, and in Problem 2, one figure has sides that cross. Ask: *What do you notice about all of the remaining shapes?* **GMP7.1** Sample answers: The shapes are all closed. All the sides are connected at the corners. The sides do not cross. All of the sides are straight. There are no holes. List children's responses on the Class Data Pad. Remind children that we call shapes with these **attributes,** or characteristics, **polygons.** Sketch and label a polygon on the Class Data Pad, and have volunteers label a **side, vertex,** and **angle.** (*See margin.*)

Together review *Student Reference Book*, pages 210–211 and highlight that the names of polygons are based on the number of sides they have. Tell children that they will continue to work with polygons throughout this unit.

▶ Introducing *What's My Polygon Rule?*

Math Masters, pp. G13–G14

WHOLE CLASS | **SMALL GROUP** | PARTNER | INDEPENDENT

Provide each small group with a set of shape cards cut from *Math Masters,* pages G13–G14. (*See Before You Begin.*) Give children time to examine and discuss the cards. Then ask the class: *What do all the shapes have in common?* **GMP7.1** Sample answers: They all are closed with straight sides that do not cross. They are all polygons.

Tell children they will be using their cards in a game called *What's My Polygon Rule?* Display a large circle on paper and use it to demonstrate a round of the game. Without stating it, model applying the rule "has equal-length sides" by placing cards A and I inside the circle and placing card G, which does not fit, outside the circle. Have children choose another shape card and predict whether it will go inside or outside the circle. **GMP7.2** Tell them whether the card fits the rule and place it accordingly (cards J, M, Q, and R fit the rule). Continue until children can guess the rule based on the patterns. **GMP7.1, GMP8.1** When children understand the game, have them make make their own circle gameboard and play several rounds in small groups, taking turns as the rule maker. Tell the rule maker to write down the rule so he or she does not forget it. If needed, refer children to game directions on *Student Reference Book,* page 262.

Observe

• How do children sort their shapes?
• Which children mention numbers of sides or angles, equal-length sides, right angles, or parallel lines?

Discuss

• *What did you look for as you figured out the rule?* **GMP7.1**
• *What rule might include cards _____ and _____?* **GMP7.2, GMP8.1**

Gather the class to discuss the vocabulary they used as they played, and illustrate attributes by displaying cards accordingly. Show cards B and J. Have a volunteer point to the **right angle** at a corner that looks like the corner of a book. Show cards H and K, and have another volunteer point out the **parallel** sides by using a ruler to show that they are the same distance apart all the way across. Ask children to identify shapes that have four sides, and remind them that they are called **quadrilaterals.**

Record *right angles, parallel sides, equal side lengths,* and *quadrilaterals* with corresponding illustrations on the Class Data Pad for future reference. Store each set of cards in a small bag for future game play.

Differentiate **Game Modifications** | Go Online Differentiation Support

---

Many key geometric definitions can evolve from children's informal observations of shapes' attributes. As children play *What's My Polygon Rule?,* allow them to use informal language to describe their rules. There will be opportunities to relate their ideas to formal vocabulary later in the lesson.

Common Misconception

Differentiate Some children may not recognize shapes that are oriented differently from their mental images. By rotating images of familiar shapes, help children recognize that orientation does not impact a shape's characteristics. For example, children may not recognize a square unless it is oriented horizontally, calling a tilted square a diamond. Help children recognize that a square is still a square by rotating square shapes. Ask questions such as: *Is this still a square? How do we know? What does it mean to be a square? Is a square still a square if it is red?*

Go Online Differentiation Support

► Representing Polygons

WHOLE CLASS SMALL GROUP **PARTNER** INDEPENDENT

Provide each partnership with a geoboard and rubber bands. Describe polygons and have partners create them on their geoboards. **GMP7.2** The polygon descriptions below provide children with the opportunity to practice using the vocabulary introduced at the end of the last activity. If children struggle to represent shapes with parallel sides, suggest that they create a set of parallel sides first and then use them to develop the rest of the shape.

Have children rotate their geoboards to examine their polygons from different perspectives, and encourage conversation about disputed representations. You may want each child to copy the polygons on Geoboard Dot Paper (*Math Masters*, page TA31).

Suggested descriptions:

- a quadrilateral
- a quadrilateral with all sides equal in length
- a triangle
- a quadrilateral with at least one right angle
- a triangle with a right angle
- a quadrilateral with a pair of parallel sides
- a hexagon (or pentagon, heptagon, octagon)

 Assessment Check-In **CCSS** 3.G.1

Circulate and observe as children represent the different polygons. Expect most children to represent triangles and quadrilaterals with equal side lengths and right angles. **GMP7.2** If children struggle, have them identify shape cards with these attributes and then copy the shape onto their geoboard. Do not expect all children to be able to represent polygons with parallel sides or less common polygons such as heptagons or octagons.

☑ Assessment and Reporting **Go Online** to record student progress and to see trajectories toward mastery for this standard.

Summarize Introduce the Two-Dimensional Shapes Poster, and have children compare and contrast the groups of polygons and discuss how they differ from the non-polygons. **GMP7.1**

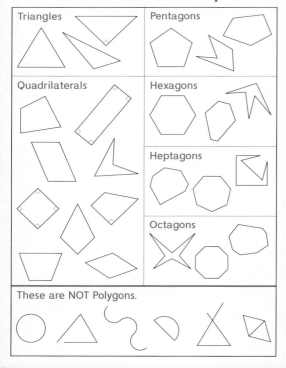

Two-Dimensional Shapes

Triangles	Pentagons
Quadrilaterals	Hexagons
	Heptagons
	Octagons

These are NOT Polygons.

3 Practice   15–20 min

Go Online

ePresentations eToolkit Home Connections

▶ Minute Math+

To practice mental math strategies, choose a *Minute Math+* activity.

▶ Playing *Multiplication Draw*

Student Reference Book, p. 248; *Math Masters,* p. G6

| WHOLE CLASS | SMALL GROUP | **PARTNER** | INDEPENDENT |

To provide additional facts practice, have children play *Multiplication Draw.* See Lesson 1-10 and *Student Reference Book,* page 248 for details.

Observe

- What strategies do children use to multiply?
- Which facts do children solve fluently? Which do they struggle to solve?

Discuss

- *Which facts do you know? For which do you use a strategy to solve?*

Differentiate Game Modifications   Go Online Differentiation Support

▶ Math Boxes 4-4

Math Journal 1, p. 111

| WHOLE CLASS | **SMALL GROUP** | PARTNER | INDEPENDENT |

Mixed Practice Math Boxes 4-4 are paired with Math Boxes 4-2.

▶ Home Link 4-4

Math Masters, p. 127

Homework Children identify whether shapes are polygons based on whether each shape's attributes fit the properties of polygons. **GMP7.1**

Planning Ahead

For Lesson 4-6, collect various small boxes, such as those for granola bars, pencils, facial tissue, or tape rolls. You will need one box per child. Boxes are also used in the Readiness activity in Lesson 4-10.

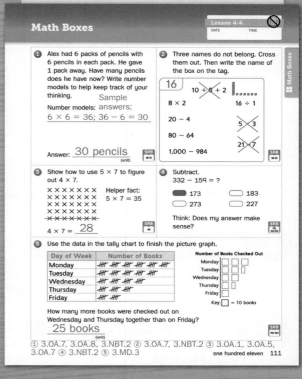

Math Journal 1, p. 111

Math Boxes   Lesson 4-4   DATE   TIME

① Alex had 6 packs of pencils with 6 pencils in each pack. He gave 1 pack away. Have many pencils does he have now? Write number models to help keep track of your thinking.
Number models: answers:
Sample
$6 × 6 = 36; 36 − 6 = 30$

Answer: __30 pencils__ (unit)

② Three names do not belong. Cross them out. Then write the name of the box on the tag.
16
$10 + 5 + 2$
$8 × 2$ $16 ÷ 1$
$20 − 4$ $5 × 3$
$80 − 64$ $21 ÷ 7$
$1,000 − 984$

③ Show how to use $5 × 7$ to figure out $4 × 7$.
× × × × × × ×
× × × × × × ×
× × × × × × ×
× × × × × × ×
× × × × × × ×
Helper fact:
$5 × 7 = 35$
$4 × 7 =$ __28__

④ Subtract.
$332 − 159 = ?$
☐ 173   ☐ 183
☐ 273   ☐ 227
Think: Does my answer make sense?

⑤ Use the data in the tally chart to finish the picture graph.

Day of Week	Number of Books
Monday	-HH- -HH- -HH- -HH- -HH-
Tuesday	-HH- -HH- -HH- -HH- -HH-
Wednesday	-HH- -HH- -HH-
Thursday	-HH- -HH- -HH-
Friday	-HH- -HH-

Number of Books Checked Out
Monday ☐☐☐
Tuesday ☐☐☐
Wednesday ☐☐
Thursday ☐
Friday ☐
Key: ☐ = 10 books

How many more books were checked out on Wednesday and Thursday together than on Friday?
__25 books__ (unit)

① 3.OA.7, 3.OA.8, 3.NBT.2 ② 3.OA.7, 3.NBT.2 ③ 3.OA.1, 3.OA.5, 3.OA.7 ④ 3.NBT.2 ⑤ 3.MD.3

one hundred eleven 111

Math Masters, p. 127

Polygons   Home Link 4-4   NAME   DATE   TIME

Family Note Today your child learned the names of different polygons. A polygon is a 2-dimensional shape with only straight sides that meet end to end to make one closed path. The sides may not cross one another. Polygons are named by the number of sides they have. Polygons are all around us. For example, a stop sign is an octagon, an 8-sided polygon, and this Home Link page is a rectangle, a 4-sided polygon with 4 right angles (square corners).
Please return this Home Link to school tomorrow.

① Cross out the shapes that are not polygons.

How do you know which shapes are not polygons?
Sample answers: Polygons have straight sides that do not cross. The shapes I crossed out have curved sides or sides that cross.

② Cut out pictures of shapes from newspapers and magazines to match each of the descriptions below. Tape or glue your pictures on the front or back of this page. Answers vary.

equal-length sides	parallel sides
at least one right angle	quadrilateral

3.G.1, SMP7   127

Special Quadrilaterals

Overview Children classify quadrilaterals.

▶ **Before You Begin**

For Part 2, prepare sketches of squares, rectangles, parallelograms, rhombuses, trapezoids, and kites. Cut out quadrilaterals from *Math Journal 1*, Activity Sheets 11–12, one set for each child. (*See Planning Ahead, Lessons 3-13 and 4-2.*)

▶ **Vocabulary**

quadrilateral • square • rectangle • parallelogram • rhombus • trapezoid • kite

Common Core State Standards

Focus Cluster
Reason with shapes and their attributes.

① Warm Up   5 min

	Materials	
Mental Math and Fluency Children solve equal-groups number stories.	slate	**3.OA.1, 3.OA.3, 3.OA.7**

② Focus   45–55 min

Math Message Children sketch a variety of quadrilaterals.	*Math Masters*, p. TA33	**3.G.1** **SMP2**
Introducing Subcategories of Quadrilaterals Children analyze similarities among quadrilaterals.	*Student Reference Book*, p. 217	**3.G.1** **SMP2, SMP7**
Exploring Quadrilateral Relationships Children consider how special quadrilaterals relate.	*Math Journal 1*, p. 112 and Activity Sheets 11–12	**3.G.1** **SMP2, SMP7**
✓ **Assessment Check-In** See page 351.	*Math Journal 1*, p. 112	**3.G.1, SMP7**
Applying Definitions of Special Quadrilaterals Children sketch quadrilaterals that do not fit into any of the special categories.	*Student Reference Book*, p. 217; *Math Masters*, pp. TA33 and G13; Class Data Pad	**3.G.1** **SMP2, SMP7**

CCSS 3.G.1 Spiral Snapshot

GMC Recognize specified subcategories of quadrilaterals.

1-3 Focus	4-5 Focus	4-6 Focus Practice	5-2 Practice	5-5 Practice	5-7 Practice	6-5 Focus Practice	8-8 Focus

/// Spiral Tracker   **Go Online**   to see how mastery develops for all standards within the grade.

③ Practice   10–15 min

Minute Math+ Children practice mental math strategies.	*Minute Math®+*	
Practicing Division Facts Children relate division to missing-factor multiplication facts.	Fact Triangles	**3.OA.6**
Math Boxes 4-5 Children practice and maintain skills.	*Math Journal 1*, p. 113	See page 353.
Home Link 4-5 **Homework** Children compare special quadrilaterals.	*Math Masters*, p. 129	**3.G.1** **SMP7**

connectED.mcgraw-hill.com ▶

Plan your lessons online with these tools.

 ePresentations   Student Learning Center   Facts Workshop Game   eToolkit   Professional Development   Home Connections   Spiral Tracker   Assessment and Reporting   English Learners Support   Differentiation Support

348   Unit 4 | Measurement and Geometry

Differentiation Options

RtI

CCSS 3.G.1

Readiness
5–10 min

| WHOLE CLASS |
| SMALL GROUP |
| PARTNER |
| INDEPENDENT |

Reviewing Attributes of Shapes

pattern blocks

To explore attributes of 2-dimensional shapes, have children review parallel and opposite sides using faces of pattern blocks. Give directions, such as: *Show me two parallel sides. Show me opposite sides. Show me two sides that are touching.* Have children point out the attributes on the pattern block faces. Lead a discussion about parallel sides and lines. Ask: *Can parallel sides touch?* No. *Can parallel sides also be opposite sides?* Yes. Remind children that parallel lines are always the same distance apart and never meet.

CCSS 3.G.1, SMP3

Enrichment
10–15 min

| WHOLE CLASS |
| SMALL GROUP |
| PARTNER |
| INDEPENDENT |

Exploring Quadrilaterals in Tangrams

Math Masters, p. 128;
Grandfather Tang's Story by Ann Tompert

To further explore relationships among quadrilaterals, have children read ***Grandfather Tang's Story*** by Ann Tompert (Dragonfly Books, 1997). This Chinese folktale uses tangrams to tell a story about two shape-changing characters. Have children complete *Math Masters,* page 128, identifying the quadrilaterals in the puzzle pieces; explaining why certain quadrilaterals, such as a square and a parallelogram, work well in the designs; and solving one of the book's puzzles.

GMP3.1

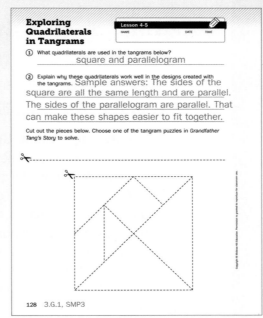

CCSS 3.G.1, SMP7

Extra Practice
10–15 min

| WHOLE CLASS |
| SMALL GROUP |
| PARTNER |
| INDEPENDENT |

Playing *Shading Shapes*

Activity Card 58;
Math Masters, p. G15

For additional practice with properties of quadrilaterals, have children shade triangles on *Math Masters,* page G15 to make the following quadrilaterals: rectangle, square, parallelogram, and trapezoid. GMP7.1 Have children check their work with cutouts from the reference portion of the page and share their strategies for making the quadrilaterals.

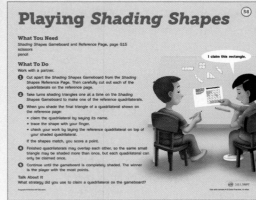

English Language Learners Support

Beginning ELL To scaffold terms in this lesson, review the vocabulary cards prepared in the previous lesson. Add similar cards for *angle, right angle,* and *parallel.* Draw or use materials, such as connecting straws and straightedges, to illustrate the different terms with examples. Use Total Physical Response prompts to model the terms, and then direct children to find examples of the terms in the classroom.

Go Online ELL English Learners Support

Standards and Goals for Mathematical Practice

SMP2 Reason abstractly and quantitatively.
GMP2.2 Make sense of the representations you and others use.

SMP7 Look for and make use of structure.
GMP7.1 Look for mathematical structures such as categories, patterns, and properties.

GMP7.2 Use structures to solve problems and answer questions.

Academic Language Development

To help children understand that *quad* means four, create a 4-column anchor chart with the headings Word, Sentence, Visual, and Word Meaning. In the Word column, write: *quadrangle, quadrilateral, quadruplets,* and *quadruped.* Write sentences in the middle column to illustrate the meanings using familiar examples. Provide visual examples of each *quad*-word from the sentences, highlighting what there are four of (four angles, four sides, four children born at one birth, and four legs). With the children, determine what *quad* defines for each word's meaning.

1 Warm Up 5 min

Go Online ePresentations eToolkit

▶ Mental Math and Fluency

Pose equal-groups number stories for children to solve on slates. *Leveled exercises:*

- ●○○ How many sides are there all together in 4 triangles? 12 sides
- ●●○ How many sides are there all together in 4 pentagons? 20 sides
- ●●● How many sides are there all together in 3 octagons? 24 sides

2 Focus 45–55 min

Go Online ePresentations eToolkit

▶ Math Message

Math Masters, p. TA33

Sketch at least three different quadrilaterals on a sheet of dot paper. What makes them different? GMP2.2

▶ Introducing Subcategories of Quadrilaterals

Student Reference Book, p. 217

| WHOLE CLASS | SMALL GROUP | PARTNER | INDEPENDENT |

Math Message Follow-Up Have children share and discuss examples of quadrilaterals, supplementing as needed. (*See Before You Begin.*) Review the definition of a **quadrilateral** as a polygon that has four sides. Look for examples of each of the following subcategories, or types, of quadrilaterals: **squares, rectangles, parallelograms, rhombuses, trapezoids,** and **kites.** If possible, select more than one example of each. Also show that quadrilaterals may fit into zero, one, or more than one subcategory. For example, when discussing rectangles, show both a rectangle that is not a square and a different rectangle that is also a square. For more information on quadrilaterals, see the Mathematical Background in the Unit Organizer.

As each subcategory of quadrilaterals is discussed:

- Display two examples, such as two different parallelograms. Do not share the name of the subcategory.
- Ask: *How are these quadrilaterals alike?* GMP2.2, GMP7.1 They have four sides. They have four parallel sides.
- Ask: *What are these types of quadrilaterals called?* Parallelograms

Once these six subcategories of quadrilaterals have been introduced, refer children to *Student Reference Book,* page 217 and discuss the descriptions provided for each subcategory. Tell children that today they will think about what these descriptions tell us about their shapes.

► # Exploring Quadrilateral Relationships

Math Journal 1, p. 112 and Activity Sheets 11–12

| WHOLE CLASS | SMALL GROUP | PARTNER | INDEPENDENT |

Distribute one set of Quadrilateral Cutouts from Activity Sheets 11–12 to each child. (*See Before You Begin.*) Invite children to examine the shapes.

Choose any two quadrilaterals of different subcategories and display them for the class to see. Ask: *What attributes do these two quadrilaterals have in common? What attributes are different?* GMP2.2, GMP7.1   Answers vary.

Have partnerships repeat the activity and record two pairs of quadrilaterals and their common and different attributes on journal page 112. Have children alternate which partner selects the two shapes.

 ## Assessment Check-In CCSS 3.G.1

Math Journal 1, p. 112

Expect most children to correctly identify the quadrilaterals they choose and to recognize and describe similarities between quadrilaterals, such as rectangles and squares.   GMP7.2   Children may have difficulty describing the relationships between the attributes of the shapes. Refer to the Common Misconception note and carefully review the defining attributes of these six subcategories of quadrilaterals. Encourage children to refer to *Student Reference Book,* page 217. Help children understand what attributes are and are not restricted by those definitions.

 Assessment and Reporting   Go Online   to record student progress and to see trajectories toward mastery for this standard.

After children have finished, have the class discuss the following examples: GMP7.2

- Hold up a square and a rhombus that is not a square. Ask: *What attributes do this square and this rhombus have in common?* All four sides are the same length. *What attributes are different?* All squares have right angles; this rhombus does not have right angles.

- Hold up a square and a rectangle that is not a square. Ask: *What attributes do this square and this rectangle have in common?* Both have four square corners. *What attributes are different?* All four sides of squares are the same length; the adjacent sides of this rectangle are not the same length.

- Hold up a parallelogram and a trapezoid that is not a parallelogram. Ask: *What attributes do this trapezoid and this parallelogram have in common?* They both have at least one pair of parallel sides. *What attributes are different?* All parallelograms have two pairs of parallel sides; this trapezoid has only one pair of parallel sides.

Common Misconception

Differentiate Watch for children who struggle to recognize that certain shapes may fit into more than one quadrilateral subcategory. For example, some may mistakenly suggest that kites must have different-length sides, not recognizing rhombuses as kites. Help them carefully review defining attributes of these shapes as listed on *Student Reference Book,* page 217. Have children look at examples of a subcategory (such as rectangle) and see whether they have all the defining attributes of another subcategory (such as parallelogram).

Go Online   Differentiation Support

Math Journal 1, p. 112

Quadrilateral Relationships   Lesson 4-5
DATE   TIME

1. Sketch your two quadrilaterals below. Record the type of quadrilaterals they are on the lines below.
Answers vary.

_____   _____

What attributes do your quadrilaterals have in common?
Answers vary.

What attributes are different?
Answers vary.

2. Sketch two more of your quadrilaterals below. Record the type of quadrilaterals they are on the lines below.
Answers vary.

_____   _____

What attributes do your quadrilaterals have in common?
Answers vary.

What attributes are different?
Answers vary.

112   one hundred twelve   3.G.1, SMP2, SMP7

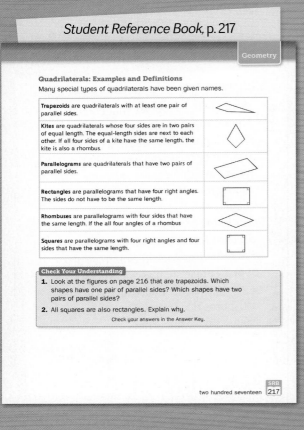
• Hold up a kite and a parallelogram that are not rhombuses. Ask: *What attributes do this kite and this parallelogram have in common?* Both have two pairs of sides that are the same length. *What attributes are different?* Sample answer: The opposite sides of a parallelogram must be parallel. The opposite sides of a kite do not have to be parallel.

Have children store their quadrilateral cutouts in their toolkits for future use.

▶ Applying Definitions of Special Quadrilaterals

Student Reference Book, p. 217; *Math Masters,* pp. TA33 and G13

WHOLE CLASS | SMALL GROUP | PARTNER | INDEPENDENT

Display card D from the *What's My Polygon Rule?* cards (*Math Masters,* page G13) and have children consider whether it has any special name besides quadrilateral. Ask: *How can we check whether it is a rectangle?* Look for four right angles. *Is it a rectangle?* No. It does not have four right angles. *How can we check whether it is a trapezoid?* Since a trapezoid has one pair of parallel sides, we can check to see if card D has parallel sides. Have partnerships ask similar questions to see whether card D matches any of the special quadrilateral attributes on *Student Reference Book,* page 217. Then elicit that it does not fit into any special quadrilateral type, or subcategory.

Have partnerships sketch quadrilaterals on dot paper (*Math Masters,* page TA33) to match the following descriptions:

• a shape that is neither a rhombus nor a rectangle Sample answer: A kite that does not have all equal-length sides

• a shape that is neither a kite nor a parallelogram Sample answer: A trapezoid that is not a parallelogram

• a shape that does not fit into any of the quadrilateral subcategories Any non-trapezoid, non-kite quadrilateral

NOTE The last prompt will likely be challenging for many children. Some children may even lose sight of what defines a quadrilateral and sketch another shape altogether. Remind them of the attributes all quadrilaterals share.

Have partnerships share their examples with the class. Prompt children to check any disputed shapes against each special quadrilateral definition.

Summarize Have children sketch a square on their dot paper. Have them name all of the other quadrilateral subcategories to which a square belongs as you list them on the Class Data Pad. GMP7.2 Rectangle, rhombus, parallelogram, kite, trapezoid

③ Practice   10–15 min   Go Online

ePresentations   eToolkit   Home Connections

▶ *Minute Math+*

To practice mental math strategies, choose a *Minute Math+* activity.

▶ Practicing Division Facts

| WHOLE CLASS | SMALL GROUP | PARTNER | INDEPENDENT |

Display a 2, 5, 10 Fact Triangle and cover the 5 with your finger. Explain that when you solve a division fact you can think of it as a multiplication fact with a missing factor. Model how to read the division fact as *10 divided by 2 is 5.* Then show how to read the multiplication fact: *Two times what number is 10?* 5 Ask: *Would this work for all multiplication and division facts? Explain.* Yes. You can read all division facts as a multiplication fact with a missing factor. Encourage children to think about multiplication facts as they practice division facts with their Fact Triangles.

▶ Math Boxes 4-5 ✏️

Math Journal 1, p. 113

| WHOLE CLASS | SMALL GROUP | PARTNER | INDEPENDENT |

Mixed Practice Math Boxes 4-5 are paired with Math Boxes 4-7.

▶ Home Link 4-5

Math Masters, p. 129

Homework Children identify and compare quadrilaterals.   GMP7.2

Math Journal 1, p. 113

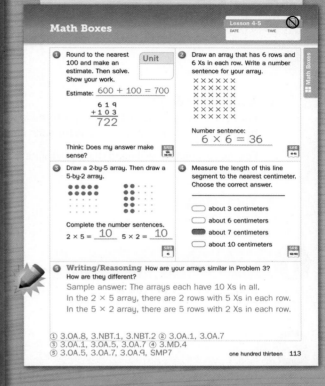

Math Masters, p. 129

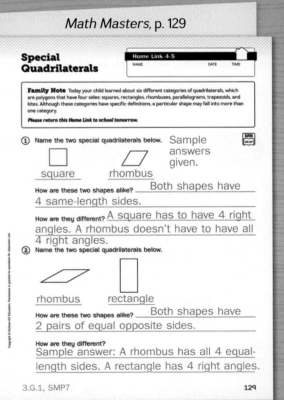

Perimeter

Overview Children identify and measure perimeters of rectangles and other polygons.

▶ **Before You Begin**

For Part 2, make an assortment of pattern blocks available for the Math Message. Gather various small boxes with rectangular faces—one for each child. (*See Planning Ahead in Lesson 4-4.*)

For Part 3, children will need their quadrilateral cutouts (*Math Journal 1*, Activity Sheets 11–12) from Lesson 4-5.

▶ **Vocabulary**

face • perimeter

Common Core State Standards

Focus Clusters
• Represent and interpret data.
• Geometric measurement: recognize perimeter.

---

1 Warm Up 5 min

	Materials	
Mental Math and Fluency Children find sums of four addends.	slate	3.NBT.2

---

2 Focus 40–50 min

Math Message Children trace a face of a pattern block and discuss ways to measure the distance around.	pattern blocks	3.MD.4, 3.G.1 SMP5
Measuring Perimeters of Polygons Children measure polygon perimeters to the nearest $\frac{1}{2}$ inch.	*Math Journal 1*, p. 114; pattern blocks; measurement tools	3.MD.4, 3.MD.8 SMP5, SMP6
Investigating Perimeters of Rectangles Children measure rectangle perimeters to the nearest $\frac{1}{2}$ inch.	small boxes, measurement tools	3.MD.4, 3.MD.8 SMP7
✓ **Assessment Check-In** See page 358.		3.MD.4, 3.MD.8, SMP5
Solving Perimeter Number Stories Children solve perimeter number stories.	*Math Journal 1*, pp. 114–115; *Student Reference Book*, pp. 174–175; *Math Masters*, p. TA35 (optional)	3.MD.8

CCSS 3.MD.8 Spiral Snapshot

GMC Solve problems involving perimeters of polygons.

4-3 Focus	4-6 Focus	4-7 Focus	4-8 Focus	4-10 Focus Practice	4-12 Practice	5-1 Warm Up Focus Practice	5-11 Practice

Spiral Tracker **Go Online** to see how mastery develops for all standards within the grade.

---

3 Practice 15–20 min

Minute Math+ Children practice mental math strategies.	*Minute Math®+*	
Feeling Quadrilaterals Children identify quadrilaterals by touch.	quadrilateral cutouts from Lesson 4-5, opaque bags or boxes	3.G.1 SMP7
Math Boxes 4-6 Children practice and maintain skills.	*Math Journal 1*, p. 116	See page 358.
Home Link 4-6 **Homework** Children solve polygon perimeter problems.	*Math Masters*, pp. 131–132	3.MD.4, 3.MD.8

---

connectED.mcgraw-hill.com

Plan your lessons online with these tools.

ePresentations · Student Learning Center · Facts Workshop Game · eToolkit · Professional Development · Home Connections · Spiral Tracker · Assessment and Reporting · English Learners Support · Differentiation Support

Differentiation Options

RtI

CCSS 3MD.4, SMP5, SMP6

Readiness

5–10 min

WHOLE CLASS
SMALL GROUP
PARTNER
INDEPENDENT

Measuring to the Nearest $\frac{1}{2}$ inch

toolkit ruler or Ruler A (*Math Masters*, p. TA30); small classroom objects

For experience with measuring to the nearest half inch, have children use a toolkit ruler or Ruler A from Lesson 4-1 to measure the lengths of small objects, such as pencils, markers, calculators, and so on. **GMP5.2, GMP6.2** You may wish to have children write the name of or draw a sketch of each object and record its length on paper.

CCSS 3.MD.8, SMP1

Enrichment

10–15 min

WHOLE CLASS
SMALL GROUP
PARTNER
INDEPENDENT

Exploring Perimeter

Math Masters, p. TA19

To further explore the concept of perimeter, have children find all possible rectangles with whole-centimeter side lengths that have a perimeter of 20 centimeters. Have children record and label the rectangles on centimeter grid paper and share their answers. **GMP1.5** There are 5 rectangles: 1-by-9, 2-by-8, 3-by-7, 4-by-6, and 5-by-5. Invite children to describe how they know they have found all the rectangles. Sample answer: I started with just one row of squares and then added more rows in order. After I got to five rows, I started to get the same rectangles again, so I knew I had found them all.

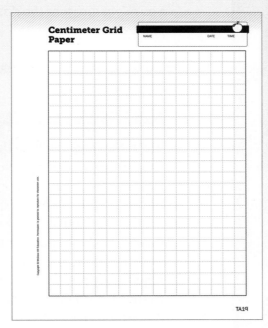

CCSS 3.MD.8, SMP7

Extra Practice

5–10 min

WHOLE CLASS
SMALL GROUP
PARTNER
INDEPENDENT

Finding the Perimeters of Polygons

Math Masters, p. 130

For additional practice, have children find perimeters of polygons when given the side lengths. Also have them find unknown side lengths when given some side lengths and the perimeter. Have children write number sentences to record their thinking and explain how they found a missing side length. **GMP7.2**

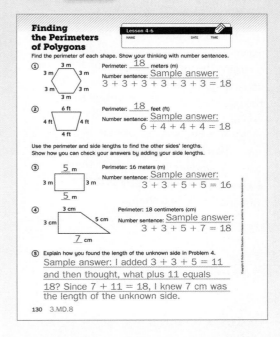

English Language Learners Support

Beginning ELL Scaffold the term *face* as a body part and as a mathematical concept. First point to your face as you say the word. Use Total Physical Response prompts to ask children to point to their own face and then to their partner's face. Then use the term while pointing to the faces of various boxes or rectangular prisms. Have children demonstrate their understanding by pointing to their face and the face of a prism in response to prompts, such as: *Show me your face. Show me a face on this* _____. Make it clear that boxes, such as those used in the Math Message, have more than one face.

Go Online **ELL** English Learners Support

Academic Language Development

For children who confuse area and
perimeter, point out that *perimeter*
contains the word *rim*. Have children
use a finger to trace around the rim of
the square saying: *The length of the
rim of the shape is the perimeter.* As
children complete the journal page,
have them circle all instances of the
word *perimeter.* This may help them
remember that perimeter is the
distance around a shape.

1 Warm Up 5 min

ePresentations eToolkit

▶ Mental Math and Fluency

Have children solve each problem mentally and write only the sums on
their slates. Then have them share their strategies. *Leveled exercises:*

⦿○○ $5 + 5 + 5 + 5$ 20; $4 + 4 + 6 + 6$ 20; $3 + 7 + 3 + 7$ 20

⦿⦿○ $18 + 18 + 2 + 2$ 40; $1 + 1 + 29 + 29$ 60; $6 + 14 + 14 + 6$ 40

⦿⦿⦿ $24 + 24 + 16 + 16$ 80; $33 + 27 + 27 + 33$ 120;
$52 + 38 + 52 + 38$ 180

2 Focus 40–50 min

ePresentations eToolkit

▶ Math Message

*Take a pattern block. Trace the shape of the block on a piece of paper.
What shape did you draw? How do you know? Talk to a partner about how
you might measure the distance all the way around the shape you drew.*
GMP5.2

▶ Measuring Perimeters of Polygons

Math Journal 1, p. 114

| WHOLE CLASS | SMALL GROUP | PARTNER | INDEPENDENT |

Math Message Follow-Up Invite volunteers to share and name the
shapes they traced. Sample answers: Square, trapezoid, triangle, hexagon
Have children share their ideas for measuring the distance around their
traced shapes. GMP5.2 Expect strategies to include wrapping a tape
measure around the block itself, because that is the same distance as the
perimeter of the shape, or the tracing (for example, by using pencil points
at each corner); measuring each side with a ruler and adding the lengths
together; or pivoting a ruler at each corner and counting on to measure
all the way around. You may want children to model each strategy and
discuss which is most efficient.

Next have children measure and record each side length on their tracings
in inches. Ask: *Why is it important to include units, such as inches or
centimeters, when we report measures?* GMP6.3 Units are important
because they let us know what the numbers mean.

Model adding side lengths of pattern blocks to find the distance around
and writing addition number models to show this work. Explain that
another name for the distance around a shape's **face,** or side, is **perimeter.**

Explain that today's lesson will focus on measuring perimeters of
2-dimensional shapes.

Have children turn to journal page 114. Ask: *How could you keep track of your measurements and units?* `GMP6.3` Sample answer: I could write them next to each side of the polygon. Ask children to complete the page and share their units and measures for Problems 1–3. `GMP6.3` Invite volunteers to share the number sentences they wrote for Problem 4. Some children may have measured around the rectangle continuously in Problem 4. Ask those who added side lengths: *What did you do with the half inches?* Sample answer: I combined them to make 1 inch and added it at the end. Remind children that 2 half inches added together are equal to 1 whole inch. Invite a few volunteers to share their number sentences.

▶ Investigating Perimeters of Rectangles

| WHOLE CLASS | SMALL GROUP | PARTNER | INDEPENDENT |

Distribute one small box to each child. (*See Before You Begin.*) Have each child trace one face of a box. Ask: *Why are the shapes all rectangles?* Sample answer: Because the faces of our boxes are polygons with four sides, and the sides meet at right angles. You may need to remind children that squares are special rectangles. Have them measure the perimeters of their shapes to the nearest $\frac{1}{2}$ inch and write number models to show their strategies. Then elicit efficient strategies for finding perimeters of rectangles.

• *What is an efficient strategy for measuring the perimeter?* Sample answer: Measure all four side lengths and add them together.

• *How could you find the perimeter of your rectangle by measuring only two sides?* `GMP7.2` Sample answers: Rectangles have opposite sides that are the same length, so I could measure two touching sides and then add each length twice or double the sum of the two sides.

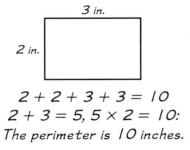

$$2 + 2 + 3 + 3 = 10$$
$$2 + 3 = 5, 5 \times 2 = 10:$$
The perimeter is 10 inches.

Use a child's tracing to model finding the perimeter by measuring only two sides. Ask: *Can we use this strategy for every rectangle? Explain.* `GMP7.2` Yes, because all rectangles have equal-length opposite sides. Then have children trace different-size faces of boxes on the back sides of their papers. They should turn or exchange their boxes as needed. Encourage children to measure and label just two sides to find the perimeters of their new rectangles.

Display one child's new tracing. Ask the class to help write number models for the perimeter of that rectangle. Sample answers: $3 + 9 = 12, 12 + 12 = 24$; $3 + 9 = 12, 12 \times 2 = 24; 3 \times 2 = 6, 9 \times 2 = 18, 6 + 18 = 24$ Have a volunteer write the perimeter with the appropriate unit. `GMP6.3` 24 inches

---

Math Journal 1, p. 114

Measuring Perimeters of Polygons   Lesson 4-6
DATE   TIME

Measure the sides of each polygon to the nearest half inch.
Use the side lengths to find the perimeters.
Write a number sentence to show how you found the perimeter.

❶
Sample answer: 3 + 3 + 1 =
Number sentence: ____7____
Perimeter: about __7__ inches

❷
Sample answer:
Number sentence: 3 + 3 + 2 = 8
Perimeter: about __8__ inches

❸
Sample answer: 1 + 3 = 4 and
Number sentence: 4 × 2 = 8
Perimeter: about __8__ inches

❹
Sample answer: 1 + 1 +
Number sentence: $2\frac{1}{2} + 2\frac{1}{2} = 7$
Perimeter: about __7__ inches

Try This
❺ Draw each shape on the centimeter grid.
   square with perimeter = 16 cm   rectangle with perimeter = 20 cm

                                          Sample
                                          answer:

114   one hundred fourteen   3.MD.4, 3.MD.8, SMP5, SMP6

Common Misconception

Differentiate Watch for children who know they only need the measures of two sides but forget to add them twice or double them. Have them trace the lengths of two same-size sides. Ask: *What is the length of this side if the other side is _____ long?* Remind children that perimeter is the measure all the way around a shape.

 Go Online Differentiation Support

Math Journal 1, p. 115

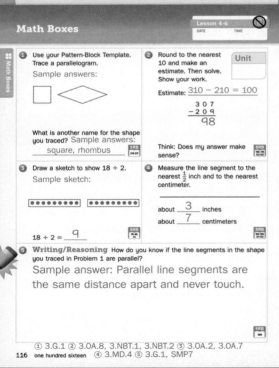

Perimeter Number Stories

Lesson 4-6

DATE   TIME

Solve each number story. Show your work.

1. Mrs. McMaster wants to add a border to a rectangular bulletin board. The top is 35 inches across, and the side is 25 inches tall. How much border does Mrs. McMaster need? You may sketch a picture.

35 in.
25 in. [ ] 25 in.
35 in.

Number model: Sample answer: 35 + 35 = 70 and 25 + 25 = 50. 70 + 50 = 120

Mrs. McMaster needs __120__ inches of border.

2. Mr. Lopez wants to put a fence around his rectangular vegetable garden. The longer sides are 14 feet long and the shorter sides are $9\frac{1}{2}$ feet long. How much fencing should Mr. Lopez buy? You may sketch a picture.

14 feet
$9\frac{1}{2}$ feet [ ] $9\frac{1}{2}$ feet
14 feet

Number model: Sample answer: 14 + 14 = 28 and 2 halves make 1 whole, so 9 + 9 = 18 and 18 + 1 = 19. 28 + 19 = 47

Mr. Lopez should buy __47__ feet of fencing.

3.MD.8   one hundred fifteen 115

Math Journal 1, p. 116

Math Boxes

Lesson 4-6

DATE   TIME

1. Use your Pattern-Block Template. Trace a parallelogram.
Sample answers:

[ ]   ◇

What is another name for the shape you traced? Sample answers:
square, rhombus

2. Round to the nearest 10 and make an estimate. Then solve. Show your work.

Unit

Estimate: 310 − 210 = 100

  3 0 7
− 2 0 9
   9 8

Think: Does my answer make sense?

3. Draw a sketch to show 18 ÷ 2.
Sample sketch:

••••••••• •••••••••

18 ÷ 2 = __9__

4. Measure the line segment to the nearest $\frac{1}{2}$ inch and to the nearest centimeter.

_____

about __3__ inches

about __7__ centimeters

5. **Writing/Reasoning** How do you know if the line segments in the shape you traced in Problem 1 are parallel?
Sample answer: Parallel line segments are the same distance apart and never touch.

① 3.G.1 ② 3.OA.8, 3.NBT.1, 3.NBT.2 ③ 3.OA.2, 3.OA.7
116 one hundred sixteen ④ 3.MD.4 ⑤ 3.G.1, SMP7

✓ **Assessment Check-In** CCSS 3.MD.4, 3.MD.8

Expect most children to correctly measure the side lengths of their traced rectangles to the nearest half inch and to write number models for the perimeter. GMP5.2 Many children may solve the number models to find the perimeter if the side lengths are whole numbers, but do not expect them to do so if the side lengths measure in half inches. Some children may double adjacent side lengths to find the perimeter. If children struggle to measure, consider implementing the Readiness activity. If they struggle to write number models for the perimeter, have them trace each side length of their shape and write its measure in a number sentence.

✓ Assessment and Reporting   (Go Online) to record student progress and to see trajectories toward mastery for these standards.

▶ Solving Perimeter Number Stories

Math Journal 1, pp. 114–115; *Student Reference Book*, pp. 174–175

| WHOLE CLASS | SMALL GROUP | PARTNER | INDEPENDENT |

Have children solve the number stories involving perimeter on journal page 115.

When most children are finished, bring the class together to discuss strategies for finding the perimeters on journal pages 114–115. Invite volunteers to share any sketches they drew and to talk about how the sketches were helpful.

Summarize Have partnerships read *Student Reference Book*, pages 174–175 and do the Check Your Understanding problems. You may want to have children record their answers on an Exit Slip (*Math Masters*, page TA35).

3 Practice
15–20 min

Go Online

ePresentations · eToolkit · Home Connections

▶ Minute Math+

To practice mental math strategies, choose a *Minute Math+* activity.

▶ Feeling Quadrilaterals

Math Journal 1, Activity Sheets 11–12

| WHOLE CLASS | SMALL GROUP | PARTNER | INDEPENDENT |

Have children take out their quadrilateral cutouts from Lesson 4-5. Place one set of quadrilaterals on a table. Without children seeing, place one of the quadrilaterals from the other set into an opaque container (such as a paper bag or empty tissue box). Have a child reach inside the container, feel the shape without looking, and find the matching shape on the table. Emphasize describing the shape and identifying it by its special category. Model one or more rounds for the class and then have partnerships work on the activity. After several rounds, bring the class together to discuss strategies for identifying the shapes. GMP7.2

▶ Math Boxes 4-6

Math Journal 1, p. 116

| WHOLE CLASS | SMALL GROUP | PARTNER | INDEPENDENT |

Mixed Practice Math Boxes 4-6 are grouped with Math Boxes 4-8 and 4-11.

▶ Home Link 4-6

Math Masters, pp. 131–132

Homework Children solve real-world and mathematical problems involving perimeters of polygons.

Planning Ahead

- For Lesson 4-7, make a square yard from newspaper or bulletin-board paper.
- For Lessons 4-7 and 4-8, children will need the 1-foot squares they made in Lesson 3-7. You may want to have some extras in different colors.
- For Lesson 4-8, use masking tape to outline a 5-by-8 foot area on the classroom or hallway floor.

Math Masters, p. 131

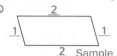

Perimeter Home Link 4-6

NAME   DATE   TIME

Family Note Today your child found the perimeters of several polygons. Perimeter is the distance around a 2-dimensional shape. Finding perimeters gives your child practice measuring to the nearest $\frac{1}{2}$ inch and the nearest whole centimeter.

Please return this Home Link to school tomorrow.

If you do not have a ruler at home, cut out and use the 6-inch ruler on the next page. Measure the sides of each polygon to the nearest $\frac{1}{2}$ inch. Use the side lengths to find the perimeter of each polygon. Write a number sentence to show how you found the perimeter.

①

Sample answer:

Number sentence: $2 + 2 + 1 + 1 = 6$

Perimeter: about **6** inches

②

Sample answer:

Number sentence: $2\frac{1}{2} + 1 + 1 + 1 = 5\frac{1}{2}$

Perimeter: about **$5\frac{1}{2}$** inches

3.MD.4, 3.MD.8   131

Math Masters, p. 132

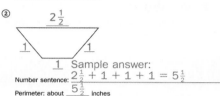

Perimeter (continued) Home Link 4-6

NAME   DATE   TIME

Find the perimeters of the square and the rectangle below.

③ 5 m

Number sentence: Sample answer: $4 \times 5 = 20$

Perimeter: **20** meters (m)

④ 5 cm   12 cm

Number sentence: Sample answer: $12 + 12 + 5 + 5 = 34$

Perimeter: **34** centimeters (cm)

⑤ Draw a quadrilateral below. Find the perimeter to the nearest $\frac{1}{2}$ inch.

Answers vary.

0 $\frac{1}{2}$ 1 2 3 4 5 6
Inches (in.)

132   3.MD.4, 3.MD.8

Area and Perimeter

Overview Children distinguish between perimeter and area.

▶ Before You Begin

For Part 2, use the 1-foot squares from Lesson 3-7. Prepare two 1-foot squares for display. In the middle of one square, write "one square foot." On the other square, darken one edge and label it "1 foot = 12 inches." (*See margin on page 362.*) Prepare a square yard using newspaper or bulletin-board paper. Draw a T chart on the Class Data Pad.

For the optional Extra Practice activity, obtain *Spaghetti and Meatballs for All!* by Marilyn Burns.

▶ Vocabulary

perimeter • length • area • square unit

Common Core State Standards

Focus Clusters
• Represent and interpret data.
• Geometric measurement: understand concepts of area and relate area to multiplication and to addition.
• Geometric measurement: recognize perimeter.

---

1 Warm Up 5 min

	Materials	
Mental Math and Fluency Children figure out missing addends in number sentences.	slate	3.NBT.2

2 Focus 40–50 min

Math Message Children determine the perimeter of a 1-foot square.	1-foot squares, measuring tools	3.MD.4 , 3.MD.8 SMP5
Finding the Perimeter of a 1-Foot Square Children share strategies for finding the perimeter.	Class Data Pad, 1-foot squares, toolkit ruler	3.MD.8 SMP5, SMP6
Measuring Perimeter and Area Children use squares to measure perimeter and area.	Class Data Pad, 1-foot squares, 1-yard square, toolkit rulers	3.MD.5, 3.MD.5a, 3.MD.5b, 3.MD.6, 3.MD.7, 3.MD.7a, 3.MD.8, SMP5, SMP6
Comparing Perimeter and Area Children use squares to compare perimeter and area.	*Math Journal 1*, p. 117; Class Data Pad; 1-foot squares; 1-yard square	3.MD.5, 3.MD.5a, 3.MD.5b, 3.MD.6, 3.MD.7, 3.MD.7a, 3.MD.8, SMP5, SMP6
✓ **Assessment Check-In** See page 365.	*Math Journal 1*, p. 117	3.MD.5, 3.MD.5a, 3.MD.5b, 3.MD.6, 3.MD.7a

CCSS 3.MD.5a Spiral Snapshot

GMC Understand that a unit square has 1 square unit of area and can measure area.

2-12 Focus Practice	3-7 Focus	4-7 Focus	4-8 Focus	4-9 Practice	4-10 Focus	4-12 Focus	5-1 Practice

Spiral Tracker   **Go Online** to see how mastery develops for all standards within the grade.

3 Practice 15–20 min

Minute Math+ Children practice mental math strategies.	*Minute Math®+*	
Playing *Name That Number* **Game** Children use different operations to name a number.	*Student Reference Book*, pp. 249–250; number cards 0–20 (4 of each); number cards 0–10	3.OA.7, 3.NBT.2 SMP2
Math Boxes 4-7 Children practice and maintain skills.	*Math Journal 1*, p. 118	See page 367.
Home Link 4-7 **Homework** Children find perimeter and area.	*Math Masters*, p. 133	3.MD.5, 3.MD.5a, 3.MD.7, 3.MD.7a, 3.MD.8, SMP5

---

connectED.mcgraw-hill.com

Plan your lessons online with these tools.

ePresentations · Student Learning Center · Facts Workshop Game · eToolkit · Professional Development · Home Connections · Spiral Tracker · Assessment and Reporting · English Learners Support · Differentiation Support

Differentiation Options RtI

| **Readiness** 5–10 min | **Enrichment** 5–10 min | **Extra Practice** 10–15 min |

Readiness · 5–10 min

Measuring Perimeter

WHOLE CLASS · **SMALL GROUP** · PARTNER · INDEPENDENT

various rectangular prisms, ruler

To provide experience with perimeter, have children measure to find the perimeters of real objects. First have them use their fingers to trace around perimeters of faces of objects, such as books, pads of stick-on notes, or tissue boxes. Have children place an object on paper and use a pencil to trace around one of the faces. Then have them measure each side of the traced shape to the nearest inch and record their measurements on paper. Discuss how perimeter can be found by adding the lengths of the sides. **GMP6.2** If time permits, have children find the perimeters of other objects.

Enrichment · 5–10 min

Exploring Area

WHOLE CLASS · SMALL GROUP · **PARTNER** · INDEPENDENT

Math Masters, p. TA19

To further explore the concept of area, have children find all possible rectangles with whole-centimeter side lengths that have an area of 20 square centimeters. Have children record the rectangles on centimeter grid paper and share their answers. **GMP1.5** There are 3 rectangles: 1-by-20, 2-by-10, and 4-by-5. Invite children to describe how they know they have found all the rectangles. Sample answer: I started with just one row of squares. Then I made 2 rows. When I tried 3 rows, I couldn't make a rectangle, so I continued on to 4 and 5 rows until I started to repeat rectangles.

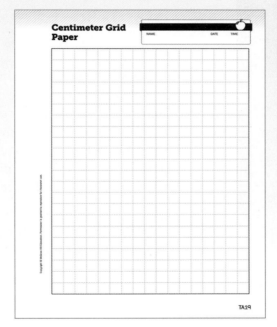

Extra Practice · 10–15 min

Reading About Area and Perimeter

WHOLE CLASS · SMALL GROUP · **PARTNER** · INDEPENDENT

Activity Card 59;
Math Masters, p. TA19;
Spaghetti and Meatballs for All! by Marilyn Burns; square pattern blocks; base-10 cubes (32 per partnership)

For additional practice with area and perimeter, have children read ***Spaghetti and Meatballs for All!*** by Marilyn Burns (Scholastic, 2008). Then have partnerships model different arrangements of tables (square pattern blocks) that can hold 32 chairs (base-10 cubes) and record their work on *Math Masters,* page TA19. **GMP1.5, GMP4.1** The square pattern blocks can be arranged into the following arrays: 15-by-1, 14-by-2, 13-by-3, 12-by-4, 11-by-5, 10-by-6, 9-by-7, and 8-by-8.

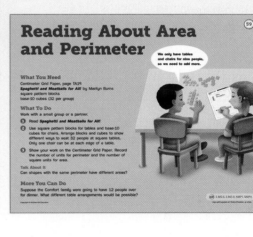

English Language Learners Support

Beginning ELL In the real world, a *cover* need not be exactly the same size and shape as the covered item. Show covering exactly: Show one stick-on note covering another, and then swap them so children see that they are the same size and shape. Show a non-example, such as a book not covering a larger notebook, and ask: *Does the book cover the notebook?* Prompt children to show you items that cover one that you display. For example: *Show me something that covers this _____.* Encourage children to repeat: *This _____ covers this _____.*

 Go Online **ELL** English Learners Support

Professional Development

The 1-foot squares are used to measure in two ways in this lesson: length measures in linear units and area measures in square units. Children will use the squares to explore and distinguish between *perimeter* as a measure of length and *area* as a measure of amount of surface inside a shape. For more information on perimeter and area, see the Mathematical Background section in the Unit Organizer.

---

1 foot = 12 inches	
	one square foot

1-foot squares on display

---

1 ▶ Warm Up 5 min Go Online ▸

ePresentations eToolkit

▶ Mental Math and Fluency

Have children write each number sentence on their slates and fill in the two matching addends that are missing. *Leveled exercises:*

● ○ ○ 4 + 4 + _____ + _____ = 10 1, 1
● ● ○ 7 + _____ + 7 + _____ = 20 3, 3
● ● ● 6 + 6 + _____ + _____ = 18 3, 3

2 ▶ Focus 40–50 min Go Online ▸

ePresentations eToolkit

▶ Math Message

Take a 1-foot square. Find its perimeter in inches. GMP5.1

▶ Finding the Perimeter of a 1-Foot Square

WHOLE CLASS	SMALL GROUP	PARTNER	INDEPENDENT

Math Message Follow-Up Invite a volunteer to remind the class of the meaning of **perimeter**. The distance around a shape On the Class Data Pad T chart (*See Before You Begin*), write *Perimeter* at the top of one column and record its meaning. Have children use their fingers to trace around the edges of their 1-foot squares. Point out that the edges of their squares make up the boundary, or outline of the squares. Have children share their answers to the Math Message, including the appropriate unit. GMP6.3
48 inches

Invite children to share the tools and strategies they used to find the perimeter. GMP5.1, GMP5.2 Children may have measured side lengths or recalled that there are 12 inches in a foot. As children share, have the class suggest number models to match the strategies and record them. Sample answers: 12 + 12 + 12 + 12 = 48; 12 + 12 = 24, 24 × 2 = 48 Invite children to share why they chose their tools. If no child mentions it, point out that a ruler is a good tool to measure the perimeter of the square because the square has straight sides.

Display two 1-foot squares. (*See Before You Begin.*) Point to the 1-foot square labeled "1 foot = 12 inches" along the edge. Ask: *How is the edge of this square like a 12-inch ruler?* Sample answers: It has a straight edge. It measures 12 inches or 1 foot. *If the **length** of each side of the square is 1 foot, what is its perimeter in feet?* 4 feet

▶ Measuring Perimeter and Area

| WHOLE CLASS | SMALL GROUP | PARTNER | INDEPENDENT |

Explain that in today's lesson, children will measure both perimeter and area with their 1-foot squares.

Perimeter Display the 1-yard square (*See Before You Begin*) and have a volunteer gesture to trace its perimeter. Ask: *How could we use our 1-foot squares to measure the perimeter of this larger square?* Answers vary.

Children may suggest placing and counting multiple 1-foot squares along the edges of the larger square. Others may suggest repeatedly placing and moving a single 1-foot square around the larger square and counting the number of moves. Emphasize that only one edge at a time should be used to measure perimeter. Remind children to think of each edge of the square as a ruler that they are using to measure the length of the sides. Choose strategies and ask volunteers to use their 1-foot squares to find the perimeter. Mention that because 12 inches are equal to 1 foot, children may either count squares to measure in feet, or count by 12s for each square to measure in inches. GMP5.2

As children work, mark the endpoint of each foot along the edge of the 1-yard square.

one square yard

Perimeter = 12 feet

Then have the class determine the perimeter in feet. 12 feet If no one mentions it, remind children that there are 3 feet in 1 yard. Each side of the 1-yard square is 1 yard long, so the perimeter can also be described as 4 yards. Some children may want to calculate the perimeter in inches. 144 inches

Area Point out the displayed square foot labeled "one square foot." Gesture inside the square and remind children that **area** is the amount of surface inside the boundary of a shape. Have children sweep their hands across the inside surface of their squares while saying the word *area.* Write *Area* at the top of the other column on the Class Data Pad T chart and record its meaning.

Note that area is usually measured in **square units.** Each standard square unit of area is built from a length unit. For example, a square unit with a side length of 1 centimeter is called a square centimeter, a square unit with a side length of 1 foot is called a square foot, and so on. Ask: *What is the area of your 1-foot square?* 1 square foot *What is the area of the larger square with each side measuring 1 yard?* GMP6.3 1 square yard

Ask: *How could we use the 1-foot squares to find the area of the square yard in square feet?* Sample answer: We could completely cover it with the 1-foot squares and count them.

> **NOTE** Some children might suggest multiplying side lengths. Acknowledge this strategy, but explain that the focus of this lesson is on tiling and unit iteration (the repetition of a single unit for a measurement). Finding area by multiplying side lengths is the focus of a later lesson in this unit.

Have children estimate how many square feet will cover a square yard.

Then have children use their 1-foot squares to tile the square yard.

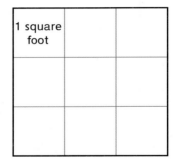

Area = 9 square feet

Ask: *Why should we avoid overlapping or leaving gaps between squares when measuring area?* GMP5.2 Sample answer: If there are gaps, the measurement is not of the entire surface; where there are overlaps, that surface is measured more than once. Have children count the number of 1-foot squares that cover the square yard. 9 Compare their estimates to the actual area.

Ask: *How could we measure the area of this large square if we only had one 1-foot square?* We could put it down, pick it up, and move it over and over again until we measure the whole shape. Discuss the path of the 1-foot square over the 1-yard square, and then have a child carefully move it over the surface. GMP5.2 Model how to keep track of the number of square feet by marking the endpoint of the square foot before moving it. Have children count aloud as the square moves across the surface. Elicit that the area is 9 square feet. Ask: *What do you notice about the two measurements?* GMP5.2 They are the same.

► # Comparing Perimeter and Area

Math Journal 1, p. 117

| WHOLE CLASS | SMALL GROUP | PARTNER | INDEPENDENT |

Ask: *How long is the top edge of the 1-yard square in feet?* **GMP6.3** 3 feet
How many 1-foot squares did we use to cover the top row of this square?
3 squares Cover the top row with squares to provide a visual reminder.
Point out that the length of a side corresponds to the number of squares
along each side, but that the length is measured by counting the top edges
of the squares.

Display the 1-yard square tiled with 1-foot squares. Have children count
along the edges. Be sure that children count both edges of the corner
squares that line up with the boundary of the 1-yard square.

Briefly remind children of the perimeter and area of the 1-yard square, and
the methods for measuring them. Emphasize that the length of the edge
of the 1-foot square measures length, and the area of the 1-foot square
measures the amount of covered space.

Have partners look at Problem 1 on journal page 117 and discuss how they
can use the squares on the rectangle to find its perimeter and area. After
a few minutes, bring the class together to share their thinking. Sample
answer: Count the lengths of the edges that make up the boundary of the
rectangle to find the perimeter. Count each square to find the area. Then
have children complete the journal page.

 ## Assessment Check-In **CCSS** 3.MD.5, 3.MD.6

Math Journal 1, p. 117

Expect most children to count unit squares to find the area of the
rectangles in Problems 1–3. If children struggle, have them mark a dot in
each square to help them keep track as they count. Do not expect all
children to successfully distinguish area and perimeter as this is an early
exposure. You may want to consider the suggestion in the Common
Misconception note and refer children to the Perimeter and Area T chart.

 Assessment
and Reporting | **Go Online** ⟩ to record student progress and to see trajectories
toward mastery for these standards.

Math Journal 1, p. 117

**Comparing Perimeter
and Area** Lesson 4-7
DATE   TIME

For Problems 1–3, find the perimeter and the area of the rectangle.

①
Key: ☐ = 1 square foot
Perimeter: __18__ feet
Area: __14__ square feet

②
Key: ☐ = 1 square meter
Perimeter: __20__ meters
Area: __24__ square meters

③
Key: ☐ = 1 square mile
Perimeter: __22__ miles
Area: __24__ square miles

Try This

④ Find the perimeter and the area of this shape.
Key: ☐ = 1 square centimeter
Perimeter: __18__ centimeters
Area: __15__ square centimeters

⑤ Nicolas says he can measure both the perimeter and the area of a rectangle
using a square. Do you agree or disagree? Explain your answer using words
or drawings.
Sample answer: I agree. You can use the edge
of the square to find the perimeter. You can tile
the rectangle with the square to find the area.

3.MD.5, 3.MD.5a, 3.MD.5b, 3.MD.6, 3.MD.7, 3.MD.7a, 3.MD.8,
SMP5, SMP6   one hundred seventeen   **117**

Common Misconception

Differentiate Watch for children who
do not understand that corner squares
have two adjacent edges that must both
be counted when measuring the
perimeter of the large square.
Emphasize that the edges of the smaller
squares make up the edges of the large
square. You may wish to have children
sketch a picture of the large square
filled in with small squares and darken
the edge of the large square to make
this visual connection.

Go Online ⟩ Differentiation
Support

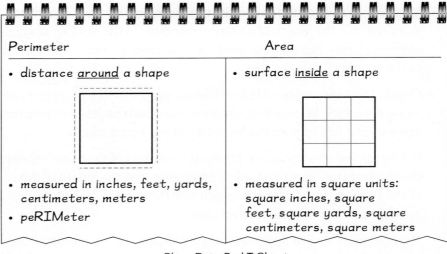

Games

Name That Number

Materials	☐ number cards 0–20 (4 of each card 0–10, and 1 of each card 11–20)
Players	2 to 4 (The game is more interesting when played by 3 or 4 players.)
Skill	Finding equivalent names for numbers
Object of the Game	To collect the most cards.

Directions

1. Shuffle the deck and place 5 cards number-side up on the table. Leave the rest of the deck number-side down. Then turn over the top card of the deck and lay it down next to the deck. The number on this card is the number to be named. This is the *target number*.

2. Players take turns. When it is your turn:
   - Try to name the target number. You can name the target number by adding, subtracting, multiplying, or dividing the numbers on 2 or more of the 5 cards that are number-side up. A card may be used only once for each turn.
   - If you can name the target number, take the cards you used to name it. Also take the target-number card. Then replace all the cards you took by drawing from the top of the deck. See the example on the next page.
   - If you cannot name the target number, your turn is over. Turn over a new card from the top of the deck and lay it down on the target-number pile. The number on this card becomes the new target number to be named.

3. Play continues until all of the cards in the deck have been turned over. The player who has taken the most cards wins.

two hundred forty-nine **SRB 249**

Games

Example

Mae and Mike take turns.

 4 10 8 12 2   6

It is Mae's turn. The target number is 6. Mae names the number with 4 + 2. She could have also used 8 − 2 or 10 − 4.

Mae takes the 4, 2, and 6 cards. Then she replaces them by drawing cards from the deck.

7 10 8 12 1   16

It is now Mike's turn. The new target number is 16. Mike sees two ways to name the target number.

- He can use 3 cards and name the target number like this:

$$7 + 8 + 1 = 16$$

- He can use 4 cards and name the target number like this:

$$12 − 10 = 2$$
$$\downarrow$$
$$2 \times 8 = 16$$
$$\downarrow$$
$$16 \div 1 = 16$$

Mike chooses the 4-card solution because he can take more cards that way. He takes the 12, 10, 8, and 1 cards. He also takes the target-number card 16. Then he replaces all 5 cards by drawing cards from the deck.

SRB 250 two hundred fifty

Summarize Revisit the Perimeter and Area T chart and ask children for suggestions of what they might add to describe and distinguish between the two measures. You may wish to add pictures to illustrate perimeter and area, tape the labeled 1-foot squares into each column, or add other helpful keywords.

Perimeter	Area
• distance <u>around</u> a shape	• surface <u>inside</u> a shape
• measured in inches, feet, yards, centimeters, meters	• measured in square units: square inches, square feet, square yards, square centimeters, square meters
• pe**RIM**eter	

Class Data Pad T Chart

3 Practice 15–20 min Go Online   ePresentations eToolkit Home Connections

▶ Minute Math+

To practice mental math strategies, select a *Minute Math+* activity.

▶ Playing *Name That Number*

Student Reference Book, pp. 249–250

| WHOLE CLASS | SMALL GROUP | PARTNER | INDEPENDENT |

Review the rules for *Name That Number* on *Student Reference Book*, pages 249–250. Encourage children to use all four operations to name the target number. **GMP2.3**

Observe

- Which children use one operation in their solutions? Which children use more than one?

Discuss

- *How did you decide which operations to use in your solutions?*

Differentiate **Game Modifications** Go Online   Differentiation Support

▶ Math Boxes 4-7 ✏️

Math Journal 1, p. 118

| WHOLE CLASS | SMALL GROUP | PARTNER | INDEPENDENT |

Mixed Practice Math Boxes 4-7 are paired with Math Boxes 4-5.

▶ Home Link 4-7

Math Masters, p. 133

Homework Children find the perimeter and area of a square and of a surface at home. **GMP5.2**

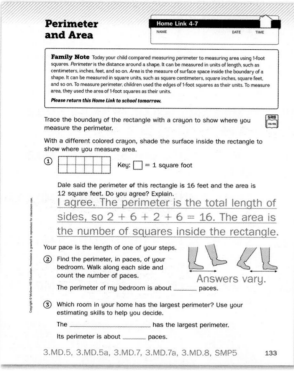

Math Masters, p. 133

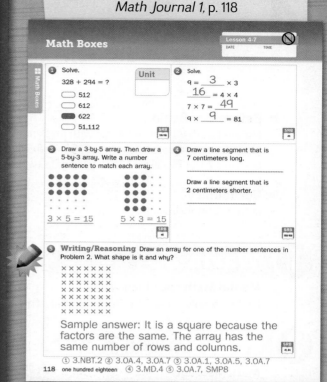

Math Boxes

Lesson 4-7

① Solve.

328 + 294 = ?

Unit

☐ 512
☐ 612
▨ 622
☐ 51,112

② Solve.

q = __3__ × 3

__16__ = 4 × 4

7 × 7 = __49__

q × __9__ = 81

③ Draw a 3-by-5 array. Then draw a 5-by-3 array. Write a number sentence to match each array.

3 × 5 = 15   5 × 3 = 15

④ Draw a line segment that is 7 centimeters long.

Draw a line segment that is 2 centimeters shorter.

⑤ **Writing/Reasoning** Draw an array for one of the number sentences in Problem 2. What shape is it and why?

x x x x x x x
x x x x x x x
x x x x x x x
x x x x x x x
x x x x x x x
x x x x x x x
x x x x x x x

Sample answer: It is a square because the factors are the same. The array has the same number of rows and columns.

① 3.NBT.2 ② 3.OA.4, 3.OA.7 ③ 3.OA.1, 3.OA.5, 3.OA.7
118 one hundred eighteen ④ 3.MD.4 ⑤ 3.OA.7, SMP8

Lesson 4-8

Area and Composite Units

Overview Children find the area of a rectangle by using composite units.

▶ **Before You Begin**

Mark off a 5-by-8 foot rectangle with masking tape in the classroom or hallway. (*See Planning Ahead in Lesson 4-6.*) Children will need their 1-foot squares from Lesson 3-7. Cut five extra 1-foot squares in two different colors.

▶ **Vocabulary**

area • composite unit

 Common Core State Standards

Focus Clusters
• Geometric measurement: understand concepts of area and relate area to multiplication and to addition.
• Geometric measurement: recognize perimeter.

1 Warm Up   5 min

	Materials	
Mental Math and Fluency Children solve multiplication number stories.	slate	3.OA.3

2 Focus   40–50 min

Math Message Children sketch rectangles and find the area and perimeter.	*Math Journal 1*, p. 119	3.MD.5, 3.MD.5a, 3.MD.5b, 3.MD.6, 3.MD.8 SMP6
Distinguishing Area and Perimeter Children compare finding area and perimeter of rectangles.	*Math Journal 1*, p. 119	3.MD.5, 3.MD.5a, 3.MD.5b, 3.MD.6, 3.MD.8 SMP6
Using Composite Units to Find Area Children use a composite unit to measure a large rectangle.	1-foot squares, tape	3.MD.5, 3.MD.5a, 3.MD.5b, 3.MD.6, 3.MD.7, 3.MD.7a SMP7
Finding Areas of Rectangles Children determine the areas of rectangles.	*Math Journal 1*, p. 120	3.MD.5, 3.MD.5a, 3.MD.5b, 3.MD.6, 3.MD.7, 3.MD.7a SMP7
✓ **Assessment Check-In** See page 372.	*Math Journal 1*, p. 120	3.MD.5, 3.MD.5a, 3.MD.5b, 3.MD.6, 3.MD.7, 3.MD.7a SMP7

CCSS 3.MD.6 Spiral Snapshot

GMC Measure areas by counting unit squares.

| 2-12
Focus
Practice | 3-7
Focus | 4-7
Focus | 4-8
Focus
Practice | 4-9
Focus
Practice | 4-10
Focus
Practice | 4-12
Practice | 5-1
Focus
Practice |

Spiral Tracker   **Go Online** to see how mastery develops for all standards within the grade.

3 Practice   15–20 min

Minute Math+ Children practice mental math strategies.	*Minute Math®+*	
Measuring Body Parts Children measure body parts to the nearest $\frac{1}{2}$ inch.	*Math Journal 1*, p. 121; tape measure	3.MD.4 SMP1, SMP5
Math Boxes 4-8 Children practice and maintain skills.	*Math Journal 1*, p. 122	See page 373.
Home Link 4-8 **Homework** Children find the areas of rectangles.	*Math Masters*, p. 137	3.MD.5, 3.MD.5a, 3.MD.5b, 3.MD.6, 3.MD.7, 3.MD.7a

connectED.mcgraw-hill.com

Plan your lessons online with these tools.

ePresentations   Student Learning Center   Facts Workshop Game   eToolkit   Professional Development   Home Connections   Spiral Tracker   Assessment and Reporting   English Learners Support   Differentiation Support

Differentiation Options RtI

Readiness   5–10 min

	WHOLE CLASS
	SMALL GROUP
	PARTNER
	INDEPENDENT

Using Squares to Find Area and Perimeter

Math Masters, p. 134; colored pencils

To provide experience finding areas and perimeters of rectangles, have children count whole-centimeter squares and the centimeter edges of squares along the borders of the rectangles on *Math Masters*, page 134.

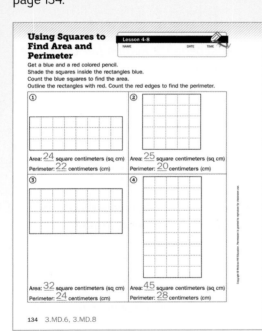

Enrichment   5–10 min

	WHOLE CLASS
	SMALL GROUP
	PARTNER
	INDEPENDENT

Exploring Area with Composite Units

Math Masters, p. 135

To further explore area, have children use different sizes of composite units to find the areas of same-size rectangles. Then have them write about which composite units are easier to use. **GMP6.1**

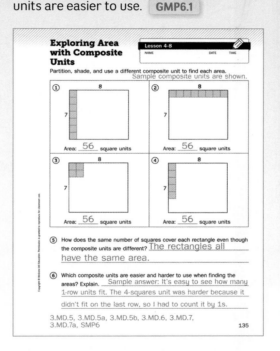

Extra Practice   5–10 min

	WHOLE CLASS
	SMALL GROUP
	PARTNER
	INDEPENDENT

Measuring Area with Composite Units

Math Masters, p. 136

For additional practice with composite units, have children find the areas of rectangles on *Math Masters*, page 136. Then have children explain their strategies for selecting composite units to determine the area.

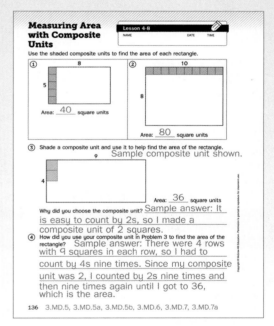

English Language Learners Support

Beginning ELL Use pictures or video clips to provide children with visual examples of rows and columns. For example, show rows found in entertainment venues and columns found in familiar buildings. Reinforce children's understanding of the terms *row* and *column* by having them "air draw" rows from side to side and columns from top to bottom as they repeat the terms and these sentences: *Rows go side to side. Columns go up and down.* Follow with show-me prompts, asking children to demonstrate a row or a column using movement or to find examples in the classroom.

Go Online   **ELL** English Learners Support

1 Warm Up   5 min

ePresentations   eToolkit

▶ Mental Math and Fluency

Have children solve the following number stories on their slates.
Leveled exercises:

- ●○○ A tic-tac-toe grid has 3 rows of spaces with 3 spaces in each row.
  How many spaces are there in all? 9 spaces
- ●●○ A checkerboard has 8 rows of squares and 8 squares in each row.
  How many squares are there in all? 64 squares
- ●●● A shelf has 7 snack bags on it. There are 7 crackers in each snack
  bag. How many crackers are there in all? 49 crackers

2 Focus   40–50 min

ePresentations   eToolkit

▶ Math Message

Math Journal 1, p. 119

*Complete the Math Message on journal page 119. Remember to include
units with your side lengths and with your area and perimeter measures.*
GMP6.3 *Be ready to explain how you found your measures.*

▶ Distinguishing Area and Perimeter

Math Journal 1, p. 119

| WHOLE CLASS | SMALL GROUP | PARTNER | INDEPENDENT |

Math Message Follow-Up Ask a volunteer to show his or her two
rectangles. Then have children share their strategies for finding the
perimeters of both rectangles. Sample answer: I counted the edges of the
squares all the way around each rectangle. I doubled the side lengths and
added them together.

Ask: *What units should we include with our perimeter measures? Why?*
GMP6.3 We should include centimeters because perimeter is a distance,
which is measured in a length unit. Emphasize that perimeter is measured
in length units because it is a measure of the distance around an object.

Next have children explain what they notice about the **area** and perimeter
measures for their rectangles. Sample answer: The perimeters are
different because they have different side lengths, but the areas are
the same. Ask: *What units should we include with our area measure?*
Square centimeter Emphasize that area is measured in square units.
Remind children that centimeter can be abbreviated as *cm*, and square
centimeters as *sq cm.* Have children share their areas and strategies
for finding them. GMP6.3 Sample answer: 15 square centimeters; I
counted the squares inside each rectangle. I skip counted by 5s for the
first rectangle.

Math Journal 1, p. 119

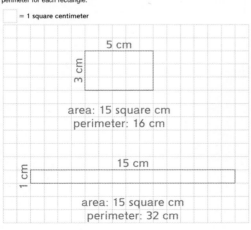

Explain that today children will find areas of rectangles without having to count every square.

► Using Composite Units to Find Area

WHOLE CLASS | **SMALL GROUP** | PARTNER | INDEPENDENT

Have children gather around the 5-by-8 foot rectangle on the floor with their 1-foot squares. (*See Before You Begin.*) Explain that they need to figure out the amount of carpet or tile needed to cover the area of the rectangle.

Have children try to tile the area with their 1-foot squares. Ask: *How can we measure the area without having enough 1-foot squares to tile the rectangle completely?* Sample answer: We could take one square unit and use it over and over to find the total number of square units that would fit.

Suggest using a **composite unit** made up of 1-foot squares. Explain that a composite unit is made from grouping smaller units together. Align 1-foot squares along the inside of the shorter side of the rectangle. (*See margin.*) Ask: *How many 1-foot squares fit along this side?* 5

Tape five 1-foot squares together to form a composite unit. Tell children to imagine another column of 5 squares. Ask: *How many square feet are in the second column?* 5 *How many square feet are in two columns all together?* 10 Explain that you want to move the 5-square foot composite unit along the longer edge of the rectangle to find the area.

Have volunteers help place and move the composite unit of 5 squares along the long side of the rectangle and count by 5s. Each time the unit is moved, have a child mark along the boundary so the next placement can be properly aligned. Ask: *What are you counting when you count by 5s?*
GMP6.3 The number of square feet of area

Ask: *How many 1-foot squares cover the surface of this rectangle?* 40 squares *What is the area of this rectangle?* 40 square feet *How many times did we place the composite unit?* 8 times *What is the length of the long side of the rectangle?* 8 feet *If we partition this rectangle into 1-foot squares so it looks like an array, how many columns would there be?* 8 *How many rows?* 5 *How do you know?* **GMP7.2** Sample answer: There are 5 squares in the composite unit, which means that there are 5 rows. We moved the composite unit 8 times, so we know there are 8 columns.

Ask: *What other composite units might we use to measure the area of this rectangle?* **GMP7.2** Sample answer: The eight 1-foot squares that make up a row Have children construct a 1-by-8 composite unit to measure the rectangle to show that the area measurement stays the same regardless of the size of the composite unit.

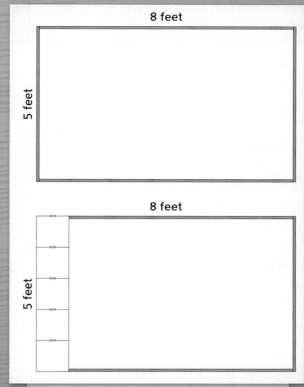

A five 1-foot square composite unit on a 5-by-8 foot rectangle

Professional Development

Guide children to think about measuring area as sweeping over or rolling across a surface. Children can imagine sweeping the composite unit over the rectangle in the same way a rug might be rolled out over a floor. Discuss other examples, such as a window shade rolling down over a window or bulletin-board paper unrolling over the bulletin board.

Adjusting the Activity

Differentiate Have children who are ready measure the area with a 3-by-3 composite unit and count by 9s. Note that part of the 3-by-3 composite unit will fall outside the area of the rectangle, so help children count only the squares inside the boundary. Invite them to compare their experiences measuring area with different composite units.

Go Online Differentiation Support

Math Journal 1, p. 120

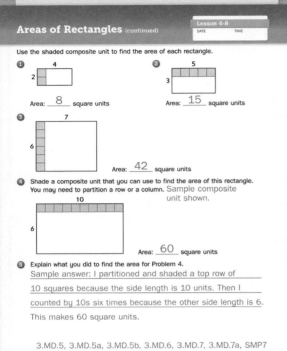

Areas of Rectangles (continued)

Lesson 4-8

DATE   TIME

Use the shaded composite unit to find the area of each rectangle.

① 4 / 2

Area: __8__ square units

② 5 / 3

Area: __15__ square units

③ 7 / 6

Area: __42__ square units

④ Shade a composite unit that you can use to find the area of this rectangle. You may need to partition a row or a column. Sample composite unit shown.

10 / 6

Area: __60__ square units

⑤ Explain what you did to find the area for Problem 4.
Sample answer: I partitioned and shaded a top row of
10 squares because the side length is 10 units. Then I
counted by 10s six times because the other side length is 6.
This makes 60 square units.

3.MD.5, 3.MD.5a, 3.MD.5b, 3.MD.6, 3.MD.7, 3.MD.7a, SMP7

120 one hundred twenty

Math Journal 1, p. 121

Body Measures

Lesson 4-8

DATE   TIME

Work with a partner to find each measurement to the nearest ½ inch.

	Me	Partner
Date		
height	about _____ in.	about _____ in.
knee to foot	about _____ in.	about _____ in.
around neck	about _____ in.	about _____ in.
waist to floor	about _____ in.	about _____ in.
forearm	about _____ in.	about _____ in.
hand span	about _____ in.	about _____ in.
arm span	about _____ in.	about _____ in.

forearm   hand span   arm span

How do you know whether your body measurements make sense?
Sample answers: I am shorter than my partner,
so my height measurement should be smaller.
I measured my knee to foot again to check.

3.MD.4, SMP1, SMP5   one hundred twenty-one 121

▶ Finding Areas of Rectangles

Math Journal 1, p. 120

| **WHOLE CLASS** | **SMALL GROUP** | **PARTNER** | INDEPENDENT |

Have children look at Problem 1 on journal page 120. Ask: *What composite unit is shaded?* Two square units *How might you use the composite unit to find the area of the rectangle?* Sample answers: The long side of the rectangle is 4 units, so I will count by 2s four times. I partitioned the rest of the rectangle into 2 rows with 4 squares in each row and that's 4 composite units. *What is the area of the rectangle?* 8 square units

Have partnerships complete the page. For Problems 2 and 3, children use given composite units to find areas of rectangles. For Problem 4, children create a unit and use it to find the area of the rectangle. GMP7.2 Circulate and observe children's strategies for finding area.

Differentiate   **Adjusting the Activity**

For children having difficulty partitioning rectangles, discuss the following strategies:

- Make tick marks along the boundary first.
- Draw lines all the way down or across to define rows or columns.
- To partition a rectangle into 2, 4, or 8 parts, divide it in half (2), divide each part in half (4), and then divide each new part in half (8).

Go Online   Differentiation Support

✓ **Assessment Check-In** CCSS 3.MD.5, 3.MD.6, 3.MD.7

Math Journal 1, p. 120

Expect children to find the areas of rectangles in Problems 2 through 4. They may count each square, while others may be ready to skip count composite units. For those who struggle to use one of these strategies, consider the suggestions in the above Adjusting the Activity note, putting dots in squares as they are counted, or tracing around each composite unit. Do not expect all children to use composite units successfully as this is their first exposure to that strategy.

✓ Assessment and Reporting   **Go Online** to record student progress and to see trajectories toward mastery for these standards.

Invite volunteers to share their strategies for finding the areas on journal page 120. Emphasize the efficiency of using composite units and skip counting. If some children multiplied side lengths, acknowledge this as an efficient strategy and tell them they will focus on this method in the next lesson.

Summarize Ask: *How does using a composite unit help us find area more quickly?* Sample answer: We don't have to count every square unit.

3 Practice   10–15 min   Go Online

ePresentations   eToolkit   Home Connections

▶ *Minute Math*+

To practice mental math strategies, select a *Minute Math*+ activity.

▶ Measuring Body Parts

Math Journal 1, p. 121

| WHOLE CLASS | SMALL GROUP | **PARTNER** | INDEPENDENT |

Have partners measure body parts using toolkit tape measures and record their measurements to the nearest $\frac{1}{2}$ inch on journal page 121. **GMP5.2** Have them discuss whether their measures make sense. For example, a taller child should generate a larger measure of height. **GMP1.4**

▶ Math Boxes 4-8

Math Journal 1, p. 122

| WHOLE CLASS | **SMALL GROUP** | PARTNER | **INDEPENDENT** |

Mixed Practice Math Boxes 4-8 are grouped with Math Boxes 4-6 and 4-11.

▶ Home Link 4-8

Math Masters, p. 137

Homework Children use composite units to find the areas of rectangles.

Planning Ahead

For Lesson 4-10, cut Action Deck and Rectangle Decks A and B from *Math Journal 1*, Activity Sheets 13–15 (1 set per partnership).

Math Journal 1, p. 122

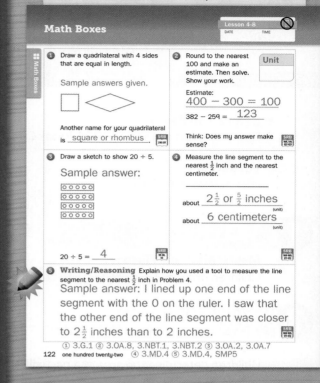

Math Boxes   Lesson 4-8
DATE   TIME

1. Draw a quadrilateral with 4 sides that are equal in length.

   Sample answers given.

   Another name for your quadrilateral is _square or rhombus_

2. Round to the nearest 100 and make an estimate. Then solve. Show your work.   Unit

   Estimate:
   $400 - 300 = 100$
   $382 - 259 = \underline{123}$

   Think: Does my answer make sense?

3. Draw a sketch to show $20 \div 5$.

   Sample answer:

   $20 \div 5 = \underline{4}$

4. Measure the line segment to the nearest $\frac{1}{2}$ inch and the nearest centimeter.

   about $2\frac{1}{2}$ or $\frac{5}{2}$ inches (unit)

   about 6 centimeters (unit)

5. **Writing/Reasoning** Explain how you used a tool to measure the line segment to the nearest $\frac{1}{2}$ inch in Problem 4.
   Sample answer: I lined up one end of the line segment with the 0 on the ruler. I saw that the other end of the line segment was closer to $2\frac{1}{2}$ inches than to 2 inches.

① 3.G.1 ② 3.OA.8, 3.NBT.1, 3.NBT.2 ③ 3.OA.2, 3.OA.7
122 one hundred twenty-two ④ 3.MD.4 ⑤ 3.MD.4, SMP5

Math Masters, p. 137   p. 113

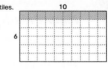

Areas of Rectangles   Home Link 4-8
NAME   DATE   TIME

Family Note Today your child found areas of rectangles using composite units. Composite units are made up of two or more square units. Using composite units to find area helps children see a rectangle as having a row-by-column structure, and it helps them measure area more efficiently.
Please return this Home Link to school tomorrow.

① Sarah tiled her floor with square tiles. This is a drawing of her floor: 10

Shade a composite unit made of 10 squares. Use the composite unit to figure out the number of tiles Sarah needs.   6

Sarah needs _60_ tiles.

② Alejandro painted a wall that is 3 yards tall and 7 yards long. This is a drawing of the wall: 7 yards

Partition the rectangle to show 3 rows with 7 squares in each row. Shade a composite unit made of 3 squares. Then figure out the area of the wall.   3 yards

How many square yards did Alejandro paint? _21_ square yards

③ Explain how you found the area of the wall in Problem 2.
Sample answer: I made a composite unit of a column of 3 squares and counted by 3s seven times to get 21.

3.MD.5, 3.MD.5a, 3.MD.5b, 3.MD.6, 3.MD.7, 3.MD.7a   137

Number Sentences for Area of Rectangles

Overview Children find areas of rectangles and write matching number sentences.

▶ **Before You Begin**
For Part 1, select and sequence Quick Look Cards 134, 136, and 146.

▶ **Vocabulary**
area • array • perimeter

CCSS **Common Core State Standards**

Focus Cluster
Geometric measurement: understand concepts of area and relate area to multiplication and to addition.

1 Warm Up 5–10 min

Materials

Mental Math and Fluency
Children practice Quick Looks with equal groups and arrays.

Quick Look Cards 134, 136, 146

3.OA.1, 3.OA.7
SMP2, SMP6

2 Focus 40–50 min

Math Message
Children determine the area of a partially visible rectangle.

Math Journal 1, p. 124

3.MD.5, 3.MD.5b, 3.MD.6, 3.MD.7, 3.MD.7a
SMP1

Reviewing Strategies for Area
Children share strategies for finding the area of a rectangle.

Math Journal 1, p. 124;
Math Masters, p. 139

3.MD.5, 3.MD.5b, 3.MD.6, 3.MD.7, 3.MD.7a, 3.MD.7b, SMP1

Using Arrays to Find Area
Children use what they know about arrays to find the areas of rectangles.

Math Journal 1, p. 124;
Math Masters, p. TA34

3.MD.5, 3.MD.5b, 3.MD.6, 3.MD.7, 3.MD.7a, 3.MD.7b
SMP2, SMP7

Multiplying Side Lengths
Children use side length measures to find the areas of rectangles.

Math Journal 1, p. 125;
Math Masters, p. TA34, p. TA35
(optional); half-sheet (optional)

3.MD.5, 3.MD.5b, 3.MD.6, 3.MD.7, 3.MD.7, 3.MD.7a, 3.MD.7b
SMP2, SMP7

✓ **Assessment Check-In**   See page 378.

Math Journal 1, p. 125

3.MD.7, 3.MD.7a, 3.MD.7b, SMP7

CCSS **3.MD.7a** **Spiral Snapshot**

GMC Show that tiling a rectangle results in the same area as multiplying its side lengths.

4-9 Focus Practice | 5-1 Practice | 5-2 Practice | 5-3 Practice | 5-9 Practice | 5-11 Practice | 8-7 Focus

Spiral Tracker   **Go Online**   to see how mastery develops for all standards within the grade.

3 Practice 15–20 min

Minute Math+
Children practice mental math strategies.

Minute Math®+

Writing Equivalent Names
Children complete name-collection boxes.

Math Journal 1, p. 123

3.OA.7, 3.NBT.2
SMP1, SMP2

Math Boxes 4-9: Preview for Unit 5
Children preview skills and concepts for Unit 5.

Math Journal 1, p. 126

See page 379.

Home Link 4-9
Homework Children find areas of rectangles using arrays.

Math Masters, p. 140

3.MD.5, 3.MD.5b, 3.MD.6, 3.MD.7, 3.MD.7, 3.MD.7a, 3.MD.7b, SMP7

---

connectED.mcgraw-hill.com

Plan your lessons online with these tools.

 ePresentations

 Student Learning Center

 Facts Workshop Game

 eToolkit

 Professional Development

 Home Connections

 Spiral Tracker

 Assessment and Reporting

 English Learners Support

 Differentiation Support

Differentiation Options

RtI

Readiness 5–10 min

Modeling Area with a Geoboard

WHOLE CLASS / **SMALL GROUP** / PARTNER / INDEPENDENT

geoboard, pennies, rubber bands

To provide concrete experience with area, have children use geoboards and rubber bands to make and then find the areas of rectangles. To ensure that children count the squares and not the pegs when counting the number of squares in the rectangle, have them place a penny in the squares. It is not necessary for children to fill in the rectangle completely because they should be encouraged to skip count by the number of rows or columns. For example, if there are 5 rows with 4 in each row, they could count by 5s or 4s to find the area.

Enrichment 10–15 min

Investigating Area and Perimeter

WHOLE CLASS / SMALL GROUP / **PARTNER** / INDEPENDENT

Activity Card 60;
Math Masters, p. TA19;
number cards 6–20; tape

To explore area and perimeter, have children draw all the possible rectangles with whole-number side lengths for a given area on Centimeter Grid Paper (*Math Masters*, page TA19). **GMP1.5** Have them record number sentences inside each rectangle for finding the area, and then discuss the relationship between their rectangles and multiplication facts.

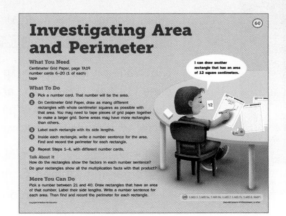

Extra Practice 5–10 min

Finding Areas of Rectangles

WHOLE CLASS / SMALL GROUP / PARTNER / **INDEPENDENT**

Math Masters, p. 138

For additional practice multiplying side lengths of rectangles to find areas, have children complete *Math Masters*, page 138.

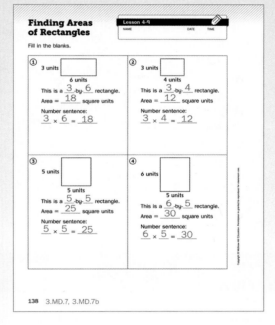

English Language Learners Support

Beginning ELL Build on children's prior experiences by using the term *array* to describe items they may have seen in everyday life, such as a muffin pan, egg carton, or checkerboard. Think aloud to name and describe the items using the terms *array*, *row*, and *column*. For example: *This muffin pan shows an array. It has 3 rows and 4 columns.* Point to each row and then to each column and ask: *How many are in each row? How many are in each column? How many muffins in all would fit in this pan?* Accept nonverbal and one-word responses, allowing children to use number cards or tell you the number.

Go Online   **ELL** English Learners Support

SMP1 **Make sense of problems and persevere in solving them.**

GMP1.6 Compare the strategies you and others use.

SMP2 **Reason abstractly and quantitatively.**

GMP2.3 Make connections between representations.

SMP7 **Look for and make use of structure.**

GMP7.2 Use structures to solve problems and answer questions.

Academic Language Development

Children are often more comfortable answering questions rather than asking them in class. Encourage children to ask one another questions about their area strategies by providing written question sentence frames, such as: *Why did you _____? Did you think about _____? Why didn't you _____? What made you use the _____ strategy? What was good about the _____ strategy?*

Math Journal 1, p. 124

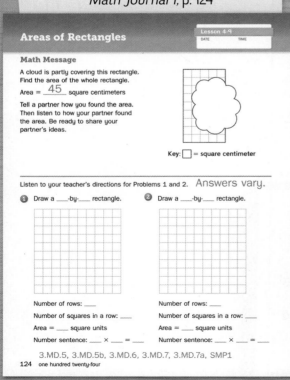

1 Warm Up 5–10 min Go Online
ePresentations   eToolkit

▶ Mental Math and Fluency

Show Quick Look Cards 134, 136, and 146 one at a time for 2–3 seconds. Ask children to share both what they saw and how they saw it. **GMP2.2, GMP6.1** Highlight equal-group or array strategies. Sample answers:

Quick Look Card 134 I saw 2 groups of 4 and 4 + 4 = 8.

Quick Look Card 136 I saw 3 groups of 5. I skip counted by 5s: 5, 10, 15.

Quick Look Card 146 I saw 2 groups of 4 that made 8 and then 2 more groups of 4 for another 8, and 8 + 8 = 16.

2 Focus 40–50 min Go Online
ePresentations   eToolkit

▶ Math Message

Math Journal 1, p. 124

Complete the Math Message on journal page 124. **GMP1.6**

▶ Reviewing Strategies for Area

Math Journal 1, p. 124; *Math Masters*, p. 139

| WHOLE CLASS | SMALL GROUP | PARTNER | INDEPENDENT |

Math Message Follow-Up Display the rectangle on *Math Masters*, page 139. Ask: *What is the **area** of the rectangle?* 45 square units Have children share their partner's strategies for finding the area. **GMP1.6** Include these strategies in the discussion:

- Draw lines over the cloud to partition the rectangle into the remaining squares. Count each square.
- Count the squares in one row (or column) to determine a composite unit. Skip count or add.

Ask children to think of the squares in the rectangle as an **array.** Ask: *How many rows of squares are there?* 9 *How many squares are in each row?* 5 Explain that the rectangle is a 9-by-5 array of squares. Ask: *How do you find the number of objects in an array?* Expect answers to include:

- Count the total number of objects.
- Skip count by the number of rows or columns.
- Multiply the number of rows by the number of objects in each row.

Ask: *How many squares are there in all?* 45 squares

Invite a volunteer to write a number sentence to represent this 9-by-5 array. $9 \times 5 = 45$

Ask: *How are these array strategies different?* Sample answer: They use different kinds of counting or multiplication. Ask: *Why do these strategies give the same answer for area?* **GMP1.6** Sample answer: They are all ways to find the total number of squares inside the rectangle.

Explain that today children will use array models and side lengths to find the areas of rectangles.

▶ Using Arrays to Find Area

Math Journal 1, p. 124; *Math Masters*, p. TA34

| WHOLE CLASS | SMALL GROUP | PARTNER | INDEPENDENT |

Draw a 10-by-8 rectangle (10 squares down, 8 squares across) on *Math Masters*, page TA34. Tell the class that this rectangle represents the front cover of a notebook you want to cover with 1-inch square stickers. Explain to children that each square represents the area of one sticker and that they are going to figure out how many stickers are needed to cover the surface of the notebook cover. Shade a row of squares along the top, shorter side of the rectangle.

Ask: *How many squares are in this row?* 8 *How many equal rows of squares are inside the rectangle?* 10 equal rows

Display $10 \times 8 = 80$. Tell the class that this number sentence represents the area of the rectangle, where 10 is the number of rows and 8 is the number of squares in each row. Ask: *How many squares are there in all?* 80 squares *How many 1-inch square stickers do you need to cover the front cover of the notebook?* **GMP2.3** Eighty 1-inch square stickers

Have children return to journal page 124. For Problems 1 and 2, dictate the number of rows and columns for each rectangle. *Suggestions:* 8-by-8 and 6-by-7.

Have children fill in blanks for rows-by-columns, and then draw each rectangle on the grid, find its area, and write a number sentence. Use array language to discuss solutions, such as: *My rectangle has 8 rows of squares with 8 squares in each row (or 8 columns), so I can find the area by solving 8 × 8. The area is 64 square units.* **GMP7.2**

NOTE In *Everyday Mathematics,* array and rectangle dimensions are written *r*-by-*c*, meaning they have *r* rows and *c* columns. However, not everyone observes this convention. An *r*-by-*c* rectangle has two opposite sides *r* units long and two opposite sides *c* units long.

Adjusting the Activity

Differentiate Scaffold the connections between arrays and area. In addition to the information to be completed below the arrays on journal page 124, add a line for children to write an addition number sentence. Sample answer: $7 + 7 + 7 + 7 + 7 = 35$ Also add a line for children to write out skip counting. Sample answer: 7, 14, 21, 28, 35 You may want to provide an enlarged template with all of these options for children to fill in for each array.

Go Online ▶ Differentiation Support

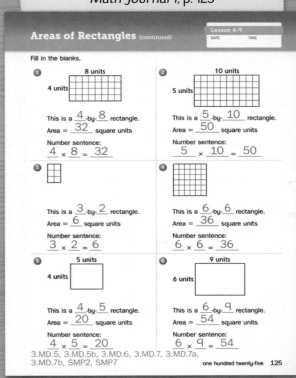

Math Journal 1, p. 125

Areas of Rectangles (continued)   Lesson 4-9

Fill in the blanks.

① 8 units / 4 units
This is a $\underline{4}$-by-$\underline{8}$ rectangle.
Area = $\underline{32}$ square units.
Number sentence:
$\underline{4} \times \underline{8} = \underline{32}$

② 10 units / 5 units
This is a $\underline{5}$-by-$\underline{10}$ rectangle.
Area = $\underline{50}$ square units.
Number sentence:
$\underline{5} \times \underline{10} = \underline{50}$

③ This is a $\underline{3}$-by-$\underline{2}$ rectangle.
Area = $\underline{6}$ square units.
Number sentence:
$\underline{3} \times \underline{2} = \underline{6}$

④ This is a $\underline{6}$-by-$\underline{6}$ rectangle.
Area = $\underline{36}$ square units.
Number sentence:
$\underline{6} \times \underline{6} = \underline{36}$

⑤ 5 units / 4 units
This is a $\underline{4}$-by-$\underline{5}$ rectangle.
Area = $\underline{20}$ square units.
Number sentence:
$\underline{4} \times \underline{5} = \underline{20}$

⑥ 9 units / 6 units
This is a $\underline{6}$-by-$\underline{9}$ rectangle.
Area = $\underline{54}$ square units.
Number sentence:
$\underline{6} \times \underline{9} = \underline{54}$

3.MD.5, 3.MD.5b, 3.MD.6, 3.MD.7, 3.MD.7a, 3.MD.7b, SMP2, SMP7

one hundred twenty-five 125

▶ Multiplying Side Lengths

Math Journal 1, p. 125; *Math Masters*, p. TA34

WHOLE CLASS | SMALL GROUP | PARTNER | INDEPENDENT

Draw attention to the 10-by-8 rectangle on display from the previous activity. Gesturing along the length of the top edge of the rectangle, have the class count the number of squares aloud. You may want to darken the top edge of each square as the class counts. Ask: *If each square represents one square inch, how long is the top side of the rectangle?* 8 inches Label the top side "8 inches." Similarly count the edges to find the longer side length and label it "10 inches." Ask: *What do you notice about each side length and the number of squares along each side?* GMP2.3 The numbers are the same. The short side has 8 square inches and represents 8 inches. The long side has 10 square inches and represents 10 inches. Help children make the connection to **perimeter** by pointing out that there is one square unit in each row for every unit of length along the side. Explain that this is because the edge of the square unit is used to measure the length of the side.

Display an 8-inch long line segment. Have children think of the line segment as a window shade that is rolled up. Ask them to imagine what would happen if you could pull that line segment (window shade) straight down 10 inches. Help them see that a rectangular space is created. For each inch you pull the line segment down, you reveal a row of 8 square inches. The total number of squares revealed when the shade is pulled down 10 inches is $10 \times 8 = 80$.

Sketch the remainder of the 10-by-8 inch rectangle window shade and label the side lengths. Ask: *How could we find the area of a rectangle that is not partitioned into unit squares?* GMP7.2 We could multiply the side lengths together.

Have children complete journal page 125. Circulate and observe children's strategies.

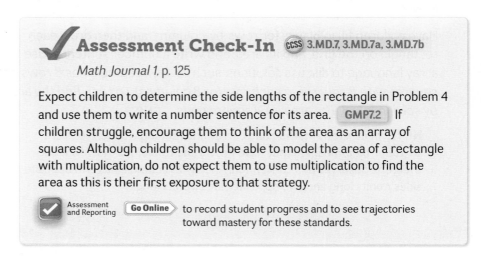

✓ **Assessment Check-In** CCSS 3.MD.7, 3.MD.7a, 3.MD.7b

Math Journal 1, p. 125

Expect children to determine the side lengths of the rectangle in Problem 4 and use them to write a number sentence for its area. GMP7.2 If children struggle, encourage them to think of the area as an array of squares. Although children should be able to model the area of a rectangle with multiplication, do not expect them to use multiplication to find the area as this is their first exposure to that strategy.

✓ Assessment and Reporting **Go Online** to record student progress and to see trajectories toward mastery for these standards.

Bring children together to share their strategies for finding area. Highlight strategies that are more efficient than counting individual squares.

Math Journal 1, p. 123

Name-Collection Boxes

Lesson 4-9

DATE   TIME

① Three names do not belong in this 100 box. Mark them with an X.

100
25 + 25 + 25 ✗ 980 − 880 80 +~~38~~ ✗
30 + 70
63 + 37   ~~1,000~~ ✗ ~~100~~
2 fifties   999 − 899
48 + 52

② Write at least 10 names for 40.

40
Answers vary.

③ Write at least 10 names for 200.

200
Answers vary.

④ Write at least 10 names for 1,000.

1,000
Answers vary.

3.OA.7, 3.NBT.2, SMP1, SMP2   one hundred twenty-three 123

Summarize Have children answer the following question orally, on a half-sheet, or an Exit Slip (*Math Masters,* page TA35): *How does multiplying side lengths work for finding the area of a rectangle?* `GMP7.2` Sample answer: The squares in a rectangle are like an array. The length of one pair of a rectangle's sides tells how many squares are in each row, and the length of the other pair of sides tells how many rows there are. So you can multiply the side lengths to find the area, just like you can multiply rows and columns to find the number of objects in an array.

3 Practice 15–20 min

Go Online

ePresentations eToolkit Home Connections

▶ *Minute Math+*

To practice mental math strategies, select a *Minute Math+* activity.

▶ Writing Equivalent Names

Math Journal 1, p. 123

| WHOLE CLASS | **SMALL GROUP** | **PARTNER** | INDEPENDENT |

Have children complete name-collection boxes. Encourage them to include expressions using addition, subtraction, multiplication, and division. `GMP1.5, GMP2.1`

▶ Math Boxes 4-9: Preview for Unit 5

Math Journal 1, p. 126

| WHOLE CLASS | **SMALL GROUP** | **PARTNER** | **INDEPENDENT** |

Mixed Practice Math Boxes 4-9 are paired with Math Boxes 4-13. These problems focus on skills and understandings that are prerequisite for Unit 5. You may want to use information from these Math Boxes to plan instruction and grouping in Unit 5.

▶ Home Link 4-9

Math Masters, p. 140

| WHOLE CLASS | SMALL GROUP | PARTNER | **INDEPENDENT** |

Homework Children find areas of rectangles using array models. `GMP7.2`

Math Journal 1, p. 126

Math Boxes Preview for Unit 5

Lesson 4-9

DATE   TIME

① Divide the shape below into four equal parts.
Shade one part.

Sample answer:
What fraction of the shape is shaded? **1-fourth**

② Use the array to show how you can use 5 × 8 to help you figure out 4 × 8.

Helper fact: 5 × 8 = 40

× × × × × × × ×
× × × × × × × ×
× × × × × × × ×
× × × × × × × ×
—×—×—×—×—×—×—×—×—

4 × 8 = ___32___

③

Select all the names that fit one of the parts. Circle the letter(s) next to the correct answer(s).

A. 1-half
B. 1-fourth
C. a quarter
D. 1 out of 2 equal parts

④ Shade the top 2 rows one color and the bottom 2 rows another color.

Area of the top 2 rows:
___12___ square units

Area of the bottom 2 rows:
___12___ square units

Area of the whole rectangle:
___24___ square units

⑤ **Writing/Reasoning** Explain how you found the area of the whole rectangle in Problem 4.
Sample answer: I counted all the squares by 2s. I added the areas of the two smaller rectangles, and 12 + 12 = 24.

① 3.NF.1, 3.G.2 ② 3.OA.1, 3.OA.5, 3.OA.7 ③ 3.NF.1, 3.G.2
④ 3.MD.5, 3.MD.5a, 3.MD.5b, 3.MD.6, 3.MD.7d ⑤ 3.MD.5, 3.MD.5a,
126 one hundred twenty-six 3.MD.5b, 3.MD.6, 3.MD.7, 3.MD.7d, SMP6

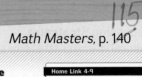

115

Math Masters, p. 140

Arrays, Side Lengths, and Area

Home Link 4-9

NAME   DATE   TIME

Family Note Today your child learned that side lengths of rectangles correspond to the number of square units in the rectangles' rows and columns. Just as rows and columns in arrays can be multiplied to find total numbers of objects, side lengths can be multiplied to find areas of rectangles.
Please return this Home Link to school tomorrow.

Make a dot inside each small square in one row. Then fill in the blanks.

① Number of rows: __7__
Number of squares in a row: __5__
Number sentence: __7__ × __5__ = __35__
Area: __35__ square units

② Number of rows: __6__
Number of squares in a row: __7__
Number sentence: __6__ × __7__ = __42__
Area: __42__ square units

Mark the dots to show each array. Then fill in the blanks.

③ Make a 4-by-8 array.
Number sentence: __4__ × __8__ = __32__

④ Make a 9-by-5 array.
Number sentence: __9__ × __5__ = __45__

3.MD.5, 3.MD.5b, 3.MD.6, 3.MD.7, 3.MD.7a,
140 3.MD.7b, SMP7

▶ **Before You Begin**

For Part 2, prepare or have children cut out *The Area and Perimeter Game* Deck A and the Action Deck from *Math Journal 1,* Activity Sheets 13–14. (*See Planning Ahead, Lesson 4-8.*) Deck B (Activity Sheet 15) may be prepared for an advanced version of the game. Plan how you will store cards for future play. For the optional Readiness activity, gather various rectangular prisms.

▶ **Vocabulary**

area • perimeter

Common Core State Standards

Focus Clusters
- Geometric measurement: understand concepts of area and relate area to multiplication and to addition.
- Geometric measurement: recognize perimeter.

---

1 Warm Up 5 min

	Materials	
Mental Math and Fluency Children solve number stories using division.	slate	3.OA.2, 3.OA.3

---

2 Focus 40–50 min

Math Message Children find the area and perimeter of a rectangle.	*Math Journal 1,* p. 127	3.MD.5, 3.MD.5a, 3.MD.5b, 3.MD.6, 3.MD.7, 3.MD.7b, 3.MD.8, SMP6
Introducing *The Area and Perimeter Game* **Game** Children discuss strategies for calculating area and perimeter and make sense of game cards.	*Math Journal 1,* p. 127 and Activity Sheets 13–14; *Student Reference Book,* pp. 230–231; *Math Masters,* p. G16; Perimeter and Area T chart from Lesson 4-7	3.MD.5, 3.MD.5a, 3.MD.5b, 3.MD.6, 3.MD.7, 3.MD.7b, 3.MD.8 SMP6, SMP7
Playing *The Area and Perimeter Game* Children practice finding the area and perimeter of rectangles.	*Math Journal 1,* Activity Sheets 13–14, 15 (optional); *Student Reference Book,* pp. 230–231; *Math Masters,* p. G16	3.MD.5, 3.MD.5a, 3.MD.5b, 3.MD.6, 3.MD.7, 3.MD.7b, 3.MD.8 SMP6, SMP7
✓ **Assessment Check-In** See page 384.	*Math Masters,* p. G16	3.MD.6, 3.MD.8
Discussing Strategies Children discuss strategies for game play.	*Math Masters,* p. G16, p. TA35 (optional); half-sheet (optional)	3.MD.5, 3.MD.6, 3.MD.7, 3.MD.8 SMP6, SMP7

CCSS 3.MD.8 Spiral Snapshot

GMC Solve problems involving perimeters of polygons.

| 4-3 Focus | 4-6 Focus Practice | 4-7 Focus Practice | 4-8 Focus | 4-10 Focus Practice | 4-12 Practice | 5-1 Warm Up Focus Practice | 5-11 Practice |

/// Spiral Tracker   Go Online   to see how mastery develops for all standards within the grade.

---

3 Practice 15–20 min

Minute Math+ Children practice mental math strategies.	*Minute Math®+*	
Taking Inventory of Known Facts Part 2 Children continue to self-assess their fact power.	*Math Journal 1,* p. 142; Fact Triangles	3.OA.7 SMP6
Math Boxes 4-10 Children practice and maintain skills.	*Math Journal 1,* p. 128	See page 385.
Home Link 4-10 **Homework** Children find areas and perimeters.	*Math Masters,* p. 142	3.MD.5, 3.MD.5a, 3.MD.5b, 3.MD.6, 3.MD.7, 3.MD.7b, 3.MD.8, SMP6

---

connectED.mcgraw-hill.com

Plan your lessons online with these tools.

 ePresentations
 Student Learning Center
 Facts Workshop Game
 eToolkit
 Professional Development
 Home Connections
 Spiral Tracker
Assessment and Reporting
English Learners Support
 Differentiation Support

380 Unit 4 | Measurement and Geometry

Readiness | 5–10 min

WHOLE CLASS
SMALL GROUP
PARTNER
INDEPENDENT

Identifying Perimeter and Area

various rectangular prisms, red and blue crayons

To provide practice identifying area and perimeter, have children trace one face of a rectangular prism, such as a tissue box, on paper. Provide a context to help children differentiate perimeter and area: if the rectangle is the floor of a room, the intersection of the floor and walls form a boundary. Have children use a blue crayon to outline the rectangle and a red crayon to shade the surface inside it. Ask: *What would you measure to find the perimeter?* The length of blue outline *The area?* The red surface inside the boundary Ask: *How do you remember the difference between area and perimeter?* Repeat the activity by tracing the faces of other rectangular prisms.

Enrichment | 10–15 min

WHOLE CLASS
SMALL GROUP
PARTNER
INDEPENDENT

Finding and Comparing Areas

Math Masters, p. 141; scissors; square pattern blocks; inch ruler

To further explore area, have children find and compare the areas of a square and the two triangles that form it. Have children cut a 4-inch square from *Math Masters,* page 141 and find its area. Then have them fold along the diagonal and cut the square into two equal-size triangles. Have them find the area of each, comparing the area of the square to the areas of the triangles and recording their findings. Help children see that the area of each triangle is half the area of the square. GMP7.1

Finding and Comparing Areas | Lesson 4-10
NAME | DATE | TIME

- Cut out the square.
- Find its area in square inches. You may tile the area with square pattern blocks or use a ruler to measure the side lengths.
- Cut the square into two equal-size triangles.
- Find the area of each triangle in square inches.

Name: _____
① Area of square: __16 square inches__ (unit)
② Area of first triangle: about __8 square inches__ (unit)
③ Area of second triangle: about __8 square inches__ (unit)
④ How do the areas of the two triangles compare? __They are the same.__
⑤ How does the area of one triangle compare to the area of the original square? __It is half the area of the square.__
⑥ How does the area of the two triangles together compare to the area of the original square? __They are the same.__

3MD.5, 3MD.5a, 3MD.5b, 3.MD.7, 3MD.7a, 3MD.7b, SMP7 | 141

Extra Practice | 10–15 min

WHOLE CLASS
SMALL GROUP
PARTNER
INDEPENDENT

Playing *The Area and Perimeter Game*

Math Journal 1, Activity Sheets 13–14; *Student Reference Book,* pp. 230–231; *Math Masters,* p. G16

For additional practice finding area and perimeter, have children play *The Area and Perimeter Game* with the Action Deck and Deck A cards (Activity Sheets 13–14). Have children record their work on *Math Masters,* page G16. GMP2.1

The Area and Perimeter Game Record Sheet
NAME | DATE | TIME

Round	Card Number	A (area) or P (perimeter)	Show how you found the area or perimeter using words, drawings, and/or a number sentence.	Score
Example:	3	P	I counted the edges of the squares along the long and short sides of the rectangle and added them: 2 + 4 + 2 + 4 = 12.	12
1				
2				
3				
4				
5				

G16

English Language Learners Support

Beginning ELL To prepare children for playing *The Area and Perimeter Game,* use Total Physical Response routines to rehearse shuffling and playing with cards. Use show-me prompts to familiarize them with the term *deck of cards.* Before beginning the game, introduce the meanings of these essential phrases: *It is your turn. It is my turn. Who is next? You win.* Demonstrate by playing a few rounds of a familiar card game and modeling the use of the phrases. Have children repeat the phrases at appropriate points during the game.

 Go Online ELL English Learners Support

SMP6 **Attend to precision.**

GMP6.1 Explain your mathematical thinking clearly and precisely.

GMP6.4 Think about accuracy and efficiency when you count, measure, and calculate.

SMP7 **Look for and make use of structure.**

GMP7.2 Use structures to solve problems and answer questions.

---

1 Warm Up   5 min

Go Online   ePresentations   eToolkit

▶ Mental Math and Fluency

Have children pretend they are forming each shape with one craft stick per side and solve the following number stories on slates.
Leveled exercises:

⬤◯◯ How many squares can you build using 16 craft sticks, one whole stick for each side?   4 squares

⬤⬤◯ How many pentagons could you build using 35 craft sticks, one whole stick for each side?   7 pentagons

⬤⬤⬤ How many hexagons could you build using 36 craft sticks, one whole stick for each side?   6 hexagons

---

2 Focus   40–50 min

Go Online   ePresentations   eToolkit

▶ Math Message

Math Journal 1, p. 127

Complete journal page 127. Be sure to clearly explain your strategies.
GMP6.1

▶ Introducing *The Area and Perimeter Game*

Math Journal 1, p. 127 and Activity Sheets 13–14; *Student Reference Book*, pp. 230–231; *Math Masters*, p. G16

| WHOLE CLASS | SMALL GROUP | PARTNER | INDEPENDENT |

Math Message Follow-Up Have children share strategies for finding the **area** and **perimeter** of the rectangle on journal page 127. Record any new strategies on the Perimeter and Area T chart from Lesson 4-7. Encourage children to clearly explain what perimeter and area are as they share their strategies. GMP6.1 Discuss the efficiency of their strategies, guiding children to understand that multiplying, doubling, or skip counting are more efficient than counting by 1s. GMP6.4

Tell children that today they will use these strategies to calculate area and perimeter while playing *The Area and Perimeter Game*.

Have children examine the Action Deck and Deck A in partnerships. (*See Before You Begin.*) Discuss features of the cards, noting the partitioned rectangles and row-by-column descriptions on Deck A and the labels A and P for area and perimeter on the Action Deck.

Math Journal 1, p. 127

Area and Perimeter   Lesson 4-10
                                          DATE   TIME

Math Message

Use the rectangle to answer Problems 1–4.
You may label the side lengths.

① Area: __42 sq cm__
              (unit)

② Perimeter: __26 cm__
                  (unit)

③ Talk to a partner about this rectangle.
List all the ways you could find
the area.
Sample answers: Count the squares to
get 42. Count by six 7 times. Multiply 6 × 7.

④ List all the ways you could find the perimeter.
Sample answers: Count the units along the
sides of the rectangle. Add 6 + 7 to get 13,
and double 13 to get 26. Double 6 to get
12, double 7 to get 14, and add 12 + 14 to
get 26. Add 6 + 6 + 7 + 7 and get 26.
Measure with a ruler.

3.MD.5, 3.MD.5a, 3.MD.5b, 3.MD.6, 3.MD.7, 3.MD.7b,
3.MD.8, SMP6   one hundred twenty-seven   127

Read the game rules together on *Student Reference Book,* pages 230–231. Then have partners read and discuss the example round. Ask: *Why do you think Liam recorded the perimeter?* GMP7.2 Sample answer: The perimeter is 14 and the area is only 12, so he will get more points if he records the perimeter.

Model playing a few rounds with a volunteer. Remind children how to calculate the perimeter and the area using the rectangle grids and row-by-column dimensions. Ask: *If you get a card that says "Player's Choice" or "Partner's Choice," what can you do?* You or your partner can choose to find and record either the area or the perimeter. Invite children to share different ways to record a few turns as you model on *Math Masters,* page G16. Children may use counting or skip-counting strategies, or number sentences for addition or multiplication.

> **Differentiate** **Common Misconception**
>
> Watch for children who think measures of area and perimeter increase or decrease in relation to each other or that one measure is always larger. Rectangles can have the same area but different perimeters or the same perimeter and different areas.
>
> **Go Online** 👥 Differentiation Support

▶ Playing *The Area and Perimeter Game*

Math Journal 1, Activity Sheets 13–14; *Student Reference Book,* pp. 230–231; *Math Masters,* p. G16

| WHOLE CLASS | SMALL GROUP | **PARTNER** | INDEPENDENT |

Have partners play *The Area and Perimeter Game.* Children should independently record their turns on *Math Masters,* page G16 and keep track of their calculations on paper. For children who are ready to multiply or add side lengths to find the areas or perimeters of rectangles, you may wish to include Deck B (Activity Sheet 15).

Observe

- Which children have difficulty distinguishing area and perimeter?
- How do children calculate the area and perimeter?

Discuss

- *What strategies do you use when finding the area? The perimeter?* GMP6.1
- *How is calculating area different from calculating perimeter?*
- *Do rectangles with larger areas always have larger perimeters? Explain.* GMP6.1, GMP7.2

> **Differentiate** **Game Modifications** **Go Online** 👥 Differentiation Support

Games

The Area and Perimeter Game

Materials	☐ 1 *The Area and Perimeter Game* Action Deck (*Math Journal 1,* Activity Sheet 13)
	☐ 1 *The Area and Perimeter Game* Deck A (*Math Journal 1,* Activity Sheet 14)
	☐ 1 *The Area and Perimeter Game* Record Sheet for each player (*Math Masters,* p. G16)
	☐ calculator (optional)
Players	2
Skill	Calculating area and perimeter
Object of the Game	To score more points by finding the areas and perimeters of rectangles.

Directions

① Shuffle *The Area and Perimeter Game* Action Deck and place it word-side down on the table. Shuffle *The Area and Perimeter Game* Deck A and place it picture-side down next to the action cards.

② Players take turns. When it is your turn, draw 1 card from each deck and place the cards faceup on the table.
- If an area (A) card is drawn, the player finds the area.
- If a perimeter (P) card is drawn, the player finds the perimeter.
- If a "Player's Choice" card is drawn, the *player* may choose to find either the area or perimeter. See the example on the next page.
- If a "Partner's Choice" card is drawn, your *partner* chooses whether you will find the area or perimeter.

③ Record your turns on your record sheet. During your turn, record the rectangle card number and write A (area) or P (perimeter). Show how you found the area or perimeter. The solution is your score for the round.

④ The player with the higher total score at the end of 6 rounds is the winner. Players may use a calculator to find their total scores.

230 two hundred thirty

Games

Example
You draw the two cards to the right. You may choose to calculate the area or the perimeter. Before you answer, figure out both the area and the perimeter in your head.

A or P
Player's Choice

You count by 4s to find the area: 4, 8.
Area = 8 square units

and

You add the side lengths of the rectangle to find the perimeter.
$2 + 4 + 2 + 4 = 12$
Perimeter = 12 units

This is a 2-by-4 rectangle.

You choose to record the perimeter, because that will earn you more points.

Round	Card Number	A (area) or P (perimeter)	Show how you found the area or perimeter using words, drawings, and/or a number sentence.	Score
Example:	3	P	*I counted the boxes along the long and short sides of the rectangle and added them:* $2 + 4 + 2 + 4 = 12$ *units.*	12

Variation

Play using *The Area and Perimeter Game* Deck B (*Math Journal 1,* Activity Sheet 15), which shows blank rectangles and two side lengths.

two hundred thirty-one **231**

Math Masters, p. G16

The Area and Perimeter Game Record Sheet

Round	Card Number	A (area) or P (perimeter)	Show how you found the area or perimeter using words, drawings, and/or a number sentence.	Score
Example:	3	P	I counted the edges of the squares along the long and short sides of the rectangle and added them: 2 + 4 + 2 + 4 = 12.	12
1				
2				
3				
4				
5				

G16

Math Journal 1, p. 142

My Multiplication Facts Inventory Part 2

Multiplication Fact	Know It	Don't Know It	How I Can Figure It Out . . .
5 × 6			
10 × 9			
1 × 0			
9 × 5			
10 × 4			
1 × 1			
2 × 1			
8 × 10			
7 × 5			
0 × 2			
5 × 8			
10 × 6			
5 × 1			
0 × 4			
7 × 10			

142 one hundred forty-two   3.OA.7, SMP6

✓ Assessment Check-In   CCSS 3.MD.6, 3.MD.8

Math Masters, p. G16

Expect children to correctly calculate the areas and perimeters of the rectangles in Deck A. If children struggle to distinguish area and perimeter, consider implementing the suggestion in the Readiness activity. If children struggle to calculate area or perimeter, refer them to the list of strategies on the Perimeter and Area T chart generated in Lesson 4-7 and the Math Message Follow-Up.

[✓] Assessment and Reporting   [Go Online] to record student progress and to see trajectories toward mastery for these standards.

▶ Discussing Strategies

Math Masters, p. G16

| WHOLE CLASS | SMALL GROUP | PARTNER | INDEPENDENT |

After children play several rounds of *The Area and Perimeter Game,* facilitate a discussion about strategies. Encourage children to explain themselves clearly. **GMP6.1** Ask:

- *For Player's Choice, why might players calculate both area and perimeter before choosing which to record?* Sample answer: To find out whether area or perimeter is greater
- *For Partner's Choice, how did you decide which measurement to tell your partner to calculate?* **GMP7.2** Sample answer: I calculated both area and perimeter and I told my partner to find the smaller one.

Academic Language Development To encourage children to justify choices in their discussions, provide written question starters, such as: *Why did you ____? Why didn't you ____? What made you use the ____ strategy? What was good about the ____ strategy?*

Have children store their decks for future play.

Summarize Display or have children find card 5 from Deck A. Ask: *If you draw a Player's Choice card, which would you find: the area or the perimeter? Why?* Have children share or record their answers on half-sheets of paper or Exit Slips (*Math Masters,* page TA35). Sample answer: The perimeter is 16 units and the area is 16 square units, so I could choose either and get the same score.

③ Practice

15–20 min

Go Online

ePresentations eToolkit Home Connections

▶ **Minute Math+**

To practice mental math strategies, select a *Minute Math+* activity.

▶ **Taking Inventory of Known Facts Part 2**

Math Journal 1, p. 142

| WHOLE CLASS | SMALL GROUP | **PARTNER** | **INDEPENDENT** |

Have children complete My Multiplication Facts Inventory Part 2 (*Math Journal 1*, page 142) by indicating whether they know each fact. Encourage children to record efficient strategies they could use to figure out the facts they do not yet know. **GMP6.4** Also remind them to work slowly and thoughtfully, being sure to read and think carefully about each fact. If children mark all the facts as known, you may wish to have them choose a few and record helpful strategies for those facts.

Then have children practice their Fact Triangles in partnerships. If needed, review the procedure for practicing with Fact Triangles.

▶ **Math Boxes 4-10**

Math Journal 1, p. 128

| WHOLE CLASS | SMALL GROUP | PARTNER | INDEPENDENT |

Mixed Practice Math Boxes 4-10 are paired with Math Boxes 4-12.

▶ **Home Link 4-10**

Math Masters, p. 142

Homework Children calculate the areas and perimeters of rectangles and describe the strategies they use. **GMP6.1**

Planning Ahead

Children complete *Math Journal 1* at the end of this unit. To prepare for Unit 5, have them cut out the six My Multiplication Facts Strategy Log pages and staple them into the back of *Math Journal 2*.

Math Journal 1, p. 128

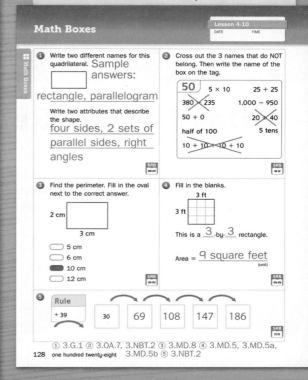

Math Masters, p. 142

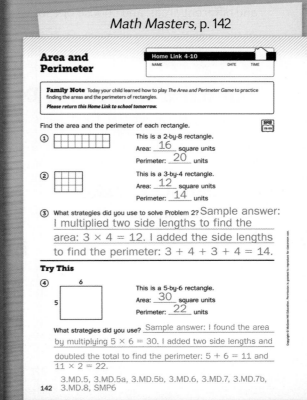

Building a Rabbit Pen

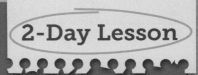
2-Day Lesson

Overview   **Day 1:** Children create and use models of a rabbit pen to solve a problem.   **Day 2:** Children compare and discuss their models and explanations and revise their work.

Day 1: Open Response

▶ **Before You Begin**
Solve the open response problem and identify possible side lengths of rectangles with a perimeter of 24 feet. Have extra copies of *Math Masters,* page TA19 available for children who need additional grid space. If possible, schedule time to review children's work and plan for Day 2 of this lesson with your grade-level team.

▶ **Vocabulary**
mathematical model • perimeter • area

Common Core State Standards

Focus Clusters
- Geometric measurement: understand concepts of area and relate area to multiplication and to addition.
- Geometric measurement: recognize perimeter.

1 Warm Up   5 min

Materials

Mental Math and Fluency
Children divide using helper facts.

slate

3.OA.7

2a Focus   55–65 min

Math Message
Children find the perimeter and the area of two dog pens.

Math Journal 1, p. 129

3.MD.7, 3.MD.7b, 3.MD.8
SMP4, SMP6

Calculating Perimeters and Areas
Children discuss strategies for calculating the perimeters and the areas of the pens.

Math Journal 1, p. 129; *Student Reference Book,* pp. 174–177 (optional)

3.MD.7, 3.MD.7b, 3.MD.8
SMP1, SMP4, SMP6

Solving the Open Response Problem
Children draw at least two rectangles with a fixed perimeter and different areas, and choose one for a rabbit pen.

Math Masters, pp. 143–144 and TA19

3.MD.7, 3.MD.7b, 3.MD.8
SMP1, SMP4, SMP6

Getting Ready for Day 2 →

Review children's work and plan discussion for reengagement.

Math Masters, p. TA6, p. TA42 (optional); children's work from Day 1

CCSS 3.MD.8 **Spiral Snapshot**

GMC Exhibit rectangles with the same perimeter and different areas or the same area and different perimeters.

 Spiral Tracker   **Go Online** to see how mastery develops for all standards within the grade.

connectED.mcgraw-hill.com ▶

Plan your lessons online with these tools.

 ePresentations

 Student Learning Center

Facts Workshop Game

 eToolkit

 Professional Development

 Home Connections

 Spiral Tracker

 Assessment and Reporting

 English Learners Support

 Differentiation Support

1 Warm Up
5 min  Go Online

ePresentations eToolkit

▶ Mental Math and Fluency

Have children solve the sequence of facts on slates and share their strategies. Highlight strategies that use the first fact to solve the second. *Leveled exercises:*

◉○○ 12 ÷ 6 = ? 2; 12 ÷ 3 = ? 4

◉◉○ 16 ÷ 4 = ? 4; 16 ÷ 2 = ? 8

◉◉◉ 24 ÷ 8 = ? 3; 24 ÷ 4 = ? 6

2a Focus
55–65 min Go Online

ePresentations eToolkit

▶ Math Message

Math Journal 1, p. 129

Complete journal page 129 and compare your work with a partner.
GMP4.1, GMP6.3

▶ Calculating Perimeters and Areas

Math Journal 1, p. 129

| WHOLE CLASS | SMALL GROUP | PARTNER | INDEPENDENT |

Math Message Follow-Up Point out to children that they used models of the dog pens to solve the problem. **Mathematical models** are representations of real-world situations or objects that help solve problems. The drawings of the pens show what the pens look like in the real world, and the rectangles are models that can help children find the areas and perimeters. GMP4.1

Discuss strategies children used to determine the perimeter and area measures for Pens A and B.

English Language Learners Support Prior to the lesson, discuss the context and vocabulary of the open response problem. Distinguish between the meaning of *pen* as a writing instrument and its use in this lesson. If possible, show a picture or drawing of a dog or rabbit pen.

CCSS Standards and Goals for Mathematical Practice

SMP1 Make sense of problems and persevere in solving them.
  GMP1.2 Reflect on your thinking as you solve your problem.

SMP4 Model with mathematics.
  GMP4.1 Model real-world situations using graphs, drawings, tables, symbols, numbers, diagrams, and other representations.

SMP6 Attend to precision.
  GMP6.3 Use clear labels, units, and mathematical language.

Professional Development

The focus for this lesson is GMP4.1. Children model with mathematics when they use mathematical ideas to represent situations in the real world. This is particularly important for solving problems. For this problem, children use grid paper to create two drawings of a rectangular rabbit pen using 24 feet of fence. They use the models to determine the areas and decide which pen is best for the rabbit.

Go Online to the *Implementation Guide* for more information about SMP4.

Math Journal 1, p. 129

Drawing Dog Pens Lesson 4-11
DATE   TIME

Brandi made drawings of her 2 dog pens. She measured the total length of each pen's fence in feet. In her drawings, each square represents 1 square foot.

Pen A   Pen B

Pen B

Pen A

├─1 ft─┤ ☐ 1 sq ft

① Calculate the perimeter and area for each pen. Record the measures using appropriate units.

Pen A
Perimeter = __20__ feet

Pen B
Perimeter = __20 feet__ (unit)

Area = __25__ square feet

Area = __21 square feet__ (unit)

② What shape are the pens? __Sample answer: Rectangles__

3.MD.7, 3.MD.7b, 3.MD.8, SMP4, SMP6   one hundred twenty-nine 129

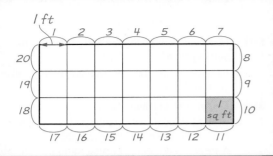

The fence around the pen measures 20 feet in length.

Look for and highlight the following strategies for finding **perimeter,** or the distance around the pens. For each strategy, model recording the side lengths of each pen.

- Add the side lengths in order (for example, $3 + 7 + 3 + 7 = 20$ feet) or add sides of equal length first (or use doubles) and then combine the sums (for example, $7 + 7 + 3 + 3 = 14 + 6 = 20$ feet).
- Count the edges of the squares that form the outer border of the rectangle. Share strategies for keeping track of the side lengths, such as darkening the edge of each square along the boundary or drawing and labeling hops with numbers while counting. (*See margin art.*)

Look for and highlight the following strategies for finding **area,** the amount of surface inside the pens:

- Count individual squares for each square foot. Write the numbers inside each square to keep an accurate count.
- Skip count by rows or columns (for example, count by 3s for Pen B).
- Multiply the number of rows by the number of columns as for an array.

As children discuss strategies, make sure they share and record the appropriate units for perimeter (feet) and area (square feet). GMP6.3 Have partners compare the perimeters, areas, and shapes of the pens. Ask: *What do you notice?* GMP1.2 Sample answers: The pens have the same perimeter but different areas and different shapes.

> **NOTE** Help children see how a 2-dimensional drawing represents a fence around the perimeter of a 3-dimensional pen by referring to the walls of the room or having children join hands in a circle. Discuss how these are like a fence around a pen.

Encourage children who have questions about perimeter and area to read *Student Reference Book,* pages 174–177. Tell children they will continue using what they know about perimeter and area to draw models of pens for a rabbit. GMP4.1

▶ Solving the Open Response Problem

Math Masters, pp. 143–144 and TA19

| WHOLE CLASS | SMALL GROUP | **PARTNER** | INDEPENDENT |

Distribute *Math Masters,* pages 143–144 and have *Math Masters,* page TA19 available. Read the introduction and Problems 1 and 2 as a class, and have partners discuss what they are asked to do. Ask:

- *What do you know after reading the introduction and the problems?* Sample answers: Miguel has 24 feet of fence to make a rabbit pen. I need to decide how to make two different rectangular pens that each use 24 feet of fence.
- *What do you need to figure out in order to draw each pen?* Sample answer: The lengths of each side of the pen
- *What else do you need to figure out for each pen?* The area
- *What is the difference between the perimeter and the area of a pen?* GMP6.3 Sample answer: The perimeter is the distance around the outside of the pen, and the area is the amount of space inside the pen.

Ask: *Problem 2 asks you to include the area measures for each rectangle. Why do you think it does not say to include the perimeter measures?* Sample answer: The perimeters for both rectangles will be 24 feet.

Tell children that they should draw at least two rectangular rabbit pens that use exactly 24 feet of fence on the centimeter grid paper. Ask them to imagine that the length of each side of a centimeter square is 1 foot. Remind them that they may use additional grid paper. GMP4.1

Have children read Problems 3 and 4. Tell them they should use mathematical language to explain which of the pens they drew would be best for Miguel's rabbit and why. Ask: *What are examples of mathematical language?* Sample answers: One pen is longer. This pen has more area. This pen is a square.

Partners may work together to share ideas about the task, but children should record their own work.

As children work, ask guiding questions to discuss their thinking, such as:

- *What helped you figure out how long to make the sides of the rectangles?* Sample answer: I thought of numbers that added to 24. I knew 20 and 4 is 24, so I drew a rectangle with 2 sides of 10 and 2 sides of 2.
- *If a pen is too small or too large, how would you know?* Sample answer: The perimeter would not be 24 feet.

> **Differentiate** **Adjusting the Activity**
>
> For children who have difficulty writing an explanation for Problem 4, ask them to describe their thinking to you or a partner and then write what they said.

Children may draw two pens with the same dimensions but different orientations. Discuss whether these are different models. GMP1.2, GMP4.1 Ask children if the two pens have the same or different areas.

NOTE The pens with whole-number side lengths that can be created using 24 feet of fence are 1-by-11, 2-by-10, 3-by-9, 4-by-8, 5-by-7, and 6-by-6. Some children may try to draw rectangles with fractional side lengths such as $1\frac{1}{2}$ feet by $10\frac{1}{2}$ feet.

Summarize Ask: *Did you draw any pens that do not use 24 feet of fence?* Answers vary. *How could a drawing that does not have a perimeter of 24 feet help you draw a model that does use 24 feet of fence?* GMP1.2 Sample answer: It could help me know whether I need to make the sides of the pen longer or shorter.

Collect children's work so that you can evaluate it and prepare for Day 2.

Math Masters, p. 143

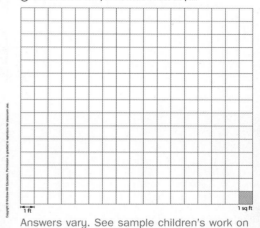

Building a Rabbit Pen

Lesson 4-11

NAME   DATE   TIME

Miguel wants to build a rectangular pen for his rabbit. He has 24 feet of fence that he can use to make the pen. He plans to use all 24 feet of fence to make the best pen he can for his rabbit.

① Use the grid to draw **at least 2 different pens** that Miguel could build.

② **Find the area** of each pen and record it inside the pen.

1 ft   1 sq ft

Answers vary. See sample children's work on page 394 of the *Teacher's Lesson Guide.*

3.MD.7, 3.MD.7b, 3.MD.8, SMP1, SMP4, SMP6   143

Math Masters, p. 144

Building a Rabbit Pen (continued)

Lesson 4-11

NAME   DATE   TIME

③ Which pen do you think would be the best for Miguel's rabbit?
Answers vary.

④ Use mathematical language to explain the reason for your choice.
Answers vary. See sample children's work on page 394 of the *Teacher's Lesson Guide.*

144   3.MD.7, 3.MD.7b, 3.MD.8, SMP1, SMP4, SMP6

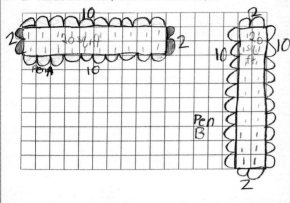

1. Use the grid to draw **at least 2 different pens** that Miguel could build.
2. **Find the area** of each pen and record it inside the pen.

Getting Ready for Day 2

Math Masters, p. TA6

Planning a Follow-Up Discussion

Review children's work. Use the Reengagement Planning Form (*Math Masters,* page TA6) and the rubric on page 392 to plan ways to help children meet expectations for both the content and practice standards. Look for common misconceptions, such as confusing perimeter and area, as well as specific ways children used mathematical language to explain the pen they chose.

Reengagement Planning Form

Common Core State Standard (CCSS): *3.MD.8 Solve real world and mathematical problems involving perimeters of polygons, including finding the perimeter given the side lengths, finding an unknown side length, and exhibiting rectangles with the same perimeter and different areas or with the same area and different perimeters.*

Goal for Mathematical Practice (GMP): *GMP4.1 Model real-world situations using graphs, drawings, tables, symbols, numbers, diagrams, and other representations.*

Organize the discussion in one of the ways below or in another way you choose. You may choose to develop a child-friendly rubric using *Math Masters,* page TA42 and facilitate a peer discussion and review as described in Lesson 3-2 on page 230. If children's work is unclear or if you prefer to show work anonymously, rewrite the work for display.

Go Online for sample children's work that you can use in your discussion.

1. Display a response, such as Child A's, that shows two rectangles with the same dimensions but different orientations. Ask:
   • *Was the correct amount of fence used for both rectangles?* **GMP1.2, GMP4.1** Sample answer: Yes. Both have a perimeter of 24 feet.
   • *Do the rectangles have different areas?* **GMP4.1** Sample answer: No. The area of both rectangles is 20 square feet.
   • *Do the rectangles have different shapes? Explain your answer.* Sample answer: No. If one was on top of the other, they would match exactly.
   • *For this problem, do you think these rectangles model two different rabbit pens?* **GMP1.2, GMP4.1** Sample answer: No. They look different, but they have the same perimeter, area, and shape. The rabbit would have the same amount of room to run.

2. Show work, such as Child B's, that indicates the child looked back at the drawing and adjusted the length or width so the rectangles would have the correct perimeter. Ask:
   • *What are the perimeters of the three rectangles in this child's work?* Sample answer: They are all 24 feet.
   • *Look at Rectangle A. Why do you think the X is there?* **GMP1.2** Sample answer: The X shows that line is not part of the fence. It was erased.
   • *Why do you think that line needed to be erased?* **GMP4.1** Sample answer: With that line, the perimeter would not have been 24 feet, so the child needed to make the sides longer.

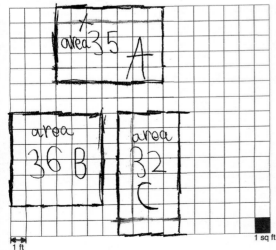

1. Use the grid to draw **at least 2 different pens** that Miguel could build.
2. **Find the area** of each pen and record it inside the pen.

- *What do you notice about Rectangle C?* **GMP4.1** Sample answer: One of the lines at the bottom of the rectangle needed to be erased, and the sides needed to be longer to make the perimeter 24 feet.
- *How could mistakes like these help you draw a correct model for the rabbit pen?* **GMP1.2** Sample answer: When the rectangles were drawn the first time, the perimeters were not large enough, but the drawings help us see that the sides needed to be longer.

3. Display a response that is correct, such as Child C's work, to discuss the models and mathematical language the child used. Ask:
   - *Look at the models of the pens on this child's work. Do you agree that the perimeter of both rectangles is 24 feet?* **GMP1.2** Yes. *How do you know?* Answers vary.
   - *What do you think the numbers inside the rectangles mean?* Sample answer: I think the 27 and 20 are the areas and the 1 and 2 are labels for the rectangles. *What could this child add to make the models easier to understand?* **GMP6.3** Sample answer: Label the areas of the pens with square feet.
   - *What mathematical language did this child use for Problem 4?* **GMP6.3** Sample answer: This child said that Pen 2 is longer than Pen 1. This child said that Pen 1 is a 3-by-9 array and that Pen 2 is a 2-by-10 array.
   - *Did this child give a reason why the chosen pen would be better for the rabbit?* **GMP1.2** Sample answer: Yes. This child said that since the pen was longer, the rabbit can run.

As different rabbit pens are discussed, make a chart that includes sketches with area and perimeter measures on the Class Data Pad or chart paper. Refer to this collection as you display and discuss children's ideas about which pen works best for Miguel's rabbit. See the example below.

Pens for Miguel's Rabbit

Sketch	Area	Perimeter
6 ft by 6 ft square	36 square feet	24 feet
10 ft by 2 ft rectangle	20 square feet	24 feet

Planning for Revisions

Have copies of *Math Masters,* pages 143–144 and TA19 available for children to use in revisions. You might want to ask children to use colored pencils so you can see what they revise.

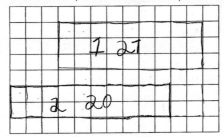

Sample child's work, Child C

1. Use the grid to draw **at least 2 different pens** that Miguel could build.
2. **Find the area** of each pen and record it inside the pen.

   1 27

   2 20

3. Which pen do you think would be the best for Miguel's rabbit?

   Pen 2

4. Use mathematical language to explain the reason for your choice.

   Pen 2 Because it is longer
   So the rabbit can run
   and it is a 2 by 10
   Array insted of a 3 by 9 Array!

Building a Rabbit Pen

Overview **Day 2:** Children compare and discuss their models and explanations and revise their work.

Day 2: Reengagement

▶ **Before You Begin**
Have extra copies available of *Math Masters,* pages 143–144 and TA19 for children to revise their work.

Common Core State Standards

Focus Clusters
- Geometric measurement: understand concepts of area and relate area to multiplication and to addition.
- Geometric measurement: recognize perimeter as an attribute of plane figures and distinguish between linear and area measures.

2b Focus 50–55 min

	Materials	
Setting Expectations Children review the open response problem and discuss what a good response includes.	Standards for Mathematical Practice Poster; Guidelines for Discussions Poster	**3.MD.7, 3.MD.7b, 3.MD.8** **SMP4**
Reengaging in the Problem Children discuss other children's work, including their models of pens and their explanations for which model they chose.	*Math Masters,* p. TA42 (optional); selected samples of children's work; Class Data Pad or chart paper (optional)	**3.MD.7, 3.MD.7b, 3.MD.8** **SMP1, SMP4, SMP6**
Revising Work Children revise their work from Day 1.	*Math Masters,* pp. 143–144 and TA19 (optional); colored pencils (optional); children's work from Day 1	**3.MD.7, 3.MD.7b, 3.MD.8** **SMP4, SMP6**

✓ **Assessment Check-In** See page 394 and the rubric below. **3.MD.8**
SMP4

Goal for Mathematical Practice **GMP4.1** Model real-world situations using graphs, drawings, tables, symbols, numbers, diagrams, and other representations.	**Not Meeting Expectations**	**Partially Meeting Expectations**	**Meeting Expectations**	**Exceeding Expectations**
	Does not draw two models of pens with the correct perimeter.	Draws two models of pens with the correct perimeter, but does not correctly label the area inside the pen, **or** does not use appropriate mathematical language to explain why the pen was chosen.	Draws two models of pens with the correct perimeter and area labeled inside the pen, **and** uses appropriate mathematical language to explain why the pen was chosen.	Meets expectations and either draws or compares more than two models of correctly labeled pens or connects the mathematical language to the real world by describing why the chosen pen would be better (for example, the pen is longer, so the rabbit can run farther).

3 Practice 10–15 min

Math Boxes 4-11 Children practice and maintain skills.	*Math Journal 1,* p. 130	See page 395.
Home Link 4-11 **Homework** Children solve problems involving perimeter and area.	*Math Masters,* p. 145	**3.MD.7, 3.MD.7b, 3.MD.8** **SMP6**

2b Focus 50–55 min | Go Online | ePresentations eToolkit

NOTE These Day 2 activities will ideally take place within a few days of Day 1. Prior to beginning Day 2, see Planning a Follow-Up Discussion from Day 1.

▶ ## Setting Expectations

| **WHOLE CLASS** | SMALL GROUP | PARTNER | INDEPENDENT |

Briefly review the open response problem from Day 1. Remind children that it is important to use what they know about perimeter and area to draw two model pens for Miguel's rabbit. Have children review **GMP4.1** on the Standards for Mathematical Practice Poster. Explain that they are going to look at others' work and think about the different pens they drew.

Remind children that if they think that someone's work is unclear or incomplete, they should be respectful when explaining why they think so. Refer to the list of discussion guidelines from earlier units, and encourage children to use sentence frames such as the following:

- I think this is a clear and complete explanation because _____.
- I think this explanation needs to include _____.

▶ ## Reengaging in the Problem

| **WHOLE CLASS** | SMALL GROUP | **PARTNER** | INDEPENDENT |

Children reengage in the problem by analyzing and critiquing other children's work in pairs and in a whole-group discussion. Have children discuss with partners before sharing with the whole group. Guide this discussion based on the decisions you made in Getting Ready for Day 2.
GMP1.2, GMP4.1, GMP6.3

▶ ## Revising Work

| **WHOLE CLASS** | SMALL GROUP | **PARTNER** | **INDEPENDENT** |

Pass back children's work from Day 1. Before children revise anything, ask them to examine their models for the rabbit pens. Encourage partnerships to discuss what they will do differently in their revised responses. Ask the following questions one at a time. Have partners discuss their responses and give a thumbs-up or thumbs-down based on their own work.

- *Did you show at least two different models for rectangular pens that used 24 feet of fence?* **GMP4.1**
- *Did you include area measures with square units for each of your drawings?* **GMP6.3**
- *Did you use clear mathematical language when you explained which pen was the best and why?* **GMP6.3**

Tell children they now have a chance to revise their work. If they did not
draw two correct pens using 24 feet of fence each, have children revise
their work to show two correct models. Children who correctly drew
two pens on Day 1 can try to draw more pens. Help children see that the
explanations presented during the discussion are not the only correct
ones. Tell children to add to their earlier work using colored pencils or to
use another sheet of paper, instead of erasing their original work.

Summarize Ask children to reflect on their work and revisions. Ask:
What did you do to improve your drawings? Answers vary. *What did you do
to improve your explanation?* Answers vary.

Assessment Check-In CCSS 3.MD.8

Collect and review children's revised work. Expect most children to
improve their work based on the class discussion. For the content
standard, expect children to draw at least two rectangular pens with a
perimeter of 24 feet that have different areas. You can use the rubric on
page 392 to evaluate children's revised work for **GMP4.1**.

 Assessment
and Reporting   Go Online to record children's progress and to see trajectories
toward mastery for this standard.

 Go Online for optional generic rubrics in the *Assessment Handbook* that
can be used to assess any additional GMPs addressed in the lesson.

Sample Children's Work—Evaluated

See the sample in the margin. This work meets expectations for the
content standard because the child drew two rectangles with a perimeter
of 24 feet but with different areas. This work meets expectations for the
mathematical practice because the child drew two correct models for the
pens and used mathematical language to explain that Pen B would be the
best because it "has the most area." GMP4.1

 Go Online for other samples of evaluated children's work.

Adjusting the Activity

Differentiate For children who found
all of the possible pens with whole-
number side lengths and wrote strong
explanations on Day 1, give this
additional prompt: *Explain how you can
be sure that you found all of the possible
rectangles for Miguel's rabbit pen.*

Sample child's work, "Meeting Expectations"

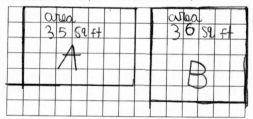

1. Use the grid to draw **at least 2 different pens** that Miguel could build.
2. **Find the area** of each pen and record it inside the pen.

3. Which pen do you think would be the best for Miguel's rabbit?
   B
4. Use mathematical language to explain the reason for your choice.
   it has the most area

3 Practice   15–20 min   Go Online

ePresentations   eToolkit   Home Connections

▶ Math Boxes 4-11

Math Journal 1, p. 130

| WHOLE CLASS | SMALL GROUP | PARTNER | INDEPENDENT |

Mixed Practice   Math Boxes 4-11 are grouped with Math Boxes 4-6 and 4-8.

▶ Home Link 4-11

Math Masters, p. 145

Homework   Children solve problems involving perimeter and area.
GMP6.3

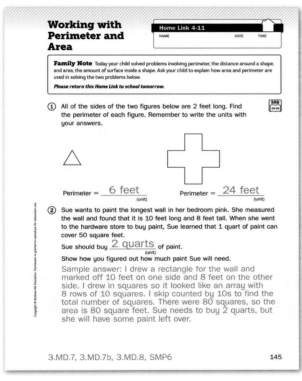

Math Masters, p. 145

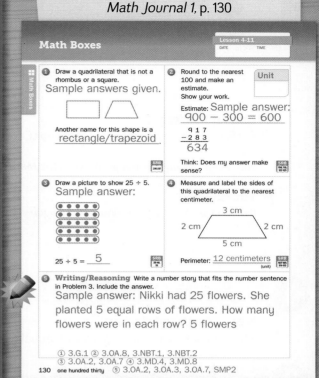

Math Journal 1, p. 130

Rectilinear Figures

Overview Children find areas of rectilinear figures.

▶ **Before You Begin**
For Part 1, select and sequence Quick Look Cards 138, 144, and 145.

For Part 2, display the image shown in the Math Message.

▶ **Vocabulary**
decompose • rectilinear figure • polygon

 Common Core State Standards

Focus Clusters
• Multiply and divide within 100.
• Solve problems involving the four operations, and identify and explain patterns in arithmetic.
• Geometric measurement: understand concepts of area and relate area to multiplication and to addition.

1 Warm Up 5–10 min

	Materials	
Mental Math and Fluency Children practice Quick Looks with equal groups and arrays.	Quick Look Cards 138, 144, 145	**3.OA.1, 3.OA.7** **SMP2, SMP6**

2 Focus 45–50 min

Math Message Children discuss ways to find the area of a rectilinear figure.		**3.MD.7, 3.MD.7d**
Finding Areas of Rectilinear Figures Children find the areas of rectilinear figures.	*Math Masters*, p. TA34	**3.OA.7, 3.OA.8, 3.MD.5, 3.MD.5a,** **3.MD.7, 3.MD.7b, 3.MD.7d** **SMP4, SMP6, SMP7**
Finding Areas of Rectilinear Animal Pens Children discuss real-world examples of rectilinear figures and find their areas.	*Math Journal 1*, p. 131; *Student Reference Book*, pp. 180–181; *Math Masters*, p. TA20 (optional)	**3.OA.7, 3.OA.8, 3.MD.5, 3.MD.5a,** **3.MD.7, 3.MD.7b, 3.MD.7d** **SMP4, SMP6, SMP7**
✔ **Assessment Check-In** See page 400.	*Math Journal 1*, p. 131	**3.MD.7, 3.MD.7d**

CCSS 3.MD.7d **Spiral Snapshot**

GMC Recognize area as additive.

4-12 Focus Practice	5-2 Practice	5-4 Practice	5-5 Focus Practice	5-6 Focus Practice	5-9 Practice	5-11 Focus Practice	6-4 Practice

III **Spiral Tracker**   **Go Online** to see how mastery develops for all standards within the grade.

3 Practice 10–15 min

Minute Math+ Children practice mental math strategies.	*Minute Math®+*	
Math Boxes 4-12 Children practice and maintain skills.	*Math Journal 1*, p. 132	See page 401.
Home Link 4-12 **Homework** Children partition and find the area of a rectilinear figure.	*Math Masters*, p. 148	**3.OA.7, 3.MD.5, 3.MD.5a, 3.MD.7,** **3.MD.7b, 3.MD.7d**

connectED.mcgraw-hill.com

Plan your lessons online
with these tools.

 ePresentations   **Student Learning Center**   **Facts Workshop Game**   **eToolkit**   **Professional Development**   **Home Connections**   **Spiral Tracker**   **Assessment and Reporting** **ELL** **English Learners Support**   **Differentiation Support**

396 Unit 4 | Measurement and Geometry

Differentiation Options
RtI

 CCSS 3.MD.7, 3.MD.7d

Readiness 5–10 min

WHOLE CLASS
SMALL GROUP
PARTNER
INDEPENDENT

Dividing Polygons into Rectangles

Math Masters, p. 146

To prepare for work with rectilinear figures, have children draw line segments to divide the polygons on *Math Masters,* page 146 into rectangles. If needed, review attributes of rectangles. Have children share their drawings.

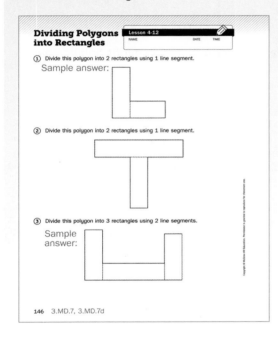

 CCSS 3.OA.7, 3.MD.5, 3.MD.5a, 3.MD.7, 3.MD.7b, 3.MD.7d, SMP1, SMP2

Enrichment 10–15 min

WHOLE CLASS
SMALL GROUP
PARTNER
INDEPENDENT

Decomposing Same-Size Rectilinear Figures

Math Masters, p. 147

To further explore area concepts, have children decompose rectilinear figures on *Math Masters,* page 147 in multiple ways. **GMP1.5** Then have children find and explain why the areas are the same. **GMP2.2**

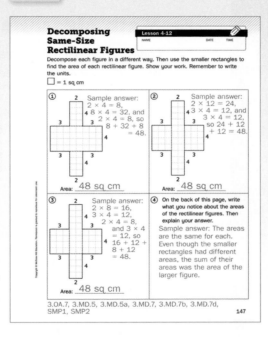

 CCSS 3.OA.7, 3.MD.5, 3.MD.5a, 3.MD.7, 3.MD.7b, 3.MD.7d

Extra Practice 10–15 min

WHOLE CLASS
SMALL GROUP
PARTNER
INDEPENDENT

Finding the Area of a Rectilinear Figure

Activity Card 61;
Math Masters, p. TA22;
scissors; tape

For additional practice finding areas of rectilinear figures, have children cut rectangles from one-inch grid paper and tape them together. Then have children find the area of their new shape.

English Language Learners Support

Beginning ELL To scaffold the term *partition,* help children relate it to the word *part.* Drop an assortment of objects into a box. Role-play sorting the objects by a category, such as color. Think aloud as you make partitions out of cardboard or paper to separate the objects. For example: *Let's separate these _____ from each other. Let's divide this box into smaller parts. Let's partition this box to keep the _____ apart from each other.* Display real-world items, such as jewelry or tackle boxes, and contrast them with similarly shaped containers that are not partitioned.

Go Online **ELL** English Learners Support

 Standards and Goals for
Mathematical Practice

SMP4 **Model with mathematics.**
  GMP4.1 Model real-world situations using graphs, drawings, tables, symbols, numbers, diagrams, and other representations.

SMP6 **Attend to precision.**
  GMP6.4 Think about accuracy and efficiency when you count, measure, and calculate.

SMP7 **Look for and make use of structure.**
  GMP7.1 Look for mathematical structures such as categories, patterns, and properties.

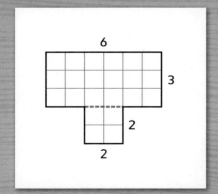

① Warm Up   5–10 min   Go Online
ePresentations   eToolkit

▶ Mental Math and Fluency

Show Quick Look Cards 138, 144, and 145 one at a time for 2–3 seconds. Ask children to share both what they saw and how they saw it.
GMP2.2, GMP6.1   Highlight equal-group and array strategies.

Quick Look Card 138   Sample answer: I saw 2 groups of 6, and $6 + 6 = 12$.

Quick Look Card 144   Sample answer: I saw 3 columns of 4, and $4 + 4 = 8$, and one more group of 4 makes 12.

Quick Look Card 145   Sample answer: I saw 4 groups of 5, and $5 + 5 = 10$, and $10 + 10 = 20$.

② Focus   45–50 min   Go Online
ePresentations   eToolkit

▶ Math Message

Look at this shape. Talk to a partner about how you might find its area. Be ready to share your ideas.

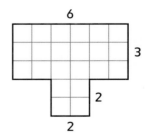

▶ Finding Areas of Rectilinear Figures

Math Masters, p. TA34

| WHOLE CLASS | SMALL GROUP | PARTNER | INDEPENDENT |

Math Message Follow-Up Invite children to share their ideas about finding the area of the shape. Expect suggestions to include counting the square units. If children suggest multiplying all the side lengths, $2 \times 2 \times 3 \times 6$, or the total side lengths, 5×6, point out that the rows in the shape do not all have the same number of squares. Explain that each row must have the same number of squares to find the area by multiplying the side lengths.

Ask: *How might we **decompose**, or separate, this shape into rectangles?* Sample answer: We can draw a line to make 2 rectangles. Have a volunteer decompose the shape into 2 rectangles. (*See margin art.*) Ask children to describe each of the rectangles. Sample answer: One has 3 rows with 6 squares in each row. The other has 2 rows with 2 squares in each row.

Explain that since each rectangle has the same number of squares in each row, we can multiply the side lengths to find the areas. Have children find the areas. $3 \times 6 = 18$ and $2 \times 2 = 4$; The areas are 18 square units and 4 square units. Ask: *How can we find the area of the entire shape?* We can add the areas of the two rectangles. *What is the area of the shape?* $18 + 4 = 22$; The area is 22 square units.

Explain that today children will use what they know about finding the areas of rectangles to find the areas of **rectilinear figures.** Rectilinear figures are **polygons** whose sides all meet at right angles.

Display a 10×10 grid (*Math Masters,* page TA34). Draw a rectilinear figure on the grid as shown below on the left. Tell children it represents an outdoor reading space you want to cover with rubber tiles. Explain that each tile measures 1 square yard and each square on the grid represents 1 square yard.

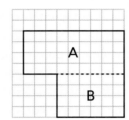

Ask: *How might you find the number of rubber tiles needed to cover an outdoor reading space of this shape?* Have children share their suggestions for partitioning the shape. GMP4.1, GMP6.4 If nobody mentions it, suggest decomposing the shape as shown above on the right. Label the rectangles as A and B. For Rectangle A, ask:

- *How many equal rows of square yards are there?* 4 equal rows
- *How many square yards are in each row?* 9 square yards

Write $4 \times 9 = 36$ below the figure and remind children that this number sentence can be used to represent the area of Rectangle A. Then determine the area of Rectangle B. $4 \times 6 = 24$; The area is 24 square yards.

Ask: *How did you find the area of the entire reading space?* GMP6.4
Sample answer: I added the areas of Rectangles A and B, $36 + 24 = 60$.

Some children may suggest finding the area of the 9-by-8 rectangle that surrounds the figure and subtracting the "cutout" area. GMP7.1
$9 \times 8 = 72$; $3 \times 4 = 12$; $72 - 12 = 60$. Acknowledge this strategy as efficient, but continue to focus on decomposing just the figure into rectangles.

Ask: *How many square yards of rubber tiles are needed to cover the entire outdoor reading space?* 60 square yards

Next display the rectilinear figure shown in the margin on page 400. Have children suggest ways to decompose it into two smaller rectangles. If no child mentions it, suggest decomposing the figure with a vertical line. Label the rectangles as C and D. Point out that because there are no unit squares, children will have to find the missing side lengths before finding the areas of the smaller rectangles. Have partners discuss and then share with the class how to find the missing side lengths for Rectangle C. GMP7.1 Sample answer: We can look at the opposite side lengths. The longer side is 7 feet and the shorter side is 4 feet.

Math Journal 1, p. 131

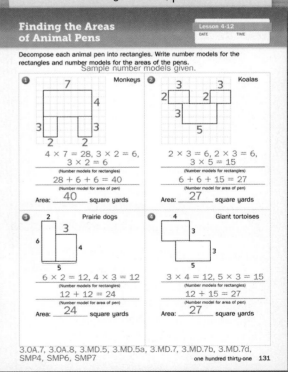

Finding the Areas of Animal Pens

Lesson 4-12

DATE   TIME

Decompose each animal pen into rectangles. Write number models for the rectangles and number models for the areas of the pens.
Sample number models given.

① Monkeys
$4 \times 7 = 28$, $3 \times 2 = 6$, $3 \times 2 = 6$
(Number models for rectangles)
$28 + 6 + 6 = 40$
(Number model for area of pen)
Area: __40__ square yards

② Koalas
$2 \times 3 = 6$, $2 \times 3 = 6$, $3 \times 5 = 15$
(Number models for rectangles)
$6 + 6 + 15 = 27$
(Number model for area of pen)
Area: __27__ square yards

③ Prairie dogs
$6 \times 2 = 12$, $4 \times 3 = 12$
(Number models for rectangles)
$12 + 12 = 24$
(Number model for area of pen)
Area: __24__ square yards

④ Giant tortoises
$3 \times 4 = 12$, $5 \times 3 = 15$
(Number models for rectangles)
$12 + 15 = 27$
(Number model for area of pen)
Area: __27__ square yards

3.OA.7, 3.OA.8, 3.MD.5, 3.MD.5a, 3.MD.7, 3.MD.7b, 3.MD.7d, SMP4, SMP6, SMP7
one hundred thirty-one 131

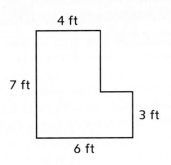

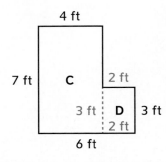

Label these side lengths. Then have children share how to find the missing side lengths for Rectangle D. Emphasize that because the length of one longer side is 3 feet, the opposite side length is also 3 feet. Model how to find Rectangle D's other side length by subtracting the length of Rectangle C's short side, 4 feet, from the entire figure's long side, 6 feet: $6 - 4 = 2$. The short side of Rectangle D is 2 feet. Label the other side lengths. Then have partners write a number sentence to represent each area, and find the area of the entire figure. **GMP6.4** $7 \times 4 = 28; 2 \times 3 = 6; 28 + 6 = 34;$ The area is 34 square feet.

▶ Finding Areas of Rectilinear Animal Pens

Math Journal 1, p. 131; *Student Reference Book,* pp. 180–181

WHOLE CLASS	SMALL GROUP	PARTNER	INDEPENDENT

Explain that different animals require different amounts of space, which zoos must consider when designing enclosures. Sometimes zoos separate sections of the animal pens to make smaller enclosures. Have children look at the shapes on journal page 131. Point out that, unlike the rabbit pens children designed in Lesson 4-11, these pens are made from multiple rectangles. Encourage children to decompose the figures into rectangles. Emphasize that there may be multiple ways to partition them, and some will need to be decomposed into more rectangles than others. **GMP4.1** Point out that the animal pen in Problem 3 has already been decomposed into two rectangles, but children will need to find the missing side lengths to calculate the area.

Circulate to observe as children work with a partner to complete the page.

> ✓ **Assessment Check-In** (CCSS) 3.MD.7, 3.MD.7d
>
> *Math Journal 1,* p. 131
>
> Expect children to decompose the rectilinear figures in Problems 1, 2, and 4 into rectangles. If children struggle to figure out where to draw lines to decompose the figures, consider implementing the Readiness activity. Because this is the first exposure to adding areas of multiple shapes, do not expect all children to be successful with this strategy.
>
> ✓ Assessment and Reporting 〈 **Go Online** 〉 to record student progress and to see trajectories toward mastery for these standards.

When most children have finished, invite the class to discuss strategies for calculating the areas of the rectilinear animal pens. Highlight strategies that involve decomposing the figures into smaller rectangles, multiplying side lengths, and adding the products to find the area. **GMP4.1, GMP7.1** Ask:

- *How did you decompose the animal pens to find the area efficiently?* **GMP6.4** Sample answer: I looked for different rectangles in the figure.

- *How else could you have decomposed the animal pens?* Answers vary.

- *How did you find the areas of the animal pens?* Sample answer: I added the areas of the smaller rectangles.

- *How did you find the missing side lengths for the rectangles in Problems 3 and 4?* Sample answer: I used the opposite side lengths to find the missing side lengths.

- *What did you notice about the giant tortoise pen and the koala pen?* Sample answer: They have the same area even though they are different shapes.

Summarize Together read about rectilinear figures on *Student Reference Book,* pages 180–181.

③ Practice   10–15 min   Go Online   ePresentations   eToolkit   Home Connections

▶ **Minute Math+**

To practice mental math strategies, select a *Minute Math+* activity.

▶ **Math Boxes 4-12**

Math Journal 1, p. 132

WHOLE CLASS   SMALL GROUP   PARTNER   INDEPENDENT

Mixed Practice Math Boxes 4-12 are paired with Math Boxes 4-10.

▶ **Home Link 4-12**

Math Masters, p. 148

Homework Children find the areas of rectilinear figures.

Math Journal 1, p. 132

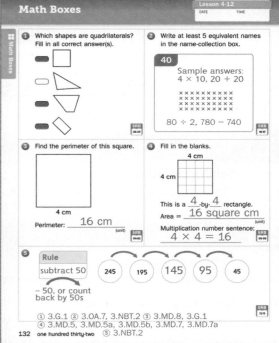

Math Masters p. 148

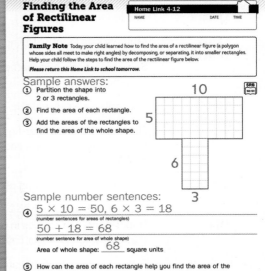

Unit 4 Progress Check

Overview Day 1: Administer the Unit Assessments.
Day 2: Administer the Cumulative Assessment.

2-Day Lesson

 Student Learning Center
Students may take
assessments digitally.

 Assessment and Reporting
Record results and track
progress toward mastery.

Day 1: Unit Assessments

① Warm Up   5–10 min

Self Assessment
Children complete the Self Assessment.

Materials

Assessment Handbook, p. 33

②a Assess   35–55 min

Unit 4 Assessment
These items reflect mastery expectations to this point.

Assessment Handbook, pp. 34–38

Unit 4 Challenge (Optional)
Children may demonstrate progress beyond expectations.

Assessment Handbook, pp. 39–40

Common Core State Standards	**Goals for Mathematical Content (GMC)**	**Lessons**	**Self Assessment**	**Unit 4 Assessment**	**Unit 4 Challenge**
3.MD.4	Measure lengths to the nearest $\frac{1}{2}$ inch, $\frac{1}{4}$ inch, or whole centimeter.	4-1 to 4-3, 4-6, 4-7	1	1	1
	Collect, organize, and represent data on line plots.	4-2	2	2	
3.MD.5, 3.MD.5a	Understand that a unit square has 1 square unit of area and can measure area.	4-7, 4-8, 4-10, 4-12	5	6b, 7–9, 10b	
3.MD.5, 3.MD.5b	Understand that a plane figure completely covered by *n* unit squares has area *n* square units.	4-7 to 4-10	5	6b, 7–9, 10b	
3.MD.6	Measure areas by counting unit squares.	4-7 to 4-10	5	6b, 7, 9, 10b	
3.MD.7, 3.MD.7a	Show that tiling a rectangle results in the same area as multiplying its side lengths.	4-9		8	
3.MD.7, 3.MD.7b	Multiply side lengths to find areas of rectangles.	4-9 to 4-12			3
	Solve real-world and mathematical problems involving areas of rectangles.	4-11		7	
3.MD.7, 3.MD.7d	Recognize area as additive.	4-12	6	10c	
	Find areas of rectilinear figures by decomposing them into non-overlapping rectangles, and apply this technique to solve real-world problems.	4-12	6	10a	
3.MD.8	Solve problems involving perimeters of polygons.	4-3, 4-6 to 4-8, 4-10	4	5a, 5b, 6a, 7–9	3
3.G.1	Understand that shapes in different categories may share attributes that can define a larger category.	4-3 to 4-5	3	3a, 3b, 4a, 4b, 5c	2
	Recognize specified subcategories of quadrilaterals.	4-5, 4-6		4a, 4b	

Goals for Mathematical Practice (GMP)	Lessons	Self Assessment	Unit 4 Assessment	Unit 4 Challenge
SMP2				
Make sense of the representations you and others use. GMP2.2	4-5			1
SMP4				
Model real-world situations using graphs, drawings, tables, symbols, numbers, diagrams, and other representations. GMP4.1	4-2, 4-11, 4-12		2	
Use mathematical models to solve problems and answer questions. GMP4.2	4-2		6–8	
SMP6				
Explain your mathematical thinking clearly and precisely. GMP6.1	4-10		5b, 7	3
Use clear labels, units, and mathematical language. GMP6.3	4-1, 4-2, 4-6 to 4-8, 4-11		1	
SMP7				
Look for mathematical structures such as categories, patterns, and properties. GMP7.1	4-3 to 4-5, 4-12		3a, 3b, 4a, 4b	2
Use structures to solve problems and answer questions. GMP7.2	4-4 to 4-6, 4-8 to 4-10		3a, 4a, 4b	
SMP8				
Create and justify rules, shortcuts, and generalizations. GMP8.1	4-4		3b	

III **Spiral Tracker** [Go Online] to see how mastery develops for all standards within the grade.

1 Warm Up 5–10 min

▶ Self Assessment

Assessment Handbook, p. 33

| WHOLE CLASS | SMALL GROUP | PARTNER | **INDEPENDENT** |

Children complete the Self Assessment to reflect on their progress in Unit 4.

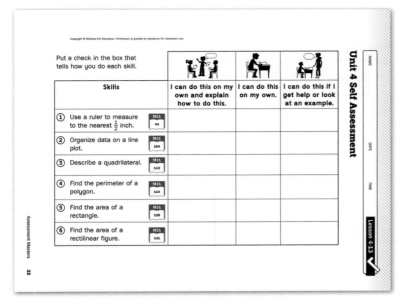

Assessment Handbook, p. 33

Assessment Handbook, p. 34

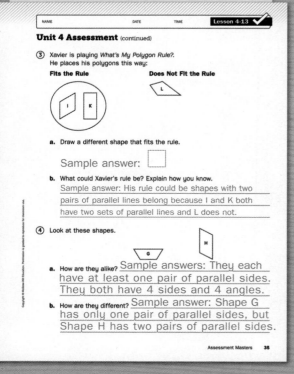

Assessment Handbook, p. 35

▶ Unit 4 Assessment

Assessment Handbook, pp. 34–38

WHOLE CLASS | SMALL GROUP | PARTNER | **INDEPENDENT**

Children complete the Unit 4 Assessment to demonstrate their progress on the Common Core State Standards covered in this unit.

The online assessment and reporting tools provide additional resources for monitoring children's progress. You may use the differentiation options to intervene as indicated.

Generic rubrics in the *Assessment Handbook* appendix can be used to evaluate children's progress on the Mathematical Practices.

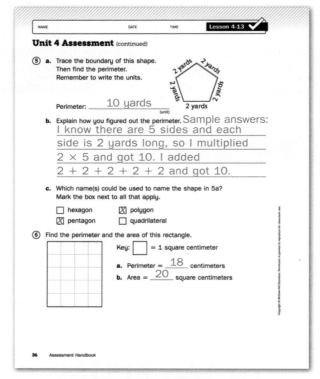

Assessment Handbook, p. 36

Differentiate   Adjusting the Assessment

Item(s)	Adjustments
1	To scaffold Item 1, have children use Ruler A from *Math Masters*, page TA30. To extend, have children use Ruler C.
2	To extend Item 2, have children generate questions with answers based on the line plot.
3, 4	To scaffold Items 3 and 4, have children refer to *Student Reference Book*, page 217.
5	To extend Item 5, have children sketch other polygons with perimeters of 10 units on Centimeter Grid Paper, *Math Masters*, page TA19.
6, 7	To scaffold Items 6 and 7, have children refer to *Student Reference Book*, pages 174–177. To extend Items 6 and 7, have children sketch a quilt with a perimeter of 16 feet and an area of 15 square feet.
8	To extend Item 8, have children sketch other rectangles with areas of 32 square units on Centimeter Grid Paper, *Math Masters*, page TA19.
9	To scaffold Item 9, have children outline the perimeter and shade the area of the rectangle on the card with two different colored pencils.
10	To extend Item 10, have children decompose the rectilinear figure in a different way and find the area.

Advice for Differentiation

All of the content included on the Unit 4 Assessment was recently introduced and will be revisited in subsequent units.

Use the online assessment and reporting tools to track children's performance. Differentiation materials are available online to help you address children's needs.

NOTE See the Unit Organizer on pages 318–319 or the online Spiral Tracker for details on Unit 4 focus topics and the spiral.

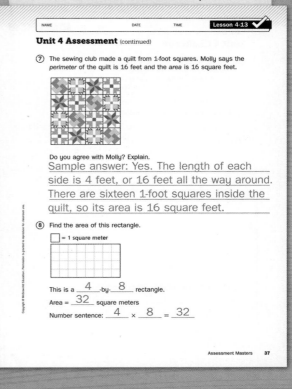

Assessment Handbook, p. 37

Assessment Handbook, p. 38

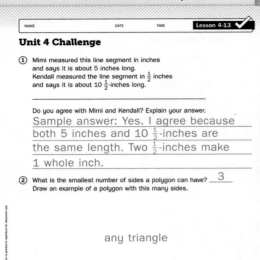

NAME   DATE   TIME   **Lesson 4-13** ✓

Unit 4 Challenge

① Mimi measured this line segment in inches
and says it is about 5 inches long.
Kendall measured the line segment in $\frac{1}{2}$ inches
and says it is about 10 $\frac{1}{2}$-inches long.

Do you agree with Mimi and Kendall? Explain your answer.
Sample answer: Yes. I agree because
both 5 inches and 10 $\frac{1}{2}$-inches are
the same length. Two $\frac{1}{2}$-inches make
1 whole inch.

② What is the smallest number of sides a polygon can have? ___3___
Draw an example of a polygon with this many sides.

any triangle

Why are there no polygons with fewer sides?
Sample answer: If you try to make a
polygon with 2 sides, it won't close. It
would be like an L or a V, and there
wouldn't be another side to connect it.

Assessment Masters   **39**

▶ # Unit 4 Challenge (Optional)

Assessment Handbook, pp. 39–40

WHOLE CLASS	SMALL GROUP	PARTNER	**INDEPENDENT**

Children can complete the Unit 4 Challenge after they complete the
Unit 4 Assessment.

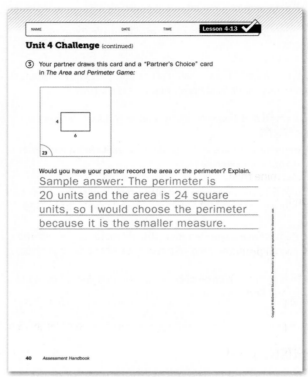

NAME   DATE   TIME   **Lesson 4-13** ✓

Unit 4 Challenge (continued)

③ Your partner draws this card and a "Partner's Choice" card
in *The Area and Perimeter Game*:

Would you have your partner record the area or the perimeter? Explain.
Sample answer: The perimeter is
20 units and the area is 24 square
units, so I would choose the perimeter
because it is the smaller measure.

40   Assessment Handbook

Assessment Handbook, p. 40

Unit 4 Progress Check ✔

Day 2: Cumulative Assessment

2b Assess 35–45 min

Materials

⭐ **Cumulative Assessment**
These items reflect mastery expectations to this point.

Assessment Handbook, pp. 41–43

CCSS

Common Core State Standards	Goals for Mathematical Content (GMC)	Cumulative Assessment
3.OA.1	Interpret multiplication in terms of equal groups.	1, 2
3.OA.4	Determine the unknown in multiplication and division equations.	3a–3c, 4, 5
3.OA.6	Understand division as an unknown-factor problem.	4, 5
3.OA.7	Multiply within 100 fluently.	5
	Know all products of 1-digit numbers $\times$ 1, $\times$ 2, $\times$ 5, and $\times$ 10 automatically.*	3a–3c, 5
	Divide within 100 fluently.	4, 5
3.NBT.1	Use place-value understanding to round whole numbers to the nearest 10.*	6a
	Use place-value understanding to round whole numbers to the nearest 100.*	6b, 6c
3.MD.1	Solve number stories involving time intervals by adding or subtracting.	7
3.MD.3	Solve 1- and 2-step problems using information in graphs.	8a–8c

	Goals for Mathematical Practice (GMP)	
SMP2	Create mathematical representations using numbers, words, pictures, symbols, gestures, tables, graphs, and concrete objects. **GMP2.1**	1, 2
	Make connections between representations. **GMP2.3**	1, 2
SMP4	Model real-world situations using graphs, drawings, tables, symbols, numbers, diagrams, and other representations. **GMP4.1**	7
	Use mathematical models to solve problems and answer questions. **GMP4.2**	8d
SMP6	Explain your mathematical thinking clearly and precisely. **GMP6.1**	6c, 8d
SMP7	Use structures to solve problems and answer questions. **GMP7.2**	4

*Instruction and most practice on this content is complete.

▥ **Spiral Tracker** 〈 **Go Online** 〉 to see how mastery develops for all standards within the grade.

3 Look Ahead 10–15 min

Materials

Math Boxes 4-13: Preview for Unit 5
Children preview skills and concepts for Unit 5.

Math Journal 1, p. 133

Home Link 4-13
Children take home the Family Letter that introduces Unit 5.

Math Masters, pp. 149–152

NAME   DATE   TIME   Lesson 4-13 ✓

Unit 4 Cumulative Assessment

① Write a multiplication number sentence for this array.

• • • • •
• • • • •
• • • • •
• • • • •

Number sentence: __4 × 5 = 20__

② Draw an array to match this number sentence.

7 × 3 = 21

• • • • • • •
• • • • • • •
• • • • • • •

③ Fill in the blanks.

a. __7__ × 2 = 14

b. 30 = 6 × __5__

c. 5 × __10__ = 50

④ Monique was solving this problem: 40 ÷ 5 = ?
She asked herself, "5 times what number is 40?"
Then she knew the answer. How did Monique figure out the answer?
Sample answer: Monique used
5 × 8 = 40 to solve 40 ÷ 5 = 8 since
both facts are in the same fact family.

Assessment Masters   **41**

NAME   DATE   TIME   Lesson 4-13 ✓

Unit 4 Cumulative Assessment (continued)

⑤ Complete.

in	out
3	15
5	25
6	30
8	40

Rule
× 5

Answers vary.

⑥ Round each number to the nearest 10 and to the nearest 100.

	a. Round to the nearest 10.	b. Round to the nearest 100.
247	250	200
489	490	500
593	590	600
303	300	300

c. Explain how you rounded 247 to the nearest 100.
Sample answer: I know that the
nearest hundreds are 200 and 300,
and 247 is closer to 200. So 247
rounded to the nearest hundred is 200.

42   Assessment Handbook

---

408   Unit 4 | Measurement and Geometry

2b **Assess**   35–45 min   Go Online ✓

Assessment   Differentiation
and Reporting   Support

▶ Cumulative Assessment

Assessment Handbook, pp. 41–43

| WHOLE CLASS | SMALL GROUP | PARTNER | **INDEPENDENT** |

Children complete the Cumulative Assessment. The items in the Cumulative Assessment address content from Units 1–3.

Monitor children's progress on the Common Core State Standards using the online assessment and reporting tools.

Generic rubrics in the *Assessment Handbook* appendix can be used to evaluate children's progress on the Mathematical Practices.

Differentiate   **Adjusting the Assessment**

Item(s)	Adjustments
1, 2	To extend Items 1 and 2, have children write a number story to fit each array.
3, 4	To scaffold Items 3 and 4, have children model facts with skip counting or counters.
5	To scaffold Item 5, have children write × 5 between the *in* and *out* columns, and read the resulting number sentences.
6	To scaffold Item 6, have children use prepared open number lines.
7	To extend Item 7, have children determine the elapsed time between 8:25 A.M. and 9:10 A.M.
8	To scaffold Item 8, have children write the number represented by each bar in the appropriate column on the bar graph.

Advice for Differentiation

All instruction and most practice is complete for the content that is marked with an asterisk (*) on page 407.

Use the online assessment and reporting tools to track children's performance. Differentiation materials are available online to help you address children's needs.

3 Look Ahead 10–15 min

Go Online ⌂
Home Connections

▶ **Math Boxes 4-13:** Preview for Unit 5

Math Journal 1, p. 133

| WHOLE CLASS | SMALL GROUP | PARTNER | INDEPENDENT |

Mixed Practice Math Boxes 4-13 are paired with Math Boxes 4-9. These problems focus on skills and understandings that are prerequisite for Unit 5. You may want to use information from these Math Boxes to plan instruction and grouping in Unit 5.

▶ **Home Link 4-13:** Unit 5 Family Letter

Math Masters, pp. 149–152

Home Connection The Unit 5 Family Letter provides information and activities related to Unit 5 content.

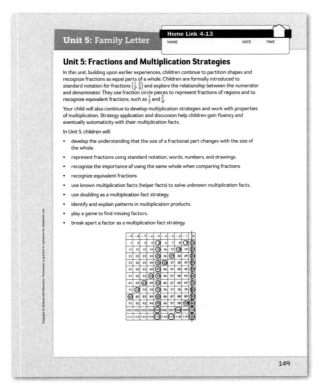

Math Masters, pp. 149–152

Mid-Year Assessment

Assessment Handbook, pp. 113–120

You may want to administer the Mid-Year Assessment after Unit 4 to check children's mastery of some of the concepts and skills in *Third Grade Everyday Mathematics.* See the *Assessment Handbook.*

Assessment Handbook, p. 43

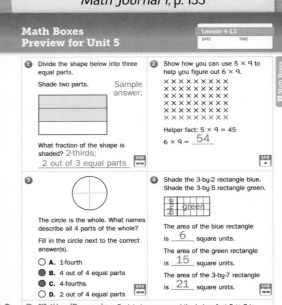

Math Journal 1, p. 133

Everyday Mathematics strives to define terms clearly, especially when those terms can be defined in more than one way.

This glossary focuses on terms and meanings for elementary school mathematics and omits details and complexities that would be required at higher levels. The definitions here are phrased for teachers. Information for explaining terms and concepts to children can be found within the lessons themselves. Additional information is available online. In a definition, most terms in italics are defined elsewhere in this glossary.

0–9

0 fact (1) The *sum* of two 1-digit numbers when one of the *addends* is 0, as in $0 + 5 = 5$. If 0 is added to any number, there is no change in the number. See *Additive Identity*. (2) The *product* of two 1-digit numbers when one of the factors is 0, as in $4 * 0 = 0$. The product of a number and 0 is always 0.

1-dimensional (1-D) (1) Having *length*, but not area or volume; confined to a curve, such as an arc. (2) A figure whose points are all on one *line*. Line segments are 1-dimensional. Compare *2-* and *3-dimensional*.

2-dimensional (2-D) (1) Having *area* but not volume; confined to a *surface*. A 2-dimensional surface can be flat or curved, such as the surface of a sphere. (2) A figure whose points are all in one *plane* but not all on one line. Examples include polygons and circles. Compare *1-* and *3-dimensional*.

3-dimensional (3-D) Having *volume*. Solids such as cubes, cones, and spheres are 3-dimensional. Compare *1-* and *2-dimensional*.

A

A.M. The abbreviation for ante meridiem, meaning "before the middle of the day" in Latin. From midnight to noon.

accurate (1) As correct as possible for a given context. An answer can be accurate without being very *precise* if the units are large. For example, the driving time from Chicago to New York is about 13 hours. See *approximate*. (2) Of a measurement or other quantity, having a high degree of correctness. A more accurate measurement is closer to the true value. Accurate answers must be reasonably precise.

addend Any one of a set of numbers that are added. For example, in $5 + 3 + 1 = 9$, the addends are 5, 3, and 1.

adding a group A *multiplication fact* strategy that involves adding one more group onto a *helper fact*. For example, 6×8 can be solved by starting with 5 groups of 8 ($5 \times 8 = 40$), then adding one more group of 8 to get 48.

addition fact Two whole numbers from 0 through 10 and their sum, such as $9 + 7 = 16$. See *arithmetic facts*.

addition/subtraction use class A category of problem situations that can be solved using addition or subtraction or other methods such as counting or direct modeling. *Everyday Mathematics* distinguishes four addition/subtraction use classes: *parts-and-total*, *change-to-more*, *change-to-less*, and *comparison situations*. The table below shows how these use classes correspond to those in the Common Core State Standards.

Everyday Mathematics	CCSS
change-to-more	add to
change-to-less	take from
parts-and-total	put together/take apart
comparison	compare

Additive Identity The number zero (0). The additive identity is the number that when added to any other number, yields that other number. See *additive inverses*.

additive inverses Two numbers whose sum is 0. Each number is called the additive inverse, or opposite, of the other. For example, 3 and −3 are additive inverses because $3 + (−3) = 0$. Zero is its own additive inverse: $0 + 0 = 0$. See *Additive Identity*.

adjacent angles Two nonoverlapping *angles* with a common *side* and *vertex*.

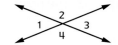

Angles 1 and 2, 2 and 3, 3 and 4, and 4 and 1 are pairs of adjacent angles.

Angle 5 is adjacent to angle 6.

adjacent sides (1) Two sides of a *polygon* with a common *vertex*. (2) Two faces of a *polyhedron* with a common *edge*.

algorithm   A set of step-by-step instructions for doing something, such as carrying out a computation or solving a problem. The most common algorithms are those for basic arithmetic computation, but there are many others. Some mathematicians and many computer scientists spend a great deal of time trying to find more efficient algorithms for solving problems.

analog clock   (1) A clock that shows the time by the positions of the hour and minute hands. (2) Any device that shows time passing in a continuous manner, such as a sundial. Compare *digital clock*.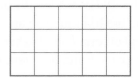

anchor chart   A classroom display that is cocreated by teacher and students and focuses on a central concept or skill.

angle   (1) A figure formed by two rays or line segments with a common endpoint called the *vertex* of the angle. The rays or segments are called the sides of the angle. Angles can be named after their vertex point alone as in ∠*A*; or by three points, one on each side and the vertex in the middle as in ∠*BCD*. One side of an angle is *rotated* about the vertex from the other side through a number of *degrees*. (2) The measure of this rotation in degrees.

240°	
∠A	∠BCD

-angle   A suffix meaning angle, or corner, for example, triangle and rectangle.

apex   (1) In a *pyramid,* the *vertex* opposite the *base*. All the nonbase faces meet at the apex. (2) The point at the tip of a *cone*.

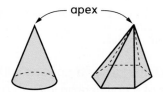
apex

approximate   Close to exact. In many situations it is not possible to get an exact answer, but it is important to be close to the exact answer. We might draw an angle that measures approximately 60° with a protractor. In this case, approximate suggests the angle drawn is within a degree or two of 60°. Compare *precise*.

area   The amount of *surface* inside a *2-dimensional* figure. The figure might be a triangle or rectangle in a *plane,* the curved surface of a cylinder, or a state or country on Earth's surface. Commonly, the area is measured in *square units,* such as square miles or square centimeters, or other units, such as acres.

  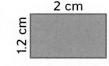

A triangle with area   A rectangle with area
21 square units   1.2 cm * 2 cm = 2.4 square centimeters

area model   (1) A *model* for multiplication in which the length and width of a *rectangle* represent the *factors,* and the *area* of the rectangle represents the *product.*

Area model for 3 × 5 = 15

(2) A model showing fractions as parts of a *whole.* The whole is a region, such as a circle or a rectangle, representing the unit whole.

Area model for $\frac{2}{3}$

arithmetic facts   The *addition facts* (*whole-number* addends 10 or less); their inverse subtraction facts; *multiplication facts* (whole-number factors 10 or less); and their inverse division facts, except there is no division by zero. Facts and their corresponding inverses are organized into *fact families.*

array (1) An arrangement of objects in a regular *pattern*, usually *rows* and *columns*. (2) A *rectangular array*. In *Everyday Mathematics*, an array is a rectangular array unless specified otherwise.

arrow rule In *Everyday Mathematics*, a rule that determines the number that goes into the next *frame* in a *Frames-and-Arrows* diagram. There may be more than one arrow rule per diagram.

arrows In *Everyday Mathematics*, the links representing the *arrow rule(s)* in a *Frames-and-Arrows* diagram.

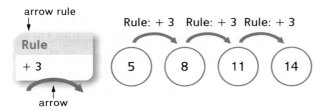

Associative Property of Addition A *property* of addition that for any numbers *a*, *b*, and *c*, $(a + b) + c = a + (b + c)$. The grouping of the three *addends* can be changed without changing the *sum*. For example, $(4 + 3) + 7 = 4 + (3 + 7)$ because $7 + 7 = 4 + 10$. Subtraction is not associative. For example, $(4 - 3) + 7 \neq 4 - (3 + 7)$ because $8 \neq -6$. Compare *Commutative Property of Addition*.

Associative Property of Multiplication A *property* of multiplication that for any numbers *a*, *b*, and *c*, $(a \times b) \times c = a \times (b \times c)$. The grouping of the three *factors* can be changed without changing the *product*. For example, $(4 \times 3) \times 7 = 4 \times (3 \times 7)$ because $12 \times 7 = 4 \times 21$. Division is not associative. For example, $(21 \div 7) \div 3 \neq 21 \div (7 \div 3)$ because $1 \neq 9$. Compare *Commutative Property of Multiplication*.

attribute A characteristic or *property* of an object or a common characteristic of a set of objects. Size, shape, color, and number of sides are attributes.

automaticity The ability to solve problems with great efficiency either by using recall or applying quick strategies. For example, one might "just know" $8 + 7 = 15$, or quickly think $8 + 2 = 10$ and 5 more is 15. Compare *fluency*.

ballpark estimate A rough *estimate*. A ballpark estimate can serve as a check of the reasonableness of an answer obtained through some other procedure, or it can be made when an exact value is unnecessary or impossible to obtain.

bar graph A graph with horizontal or vertical bars that represent (typically categorical) *data*. The lengths of the bars may be *scaled*.

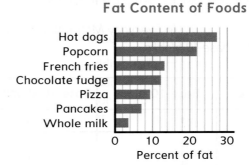

base The *side* of a *polygon* or *face* of a polyhedron from which the *height* is measured.

base angles of a trapezoid Two *angles* that share a *base* of a trapezoid.

base of a number system The foundation number for a *place-value* based *numeration* system. For example, our usual way of writing numbers uses a *base-10* place-value system. In programming computers or other digital devices, bases of 2, 8, 16, or other powers of 2 are more common than base 10.

base of a trapezoid (1) Either of a pair of *parallel sides* in a *trapezoid*. (2) The *length* of this side. The area of a trapezoid is the average of a pair of bases times the corresponding height.

base ten (1) Related to powers of 10. (2) The most common system for writing numbers, which uses 10 symbols 0, 1, 2, 3, 4, 5, 6, 7, 8, and 9, called *digits*. One can write any number using one or more of these 10 digits, and each digit has a value that depends on its place in the number (its *place value*). In the base-10 system, each place has a value 10 times that of the place to its right, and one-tenth the value of the place to its left.

comparison diagram In *Everyday Mathematics*, a diagram used to model situations in which two quantities are compared. The diagram represents two quantities and their *difference*. See *situation diagram*.

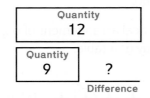

A comparison diagram for 12 = 9 + ?

comparison situation A situation involving two quantities and the *difference* between them. See *addition/subtraction use class*.

compose To make up or form a number or shape by putting together smaller numbers or shapes. For example, one can compose a 10 by putting together ten 1s: 1 + 1 + 1 + 1 + 1 + 1 + 1 + 1 + 1 + 1 = 10. One can compose a pentagon by putting together an equilateral triangle and a square.

composite number A *counting number* that has more than two *factors*. For example, 10 is a composite number because it has four factors: 1, 2, 5, and 10. Compare *prime number*.

composite unit A *unit* of measure made up of multiple copies of a smaller unit. For example, a foot is a composite unit of 12 inches used to measure length, and a row of unit squares can be used to measure area.

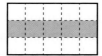

3 rows of 5 square units each gives an area of 15 square units.

concave polygon A *polygon* on which there are at least two points that can be connected with a *line segment* that passes outside the polygon. For example, segment *AD* is outside the hexagon between *B* and *C*. Informally, at least one *vertex* appears to be "pushed inward." At least one interior angle has measure greater than 180°. Same as *nonconvex polygon*. Compare *convex polygon*.

cone A *geometric solid* comprising a circular *base*, an *apex* not in the *plane* of the base, and all line segments with one endpoint at the apex and the other endpoint on the circumference of the base.

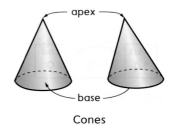

Cones

congruent figures Figures having the same size and shape. Two figures are congruent if they match exactly when one is placed on top of the other after a combination of isometric transformations (slides, flips, and/or turns). In diagrams of congruent figures, the *corresponding* congruent *sides* may be marked with the same number of hash marks. The symbol ≅ means "is congruent to".

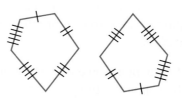

Congruent pentagons

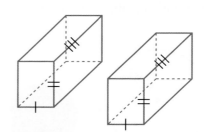

Congruent right rectangular prisms

conjecture A claim that has not been proved, at least by the person making the conjecture.

continuous model of area   A way of thinking about *area* as sweeping one dimension of a plane figure across the other dimension. For example, the paint roller below shows how the area of a rectangle can be modeled continuously by sweeping the shorter side across the longer side. Compare *discrete model of area*.

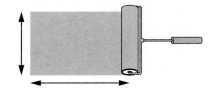

A continuous model of area

convex polygon   A *polygon* on which no two points can be connected with a *line segment* that passes outside the polygon. Informally, all *vertices* appear to be "pushed outward". Each *angle* in the polygon measures less than 180°. Compare *concave polygon*.

corner   Informal for *vertex* or *angle*.

counterclockwise rotation   Opposite the direction in which the hands move on a typical *analog clock;* a turn to the left.

counting numbers   The numbers used to count things. The set of counting numbers is {1, 2, 3, 4, . . .}. Sometimes 0 is included, but not in *Everyday Mathematics*. Counting numbers are also known as *natural numbers*.

counting-up subtraction   A subtraction strategy in which a *difference* is found by counting or adding up from the smaller number to the larger number. For example, to calculate 87 − 49, one could start at 49, add 30 to reach 79, and then add 8 more to reach 87. The difference is 30 + 8 = 38.

cube   (1) A *regular polyhedron* with 6 square *faces*. A cube has 8 *vertices* and 12 *edges*.

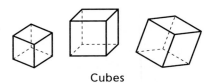

Cubes

(2) In *Everyday Mathematics*, the smaller cube of the *base-10 blocks*, measuring 1 cm on each edge.

curved surface   A *2-dimensional surface* that does not lie in a *plane*. Spheres, cylinders, and cones have curved surfaces.

customary system of measurement   In *Everyday Mathematics*, same as *U.S. customary system of measurement*. See *Tables of Measures*.

cylinder   A *geometric solid* with two *congruent, parallel* circular regions for *bases* and a curved *face* formed by all the *segments* that have an endpoint on each *circle* and that are parallel to a segment with endpoints at the *centers of the circles*. Also called a circular cylinder.

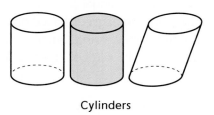

Cylinders

D

data   Information that is gathered by counting, measuring, questioning, or observing. Strictly, data is the plural of datum, but data is often used as a singular word.

decagon   A 10-sided *polygon*.

decimal   (1) A number written in standard *base-10* notation containing a *decimal point*, such as 2.54. (2) Any number written in standard base-10 notation. See *decimal fraction, repeating decimal,* and *terminating decimal*.

decimal fraction   (1) A *fraction* or mixed number written in standard *decimal notation*. (2) A fraction $\frac{a}{b}$ where b is a positive power of 10, such as $\frac{84}{100}$.

decimal notation   Same as *standard notation*.

decimal point   A mark used to separate the ones and tenths places in *decimals*. A decimal point separates dollars from cents in dollars-and-cents notation. The mark is a dot in the U.S. customary system and a comma in Europe and some other countries.

decompose   To separate a number or shape into smaller numbers or shapes. For example, 14 can be decomposed into 1 ten and 4 ones. A square can be decomposed into two isosceles right triangles. Any even number can be decomposed into two equal parts: $2n = n + n$.

defining attributes of a shape   Characteristics of a shape that are consequences of the definition. The shape will always have those characteristics. For example, four right angles is a defining *attribute* of a square, but being orange or having an area of 4 square inches are not defining attributes of a square. Compare *nondefining attributes of a shape*.

degree (°)   (1) A unit of measure for *angles* based on dividing a *circle* into 360 equal parts. Latitude and longitude are measured in degrees based on angle measures. (2) A unit for measuring *temperature*. See *Celsius* and *Fahrenheit*. The symbol ° means degrees of any type.

denominator   The nonzero *divisor b* in a *fraction* $\frac{a}{b}$. In a *part-whole fraction*, the denominator is the number of equal parts into which the *whole* has been divided. The denominator determines the size of each part. Compare *numerator*.

difference   (1) The distance between two numbers on a *number line*. The difference between 5 and 12 is 7. (2) The result of subtracting one number from another. For example, in $12 - 5 = 7$ the difference is 7, and in $5 - 12$ the difference is −7. Compare *minuend* and *subtrahend*.

digit   (1) Any of the symbols 0, 1, 2, 3, 4, 5, 6, 7, 8, and 9 in the *base-10 numeration* system. For example, the *numeral* 145 is made up of the digits 1, 4, and 5. (2) Additional symbols in other *place-value* systems, such as, A, B, C, D, E, and F in base-16 notation.

digital clock   A clock that shows the time with numbers of hours and minutes, usually separated by a colon. This display is discrete, not continuous, meaning that the display jumps to a new time after a minute delay has elapsed. Compare *analog clock*.

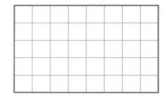

dimension   (1) A measurable extent such as *length*, width, or *height*. Having two makes the measured figure 2-dimensional. See *1-, 2-*, and *3-dimensional*. (2) The measures of those extents. For example, the dimensions of a box might be 24 cm by 20 cm by 10 cm. (3) The number of coordinates necessary to locate a point in a geometric space. A plane has two dimensions because an ordered pair of two coordinates uniquely locates any point in the plane.

discrete model of area   A way of thinking about *area* as filling a figure with unit squares and counting them. For example, the rectangle below has been filled with 40 square units. Compare *continuous model of area*.

disk   A *circle* and its *interior* region.

displacement method   A method for measuring the *volume* of an object by submerging it in water and then measuring the volume of water it displaces. The method is especially useful for finding the volume of an irregularly shaped object.

Distributive Property of Multiplication over Addition and Subtraction   A *property* that for any numbers *a*, *b*, and *c*:

$$a * (b + c) = (a * b) + (a * c)$$
$$\text{or } a(b + c) = ab + ac$$
$$\text{and } a * (b - c) = (a * b) - (a * c)$$
$$\text{or } a(b - c) = ab - ac$$

This property relates multiplication to a *sum* or *difference* of numbers by distributing a *factor* over the terms in the sum or difference. For example,

$$2 * (5 + 3) = (2 * 5) + (2 * 3) = 10 + 6 = 16.$$

dividend   The number in division that is being divided. For example, in $35 / 5 = 7$, the dividend is 35. Compare *divisor* and *quotient*.

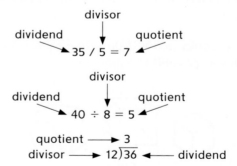

division symbols The number a divided by the number b is written in a variety of ways. In *Everyday Mathematics*, $a \div b$, a / b, and $\frac{a}{b}$ are the most common notations, while $\overline{)}$ is used to set up some division algorithms. $a{:}b$ is sometimes used in Europe, $\div$ is common on calculators, and / is common on computer keyboards.

divisor In division, the number that divides another number. For example, in $35 / 7 = 5$, the divisor is 7. See the diagram with dividend. Compare *dividend* and *quotient*.

double (1) Two times an amount; an amount added to itself. (2) A multiplication strategy that involves halving one factor to create a helper fact, and then doubling the product of the helper fact. For example, 4×8 can be solved by using 2×8 as a *helper fact* and doubling its product, 16, to get 32.

doubles fact The *sum* of a number 0 through 10 added to itself, such as $4 + 4 = 8$, sometimes written as that number multiplied by 2, $2 \times 4 = 8$. These are key *helper facts*.

E

edge (1) Any *side* of a *polyhedron's* faces.

edges

(2) A line segment or curve where two *surfaces* of a *geometric solid* meet.

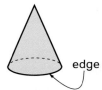

edge

efficient strategy A method that can be applied easily and quickly. For example, adding a group and doubling are usually efficient strategies for solving multiplication facts.

elapsed time The amount of time that has passed from one point in time to the next. For example, between 12:45 P.M. and 1:30 P.M., 45 minutes have elapsed.

equal (1) Identical in number or measure; neither more nor less. (2) *Equivalent*.

equal-grouping situation A situation in which a quantity is divided into equal groups. The total and size of each group are known and the number of groups is unknown. For example, "How many tables seating 4 people each are needed to seat 52 people?" is an equal-grouping situation. Often division can be used to solve equal-grouping situations. Compare *equal-sharing situation*.

equal groups Sets with the same number of elements, such as cars with 5 passengers each, rows with 6 chairs each, and boxes containing 100 paper clips each.

equal-groups notation In *Everyday Mathematics*, a way to denote a number of equal-size groups. The size of each group is shown inside square brackets and the number of groups is written in front of the brackets. For example, 3 [6s] means 3 groups with 6 in each group. In general, n [ks] means n groups with k in each group.

equal parts *Equivalent* parts of a *whole*. For example, dividing a pizza into 4 equal parts means each part is $\frac{1}{4}$ of the pizza and is equal in size to each of the other 3 parts.

equal share One of several parts of a whole, each of which has the same amount of area, volume, mass, or other measurable or countable quantity. Sometimes called fair share. See *equal parts*.

equal-sharing situation A situation in which a quantity is shared equally. The total quantity and the number of groups are known. For example, "There are 10 toys to share equally among 4 children. How many toys will each child get?" is an equal-sharing situation. Often division can be used to solve equal-sharing situation. Compare *equal-grouping situation*.

equation A *number sentence* that contains an equal sign. For example, $5 + 10 = 15$ and $P = 2l + 2w$ are equations.

equilateral polygon A *polygon* in which all sides are the same length.

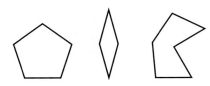

Equilateral polygons

equilateral triangle   A *triangle* with all three sides equal in length. Each angle of an equilateral triangle measures 60°, so it is also called an equiangular triangle. All equilateral triangles are *isosceles triangles*.

equivalent   *Equal* in value but possibly in a different form. For example, $\frac{1}{2}$, 0.5, and 50% are all equivalent.

equivalent fractions   *Fractions* that name the same number, such as $\frac{1}{2}$, $\frac{4.5}{9}$, and $\frac{28}{56}$.

equivalent names   Different ways of naming the same number. For example, 2 + 6, 4 + 4, 12 − 4, 18 − 10, 100 − 92, 5 + 1 + 2, eight, VIII, and ⊬⊬ /// are all equivalent names for 8. See *name-collection box*.

estimate   (1) An answer close to, or *approximating*, an exact answer. (2) To make an estimate.

evaluate a numerical expression   To carry out the *operations* in a numerical *expression* to find a single value for the expression.

even number   (1) A *counting number* that is divisible by 2: 2, 4, 6, 8 . . .. (2) An *integer* that is divisible by 2. Compare *odd number*.

expand-and-trade subtraction   A subtraction *algorithm* in which *expanded notation* is used to facilitate *place-value* exchanges.

expanded form   Same as *expanded notation*.

expanded notation   A way of writing a number as the *sum* of the values of each *digit*. For example, 356 is 300 + 50 + 6 in expanded notation. Same as *expanded form*. Compare *standard notation* and *number-and-word notation*.

Explorations   In *First* through *Third Grade Everyday Mathematics*, independent or small-group activities that focus on concept development, manipulatives, data collection, problem solving, games, and skill reviews.

expression   (1) A mathematical phrase made up of numbers, *variables, operation symbols,* and/or *grouping symbols*. An expression does not contain *relation symbols* such as =, >, and ≤. (2) Either side of an *equation* or *inequality*.

extended facts   Variations of basic *arithmetic facts* involving *multiples* of 10, 100, and so on. For example, 30 + 70 = 100, 40 * 5 = 200, and 560 / 7 = 80 are extended facts. See *fact extensions*.

F

face   (1) A flat *surface* on a closed, *3-dimensional* figure. Some special faces are called *bases*.

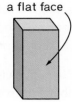

a flat face

(2) More generally, any *2-dimensional* surface on a 3-dimensional figure.

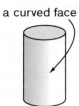

a curved face

fact extensions   Calculations with larger numbers using knowledge of basic *arithmetic facts*. For example, knowing the addition fact 5 + 8 = 13 makes it easier to solve problems such as 50 + 80 = ? and 65 + ? = 73. Fact extensions apply to all four basic arithmetic operations. See *extended facts*.

fact family   A set of related *arithmetic facts* linking two inverse operations. For example,

$$5 + 6 = 11 \qquad 6 + 5 = 11$$
$$11 - 5 = 6 \qquad 11 - 6 = 5$$

are an addition/subtraction fact family. Similarly,

$$5 * 7 = 35 \qquad 7 * 5 = 35$$
$$35 / 7 = 5 \qquad 35 / 5 = 7$$

are a multiplication/division fact family. Same as *number family*.

fact power   In *Everyday Mathematics, automaticity* with basic *arithmetic facts*. Automatically knowing the facts is as important to arithmetic as knowing words by sight is to reading.

Fact Triangle   In *Everyday Mathematics,* a triangular flash card labeled with the numbers of a *fact family* that children can use to practice addition/subtraction and multiplication/division facts. The two addends or factors and their sum or *product* (marked with a dot) appear in the corners of each triangle.

factor   (1) Each of the two or more numbers or *variables* in a *product*. For example, in 6 * 0.5, 6 and 0.5 are factors; in 7b, 7 and b are factors. Compare *factor of a counting number* n. (2) To represent a number as a product of factors. For example, factor 21 by rewriting as 7 * 3.

factor of a counting number *n*   A *counting number* whose product with another counting number equals *n*. For example, 2 and 3 are *factors* of 6 because $2 * 3 = 6$. But 4 is not a factor of 6 because $4 * 1.5 = 6$, and 1.5 is not a counting number.

factor pair   Two *factors of a counting number* n whose *product* is *n*. A number may have more than one factor pair. For example, the factor pairs for 18 are 1 and 18; 2 and 9; 3 and 6.

facts table   A chart showing *arithmetic facts*. An addition/subtraction facts table shows addition and subtraction facts. A multiplication/division facts table shows multiplication and division facts.

Fahrenheit   A *temperature* scale on which pure water at sea level freezes at 32° and boils at 212°. The Fahrenheit scale is widely used in the United States but in few other places. Compare *Celsius*.

false number sentence   A *number sentence* that is not true. For example, $8 = 5 + 5$ is a false number sentence. Compare *true number sentence*.

figurate numbers   Numbers that can be illustrated by specific geometric *patterns*. *Square numbers* and *triangular numbers* are figurate numbers.

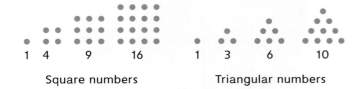

1	4	9	16		1	3	6	10

Square numbers   Triangular numbers

flat   In *Everyday Mathematics*, the *base-10 block* that is equivalent to one hundred 1-cm cubes.

fluency   The ability to compute using efficient, appropriate, and flexible strategies. Compare *automaticity*.

fraction   (1) A number in the form $\frac{a}{b}$ or a/b, where *a* and *b* are *integers* and *b* is not 0. A fraction may be used to name part of an object or part of a collection of objects, to compare two quantities, or to represent division. For example, $\frac{12}{6}$ might mean 12 eggs divided in groups of 6, a ratio of 12 to 6, or 12 divided by 6. Also called a common fraction. (2) A fraction that satisfies the previous definition and includes a unit in both the *numerator* and the *denominator*. For example, the rates $\frac{50 \text{ miles}}{1 \text{ gallon}}$ and $\frac{40 \text{ pages}}{10 \text{ minutes}}$ are fractions. (3) A number written using a fraction bar, where the fraction bar is used to indicate division. For example, $\frac{2.3}{6.5}, \frac{1\frac{4}{5}}{12}, \frac{\pi}{4}$, and $\frac{\frac{3}{4}}{\frac{5}{8}}$. Compare *decimal*.

Fraction Circle Pieces   In *Third* through *Fifth Grade Everyday Mathematics*, a set of colored circles each divided into equal-size slices, used to represent *fractions*.

Fraction Quick Looks   *Quick Looks* that particularly address how fractions relate to wholes. For example, this Fraction Quick Look image represents $\frac{3}{2}$ when the whole is a full circle.

fractional part   Part of a whole. *Fractions* represent fractional parts of numbers, sets, or objects.

frames   In *Everyday Mathematics*, the empty shapes in which numbers are written in a *Frames-and-Arrows* diagram.

Frames and Arrows   In *Everyday Mathematics*, diagrams consisting of *frames* connected by *arrows*. Frames-and-arrows diagrams are used to represent number sequences. Each frame contains a number, and each arrow represents a rule that determines which number goes in the next frame. There may be more than one rule, represented by different-color arrows. Frames-and-Arrows diagrams are also called chains.

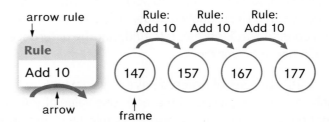

frequency   (1) The number of times a value occurs in a set of *data*. (2) A number of repetitions per unit of time, such as the vibrations per second in a sound wave.

frequency graph   A graph showing how often each value occurs in a *data* set.

Colors in a Bag of Marbles

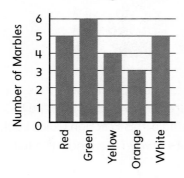

frequency table   A table in which *data* are *tallied* and organized, often as a first step toward making a *frequency graph*.

Color	Number of Marbles
Red	⊬⊬⊦
Green	⊬⊬⊦ /
Yellow	////
Orange	///
White	⊬⊬⊦

friendly numbers   An addition/subtraction *strategy* that uses a number that is easy to work from, typically 10 or a multiple of 10. For example, to solve 16 − 9, one might recognize that the friendly number 10 is 6 less than 16, then count down 1 more to 9 to find that the difference is 7. Compare *helper facts*.

function   (1) A set of *ordered pairs* (*x, y*) in which each value of *x* is paired with exactly one value of *y*. A function is typically represented in a table, by points on a coordinate graph, or by a rule such as an *equation*. (2) A rule that pairs each *input* with exactly one *output*. For example, for a function with the rule "Double," 1 is paired with 2, 2 is paired with 4, 3 is paired with 6, and so on. See *"What's My Rule?"*

function machine   An imaginary device that receives *inputs* and pairs them with *outputs* using a rule that is a *function*. For example, the function machine below pairs an input number with its double. See *function*.

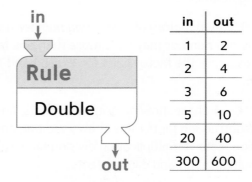

in	out
1	2
2	4
3	6
5	10
20	40
300	600

A function machine and function table

G

geoboard   (1) A small wooden or plastic board with nails or other posts, usually arranged at equally spaced intervals in a *rectangular array*. Geoboards and rubber bands are useful for exploring basic concepts in plane geometry.

(2) A digital version of a geoboard.

geometric solid   The *surface* or surfaces that make up a *3-dimensional* figure such as a *prism, pyramid, cylinder, cone,* or *sphere*. Despite its name, a geometric solid is hollow; that is, it does not include the points in its *interior*. Informally, and in some dictionaries, a solid is defined as both the surface and its interior.

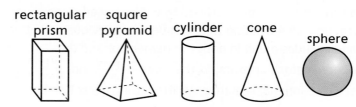

Geometric solids

going through 10 A subtraction fact strategy that involves using 10 as a benchmark to simplify the subtraction. For example, one might solve $16 - 9$ by either going up through 10 and thinking $9 + 1 = 10$ and $10 + 6 = 16$ so the *difference* is 7, or by going back through 10 by thinking 16 take away 6 is 10, and 10 take away 3 more is 7, so the difference is 7. Compare *making 10*.

-gon A suffix meaning *angle*. For example, a *hexagon* is a plane figure with six angles.

grouping addends An addition strategy that involves adding three or more numbers in an order that makes the addition simpler, such as recognizing and adding a combination of 10 or a doubles fact first. See *Associative* and *Commutative Properties of Addition*.

grouping symbols Parentheses ( ), brackets [ ], braces { }, and similar symbols that define the order in which operations in an *expression* are to be done. *Nested* grouping symbols are groupings within groupings, and the innermost grouping is done first. A vinculum is a bar or line used to group numbers $\left(\text{as in } \frac{3+5}{2}\right)$ or in conjunction with a radical $\left(\text{as in } \frac{3+5}{\sqrt{1+3}}\right)$ or in a variety of other ways beyond elementary school mathematics.

H

height (1) The *length* of a perpendicular segment from one *side* of a geometric figure to a *parallel* side or from a *vertex* to the opposite side. (2) The line segment itself.

Height of 2-D figures are shown in red.

helper facts Well-known facts used to derive unknown facts. Doubles and combinations of 10 are key addition/subtraction helper facts. For example, knowing the doubles fact $6 + 6$ can help one derive $6 + 7$ by thinking $6 + 6 = 12$ and 1 more makes 13.

heptagon A 7-sided *polygon*.

Heptagons

hexagon A 6-sided *polygon*.

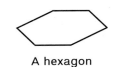

A hexagon

hierarchy of shapes A classification in which shapes are organized into categories and subcategories. For each category, every defining *attribute* of a shape in that category is a defining attribute of all shapes in its subcategories. A hierarchy is often shown in a diagram with the most general category at the top and arrows or lines connecting categories to their subcategories. See *quadrilateral* and below for examples.

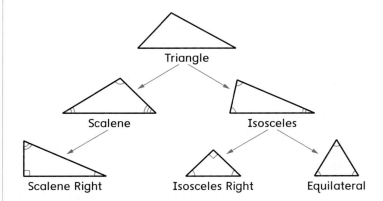

Hierarchy of triangles by angle size

Home Link In *Everyday Mathematics*, a suggested follow-up or enrichment activity to be done at home.

I

image A figure that is produced by a transformation of another figure called the *preimage*.

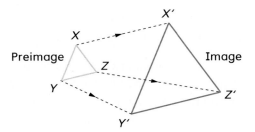

improper fraction A *fraction* with a numerator that is greater than or equal to its denominator. For example, $\frac{4}{3}, \frac{5}{2}, \frac{4}{4}$, and $\frac{24}{12}$ are improper fractions. *Everyday Mathematics* does not use this term. Improper fractions are referred to as fractions greater than or equal to 1.

inequality   A *number sentence* with a *relation symbol* other than =, such as >, <, ≥, ≤, or ≠. Compare *equation*.

input   (1) A number inserted into a *function machine*, which applies a rule to pair the input with an *output*. (2) Numbers or other information entered into a calculator or computer.

integer   A number in the set {. . . , −4, −3, −2, −1, 0, 1, 2, 3, 4, . . .}. A *whole number* or its opposite, where 0 is its own opposite. Compare *rational numbers, irrational numbers,* and *real numbers*.

interior of a figure   (1) The set of all points in a *plane* bounded by a closed *2-dimensional* figure such as a polygon or circle. (2) The set of all points in space bounded by a closed *3-dimensional* figure such as a polyhedron or sphere. The interior is usually not considered to be part of the figure.

interval   (1) The set of all numbers between two numbers *a* and *b*, which may include one or both of *a* and *b*. (2) All points and their coordinates on a *segment* of a *number line*. The interval between 0 and 1 on a number line is the unit interval.

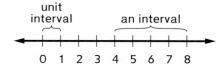

inverse operations   Two *operations* that undo the effects of each other. Addition and subtraction are inverse operations, as are multiplication and division.

irrational numbers   Numbers that cannot be written as *fractions* where both the numerator and denominator are *integers* and the denominator is not zero. For example, $\sqrt{2}$ and π are irrational numbers. In *standard notation,* an irrational number can only be written as a nonterminating, nonrepeating decimal. For example, $\pi = 3.141592653$ . . . continues forever without a repeating pattern. The number 1.10100100010000 . . . is irrational because its pattern does not repeat. Compare *rational numbers*.

isosceles trapezoid   A *trapezoid* with a pair of *base angles* that have the same measure. See *quadrilateral*.

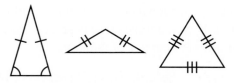

An isosceles trapezoid

isosceles triangle   A *triangle* with at least two equal-length *sides. Angles* opposite the equal-length sides are equal in measure.

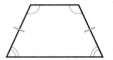

Isosceles triangles

iterate units   To repeat a *unit* without gaps or overlaps in order to measure. To measure *length,* units are placed end-to-end along a path. Unit iteration can also be used to measure *area* (by tiling) or volume (by filling).

K

key sequence   The order in which calculator keys are pressed to perform a calculation.

kilogram   A metric unit of *mass* equal to 1,000 grams. Though for over a century the kilogram has been defined based on platinum and iridium cylinder kept in Sevres, France, the National Institute of Standards and Technology has been working to define it by unchanging quantum properties of nature. A kilogram is about 2.2 pounds. See *Tables of Measures*.

kite   A *quadrilateral* that has two nonoverlapping pairs of *adjacent,* equal-length *sides.* Note that all four sides might be of equal length, so a *rhombus* is a kite.

Kites

L

label (1) A descriptive word or phrase used to put a number or numbers in context. Labels encourage children to associate numbers with real objects. (2) In a spreadsheet, a table, or graph, words or numbers providing information such as the title of the spreadsheet, the heading for a row or column, or the variable on an axis.

length The distance between two points on a *1-dimensional* figure. For example, the figure might be a line segment, an arc, or a curve on a map modeling a hiking path. Length is measured in units such as inches, kilometers, and miles.

length of day The *elapsed time* between sunrise and sunset.

line A *1-dimensional* straight path of points that extends forever in opposite directions. A line is named using two points on it or with a single, italicized lower-case letter such as *l*. In formal Euclidean geometry, line is an undefined geometric term.

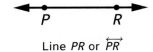

Line *PR* or $\overleftrightarrow{PR}$

line graph A graph in which *data* points are connected by line segments. Also known as broken-line graph.

line plot A sketch of *data* in which check marks, Xs, or other symbols above a labeled line show the *frequency* of each value.

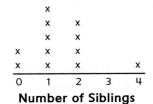

A line plot

line segment A part of a *line* between and including two points called endpoints of the *segment*. Same as *segment*. A line segment is often named by its endpoints.

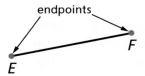

Segment *EF* or $\overline{EF}$

liquid volume An amount of liquid measured in units such as liters and gallons. Units of liquid *volume* are frequently used to measure *capacity*.

liter (L) A metric unit of *volume* or *capacity* equal to the volume of a cube with 10 cm long edges. 1 L = 1,000 mL = 1,000 cm³. A liter is a little larger than a quart. See *Tables of Measures*.

long In *Everyday Mathematics*, the *base-10 block* that is equivalent to ten 1-cm cubes. Sometimes called a rod.

long-term memory *Memory in a calculator* used by keys with an M on them, such as [M-] and [M+]. Numbers in long-term memory are not affected by calculations with keys without an M, which use *short-term memory*.

M

mass (1) A measure of the amount of matter in an object. Mass is not affected by gravity, so it is the same on Earth, the moon, or anywhere else in space. Mass is usually measured in grams, kilograms, and other metric units. Compare *weight*. (2) A standard object used in measuring weight or mass.

Math Boxes In *Everyday Mathematics*, a collection of problems to practice skills. Math Boxes for each lesson are in the *Math Journal.*

Math Message In *Everyday Mathematics,* an introduction to the day's lesson designed for students to complete independently.

mathematical argument An explanation that shows why a claim or *conjecture* is true or false using words, pictures, symbols, or other representations. For example, if a student makes a conjecture that $\frac{1}{2} + \frac{3}{5} = \frac{4}{7}$ is not true, the student might support that conjecture by arguing that $\frac{3}{5}$ is more than $\frac{1}{2}$, so the answer to $\frac{1}{2} + \frac{3}{5}$ is greater than 1. Since $\frac{4}{7}$ is less than 1, $\frac{1}{2} + \frac{3}{5} = \frac{4}{7}$ must not be true.

mathematical practice Ways of working with mathematics. Mathematical practices are habits and actions that help people use mathematics to solve problems, such as perseverance, abstract reasoning, and pattern generation.

mathematical structure A relationship among mathematical objects, operations, or relations; a mathematical *pattern,* framework, category, or *property.* For example, the *Distributive Property of Multiplication over Addition* is a key structure of arithmetic. The number grid illustrates some patterns and structures that exist in our base-ten number system.

maximum The largest amount; the greatest number in a set of *data.* Compare *minimum.*

measurement scale See *scale of a number line.*

measurement unit The reference unit used when measuring. Examples of basic units include inches for length, grams for mass or weight, cubic inches for volume or capacity, seconds for elapsed time, and degrees Celsius for change of temperature. Compound units include square centimeters for area and miles per hour for speed.

memory in a calculator Where numbers are stored in a calculator for use in later calculations. Most calculators have both a *short-term memory* and a *long-term memory.*

mental arithmetic Computation done by people "in their heads," either in whole or in part. In *Everyday Mathematics,* children learn a variety of mental-calculation *strategies* as they develop *automaticity* with basic facts and *fact power.*

Mental Math and Fluency In *Everyday Mathematics,* short, leveled exercises presented at the beginning of lessons. Mental Math and Fluency problems prepare children to think about math, warm up skills they need for the lesson, and build mental-arithmetic skills. They also help teachers assess individual strengths and weaknesses.

meter (m) The basic metric unit of *length* from which other metric units of length are derived. Originally, the meter was defined as $\frac{1}{10,000,000}$ of the distance from the North Pole to the equator along a meridian passing through Paris. From 1960 to 1983, the meter was redefined as 1,630,763.73 wavelengths of orange-red light from the element krypton. Today, the meter is defined as the distance light travels in a vacuum in $\frac{1}{299,792,458}$ second. One meter is equal to 10 decimeters, 100 centimeters, or 1,000 millimeters.

metric system The measurement system used in most countries and by virtually all scientists around the world. *Units* within the metric system are related by powers of 10. Units for *length* include millimeter, centimeter, meter, and kilometer; units for *mass* and *weight* include gram and kilogram; units for *volume* and *capacity* include milliliter and liter; and the unit for *temperature* change is degrees Celsius. See *Tables of Measures.*

minimum The smallest amount; the smallest number in a set of *data.* Compare *maximum.*

minuend In subtraction, the number from which another number is subtracted. For example, in $19 - 5 = 14$, the minuend is 19. Compare *subtrahend* and *difference.*

missing addend An *addend* that is unknown within an addition *equation.* A subtraction problem can be represented by an addition number sentence with a missing addend. See *unknown.*

missing factor A factor that is unknown within a multiplication equation. A division problem can be represented by a multiplication number sentence with a missing factor. See *unknown.*

mixed number A number that is written using both a *whole number* and a *fraction.* For example, $2\frac{1}{4}$ is a mixed number equal to $2 + \frac{1}{4}$.

model A mathematical representation or description of an object or a situation. For example, 60×3 can be a model for how much money is needed to buy 3 items that cost 60 cents each. A circle can be a model for the rim of a wheel. See *represent*.

multiple of a number *n* (1) A *product* of *n* and a *counting number*. For example, the multiples of 7 are 7, 14, 21, 28, . . . and the multiples of $\frac{1}{5}$ are $\frac{1}{5}, \frac{2}{5}, \frac{3}{5}$ . . . . (2) A product of *n* and an *integer*. For example, the multiples of 7 are . . . , −21, −14, −7, 0, 7, 14, 21, . . . and the multiples of π are . . . −3π, −2π, −π, 0, π, 2π, 3π, ...

multiplication counting principle The principle that one can determine the total number of ways to combine two or more independent possibilities by multiplying. For example, 5 shirts and 3 pairs of pants can be combined $5 \times 3 = 15$ different ways: (purple shirt, gray pants), (purple shirt, black pants), (purple shirt, tan pants), (green shirt, gray pants), (green shirt, black pants), (green shirt, tan pants), and so on.

multiplication fact The product of two *whole numbers* 0 through 10, such as $6 * 7 = 42$. See *arithmetic facts*.

multiplication square Same as *square number*.

multiplication symbols The number *a* multiplied by the number *b* is written in a variety of ways. Many mathematics textbooks and *Second* and *Third Grade Everyday Mathematics* use $\times$ as in $a \times b$. Beginning in fourth grade, *Everyday Mathematics* uses $*$ as in $a * b$. Other common ways to indicate multiplication are by a dot as in $a \cdot b$ and by juxtaposition as in *ab*, which is common in formulas and in algebra.

multiplication/division diagram A diagram used in *Everyday Mathematics* to *model* situations in which a total number is made up of equal-size groups. The diagram contains a number of groups, a number in each group, and a total number. Also called a multiplication diagram for short. See *situation diagram*.

rows	chairs per row	total chairs
15	25	?

A multiplication/division diagram

multiplication/division use class A category of problem situations that can be solved using multiplication or division or other methods such as counting or direct modeling. In *Everyday Mathematics,* these include *equal grouping/sharing, arrays* and *area*, rates and ratio, *scaling*, and *multiplication counting* situations.

multiplicative identity The number 1. The multiplicative identity is the number that when multiplied by any other number yields that other number. See *multiplicative inverse*.

multiplicative inverses Same as *reciprocals*.

N

name-collection box In *Everyday Mathematics,* a diagram that is used for collecting *equivalent names* for a number.

25
37 − 12   20 + 5
∕∕∕∕ ∕∕∕∕ ∕∕∕∕ ∕∕∕∕ ∕∕∕∕
twenty-five   veinticinco

natural numbers Same as *counting numbers*.

near doubles An addition fact strategy that involves relating a given fact to a nearby *doubles fact* to help solve the fact. For example, $7 + 8$ can be solved by thinking $7 + 7 = 14$, then $14 + 1 = 15$. It can also be solved by thinking $8 + 8 = 16$, then $16 − 1 = 15$.

near squares A special case of adding or subtracting a group involving using a *multiplication square* as a *helper fact*. For example, to solve 7×8, children may use 8×8 as a helper fact and then subtract a group of 8 from the product, 64, to get 56.

negative numbers Numbers less than 0; the opposites of the *positive numbers,* commonly written as a positive number preceded by a −. Negative numbers are plotted left of 0 on a horizontal *number line* or below 0 on a vertical number line.

nested parentheses   *Parentheses* within parentheses in an *expression*. Expressions are evaluated from within the innermost parentheses outward. For example: $4 * (4 - [2 + 1]) = 4 * (4 - 3) = 4 * 1 = 4$.

net   A *2-dimensional* figure created to represent a *3-dimensional* figure by cutting and unfolding or separating its faces and sides. A 2-dimensional figure that can be folded to form all the faces of a closed 3-dimensional figure is called a net. For example, if a cereal box is cut along some of its edges and laid out flat, it will form a net for the box.

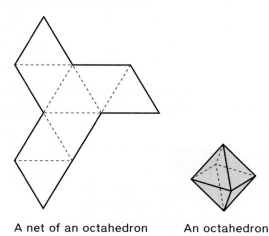

A net of an octahedron   An octahedron

n-gon   A *polygon,* where *n* is the number of *sides.* Polygons that do not have special names like squares and pentagons are usually named using *n*-gon notation, such as 13-gon or 100-gon.

nonagon   A 9-sided *polygon.*

nonconvex polygon   Same as *concave polygon.*

nondefining attributes of a shape   Characteristics of a shape that are not required by the definition of the shape. Size, color, and orientation are nondefining attributes of shapes. Compare *defining attributes of a shape.*

number family   Same as *fact family.*

number grid   A table in which consecutive numbers are arranged in *rows,* usually 10 *columns* per row. A move from one number to the next within a row is a change of 1; a move from one number to the next within a column is a change of 10.

−9	−8	−7	−6	−5	−4	−3	−2	−1	0
1	2	3	4	5	6	7	8	9	10
11	12	13	14	15	16	17	18	19	20
21	22	23	24	25	26	27	28	29	30
31	32	33	34	35	36	37	38	39	40
41	42	43	44	45	46	47	48	49	50
51	52	53	54	55	56	57	58	59	60
61	62	63	64	65	66	67	68	69	70
71	72	73	74	75	76	77	78	79	80
81	82	83	84	85	86	87	88	89	90
91	92	93	94	95	96	97	98	99	100
101	102	103	104	105	106	107	108	109	110

A number grid

number line   A *line* on which points are indicated by *tick marks* that are usually at regularly spaced intervals from a starting point called the *origin,* the zero point, or simply 0. Numbers are associated with the tick marks on a *scale* defined by the unit interval from 0 to 1. Every *real number* locates a point on the line, and every point corresponds to a real number. See *real numbers.*

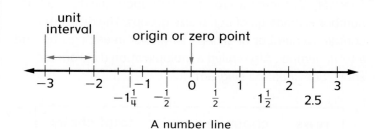

A number line

number model A *number sentence, expression,* or other representation that fits a *number story* or situation. For example, the number story "Sally had $5, and then she earned $8" can be modeled as the number sentence $5 + 8 = 13$, as the expression $5 + 8$, or by

$$\begin{array}{r} 5. \\ + 8 \\ \hline 13 \end{array}$$

number sentence Two *expressions* with a relation symbol, such as $=$, $<$, or $>$.

$$5 + 5 = 10 \qquad 16 \leq a * b$$
$$2 - ? = 8 \qquad a^2 + b^2 = c^2$$

Number sentences

number sequence A list of numbers, often generated by a rule. In *Everyday Mathematics*, children explore number sequences using *Frames-and-Arrows* diagrams.

$$1, 2, 3, 4, 5, \ldots \qquad 1, 4, 9, 16, 25, \ldots$$
$$1, 2, 1, 2, 1, \ldots \qquad 1, 3, 5, 7, 9, \ldots$$

Number sequences

number story A story that involves numbers and one or more explicit or implicit questions. For example, "I have 7 crayons in my desk; Carrie gave me 8 more crayons," is a number story.

number-and-word notation A notation consisting of the significant digits of a number and words for the *place value*. For example, 27 billion is number-and-word notation for 27,000,000,000. Compare *standard notation*.

numeral (1) A combination of *base-10 digits* used to express a number. (2) A word, symbol, or figure that represents a number. For example, six, VI, ⅲⅰⅰ, and 6 are all numerals that represent the same number.

numeration A method of numbering or of reading and writing numbers. In *Everyday Mathematics*, numeration activities include counting, writing numbers, identifying equivalent names for numbers in *name-collection boxes*, exchanging coins such as 5 pennies for 1 nickel, and renaming numbers in computation.

numerator The *dividend a* in a *fraction* $\frac{a}{b}$ or a/b. In a *part-whole fraction,* the *whole* is divided into a number of equal parts and the numerator is the number of equal parts being considered. Compare *denominator.*

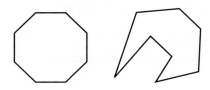

octagon An 8-sided *polygon.*

Octagons

octahedron A *polyhedron* with 8 *faces.* An octahedron with 8 *equilateral triangle* faces is one of the five *regular polyhedrons.*

odd number (1) A *counting number* that is not divisible by 2. (2) An *integer* that is not divisible by 2. Compare *even number.*

open number line A line on which one can indicate points by *tick marks* and labels that are not spaced at regular intervals. Like *number lines,* there is an order and an implied *origin,* but unlike number lines, there is no *scale* or unit interval. Open number lines are useful *tools* for solving problems.

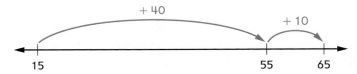

An open number line used to solve $15 + 50$

open sentence A *number sentence* with one or more *variables* that is neither true nor false. For example, $9 + \underline{\quad} = 15$, $? - 24 < 10$, and $7 = x + y$ are open sentences. See *variable* and *unknown.*

operation An action performed on one or more mathematical objects such as numbers, *variables,* or *expressions* to produce another mathematical object. Addition, subtraction, multiplication, and division are the four basic arithmetic operations. Taking a square root, squaring a number, and multiplying both sides of an *equation* by the same number are also operations. In *Everyday Mathematics,* children learn about many operations along with procedures, or *algorithms,* for carrying them out.

operation symbol   A symbol used in *expressions* and *number sentences* to stand for a particular mathematical operation. Symbols for common arithmetic operations are: addition $+$; subtraction $-$; multiplication $\times$, $*$, $\bullet$; division $\div$, $/$; powering$^\wedge$. See *General Reference*.

opposite sides in a quadrilateral   Two sides in a *quadrilateral* that do not share a vertex.

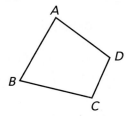

Sides *AB* and *DC*; sides *BC* and *AD* are pairs of opposite sides.

opposite-change rule for addition   An addition *algorithm* in which a number is added to one *addend* and subtracted from the other addend. Compare *same-change rule for subtraction*.

order   To arrange things according to a specific rule, often from smallest to largest, or from largest to smallest. See *sequence*.

order of operations   A set of rules that tell the order in which operations in an expression should be carried out. See *General Reference*.

ordered pair   (1) Two numbers, or coordinates, used to locate a point on a rectangular coordinate grid. The first coordinate *x* gives the position along the horizontal axis of the grid, and the second coordinate *y* gives the position along the vertical axis. The pair is written (x, y). (2) Any pair of objects or numbers in a particular order, as in letter-number spreadsheet cell names or map coordinates or functions given as sets of pairs of numbers.

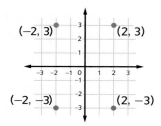

Ordered pairs

ordinal number   A number describing the position or order of something in a *sequence*, such as first, third, or tenth. Ordinal numbers are commonly used in dates, as in "May fifth" instead of "May five". Compare *cardinal number*.

origin   The zero point in a coordinate system. On a *number line*, the origin is the point at 0. On a coordinate grid, the origin is the point $(0, 0)$ where the two axes intersect.

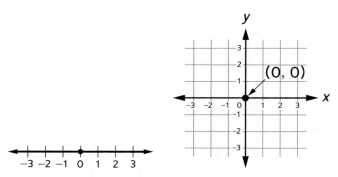

The points at 0 and $(0, 0)$ are origins.

outcome   A possible result of a chance experiment or situation. For example, HEADS and TAILS are the two possible outcomes of flipping a coin.

output   (1) A number paired to an *input* by a *function machine* applying a rule. (2) Numbers or other information displayed or produced by calculator or computer.

P

P.M.   The abbreviation for post meridiem, meaning "after the middle of the day" in Latin. From noon to midnight.

pan balance   A measuring device used to weigh objects or compare *weights* or *masses*. Simple pan balances have two pans suspended at opposite ends of a bar resting on a fulcrum at its midpoint. When the weights or masses of the objects in the pans are *equal*, the bar is level.

A pan balance

parallel   *Lines,* line segments, or rays in the same *plane* are parallel if they never cross or meet, no matter how far they are extended. Two planes are parallel if they never cross or meet. A line and a plane are parallel if they never cross or meet. The symbol ∥ means is parallel to.

parallelogram   A *trapezoid* that has two pairs of *parallel* sides. See *quadrilateral.*

Parallelograms

parentheses   See *grouping symbols.*

partial-products multiplication   (1) A multiplication *algorithm* in which partial products are computed by multiplying the value of each digit in one factor by the value of each digit in the other factor. The final *product* is the sum of the partial products. (2) A similar method for multiplying mixed numbers.

partial-sums addition   An addition *algorithm* in which separate *sums* are computed for each *place value* of the numbers and then added to get a final sum.

partition   In geometry, to divide a shape into smaller shapes. For example, a *polygon* can be partitioned into triangles. Shapes can be partitioned *into equal shares* to represent *fractions.* Partitioning can also be used to find *length, area,* or *volume.*

parts-and-total diagram   In *Everyday Mathematics,* a diagram to *model* situations in which two or more quantities (parts) are combined to make a total quantity. See *situation diagram.*

Total	
13	
Part	Part
8	**?**

Parts-and-total diagram for 13 − 8 = ?

parts-and-total situation   A situation in which a quantity is made up of two or more distinct parts. For example, the following is a parts-and-total situation: "There are 15 girls and 12 boys in Mrs. Dorn's class. How many children are there in all?". See *addition/subtraction use class.*

part-whole fraction   A *fraction* that describes a portion of an object or collection divided into equal parts. In *Everyday Mathematics,* the object or collection is called the *whole* and is the *denominator* of the fraction. The *numerator* is the number of parts of the whole. For example, in the situation Padma ate $\frac{2}{5}$ of the pizza, the whole is 5 pieces of pizza (a whole pizza divided into 5 parts) and Padma ate 2 of the 5 parts.

pattern   A repetitive order or arrangement. In *Everyday Mathematics,* children mainly explore visual and number patterns in which elements are arranged so that what comes next can be predicted.

pentagon   A 5-sided *polygon.*

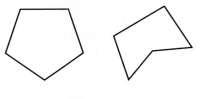

Pentagons

per   For each, as in ten chairs per row or six tickets per family.

perimeter   The distance around the boundary of a *2-dimensional* figure. The perimeter of a circle is called its circumference. Perimeter comes from the Greek words for "around measure".

pictograph   See *picture graph.*

picture graph   A graph constructed with icons representing *data* points. They are sometimes called scaled picture graphs when each icon represents more than 1 data point.

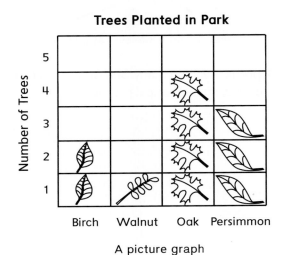

A picture graph

place value A system that gives a *digit* a value according to its position, or place, in a number. In our standard, *base-ten (decimal)* system for writing numbers, each place has a value 10 times that of the place to its right and one-tenth the value of the place to its left.

thousands	hundreds	tens	ones	.	tenths	hundredths

plane A *2-dimensional* flat *surface* that extends forever in all directions. In formal Euclidean geometry, plane is an undefined geometric term.

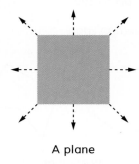

A plane

plane figure A set of points that is entirely contained in a single plane. For example, squares, pentagons, circles, parabolas, lines, and rays are plane figures; cones, cubes, and prisms are not.

plot To draw a point or a curve on a number line, coordinate grid, or graph. The points plotted can come from lists, mathematical relationships, or *data*.

point An exact location in space. Points are usually labeled with capital letters. In formal Euclidean geometry, point is an undefined geometric term.

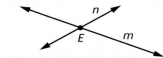

Lines *m* and *n* intersect at point *E*.

poly- A prefix meaning many. See *General Reference, Prefixes* for specific numerical prefixes.

polygon A plane figure formed by *line segments (sides)* that meet only at their endpoints (*vertices*) to make a closed path. The sides may not cross one another.

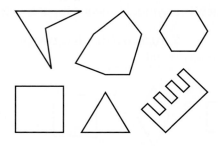

Polygons

polyhedron A closed *3-dimensional* figure formed by *polygons* with their *interiors (faces)* that may meet but do not cross. Plural is polyhedrons or polyhedra.

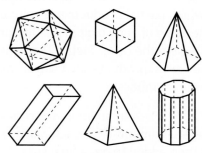

Polyhedrons

positive numbers Numbers greater than 0; the opposites of the *negative numbers*. Positive numbers are plotted to the right of 0 on a horizontal *number line* or above 0 on a vertical number line.

poster In *Everyday Mathematics*, a page displaying a collection of illustrated numerical data. A poster may be used as a source of *data* for developing *number stories*.

precise Of a measurement or other quantity, having a high degree of exactness. A measurement to the nearest inch is more precise than a measurement to the nearest foot. A measurement's precision depends on the *unit* scale of the *tool* used to obtain it. The smaller the unit is, the more precise a measure can be. For instance, a ruler with $\frac{1}{8}$ inch markings can give a more precise measurement than a ruler with $\frac{1}{2}$-inch markings. Compare *accurate*.

preimage The original figure in a transformation. Compare *image*.

prime number A *counting number* greater than 1 that has exactly two *whole-number factors,* 1 and itself. For example, 7 is a prime number because its only factors are 1 and 7. The first five prime numbers are 2, 3, 5, 7, and 11. Compare *composite number.*

prism A polyhedron with two *parallel* and *congruent polygonal bases* and lateral *faces* shaped like *parallelograms*. Right prisms have rectangular lateral faces. Prisms get their names from the shape of their bases.

A triangular prism   A rectangular prism   A hexagonal prism

product The result of multiplying two or more numbers, called *factors*. For example, in $4 * 3 = 12$, the product is 12.

property (1) A generalized statement about a mathematical relationship, such as the *Distributive Property of Multiplication over Addition.* (2) Same as *attribute*.

pyramid A *polyhedron* with a polygonal *base* and *triangular* other *faces* that meet at a common *vertex* called the *apex*. Pyramids get their names from the shapes of their bases.

quadrangle Same as *quadrilateral.*

quadrilateral A 4-sided *polygon*. Squares, rectangles, *parallelograms, rhombuses, kites,* and *trapezoids* are organized by *defining attributes* into a *hierarchy of shapes.*

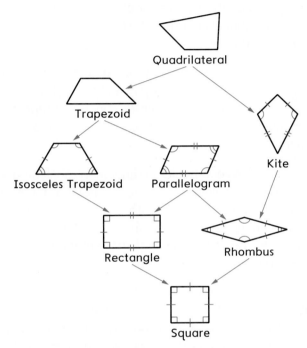

A hierarchy of quadrilaterals

quantity A number with a unit, usually a measurement or count.

Quick Looks An *Everyday Mathematics* routine in which an image of a quantity is displayed for 2-3 seconds and then removed. Quick Looks encourage children to *subitize, compose* and *decompose* numbers in flexible ways, and to develop strategies for *addition* and *multiplication facts.*

quotient The result of dividing one number by another number. For example, in $10 / 5 = 2$, the quotient is 2. Compare *dividend* and *divisor.*

$$\text{dividend} \quad \overset{\text{divisor}}{\underset{35 / 5 = 7}{\downarrow}} \quad \text{quotient}$$

$$\text{dividend} \quad \overset{\text{divisor}}{\underset{40 \div 8 = 5}{\downarrow}} \quad \text{quotient}$$

quotient ⟶ 3
divisor ⟶ 12)‾36‾ ⟵ dividend

R

range (1) The *difference* between the *maximum* and the *minimum* in a *data* set. The range is a measure of how spread out a distribution is. (2) The interval between the maximum and the minimum in a set of data.

rational counting Counting using one-to-one matching. For example, counting a number of chairs, people, or crackers. In rational counting, the last number gives the *cardinality* of the set.

rational numbers Numbers that can be written in the form $\frac{a}{b}$, where *a* and *b* are *integers* and $b \neq 0$. The *decimal* form of a rational number either terminates or repeats. For example, $\frac{2}{3}$, $-\frac{2}{3}$, 0.5, 20.5, and 0.333 . . . are rational numbers.

r-by-c array A rectangular arrangement of elements with *r* rows and *c* elements per row. Among other things, an *r*-by-*c* array models *r* sets with *c* objects per set. Although listing rows before *columns* is arbitrary, it is in keeping with the order used in matrix notation, which children will study later in school.

real numbers All *rational* and *irrational numbers;* all numbers that can be written as *decimals.* For every real number there is a corresponding point on a *number line,* and for every point on the number line there is a real number.

reciprocals Two numbers whose *product* is 1. For example, 5 and $\frac{1}{5}$, $\frac{3}{5}$ and $\frac{5}{3}$, and 0.2 and 5 are pairs of reciprocals. Same as *multiplicative inverses.*

rectangle A *parallelogram* with four *right angles.* All rectangles are both parallelograms and *isosceles trapezoids.* See *quadrilateral.*

rectangular array An arrangement of objects in *rows* and *columns* that form a rectangular shape. All rows have the same number of objects, and all columns have the same number of objects. See r-*by-*c *array.*

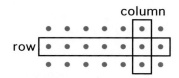

A rectangular array

rectangular prism A *prism* with rectangular *bases.* The four *faces* that are not bases are formed by either *rectangles* or *parallelograms.* For example, a rectangular prism in which all sides are rectangular models a shoebox.

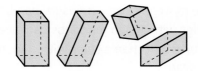

Rectangular prisms

rectangular pyramid A *pyramid* with a rectangular *base.*

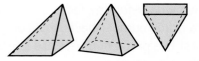

Rectangular pyramids

rectilinear figure In *Everyday Mathematics,* a *polygon* with a right angle at each vertex.

Rectilinear figures

reference frame A system for locating numbers within a given context, usually with reference to an *origin* or zero point. For example, *number lines,* clocks, calendars, temperature scales, and maps are reference frames.

regular polygon A *polygon* in which all sides are the same *length* and all interior *angles* have the same measure.

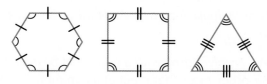

Regular polygons

regular polyhedron A *polyhedron* whose *faces* are all formed by *congruent regular polygons* and in which the same number of faces meet at each *vertex*. There are only five. They are called the Platonic solids, and are shown below.

Tetrahedron	Cube	Octahedron
(4 equilateral triangles)	(6 squares)	(8 equilateral triangles)

Dodecahedron	Icosahedron
(12 regular pentagons)	(20 equilateral triangles)

relation symbol A symbol used to express a relationship between two quantities, figures, or sets, such as $\leq$, $\parallel$, or $\subset$. See *General Reference, Symbols*.

remainder An amount left over when one number is divided by another number. For example, in $16 / 3 \rightarrow 5$ R1, the *quotient* is 5 and the remainder is 1.

repeating decimal A *decimal* in which one digit or block of digits is repeated without end. For example, 0.3333. . . and $0.\overline{147}$ are repeating decimals. Compare *terminating decimal*.

represent To show, symbolize, or stand for something. For example, numbers can be represented using base-10 blocks, spoken words, or written numerals. See *model*.

rhombus A *parallelogram* with four sides of the same length. All rhombuses are both parallelograms and *kites*. See *quadrilateral*.

Rhombuses

right angle An *angle* with a measure of 90°.

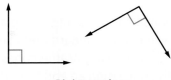

Right angles

right triangle A *triangle* with a right angle.

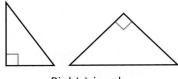

Right triangles

rote counting Reciting a string of number words by rote, without necessarily understanding their significance. See *skip counting*.

rotation (1) A turn about an axis or point. (2) Point P′ is a rotation *image* of point P around a center of rotation C if P′ is on the *circle* with center C and radius CP. If all the points in one figure are rotation images of all the points in another figure around the same center of rotation and with the same *angle* of rotation, then the figures are rotation images. The center can be inside or outside of the original image. Reflections, rotations, and translations are types of isometric transformations. (3) If all points on the image of a 3-dimensional figure are rotation images through the same angle around a point or a line called the axis of rotation, then the image is a rotation image of the original figure.

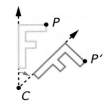

round (1) To *approximate* a number to make it easier to use, or to make it better reflect the *precision* of the data. "Rounding up" means to approximate larger than the actual value. "Rounding down" means to approximate smaller than the actual value. (2) Circular in shape.

round to the nearest To round a number up or down in a particular place, depending on which approximation is closer to the actual value. For example, 1,647 rounded to the nearest hundred is 1,600. Rounding 1.376 to the nearest tenth yields 1.4.

row (1) A horizontal arrangement of objects or numbers in an *array* or table. (2) A horizontal section of cells in a spreadsheet.

rubric   A tool used to categorize work based on its quality.

ruler   (1) Traditionally, a wood, metal, or plastic strip *partitioned* into same-size standard *units*, such as inches or centimeters. (2) In *Everyday Mathematics,* a tool for measuring length comprising an end-to-end collection of same-size units.

S

same-change rule for subtraction   A subtraction *algorithm* in which the same number is added to or subtracted from both numbers.

scale   (1) A multiplicative comparison between the relative sizes or numbers of things. (2) Same as scale factor. (3) A tool for measuring *weight* and *mass*.

scale of a number line   The unit interval on a *number line* or measuring device. The scales on this ruler are 1 millimeter on the left side and $\frac{1}{16}$ inch on the right side.

scaled picture graph   A graph constructed with icons each representing the same number of multiple *data* points. For example, each icon of a car on a graph may stand for 1,000 cars. See *picture graph*.

scalene triangle   A *triangle* with *sides* of three different lengths. The three *angles* of a scalene triangle have different measures.

segment   Same as *line segment*.

sequence   An *ordered* list of numbers, often with an underlying rule that may be used to generate numbers in the list. *Frames-and-Arrows* diagrams can be used to represent sequences.

set   A collection or group of objects, numbers, or other items.

short-term memory   *Memory in a calculator* used to store values for immediate calculation. Short-term memory is usually cleared with a [C], [AC], [Clear], or similar key. Compare *long-term memory*.

side   (1) One of the *line segments* that make up a *polygon*. (2) One of the rays or segments that form an *angle*. (3) One of the *faces* of a *polyhedron*.

situation diagram   In *Everyday Mathematics,* a diagram used to organize information in a problem situation in one of the *addition/subtraction* or *multiplication/division use classes*.

Total
7

Part	Part
2	5

Susie has 2 pink balloons and 5 yellow balloons.
She has 7 balloons in all.

skip counting   Counting by intervals, such as 2s, 5s or 10s. See *rote counting*.

slate   In *Everyday Mathematics,* a lap-size (about 8 inches by 11 inches) chalkboard or whiteboard that children use for recording responses during group exercises and informal group assessments.

solid   See *geometric solid*.

solution of a problem   (1) The answer to a problem. (2) The answer to a problem together with the method by which that answer was obtained.

solution of an open sentence   A value or values for the *variable(s)* in an *open sentence* that make the sentence true. For example, 7 is a solution of $5 + n = 12$. Although equations are not necessarily open sentences, the solution of an open sentence is commonly referred to as a solution of an equation.

sphere   The set of all points in space that are an equal distance from a fixed point called the center of the sphere. The distance from the center to the sphere is the radius of the sphere. The diameter of a sphere is twice its radius. Points inside a sphere are not part of the sphere.

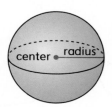

A sphere

Spiral Snapshot   In *Everyday Mathematics,* an overview of nearby lessons that address one of the Goals for Mathematical Content in the Focus part of the lesson. It appears in the Lesson Opener.

Spiral Trace   In *Everyday Mathematics,* an overview of work in the current unit and nearby units on selected Standards for Mathematical Content. It appears in the Unit Organizer.

Spiral Tracker   In *Everyday Mathematics,* an online database that shows complete details about learning trajectories for all goals and standards.

square   A *rectangle* with four sides of equal length. All squares are both rectangles and *rhombuses.* See *quadrilateral.*

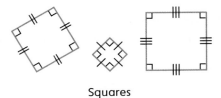

Squares

square array   A *rectangular array* with the same number of rows as columns. For example, 16 objects will form a square array with 4 objects in each row and 4 objects in each column.

A square array

square corner   Same as *right angle.*

square number   A *figurate number* that is the *product* of a counting number and itself. For example, 25 is a square number because $25 = 5 * 5$. A square number can be represented by a *square array* and as a number squared, such as $25 = 5^2$.

square of a number *n*   The product of *n* and itself, commonly written n^2. For example, $81 = 9 * 9 = 9^2$ and $3.5^2 = 3.5 * 3.5 = 12.25$.

square pyramid   A *pyramid* with a square *base.*

square unit   A *unit* to measure *area.* A model of a square unit is a square with each side a related unit of *length.* For example, a square inch is the area of a square with 1-inch sides. Square units are often labeled as the length unit squared. For example, 1 cm^2 is read "1 square centimeter" or "1 centimeter squared".

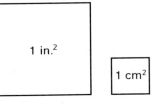

standard form   Same as *standard notation.*

standard notation   The most common way of representing *whole numbers, integers,* and decimals. Standard notation for real numbers is *base-ten place-value* numeration. For example, standard notation for three hundred fifty-six is 356. Same as *decimal notation.* Compare *number-and-word notation.*

standard unit   A *unit* of measure that has been defined by a recognized authority, such as a government or National Institute of Standards and Technology. For example, inches, meters, miles, seconds, pounds, grams, and acres are all standard units.

straightedge   A tool used to draw *line segments* more accurately than by freehand. Strictly speaking, a straightedge does not have a measuring *scale* on it, so one ignores the marks if using a ruler as a straightedge.

strategy   An approach to a problem that may be general, like "divide and conquer," or more specific, like "adding a group". Compare *algorithm.*

subitize   To recognize a quantity without needing to count. For example, many children can instantly recognize the number of dots on a rolled die without needing to count them. In *Everyday Mathematics, Quick Looks* help children develop the ability to subitize and use relationships between quantities to find more complex totals.

subtracting a group   A *multiplication fact* strategy that involves using a *helper fact* with a larger factor. For example, 9×6 can be solved by starting from the helper fact 10×6 and subtracting one group of 6 from the product, 60, to get 54. This makes use of the *Distributive Property of Multiplication over Addition.*

subtrahend   The number being taken away in a subtraction problem. For example, in $15 - 5 = 10$, the subtrahend is 5. Compare *difference* and *minuend.*

sum   The result of adding two or more numbers. For example, in $5 + 3 = 8$, the sum is 8.

surface   (1) The boundary of a *3-dimensional* object. (2) Any *2-dimensional* layer, such as a *plane* or a *face* of a polyhedron.

survey   (1) A study that collects *data* by asking people questions. (2) Any study that collects data. Surveys are commonly used to study demographics such as people's characteristics, behaviors, interests, and opinions.

Tables of Measures

Metric System

Units of Length

1 kilometer (km)	= 1,000 meters (m)
1 meter	= 10 decimeters (dm)
	= 100 centimeters (cm)
	= 1,000 millimeters (mm)
1 decimeter	= 10 centimeters
1 centimeter	= 10 millimeters

Units of Area

1 square meter (m²)	= 100 square decimeters (dm²)
	= 10,000 square centimeters (cm²)
1 square decimeter	= 100 square centimeters
1 are (a)	= 100 square meters
1 hectare (ha)	= 100 ares
1 square kilometer (km²)	= 100 hectares

Units of Volume and Capacity

1 cubic meter (m³)	= 1,000 cubic decimeters (dm³)
	= 1,000,000 cubic centimeters (cm³)
1 cubic centimeter	= 1,000 cubic millimeters (mm³)
1 kiloliter (kL)	= 1,000 liters (L)
1 liter	= 1,000 milliliters (mL)

Units of Mass and Weight

1 metric ton (t)	= 1,000 kilograms (kg)
1 kilogram	= 1,000 grams (g)
1 gram	= 1,000 milligrams (mg)

U.S. Customary System

Units of Length

1 mile (mi)	= 1,760 yards (yd)
	= 5,280 feet (ft)
1 yard	= 3 feet
	= 36 inches (in.)
1 foot	= 12 inches

Units of Area

1 square yard (yd²)	= 9 square feet (ft²)
	= 1,296 square inches (in.²)
1 square foot	= 144 square inches
1 acre	= 43,560 square feet
1 square mile (mi²)	= 640 acres

Units of Volume and Capacity

1 cubic yard (yd³)	= 27 cubic feet (ft³)
1 cubic foot	= 1,728 cubic inches (in.³)
1 gallon (gal)	= 4 quarts (qt)
1 quart	= 2 pints (pt)
1 pint	= 2 cups (c)
1 cup	= 8 fluid ounces (fl oz)
1 fluid ounce	= 2 tablespoons (tbs)
1 tablespoon	= 3 teaspoons (tsp)

Units of Mass and Weight

1 ton (T)	= 2,000 pounds (lb)
1 pound	= 16 ounces (oz)

System Equivalents (Conversion Factors)

1 inch ≈ 2.5 centimeter (2.54)	1 liter ≈ 1.1 quarts (1.057)
1 kilometer ≈ 0.6 mile (0.621)	1 ounce ≈ 28 grams (28.350)
1 mile ≈ 1.6 kilometers (1.609)	1 kilogram ≈ 2.2 pounds (2.21)
1 meter ≈ 39 inches (39.37)	1 hectare ≈ 2.5 acres (2.47)

Body Measures

1 *digit* is about the width of a finger.

1 *hand* is about the width of the palm and thumb.

1 *span* is about the distance from the tip of the thumb to the tip of the first (index) finger of an outstretched hand.

1 *cubit* is about the length from the elbow to the tip of the extended middle finger.

1 *yard* is about the distance from the center of the chest to the tip of the extended middle finger of an outstretched arm.

1 *fathom* is about the length from fingertip to fingertip of outstretched arms. Also called an arm span.

Units of Time

1 century	= 100 years
1 decade	= 10 years
1 year (yr)	= 12 months
	= 52 weeks (plus one or two days)
	= 365 days (366 days in a leap year)
1 month (mo)	= 28, 29, 30, or 31 days
1 week (wk)	= 7 days
1 day (d)	= 24 hours
1 hour (hr)	= 60 minutes
1 minute (min)	= 60 seconds (s or sec)

Unpacking the Common Core State Standards

The **Common Core State Standards** include two groups of standards: Standards for Mathematical Content and Standards for Mathematical Practice. The Content Standards define the mathematical content to be mastered at each grade. The Practice Standards define the processes and habits of mind students need to develop as they learn the content for their grade level.

The Content Standards are organized into **Domains**, large groups of related standards. Within each Domain are **Clusters**, smaller groups of related standards. The **Standards** themselves define what students should understand and be able to do by the end of that grade.

The summary page from the Common Core State Standards for Grade 3 is on the following page. This page summarizes the mathematical content that children should learn in Grade 3.

The chart beginning on page EM3 lists the Common Core State Standards for Mathematical Content with corresponding *Everyday Mathematics* **Goals for Mathematical Content (GMC)**.

The chart beginning on page EM8 lists the Common Core State Standards for Mathematical Practice with corresponding *Everyday Mathematics* **Goals for Mathematical Practice (GMP)**.

Common Core State Standards

Standards for Mathematical Content

Domain Operations and Algebraic Thinking 3.OA	*Everyday Mathematics* **Goals for Mathematical Content**
Cluster Represent and solve problems involving multiplication and division.	
3.OA.1 Interpret products of whole numbers, e.g., interpret 5 × 7 as the total number of objects in 5 groups of 7 objects each. *For example, describe a context in which a total number of objects can be expressed as 5 × 7.*	**GMC** Interpret multiplication in terms of equal groups.

"…larger groups of related standards. Standards from different domains may…be…related."

"…groups of related standards… Standards from different clusters may…be… related, because mathematics is a connected subject."

the first standard under this Domain

program goals for finger-grained tracking of student progress

The table on pages EM8–EM11 may be used to trace the *Everyday Mathematics* **Goals for Mathematical Practice** as they unpack the Standards for Mathematical Practice.

The Grade 3 Content Standards are introduced in the CCSS document on page 21, as follows:

In Grade 3, instructional time should focus on four critical areas: (1) developing understanding of multiplication and division and strategies for multiplication and division within 100; (2) developing understanding of fractions, especially unit fractions (fractions with numerator 1); (3) developing understanding of the structure of rectangular arrays and of area; and (4) describing and analyzing two-dimensional shapes.

(1) Students develop an understanding of the meanings of multiplication and division of whole numbers through activities and problems involving equal-sized groups, arrays, and area models; multiplication is finding an unknown product, and division is finding an unknown factor in these situations. For equal-sized group situations, division can require finding the unknown number of groups or the unknown group size. Students use properties of operations to calculate products of whole numbers, using increasingly sophisticated strategies based on these properties to solve multiplication and division problems involving single-digit factors. By comparing a variety of solution strategies, students learn the relationship between multiplication and division.

(2) Students develop an understanding of fractions, beginning with unit fractions. Students view fractions in general as being built out of unit fractions, and they use fractions along with visual fraction models to represent parts of a whole. Students understand that the size of a fractional part is relative to the size of the whole. For example, 1/2 of the paint in a small bucket could be less paint than 1/3 of the paint in a larger bucket, but 1/3 of a ribbon is longer than 1/5 of the same ribbon because when the ribbon is divided into 3 equal parts, the parts are longer than when the ribbon is divided into 5 equal parts. Students are able to use fractions to represent numbers equal to, less than, and greater than one. They solve problems that involve comparing fractions by using visual fraction models and strategies based on noticing equal numerators or denominators.

(3) Students recognize area as an attribute of two-dimensional regions. They measure the area of a shape by finding the total number of same size units of area required to cover the shape without gaps or overlaps, a square with sides of unit length being the standard unit for measuring area. Students understand that rectangular arrays can be decomposed into identical rows or into identical columns. By decomposing rectangles into rectangular arrays of squares, students connect area to multiplication, and justify using multiplication to determine the area of a rectangle.

(4) Students describe, analyze, and compare properties of two-dimensional shapes. They compare and classify shapes by their sides and angles, and connect these with definitions of shapes. Students also relate their fraction work to geometry by expressing the area of part of a shape as a unit fraction of the whole.

Common Core State Standards

Standards for Mathematical Content

Domain Operations and Algebraic Thinking 3.OA	*Everyday Mathematics* Goals for Mathematical Content

Cluster Represent and solve problems involving multiplication and division.

3.OA.1 Interpret products of whole numbers, e.g., interpret 5×7 as the total number of objects in 5 groups of 7 objects each. *For example, describe a context in which a total number of objects can be expressed as 5×7.*	**GMC** Interpret multiplication in terms of equal groups.
3.OA.2 Interpret whole-number quotients of whole numbers, e.g., interpret $56 \div 8$ as the number of objects in each share when 56 objects are partitioned equally into 8 shares, or as a number of shares when 56 objects are partitioned into equal shares of 8 objects each. *For example, describe a context in which a number of shares or a number of groups can be expressed as $56 \div 8$.*	**GMC** Interpret division in terms of equal shares or equal groups.
3.OA.3 Use multiplication and division within 100 to solve word problems in situations involving equal groups, arrays, and measurement quantities, e.g., by using drawings and equations with a symbol for the unknown number to represent the problem.[1]	**GMC** Use multiplication and division to solve number stories. **GMC** Model number stories involving multiplication and division.
3.OA.4 Determine the unknown whole number in a multiplication or division equation relating three whole numbers. *For example, determine the unknown number that makes the equation true in each of the equations $8 \times ? = 48$, $5 = \_\_ \div 3, 6 \times 6 = ?$*	**GMC** Determine the unknown in multiplication and division equations.

Cluster Understand properties of multiplication and the relationship between multiplication and division.

3.OA.5 Apply properties of operations as strategies to multiply and divide.[2] *Examples: If $6 \times 4 = 24$ is known, then $4 \times 6 = 24$ is also known. (Commutative property of multiplication.) $3 \times 5 \times 2$ can be found by $3 \times 5 = 15$, then $15 \times 2 = 30$, or by $5 \times 2 = 10$, then $3 \times 10 = 30$. (Associative property of multiplication.) Knowing that $8 \times 5 = 40$ and $8 \times 2 = 16$, one can find 8×7 as $8 \times (5 + 2) = (8 \times 5) + (8 \times 2) = 40 + 16 = 56$. (Distributive property.)*	**GMC** Apply properties of operations to multiply or divide.
3.OA.6 Understand division as an unknown-factor problem. *For example, find $32 \div 8$ by finding the number that makes 32 when multiplied by 8.*	**GMC** Understand division as an unknown factor problem.

Cluster Multiply and divide within 100.

| 3.OA.7 Fluently multiply and divide within 100, using strategies such as the relationship between multiplication and division (e.g., knowing that $8 \times 5 = 40$, one knows $40 \div 5 = 8$) or properties of operations. By the end of Grade 3, know from memory all products of two one-digit numbers. | **GMC** Multiply within 100 fluently.
GMC Know all products of 1-digit numbers $\times 1$, $\times 2$, $\times 5$, and $\times 10$ automatically.
GMC Know all square products of 1-digit numbers automatically.
GMC Know all products of 1-digit numbers $\times 0$, $\times 3$, and $\times 9$ automatically.
GMC Know all products of 1-digit numbers $\times 4$, $\times 6$, $\times 7$ and $\times 8$ automatically.
GMC Divide within 100 fluently. |

[1] See Glossary, Table 2. http://www.corestandards.org/assets/CCSSI_Math%20Standards.pdf
[2] Students need not use formal terms for these properties.

Common Core State Standards

Standards for Mathematical Content

Cluster Solve problems involving the four operations, and identify and explain patterns in arithmetic.

3.OA.8 Solve two-step word problems using the four operations. Represent these problems using equations with a letter standing for the unknown quantity. Assess the reasonableness of answers using mental computation and estimation strategies including rounding.[3]	**GMC** Assess the reasonableness of answers to problems.
	GMC Solve 2-step number stories involving two of the four operations.
	GMC Model 2-step number stories with equations, using a letter or symbol for the unknown.
	GMC Understand that grouping symbols affect the order in which operations are performed.
	GMC Apply the order of operations when grouping symbols are not present.
3.OA.9 Identify arithmetic patterns (including patterns in the addition table or multiplication table), and explain them using properties of operations. *For example, observe that 4 times a number is always even, and explain why 4 times a number can be decomposed into two equal addends.*	**GMC** Identify arithmetic patterns and explain them using properties of operations.

Domain Number and Operations in Base Ten 3.NBT

Cluster Use place value understanding and properties of operations to perform multi-digit arithmetic.[4]

3.NBT.1 Use place value understanding to round whole numbers to the nearest 10 or 100.	**GMC** Use place-value understanding to round whole numbers to the nearest 10.
	GMC Use place-value understanding to round whole numbers to the nearest 100.
3.NBT.2 Fluently add and subtract within 1000 using strategies and algorithms based on place value, properties of operations, and/or the relationship between addition and subtraction.	**GMC** Add within 1,000 fluently.
	GMC Subtract within 1,000 fluently.
3.NBT.3 Multiply one-digit whole numbers by multiples of 10 in the range 10–90 (e.g., $9 \times 80, 5 \times 60$) using strategies based on place value and properties of operations.	**GMC** Multiply 1-digit numbers by multiples of 10.

Domain Number and Operations—Fractions[5] 3.NF

Cluster Develop understanding of fractions as numbers.

3.NF.1 Understand a fraction *1/b* as the quantity formed by 1 part when a whole is partitioned into b equal parts; understand a fraction *a/b* as the quantity formed by a parts of size *1/b*.	**GMC** Understand, identify, and represent unit fractions as 1 part when a whole is divided into *b* equal parts.
	GMC Understand, identify, and represent non-unit fractions as the quantity formed by *a* parts of size $\frac{1}{b}$.
	GMC Represent fractions by sharing collections of objects into equal shares.

[3] This standard is limited to problems posed with whole numbers and having whole number answers; students should know how to perform operations in the conventional order when there are no parentheses to specify a particular order (Order of Operations).
[4] A range of algorithms may be used.
[5] Grade 3 expectations in this domain are limited to fractions with denominators 2, 3, 4, 6, and 8.

Common Core State Standards

Standards for Mathematical Content

3.NF.2 Understand a fraction as a number on the number line; represent fractions on a number line diagram.

3.NF.2a Represent a fraction 1/b on a number line diagram by defining the interval from 0 to 1 as the whole and partitioning it into b equal parts. Recognize that each part has size 1/b and that the endpoint of the part based at 0 locates the number 1/b on the number line.	**GMC** Represent unit fractions on a number-line diagram.
3.NF.2b Represent a fraction a/b on a number line diagram by marking off a lengths 1/b from 0. Recognize that the resulting interval has size a/b and that its endpoint locates the number a/b on the number line.	**GMC** Represent non-unit fractions on a number-line diagram.

3.NF.3 Explain equivalence of fractions in special cases, and compare fractions by reasoning about their size.

3.NF.3a Understand two fractions as equivalent (equal) if they are the same size, or the same point on a number line.	**GMC** Understand that equivalent fractions are the same size.
	GMC Understand that equivalent fractions name the same point on a number line.
3.NF.3b Recognize and generate simple equivalent fractions, e.g., 1/2 = 2/4, 4/6 = 2/3. Explain why the fractions are equivalent, e.g., by using a visual fraction model.	**GMC** Recognize and generate simple equivalent fractions.
3.NF.3c Express whole numbers as fractions, and recognize fractions that are equivalent to whole numbers. *Examples: Express 3 in the form 3 = 3/1; recognize that 6/1 = 6; locate 4/4 and 1 at the same point of a number line diagram.*	**GMC** Express whole numbers as fractions.
	GMC Recognize fractions that are equivalent to whole numbers.
3.NF.3d Compare two fractions with the same numerator or the same denominator by reasoning about their size. Recognize that comparisons are valid only when the two fractions refer to the same whole. Record the results of comparisons with the symbols >, =, or <, and justify the conclusions, e.g., by using a visual fraction model.	**GMC** Compare fractions with the same numerator or the same denominator.
	GMC Recognize that fraction comparisons require the wholes to be the same size.
	GMC Record fraction comparisons using >, =, or <.
	GMC Justify the conclusions of fraction comparisons.

Domain Measurement and Data 3.MD

Cluster Solve problems involving measurement and estimation.

3.MD.1 Tell and write time to the nearest minute and measure time intervals in minutes. Solve word problems involving addition and subtraction of time intervals in minutes, e.g., by representing the problem on a number line diagram.	**GMC** Tell and write time.
	GMC Measure time intervals in minutes.
	GMC Solve number stories involving time intervals by adding or subtracting.
3.MD.2 Measure and estimate liquid volumes and masses of objects using standard units of grams (g), kilograms (kg), and liters (l).[6] Add, subtract, multiply, or divide to solve one-step word problems involving masses or volumes that are given in the same units, e.g., by using drawings (such as a beaker with a measurement scale) to represent the problem.[7]	**GMC** Measure and estimate masses of objects using grams and kilograms.
	GMC Measure and estimate liquid volumes using liters and other units.
	GMC Solve 1-step number stories involving mass.
	GMC Solve 1-step number stories involving volume.

[6] Excludes compound units such as cm³ and finding the geometric volume of a container.
[7] Excludes multiplicative comparison problems (problems involving notions of "times as much"; see Glossary, Table 2).

Common Core State Standards

Standards for Mathematical Content

Cluster Represent and interpret data.

3.MD.3 Draw a scaled picture graph and a scaled bar graph to represent a data set with several categories. Solve one- and two-step "how many more" and "how many less" problems using information presented in scaled bar graphs. *For example, draw a bar graph in which each square in the bar graph might represent 5 pets.*	GMC	Organize and represent data on scaled bar graphs and scaled picture graphs.
	GMC	Solve 1- and 2-step problems using information in graphs.
3.MD.4 Generate measurement data by measuring lengths using rulers marked with halves and fourths of an inch. Show the data by making a line plot, where the horizontal scale is marked off in appropriate units—whole numbers, halves, or quarters.	GMC	Measure lengths to the nearest $\frac{1}{2}$ inch, $\frac{1}{4}$, or whole centimeter.
	GMC	Collect, organize, and represent data on line plots.

Cluster Geometric measurement: understand concepts of area and relate area to multiplication and to addition.

3.MD.5 Recognize area as an attribute of plane figures and understand concepts of area measurement.

3.MD.5a A square with side length 1 unit, called "a unit square," is said to have "one square unit" of area, and can be used to measure area.	GMC	Understand that a unit square has 1 square unit of area and can measure area.
3.MD.5b A plane figure which can be covered without gaps or overlaps by *n* unit squares is said to have an area of *n* square units.	GMC	Understand that a plane figure completely covered by *n* unit squares has area *n* square units.
3.MD.6 Measure areas by counting unit squares (square cm, square m, square in, square ft, and improvised units).	GMC	Measure areas by counting unit squares.

3.MD.7 Relate area to the operations of multiplication and addition.

3.MD.7a Find the area of a rectangle with whole-number side lengths by tiling it, and show that the area is the same as would be found by multiplying the side lengths.	GMC	Find the area of a rectangle by tiling it.
	GMC	Show that tiling a rectangle results in the same area as multiplying its side lengths.
3.MD.7b Multiply side lengths to find areas of rectangles with whole-number side lengths in the context of solving real world and mathematical problems, and represent whole-number products as rectangular areas in mathematical reasoning.	GMC	Multiply side lengths to find areas of rectangles.
	GMC	Solve real-world and mathematical problems involving areas of rectangles.
	GMC	Represent whole-number products as rectanglular areas.
3.MD.7c Use tiling to show in a concrete case that the area of a rectangle with whole-number side lengths *a* and *b* + *c* is the sum of *a* × *b* and *a* × *c*. Use area models to represent the distributive property in mathematical reasoning.	GMC	Use tiling to concretely demonstrate the distributive property.
	GMC	Use area models to represent the distributive property.
3.MD.7d Recognize area as additive. Find areas of rectilinear figures by decomposing them into non-overlapping rectangles and adding the areas of the non-overlapping parts, applying this technique to solve real world problems.	GMC	Recognize area as additive.
	GMC	Find areas of rectilinear figures by decomposing them into non-overlapping rectangles, and apply this technique to solve real-world problems.

Cluster Geometric measurement: recognize perimeter.

3.MD.8 Solve real world and mathematical problems involving perimeters of polygons, including finding the perimeter given the side lengths, finding an unknown side length, and exhibiting rectangles with the same perimeter and different areas or with the same area and different perimeters.	GMC	Solve problems involving perimeters of polygons.
	GMC	Exhibit rectangles with the same perimeter and different areas or the same area and different perimeters.

Common Core State Standards

Standards for Mathematical Content

Domain Geometry 3.G

Cluster Reason with shapes and their attributes.

3.G.1 Understand that shapes in different categories (e.g., rhombuses, rectangles, and others) may share attributes (e.g., having four sides), and that the shared attributes can define a larger category (e.g., quadrilaterals). Recognize rhombuses, rectangles, and squares as examples of quadrilaterals, and draw examples of quadrilaterals that do not belong to any of these subcategories.	**GMC** Understand that shapes in different categories may share attributes that can define a larger category. **GMC** Recognize specified subcategories of quadrilaterals. **GMC** Draw quadrilaterals that do not belong to specified subcategories.
3.G.2 Partition shapes into parts with equal areas. Express the area of each part as a unit fraction of the whole. *For example, partition a shape into 4 parts with equal area, and describe the area of each part as 1/4 of the area of the shape.*	**GMC** Partition shapes into parts with equal areas. **GMC** Express the area of each part as a unit fraction of the whole.

Common Core State Standards

Standards for Mathematical Practice	*Everyday Mathematics* **Goals for Mathematical Practice**

1 Make sense of problems and persevere in solving them.

Mathematically proficient students start by explaining to themselves the meaning of a problem and looking for entry points to its solution. They analyze givens, constraints, relationships, and goals. They make conjectures about the form and meaning of the solution and plan a solution pathway rather than simply jumping into a solution attempt. They consider analogous problems, and try special cases and simpler forms of the original problem in order to gain insight into its solution. They monitor and evaluate their progress and change course if necessary. Older students might, depending on the context of the problem, transform algebraic expressions or change the viewing window on their graphing calculator to get the information they need. Mathematically proficient students can explain correspondences between equations, verbal descriptions, tables, and graphs or draw diagrams of important features and relationships, graph data, and search for regularity or trends. Younger students might rely on using concrete objects or pictures to help conceptualize and solve a problem. Mathematically proficient students check their answers to problems using a different method, and they continually ask themselves, "Does this make sense?" They can understand the approaches of others to solving complex problems and identify correspondences between different approaches.

GMP1.1	Make sense of your problem.
GMP1.2	Reflect on your thinking as you solve your problem.
GMP1.3	Keep trying when your problem is hard.
GMP1.4	Check whether your answer makes sense.
GMP1.5	Solve problems in more than one way.
GMP1.6	Compare the strategies you and others use.

2 Reason abstractly and quantitatively.

Mathematically proficient students make sense of quantities and their relationships in problem situations. They bring two complementary abilities to bear on problems involving quantitative relationships: the ability to *decontextualize*—to abstract a given situation and represent it symbolically and manipulate the representing symbols as if they have a life of their own, without necessarily attending to their referents—and the ability to *contextualize*, to pause as needed during the manipulation process in order to probe into the referents for the symbols involved. Quantitative reasoning entails habits of creating a coherent representation of the problem at hand; considering the units involved; attending to the meaning of quantities, not just how to compute them; and knowing and flexibly using different properties of operations and objects.

GMP2.1	Create mathematical representations using numbers, words, pictures, symbols, gestures, tables, graphs, and concrete objects.
GMP2.2	Make sense of the representations you and others use.
GMP2.3	Make connections between representations.

Common Core State Standards

Standards for Mathematical Practice	***Everyday Mathematics*** **Goals for Mathematical Practice**

3 Construct viable arguments and critique the reasoning of others.

Mathematically proficient students understand and use stated assumptions, definitions, and previously established results in constructing arguments. They make conjectures and build a logical progression of statements to explore the truth of their conjectures. They are able to analyze situations by breaking them into cases, and can recognize and use counterexamples. They justify their conclusions, communicate them to others, and respond to the arguments of others. They reason inductively about data, making plausible arguments that take into account the context from which the data arose. Mathematically proficient students are also able to compare the effectiveness of two plausible arguments, distinguish correct logic or reasoning from that which is flawed, and—if there is a flaw in an argument—explain what it is. Elementary students can construct arguments using concrete referents such as objects, drawings, diagrams, and actions. Such arguments can make sense and be correct, even though they are not generalized or made formal until later grades. Later, students learn to determine domains to which an argument applies. Students at all grades can listen or read the arguments of others, decide whether they make sense, and ask useful questions to clarify or improve the arguments.	**GMP3.1** Make mathematical conjectures and arguments. **GMP3.2** Make sense of others' mathematical thinking.

4 Model with mathematics.

Mathematically proficient students can apply the mathematics they know to solve problems arising in everyday life, society, and the workplace. In early grades, this might be as simple as writing an addition equation to describe a situation. In middle grades, a student might apply proportional reasoning to plan a school event or analyze a problem in the community. By high school, a student might use geometry to solve a design problem or use a function to describe how one quantity of interest depends on another. Mathematically proficient students who can apply what they know are comfortable making assumptions and approximations to simplify a complicated situation, realizing that these may need revision later. They are able to identify important quantities in a practical situation and map their relationships using such tools as diagrams, two-way tables, graphs, flowcharts and formulas. They can analyze those relationships mathematically to draw conclusions. They routinely interpret their mathematical results in the context of the situation and reflect on whether the results make sense, possibly improving the model if it has not served its purpose.	**GMP4.1** Model real-world situations using graphs, drawings, tables, symbols, numbers, diagrams, and other representations. **GMP4.2** Use mathematical models to solve problems and answer questions.

Common Core State Standards

Standards for Mathematical Practice	Everyday Mathematics Goals for Mathematical Practice

5 Use appropriate tools strategically.

Mathematically proficient students consider the available tools when solving a mathematical problem. These tools might include pencil and paper, concrete models, a ruler, a protractor, a calculator, a spreadsheet, a computer algebra system, a statistical package, or dynamic geometry software. Proficient students are sufficiently familiar with tools appropriate for their grade or course to make sound decisions about when each of these tools might be helpful, recognizing both the insight to be gained and their limitations. For example, mathematically proficient high school students analyze graphs of functions and solutions generated using a graphing calculator. They detect possible errors by strategically using estimation and other mathematical knowledge. When making mathematical models, they know that technology can enable them to visualize the results of varying assumptions, explore consequences, and compare predictions with data. Mathematically proficient students at various grade levels are able to identify relevant external mathematical resources, such as digital content located on a website, and use them to pose or solve problems. They are able to use technological tools to explore and deepen their understanding of concepts.

GMP5.1 Choose appropriate tools.

GMP5.2 Use tools effectively and make sense of your results.

6 Attend to precision.

Mathematically proficient students try to communicate precisely to others. They try to use clear definitions in discussion with others and in their own reasoning. They state the meaning of the symbols they choose, including using the equal sign consistently and appropriately. They are careful about specifying units of measure, and labeling axes to clarify the correspondence with quantities in a problem. They calculate accurately and efficiently, express numerical answers with a degree of precision appropriate for the problem context. In the elementary grades, students give carefully formulated explanations to each other. By the time they reach high school they have learned to examine claims and make explicit use of definitions.

GMP6.1 Explain your mathematical thinking clearly and precisely.

GMP6.2 Use an appropriate level of precision for your problem.

GMP6.3 Use clear labels, units, and mathematical language.

GMP6.4 Think about accuracy and efficiency when you count, measure, and calculate.

Common Core State Standards

Standards for Mathematical Practice	*Everyday Mathematics* Goals for Mathematical Practice

7 Look for and make use of structure.

Mathematically proficient students look closely to discern a pattern or structure. Young students, for example, might notice that three and seven more is the same amount as seven and three more, or they may sort a collection of shapes according to how many sides the shapes have. Later, students will see 7×8 equals the well remembered $7 \times 5 + 7 \times 3$, in preparation for learning about the distributive property. In the expression $x^2 + 9x + 14$, older students can see the 14 as 2×7 and the 9 as $2 + 7$. They recognize the significance of an existing line in a geometric figure and can use the strategy of drawing an auxiliary line for solving problems. They also can step back for an overview and shift perspective. They can see complicated things, such as some algebraic expressions, as single objects or as being composed of several objects. For example, they can see $5 - 3(x - y)^2$ as 5 minus a positive number times a square and use that to realize that its value cannot be more than 5 for any real numbers x and y.	**GMP7.1** Look for mathematical structures such as categories, patterns, and properties. **GMP7.2** Use structures to solve problems and answer questions.

8 Look for and express regularity in repeated reasoning.

Mathematically proficient students notice if calculations are repeated, and look both for general methods and for shortcuts. Upper elementary students might notice when dividing 25 by 11 that they are repeating the same calculations over and over again, and conclude they have a repeating decimal. By paying attention to the calculation of slope as they repeatedly check whether points are on the line through (1, 2) with slope 3, middle school students might abstract the equation $(y - 2)/(x - 1) = 3$. Noticing the regularity in the way terms cancel when expanding $(x - 1)(x + 1)$, $(x - 1)(x^2 + x + 1)$, and $(x - 1)(x^3 + x^2 + x + 1)$ might lead them to the general formula for the sum of a geometric series. As they work to solve a problem, mathematically proficient students maintain oversight of the process, while attending to the details. They continually evaluate the reasonableness of their intermediate results.	**GMP8.1** Create and justify rules, shortcuts, and generalizations.

3–4 Games Correlation

Game	Grade 3 Lesson	Grade 4 Lesson	Operations and Algebraic Thinking	Number and Operations in Base Ten	Number and Operations—Fractions	Measurement and Data	Geometry
Addition Top-It	2-1	1-1, 1-3, 1-12		●			
Angle Add-Up		6-11, 7-12, 8-2, 8-11		●		●	
Angle Race		6-9				●	
Angle Tangle		6-10, 7-4		●		●	
The Area and Perimeter Game	4-10, 5-11, 7-10					●	
Array Bingo	2-7, 3-10, 8-3		●	●			
Baseball Multiplication	6-2, 6-3, 6-5, 7-6		●				
Baseball Multiplication (with Tens)	6-2		●				
Beat the Calculator	6-4, 6-10, 7-12, 8-6, 9-2	4-13, 6-4	●	●			
Beat the Calculator (Extended Facts)		4-1, 6-4		●			
Buzz and Bizz-Buzz		2-4, 2-9, 3-3, 6-3	●	●			
Coin Top-It		3-13			●		
Decimal Top-It		3-13, 5-4, 6-13, 7-11			●		
Divide and Conquer		6-1, 6-7, 7-5		●			
Division Arrays	2-10, 2-12		●	●			
Division Dash		6-8, 6-10, 8-6		●			
Division Top-It		6-4, 6-7		●			
Dollar Exchange		4-8		●		●	
Factor Bingo	8-5, 8-7, 9-4	2-3, 2-5	●	●			
Factor Captor		2-3, 2-8, 4-3	●	●			
Finding Factors	8-3, 9-4		●				
Fishing for Digits		1-4, 1-13, 2-3		●			
Fishing for Fractions (Addition)		5-10, 6-9, 7-8			●		
Fishing for Fractions (Mixed-Number Addition)		6-1, 8-7			●		
Fishing for Fractions (Mixed-Number Subtraction)		6-3, 8-9			●		
Fishing for Fractions (Subtraction)		5-13, 7-2, 8-1			●		
Fraction/Decimal Concentration		4-7, 5-8			●		

McGraw-Hill Education

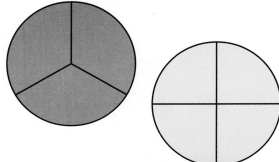

Game	Grade 3 Lesson	Grade 4 Lesson	Operations and Algebraic Thinking	Number and Operations in Base Ten	Number and Operations—Fractions	Measurement and Data	Geometry
Fraction Match		3-2, 3-9, 3-13, 4-11, 5-2, 6-7, 6-12			●		
Fraction Memory	5-3, 6-4, 7-2, 7-5, 9-5				●		
Fraction Multiplication Top-It		7-7, 7-13, 8-5			●		
Fraction Number-Line Squeeze	8-7, 9-5				●		
Fraction Top-It	7-7, 7-9, 7-10, 9-5	3-7, 3-11, 4-9, 5-11, 6-6			●		
Hit the Target	1-3			●			
How Much More?		2-9, 2-12, 4-8, 6-11	●	●			
Multiplication Draw	1-10, 1-12, 2-2, 3-11, 4-4, 5-4, 6-5		●				
Multiplication Top-It	6-7	4-1, 5-1	●	●			
Multiplication Top-It (with Extended Facts)	9-3, 9-5	4-9	●	●			
Multiplication Wrestling		4-10, 5-7, 6-2, 7-3, 8-8		●			
Name That Number	3-13, 4-3, 4-7, 6-8, 9-7	8-13	●	●			
Number-Grid Difference	1-2, 1-3			●			
Number Top-It		1-2, 1-5, 1-11, 2-11, 4-12		●			
Polygon Capture		2-11, 3-10, 4-4					●
Product Pile-Up	9-1, 9-4		●				
Roll to 1,000	2-5, 3-1		●	●			
Roll to 1,000 (with Multiplication)	8-2			●			
Rugs and Fences		2-2, 2-10, 3-8, 4-1, 4-11, 6-2		●		●	
Salute!	2-1, 5-8, 6-1, 6-5, 7-3		●	●			
Shading Shapes	4-5						●
Shuffle to 100	3-3, 3-7			●			

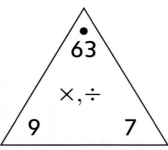

Game	Grade 3 Lesson	Grade 4 Lesson	Operations and Algebraic Thinking	Number and Operations in Base Ten	Number and Operations—Fractions	Measurement and Data	Geometry
				CCSS Domain			
Shuffle to 1,000	3-3			•			
Speed Factor Bingo	8-5		•				
Spin and Round	1-7, 1-13	1-3, 1-6, 1-10, 2-2, 3-7, 4-2		•			
Subtraction Target Practice		2-1		•			
Subtraction Top-It	2-1	1-2, 1-4		•			
What's My Polygon Rule?	4-4, 6-8						•

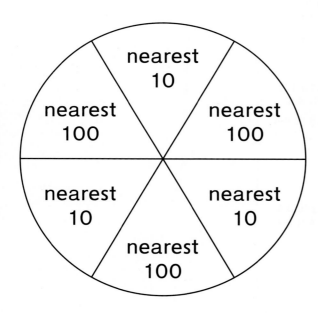

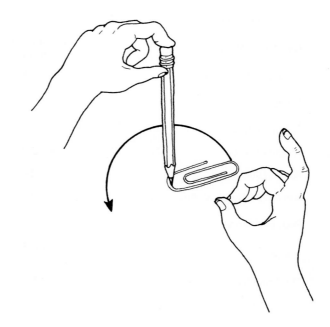

Sample Work from Child A

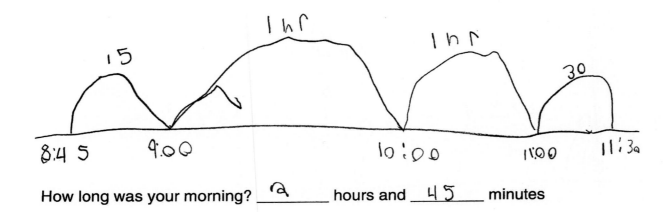

How long was your morning? ___a___ hours and ___45___ minutes

Sample Work from Child B

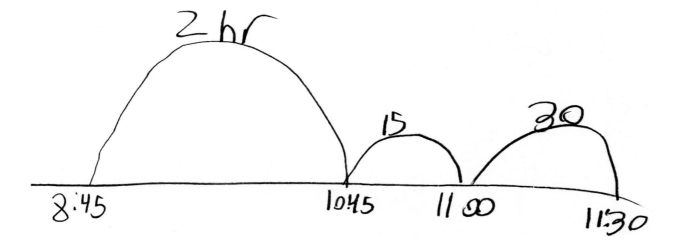

How long was your morning? ___2___ hours and ___45___ minutes

Sample Work from Child C

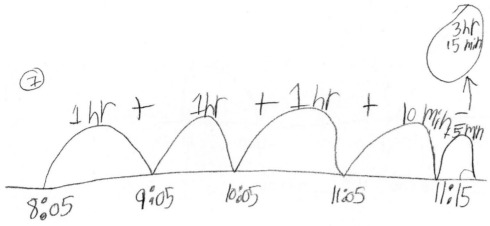

⑦

How long was your morning? ___3___ hours and ___15___ minutes

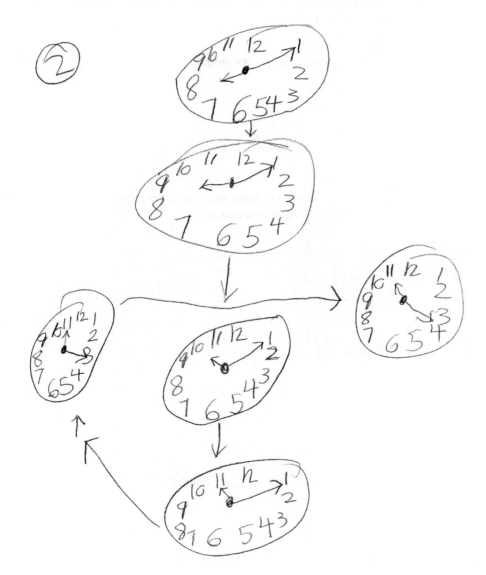

Sample Work from Child D

How long was your morning? ___3___ hours and ___15___ minutes

Lesson 2-8

Sample Work from Child A

1. There are 20 children in art class. If 4 children can sit at each table, how many tables do they need?

_____5_____ tables

2. There are 20 children in music class. If 6 children can sit at each table, how many tables do they need?

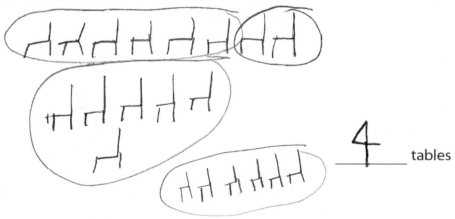

_____4_____ tables

Sample Work from Child B

1. There are 20 children in art class. If 4 children can sit at each table, how many tables do they need?

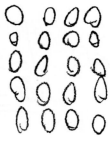

_____5_____ tables

2. There are 20 children in music class. If 6 children can sit at each table, how many tables do they need?

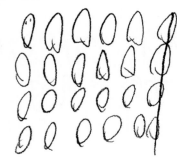

$20 \div 5 = 4$

_____4_____ tables

Sample Work from Child C

2. There are 20 children in music class. If 6 children can sit at each table, how many tables do they need?

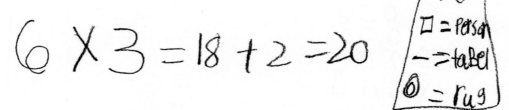

$6 \times 3 = 18 + 2 = 20$

key
□ = person
— = table
⊙ = rug

_____3_____ tables + 2 people

left over can sit on the rug

Sample Work from Child A

2. Write your estimate for
how much money the club has left over. $ _____40_____

3. Use your estimate to decide if Ann's answer is reasonable.
Is Ann's answer reasonable? _____not reasonabl_____

4. Show your thinking and how you used an estimate in the thought
bubble below.

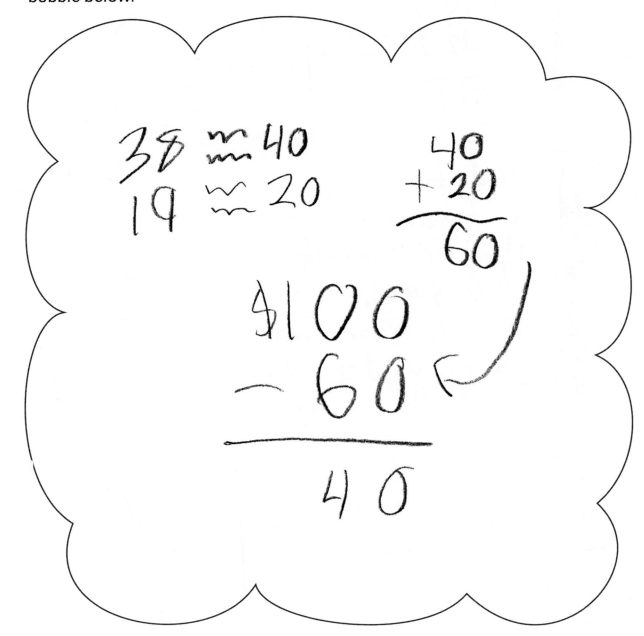

Sample Work from Child B

3. Use your estimate to decide if Ann's answer is reasonable.
Is Ann's answer reasonable? _____No_____

4. Show your thinking and how you used an estimate in the thought
bubble below.

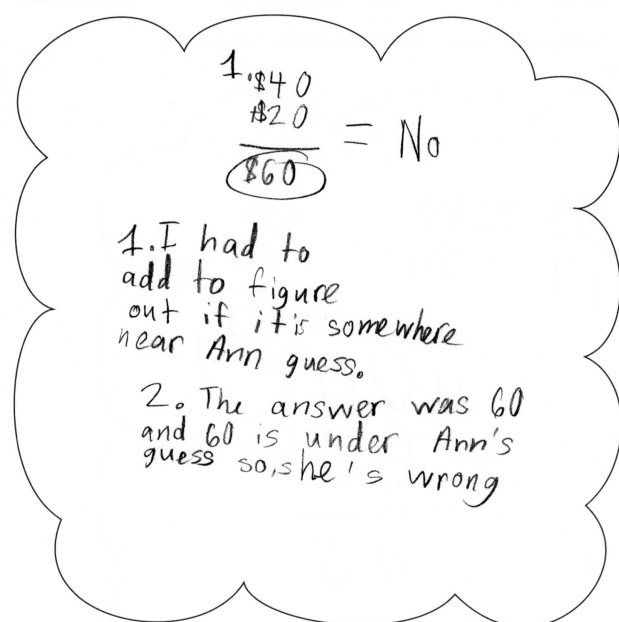

1. $40
$20
———— = No
$60

1. I had to add to figure out if it is somewhere near Ann guess.

2. The answer was 60 and 60 is under Ann's guess so, she's wrong

Sample Work from Child C

3. Use your estimate to decide if Ann's answer is reasonable.
   Is Ann's answer reasonable? ___Yes___

4. Show your thinking and how you used an estimate in the thought
   bubble below.

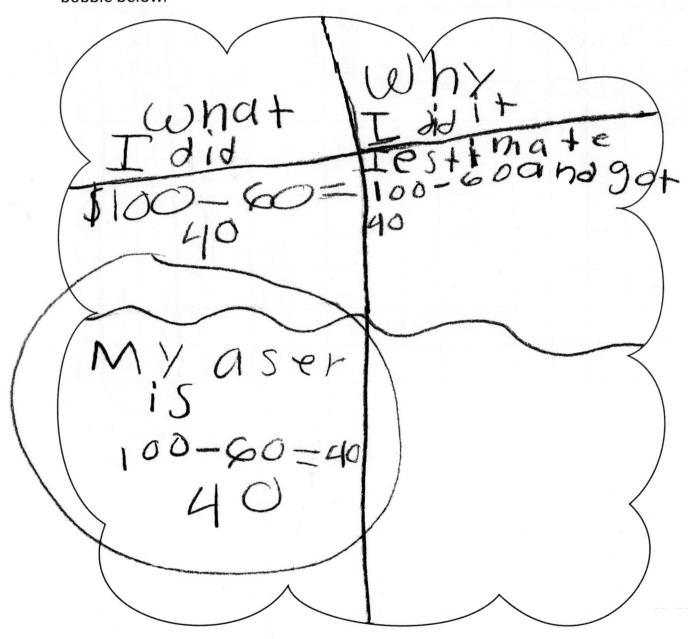

what
I did
$100 – 60 =
40

why
I did it
I estimate
100 – 60 and got
40

My aser
is
100 – 60 = 40
40

Sample Work from Child A

1. Use the grid to draw **at least 2 different pens** that Miguel could build.
2. **Find the area** of each pen and record it inside the pen.

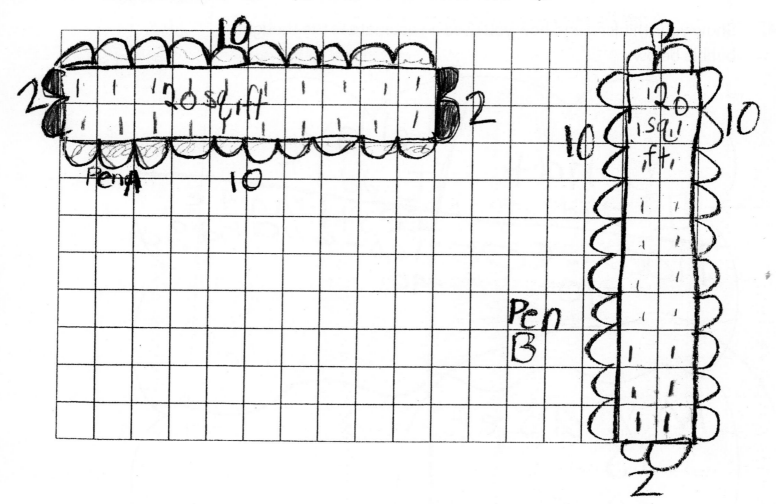

Sample Work from Child B

1. Use the grid to draw **at least 2 different pens** that Miguel could build.
2. **Find the area** of each pen and record it inside the pen.

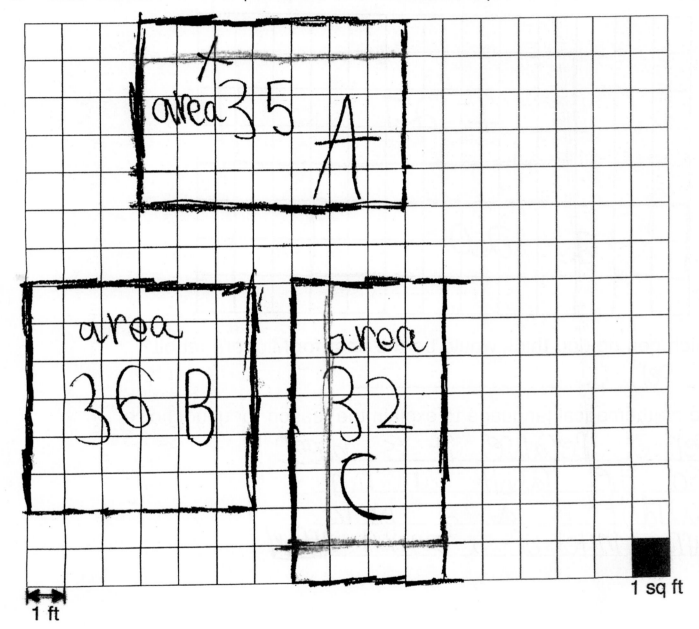

1 ft

1 sq ft

Lesson 4-11

Sample Work from Child C

1. Use the grid to draw **at least 2 different pens** that Miguel could build.

2. **Find the area** of each pen and record it inside the pen.

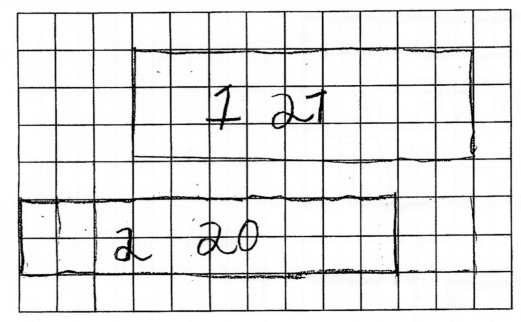

3. Which pen do you think would be the best for Miguel's rabbit?

   Pen 2

4. Use mathematical language to explain the reason for your choice.

   Pen 2 Because it is longer
   So the rabbit can run
   and it is a 2 by 10
   Array insted of a 3 by 9 Array!

CCSS 3.MD.1

Work Sample #1—
Partially Meeting Expectations

This sample work does not meet expectations for the content standard and partially meets expectations for the mathematical practice. This child does not add the intervals of time shown on the number line to solve the problem. **3.MD.1** The child drew a number line that accurately represents the elapsed time, but the number line was not used to solve the problem. The written description indicates thinking that the problem can be solved by "counting how many numbers it is." This statement provides evidence of an incomplete understanding of how to use the number line to determine elapsed time. **GMP4.2**

Write the times:

We start at __8 : 40__.

We go to lunch at __12 : 25__.

Use at least one strategy to find how long you are in school in the morning. Show how you solve the problem.

8:40   9:00   10:00   11:00   12:00   12:25

I figerd it out by making a numbe line and counting how many numbers it is.

How long was your morning? _____ hours and _____ minutes

Work Sample #2—Meeting Expectations

This sample work meets expectations for the content standard and for the mathematical practice. With revision, this child correctly found that the morning lasted 2 hours and 45 minutes by adding the intermediate times shown on the number line. **3.MD.1** The number line correctly models the elapsed time and the written description provides evidence that the number line was used successfully to determine the elapsed time. Note that the explanation would be clearer if the child had written two number sentences: 1 hr 30 min + 1 hr = 2 hr 30 min and 2 hr 30 min + 15 min = 2 hr 45 min. **GMP4.2**

Write the times:

We start at __8:45__.

We go to lunch at __11:30__.

Use at least one strategy to find how long you are in school in the morning. Show how you solve the problem.

1hr   15m   1hr and 30m

8:45   9:45   10:00   11:30

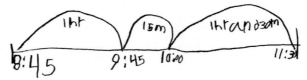
frist I added 130m + 1h = 2h30m + 15m = 2h45

How long was your morning? __2__ hours and __45__ minutes

CCSS 3.MD.1

Work Sample #3—
Exceeding Expectations

This sample work meets expectations for the content standard and exceeds expectations for the mathematical practice. The child correctly solved the problem by adding the intermediate times to find that the morning lasted 3 hours and 15 minutes. **3.MD.1** The child used two different models to determine the elapsed time. The first model, a number line starting at 8:05 and ending at 11:20, is used to correctly answer the question. (Although 11:20 is not labeled because the child seemed to run out of room, the final 5 min is shown above the last hop.) In the second model, a series of clocks shows the elapsed time. All of the times shown on the clocks correspond to times on the number line, with both models showing an elapsed time of 3 hours and 15 minutes. **GMP4.2**

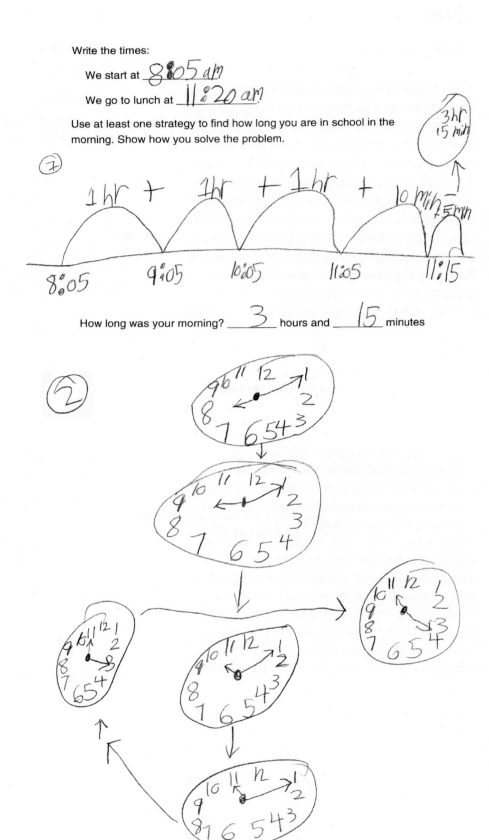

Write the times:

We start at ___8:05 am___

We go to lunch at ___11:20 am___

Use at least one strategy to find how long you are in school in the morning. Show how you solve the problem.

How long was your morning? ___3___ hours and ___15___ minutes

CCSS 3.OA.2, 3.OA.3

Work Sample #1—
Partially Meeting Expectations

This sample work meets expectations for the content standards and partially meets expectations for the mathematical practice. This child found the correct number of tables for Problem 1 using an equal-grouping strategy. **3.OA.2, 3.OA.3** The drawing for Problem 1 uses tallies to show 5 tables with 4 children at each table. Although the picture in Problem 2 shows 4 tables with 5 children each, it is not clear how this representation was used to solve the problem since the answer given is 3 tables.
GMP2.1

1. There are 20 children in art class. If 4 children can sit at each table, how many tables do they need?

_____ tables

2. There are 20 children in music class. If 6 children can sit at each table, how many tables do they need?

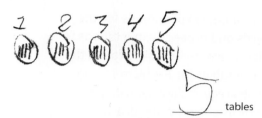

_____ tables

Work Sample #2—Meeting Expectations

This sample work meets expectations for the content standards and for the mathematical practice. This child found the correct number of tables for Problem 1 using an equal-grouping strategy. **3.OA.2, 3.OA.3** For Problem 1, the drawing clearly shows 5 tables with 4 children at each table. In revisions for Problem 2, the child added a table to the picture (see the small table in blue) and to the answer for the 2 children previously pictured on a rug. With these revisions, both drawings are clear and complete. Note that the number model is not a true number sentence because (6×3) does not equal $18 + 2$. It would improve the work if the child wrote two correct number sentences ($6 \times 3 = 18$ and $18 + 2 = 20$).
GMP2.1

1. There are 20 children in art class. If 4 children can sit at each table, how many tables do they need?

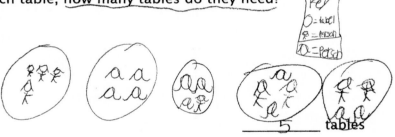

_____ tables

2. There are 20 children in music class. If 6 children can sit at each table, how many tables do they need?

$$(6 \times 3) = 18 + 2 = 20$$

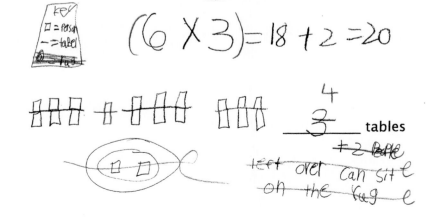

_____ tables

left over can site on the rug

Evaluated Children Work Samples

Lesson 2-8

CCSS 3.OA.2, 3.OA.3

Work Sample #3— Exceeding Expectations

This sample work meets expectations for the content standards and exceeds expectations for the mathematical practice. This child found the correct number of tables for Problem 1 using more than one strategy, including an equal-grouping strategy as shown in the drawing. **3.OA.2, 3.OA.3** The pictures and number models in Problems 1 and 2 clearly indicate that more than one strategy was used to solve each problem. Additionally, with the revisions in Problem 2, the child provided an explanation of how he or she interpreted the remainder and chose to add a fourth table for the remaining 2 children. **GMP2.1**

1. There are 20 children in art class. If 4 children can sit at each table, how many tables do they need?

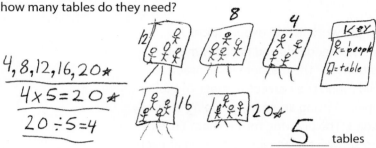

$$4, 8, 12, 16, 20 *$$
$$4 \times 5 = 20 *$$
$$20 \div 5 = 4$$

5 tables

2. There are 20 children in music class. If 6 children can sit at each table, how many tables do they need?

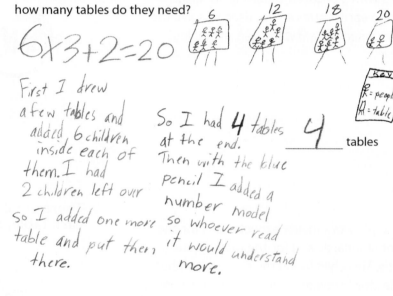

$$6 \times 3 + 2 = 20$$

First I drew a few tables and added 6 children inside each of them. I had 2 children left over so I added one more table and put them there.

So I had **4** tables at the end. Then with the blue pencil I added a number model so whoever read it would understand more.

4 tables

3.OA.8

Work Sample #1—Partially Meeting Expectations

This sample work does not meet expectations for the content standard and partially meets expectations for the mathematical practice. This child did not subtract 60 from 100, the second step needed to determine the reasonableness of Ann's answer. **3.OA.8** Although this work shows close-but-easier numbers, it does not show both of the calculations needed to estimate how much money the club has left. **GMP6.1**

2. Write your estimate for how much money the club has left over. $ 20.00

3. Use your estimate to decide if Ann's answer is reasonable. Is Ann's answer reasonable? No

4. Show your thinking and how you used an estimate in the thought bubble below.

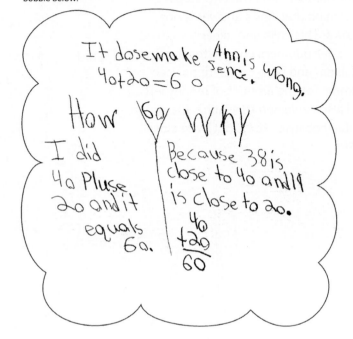

Work Sample #2—Meeting Expectations

This sample work meets expectations for the content standard and for the mathematical practice. The work shows close-but-easier numbers and the two steps needed to determine that Ann's answer is not reasonable. **3.OA.8** This child clearly showed the close-but-easier numbers and both calculations used to estimate the amount of money left over. **GMP6.1**

2. Write your estimate for how much money the club has left over. $ 40

3. Use your estimate to decide if Ann's answer is reasonable. Is Ann's answer reasonable? no

4. Show your thinking and how you used an estimate in the thought bubble below.

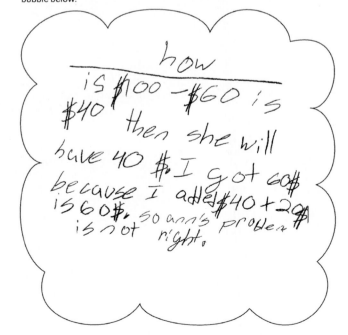

CCSS 3.OA.8

Work Sample #3—Exceeding Expectations

This sample work meets expectations for the content standard and exceeds expectations for the mathematical practice. The work shows close-but-easier numbers and the two steps needed to determine that Ann's answer is not reasonable. 3.OA.8 This child very clearly showed the close-but-easier numbers chosen for the first step of the problem and both calculations used to find an estimate for the amount of money left over. This child also explained that Ann's answer is not reasonable because "$67 is not even close to $40!" GMP6.1

2. Write your estimate for how much money the club has left over. $ __40__

3. Use your estimate to decide if Ann's answer is reasonable. Is Ann's answer reasonable? ___No___

4. Show your thinking and how you used an estimate in the thought bubble below.

> I thought that 38 was closer to 40 and that 19 was closer to 20. 40+20=60$ how much they spent. Then I remembered that they had $100 in all. 60+40=100. I think that they have $40 left over. That shows that Ann's answer is incorrect because $67 is not even close to $40!

3.MD.8

Work Sample #1—
Partially Meeting Expectations

This sample work meets expectations for the content standard and partially meets expectations for the mathematical practice. This work shows two rectangles with a perimeter of 24 feet, but with different areas. **3.MD.8** While this child drew two correct models for the pens, the area was not included in the models. Furthermore, the child's use of mathematical language is not clear because the answer to Problem 4 argues that Pen B, the pen with the smaller area, is the best because it has "a lot of space for a rabbit to hop around." **GMP4.1**

1. Use the grid to draw **at least 2 different pens** that Miguel could build.
2. **Find the area** of each pen and record it inside the pen.

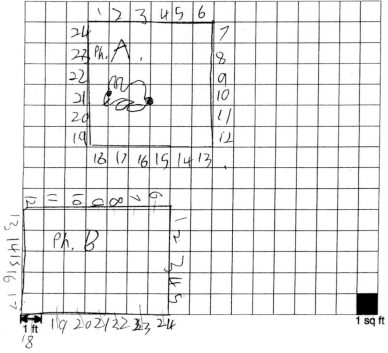

3. Which pen do you think would be the best for Miguel's rabbit?

eh B

4. Use mathematical language to explain the reason for your choice.

because I know rabbits like to hop, arr ph. b has 24ft. and it almost a square but still a rectangul. Ph. b has a lot of space for a rabbit to hop around

3.MD.8

Work Sample #2—Meeting Expectations

This sample work meets expectations for the content standard and for the mathematical practice. This work shows two rectangles with a perimeter of 24 feet, but with different areas. 3.MD.8 This work shows two correct models for the pen with the areas and sides correctly labeled with units. The child also used mathematical language to explain which pen would be best by saying, "The second one has 1 less space than the first one." GMP4.1

1. Use the grid to draw **at least 2 different pens** that Miguel could build.
2. **Find the area** of each pen and record it inside the pen.

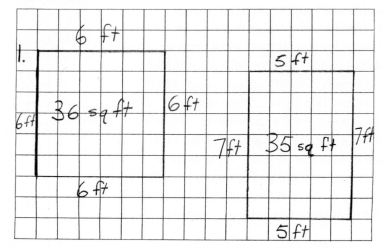

3. Which pen do you think would be the best for Miguel's rabbit?

   The 1st one.

4. Use mathematical language to explain the reason for your choice.

   Because it has more room inside of it. The 2nd one has 1 less space than the 1st one.

3.MD.8

Work Sample #3—
Exceeding Expectations

This sample work meets expectations for the content standard and exceeds expectations for the mathematical practice. This work shows two rectangles with a perimeter of 24 feet, but with different areas. 3.MD.8 This child drew two correct models for the pen with the areas labeled with correct units and used mathematical language to explain which pen would be best by saying, "it has more space." The child connects the mathematical language to the real world by explaining that the pen is better because the rabbit "can sleep well and to run." GMP4.1

1. Use the grid to draw **at least 2 different pens** that Miguel could build.

2. **Find the area** of each pen and record it inside the pen.

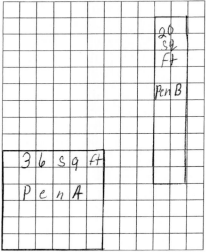

3. Which pen do you think would be the best for Miguel's rabbit?

   _____ Pen A _____

4. Use mathematical language to explain the reason for your choice.

   because it has more space
   for he can sleep well and
   to run.

Gram (g), 77, 95, 99, 100–101, 103, 814. *See also* Mass

Grandfather Tang's Story (Literature Link), 349

Graphing/graphs. *See also* Data
 comparing graphs, 804, 805, 851–852
 Length-of-Day Graph, 71, 90–91, 804, 805, 850, 851
 line plots, 312, 320, 330–335, 529, 565–566, 743
 scaled bar graphs, 58–63, 211, 218, 259, 261, 477
 scaled picture graphs, 266–271, 335
 tally charts, 59, 61, 62, 764

Greater than (>), 656, 665, 675. *See also* Comparing

Grids. *See* Number grids

Grouping symbols. *See* Parentheses

Guidelines for discussion. *See* Discussion guidelines

Guide to Solving Number Stories
 background information, 122, 123
 making sense of problems, 157, 158, 180, 571, 574, 606, 704, 769, 815–816
 multistep problems, solving, 145–146
 number models, writing, 140, 610
 organizing information, 138–140
 problem solving, process of, 132–134
 using, 157, 329, 648–649, 650
 using diagrams with, 573

Half inch. *See also* Inch (in.)
 data interpretation, 334
 exploring rulers, 326–327, 328–329
 graphing measurements on line plots, 331, 332–333
 identifying, 337
 measuring to nearest, 324–329, 340, 355, 357–358, 373

Height, 743. *See also* Length

Helper facts, in multiplication, 287, 295, 466
 adding a group (*See* Add a group/adding a group)
 background information, 12, 218, 286, 441, 442, 443
 breaking apart factors, 515–516, 517, 525, 579, 580
 doubling, 472, 481–482
 identifying, 465, 467–468, 551
 near squares, 497, 498–500
 purpose of, 82, 552–553
 subtracting a group (*See* Subtract a group/ subtracting a group)

Heptagons, 346

Hexagonal prisms, 730, 781

Hexagons, 346

Hit the Target, 27

Home Links, *All lessons contain a Home Link activity.*

Homophones, 196, 445, 545

Hours, 29, 41, 42–45, 489. *See also* Time

Identity Property of Addition, 158

Identity Property of Multiplication, 157

Implementation Guide, 13, 47, 49, 50, 107, 123, 167, 219, 227, 323, 387, 443, 503, 537, 589, 633, 679, 731, 751, 805, 839

Inch (in.), 29, 325, 326–327, 328, 356, 363

Information. *See* Data

Input, 221, 222, 680. *See also* "What's My Rule?"

Integers, 631

Intervals
 in graphing, 332
 in measurement, 328

Key, 267, 269, 270

Kilogram (kg), 77, 95, 99, 100–101, 103, 339, 814. *See also* Mass

Kites, 350, 351, 352

Length, 329. *See also* Measurement; Perimeter
 comparing, 320
 finding missing side lengths (*See* Sides (area/perimeter))
 measuring, 29–30, 31, 320, 321, 325, 337, 362, 370, 659, 728, 732–737, 743
 number stories with, 329
 precision in, 323, 728, 735
 units for, 647

Length-of-Day Graph, 71, 90–91, 804, 805, 850, 851

Length-of-Day Project, 13, 89–91, 804, 848–853

Lesson materials. *See* Materials

Lesson overviews, 3, 113, 209, 313, 433, 527, 623, 721, 795

Less than (<), 656, 665, 675. *See also* Comparing

Line plots, 312, 320, 330–335, 529, 565–566, 743. *See also* Number lines

Line segments, 29–30, 328, 702, 728, 735–736

Liquid volume, 636
 background information, 630
 benchmarks in, 633, 637, 638, 639
 comparing, 115, 198, 622, 630, 636–637
 estimating, 198, 622, 630, 635, 637, 638, 639, 774, 783
 exploring, 195, 199, 638–639, 677
 measuring, 198, 622, 625, 630, 633, 635, 637, 638, 643, 783
 number stories, 630, 649
 units for, 637, 647

Liter (L), 198, 630, 637

Literature Link
 Doorbell Rang, The, 73

Each Orange Had 8 Slices: A Counting Book, 155

Eating Fractions, 451

Grandfather Tang's Story, 349

One Grain of Rice, 819

Remainder of One, A, 73

Sea Squares, 273

Spaghetti and Meatballs for All!, 361

Manipulatives. *See also, for example,* Base-10 blocks; Calculators; Clocks; Concrete modeling; Fact Triangles; Fraction circles; Fraction strips; Pattern blocks
 counters, 149, 162, 168, 179, 221, 297, 524, 752, 753
 cubes, 445, 459, 472, 516, 773
 geoboards, 315, 343, 346, 375, 731, 776
 tape measures, 320 (*See also* Rulers)
 using, 169

Mass, 12, 94
 benchmarks for, 315, 337, 339, 581
 comparing, 5, 94–95, 315, 339, 805, 820
 estimating, 5, 99, 101, 102, 337, 339, 581
 exploring, 12, 797, 804, 814–815, 829
 measuring, 13, 98–103, 337, 581, 825
 number stories with, 102, 103, 802, 805, 813, 825
 ordering objects, 99, 102
 predicting, 97
 units for, 647

Masses, standard, using, 95. *See also* Pan balance

Mass Museum, 99, 100, 102, 181

Materials, 4, 114, 210, 314, 434, 528, 624, 722, 796

Math Boxes, *Nearly all lessons contain a Math Boxes activity.*

Mathematical argument. *See* Arguments

Mathematical Background
 Content, 10–12, 120–122, 216–218, 320–322, 440–442, 534–536, 630–632, 728–730, 802–804
 Practices, 13, 123, 219, 323, 443, 537, 633, 731, 805

Mathematical model, 50, 387, 805. *See also* Modeling

Mathematical reasoning. *See* Arguments; Conjectures; Sentence frames, using; Sentence starters, using

Mathematical tools, 2, 13, 26–31, 323, 731. *See also specific tools*

Math Message, *An introductory activity that appears in every lesson except the Progress Check lessons.*
 general information, 5, 115, 211, 315, 435, 529, 625, 723, 797

Measurement. *See also* Metric system; U.S. Customary system
 applications of, 720, 728
 of area (*See* Area)
 background information, 320
 bar graphs of (*See* Bar graphs)
 collecting data, 566

Notes

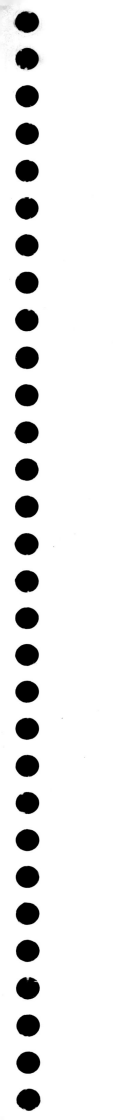